KU-766-547

Business and Society

Corporate Strategy, Public Policy, Ethics

Ninth Edition

Business and Society

Corporate Strategy, Public Policy, Ethics

James E. Post
Boston University

Anne T. Lawrence
San Jose State University

James Weber
Duquesne University

Boston   Burr Ridge, IL   Dubuque, IA   Madison, WI   New York   San Francisco   St. Louis
Bangkok   Bogotá   Caracas   Lisbon   London   Madrid
Mexico City   Milan   New Delhi   Seoul   Singapore   Sydney   Taipei   Toronto

Irwin/McGraw-Hill

A Division of The **McGraw·Hill** *Companies*

Business and Society: Corporate Strategy, Public Policy, Ethics
Copyright © 1999 by The McGraw-Hill Companies, Inc. All rights reserved, Previous editions © 1975, 1980, 1984, 1988, 1992, and 1996. Printed in the United States of America. Except as permitted under the United States Copyright Act of 1976, no part of this publication may be reproduced or distributed in any form or by any means, or stored in a data base or retrieval system, without the prior written permission of the publisher.

This book is printed on recycled, acid-free paper containing 10% post consumer waste.

2 3 4 5 6 7 8 9 0 DOC/DOC 9 3 2 1 0 9 8

ISBN 0-07-292447-0

Vice president and editorial director: *Michael W. Junior*
Publisher: *Craig D. Beytien*
Sponsoring editor: *Karen M. Mellon*
Marketing manager: *Kenyetta Giles*
Project manager: *Kimberly D. Hooker*
Production supervisor: *Lori Koetters*
Designer: *Kiera Cunningham*
Supplement coordinator: *Linda Huenecke*
Compositor: *York Graphic Services*
Typeface: *10/12 Times Roman*
Printer: *R. R. Donnelley & Sons Company*

Library of Congress Cataloging-in-Publication Data
Business and society : corporate strategy, public policy, ethics.—9th
  ed. / James E. Post, Anne T. Lawrence, James Weber.
    p. cm
  ISBN 0-07-292447-0 (acid free paper)
  Includes bibliographical references and indexes.
    1. Social responsibility of business. I. Post, James E. II. Lawrence,
Anne T. III. Weber, James.
HD60.B879   1999
  658.4/08dc—21   98-17649

http://www.mhhe.com

Dedication

To William C. Frederick

Scholar, Mentor, Colleague, Friend

**Founder of the field, researcher, and coauthor of
Business and Society fourth through eighth editions**

About the Authors

James E. Post   is a professor of management at Boston University. His primary areas of teaching and research are business and public affairs management, public policy, and corporate citizenship. He is the author or coauthor of such books as *Private Management and Public Policy* (with Lee E. Preston) and *Managing Environmental Issues: A Casebook* (with Rogene Buchholz and Alfred Marcus) and is series editor of *Research in Corporate Social Performance and Policy,* an international research annual. He has been an adviser to business, nongovernmental organizations, and government agencies on a range of issues involving business practices and responsibilities. He has been an expert witness before the U.S. Congress and regulatory agencies and served as a research director of The Conference Board's business and society program. He has been chairperson of the Social Issues in Management division of the Academy of Management, served as a reviewer and member of editorial boards for many management journals, and published articles in leading business journals. In 1989, his book *Private Management and Public Policy* was cited by the Academy of Management for "its lasting contribution to the study of business and society."

Anne T. Lawrence   is a professor of organization and management at San Jose State University. She holds a Ph.D. from the University of California, Berkeley, and completed two years of postdoctoral work at Stanford University. Her articles, cases, and reviews have appeared in many journals, including the *Academy of Management Review, Administrative Science Quarterly, Journal of Management Education, Case Research Journal, Business and Society Review,* and *Research in Corporate Social Performance and Policy.* Her cases in business and society have also been reprinted in many textbooks and anthologies. She is associate editor of the *Case Research Journal* and has served as president of the Western Casewriters Association and as an officer of the North American Case Research Association. At San Jose State University, she was named Outstanding Undergraduate Instructor in the College of Business and received the Dean's Award for Faculty Excellence.

James Weber   is an associate professor and the director of the Beard Center for Leadership in Ethics at Duquesne University. He has a Ph.D. from the University of Pittsburgh and has taught at the University of San Francisco, University of Pittsburgh, and Marquette University. His areas of interest and research include managerial and organizational values, cognitive moral reasoning, business ethics, and ethics training and education. He has conducted corporate training workshops in the areas of ethical decision making and corporate-community relations for various businesses and professional associations. He has published works in numerous management and ethics journals, such as *Organization Science, Human Relations,* the *Journal of Business Ethics,* and *Research in Corporate Social Performance and Policy.* He was recognized by the Social Issues in Management division of the Academy of Management with the Best Paper Award in 1989 and 1994. He is a member of and has served as division and program chair of the Social Issues in Management division of the Academy of Management; he has also served as president and program chair of the International Association of Business and Society (IABS). In addition, he is a member of and has served in various leadership roles in the Society for the Advancement of Socio-Economics (SASE) and the Society for Business Ethics.

Brief Contents

Contents

4
Socially Responsive Management 78

5
Ethical Dilemmas in Business 96

6
Ethical Reasoning and Corporate Programs 119

7

Global Challenges to Corporate Responsibility   144

9

Managing Business-Government Relations   197

10

Antitrust, Mergers, and Global Competition   218

11

Ecology, Sustainable Development, and Global Business   242

12

Managing Environmental Issues   264

PART SIX
Responding to Stakeholders

13
Stockholders and Corporate Governance   288

14
Consumer Protection   309

15
The Community and the Corporation   330

16
The Employee-Employer Relationship   358

PART SEVEN
Social Issues

17
Women, Work, and the Family   384

18
Technology as a Social Force   406

Case Studies in Corporate Social Policy

Preface

The relationship between business and society is changing in new and profound ways. At the beginning of the twenty-first century, the global economy is an intricate landscape of social, political and economic entities: highly advanced industrial nations such as the United States, Japan, and Germany; emerging economies in Asia and Latin America; Eastern European economies that are free after decades of political repression; and countries that are still struggling to devise economic strategies that will help produce prosperity and an improved quality of life for their citizens.

The prosperity that accompanies such growth is not shared equally among the countries in each group. Income and quality of life are unevenly distributed. People with education tend to gain a larger share of a nation's wealth than those who lack schooling. Knowledge commands a premium in a world of new and powerful technologies, and education is a powerful source of economic well-being. People who understand the complex interplay of economic, political, and social forces are better able to appreciate the impact of globalization of markets, advances in science, and the changing relationships between humans and nature. As we enter a new century, we are called to understand a very complicated and rapidly changing world. In the midst of this social change, the realities of managing a business are also changing.

Businesses have new roles and new responsibilities in the modern economy. Decisions are not made in the same ways as they were 10 or 20 years ago. The impact of business decisions is felt by more people, in more ways than in an earlier time. And because so many other things have changed in the new global economy, business leaders are required to think more carefully than ever about the effects of their actions on their company's employees, customers, suppliers, and investors. The actions of business are watched carefully by the media, government officials, and the communities in which business is conducted. In a very real sense, the world is watching as business executives chart their companies' future direction.

This new edition of *Business and Society* is about how we as stakeholders—managers, consumers, employees, and community members—try to understand, influence, and shape business behavior and social change. Consider these factors:

- Businesses in the United States and other nations are once again transforming the employment relationship, abandoning practices that once provided job security to employees, in favor of highly flexible but less secure forms of employment. This historic shift in the social contract is driven by complex economic, technological, and social factors.

- The restructuring and redesign of businesses has been driven by vigorous competition in global markets, pressure to improve the quality of products and services, and the creation of information networks that facilitate rapid transfer of economic, social, and political information. Geography, technology, and time once provided buffers that protected companies and people from change. Today, those buffers are disappearing.

- Government policies toward individual industries and sectors of the economy have shaped and reshaped markets for goods and services. International trade policies are now critical to the competitive future of businesses everywhere and to the well-being of more than 5 billion people that now inhabit the earth.

- Ecological and environmental problems have forced businesses and governments to take action. Crises, accidents, and better understanding of how human activities affect natural resources is producing a consensus that environmental protection must be achieved *with* economic growth if development is to be sustainable.

- Public concern is growing about the ethical and moral behavior of business executives and government officials. As standards change, businesses are challenged to understand new public standards and norms, adjust business practices, and reconcile sometimes conflicting ethical messages. Social values differ from country to country, which challenges accepted notions of the moral order. Business executives must operate in many nations whose people hold very different values about the workplace and the marketplace.

- The challenge of corporate responsibility and ethical behavior is made more complex when companies conduct business in countries with very different social and political cultures. Companies are challenged to function in a world community where great differences still exist. For example, China's role as a powerful economic and political actor has produced conflict in light of the country's unwillingness to conform to Western views of human rights. Human rights advocates pressure governments to link trade policies to human rights, while others argue that unfettered trade with China will eventually produce a freer, more democratic Chinese society.

- A host of new technologies have become part of the everyday lives of billions of the world's population. Advances in basic sciences—physics, biology, and chemistry—are stimulating extraordinary changes in agriculture, telecommunications, and pharmaceuticals. The media uses superlatives such as *biotechnology revolution* and the *information age* to convey some of the exciting possibilities that these scientific and technological developments promise. New industries emerge, and new approaches to living and working follow from these advances. But serious public issues also arise, as with genetically cloned animals or use of the Internet for pornographic and exploitative purposes.

This Book

This edition of *Business and Society* addresses this complex agenda of issues and their impact and influence on business and its stakeholders. The authors bring a broad background of business and society teaching, research, and case development to this endeavor. The development of this edition began by asking current users of the book to share their suggestions and insights with the author team. Many recommended changes are integrated into this new edition.

Since the 1960s, when Professors Keith Davis and Robert Blomstrom wrote the first edition of this book, *Business and Society* has maintained a position of leadership by discussing central issues of business performance in a form that students and faculty have found engaging and stimulating. The leadership of Professor Davis and Professor William C. Frederick helped *Business and Society* to consistently achieve a high standard of quality and market acceptance in the field. Thanks to the authors' remarkable eye for the emerging issues that shape the organizational, social, and public policy environments in which students will soon live and work, the book has added value to the business education of many thousands of students.

The ninth edition of *Business and Society* builds on this legacy of market leadership by reexamining such central issues as the role of business in society, the nature of corporate responsibility, business ethics practices, and the complex roles of government and business in the global economic community. Examples of individuals and companies of all sizes illustrate the concepts, theories, and ideas for action in each topical area.

New Themes

This edition also addresses important new themes in modern business and management education.

- The rise of *cross-disciplinary* teaching has created a need for books that span the breadth of business activity, including strategic and operational management. *Business and Society,* ninth edition, helps meet this need by illustrating how all types of business decisions impact stakeholders within and outside the firm.

- Business schools often teach today's students how to *manage across business functions*. This edition presents examples of companies that have managed social issues across the business functions in a strategic, stakeholder-oriented manner.

- The growth of the *Internet* and the proliferation of *World Wide Web sites* creates new opportunities for students and faculty to enrich courses with information drawn from a nearly infinite universe of sources. A list of useful Web sites is included at the end of each chapter, and many text references include Web site references.

This is a book with a vision. It is not simply a compendium of information and ideas. This ninth edition of *Business and Society* articulates the view that in a global community, where traditional buffers against change no longer protect business from external change, managers *can* create strategies that integrate stakeholder interests, respect personal values, support community development, and are implemented fairly. Most important, these goals can be achieved while also being economically sound and successful.

Acknowledgments

We are grateful for the assistance of many colleagues at universities in the United States and abroad who have made suggestions and shared ideas for this edition. We also note the feedback from students in our classes and from other colleges and universities that have helped make this book as user-friendly as possible. Among the special contributors to this project are Carla Galisin, Boston University; Stephanie Glyptis, Duquesne University; and Carol Anderson and Lisa Iha, San Jose State University, who helped with numerous research and developmental tasks. Sandra Waddock and Michael Ames of Boston College contributed the Unum case study. We also appreciate the efforts of the following reviewers: Leslie Conley, University of Central Florida; Susan Esiner, Ramapo College of New Jersey; Katharine Harrington, University of Southern California; Norma J. Carr-Rufino, San Francisco State University; Joseph Ford, Iona College; David Jacobs, American University; Harvey Nussman, Wayne State University; William Soderman, Southern Indiana University; Kurt Parkum, Pennsylvania State University, Harrisburg; Robert Boewaldt, Georgia College; and Marsha Silverman, University of Miami.

We are grateful to the excellent editorial and production team at Irwin/McGraw-Hill. Special thanks to Karen Mellon, sponsoring editor, for her leadership in this project. Kimberly Hooker, project manager; Linda Huenecke, supplement coordinator; and Steven Gomes, copyeditor have made contributions that we very much appreciate. You have given much meaning to the term *team*.

Finally, we wish to acknowledge the support and inspiration of Keith Davis and Bill Frederick, two pioneers in the business and society field, whose legacy of intellectual and editorial leadership we proudly continue in this edition.

James E. Post
Anne T. Lawrence
James Weber

Introduction and Overview

The book is divided into parts that are organized around major themes. In this introduction, we explain the overall design. Each chapter contains a number of common featues designed to enhance student learning.

Part One   The Corporation in Society

Readers are introduced to the basic conceptual themes and ideas of the interaction of business and society. Chapter 1 introduces the corporation and its stakeholders and provides a focused way of mapping the relationships between an organization and its stakeholders. The chapter also discusses the central forces that are shaping business and society relations as we move into the new century. The role of the firm in its social, economic, and political setting is discussed.

Chapter 2 introduces a strategic management approach that executives use in dealing with public issues. By understanding the relationship between stakeholder expectations and corporate performance, it is possible to follow the evolution of public issues through a normal life cycle. Business responses to public issues are discussed, with a close look at the corporate public affairs function and the development of issues management systems. The chapter concludes with a discussion of crisis management and ways to strategically manage an organization's stakeholder relations.

Part Two   Business and the Social Environment

Chapter 3 discusses public expectation that business will act in a socially responsible manner. This chapter looks at how corporate social responsibility is practiced around the world and the various limits to a firm's social obligations. Balancing its economic, legal, and social responsibilities is a major challenge for modern businesses.

Chapter 4 describes how a socially responsive firm manages its relations with stakeholders. Firms must address environmental forces before shaping a successful social strategy. This chapter provides a model for determining if a firm is acting in a socially responsive manner.

Part Three   Business and the Ethical Environment

Chapters 5 and 6 introduce the concept of business ethics. Learning how to recognize ethical issues and understanding their importance to business are emphasized in Chapter 5. International efforts to curtail unethical practices are described. Chapter 6 focuses on business efforts to promote an ethical environment in the workplace. An ethical decision-making framework and ethical safeguards are discussed in this chapter.

Chapter 7 focuses on the powerful global changes are reshaping the business world. The influence of the multinational corporation, demise of communism, emergence of market economies, and the rise of ethnic, religious, and radical forces in the geopolitical world are all shaping the global processes of commerce. The business challenge of acting responsibly, managing issues well, and living by ethical norms is clearly developed for students.

Part Four   Business and Government in a Global Society

Chapters 8 and 9 discuss the changing role of government in the global economy, especially its role as a strategist for national economic growth and social welfare. The many roles and responsibilities of government in advanced industrial nations are explored in comparative form, and the essential roles of governments in developing and newly industrialized countries is also discussed.

Chapter 10 revisits the century-old issue of antitrust in the context of today's rapid technological change and the globalization of markets. As the world economy has changed, policymakers have confronted new challenges in promoting free competition and curbing monopoly power.

Part Five   The Corporation and the Natural Environment

Chapters 11 and 12 address the ecological and natural resource issues that will reshape entire industries as the next century unfolds. Rapid population growth and the explosive development of many of the world's economies have placed new pressures on scarce resources. Water, air, and land pollution have created new constraints for business around the globe. These chapters explore both the challenges and the opportunities presented by the need to move to a more sustainable business model.

Part Six   Responding to Stakeholders

The central concepts and themes discussed in earlier chapters are applied to managing relations with the corporation's primary stakeholders and to a number of emerging social issue areas. Chapter 13 explores the changing roles and responsibilities of stockholders, managers, boards of directors, and other stakeholders in contemporary corporate governance. It also takes up the controversial debate over executive compensation.

Chapter 14 focuses on consumer protection, including such current topics as the social dimensions of advertising, product liability reform, and recent business efforts to use new technologies to communicate more effectively with their customers. It also explores issues of consumer privacy in the new information age.

The role of the corporation in the community is examined in Chapter 15. The chapter looks at business's role in the community, addressing such issues as education reform. The importance of corporate giving, charitable contributions, and employee volunteerism to community life are also discussed.

Chapter 16 focuses on the evolving employee-employer relationship. Governmental influences on this relationship from countries around the world are described in this chapter. Ethical challenges concerning employees' and employers' rights in the workplace are discussed.

Part Seven   Social Issues

Chapter 17 addresses the special issue of women at work. Where do women work? To what extent have women moved into the ranks of top management, and do women as a group manage differently than men? This chapter also explores programs companies have developed to support working parents and eliminate sex discrimination.

Chapter 18 is a new chapter that examines technology as a social force. The complex relationships between science, technology, and society are creating numerous ethical and political issues for business. If the information superhighway emerges as experts believe it will, the careers of future managers will be inextricably tied to its features. Technological advances in many other fields promise equally complicated decisions for managers and companies. Business and society will be profoundly affected by this new age of science and technological change.

Case Studies in Corporate Social Policy

The book features nine full-length case studies, including a number of new cases prepared especially for this edition. The cases are written to provide rich discussion material and present a variety of opportunities for instructors to connect topics raised across individual chapters.

PART ONE

The Corporation in Society

1

The Corporation and Its Stakeholders

Business has complex relationships with many segments of society. The existence and power of these stakeholders require careful management attention and action. A company's success can be affected—negatively or positively—by its stakeholders. In an era when business strategies are changing because of such forces as global competition, new political arrangements, shifting public values, and ecological concerns, managers are challenged to achieve good economic results while also considering the needs and requirements of their business's stakeholders.

This chapter focuses on these key questions and objectives:

- Why are business, government, and society an interactive system?
- What kind of involvement does business have with other segments of society?
- Who are a corporation's primary and secondary stakeholders?
- Why are stakeholders important to a corporation, and how can they affect its success?
- What major forces of change are reshaping the business environment for companies?
- How do globalization, ecological concerns, and ethical norms affect corporate stakeholders?

Each day, hundreds of newsworthy stories are made by businesses and managers making decisions on new products, employment policies, advertising campaigns, locations for production and manufacturing, and directions for future research and development. The face of business in today's society is ever-changing, highly dynamic, and extraordinarily diverse. Some events are exciting, others depressing. But many reflect the basic trends and underlying forces that are shaping business and society, as illustrated by the following examples.[1]

- In what was described as the largest merger and acquisition in U.S. business history, MCI, a global communications company, was acquired by WorldCom, a smaller but more prosperous global communications firm. The merger was valued at more than $34 billion, well beyond the previous high (the $22 billion merger of R.J. Reynolds and Nabisco). Other bidders for MCI included the British Telephone (BT), a European telecommunications giant, and GTE, a U.S. company with a vast domestic telephone market. The completed merger will affect hundreds of thousands of employees, thousands of suppliers of equipment, and millions of customers.

- Unionized workers at United Parcel Service (UPS), the world's largest package delivery company, went on strike for several weeks to protest the company's contract offer. A major issue in the dispute, which disrupted package delivery in the United States and abroad, involved the company's two-tier wage structure in which part-time employees received lower hourly wages than full-time employees and no benefits while doing the same work. The union argued that this system was fundamentally unfair since both types of workers were performing comparable tasks. The company claimed that the two-tier system was essential if it was to have needed flexibility in a very competitive marketplace. Direct mail and catalog retailers such as Lands' End and L.L. Bean desperately sought to meet delivery schedules. The U.S. Postal Service was a big winner: Its business grew substantially, and many new customers said they would stay with the Post Office rather than return to UPS. Throughout the strike, public sentiment and opinion polls firmly supported the strikers. Pollsters speculated that the strike was a way for the public to lash out at the uncertainty caused by a decade of downsizing and restructuring. News commentators and labor relations experts called the strike a watershed event in modern employer–union relations.

- Warner-Lambert, a global pharmaceutical company with headquarters in Morris Plains, New Jersey, was fined $3 million after pleading guilty to falsifying reports on the levels of pollutants released from a wastewater treatment plant in Puerto Rico, according to the U.S. Justice Department. The company will also pay a $670,000 civil penalty for releasing excessive levels of pollutants from 1992 to 1995, violating its wastewater discharge permit 347 times. The plant's supervisor, Juan Ruiz Orengo, pleaded guilty to similar charges and could be sentenced to up to 27 months in jail. He was responsible for collecting and

---

[1]Based on published material in *The Wall Street Journal,* the *New York Times,* and other business journals. See, for example, "Warner-Lambert Is Fined $3 Million," *New York Times,* October 24, 1997, p. D2; and "Deferring to Company's Will: Kodak Workers Say Layoffs May Be Needed Tonic," *New York Times*, November 16, 1997, pp. 41, 46.

analyzing wastewater samples for 34 pollutants, including fecal coliform, metals, oil, and grease.

- In Rochester, New York, officials at Eastman Kodak Company announced a reorganization and downsizing. The global photography company is Rochester's largest employer, taxpayer, and purchaser of goods and services. Its photographic film and imaging equipment is sold throughout the world, and the Kodak label is one of the world's best-known logos. For decades, Kodak "owned" the photographic film business and exercised its market power by charging relatively high prices for its products. Although profitable, the pricing strategy exposed the company to potential competition. In the 1990s, Fuji, a Japanese film manufacturer, introduced high-quality films that compared favorably with Kodak's and sold for much less. Big Father Yellow, as Kodak is called in Rochester, began to suffer sharply declining sales and plummeting profits. The problem worsened until late 1997, when CEO George Fisher, announced a major restructuring that included the elimination of 10,000 jobs. The company promised job placement assistance and generous benefits for displaced workers. Although shaken by the bad news, Rochester's mayor expressed both admiration for Kodak's commitment to the community and confidence that unemployed workers would find jobs in the local economy.

These examples highlight some of the powerful and central forces in the modern economy. The changing shape of competition is reflected in the MCI/WorldCom merger and in Kodak's failing film business. Technological change is evident in the merger case and the global package delivery business. The complex relationship between labor, capital, and competition in the modern global economy is illustrated by the changing employer–employee relations at UPS and Kodak. The importance of the natural environment and the need for government regulation to protect the public against unethical actions by companies and managers is clearly illustrated in the Justice Department's actions against Warner-Lambert. All of these issues, and many others as well, underline the complicated and challenging relationships that exist between modern businesses, the people they affect, and the society in which they operate.

Every business has complex involvements with other people, groups, and organizations in society. Some are intended and desired; others are unintentional and not desired. The people and organizations with which a business is involved have an interest in the decisions, actions, and practices of the firm. Customers, suppliers, employees, owners, creditors, and local communities are among those affected by the profitability and economic success of the business. Their support can be critical to a company's success or failure.

The modern business, whether small or large, *is* part of the global business environment. It will be affected by social issues, events, and pressures from around the world. Whether the company has 50 employees or 50,000, its links to customers, suppliers, employees, and communities are likely to be numerous, diverse, and vital to its success. This is why the relationship between business, government, and society is so important to understand as both a citizen and a manager. Whether looked at from outside business—as a member of the community—or from within business—as a manager, employee, or entrepreneur—it is important to see how businesses can blend economic and social purposes together, with minimum conflict and maximum benefits for all.

Business-Government-Society: An Interdependent System

As the introductory examples illustrate, business, government, and other elements of society are highly interdependent. Few business actions are without an impact on others in society, just as few actions by government are without direct or indirect impact on business. And, of course, business and government decisions continuously affect all segments of the general public. To manage these interdependencies, corporate managers need a conceptual understanding of the relationships and ideas for responding to issues.

A Systems Perspective

Management thinking has been greatly influenced by general systems theory. According to this theory, all living organisms (systems) interact with, and are affected by, other forces in their host environments. The key to survival is the ability to adapt—to be responsive to the changing conditions in the environment. For an organism such as the modern business corporation, systems thinking provides a powerful tool to help managers appreciate the relationships between their companies and the rest of the world.

Figure 1–1 illustrates the "systems" connections between broad, abstract ways of thinking about business-government-society relationships and specific, practical ways of doing so. The broadest view of that relationship is a societal perspective that emphasizes the systems connections between a nation's economic activity, its political life, and its culture. Every society is a mixture of economic, political, and cultural influences, each generated by its own system of people, institutions, and ideas.[2] In other words, reality for all of us is a mixture of economic, political, and cultural influences.

A somewhat narrower perspective is illustrated in the middle panel of Figure 1–1. *Business* is composed of many segments, industries, and sectors; *government* involves political life at the national, state, local, and, increasingly, international levels; and *society* is composed of many segments, ethnic and other groups, and stakeholders. Once, it was widely believed that business interacted with others in society only through the marketplace. But that view has long since been replaced by an understanding that business and society have many nonmarket interactions as well. Many social influences on business come from cultural and political forces in society; business also has an influence on the political life and culture of any society.

> *About a decade ago, Bell Atlantic, a U.S. telecommunications company, formed a joint venture with the national telecommunications company of New Zealand. The joint venture made possible an expanded array of telecommunications services for citizens and businesses in New Zealand. Faxes between New Zealanders and others throughout the Pacific grew exponentially; the number of international telephone calls exploded. New Zealanders quickly became more connected to the rest of the world. Despite large geographic distances, New Zealand businesses were linked to important markets in the global economy in ways that had never before occurred.*

Computer technology has also had pervasive effects on cultures and societies everywhere. These cultural effects are largely due to the success of computer pioneers such as IBM, Apple Computer, Microsoft, and others in developing technology (hardware and

---

[2]See, for example, Amitai Etzioni, *The New Golden Rule* (New York: Basic Books, 1996); and Amitai Etzioni, *The Spirit of Community* (New York: Crown Publishers, 1993).

Figure 1–1

A range of levels for understanding business–government–society relationships.

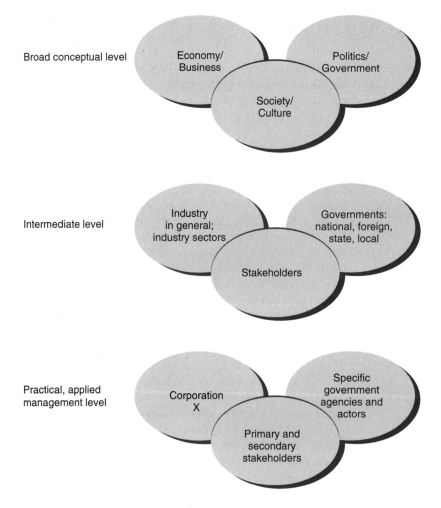

Broad conceptual level

Economy/Business

Politics/Government

Society/Culture

Intermediate level

Industry in general; industry sectors

Governments: national, foreign, state, local

Stakeholders

Practical, applied management level

Corporation X

Specific government agencies and actors

Primary and secondary stakeholders

software), marketing it to many types of customers, and encouraging the public to use it for work and entertainment.

One result of this close, inseparable relationship between business and society is that all business decisions have a social impact, much as a pebble thrown into a pond creates ever-widening ripples. Another result is that the vitality and survival of business depend on society's actions and attitudes. Business can be smothered under a heavy blanket of social demands. Taxes can be set at levels that limit available funds for capital investment or encourage relocation to communities in countries with lower tax burdens. Environmental regulations may prove technically impossible or too costly to allow certain industries to continue operating, leading to plant closures and job losses. Labor unions can demand wages or working conditions that exceed a company's ability to pay or its ability to compete in the marketplace. So, while business decisions can have both positive and negative impacts on society, the actions of a society can also influence and affect whether a business firm will prosper or fail.[3]

---

[3]William C. Frederick, *Values, Nature, and Culture in the American Corporation* (New York: Oxford University Press, 1995).

That is why business and society,
Each needs the other; each influences the
action taken by one will inevitably affec
blurred and indistinct. Business is part of s
business. They are both separate and conne
cation is rapidly expanding, the connections
of the twentieth century, most travel was dor
Fifty years later, autos and airplanes were tl
twenty-first century, equally momentous tran
politics. Throughout this book are examples of
the business-society relationships of the twenty

The Stakeholder Concept

When business interacts so often and so closely ~~~ society, a shared interest and interdependence develops between a company and other groups—the organization is interacting with its stakeholders.[4] **Stakeholders** are all the people and groups affected by, or that
can affect, an organization's decisions, policies, and operations. The number of stakeholders and the variety of their interests can be quite large; thus, a company's decisions
can become very complex.

Government, a stakeholder, creates conditions that can influence a company to stay
in or withdraw from a particular market; still, the decision is ultimately the company's to
make. However, a business cannot act without regard to its stakeholders' interests. In addition to profit and economic considerations, for example, the company must consider its
customers, suppliers, employees, owners, and creditors. Simply stated, good managerial
decisions are made by paying attention to the effects of those decisions—pro and con—
on the people and interests that are affected. Weighing conflicting considerations such as
these is a part of any manager's job.

The Three-Legged Stool

The relationships between companies and their stakeholders have changed over the years.
Previously, managers had only to focus their attention on the product-market framework;
they could concentrate on bringing products and services to market as efficiently and effectively as possible. The number of stakeholders was limited. Thomas J. Watson, Sr.,
chairman of IBM in the 1950s, described management's role as one of balancing a three-
legged stool consisting of employees, customers, and shareholders. To emphasize their
equality, he routinely changed the order in which he mentioned the three groups in his
talks and speeches. In those days, it could be assumed that these were the important stakeholders. In contrast, the 1990 book about IBM by Thomas J. Watson, Jr., son of the senior Watson, emphasized the large number and variety of other stakeholders—communities, arts organizations, colleges and universities, foreign governments, and many more—
with which the company interacted during the era of the younger Watson's leadership.
Ironically, John Akers, one of the Watsons' successors as IBM chairman, was deposed as

[4]R. Edward Freeman, *Strategic Management: A Stakeholder Approach* (Marshfield, MA: Pitman, 1984); and
Thomas Donaldson and Lee E. Preston, "The Stakeholder Theory of the Corporation: Concepts, Evidence,
Implications," *Academy of Management Review*, January 1995, pp. 71–83.

s chief executive in 1993 because he was unable to meet expectations of critical holders such as shareholders and creditors. The multilegged stool had become imbalanced and cost Akers his job as the economic stakeholders (i.e., investors) reasserted their importance and power. His successor, Lewis V. Gerstner, Jr., emphasized the importance of *all* the company's stakeholders and orchestrated a massive turnaround in IBM's fortunes by the end of the 1990s. The results benefited all of IBM's stakeholders, including investors, employees, customers, communities, and the many educational institutions the company supports through its philanthropic giving.

Managers have the challenge of weighing and balancing the interests of the corporate stakeholders. If their concerns are disregarded, the stakeholders may damage or halt the company's operations. The key point about corporate stakeholders is that they may, and sometimes do, share decision-making power with a company's managers. Their justification for seeking a voice is that they are affected by the company's operations. The interest created between a company and its stakeholders can be a powerful aid to business, or it can be turned against a company. When stakeholders demand a voice in decision making and policy making, the company's managers need to respond with great skill if their primary business mission—producing goods and services—is to be achieved.

On the positive side, a corporation's stakeholders can also be enlisted to aid and support a company that is in trouble.

For example, when Malden Mills, a textile manufacturer located in Methuen, Massachusetts, suffered a devastating fire that destroyed its mill, employees, community officials, the governor, state legislative leaders, and prominent business leaders were ready to help. The family-owned company and its chief executive, Aaron Feuerstein, had defied the odds for years by producing special textiles for the furniture and clothing industries. Malden Mills was New England's last textile producer, in large measure because of Feuerstein's refusal to walk away from the company's 1,400 employees. When the fire damage was surveyed, it appeared that the company could not continue. Feuerstein refused advice to close. He insisted that production continue in the buildings that were not damaged. Immediate repairs were made to equipment and additional space was rented. Injured workers were promised top medical care, and Feuerstein's daughter personally oversaw arrangements for families whose members had been transferred to Boston burn-treatment centers. Most important, Feuerstein promised all workers that he would continue their pay and medical benefits for one month despite the lack of actual work. He later extended these benefits for additional months, enabling many of the families to meet critical emergency expenses.

Feuerstein prepared an ambitious schedule to get the mill rebuilt. But he couldn't do it alone. Industrial facilities take many months, even years, to complete. Regulations are complex and extensive. At Malden Mills, the reconstruction occurred in record time. The state legislature quickly passed needed legislation, and local banks extended credit to the company, despite its immediate inability to pay. Customers, including clothing and furniture manufacturers with unforgiving seasonal demands, tried to reserve their business for Malden Mills. The Malden Mills stakeholder network was concerned and eager to help the company. The state's congressional representatives and senators urged the secretary of labor and president of the United States to invoke federal law to help the company. In the end, the company did reopen and virtually all employees were offered jobs at the new facility. Aaron Feuerstein was hailed as a business hero and received many prizes, honorary degrees, and commendations. He insisted the credit belonged to others and always thanked the company's many friends and supporters.

There are many examples of companies disregarding their stakeholders' wishes, either out of the belief that the stakeholder is wrong or out of arrogance reflected in the attitude that one unhappy customer, employee, or regulator doesn't matter. Such attitudes are foolish and often prove costly to the company involved. Today, for example, builders know that they cannot locate a plant in a community that strongly objects. The only way to build a power plant or incinerator, for example, is to work with the community, to respond to concerns, and to invest in creating and maintaining a relationship of trust. John deButts, who once served as chairman of AT&T, commented about the three-legged stool in this way: "The only image which recurs with uncomfortable persistence is not a piece of furniture at all. It is a porcupine, with quills reversed!"[5]

Today, many stakeholders have the ability to stick quills into business. But, as the Malden Mills example suggests, stakeholder relationships are also a vital part of the company's assets. Companies need comprehensive approaches that take into account the needs of a larger and more diverse group of stakeholders. Business cannot be done in a social and political vacuum, and good management planning must take into account this web of stakeholder considerations.

Primary and Secondary Stakeholders

Business interacts with society in a variety of different ways, and a company's relations differ with different stakeholders. Figure 1–2 shows business interacting with groups that affect its ability to carry out its primary purpose of providing society with goods and services. Investors (stockholders) and creditors provide financial capital to the company; employees contribute their work skills and knowledge; suppliers provide raw materials, energy, and other supplies; and wholesalers, distributors, and retailers help move the product from plant to sales offices to customers. All businesses need customers who are willing to pay for the products or services being produced, and most companies compete against others offering similar products and services in the marketplace. These are the fundamental interactions every business has with society, and they help us define the primary economic mission of the company.

A business's primary involvements with society include all the direct relationships necessary for it to perform its major mission of producing goods and services for customers. These interactions normally occur in the marketplace and involve processes of buying and selling. The primary involvements shape a company's strategy and the policy decisions of its managers and reveal the importance of its **primary stakeholders.** These stakeholders, who are critical to the company's existence and activities, include customers, suppliers, employees, and investors.

However, as Figure 1–3 on page 12 reveals, a business's relationships go beyond those primary involvements to others in society. Secondary interactions and involvements

[5]John deButts, "A Strategy of Accountability," in William Dill, ed., *Running the American Corporation* (Englewood Cliffs, NJ: Prentice Hall, 1978), p. 141.

Figure 1–2

Relations between a business firm and its primary stakeholders.

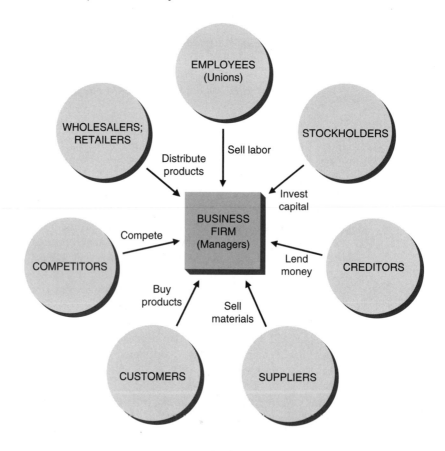

occur when other groups express interest in or concern about the organization's activities. **Secondary stakeholders** are those people and groups in society who are affected, directly or indirectly, by the company's primary activities and decisions. They include the general public, various levels of government, social activist groups, and others.

Calling these involvements and stakeholders *secondary* does not mean that they are less important than business's primary relationships with society. It means that they occur *as a consequence* of the normal activities of conducting business. Moreover, primary and secondary areas of involvement are not always sharply distinguished; often, one area shades into the other. For example, while the safety or environmental effect of a product (e.g., an automobile) is a primary concern to a customer, the cumulative effect of the use of the product may represent a secondary safety or environmental concern for the entire community (e.g., smog from automobile emissions).

Combining a business's primary and secondary interactions gives an **interactive model of business and society.** The interactive model of business and society recognizes the fundamental role of business as an economic contributor to society. But it also suggests that managers must make decisions and take actions that benefit the society as a whole as well as the company's economic interests. The net effect is to enhance the quality of life in the broadest possible way, as that quality of life is defined by society. Business acts to produce the goods and services that society wants, recognizes the social effects of its activities, and is concerned with the social and economic effects on society.

Figure 1–3

Relations between a business firm and some of its other (secondary) stakeholders.

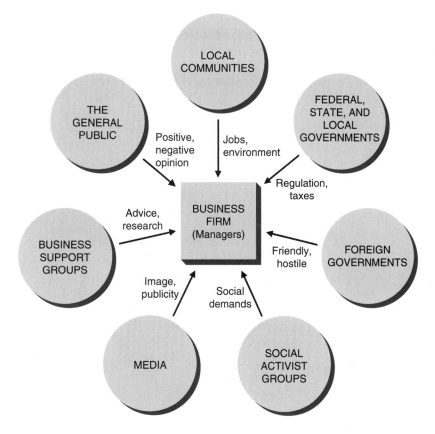

Stakeholder Interests and Power

Stakeholder groups exist in many forms, some well organized, others much less so. This variety makes it more difficult for a company's managers to understand and respond to stakeholder concerns. Each stakeholder has a unique connection with the organization, and managers must understand these involvements and respond accordingly. For example, stockholders have an ownership interest in the organization. The economic health and success of the corporation affect these people financially; their personal wealth is at stake. Customers, suppliers, and retailers have different interests. Owners are most interested in realizing a return on their investment, whereas customers and suppliers are most interested in gaining fair value in the exchange of goods and money. Neither has a great interest in the other's stake. And when we recognize that there are different kinds of owners, ranging from pension funds with large holdings to individual owners with small holdings, the picture grows more complicated.

Governments, public interest groups, and local communities have another sort of relationship with the company. In general, their stake is broader than the financial stake of owners or persons who buy products and sell services to the company. They may wish to protect the environment, assure human rights, or advance other broad social interests. Managers need to track these stakeholder interests with great care.

Different stakeholders also have different types and degrees of power. Stakeholder power, in this instance, means the ability to use resources to make an event happen or to secure a desired outcome. Most experts recognize three types of stakeholder power: voting power, economic power, and political power.

Voting power (not referring to political, electoral voting) means that the stakeholder has the legitimate right to cast a vote. For example, each stockholder has a voting power proportionate to the percentage of the company's stock he or she owns. Stockholders typically have an opportunity to vote on such major decisions as mergers, acquisitions, and other extraordinary issues. Through the exercise of informed, intelligent voting, they may influence company policy so that their investment is protected and produces a healthy return.

Customers, suppliers, and retailers have *economic power* with the company. Suppliers can withhold supplies or refuse to fill orders if a company fails to meet its contractual responsibilities. Customers may refuse to buy a company's products if the company enacts an improper policy. Customers can boycott products if they believe the goods are too expensive, poorly made, unsafe, or inappropriate for consumption.

Government exercises *political power* through legislation, regulations, or lawsuits. Other stakeholders also exercise political power, using their resources to pressure government to adopt new laws or regulations or to take legal action against a company.

> In a landmark case, a group of citizens in Woburn, Massachusetts, sued W.R. Grace and Company and Beatrice Foods for allegedly dumping toxic chemicals that leaked into underground wells used for drinking water. The deaths and illnesses of family members led the survivors to mobilize political power against the two companies. Investigations were conducted by private groups and public agencies. The lawsuits and political pressure helped make toxic dumping and the protection of water supplies very important political issues. (This case is the basis of Jonathan Haar's book A Civil Action and the 1998 John Travolta movie of the same name.)

Of course, a single stakeholder is capable of exercising more than one type of power. The Woburn families sued the two companies (political power), but they had other powers too. They could have led a boycott of the companies' products (economic power) or purchased shares of stock in the companies and attempted to oust the directors and management through a proxy fight (voting power).

Stakeholder Coalitions

Stakeholder coalitions are not static. Stakeholders that are highly involved with a company today may be less involved tomorrow. Issues that are most salient at one point in time may be replaced by other issues at another time; stakeholders who are most dependent on an organization at one time may be less so at another. To make matters even more complex, the process of shifting coalitions may not occur uniformly in all parts of a large corporation. Stakeholders involved with one part of a large company often have little or no involvement with other parts of the organization.

Groups are always changing their relationships to one another in society. Stakeholder coalitions are the temporary unions of stakeholder groups that come together and share a common point of view on a particular issue or problem. There are very broad coalitions whose member organizations span the nation and the world. Movements such as the environmental movement or the human rights movement involve hundreds of state, national, and international organizations and may operate with little or no coordination and policy making. Other movements may be very diverse but operate in a coordinated manner through a central policy-making board or group.

Coalitions of stakeholders have become increasingly internationalized as well. Sophisticated communications technology has enabled like-minded people to communicate quickly, irrespective of political boundaries. Telephones, fax machines, computers, and the Internet have become powerful tools in the hands of activist groups trying to monitor how multinational businesses are operating in different locations around the world.

For example, the Scott Paper Company, a U.S. multinational corporation headquartered in Philadelphia, negotiated an agreement with the government of Indonesia to build a new paper mill and pulp-processing plant on Sumatra, one of Indonesia's principal islands. Indonesian environmental activists were outraged at the proposal, however, and fought to prevent it. They feared that the paper mill would inevitably lead to destruction of Sumatra's rain forest. Since pulp and paper mills are also notorious for their air and water pollution, the Indonesian environmentalists contacted friends in the United States, including the Natural Resources Defense Council (NRDC). NRDC staff focused on what kind of pressure they could apply against Scott. They concluded that a national boycott of Scott paper products, including such highly visible consumer products as Scotties tissues, was possible. Once this was communicated to Scott Paper's executives, they recognized the company's vulnerability to a consumer boycott and decided to withdraw from the Indonesia project. The Indonesian government was disappointed, having anticipated tax revenues and the creation of jobs. The government eventually turned to a Japanese company to build and operate the pulp and paper mill.[6]

This example illustrates how national and international networks of experienced activists, and the media's interest in a wide range of local, national, and international issues, make coalition development and issue activism an increasingly powerful factor in business.

Forces Shaping Business-Society Relations

Today's business firms do not operate in a social or political vacuum; rather, they find themselves in a virtual whirlwind of social and political problems and controversies. Business managers are buffeted by complicated and threatening forces, many of them global in scope. These trends now intrude into the very core of business operations, thus requiring careful attention and planning. Even small business firms that serve local markets are affected by disruptions in supply, price fluctuations, regional warfare, and uncertainty stemming from international political and economic events. Figure 1–4 illustrates six critical forces that are shaping business-society relations in the 1990s. Each of these forces is introduced below; other chapters in this book discuss each of these topics in further detail.

Force 1: Strategic and Social Challenges

Throughout the world, companies of all sizes and in all industries are rethinking critical business assumptions about where to compete and how. **Strategic rethinking** has produced major changes in virtually every company in every industry. Many companies have

---

[6]Based on an interview conducted by one of the authors with the head of the Indonesian Environmental Federation.

Figure 1–4

Six forces shaping
business-society
relations.

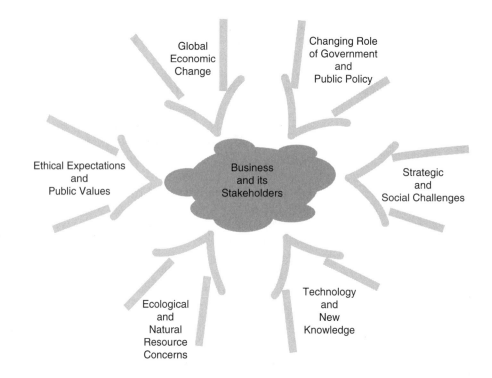

Figure 1–4

Six forces shaping business-society relations.

restructured their business operations, often eliminating those activities that seem too distant from the company's strengths or too vulnerable to competitors. Reorganization of business operations occurs frequently as companies have tried to improve the quality of their products and services, reduce costs, and improve the speed with which they respond to customers. This redesign of business operations is also known as **reengineering.**[7]

This broad process of reinventing the corporation has many social consequences. Employees are dismissed from jobs that no longer exist in a redesigned manufacturing or service-delivery system. People who have made long-term career commitments to one firm are asked to take an early retirement or face dismissal. The impact can be tempered by financial arrangements and efforts to train and relocate former employees in new jobs. But the overwhelming sense of loss that people feel in such circumstances is reflected in social indicators such as increased suicide, alcoholism, mental illness, and child and spouse abuse.

Strategic changes in a company's business also affect its relationships with other segments of society. External stakeholders are hurt when a business closes: suppliers, competitors, and other businesses (restaurants, retailers, banks, movie theaters) suffer. A multiplier effect leaves the community short on jobs, tax revenues, and morale.

Traditional concepts of the corporation's responsibility to its stakeholders may be challenged when a company begins to rethink its strategy. Many experts describe the

---

[7]Michael Hammer and James Champy, *Reengineering the Corporation* (New York: Harper Business, 1993). The popularity of the concept led to many abuses by companies and, in time, a reconsideration of the concept by the authors. See Michael Hammer, *Beyond Reengineering: How the Process-Centered Organization Is Changing Our Work and Our Lives* (New York: Harper Business, 1996).

corporation-stakeholder relationship as a **social contract,** an implied understanding between a business and stakeholders as to how they will act toward one another. Social contracts are often affected when a company's business strategy changes. Commitments to
employees may change in bad times. A company's community involvements and charitable contributions may decline when it encounters severe economic problems. Such changes
in the social contract between companies and their stakeholders occurred frequently during the 1990s, leading some observers to conclude that the "good corporation" is dead.[8]

What is emerging in the view of some experts, however, is a **new social contract**
between the corporation, its employees, and other stakeholders.[9] As the dynamics of a
business change, relationships with stakeholders also change. The roles and responsibilities a company acknowledges and accepts must necessarily change. The new social contract implies that stakeholders can reasonably expect that managers will acknowledge those
relationships, deal with the impacts of their decisions, and respond to the people who are
touched by the corporation's activities. That is the essence of "doing the right thing."

> *During the 1990s, more than four million job losses were announced by large
> American companies. Downsizing occurred in virtually every sector of the
> economy. Manufacturing, financial services, retailing, and transportation were
> among the industries greatly affected. A package of benefits was typically of-
> fered to departing employees, including compensation based on years of ser-
> vice, continuation of health care benefits for a period of time (ranging from 30
> days to one or more years), and support for retraining or education. Research
> showed that surviving employees also felt the psychological impact of staff re-
> ductions, including fears of how management would act in the future. Compa-
> nies such as Levi Strauss recognized the need to do the right thing for employ-
> ees and responded to these concerns by stating in writing the commitments on
> which continuing employees could count. In some companies, these statements
> of commitment are called* compacts, covenants, *or* social contracts, *symbolizing
> the special nature of the employee-employer relationship.*

Reinventing corporate strategy along these lines is often more a matter of mind and
managerial attitude than anything else. It takes a business executive who is willing to look
at more than the bottom line. Social sensitivity is possessed by a manager who realizes
that employees are people first and producers second. Employees may take pride in their
work, but at the same time they are family members, citizens of communities, members
of churches, political adherents, and people with aspirations, problems, hopes, and desires
who are often emotional, sometimes rational, and frequently confused.

Research has shown that companies with the best social reputations and the best social performance records have top managers who take a broad view of their company's
place in society.[10] In fact, these managers often believe that their companies should take

---

[8]Robert J. Samuelson, "R.I.P.: The Good Corporation," *Newsweek,* July 5, 1993, p. 41; and John W. Houck and
Oliver Williams, eds., *Is the Good Corporation Dead?* (South Bend, IN: University of Notre Dame Press, 1996).

[9]James E. Post, "The New Social Contract," in Oliver Williams and John Houck, eds., *The Global Challenge
to Corporate Social Responsibility* (New York: Oxford University Press, 1995); and Severyn T. Bruyn, *A Future for the American Economy: The Social Market* (Stanford, CA: Stanford University Press, 1991).

[10]Charles J. Fombrun, *Reputation: Realizing Value from the Corporate Image* (Boston, MA: Harvard Business
School Press, 1996). See also *Corporate Reputation Review* 1, nos. 1 and 2 (1997), which focus on reputation
as one of an organization's strategic assets.

the lead in helping society solve its problems. Corporations with this attitude generally take a long-run view of the company rather than focusing exclusively on short-run gains. Social goals, as well as economic goals, are given a high priority in planning the company's future. Such an attitude will not prevent the company from facing the stern pressures of marketplace competition or enable them to avoid difficult issues of restructuring, reorganizing, and refocusing, but it will help ensure that the interests of the company and all of its stakeholders are integrated into the corporate strategy.

There are many companies, large and small, that are committed to finding ways to operationalize this new social contract. Anita Roddick, founder and managing director (CEO) of the Body Shop International, a company that manufactures and markets natural cosmetics, soaps, and toiletries through franchise stores, expressed a sentiment shared by members of such businesses:

> [O]ver the past decade, while many businesses have pursued what I call "business as usual," I have been part of a different, smaller business movement—one that has tried to put idealism back on the agenda. We want a new paradigm, a whole new framework, for seeing and understanding [that] business can and must be a force for positive social change. It must not only avoid hideous evil—it must actively do good.[11]

Whether or not this attitude will yield consistent, high levels of economic performance is not yet clear. What is clear is that the business-society relationship is always dynamic; it has been changing very rapidly in recent years and is likely to continue doing so in the next decade. Creating a successful business strategy will require managers who are concerned that business continue to perform a positive role in society. These issues are discussed further in Chapters 3 and 4.

Force 2: Ethical Expectations and Public Values

Ethical expectations are a vital part of the business environment. The public expects business to be ethical and wants corporate managers to apply **ethical principles**—in other words, guidelines about what is right and wrong, fair and unfair, and morally correct—when they make business decisions.

In the global arena, ethical standards—and even what is meant by *ethics*—can vary from one society to another. These kinds of problems and how to deal with them are discussed in Chapters 5 and 6. In spite of differences in ethical meanings, cultural variation does not automatically rule out common ethical agreement being reached among people of different societies. For example, the European Union's Social Charter promotes common job rights and humane workplace treatment among its member-nations. The International Chamber of Commerce has promoted a common code of environmental practices and principles to protect natural resources around the world. And the 29 member-nations of the Organization for Economic Cooperation and Development (OECD), the world's leading industrial economies, adopted a treaty banning bribery of foreign officials in international commerce.[12]

[11]Anita Roddick, "Corporate Responsibility: Good Works Not Good Words," Speech to the International Chamber of Commerce, October 21, 1993; reprinted in *Vital Speeches of the Day* 60, no. 7, (January 15, 1994), pp. 196–99.
[12]Edmund Andrews, "29 Nations Agree to Outlaw Bribing Foreign Officials," *New York Times*, November 21, 1997, pp. A1, C2.

Human rights issues have become more prominent and important for business. For many years, great pressure was exerted on South Africa's political leaders to halt racially discriminatory practices of apartheid and its business leaders to challenge the South African government's enforcement of the policy. More recently, pressures from many sources have focused on alleged abuses of human rights in countries such as China, Burma (Mynamar), and Nigeria. And religious organizations in the United States, Canada, and Britain have proposed Principles for Global Corporate Responsibility (see Chapters 5 and 7).

The question is not, Should business be ethical? Nor is it, Should business be economically efficient? Society wants business to be both at the same time. Ethical behavior is a key aspect of corporate social performance. To maintain public support and credibility—that is, **business legitimacy**—businesses must find ways to balance and integrate these two social demands: high economic performance and high ethical standards. When a company and its employees act ethically in dealings with other stakeholders, they are improving the organization's contribution as a social actor. When they fail to act ethically, there is the risk of losing the public support an organization needs to be credible and successful.

> *For example, in the early 1990s it was disclosed that William Aramony, chief executive officer of United Way of America, a nonprofit organization, was being paid a salary in excess of $400,000 per year, plus other expensive benefits. Moreover, there was alleged evidence that directors and others were misled by Aramony as to the extent of his compensation and spending habits. This was viewed as unethical and scandalous for a nonprofit organization that pays no taxes because it is a charitable institution. The negative publicity resulted in Aramony's dismissal, a shake-up of officers at United Way, and the naming of a new CEO at a significantly lower salary. Public financial support for United Way fell dramatically. It took more than five years for the organization—which supports a wide range of community groups—to restore its reputation and rebuild its donor support.*

Business leaders are faced with the continuing challenge of meeting public expectations that are, themselves, always changing. Yesterday's acceptable behavior may not be tolerated today. Many forms of harassment and discrimination were once common. Today, however, social standards make such actions unacceptable. Public expectations of service and ethical behavior are as relevant to a business as customer expectations regarding products such as automobiles and computers.

Force 3: Global Economic Change

Foremost among the factors affecting business is **global economic change.** Dramatic changes have transformed the world's economic scene in recent times. Consider the following events: Asian economic growth, third-world economic development, Western European economic integration, the experiments of Eastern European economies with free markets and competition, and the North American Free Trade Agreement (NAFTA). Global changes of this magnitude create more than just new economic competition. As economies have changed, so have governments, politics, and social systems. Achieving business goals in the midst of such global change requires a keen understanding of interrelated social, economic, political, and cultural trends (see Exhibit 1–A).

EXHIBIT
1–A

General Motors Catches the Asian Flu

The General Motors Corporation is the world's largest automobile company. It operates around the world and has vast experience in dealing with the economic and political ups and downs of countries. As 1998 began, however, General Motors executives were stunned to see what happened to their business in many Asian countries. In what business observers were calling the Asian flu and Asian contagion, the economies of Thailand, South Korea, and Indonesia suffered huge economic losses.

For Ronald Frizzell, president of GM's Thailand subsidiary, the story began in July 1997, while he was on vacation in Scotland. One day, he received a fax requiring his immediate return to Thailand.

Thailand had been forced to devalue its currency, the baht, plunging the nation into financial turmoil. And as the crisis spread to other Asian countries, Frizzell and his GM colleagues faced a crisis of their own: They were in the midst of building a $500 million factory in Rayong, Thailand, on a former pineapple plantation to supply what they thought would be an endlessly booming Asian market.

"In the annals of poorly timed corporate investments, GM's history in Thailand looks at the moment like a doozy," opined *The Washington Post*. Along with other U.S. automakers, GM withdrew from Thailand and other Southeast Asian markets in the late 1970s, leaving Japanese competitors who quickly gained 90 percent of the market and reaped handsome profits as the Asian economic "miracle" generated the world's fastest growth in auto sales. A long decision process finally produced GM's decision to reenter the Asian car market in a big way.

GM's rush back into the market came just as auto sales slumped and an economic crunch gripped the region. At the the Tokyo Auto Show in October 1997, GM chairman Jack Smith said that the company was looking to the long term, not short-term gain. The plant's construction will continue although the product portfolio might change. The original plan called for production of 100,000 low- to-medium-end passenger cars annually. GM executives now believe production will be lower, and the models may be changed in light of new market conditions.

Across Asia, economic experts are changing their growth forecasts for what were called the tiger economies because of their high economic growth rates throughout the 1990s. Thailand seems to be slipping into an outright recession because of the flight of investment funds by investors who are concerned that the nation is laden with unproductive real estate, wasteful pork-barrel projects, and overly ambitious industrial investments. Car sales in July and August 1997 dropped 75 percent below year-earlier levels. Wealthy Thais were selling off their luxury vehicles at auction just to raise cash.

When Frizzell flew back to Detroit for meetings with GM's top brass to discuss options. Nobody in a position of authority wanted to pull the plug on the factory. "Detroit was concerned, as we are, but they realize this is a strategic decision, and if we're going to participate in Asian markets, we've got to build in Asia."

The timing could work in Frizzell's favor. The plant was not scheduled to be fully operational until 1999. As Frizzell said, "I anticipate that by the time we come to market, the economy might then be starting to recover. And what better time to come to market with a new product than when a recovery is taking place?"

Source: Paul Blustein, "GM's New Factory in Thailand Rises as Car Sales Fall," *Washington Post*, November 10, 1997, pp. A1, A33.

The emergence of Japan as a global economic power dramatically illustrates the nature of global economic change as a force in business-society relations. Japan was known for its success in steel, electronics, and automobile production in the 1970s and 1980s; so by the 1990s, no business leader anywhere in the world could ignore Japan's emergence as a leading competitor in major sectors of the global economy. Japan also became a large investor in the economies of other nations. For example, Japanese interests doubled their investment in Europe during the late 1980s and grew from 10 percent of foreign-owned business in the United States to more than 20 percent in less than a decade. Japan also became the dominant lender to other Asian economies and invested in industrial projects in the developing nations of Latin America and Africa. In the 1990s, Japan became a primary actor in the world's financial markets.

While Japan continued to grow, some of the world's less developed nations also began to make their economic influence felt. Nations that earlier had occupied only the outer margins of the world economy emerged as strong competitors in the 1990s. South Korea, Taiwan, Singapore, Brazil, Spain, and Mexico became world-class competitors in clothing, footwear, toy, and electronic assembly industries. As they shifted production into basic industries such as steel and other capital-intensive manufacturing industries, even poorer countries with lower wage rates began to produce consumer items such as clothing and footwear.

The new players in the world economy have greatly intensified competition. Their competitive success has disrupted social and economic relations in other countries. The jobs that have gone to people willing to work for low wages in poor nations have sometimes taken away jobs from workers in the wealthier, developed countries. By opening plants in the third world, companies have closed older operations in Europe and North America, creating economic and social distress there. The effects have been dramatic, signaling economic hope for poorer nations but sending a competitive chill through the highly industrialized nations. This new and intense competition from developing countries has helped reshape the economic and social strategies of the advanced industrial nations, as discussed above.

One exceptionally important development has been the opening of societies previously closed to trade and international competition. The opening of the People's Republic of China (PRC) to foreign investment and economic development, for example, stimulated an impressive boom of commercial activity. Billions of dollars of foreign investment have flooded into China to support infrastructure projects such as new roads, power plants, water systems, and investment in industries such as steel, electronics, textiles, and consumer products. With a population of 1.4 billion people, the PRC represents one of the world's largest potential markets for goods and services and an economic colossus as a producer.

> *During the 1990s, for example, China's gross domestic product grew by nearly 10 percent per year, the highest rate of any nation in the world. Its industrial production soared as well. Such success led many nations that once disdained economic trade with the capitalist world to rethink their policies. China's growth has led businesses everywhere to investigate how they too can do business with Chinese entrepreneurs, traders, and businesses.*

Political reorganization and changes have also stimulated major economic changes during the past decade. Western European nations pursued the opening and integration of their economies as a way to establish a vibrant economic base that would create jobs and well-being for more than 300 million people, a population larger than the combined total of the United States, Canada, and Mexico. The member-nations of the European Economic Community (EEC) agreed to create a common market by the end of 1992. Since then, these nations have taken other steps—including creation of a common currency—to expand trade. As the 1990s end, such steps have produced a larger European market and encouraged additional countries to join the renamed European Union (EU).

The remarkable economic, political, and ideological upheavals that occurred in Eastern Europe, beginning with the fall of the Berlin Wall and including the breakup of the former Soviet Union, have also created a mixture of opportunities and threats to business. The opening of Eastern European nations to democracy and trade with the rest of the world provides economic opportunities, but it is also producing social strains as old ways crumble.

The basic lesson to be drawn from these examples is clear: Fundamental social and political change pressures businesses to adjust the way they conduct operations. A firm's economic and financial strategy is vitally affected by political events and changing public attitudes. In these rapidly changing political and social settings, a company's short-term and long-term success may depend greatly on how well its social and economic strategy work together.

Since the end of World War II in 1945, numerous international agreements have been crafted to encourage trade among nations. Much of this effort was coordinated through the General Agreement on Tariffs and Trade (GATT). Many nations have also established trade agreements with other nations with which they are economically interdependent. This drive to open markets and integrate economic activity across national borders in North America started in the late 1980s when the leaders of Canada, Mexico, and the United States began shaping a North American Free Trade Agreement to remove trade and investment restrictions. The agreement, which went into effect on January 1, 1994, will lower trade barriers among the three nations for the next decade.

The reorganization of global markets has not occurred without difficulties. People who think of themselves as citizens of France, Germany, the Netherlands, or any other nation will not quickly give up that sense of cultural identity simply because the European Union exists. Former Communists will not embrace capitalism just because the new political leadership thinks it is a good idea. American workers will remain concerned that high-paying jobs might be exported to Mexico by firms seeking to reduce labor costs. And the businesspeople of South Korea, Indonesia, and Thailand will not quickly forget the pain that they and their fellow citizens endured in 1998 as their economies collapsed under the weight of too much debt and heavy international financial burdens. The world economy may improve by establishing free trade and uniform economic standards and regulations, but the social and political environment will remain quite complex. Firms planning to do business in this challenging environment will need a sophisticated understanding of local customs, social institutions, and political systems. That is another way of saying they will need a sound social strategy at home and abroad.

Force 4: The Changing Role of Government and Public Policy

Beginning in the 1970s, new winds of reform began to blow through many of the world's economic, political, and social institutions. No one knew exactly what had set these new currents in motion. They were not felt with the same strength in all nations, nor in all kinds of institutions in any one nation. But wherever these currents blew, the focal points seemed to be centralized power and authority. Governmental power and, especially, the role of government in society were challenged.

Demands were made to disperse power more widely within many societies and nations. "Power to the people" became a popular rallying cry that captured the essence of this new social force. Leaders discovered that their grip on institutional power was not as secure as it had been in earlier times. The public, less trusting of its leaders, wanted a piece of the action. Believing that too much power had been concentrated at the top of society's major institutions, the public demanded democratic reforms.

The best known of these political changes were deregulation and privatization in the Western world; **glasnost** (openness) and **perestroika** (reform, reconstruction, renewal) in the former Soviet Union; freer markets and a more decentralized economic system in China; and sweeping political upheavals in Eastern Europe. In each of these cases, centralized governmental power was being dispersed and moved out from the center toward the periphery. In many countries, this has been called the *devolution* of governmental power.

What does this global reform movement mean for business? First, and foremost, it creates new business opportunities. But it also poses new business risks. When free markets open up where none existed before, corporations can take advantage of profit opportunities. European, Japanese, and American business firms flocked to China in the early days of its reform movement. But just as quickly, they became more cautious when government authorities showed signs of reinstalling centralized power over all business decisions. When the nations of the former Soviet Union and Eastern European nations relaxed government controls and welcomed economic ties with Western nations, many corporations crossed over into that formerly forbidden territory, seeking profitable opportunities. The business risks were considerable, because these former socialist nations lacked free and open market systems, stable currencies, and competitive traditions.

As Eastern Europe struggled to transform its economic and political institutions, its governments faced formidable problems such as inflation, unemployment, and declining national income. Speaking of this difficult period, a Hungarian political scientist said, "The cold war is over, but this will be a very dangerous peace. . . . Conflicts are growing between nationalities, between rich people and poor, between the government and street protesters, between industrialists and laborers."[13] The view was prophetic: Ethnic, ideological, and economic conflicts have raged in Eastern Europe (e.g., Bosnia, Serbia) since the early 1990s, and the political winds have blown in different, often contradictory directions.

The global movement from centralized governmental authority toward freedom and democracy carries both pluses and minuses for business. Once again, corporations have found themselves facing large measures of uncertainty and risk.

Russia is one of the world's largest and most resource-abundant countries in the world. Since the fall of communism, Russia has suffered political convulsions as Mikhail Gorbachev, Boris Yeltsin, and Vladimir Zhiranovsky have contested for power. This political uncertainty has influenced the way Central

---

[13]"East Europe Offers Investors Big Profits and Big Perils," *The Wall Street Journal*, January 11, 1991, p. A6.

Asia's oil industry has been developing. Chevron Corporation, a U.S. multinational oil company, has invested heavily in Kazhakistan, a former Soviet republic. As the political fortunes of the republics have ebbed and flowed, Chevron's political risk has also grown. Its traditional multinational oil competitors such as Royal Dutch Shell (Netherlands) and Total (France) are trying to acquire drilling rights in the area where Chevron has conducted explorations. Each company has its political friends. New state oil companies from Russia (Gazprom) and Malaysia (Petronas) are working to foreclose U.S. companies. Chevron executives know how bad it can get: In the 1980s, Chevron invested $1 billion in Sudan. But as that nation slid into anarchy, Chevron was forced to abandon its wells, refineries, and pipelines. Although Chevron sees business potential in Kazhakistan and Central Asia, its executives also recognize that political risk may overwhelm the business opportunity.[14]

Such volatile political and ideological forces have become a central part of the world business climate. Corporations and their managers cannot ignore them; to do so could be fatal. Learning how to integrate changing political realities into a corporate business strategy has become a basic requirement for companies and managers. Looking ahead, it seems to loom even more important in the future.

The role of government has also changed in the United States. Deregulation of segments of the economy created change for the airlines, trucking, and communications industries in the 1970s. In the 1980s, presidents Ronald Reagan (1981–89) and George Bush (1989–93) pressed for an approach that would limit the role of the federal government and leave more responsibility with state and local governments to meet public needs. During the 1992 presidential campaign, candidates George Bush, Bill Clinton, and Ross Perot argued sharply different positions on the role government should play in education, environmental protection, and most important, creating a healthy economy. The election of President Clinton did not settle the debate. In 1994, Republicans swept into Congress on a campaign platform that called for downsizing the role of the federal government. Subsequent national elections have not clarified the picture, insofar as Clinton and many of his congressional opponents won reelection. As political pundit Chris Matthews suggested, "perhaps Americans *like* political gridlock."

The role of government and public policy, including regulation and antitrust, and the role of business in politics are discussed in Chapters 8, 9, and 10. The importance of these issues in the modern world was succinctly expressed by Milton Friedman, a Nobel Prize-winning economist who has long urged that government not interfere with free markets:

It is today possible, to a greater extent than at any time in the world's history, for a company to locate anywhere, to use resources from anywhere to produce a product that can be sold anywhere. . . . [The challenge] is to use our influence to make sure governments are not short-sighted and do not short-circuit the process.[15]

---

[14]Sheila N. Heslin, "The New Pipeline Politics," *New York Times*, November 10, 1997, p. A37.

[15]Milton Friedman, quoted in Lindley H. Clark, Jr., "The New Industrial Revolution," *The Wall Street Journal*, November 23, 1993, p. A16.

Force 5: Ecological and Natural Resource Concerns

One of the most important social challenges to business is to strike a balance between industrial production and nature's limits. Industrial production, mining, and farming are bound to produce waste and pollution, along with needed goods and services. Waste and pollution are a price society pays for rising populations, urbanization, and more goods and services. All industrial societies—whether the United States, Japan, Germany, Russia, or South Korea—create a disproportionate (relative to population) share of the world's pollution and waste because these are the unavoidable by-products of a high level of economic activity. The emerging nations of the third world, with their rapid growth rates and limited pollution controls, also contribute to global ecological problems as their economies become more industrialized.

Consumers too are responsible for much solid waste and pollution because they demand, buy, and use pollution-generating products such as automobiles, refrigerators, air conditioners, and computers. The widespread use of product packaging and the proliferation of toxic products such as cleaners, lawn chemicals, batteries, and antifreeze all contribute to global pollution issues.

Ecological impacts extend far beyond national boundaries. Stratospheric ozone depletion potentially threatens health and agriculture on a worldwide basis. The industrial accident at the Chernobyl nuclear power station spread dangerous radiation across several European nations and sent a radiation cloud around the globe. Oil spills have fouled the oceans and beaches of many nations. The cutting and burning of tropical rain forests has the potential to affect weather climates throughout the world.

Environmental protection, involving pollution control, waste minimization, and natural resource conservation, has become a high priority for developing nations as well as the advanced industrialized nations. International agreements have been created to address the most pressing issues, such as ozone depletion, biodiversity, and global warming. But government and industry leaders recognize that this is just the beginning of what must be done to achieve a sustainable balance between economic activity, which requires the use of resources, and global environmental protection, which requires the preservation of resources. Business leaders and managers at every level of business activity from corporate headquarters to the local retail outlet are being challenged by the need to integrate ecological thinking into their decision making. These issues are discussed in Chapters 11 and 12.

Today, companies are learning how to adjust their products, manufacturing processes, purchasing activities, and business strategies to the need for sustainable economic and ecological practices. Although much has already been improved, there is no doubt that reducing harmful ecological effects will continue to be a major social challenge for corporate managers. Pollution and waste cannot be stopped entirely, but their volume can be reduced through improved product designs, better controls, and the recycling of reusable materials. Environmental accidents such as oil spills can be prevented by careful planning, and cleanup efforts can be pursued vigorously with new techniques and technologies. The basic goal is to achieve a livable balance between human needs and nature's limits.[16]

---

[16] Andrew J. Hoffman, *From Heresy to Dogma* (San Francisco: New Lexington Press, 1997); and A. J. Hoffman, ed., *Global Climate Change* (San Francisco: New Lexington Press, 1997).

Force 6: Technology and New Knowledge

Technology is one of the most powerful forces affecting business and society. Improved technology includes machines of all sizes, shapes, and functions; processes that enable business to produce goods at faster speeds, with lower costs, and with less waste; and software that incorporates new forms of learning into formats that direct machines (hardware) to perform functions that would have taken much longer, and been less reliable, if done by other means. Technology involves harnessing human imagination to create new devices and new approaches to the needs, problems, and concerns of a modern society. Indeed, a government study showed that sales by the computing and telecommunications industries grew by 57 percent during the 1990s to more than $866 billion, making those businesses the nation's largest industry, ahead of construction, food products, and automotive manufacturing.[17]

Technology also involves drawing together fields of knowledge that converge, enabling new ways to solve problems or perform tasks. An example of such a convergence technology is biometrics.

Biometrics is a field that integrates biological science and computer science. One application of this new field of knowledge involves identification procedures. Scientists know that no two persons have the same fingerprint. This makes fingerprints a nearly foolproof method of identification. In the past, an individual's fingers were coated with ink, and impressions were made on paper, then compared with impressions made by others. Laboratories such as the Federal Bureau of Investigation (FBI) kept files containing thousands of fingerprints. In time, computers enabled researchers to digitalize fingerprints and reproduce them on computer screens. This enabled searches to occur much faster once fingerprints were on file. Biometrics has now made possible the next step in this evolution of identification science. New scanners enable a person to place his or her finger on an imaging surface and instantaneously receive confirmation that the fingerprint matched that of the owner of an identification card. This technology of identification has been used to speed health-care identification, eligibility for welfare benefits, and credit-card approvals.

Although new technologies have the potential to benefit large portions of the population, they may also negatively affect some people. If biometric scanners are generally adopted, for example, ink-based print systems will be rendered obsolete, costing manufacturers of inkpads and employees of inkpad companies their livelihood. Still, for society as a whole, biometric identification may prove to be a highly efficient and productive use of resources. It is in this way that new technologies put pressure on today's companies to understand and respond to new knowledge and its applications.

Many technologies have broader social impacts as well as competitive effects. As discussed in Chapter 18, new technologies force managers and organizations to examine all of the ethical implications of their use.

---

[17]Steve Lohr, "Information Technology Field Is Rated Largest U.S. Industry," *New York Times*, November 18, 1997, p. D12.

For example, as medical experts learned h(
as kidneys and hearts from one person to
about the criteria that hospitals would fol
what conditions, transplants would occui
donors and the recipients. When is a pe(
be removed before the donor is dead bu
death will soon occur? Is it safe for a
lung, or other organ?

As new technologies become availabl(
come even more ethically complicated. As experiment
possible to regenerate cells that once were thought to be dead, hospit...
struggle to decide whether the tissue of aborted fetuses can be used to treat strokes,
cord injuries, and other health problems once thought to be beyond hope.

Technology is creating what experts call the *knowledge economy*. This is an economy in which new knowledge, in all of its many forms, is reshaping and transforming old industries and businesses, creating new industries and businesses, and ultimately affecting individuals, families, communities, and institutions throughout the world. For these reasons, technology must be understood as one of the major drivers of change in both business and society.

Corporate Strategy for the Twenty-First Century

Business, government, and society are interdependent and their relationship is complex in every nation. General systems theory tells us that all organisms or systems are affected by their host environments; thus, an organization must be appropriately responsive to changes and conditions in its environment to survive and succeed.

This web of interactions between business, government, and society creates a system of stakeholders—groups affected by and influential in corporate decisions and actions. The analysis of these stakeholders—who they are, what power they hold, and the ways in which they interact with one another—helps managers understand the nature of their concerns and needs and how these relationships are changing. If the creation of stakeholder networks is a natural process for organizations, managers must learn how to understand and utilize these relationships. The business of the twenty-first century must have managers who understand the importance of creating business strategies that include these considerations.

The relationship between business and society is also continuously changing. People, organizations, and social issues change; inevitably, new issues will arise and challenge managers to develop new solutions. To be effective, corporate strategy must respond to the biggest and most central questions in the public's mind. People expect businesses to be competitive, to be profitable, and to act responsibly by meeting the reasonable expectations of stakeholders. The corporation of the twenty-first century is certain to be affected by global economic and political trends, powerful new technologies, and a global population of stakeholders who will expect their interests to be integrated into the thinking of the companies from which they buy goods and services, to which they contribute labor and ideas, and to which they extend the hospitality and support of their communities.

of This Chapter

- Business, government, and society form an interactive system because each affects and influences the other and because neither can exist without the others. Economic, political, and cultural life are thoroughly entwined with one another in every nation. Together, they define the uniqueness of a society.

- Every business firm has economic and social involvements and relationships with others in society. Some are intended, some unintended; some are positive, others negative. Those related to the basic mission of the company are its primary involvements; those that flow from those activities but are more indirect are secondary involvements.

- The people, groups, and organizations that interact with the corporation and have an interest in its performance are its stakeholders. Those most closely and directly involved with a business are its *primary* stakeholders; those who are indirectly connected are its *secondary* stakeholders.

- Stakeholders can exercise their economic, political, and other powers in ways that benefit or challenge the organization. Stakeholders may also act independently or create coalitions to influence the company.

- Six key forces are affecting the business-society relationship as companies move into the late 1990s: strategic refocusing and restructuring of businesses; changing ethical expectations and public values; global economic change; a global trend toward rethinking the role of government; ecological and natural resource concerns; and the transformational role of technology.

- To deal effectively with globalization, ecological concerns, and ethical issues, a corporate strategy must take into account the interests, needs, and expectations of all of the company's stakeholders. Companies should have a strategy that combines business goals and broad social interests.

Key Terms and Concepts Used in This Chapter

- Stakeholders
- Primary stakeholders
- Secondary stakeholders
- Interactive model of business and society
- Strategic rethinking
- Reengineering
- Social contract

- New social contract
- Ethical principles
- Business legitimacy
- Global economic change
- Glasnost
- Perestroika
- Environmental protection

Internet Resources

- http://www.businessweek.com   *Business Week*—broad range of business topics
- http://www.economist.com   *The Economist*—strong international coverage
- http://www.fortune.com   *Fortune*—useful profiles of large corporations
- http://www.ethics.org   Ethics Resource Center
- http://www.whitehouse.gov/fsbr/ssbr.html Executive Office of the President of the United States

Discussion Case   Inland National Bank

Amy Miller, manager of community affairs at Inland National Bank (INB), was facing a problem. Inland had recently acquired another local bank, Home Savings Bank. INB's senior management was in the process of reorganizing the company's retail banking operations, and some branches were sure to be consolidated. Located in a medium-sized city in the midwestern United States, Inland National Bank had a good reputation for community involvement and solid financial performance. The decision to reorganize the bank's branches made economic sense, but Amy was troubled by how it would affect a number of local neighborhoods. She was especially concerned about two branches in her district.

Rockdale Branch

This was a small Home Savings branch. The problem here was obvious: The neighborhood was old and on the decline. Home Savings had not modernized the facility for many years, and a major upgrade was essential to improve the rundown facility. Miller thought the cost could be as much as $500,000. It was unclear whether the financial potential of the neighborhood warranted such an investment. Home Savings was the last bank to have a Rockdale branch; all of the other banks had closed their branch offices at least five years ago. If the local office was closed, Rockdale customers could use INB's branch in Culver Heights, about a 10-minute auto or bus ride from Rockdale. The Culver Heights branch was conveniently located on a local bus route.

North Madison Branch

Miller was also concerned about a branch office located in North Madison, a neighborhood adjacent to Rockdale. This was a poor neighborhood, with an average income about $2,000 per household below that of any other neighborhood in the city. Many of North Madison's residents were on welfare and public assistance. Home Savings Bank also had a branch office in North Madison's main commercial main district. INB had not offered local branch banking here in more than a decade. One of INB's senior executives had talked about closing the branch, replacing it with four automatic teller machines conveniently located in the North Madison shopping district. The move would eliminate a total of 20 jobs at the branch. Only a few of these employees were likely to find other jobs within the bank. Miller understood that about half of the employees in the two branches lived in or near North Madison.

Other Factors

Rockdale residents had organized a group of picketers in front of the Home Savings branch a few days after the merger announcement was made. A local television station sent a crew to cover the story. One local resident who was interviewed said, "INB just hates old people, and old people is all that lives in Rockdale! They care more about money than people."

INB had also received angry telephone calls from several city officials. Sheila Thomas, an elected member of the city council whose district included both the Rockdale and North Madison neighborhoods, was especially vocal about the bank's plan. She questioned whether the bank was acting in good faith toward all of the city's residents. During a television interview she said, "It's wrong for this bank to cut the heart out of neighborhoods by replacing people with ATMs." Amy Miller knew and respected Sheila Thomas, but also recognized the political visibility this issue was providing an ambitious elected official.

Inland National Bank operated under the regulatory supervision of several federal and state banking agencies. The bank had a good record with these authorities, but the branch reorganization plan clouded the picture. Under the federal Community Reinvestment Act, INB had to disclose where its deposits came from and where they were being invested. This was to help ensure that money was being fairly reinvested in communities where depositors lived and worked. The law gave banking officials some leverage to force banks to pay attention to local community needs.

The Rockdale protest and phone calls from North Madison residents and merchants had gotten the attention of state banking officials who needed to approve INB's branch closings. The state's banking commissioner had given a number of speeches urging banks to invest "at home," and "in people, as well as technology." The traditional test for banking officials was whether the financial solvency of the bank would be improved or harmed by the proposed action. These communities were raising different issues.

The Decision

At a recent meeting with INB's president and senior management committee, Miller learned that the state banking officials had told INB to submit a plan that responded to the issues raised by the residents of Rockdale and North Madison. She was named to a team that had to recommend a course of action to INB's president by the end of the week.

The team's leader had called a meeting for this afternoon. He had suggested that one way for INB to get out of this problem was to close just one of the branches. Miller had been asked to bring her analysis of Rockdale and North Madison to the meeting.

Discussion Questions

1. Who are the stakeholders in this case? Which are primary, and which are secondary? What influence do they have? How are they related to each other? Draw a diagram of the stakeholder relationships to INB.
2. If INB decides to close the Rockdale and North Madison branches, how will the business-government-society relationship come into play? How might the issue develop? What considerations must be weighed by INB's management?
3. What should Amy Miller recommend to her team? Are there steps that can be taken to soften the impact of the closings? Should she recommend against closing the branches?
4. Compare the business and social considerations in the Rockdale and North Madison communities. Which branch seems to be more important to the community? Are there any meaningful differences between the two situations?
5. Identify the key terms and concepts in this chapter that apply to this discussion case.

2

Business and Public Issues

Businesses face a large number of public and social issues. Each business must deal with a unique set of relationships and issues that are tied to its activities. Senior executives often spend large amounts of time managing relationships with their organization's stakeholders. Many companies also designate specific managers to the job of public affairs management; others believe that managing public and social issues effectively is a job that all managers must perform.

This chapter focuses on these key questions and objectives:

- Why do the expectations of stakeholders matter to organizations and managers?
- What is the life cycle through which public issues evolve?
- What is the mission and purpose of a company's public affairs function?
- What strategies can an organization use to cope with specific public issues?
- What activities make up an issues management system?
- What are the elements of effective crisis management?
- What must a company do to strategically manage its stakeholder relations?

T he Ford Motor Company is one of the world's largest and most successful automobile manufacturers. Building and selling cars, trucks, and other motorized vehicles of all sizes throughout the world, the company has earned a reputation as a high-quality manufacturer. Still, there are times when Ford vehicles fail to meet customer expectations. Such is the case in what some disgruntled Ford customers call the case of the Flaming Fords.[1]

Ford Motor Company has long manufactured a range of automobiles and light trucks. The popularity of these vehicles has led to many millions being sold in the North American market. Between 1988 and 1993, for example, Ford sold more than 26 million vehicles in North America. That five-year period is important for other reasons as well.

The problem that angered Ford customers involved an ignition system that appears to have experienced an internal short circuit, thereby overheating and creating smoke and fire in the steering column of the vehicle. By 1993, Ford received reports of at least 300 such fires among Canadian owners and more than 800 from owners in the United States. In many of these cases, the entire vehicle had been engulfed and the driver injured.

Lawyers representing victims of these fires sued Ford and charged that the company knew, or should have known, about risks involved with the ignition system. Ford denied that the ignition system was defective and defended its overall safety. To advance their case, lawyers for some of the victims tried to locate other Ford owners who have experienced such problems in the hope of joining forces in a class action lawsuit against Ford. To identify and inform prospective members of the class (Ford owners), the lawyers created a Web site entitled "Association of Flaming Ford Owners." One page on the site showed a burnt out truck and asked, "Are you one of the 26 million owners of a Ford manufactured vehicle that contains an ignition switch that starts fires?" The reader was prompted to click onto the model and year of Ford vehicle owned for information in the database.

The Web site was a boon to Ford owners. They have been able to access current information about the ignition system, pending lawsuits, and new plaintiffs. According to one attorney involved in the litigation, the Web site made it possible for customers to proceed much faster and with more complete information than in the past. In this respect, Flaming Fords story shows how a conflict between a manufacturer and some of its customers can be transformed into a larger, faster-developing, and more potent public issue.

Each year, hundreds of millions of dollars of new products and services are sold through the Internet. Digital commerce is a powerful commercial force. Indeed, in the late 1990s, Ford Motor Company is promoting and selling vehicles through Web-based marketing strategies. Technology such as the World Wide Web is changing the way both commerce and social issues must be managed. But customers and citizens are also using the Internet to learn about public issues and, as in the case of the Flaming Fords, to organize large numbers of other people into a powerful force for action. The Internet, then, is a tool for promoting commerce and for expanding public awareness of problems and issues involving products, business practices, and social impacts. In terms of the forces discussed in Chapter 1, the case of the Flaming Fords underscores how technology is forcing ethics and business strategy closer together. For business today, there is no hiding from a world of stakeholders who are capable of closely observing every decision and every mistake a company makes.

---

[1]See http://www.flamingfords.com/flaming1.cgi.

Why Public Issues Matter

As the case of the Flaming Fords illustrates, companies cannot afford to ignore their stakeholders. Customers, suppliers, and competitors are capable of quickly organizing forces to pressure a company's managers. Of course, not every claim is legitimate, and not every stakeholder has a request that is reasonable. But managers who ignore the concerns of their company's stakeholders do so at their peril and may place the company at risk.

In the modern business environment, no organization can long ignore legitimate stakeholders whose lives are entwined with the activities of the business. First, many stakeholders (e.g., owners, employees, suppliers) have a legitimate connection to the business, often sacrificing something of value for the success of the enterprise. Second, to ignore stakeholders is to risk the kind of campaign that Ford faced with the Flaming Fords. For this reason, many organizations have created systematic ways of responding to stakeholder issues as they arise and have developed more strategic, longer-term business approaches to their key stakeholder relationships.

Emergence of Public Issues

One reason companies are exploring new ways to build positive relationships with stakeholders is that other, more adversarial approaches have often failed. The first sign of a problem is often a complaint, objection, or protest from a stakeholder or stakeholder group whose expectations are not being met.

For example, a group of residents may object to the odor or smoke from a local plant. Citizens may protest the use of monkeys or mice for scientific research at a local university. Employees may claim that they became ill after eating food prepared in a company's cafeteria or breathing fumes from chemicals used in a manufacturing process. In each case, the complaint serves as an early warning of a problem that the company's management should examine more closely.

The Performance-Expectations Gap

In each of the instances described above, a gap has developed between the expectations of the stakeholder (person or group) and the actual performance of the corporation (see Figure 2–1). Stakeholder expectations are a mixture of the opinions, attitudes, and beliefs

Figure 2–1

The performance-expectations gap: A measure of stakeholder wants versus company actions and results.

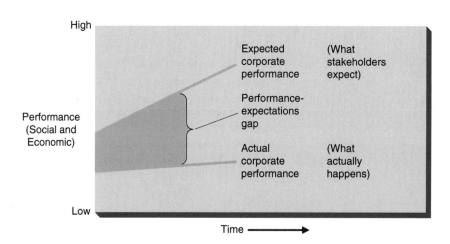

of people about what constitutes reasonable business behavior. The residents do not believe that air emissions constitute reasonable behavior; some people who care about animals do not believe it is morally responsible to inflict pain on animals in the name of scientific research; employees who get sick from food or choke on fumes do not believe it is ethically responsible for a company to endanger their health in this way. The following example illustrates how one company has read the signs of stakeholder sentiment and decided to act before the **performance-expectations gap** grew any wider.[2]

> *A few days before Thanksgiving in 1997, the Mattel Toy Co. joined a number of other retailers in adopting a labor code of conduct. The company, which does a huge portion of its annual sales during the Christmas season, had been under pressure from consumers and activist organizations to ensure that the workers who manufacture these toys in countries such as India, Malaysia, and China were not being exploited by suppliers who have been shown to pay slave wages and operate in dangerous conditions. In announcing a code of conduct for its suppliers, Mattel pledged to monitor the conditions in its supplier's plants and halt contracts if they violated the company's wage and safety standards.*

Managers and organizations have a responsibility to identify the beliefs and expectations of their stakeholders as early as possible. Failure to understand their concerns, and to respond appropriately, will permit the performance-expectations gap to grow larger. This gap shows the magnitude of the difference between what the stakeholder expects and the firm's actual performance. The larger the gap, the greater the risk of stakeholder backlash.

The Public Issue Life Cycle

Effective management of stakeholder concerns begins with the understanding that public issues often develop in predictable ways. In other words, it is possible for managers to anticipate how pressures will build around an issue and possibly turn it into a high profile problem that attracts the attention of media and political figures.

A **public issue** exists when there is a gap between the *stakeholder expectations* of what an institution should do and the *actual performance* of those businesses, government agencies, or nonprofit organizations. Ford executives could have anticipated how the Flaming Ford members would act and responded to problems with the defective ignition issue when they were first recognized. One way companies can do so is to study the **public issue life cycle,** shown in Figure 2–2. This model illustrates the basic phases through which a public issue passes as it matures.

Phases of the Public Issue Life Cycle

Social concerns generally evolve through a series of phases that, because of their natural evolution, can be thought of as a life cycle. By recognizing the pattern through which issues evolve and spotting the early warning signs, managers can anticipate problems and work to resolve them before they reach crisis proportions. As shown in Figure 2–2, the public issue life cycle contains four phases: the changing of stakeholder expectations; po-

---

[2]"Mattel Adopts Standards," *New York Times*, November 20, 1997, p. D5; and CNBC, "Nightly Business Report," November 20, 1997, interview with Prakash Sethi, chairman of Mattel's commission.

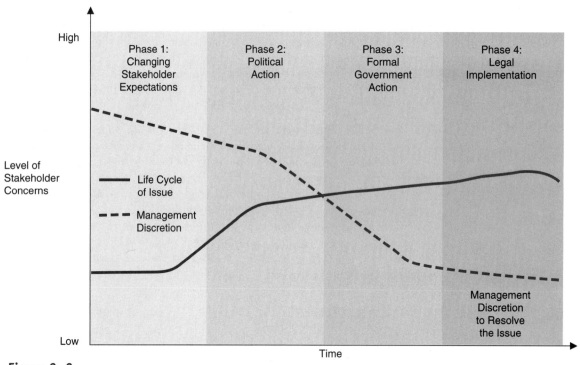

Figure 2–2

The Public issue life cycle.

litical action; formal government action; and legal implementation. Each phase is discussed below.

Phase 1: Changing stakeholder expectations

Public issues develop as stakeholder expectations of how business or government should behave are not met. This failure can take many forms, ranging from small groups of residents objecting to a local manufacturer's fouling of the air, to the concern of animal lovers for the welfare of monkeys being used in scientific research in a laboratory, to the anger of voters at officials who raise taxes. As discussed above, once a gap develops, the seeds of a public issue have been sown.

> *Few industries have faced as large a legitimacy gap in the 1990s as the American tobacco industry. The industry has battled an increasingly pervasive antismoking climate. For decades, smoking was considered to be glamorous and sophisticated. Advertisements during the 1940s featured movie stars dressed in military uniforms, which gave the impression that smoking was not only glamorous but patriotic. The perception of smokers and smoking is very different today. Smoking has become an unacceptable social behavior. Although the industry has argued that smokers are being unfairly turned into social pariahs, health experts argue that the public has a right to live free from smoke and its negative health effects. Cities, states, and even the federal government have taken steps to ensure that nonsmokers were free of unwanted smoke. In 1993, for example, antismoking advocates proposed legislation (the Smoke-Free*

Environment Act) in both houses of Congress to prohibit smoking in any build-
ing (other than private homes) that is regularly used by 10 or more workers a
week.[3] *And in 1998, California started implementing a law that banned smok-*
ing in bars and nightclubs.

Cigarette manufacturers, such as Philip Morris and R. J. Reynolds, have lived with
the health effects issue for many years. As criticism mounted, the companies identified
segments of the population that oppose and those that support smoking restrictions. Although nonsmokers want restrictions, the companies have effectively argued that smokers have rights too. By campaigning heavily on this theme, the companies have tried to
frame the debate in terms of nonsmokers' reasonable expectations, balancing the rights of
smokers and nonsmokers and finding ways to create accommodation.

What does it take to put a problem on the agenda for action by government? The
agenda of public issues on which officials are asked to act is enormous, and not all public issues warrant action by government. Of the thousands of issues to which government
is asked to respond each year, most fail to get needed support.

Strong and effective leadership is always needed to capture enough public attention
to lead a reform movement. The American civil rights movement, for example, had charismatic leadership in Dr. Martin Luther King, Jr., during the 1960s. Dr. King, a brilliant
public speaker whose speeches attracted large audiences and media coverage, helped to
build powerful support for the expansion of equal opportunity to citizens of all races. Other
movements have had leaders with very different personalities. Ralph Nader's fight for automobile safety won public support with detailed technical analyses of dangerous products, including his famous book, *Unsafe at Any Speed*,[4] Gloria Steinem and Betty Friedan
were effective advocates for women's rights. Cesar Chavez, a quiet and determined leader,
drew public attention to the plight of farm workers through hunger strikes and product
boycotts. Each of these leaders used his or her personality and knowledge to keep issues
in front of the public and its political leaders. There are times when a reform movement's
leadership comes from within the political system itself. In the mid-1990s, Congressman
Newt Gingrich led a political crusade to reduce the power of the federal government, and
more recently, U.S. Senator John McCain led a campaign to change the rules surrounding political campaign financing.

Dramatic events can also prompt government to act. Environmental crises such as
the nuclear power plant accident at Three Mile Island, the tragedy at Union Carbide's
chemical plant in Bhopal, India, or the discovery of chemical dangers in places such as
Love Canal (Niagara Falls, New York) or Times Beach, Missouri, all served to generate
public pressure on government to strengthen environmental protection laws (see Chapters
11 and 12).

Interest groups may signal the emergence of an issue by advocating government action to protect members. Managers must understand what others are asking government
to do and be prepared to ask government to act on behalf of their business. International

---

[3]Philip Morris and R. J. Reynolds developed advertising campaigns using the accommodation theme. In one
RJR-sponsored advertisement, three picture captions read, respectively, "The Berlin Wall Crumbles," "Russia
Approves New Constitution," and "Democracy's Victory in South Africa." The fourth caption provided a contrast: "Nationwide, Reins on U.S. Smokers' Freedom Tightens." The title to the ad read: "Where Exactly Is
the Land of the Free?" See *New York Times*, October 25, 1994, p. A17. For a discussion of cigarette companies' business strategies see, Richard McGowan, *Business, Politics, and Cigarettes* (Westport, CT:
Praeger/Quorum Books, 1995).
[4]Ralph Nader, *Unsafe at Any Speed* (New York: Grossman, 1965).

trade conflicts, for example, prompted American companies to ask the federal government to challenge the unfair trade practices of foreign competitors.

> *U.S. auto manufacturers sought the assistance of the federal government in getting Japan to allow more U.S. vehicles to be sold in that country. The unwillingness of Japan to open its domestic market to the sale of more General Motors, Ford, and Chrysler automobiles contrasted sharply with the U.S. market, where Japanese auto companies have established major market positions with their Toyota, Nissan, and Honda vehicles. U.S. firms claimed Japanese governmental policy was behind the closed market. Hence, only the U.S. government could move Japan to change.*

Phase 2: Political action

It may take months or even years for a concerned group of stakeholders to build a base of support sufficient to challenge a corporation. If an issue persists, however, the group may organize formally and campaign for its point of view through pamphlets, newsletters, Web pages, and other forms of print and electronic communication. They may attract the attention of the media, which will result in newspaper, television, or radio coverage. This moves the issue from one of citizen concern to one of political importance.

> *The political drive against passive smoking took off when the Civil Aeronautics Board ruled that smokers had to be separated from nonsmokers on airline flights. Political developments included the formation of various antismoking groups, including Group Against Smoking Pollution (GASP). GASP received calls from people complaining of illness caused by passive smoke—smoke from other people's cigarettes. They assisted companies that wished to establish smoking restrictions. Antismoking activists attribute corporate willingness to set up such policies to dozens of legal cases in which nonsmokers have sued companies for failing to protect them from passive smoke. The Environmental Protection Agency issued statistics that showed passive smoke kills thousands of people each year, and courts increasingly sided with nonsmokers in passive smoking lawsuits. In 1997, for example, 60,000 airline attendants sued tobacco companies to recover damages for injuries from passive smoke. Trial of the case began, but it ended when the companies negotiated a settlement with the airline attendants. The attendants claimed victory. Governments have also sued tobacco companies for the costs of smoking-related disease. Florida, for example, was the first state to sue tobacco product manufacturers to recover the costs of treating the tobacco-related illnesses of Florida Medicaid patients. Other states followed and the financial risk of such lawsuits led the industry to negotiate with states' attorneys general. (See "The Tobacco Deal" case study at the end of the book.)*

Politicians are interested in citizens' concerns and often are anxious to advocate action on their behalf. The government officials become new stakeholders with different types of power to use in closing the gap between public expectations and business performance. The tobacco lobby once had the support of a powerful coalition of elected representatives and senators in Washington. But as antismoking pressures have grown, more elected officials and political candidates have spoken in favor of antismoking laws. Some have also become outspoken critics of the tobacco lobby. The involvement of political actors creates more stakeholders and, hence, makes the issue more complex for the company and its managers.

Phase 3: Formal government action

As more people are drawn into a political conflict, ideas may emerge about how to use laws or regulations to solve the problem. When legislative proposals or draft regulations emerge, the public issue moves to a new level of action.

Much legislative action has been taken in favor of antismoking activists during the past decade. Antismoking legislation has been enacted nationally and in many states and cities. The federal government has required that health warnings on cigarette labels be in larger print and that messages be rotated quarterly to provide more effective warnings. Many communities set limits on the areas in restaurants that can be used by smokers, and nonsmokers in the workplace can legally declare their immediate work area a no-smoking zone. Some cities have even outlawed smoking entirely in office buildings, restaurants, and public buildings.

Companies involved in legislative actions are usually represented by lawyers, lobbyists, and professional political consultants. Top management may be called to testify before government committees or regulatory agencies; corporate lawyers and lobbyists decide what proposals are best and worst for the company, and they make efforts to slow or alter legislative proposals that work against the company's interests.

Tobacco companies have hired dozens of lobbyists, lawyers, and political advisers to fight antismoking efforts. In 1997, it was estimated that the tobacco industry was spending $650 million dollars per year in legal and lobbying fees. Individually, and through the Tobacco Institute, an industry association, they have challenged scientific findings and worked to defeat antismoking proposals. Two powerful counterarguments have been used: first, that 50 million U.S. smokers are citizens who also have rights, including the personal freedom to smoke; and second, that taxes on tobacco products are an important source of revenue for cities and states, accounting for many millions of dollars. Legislators who might vote for an antismoking law are sometimes stopped by fears of what it will mean for government to lose tobacco tax revenue or to have angry smokers campaigning against them in the next election.

Phase 4: Legal implementation

Making a public policy decision does not mean that the policy will be carried out automatically. The validity of new laws and regulations is often challenged through law suits. Once the legal issues are settled, however, the company must comply with the law.

Stakeholder interest in an issue tends to plateau or even decline as a new law or regulation is implemented. New laws often spark lawsuits to test the interpretation and limits of the statute. Once the test cases are over, affected parties will normally abide by the law and compliance will reduce public interest in the issue. If the law is violated or ignored, however, the issue may reemerge, as a new gap develops between stakeholder expectations and the corporation's actual performance.

Business still has a chance to influence how government policy is implemented at this stage of the process. A company may negotiate with a regulatory agency for extending compliance deadlines, as steel companies have done regarding pollution controls and auto manufacturers have done in introducing air bags and other safety devices. Legal steps can also be taken by appealing to a court to review the law or regulation's constitutionality. Or an industry may play off one branch of government against another. For example, presidential decisions can sometimes be overridden by congressional votes.[5]

Continuing Issues

Debates about some public issues may continue long after the implementation of policy. Advocacy groups may keep the issue alive, knowing that new government officials may be receptive to changing the law or interpreting it differently. Groups opposed to a policy may work to document its negative effects, whereas supporters work to document the positive effects. Government officials may try to find out whether the benefits have been worth more than the costs and whether the policy goals could have been achieved in other, more efficient or less expensive ways.

Public issues often overlap and interweave with one another, creating a complex web of advocacy groups, coalitions, government policies, programs, laws, regulations, court orders, and political maneuvers. Something is always happening in each stage, often involving issues of concern to the company and its management. Thus, the business, or any other interest group, must anticipate and respond to issues in a timely way. That is the essence of good management.

The Public Affairs Function

The pressures on business firms that arise from public issues, plus the increasingly complex relationships organizations have with stakeholders, have led many companies to create specialized staff departments to manage external affairs. The emergence of the corporate public affairs function has been a major innovation in U.S. management in the past two decades, especially as the number of stakeholder issues has grown and issues have become more complex and important to business.[6]

Public affairs management refers to the active management of a company's external relations, especially its relations with external stakeholders such as government, regulatory agencies, and communities. Other names that are sometimes used to describe the function are *external affairs* or *corporate relations*. Some companies have also created separate departments for *community relations, government relations,* and *media relations.* The creation of public affairs units appears to be a global trend as well, with many companies in Canada, Australia, and Europe developing sophisticated public affairs operations.[7]

---

[5]Hedrick Smith, *The Power Game: How It Works* (New York: Random House, 1988); and Haynes Johnson and David S. Broder, *The System: The American Ways of Politics at the Breaking Point* (Boston, MA: Little, Brown, 1996).

[6]The data for this discussion are reported in James E. Post and Jennifer J. Griffin, *The State of Corporate Public Affairs* (Washington, D.C.: Foundation for Public Affairs, 1997). These data are also discussed in James E. Post and Jennifer J. Griffin, "Corporate Reputation and External Affairs Management," *Corporate Reputation Review* 1 (1997), pp. 165–71.

[7]The survey of Australian companies can be found in James E. Post and Australian Centre for Corporate Public Affairs, "Australian Public Affairs Practice: Results of the 1992 National Public Affairs Survey," in J.E. Post, ed., *Research in Corporate Social Performance and Policy*, vol. 14 (Greenwich, CT: JAI Press, 1993), pp. 93–103.

Although many names are used to describe the function, there is broad agreement among companies as to what activities have to be managed if an organization is to effectively address its external stakeholders. Figure 2–3 shows the profile of activities performed by public affairs units in more than 250 large and medium-sized companies in the United States.

These activities may seem quite diverse, but they are linked by a company's need to relate to its many stakeholders. Notice how many of the activities refer to a named stakeholder group (e.g., federal, state, and local government relations; community relations; media relations; employee communications; and investor relations). Others refer to activities that are clearly connected to one stakeholder or more (e.g., political action committees, grassroots programs, environmental affairs).

Organizations typically seek three distinct types of contribution from their public affairs operations. As one group of scholars has written,

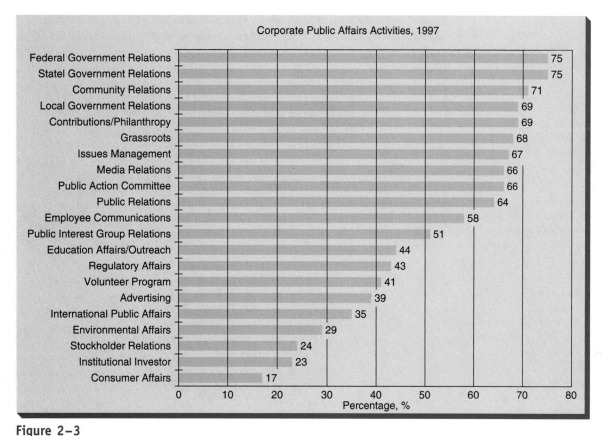

Figure 2–3

Public affairs activities in a sample of U.S. corporations, 1997.

Source: James E. Post and Jennifer J. Griffin, *The State of Corporate Public Affairs: Final Report* (Washington, DC: Foundation for Public Affairs, 1997). Used with permission.

[T]he essential role of public affairs units appears to be that of a window out of the corporation through which management can perceive, monitor, and understand external change, and simultaneously, a window in through which society can influence corporate policy and practice. This boundary spanning role primarily involves the flow of information to and from the organization. In many firms it also involves the flow of financial resources in the form of political contributions to various stakeholder groups in society.[8]

As shown in Figure 2–4, three critical elements help define the responsibility of public affairs in relating to stakeholder issues and concerns. These include social and political intelligence, internal communication, and external action programs. Each is discussed below.

- *Social and political intelligence.* Public affairs is responsible for collecting, analyzing, and preparing social and political intelligence for other managers. Issues are identified, trends forecasted, and activists in the external environment are studied. If there is no public affairs unit or staff, the organization must develop alternative ways to gather such information.

- *Internal communication.* Public affairs must communicate what it learns to other managers throughout the company. Public affairs units typically produce daily

Figure 2–4

Three functions of public affairs management.

The "value added" that public affairs delivers to an organization consists of three parts:

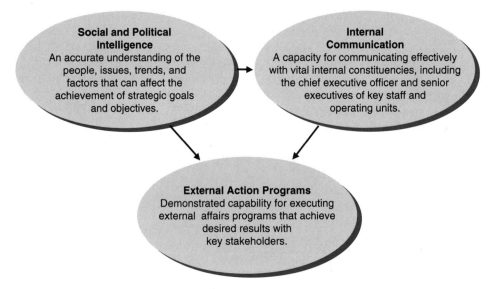

[8]Boston University Public Affairs Research Group, *Public Affairs Offices and Their Functions: A Summary of Survey Results* (Boston, MA: Boston University School of Management, 1981), p. 1.

reports for the CEO and regular reports for the board of directors and senior executives. Special reports are frequently prepared for strategic planners, heads of business units, and operating managers. Many public issues require that the interests and ideas of managers in many different parts of the organization be coordinated. This coordination is vital to the development of sound positions on complex issues.

- *External action programs.* Public affairs is responsible for developing and executing action programs that target key external stakeholders. Thus, a public affairs department will often have a media contacts program for building regular interaction with the press; a local community affairs program for strengthening contacts with the local community; and state and federal government lobbying operations that ensure the company's voice will be heard by legislators or other government officials.

Many companies have drafted a public affairs mission statement to define that function's purpose and focus. Most companies have appointed a senior manager or executive to lead the public affairs department, providing a direct voice and perspective on the company's major strategy and policy decisions. The size of the department and the support staff vary widely across companies. Many companies assign employees from other parts of the business to work on public affairs issues and to help plan, coordinate, and execute public affairs activities. In this way, the formulation and implementation of the policies and programs developed by a company's public affairs unit are closely linked to the primary business activities of the firm. The organization chart for the public affairs organization of a modern global corporation is illustrated in Figure 2–5.

Figure 2–5

Public affairs organization for a global corporation.

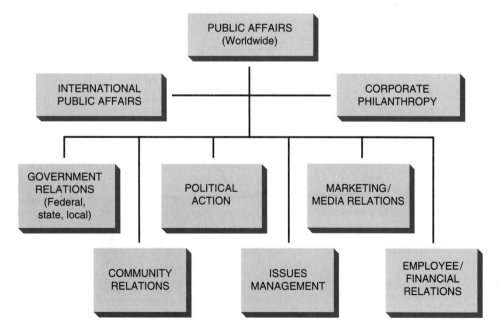

Managing Issues

The Process

Issues management is a structured and systematic method through which companies respond to those public issues that are of greatest importance to the business. Companies rarely have full control of a public issue because of the many factors involved. But it is possible for an organization to create a management system that monitors issues as they emerge and involves managers in action to minimize the negative effects of a public issue or to maximize the positive effects to the organization's advantage. One of the foremost practitioners of systematic issues management is the Dow Chemical Company.

> *According to its executives, Dow Chemical created an issues management system to provide an early warning/early response capability so that a public issue's positive potential can be encouraged and enhanced and its negative potential can be discouraged or inhibited. "The objective is to identify issues in the early stages of development before options are narrowed and liabilities expanded. The difference between issues management and crisis management is timing."[9]*

Managers have less influence on a public issue as it evolves. That is another way of saying that the sooner a company can become involved in managing an issue, the more likely it can shape an outcome that is acceptable to the organization and others. The issues management process is a basic tool used to achieve this objective. Figure 2–6 illustrates the components of a typical issues management system.

Figure 2–6

The issues management process.

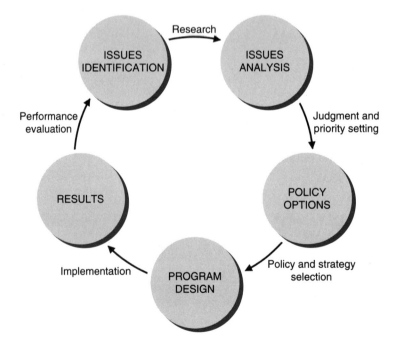

---

[9]Tony Jacques, Public Affairs Manager, Dow Chemical (Australia) Limited. Presentation at Public Affairs Institute, Melbourne, Australia, July 1994.

Issues identification

This involves the active scanning of newspapers, other media, experts' views, and community concerns to identify issues of concern to the public. Because there are many ways to spot emerging issues, managers must decide how best to focus their efforts. Companies often use electronic databases, including the Internet, to track ideas, themes, and issues that may be relevant to their public policy interests.

Issues analysis

Once identified, the facts and implications of the issue must be analyzed. For example, an analysis of the dioxin issue would show that there is much discussion among scientists as to the chemical process of dioxin exposure and much debate as to whether, or how, dioxin contamination can be cleaned up. Similarly, tobacco companies have invested in having researchers examine every study that claims a link between passive smoking and health effects. Issue analysis is guided by management's need to answer two basic questions: (1) What impact can this issue have on our business? and (2) What is the probability that this issue will evolve into later stages of the public issue life cycle?

Policy options

An issue's impact and probability of occurrence tell managers how significant the issue is for the company; but they do not tell management what to do. Developing policy options involves creating choices. It requires complex judgments that incorporate ethical considerations, the company's reputation and good name, and other nonquantifiable factors. Management may decide to change internal practices, operating procedures, or even the product itself. Companies in the pulp and paper industry, for example, have invested in developing new bleaching technologies to eliminate chlorine from their manufacturing processes.[10] Management may also focus on changing the views of officials, the public, or the media. Doing nothing may also be an option if an issue is not ripe for immediate action. Research organizations, such as think tanks, can be useful sources of ideas about alternative policy options. These groups issue papers on many public policy topics, including environmental practices, taxation, minimum wages, and regulation.[11]

Program design

Once the policy option has been chosen, the company must design and implement an appropriate program. For example, tobacco companies made a policy choice to fight antismoking proposals in every city, state, and political district in which such proposals are made. Their program was designed to ensure that no antismoking law is created without efforts by the industry to shape, influence, or kill the proposal. This "fight on every front" policy requires a very expensive program, but it has been an integral part of the tobacco companies' strategy for years.

Early issues identification enables a company to build political capital before it is needed. Often, a company creates goodwill by helping other organizations, which, in time, can lead those organizations into becoming the company's allies.

---

[10]See Chapters 11 and 12 for additional examples.

[11]David Ricci, *The Transformation of American Politics: The New Washington and the Rise of Think Tanks* (New Haven, CT: Yale University Press, 1993).

For many years, Philip Morris has been a patron of the arts. Millions of its dollars have supported museums, art galleries, and performing arts organizations across the nation. Philip Morris, which has its corporate headquarters in New York, faced the prospect of a complete ban on cigarettes in restaurants and other public places under an ordinance proposed by the New York City Council. Philip Morris executives telephoned arts institutions that had benefited from the company grants and asked them to put in a good word with the city council. The company said it would have to move away from New York if such a ban were passed, with inevitable loss of support for the arts organizations. The arts groups were asked to tell the city council how much that would mean to their organizations.[12]

Results

Once a company has tried an issues management program, it must study the results and make adjustments if necessary. Because political issues may take considerable time to evolve, it is important that the manager entrusted with a particular issue regularly update senior managers as to the actions and effectiveness of other stakeholders. The company may reposition or even rethink its approach to the issue.

Managing a Single Issue

Traditionally, public issues are managed by the company's public affairs or government relations staff. A new trend is for responsibility of managing an issue to be placed in the hands of managers from the area of the business most affected by the problem. For example, an issue involving tax rates or depreciation schedules would be assigned to an issues manager from the company's tax department; an issue involving local protests of truck traffic at a plant in Tulsa, Oklahoma, would properly be assigned to the plant manager of the Tulsa facility. TRW, a global manufacturer of defense and industrial products, pioneered the management of issues by operating managers when it created its "quarterback system," in which one manager coordinates the efforts of a team of people from across the company.

When an issue involves several areas of a company's business, an *issues management team* may be created to deal with the issue. Building on the quarterback concept, these teams are led by a manager from the area most directly affected by the problem. She or he will "own" the issue and be responsible for ensuring that the company is acting appropriately to manage the problem. Experts from other areas within the company will be included in the team as needed. Through the use of electronic mail and other technologies, teams can be organized from personnel at different locations.

For example, Dow Chemical created a global issues management team in the 1990s to deal with public issues surrounding chlorine. As one of the world's largest producers of chlorine, Dow had a very large stake in proposals to ban or regulate the use of chlorine, a widely used chemical in modern manufacturing. Members of the global issues management team were drawn from the United States, Europe, and Asia-Pacific and included scientists, plant man-

---

[12]"Hooked on Tobacco Sponsorships," *New York Times,* January 13, 1998, p. A22; for more background, see Maureen Dowd, "Philip Morris Calls in I.O.U.'s in the Arts," *New York Times,* October 5, 1994, pp. A1, C4.

agers, and managers from Dow's manufacturing businesses that would be affected by any changes in the availability of chlorine. The global issues management team analyzed scientific studies of chlorine, followed government actions across the world, coordinated research into various aspects of the problem, and worked with the company's lobbyists and government relations staff to ensure Dow spoke with one voice when talking about chlorine.

Issues management teams usually exist only as long as the issue is a high priority for the company. This mirrors the modern management trend toward using task forces and other temporary team assignments to manage issues in companies. Rather than create large staffs and costly bureaucracies, companies have learned that flexibility is the key to managing public issues as well as other aspects of the business.

Managing Multiple Issues

Companies facing many public issues need to set priorities about which ones will receive the most attention. Many companies use an *issues priority matrix* such as that shown in Figure 2–7. The number of issues that a company can actively work on is limited by resources. If resources are limited, only high-priority issues (those with the greatest impact on the firm and highest chance of occurring) will be assigned for managers to work on; the company may use trade associations or consultants to follow less important issues.

Crisis Management

Crisis management is the process companies use to respond to short-term and immediate shocks, such as accidents, disasters, catastrophes, and injuries. It is not easy to generalize about how to manage in a crisis. As one crisis management

Figure 2–7

The issues priority matrix.

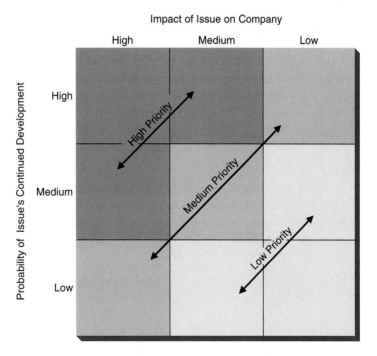

adviser has written, "It is true that every corporate crisis is unique; that is to say, the underlying circumstances are unique, the individuals who are involved are unique to that company or to that organization, the facts, the timing and anything else going on in the marketplace is unique. Therefore, every situation has to be managed on its own terms."[13] There are, however, certain characteristics that emerge time and again. (See Exhibit 2A)

What Is a Crisis?

According to the consultant quoted above, four characteristics define a crisis.

1. *Surprise.* Surprise is the single-most defining characteristic of a crisis. The organization is not ready for the event, it happens without warning, and managers are left trying to react to events beyond their control. "Expect the unexpected," said one experienced observer of organizational crises.

2. *Lack of information.* Crises often put managers in the position of needing to act, but having to do so without reliable information. Today, most managers operate in an information-rich environment. But when a crisis strikes, managers may be forced to act quickly without full and complete information. When TWA Flight 800 crashed on takeoff over the Long Island Sound, for example, TWA executives and employees were caught without vital information about the aircraft and its passengers. Without an accurate passenger list, TWA could not confirm the number of people on board and presumed dead. Sixteen hours passed before the company's CEO arrived in New York and was able to speak to the media. Lack of information slowed communications between the airline, government officials, rescue workers, and the families of passengers on board.

3. *Escalating pace of events.* A crisis does not wait until a company is ready for it. Once a crisis begins, it often sets in motion a chain of events that increases in number and complexity for the company. For example, when the *Exxon Valdez* oil spill occurred in Alaska, government agencies and environmental groups were on the scene at Prince William Sound well before Exxon was able to establish its communications command center. Government officials and environmental spokespersons were able to hold press conferences and define the crisis their way. This enabled them to create expectations and set the agenda for what would be an adequate response by Exxon. All of this occurred before any Exxon officials were on site to make their own determination of the oil spill.

4. *Intense scrutiny.* During a crisis, the world is watching every move executives make. In the normal course of business, managers make decisions on the basis of research and analysis, extensive consultation within experts within the company, and careful deliberation, and they do so *in private*. During a crisis, every single decision is closely scrutinized and subject to immediate assessment by the media, government officials, and many other external stakeholders. Crisis management is management in a fishbowl. Feedback comes quickly, whether as praise, criticism, or condemnation. This makes it very hard for managers to internalize the feedback they are receiving and evaluate what others are saying.

---

[13]Ray O'Rourke, "Managing in Times of Crisis," *Corporate Reputation Review* 1 (1997), pp. 120–25.

EXHIBIT
2-A

Key Principles of Crisis Management

What does one do when a crisis occurs? According to experts, there are some principles, not *rules*, that can be useful to managers facing a crisis.

Define the Real Problem

Crises tend to force managers to think short term and focus on the narrow problem at hand. Experience suggests that the crisis management team should ask several reflective questions: What would constitute a good job in managing this crisis? What can we accomplish? What is impossible?

Set Goals and Define the Crisis Strategy in Light of Those Goals

The urge to act first, think later is hard to resist when facing a crisis. Experts suggest that the better course is to have some managers actively thinking about the goals—What do we want to accomplish? How do we want to be perceived by the media? By our shareholders? By our employees and customers?

Manage the Flow of Information

Experts advise managers to tell the story their way, consistently, and frequently. Because electronic media repeat crisis stories quite frequently in a typical news day, managers have an opportunity to correct errors and should not permit an erroneous statement to stand unchallenged.

Adopt a Team Approach

It is important to have one spokesperson designated at the outset and available to act on the company's behalf immediately. Successful companies have thought in advance about the skills each crisis team should possess. Legal, media, and government relations skills are essential in many crisis situations.

Plan for the Worst Case

A crisis always has the potential to worsen, and managers need to anticipate the worst-case possibility. It is tempting to assume a crisis will pass and the world will return to normal. Experience suggests it is wise to prepare for the worst.

Plan on the Situation Getting Worse

By doing so, an organization can begin to see ahead and create contingency plans for communicating with key stakeholders, deploying resources, and organizing other companies and people for action.

Follow Up after the Crisis is Over

Many contacts with stakeholders occur during a crisis. Experience suggests that a company can restore its image and reputation by dedicated follow-up to stakeholders.

Use Technology

Information technology can be a powerful aid to a company facing a crisis and needing to communicate with stakeholders. Experts also advise that a company should measure the effectiveness of communication messages through polling, surveys, and focus-group interviews.

Don't Give Up

As bad as it can be for an organization, a crisis rarely destroys a well-managed business. Leadership is vital if an organization's internal and external stakeholders are to believe that there is a bright future beyond the crisis.

Source: Adapted from Ray O'Rourke, "Managing in Times of Crisis," *Corporate Reputation Review* 1 (1997), pp. 120–25.

Is it possible to really manage a crisis? Although managers are at a disadvantage, there are a number of principles that experts believe help minimize the impact of a crisis on the organization. And since no two crises are ever alike, managers can only try to learn the lessons from past crises to be more prepared for the future. As shown in Exhibit 2–A, advisers to companies that have been caught in crises have learned some lessons that enable us to define some guidelines and suggestions. Still, a company's executives often have to rely on their own good sense and instincts for dealing with stakeholders when facing a crisis.

Strategic Management of Stakeholder Relations

Companies are learning that it is important to take a strategic approach to stakeholder relations. That requires thinking ahead, understanding what is important to each stakeholder, and determining when it is possible to cooperate and when it is necessary to disagree. Strategic thinking recognizes that while some disagreement may be inevitable, a company's long-term well-being is dependent on the continued support and cooperation of its many stakeholders.

To manage stakeholder relations in a strategic way, three types of actions must be undertaken. As illustrated in Figure 2–8, management must first be aware of the company's stakeholders and demonstrate an acceptance of their legitimate right to participate in decisions affecting them. Second, the company must think proactively about how its

Figure 2–8

Strategic management approach to managing external relations.

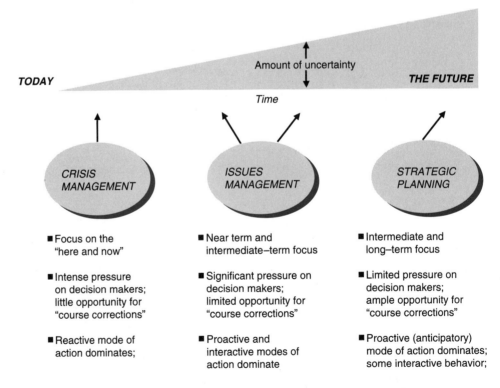

plans will affect, positively and negatively, its many stakeholders. Plans should be developed to build support whenever possible and creatively address negative impacts when they occur. Third, the firm should manage issues carefully and consistently, recognizing the possibility that issues may explode if mishandled, possibly creating other unanticipated and unforeseen problems.

> *For example, Ford Motor Company has developed important relationships with suppliers, dealers, and customers. The company regularly surveys purchasers of its products, for example, to determine customer satisfaction with the automobiles and trucks, service problems, and other concerns. This approach helps the company meet the second principle of anticipating the impact of decisions on stakeholders and the reaction of those stakeholders. Ford knows its customers, many of whom are repeat purchasers of Ford products. Still, unexpected surprises can and do occur. Ford claims it was greatly surprised by the reactions of its customers when it refused to settle the ignition fire cases.*

Strategies of Response

Businesses respond to stakeholder pressures in various ways. Some firms steadfastly adhere to their plans, no matter how strong the opposition or pressure from others. Some firms change only when forced to do so by strong outside pressures. Others actively attempt to move stakeholders in directions that will be to the company's advantage. And some try to find ways to harmonize the company's goals and objectives with the changing needs, goals, and expectations of the public. These approaches are respectively referred to as **inactive, reactive, proactive,** and **interactive strategies of response,** as illustrated in Figure 2–9.

Figure 2–9

Four basic strategies of response to stakeholder issues.

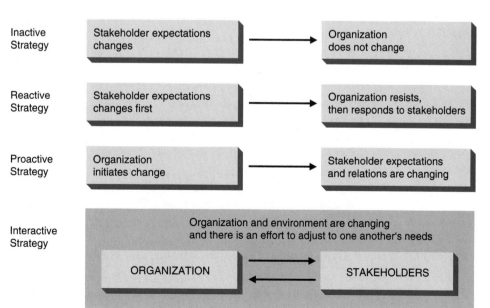

Inactive Strategy	Stakeholder expectations changes	Organization does not change
Reactive Strategy	Stakeholder expectations changes first	Organization resists, then responds to stakeholders
Proactive Strategy	Organization initiates change	Stakeholder expectations and relations are changing
Interactive Strategy	Organization and environment are changing and there is an effort to adjust to one another's needs	
	ORGANIZATION	STAKEHOLDERS

Companies may use any of these strategies in responding to a particular issue or problem. Sometimes a company will quite deliberately be slow to respond (reactive) to an issue. At other times, the same company may be deliberately proactive in trying to head off an issue before it develops into a major problem. Some companies display a general preference for one or another of these strategies in dealing with many types of issues, although it is unclear whether this is just a style of management or a conscious strategy for use in responding to a particular issue. As the following example suggests, today's strategy may have to change—perhaps dramatically—if the business environment changes.

> *Petroleum companies have long explored for oil in remote and difficult-to-reach places. Offshore exploration has been one great challenge, as companies have sought to build and operate drilling rigs in deep ocean waters amidst hurricane winds, blizzard storms, and waves the size of high-rise buildings. And in the remote jungles of African, Asian, and Latin American nations another kind of problem has arisen. Having long been accused of operating with disregard for the enormous environmental impact of drilling and production activities and running roughshod over the rights of native peoples, companies such as Royal Dutch/Shell and Mobil have been the target of boycotts and other protests by global activist organizations. Stymied by such protests, Shell and Mobil are pursuing a different approach in developing the rich gas resources of Camisea, a remote area in Peru with enormous potential. Working with government officials, local environmental groups, and international advisers, the companies are making a major effort to work with local Indian tribes and critics. Plans have been adapted to local conditions, and the companies are earning respect for listening and changing their traditional practices.*[14]

Summary Points of This Chapter

- Stakeholder expectations can, if unmet, trigger action to transform social concern into pressure on business and government. The existence of a gap between what is expected and actual performance stimulates the formation of a public issue.

- The public issue life cycle describes the evolution of a social concern through stages of politicalization, formal government action, and implementation of legally mandated change. Every public issue passes through these stages, and managers can predict what will happen if the performance-expectations gap is not closed.

- An organization's public affairs function is charged with collecting and analyzing information about the social and political environment, communicating with internal audiences, and interacting with stakeholders to achieve the organization's objectives.

- Companies can develop reactive, proactive, or interactive strategies to respond to public issues. Some steadfastly adhere to inactive strategies. Most organizations will develop separate strategies for each issue they are trying to manage.

[14]Jonathan Friedland, "Green Acres: Oil Companies Strive to Turn a New Leaf to Save Rain Forest," *The Wall Street Journal*, July 17, 1997, pp. A1, A8.

- Issues management includes identification and analysis of issues; development of policy options; program design; implementation; and evaluation of the results of such activities.

- Crisis management is the process organizations use to respond to short-term and immediate shocks, such as accidents, distress, and catastrophes. A number of practical guidelines have emerged through experience. Effective crisis management always begins with the proactive step of being prepared.

- Strategic management of stakeholder relations involves awareness of stakeholders and their interests, proactive planning of relationship development with them, and readiness to respond quickly and effectively to issues and crises.

Key Terms and Concepts Used in This Chapter

- Performance-expectations gap
- Public issue
- Public issue life cycle
- Public affairs management

- Issues management
- Crisis management
- Inactive, reactive, proactive, interactive strategies of response

Internet Resources

- http://allpolitics.com
- http://nationaljournal.com

CNN/*Time* review of emerging social-political issues
National Journal index of current events

Discussion Case   McDonald's Plays Tough in UK

Dave Morris and Helen Steel didn't look like they were capable of challenging a multibillion (U.S.) corporation in the court of world opinion. But that's just what they did, and in doing so, they held their own against one of the world's best marketing organizations.

The Problem

Morris (age 43) and Steel (age 31) were accused of libeling McDonald's by passing out leaflets on London streets that charged the company with exploiting underpaid workers, despoiling the environment, and endangering human health. Entitled "What's Wrong with McDonald's?" the leaflet claimed that McDonald's sells products that are high in fat, sugar, and salt, and low in fiber, vitamins, and minerals, all factors associated with breast cancer and bowel and heart disease. It also charged that the company exploits children by using gimmicks to get them to eat junk food, underpays its staff, creates mountains of waste through discarded packaging, is cruel to animals, and helps destroy South American rain forests to make way for cattle ranches.

Following its worldwide strategy of defending its brand name and reputation, McDonald's decided to go to court to secure an injunction. To do so, it was necessary to sue Morris and Steel for damages to get a court hearing. The London media publicized the controversy and quickly christened the case, "McLibel." The David-and-Goliath imagery was enhanced when it was disclosed that the leafleteers were a $105-a-week welfare recipient and a part-time bartender.

Strategy and Counterstrategy

British libel law is relatively restrictive unlike U.S. law where free speech protections have created a broad immunity to libel suits. McDonald's decided to press its case in the British courts and hired Richard Rampton, a libel specialist, to head its legal team. Rampton, it was later disclosed, charges more than $3,285 (U.S.) per day. The proceedings involved 313 days of hearings and the testimony of more than 130 witnesses (some testified for as long as two weeks). The trial produced 40,000 documents and more than 20,000 pages of transcripts.

If McDonald's thought the lawsuit would discourage criticism of its business activities, it was badly mistaken. The McLibel Support Campaign raised donations for the defense and conducted a public campaign against the company by handing out two million leaflets in Britain since the controversy began in 1990. The group also used the World Wide Web (http://www.mcspotlight.org) to post such documents as the transcript of the trial, McDonald's 500-page summing-up document, film clips, and other documentation in 15 different languages.

Morris and Steel were unable to afford lawyers and chose to fight their own case. They flew in witnesses from around the world with donations from supporters. They cross-examined McDonald's executives and filed a countersuit for libel against McDonald's after the company issued leaflets that accused them of spreading lies.

Negotiations

McDonald's tried to reach a negotiated settlement with Morris and Steel. A McDonald's spokesman said there were two separate attempts to reach a mutually acceptable resolution. Morris and Steel said that McDonald's asked them for between $130,000 and $190,000 damages; but McDonald's stated it only wanted to ensure that the pair does not continue to libel the company, calling the claim for damages a legal formality. Morris and Steel claimed that McDonald's executives from corporate headquarters (Oak Brook, Illinois) tried on three occasions to persuade them to agree to an out-of-court settlement. They said they refused to do so unless McDonald's guaranteed to refrain from suing other people who make similar allegations, a condition the company rejected.

The Verdict

Morris and Steel said that if they lost the court proceeding to McDonald's, they would exercise their right to appeal the case. In addition, they threatened to bring the case before the European Court of Human Rights. A McDonald's spokesperson said that if the company lost the first round to Morris and Steel, it would appeal the decision to a higher court.

On June 19, 1997, Judge Rodger Bell handed down his verdict. The judge found that Morris and Steel had libeled McDonald's by making certain untrue statements regarding environmental damage in third-world countries and claiming that the company's food was unhealthy and dangerous for public consumption.

The judge also found that Morris and Steel had *not* libeled McDonald's on such issues as child labor, wages rates, and some food-related claims. Finally, the judge ordered that Morris and Steel pay McDonald's the sum of $100,000 in damages.

The trial itself took over three years, making it the longest-running case in British history. Morris and Steel immediately declared victory.

Sources: Ray Moseley, "Three-year Trial Pits Burger Giant against a Pair of Leafleteers," *Boston Globe,* June 15, 1997, p. A23. Also, John Vidal, *Burger Culture on Trial* (New York: New Press, 1997).

Discussion Questions

1. Whose expectations are at stake in this case? What performance changes could McDonald's conceivably make to close the gap?
2. How did this issue evolve through the public issues life cycle? What were the drivers?
3. What kind of an issues management team would you want to assemble if you were an executive at McDonald's? What skills would you want represented on the team?
4. Using the suggested guidelines in Exhibit 2–A, describe what steps McDonald's might have taken to deal with Morris and Steel.

PART TWO

Business and the Social Environment

3

Corporate Social Responsibility

Corporate social responsibility challenges businesses to be accountable for the consequences of their actions affecting the firm's stakeholders while they pursue traditional economic goals. The general public expects businesses to be socially responsible, and many companies have responded by making social goals a part of their overall business operations. Guidelines for acting in socially responsible ways are not always clear, thus producing controversy about what constitutes such behavior, how extensive it should be, and what it costs to be socially responsible.

This chapter focuses on these key questions and objectives:

- What is the basic meaning of corporate social responsibility?

- Where and when did the idea of social responsibility originate? *Background* ✓

- What must a company do to be considered socially responsible?

- Is corporate social responsibility practiced by businesses around the world?

- What are the limits of corporate social responsibility?

- How does business meet its economic and legal obligations while being socially responsible?

Do managers have a responsibility to their stockholders? Certainly, for the owners of the business have invested their capital in the firm. Do managers also have a responsibility, a social responsibility, to their employees? Since worker satisfaction appears closely related to productivity, being socially supportive of employees seems to make good economic sense; thus, social responsibility to employees may also benefit the firm's stockholders. What happens when these, and other, responsibilities seem to clash? The following two stories reflect different views of managerial responsibility, particularly to the firm's employees. The approaches are at different ends of the spectrum in the debate over corporate social responsibility.

At Caterpillar Inc., the chief executive officer, Donald V. Fites, was accused by many of his own employees of various antiworker practices. The workers claimed that Fites eliminated unions by beating back a strike attempt, closed plants, and provided management with huge paychecks while holding down wage increases for blue-collar employees. Yet, many of his colleagues cited his company's behavior as being a model of social responsibility. Fites was credited with turning around Caterpillar. His strategy may have saved tens of thousands of jobs for Americans when many of his competitors were shifting employment to low-wage sites abroad. "The first and most important responsibility of any corporation is to be economically viable," said Peter Feuille, the director of the Institute for Labor and Industrial Relations at the University of Illinois. Caterpillar's Fites seemed to embody that form of social responsibility.

Employees experienced a different version of corporate social responsibility at Harman International, a speaker manufacturing company. Recently President Clinton held up Sidney Harman, chief executive of Harman International, as a model of how treating workers well is not only the right thing to do but also good for business. Harman offered extensive training programs for his employees and experimented with allowing workers to share in the proceeds of cost savings they proposed to management. Despite a downturn in the industry in 1996, when layoffs at the company were inevitable, Harman sought to keep his workers employed by putting them on the payroll of a firm he called Off Line Enterprises. This firm made wiring for Harman International that would otherwise be purchased from suppliers. Laid-off employees also worked as security officers and gardeners at Harman International plants, jobs that would normally have gone to outside contractors. Keeping these 250 workers on the payroll cost the company $130,000 a week. Yet, Harman noted that most of the cost was made up in savings on what the company would otherwise have paid outside suppliers for parts and service. Harman planned to have these workers go back to their regular jobs as soon as industry demand picked up.[1]

Which firm, Caterpillar or Harman International, is practicing corporate social responsibility? Which firm will survive in the long run and why? Which firm would you want to work for?

In this chapter we discuss the advantages and drawbacks of being socially responsible. Most of all, though, we argue that social responsibility is an inescapable demand made by society. Whether businesses are large or small, make goods or provide services, operate at home or abroad, willingly try to be socially responsible or fight against it all the way—there is no doubt about what the public expects. Many business leaders also

---

[1]Richard W. Stevenson, "Do People and Profits Go Hand in Hand? Different Views of Corporate Responsibility, but Companies Share Goals," *New York Times,* May 9, 1996, pp. C1, C2.

subscribe to the idea of social responsibility. A *Business Week*/Harris poll revealed that U.S. top-level corporate executives (69 percent of those polled) and MBA students (89 percent) believe that corporations should become more involved in solving social problems. Similar beliefs were recorded in a study of 107 European corporations, in which a majority of CEOs surveyed agreed that addressing social issues, such as substance abuse, health care, and education, was needed.[2]

The Meaning of Corporate Social Responsibility

Corporate social responsibility means that a corporation should be held accountable for any of its actions that affect people, their communities, and their environment. It implies that negative business impacts on people and society should be acknowledged and corrected if at all possible. It may require a company to forgo some profits if its social impacts are seriously harmful to some of its stakeholders or if its funds can be used to promote a positive social good.

The Many Responsibilities of Business

However, being socially responsible does not mean that a company must abandon its other primary missions. As discussed later in this chapter, a business has many responsibilities: economic, legal, and social. The challenge for management is the blending of these responsibilities into a comprehensive corporate strategy while not losing sight of any of its obligations. At times these responsibilities will clash; at other times they will work together to better the firm. Thus, having multiple and sometimes competing responsibilities does not mean that socially responsible firms cannot be as profitable as others less responsible; some are and some are not.

Social responsibility requires companies to balance the benefits to be gained against the costs of achieving those benefits. Many people believe that both business and society gain when firms actively strive to be socially responsible. Others are doubtful, saying that business's competitive strength is weakened by taking on social tasks. The arguments on both sides of this debate are presented later in this chapter.

Social Responsibility and Corporate Power

The social responsibilities of business grow directly out of two features of the modern corporation: (1) the essential functions it performs for a variety of stakeholders and (2) the immense influence it has on the lives of the stakeholders. We count on corporations for job creation, much of our community well-being, the standard of living we enjoy, the tax base for essential municipal, state, and national services, and our needs for banking and financial services, insurance, transportation, communication, utilities, entertainment, and a growing proportion of health care. These positive achievements suggest that the corporate form of business is capable of performing a great amount of good for society, such as encouraging economic growth, expanding international trade, and creating new technology.

---

[2]David L. Mathison, "European and American Executive Values," *Business Ethics: A European Review,* April 1993, pp. 97–100.

The following well-known quotation, frequently appearing in journals for business executives, challenges the readers to assume a responsible role for business in society:

> *Business has become, in the last half century, the most powerful institution on the planet. The dominant institution in any society needs to take responsibility for the whole. . . . Every decision that is made, every action that is taken, must be viewed in light of that kind of responsibility.*[3]

Consider the following statistics: the world's largest industrial corporations employ only .05 of 1 percent of the world's population, yet they control 25 percent of the world's economic output. The top 300 transnationals own nearly 25 percent of the world's productive assets. Of the world's 100 largest economies, 50 are corporations. In the world's international currency markets, more than $1 trillion changes hands each day; the traders are seeking instant profits unrelated to the production or trade of real goods and services.[4]

Many people are concerned about potential corporate influence. The focused power found in the modern business corporation means that every action it takes can affect the quality of human life—for individuals, for communities, and for the entire globe. This obligation is often referred to as the **iron law of responsibility.** The iron law of responsibility says that in the long run, those who do not use power in ways that society considers responsible will tend to lose it.[5] With such technology as computers, communications satellites, and television networks drawing the world into a tighter and tighter global village, the entire Planet Earth has become a stakeholder in all corporations. All societies are now affected by corporate operations. As a result, social responsibility has become a worldwide expectation.

How Corporate Social Responsibility Began

In the United States, the idea of corporate social responsibility appeared around the turn of the twentieth century. Corporations at that time came under attack for being too big, too powerful, and guilty of antisocial and anticompetitive practices. Critics tried to curb corporate power through antitrust laws, banking regulations, and consumer-protection laws.

Faced with this kind of social protest, a few farsighted business executives advised corporations to use their power and influence voluntarily for broad social purposes rather than for profits alone. Some of the wealthier business leaders—steelmaker Andrew Carnegie is a good example—became great philanthropists who gave much of their wealth to educational and charitable institutions. Others, like automaker Henry Ford, developed paternalistic programs to support the recreational and health needs of their employees. The point to emphasize is that these business leaders believed that business had a responsibility to society that went beyond or worked in parallel with their efforts to make profits.[6]

---

[3]David C. Korten, "Limits to the Social Responsibility of Business," The People-Centered Development Forum, no. 19, June 1, 1996.

[4]David C. Korten, *When Corporations Rule the World* (San Francisco: Kumarian Press, 1995).

[5]This concept first appeared in Keith Davis and Robert Blomstrom, *Business and Its Environment* (New York: McGraw-Hill, 1966).

[6]Harold R. Bowen, *Social Responsibilities of the Businessman* (New York: Harper, 1953); and Morrell Heald, *The Social Responsibility of Business: Company and Community, 1900–1960* (Cleveland: Case-Western Reserve Press, 1970). For a history of how some of these business philanthropists acquired their wealth, see Matthew Josephson, *The Robber Barons: The Great American Capitalists* (New York: Harcourt Brace, 1934).

As a result of these early ideas about business's expanded role in society, two broad principles emerged. These principles have shaped business thinking about social responsibility during the twentieth century and are the foundation stones for the modern idea of corporate social responsibility.

(FOUNDATIONS)
← ORIGINS

The Charity Principle

The **charity principle,** the idea that the wealthier members of society should be charitable toward those less fortunate, is a very ancient notion. Royalty through the ages has been expected to provide for the poor. The same is true of those with vast holdings of property, from feudal times to the present. Biblical passages invoke this most ancient principle, as do the sacred writings of other world religions. When Andrew Carnegie and other wealthy business leaders endowed public libraries, supported settlement houses for the poor, gave money to educational institutions, and contributed funds to many other community organizations, they were continuing this long tradition of being "my brother's keeper."

> *Andrew Carnegie and John D. Rockefeller are usually credited with pioneering the path of the giant givers of modern philanthropy. For some years, the world's newspapers kept score on the giving. The* London Times *reported that in 1903 Carnegie had given away $21 million, Rockefeller $10 million. By 1913, the* New York Herald *ran a final box score: Carnegie, $332 million; Rockefeller, $175 million. All this was before the income tax and other tax provisions had generated external incentives to giving. The feeling of duty to the public good arose from inner sources.*[7]

little welfare

This kind of private aid to the needy members of society was especially important in the early decades of this century. At that time, there was no Social Security system, no Medicare for the elderly, no unemployment pay for the jobless, and no United Way to support a broad range of community needs. There were few organizations capable of counseling troubled families, sheltering women and children who were victims of physical abuse, aiding alcoholics, treating the mentally ill or the physically handicapped, or taking care of the destitute. When wealthy industrialists reached out to help others in these ways, they were accepting some measure of responsibility for improving the conditions of life in their communities. In doing so, their actions helped counteract the critics who claimed that business leaders were uncaring and interested only in profits.

Before long, these community needs outpaced the riches of even the wealthiest persons and families. When that happened, beginning in the 1920s, much of the charitable load was taken on by business firms themselves rather than by the owners alone. The symbol of this shift from individual philanthropy to corporate philanthropy was the Community Chest movement in the 1920s, the forerunner of today's United Way drives that are widespread throughout the United States. Business leaders gave vigorous support to this form of corporate charity, urging all firms and their employees to unite their efforts to extend aid to the poor and the needy. Business leaders established pension plans, employee stock ownership and life insurance programs, unemployment funds, limitations on working hours, and higher wages. They built houses, churches, schools, and libraries, provided medical and legal services, and gave to charity.

---

[7]Michael Novak, *Business as a Calling: Work and the Examined Life* (New York: Free Press, 1996), p. 197.

For some of today's business firms, corporate social responsibility means participating in community affairs by making paternalistic, charitable contributions. Ted Turner's sensational pledge of $1 billion ($100 million a year for 10 years) to the United Nations in October 1997 served as a gauntlet for other millionaire business leaders, challenging them to contribute in a similar fashion.[8] However, charitable giving is not the only form that corporate social responsibility takes.

The Stewardship Principle

Many of today's corporate executives see themselves as stewards, or trustees, who act in the general public's interest. Although their companies are privately owned and they try to make profits for the stockholders, business leaders who follow the **stewardship principle** believe they have an obligation to see that everyone—particularly those in need—benefits from the company's actions. According to this view, corporate managers have been placed in a position of public trust. They control vast resources whose use can affect people in fundamental ways. Because they exercise this kind of crucial influence, they incur a responsibility to use those resources in ways that are good not just for the stockholders alone but for society generally. In this way, they have become stewards, or trustees, for society. As such, they are expected to act with a special degree of social responsibility in making business decisions.[9]

This kind of thinking eventually produced the modern theory of stakeholder management, which was described in the opening chapter of this book. According to this theory, corporate managers need to interact skillfully with all groups that have a stake in what the corporation does. If they do not do so, their firms will not be fully effective economically or fully accepted by the public as a socially responsible corporation. As one former business executive declared, "Every citizen is a stakeholder in business whether he or she holds a share of stock or not, is employed in business or not, or buys the products and services of business or not. Just to live in American society today makes everyone a stakeholder in business."[10]

Modern Forms of Corporate Social Responsibility

These two principles—the charity principle and the stewardship principle—established the original meaning of corporate social responsibility. Figure 3–1 shows how these two principles have evolved to form the modern idea of corporate social responsibility.

[8]For a comprehensive discussion of millionaire business leaders turning philanthropists, see "A New Breed of Philanthropist," *Business Week,* October 6, 1997, pp. 40–44. Two sizable donations are discussed in Monica Langley, "How Turner Decided to Give Away $1 Billion," *The Wall Street Journal,* September 22, 1997, pp. B1, B18; and Karen Kaplan, "Microsoft's Gates to Donate $200 Million to Libraries," *Los Angeles Times,* June 24, 1997, p. A1.

[9]Two early statements of this stewardship-trustee view are Frank W. Abrams, "Management's Responsibilities in a Complex World," *Harvard Business Review,* May 1951, pp. 29–34; and Richard Eells, *The Meaning of Modern Business* (New York: Columbia University Press, 1960).

[10]James E. Liebig, *Business Ethics: Profiles in Civic Virtue* (Golden, CO: Fulcrum, 1990), p. 217. For stakeholder theory, see R. Edward Freeman, *Strategic Management: A Stakeholder Approach* (Boston: Pitman, 1984).

Figure 3-1

Foundation principles of corporate social responsibility and their modern expression.

	Charity Principle	Stewardship Principle
Definition	Business should give voluntary aid to society's needy persons and groups.	Business, acting as a public trustee, should consider the interests of all who are affected by business decisions and policies.
Modern Expression	■ Corporate philanthropy ■ Voluntary actions to promote the social good	■ Acknowledging business and society interdependence ■ Balancing the interests and needs of many diverse groups in society
Examples	■ Corporate philan-thropic foundations ■ Private initiatives to solve social problems ■ Employee volunteerism ■ Social partnerships with needy groups	■ Enlightened self-interest ■ Meeting legal requirements ■ Stakeholder approach to corporate strategic planning

Corporate Philanthropy

Corporate philanthropy is the modern expression of the charity principle. The steward-ship principle is given meaning today when corporate managers recognize that business and society are intertwined and interdependent, as explained in Chapter 1. This mutual-ity of interests places a responsibility on business to exercise care and social concern in formulating policies and conducting business operations. Exhibit 3–A shows a few of the many organizations that foster modern day corporate philanthropy. Figure 3–2 on page 64 shows a list of social priorities from the early 1970s developed by the Committee for Eco-nomic Development (CED), a group of about 200 top-level business executives. These recommendations were some of the first industrywide suggestions for social responsibility programs.

Most recent surveys identifying areas of corporate social involvement generally re-flect the CED's 1971 list. Employment and training has expanded to include various health and wellness issues, such as employee fitness, AIDS education and treatment, and de-pendence on cigarettes, alcohol, and drugs.

Corporate Employee Volunteerism

Corporate employee volunteerism is a relatively new phenomenon. Many large corpo-rations developed charitable contribution programs but left employee involvement in community service up to the individual. In the early 1970s, companies began to see

EXHIBIT 3–A	**Helping Business with Philanthropic Activities**

Numerous organizations exist that seek to help business in their expressions of modern-day corporate philanthropy.

- **Business for Social Responsibility** Was formed in 1992 to work with its members to integrate a full range of socially responsible practices into the strategic, long-term vision of the firm. It recognizes the best practices of its members in the areas of the workplace, the community, and the environment.

- **The Cygnus Group** Helps businesses integrate environmental concepts into their strategic planning, marketing, and communications activities. The Cygnus Group is a pioneer in the use of the Internet for business information retrieval, analysis, and dissemination.

- **Business Council for Sustainable Development in the Gulf of Mexico** Was established by a group of Mexican and American corporate leaders to promote new partnerships, develop policy initiatives, and undertake regional sustainable development endeavors to support sound and sustained economic growth.

- **Prince of Wales Business Leaders Forum** Was established in 1990 to provide a focus for international business leaders who recognize that good corporate citizenship is important to global business success. It includes an international charity supported by business from North America, Europe, and the Far East.

Source: Key Organizations Focused on Business and Industry, compiled by IISD, © 1996, http://iisdl.iisd.ca/ic/sb/direct/SDBUSIN.HTM (June 27, 1997).

dual benefit.

community service as a way to improve their images—internally and externally—as well as to serve the communities in which the business operates. According to The National Volunteer Center, more than 1,100 major U.S. corporations had established structured activities to involve their workers in community volunteerism by 1990. A 1996 survey of 180 leading U.S. companies found that 79 percent had volunteer programs.[11]

Today, workplace employee volunteer programs generally take two forms:

- The team model, in which a team of employees plan and implement group volunteer activities.

- The volunteer clearinghouse model, in which a full-time coordinator or a part-time employee provides volunteer opportunities to employees.[12]

rationale + reward

Employee volunteer programs help companies attract and retain good employees, according to a study conducted by the Conference Board. Volunteerism helps develop characteristics such as creativity, trust, teamwork, and persistence. It builds skills and attitudes that foster commitment, company loyalty, and job satisfaction. Morale is as much as three

[11]Steve Levin, "Volunteer Spirit Lifts Morale, Bottom Line for Corporations," *Pittsburgh Post-Gazette,* May 25, 1997, pp. A1, A12–13.

[12]Loyce Haran, Siobhan Kenney, and Mark Vermilion, "Contract Volunteer Services: A Model for Successful Partnerships, Sun Microsystems, Jobs and Corporate Information," http://www.sun.com (June 27, 1997).

Figure 3-2

Recommended social responsibility actions—Committee for Economic Development.

Source: Social Responsibilities of Business Corporations (New York: Committee for Economic Development, 1971).

- ■ **Economic growth and efficiency**
  Improving productivity
  Cooperating with government

- ■ **Education**
  Giving aid to schools and colleges
  Assisting in managing schools and colleges

- ■ **Employment and training**
  Training disadvantaged workers
  Retraining displaced workers

- ■ **Civil rights and equal opportunity**
  Ensuring equal job opportunities
  Building inner-city plants

- ■ **Urban renewal and development**
  Building low-income housing
  Improving transportation systems

- ■ **Pollution abatement**
  Installing pollution controls
  Developing recycling programs

- ■ **Conservation and recreation**
  Protecting plant and animal ecology
  Restoring depleted lands to use

- ■ **Culture and the arts**
  Giving aid to art institutions

- ■ **Medical care**
  Helping community health planning
  Designing low-cost medical care programs

- ■ **Government**
  Improving management in government
  Modernizing and reorganizing government

times higher in companies with volunteer programs.[13] Research has found a positive association between employees involved in corporate volunteer programs and better physical health, mental health, and social interaction. An example of an employee volunteer program is described in Exhibit 3–B. A study conducted by IBM and the Graduate School of Business at Columbia University showed a clear link between volunteerism and return on assets, return on investment, and employee productivity. A company with a strong community involvement program is likely to score high in profitability and employee morale.

[13]Shari Caudron, "Volunteer Efforts Offer Low-Cost Training Options," *Personnel Journal,* June 1994, pp. 38, 40, 42, 44.

EXHIBIT 3–B

Community Service Improves Employee Job Skills

Helene Curtis, a Chicago-based personal care company, integrated community volunteerism into its management development program. The results benefited both the employees and the business. "The program gives employees the chance to learn and apply experiences gained through community service to their personal and professional growth," explained Ann Schwartz, manager of community relations at Helene Curtis. "Our goal is to help employees identify the skills they want to develop and then work with them to identify ways and venues in which to practice those skills."

The goals of the program are to formally recognize the value of business skills gained through community service, transfer practical skills from community work to business application, provide managers and employees with alternative ways to develop business skills, provide a low-risk learning experience for both the employees and the corporation, and contribute to the betterment of the organization and community. Managers at Helene Curtis see employee volunteerism as reinforcing the values at the firm. As one employee pointed out, "This program is such a natural fit with the Helene Curtis culture and reflects the values of our CEO."

Source: "Using Community Service Projects to Improve Employee Job Skills," *Issues in Corporate Social Responsibility,* Barnes and Associates publication, Spring 1996, p. 9.

Corporate Awards for Social Responsibility

Recognition of socially responsible behavior by business has increased dramatically. One of the first award programs was sponsored by the Council on Economic Priorities (CEP). The CEP is a corporate watchdog organization that reports periodically on the social behavior of large corporations. In 1987 the council began to accentuate the positive by citing companies that had demonstrated an outstanding record of socially responsible behavior. A selective list of the CEP award recipients is provided in Figure 3–3. In addition, companies have been given dishonorable mentions for a variety of socially irresponsible actions.

> *The Business Enterprise Trust, founded in 1989 by prominent leaders in business, academia, labor, and the media, recognizes business leaders and other individuals who have significantly advanced the cause of social responsibility through "acts of courage, integrity, and social vision." The Trust's annual awards have been presented to Merck & Company for developing a drug to combat river blindness, McKay Nursery Company for their employee stock ownership plan that included 60 migrant workers hired for eight months a year, DAKA International—a restaurant and food service business—for pioneering an aggressive AIDS education program, and Julia Stasch for developing the Female Employment Initiative to assist women in the pursuit of careers in the construction industry.*[14]

[14]A thorough analysis of the Business Enterprise Trust program can be found in James O'Toole, "Do Good, Do Well: The Business Enterprise Trust Awards," *California Management Review,* Spring 1991, pp. 9–24.

Figure 3–3

Social responsibility honored by the Council on Economic Priorities.

Source: America's Corporate Conscience Awards, Council on Economic Priorities, http://www.accesspt.com/cep/research/cca/pastawards.html.

America's Corporate Conscience Awards, 1993–1997

Community Involvement

Brooklyn Union Gas	Kellogg
Clorox	Pfizer
Colgate-Palmolive	Timberland
Community Pride Food Stores	Working Assets

Employee Issues

Coca-Cola	Pitney Bowes
Cooperative Home Care	Polaroid
Federal National Mortgage	Quad Graphics
Hewlett-Packard	SAS Institute
Merck & Co.	

Environmental Stewardship

Aveda Corp.	New England Electric System
Digital Equipment	Novo Nordisk
Enron	S.C. Johnson
J. Sainsbury	Stoneyfield
Natural Cotton Colours	Wilkhahn Wilkening

Global Ethics

Cooperative Bank	Starbucks Coffee
Levi Strauss & Co.	Toys 'R' Us
Merck & Co.	

President Clinton announced in 1996 the establishment of the Ron Brown Award for Corporate Leadership, which is to be given each year by the president of the United States to corporations that demonstrate good corporate citizenship. The key criteria for receiving the award include: be at the "best practice" level—distinctive, innovative, and effective; have a significant, measurable impact on the people served; offer broad potential for social and economic benefits; be sustainable and feasible within a business environment and mission; and be adaptable to other businesses and communities.

Corporate Social Responsibility Around the World

Social responsibility, however, reflects cultural values and traditions and takes different forms in different societies. What may be the accepted custom in the United States, Japan, or South Korea may not be in Germany, Brazil, Indonesia, or the Ukraine. Determining what is socially acceptable around the world often is a difficult process.

Japanese firms have proven themselves to be model citizens on many dimensions of corporate social responsibility. Their support of local community activities and other philanthropic endeavors has led to increased goodwill in the communities where they operate. The firms help society in areas directly related to the operations of the business. Thus, Japanese firms clearly help themselves while helping others, showing a strong commitment to the harmonious relations between the corporation and society.

From a U.S. perspective, however, this may seem to be a narrow understanding of corporate social responsibility. Victims of environmental disasters have been treated as outcasts when seeking compensation for harm caused by Japanese business. Employment practices that may favor certain groups have been generally accepted as a social practice in Japan.[15] However, as Japanese firms have become more integrated with the international community, a broader view of corporate social responsibility has begun to emerge.

> *The Japan External Trade Organization (JETRO) conducted a survey of Japanese philanthropy in the United States. They reported that approximately 80 percent of Japanese-affiliated operations in the United States responding to their survey engaged in corporate philanthropy. Making cash contributions was the most common form of philanthropy (91 percent), followed by participation in community organizations (57 percent). Community development and education were the primary beneficiaries of cash donations, and encouragement of employee volunteerism was up 36 percent from 1992. Over 95 percent of responding organizations maintained or increased both cash donations, and other philanthropic activities since the last survey in 1992.[16]*

Dong Ah Company, a South Korean construction firm, demonstrated its belief in corporate social responsibility in October 1994. One week after a 17-year-old bridge in Seoul, South Korea, collapsed killing 32 people, Dong Ah pledged to build a new bridge even though the company was not blamed for the accident. (Several Seoul officials were arrested on charges of neglecting to maintain the bridge.) The cost of replacing the structure was 150 billion won, or $188.1 million. In addition, the company donated 10 billion won, about $12.5 million, to a program designed to improve South Korean commuters' safety.

Corporate social responsibility has assumed a different form in European countries. Governments have provided many social services often received as benefits from private employers in the United States. For example, debate by government representatives over social responsibility issues resulted in the adoption of a social policy for the European Union countries, called the Social Charter. Rather than relying on private corporate initiatives, governments represented in the EU drafted a public policy that provided incentives and rewards for corporate social actions within the EU.

Embodied within the Social Charter is the Social Action Programme (SAP). The SAP established health and safety guidelines, regulations on working hours, Europe-wide rules for worker consultation, and rules for gender equality at work. Thus, European businesses' response toward social responsibility is actually often a matter of compliance with various governmental policy guidelines and program initiatives.

> *Other acts of corporate social responsibility are performed by McCarthy Retail, a South African firm. The company has an active Corporate Social Involvement program aimed at supporting and facilitating community*

---

[15]For a thorough discussion of corporate social responsibility Japanese style, see Richard E. Wokutch and Jon M. Shepard, "Corporate Social Responsibility, Moral Unity, and the Maturing of the Japanese Economy," http://www.nd.edu/~isbee/p_wokut.htm (June 27, 1997); and "Kyosei: Japanese Firms Must Pick Up the Social Tab as Well," *Tokyo Business Today,* January–February 1993, pp. 33–34.

[16]Japanese External Trade Organization, "Executive Summary," http://www.jetro.go.jp/JETROINFO/SURVEY/PHILAN/lexe.html (June 27, 1997).

development. According to the firm, the programs exist because the company sees pressing needs at the community level and is in a position to contribute to the long-term development of communities; the company realizes that its future business success depends on stable and thriving communities. Education has become the main focus of the company's efforts, particularly by establishing networking computer centers in schools in disadvantaged communities and actively supporting classroom-building projects in rural communities.[17]

In many of the world's developing nations where poverty is widespread or civil strife is frequent, economic goals and military activities tend to be given a higher priority than the pursuit of social goals. Environmental protection, for example, may be considered less critical than having a polluting steel plant that creates jobs. In these cases, social responsibility initiatives by business may be slow in coming.

The Limits of Corporate Social Responsibility

Social responsibility is widely expected of business. It can benefit both the business and the stakeholders of the firm. There are strong arguments in favor of corporate social responsibility; however, corporate social responsibility has its critics. The key arguments for and against social responsibility are noted in Figure 3–4.

Even if corporate social responsibility is a welcomed business strategy, it has limits. The main limits are legitimacy, cost, efficiency, and scope and complexity. As a result of these constraints, the amounts and kinds of social actions pursued by businesses are sometimes less than the public wants to see.

Figure 3–4

The pros and cons of corporate social responsibility.

Arguments for corporate social responsibility	Arguments against corporate social responsibility
■ Balances corporate power with responsibility.	■ Lowers economic efficiency and profit.
■ Discourages government regulation.	■ Imposes unequal costs among competitors.
■ Promotes long-term profits for business.	■ Imposes hidden costs passed on to stakeholders.
■ Responds to changing stakeholders' demands.	■ Requires social skills business may lack.
■ Corrects social problems caused by business.	■ Places responsibility on business rather than individuals.

[17]The McCarthy Retail social programs are described in the company's Web site, http://www.mccarthy.co.za/corporate/community.html (July 9, 1997).

Legitimacy

Is this social problem any of our affair? Is it seriously affecting our business? Do we have the needed in-house talent? Can solving it help us, as well as others? These are questions corporate officials would be wise to ask. A yes answer to these questions might lead a company to an understanding that it has a legitimate obligation to take socially responsible action. If, for example, drug use is causing serious safety problems in a plant, a company might be justified in spending money on a drug education and treatment center that can help its employees and others in the community.

However, a no or a not sure answer to the questions should cause company executives to think twice. Social expenditures by corporations can be justified, and are considered to be a lawful use of stockholders' funds, if they promote the interests of the company while simultaneously helping society. This legal principle was established in a famous 1951 lawsuit when a judge ruled that corporations were justified in contributing company funds to a university because these corporate gifts benefited the company in the long run. Judgments about the legitimacy of any social activity are usually made by a firm's top-level executives who, in the words of the court, must take "a long-range view of the matter" and exercise "enlightened leadership and direction."[18]

Costs

Every social action is accompanied by costs of one kind or another. Consider, for instance, a company's contributions to a worthy charity or its establishing a child-care center for its employees. A United Way contribution could have been paid instead to company stockholders as a dividend. Money spent on a child-care center could have been used instead to boost employees' wages. As worthy as some social actions may be, they do impose costs either on the business firm or on some groups in society, or both.

Efficiency

The costs of social responsibility, like all business expenses, can potentially reduce a company's efficiency and affect its ability to compete in the marketplace. For example, if a company is pressured by a local community to keep an outmoded, inefficient plant in operation because closing it would mean a big job loss for local people, while its competitors close their old plants and move operations to foreign nations where wage rates are lower, which company is more likely to survive in the long run? The managers who make what seems to be a socially responsible decision by putting the interests of their local employees first may not be able to compete with their lower-cost, more efficient competitors.

Scope and Complexity

Some of society's problems are simply too massive, too complex, and too deep-seated to be solved by even the most socially conscientious company or by all companies acting together.

---

[18]*Barlow et al.* v. *A.P. Smith Manufacturing Company* (1951, New Jersey Supreme Court), discussed in Clarence C. Walton, *Corporate Social Responsibility* (Belmont, CA: Wadsworth, 1967), pp. 48–52.

co-operate

Examples are environmental problems such as acid rain, ozone depletion in the upper atmosphere, and destruction of rain forests. What is required is joint action by corporations and governments in several nations, as happened when companies producing the chemicals that destroy the planet's ozone layer agreed to phase out production gradually.[19]

Some of today's health problems—AIDS, on-the-job drug abuse, and tobacco use—frequently reflect complex social conditions. Although socially responsive businesses can adopt workplace policies and programs regarding these and other health problems, solutions are most likely to be found through joint actions of government, business, community groups, and the individuals involved.

Other social problems are even more persistent. These may include the deep-seated issues of race relations, sex discrimination, and ethnic and religious animosities. No single business firm can be expected to root out these long-standing features of society. The most it can do is to adopt socially responsible attitudes and policies about these issues, being certain that company practices do not make things worse.

These four limits often produce disagreements among those who want corporations to be socially responsible and those who think business is doing enough. The latter group usually declares, Business cannot do more because of these limits. Their opponents in the debate usually respond by saying, Business should be socially active in spite of these constraints, because it is obligated to help society solve its problems.

Balancing Economic, Legal, and Social Responsibilities

Any organization and manager must seek to juggle multiple responsibilities. The popular belief that the business of business is solely profit making was dispelled by a 1997 *Business Week*/Harris poll in which 95 percent of the American adults surveyed rejected that corporations' only role was to make money. As shown in Figure 3–5, business is challenged by managing its economic responsibilities to its stockholders, its legal requirements to societal laws and regulations, and its social responsibilities to various stakeholders. Although these obligations may conflict at times, a successful firm is one for which management finds ways to meet each of its critical responsibilities and develops strategies to enable these obligations to help each other.

Triple bottom line

Figure 3–5
The multiple responsibilities of business.

[19]The Montreal Protocol, the multinational government-business agreement that banned or phased out the use of various materials harmful to the earth's ozone layer, is discussed in Chapter 11.

Enlightened Self-Interest

Being socially responsible by meeting the public's continually changing expectations requires wise leadership at the top of the corporation. Companies with an ability to recognize profound social changes and anticipate how they will affect operations have proven to be survivors. They get along better with government regulators, are more open to the needs of the company's stakeholders, and often cooperate with legislators as new laws are developed to cope with social problems. Corporate leaders who possess this kind of social vision believe that business should help create social change rather than block it. With such an attitude, they know that their own companies will have a better chance of surviving in the turbulent social currents of today's world.[20]

Companies with this outlook are guided by **enlightened self-interest,** which means that they are socially aware without giving up their own economic self-interest. According to this view, profits are the reward for the firm as it continues to provide true value to its customers, to help its employees to grow, and to behave responsibly as a corporate citizen.[21] These goals are reflective of the fastest-growing, most-profitable firms in the United States.

> *An emphasis on social responsibility can attract customers. A poll conducted by Opinion Research Corporation shows that 89 percent of purchases by adults are influenced by a company's reputation. Social responsibility also benefits companies by enabling them to recruit a high-quality labor force. The reputation of the firm and the goodwill associated with socially responsible actions attract talented prospective employees, people seeking an employer for which they would be proud to work.*

Economic Obligations and Social Responsibility

Do socially responsible companies sacrifice profits by working conscientiously to promote the social good? Do they make higher profits, better-than-average profits, or lower profits than corporations that ignore or flout the public's desires for a high and responsible standard of social performance? Efforts to discover an observed relationship between a company's financial performance and its social performance have produced mixed results.

Some studies seem to demonstrate that good social performers also tend to have good records of profit making, which could be an example of enlightened self-interest. For example, scholars found no support for the belief that social responsibility and profitability were trade-offs for businesses. In fact, they discovered "a positive association between social and financial performance in large U.S. corporations." However, other research reported that the relationship between profits and social responsibility is sequential. In this view, once the company is profitable, it can "afford" to be socially responsible in its actions. Others have argued that being socially responsible attracts investors to the firm.

---

[20]Robert H. Miles, *Managing the Corporate Social Environment: A Grounded Theory* (Englewood Cliffs, NJ: Prentice Hall, 1987).

[21]Jeff Frooman, "Socially Irresponsible and Illegal Behavior and Shareholder Wealth," *Business and Society,* September 1997, pp. 221–49, he argues that negative effects on shareholder wealth when a firm acts irresponsibly support the enlightened self-interest view: Act responsibly to promote shareholders' interests.

The relationship between social responsibility and profitability is extremely complex and difficult to prove.[22]

Any social program—for example, an in-company child-care center, a drug education program for employees, or the lending of company executives as advisers to community agencies—will usually impose immediate monetary costs on the participating company. These short-run costs certainly have a potential for reducing the company's profits unless the social activity is designed to make money, which is not usually the purpose of these programs. Therefore, a company may sacrifice short-run profits by undertaking social initiatives. But what is lost in the short run may be gained back over a longer period. For example, if a drug education program prevents and reduces on-the-job drug abuse, the firm's productivity may be increased by lower employee turnover, fewer absences from work, a healthier workforce, fewer accidents and injuries, and lower health insurance costs. In that case, the company may actually experience an increase in its long-run profits, although it had to make an expensive outlay to get the program started.

Legal Requirements versus Corporate Social Responsibility

Accompanying a firm's economic responsibility to its stockholders are its **legal obligations.** As a member of society, a firm must abide by the laws and regulations governing the society. How are a firm's legal obligations related to its social responsibilities? Laws and regulations are enacted to ensure socially responsible conduct by businesses. The high standard of social behavior expected by society are embodied in the society's laws. Can't businesses voluntarily decide to be socially responsible? Of course, but legal rules set standards for businesses to follow. Some firms go beyond the law; others seek to change the law to require its competitors to be more socially responsible.

Laws and regulations help create a level playing field for businesses that compete against one another. By requiring all firms to meet the same social standards—for example, the safe disposal of hazardous wastes—one firm cannot gain a competitive advantage over its rivals by dumping its wastes carelessly without the risk of lawsuits, fines, possible jail terms for some of its managers and employees, and unfavorable publicity for its actions.

Businesses that comply with laws and public policies are meeting a minimum level of social responsibility expected by the public. According to one leading scholar of corporate social performance, even legal compliance is barely enough to satisfy the public:

> *The traditional economic and legal criteria are necessary but not sufficient conditions of corporate legitimacy. The corporation that flouts them will not*

---

[22]The positive relationship between social and financial performance is reported in Lee E. Preston and Douglas P. O'Bannon, "The Corporate Social–Financial Performance Relationship," *Business and Society,* December 1997, pp. 419–29. The "profits first, then social action" argument is discussed by Jean B. McGuide, Alison Sundgeon, and Thomas Schneeweis, "Corporate Social Responsibility and Firm Financial Performance," *Academy of Management Journal* 31 (1988), pp. 854–72. The "social responsibility attracts investors" argument is supported by research reported in Samuel B. Graves and Sandra A. Waddock, "Institutional Owners and Corporate Social Performance," *Academy of Management Journal* 37 (1994), pp. 1034–46. Prior studies investigating this relationship are summarized in Jennifer J. Griffin and John F. Mahon, "The Corporate Social Performance and Corporate Financial Performance Debate," *Business and Society,* March 1997, pp. 5–31.

survive; even the mere satisfaction of these criteria does not ensure the corpo-
ration's continued existence. . . .

Thus, social responsibility implies bringing corporate behavior up to a
level where it is in congruence with currently prevailing social norms, values,
and performance expectations. . . . [Social responsibility] is simply a step
ahead—before the new societal expectations are codified into legal require-
ments.[23]

Stockholder Interests versus Other Stakeholder Interests

Top-level managers, along with a corporation's board of directors, are generally expected
to produce as much value as possible for the company's owners and investors. This can
be done by paying high dividends regularly and by running the company in ways that
cause the stock's value to rise. Not only are high profits a positive signal to Wall Street
investors that the company is being well run—thereby increasing the stock's value—but
those profits make possible the payment of high dividends to stockholders. Low profits
have the opposite effects and put great pressure on managers to improve the company's
financial performance.

However, stockholders are not the only stakeholder group that management must
keep in mind. The leaders of the world's largest organizations from Europe, Asia, and
North America have formed the Caux Roundtable. In its publications, these corporate
leaders have recognized that all the stakeholders must be considered; none can be
ignored. A top manager's job is to interact with the totality of the company's stakeholders, including those groups that advocate high levels of social responsibility by business. Management's central goal is to promote the interests of the entire company, not
just any single stakeholder group, and to pursue multiple company goals, not just profit
goals. These two contrasting views of corporate social responsibility are shown in
Exhibit 3–C.

This broader and far more complex task tends to put more emphasis on the long-
run profit picture rather than an exclusive focus on immediate returns. When this happens, dividends paid to stockholders may be less than they desire, and the value of their
shares may not rise as rapidly as they would like. These are the kinds of risks faced by
corporate managers who have a legal responsibility to produce high value for the company's stockholder-owners but who also must try to promote the overall interests of the
entire company. Putting all of the emphasis on short-run maximum profits for stockholders can lead to policies that overlook the interests and needs of other stakeholders.
Managers may also downgrade social responsibility programs that increase short-run
costs, although it is well-known that the general public strongly approves socially responsible companies.

As a response to the conflict between long- and short-term profit making, an enlightened self-interest point of view may be the most useful and practical approach. That
means incurring reasonable short-run costs to undertake socially responsible activities that
benefit both the company and the general public in the long run.

---

[23]S. Prakash Sethi, "A Conceptual Framework for Environmental Analysis of Social Issues and Evaluation of
Business Response Patterns," in S. Prakash Sethi and Cecilia M. Falbe, eds., *Business and Society: Dimensions of Conflict and Cooperation* (Lexington, MA: Lexington Books, 1987), pp. 42, 43.

EXHIBIT
3–C

Two Views of Corporate Social Responsibility

Shareholder Wealth

In a market-based economy that recognizes the rights of private property, the only social responsibility of business is to create shareholder value and to do so legally and with integrity. Yet we do have important unresolved social challenges—from drug abuse to education and the environment—that require collective action. Corporate management however has neither the political legitimacy nor the expertise to decide what is in the social interest. It is our form of government that provides the vehicle for collective choice via elected legislators and the judicial system.

Whether corporate social responsibility is advocated by political activists or the chief executive officer, the costs of these expenditures, which don't increase the value of the company or its stock, will be passed on to consumers by way of higher prices, or to employees as lower wages, or to shareholders as lower returns.

Source: Alfred Rappaport, "Let's Let Business Be Business," *New York Times,* February 4, 1990, p. F13. Copyright © 1990 By The New York Times Company. Reprinted by Permission.

Multiple Stakeholders

We believe in treating all customers with dignity irrespective of whether they purchase our products and services directly from us or otherwise acquire them in the market. . . .

We believe in the dignity of every employee and in taking employee interests seriously. . . .

We believe in honoring the trust our investors place in us. . . .

Our relationship with suppliers and subcontractors must be based on mutual respect. . . .

We believe that fair economic competition is one of the basic requirements for increasing the wealth of nations and, ultimately for making possible the just distribution of goods and services. . . .

We believe that as global corporate citizens, we can contribute to such forces of reform and human rights . . . at work in the communities [where we operate]. . . .

Source: "The Caux Principles," Section 3, *The Caux Roundtable,* http://www.arq.co.uk/ethicalbusiness/archive/caux/caux3.htm (July 9, 1997).

Summary Points of This Chapter

- Corporate social responsibility means that a corporation should be held accountable for any of its actions that affect people, their communities, and their environment. Businesses must recognize their vast power and wield it to better society.

- The idea of corporate social responsibility in the United States was adopted by business leaders in the early twentieth century. The central themes of social responsibility have been charity—which means giving aid to the needy—and stewardship—acting as a public trustee and considering all corporate stakeholders when making business decisions.

- Social responsibility most often is demonstrated through philanthropic contributions and employee volunteerism.

- Examples of corporate social responsibility are increasing around the world. However, some cultures, such as Japan, take a more limited view of social responsibility.

- Business firms are limited in their efforts to be socially responsible. Usually excluded are actions that are unrelated to company goals and abilities, are too costly, impair business efficiency, and are highly complex.

- Socially responsible businesses should attempt to balance economic, legal, and social obligations. Following an enlightened self-interest approach, a firm may be economically rewarded while society benefits from the firm's actions. Abiding by legal requirements can also guide businesses in serving various groups in society. Managers should consider all of the company's stakeholders and their interests.

Key Terms and Concepts Used in this Chapter

- Corporate social responsibility
- Iron Law of Responsibility
- Charity principle
- Stewardship principle

- Corporate philanthropy
- Corporate employee volunteerism
- Enlightened self-interest
- Legal obligations

Internet Resources

- http://www.capitalresearch.org/crc/patterns   Patterns in Corporate Philanthropy
- http://www.rpbooks.com/visitors/newsroom   Corporate Philanthropy News
- http://www.iquest.com/~hats/promos.html   Corporate Aspects of Volunteerism
- http://www.bsr.org   Business for Social Responsibility

Discussion Case   Cummins Engine Company

One admirer called it "capitalism at its best." Another said its chief executive officer "believed in superb products, concern for employees, involvement in the community—all those qualities that made American corporations the envy of the world."

The subject of this commentary was Cummins Engine Company, a leading maker of heavy-duty diesel engines for trucks. From its founding in 1919, Cummins was known for a benevolent attitude, mainly a result of the religious convictions and social philosophy of Clessie Cummins, the founder. It also was famous for high-quality, reliable, and efficient engines.

Cummins's long record of social responsibility is well-known. Its headquarters town of Columbus, Indiana, is sprinkled with public buildings designed by some of the world's leading architects whose fees were paid by Cummins. The management staff was racially integrated as early as the 1960s, and Cummins became an early leader in reducing pollution caused by its engines. Employees are protected against unwarranted use of personal data in company files, and Cummins's chairman helped develop privacy guidelines for other employers. Many local causes draw upon the company's charitable funds, along with the voluntary help of company executives and employees. Townspeople remained fiercely loyal to the company, even after over 4,000 were laid off during the 1980s. Cummins employees receive good wages and benefits and take much pride in producing high-quality engines.

But as the 1990s began, this paragon of social responsibility appeared to be in trouble. It had lost over $100 million in 1986, almost as much in 1988, and had only a tiny net profit in 1987. It had fended off one British corporate raider at a cost of $72 million but faced another potential hostile takeover by a Hong Kong investor who held around 15 percent of the company's stock. In spite of shaky profits, the company refused to cut long-term research spending to improve its products or to reduce charitable contributions which were among the highest in industrial America. Neither would company officials listen to those who urged a move from its midwestern home to nonunion lower-cost areas in the South. When Hurricane Hugo devastated large sections of South Carolina in 1989, the company sent free engines and generators to some of the victims. Near its new factory in Brazil, it helped build a school, a clinic, and a gymnasium in a poor neighborhood. Viewing this situation, one financial analyst declared, "Cummins is one big social slush fund. An incredibly naive attitude exists at the company."

Henry B. Schacht, Cummins's chairman, disagreed. He commented: "Some say the company's main goal should be to maximize shareholder value . . . I say no. [The company's goal is] being fair and honest and doing what is right even when it is not to our immediate benefit." Hearing this, a Wall Street skeptic declared that Cummins has been "in a long-term mode for 10 years. . . . Schacht sounds great, but at some point there's got to be a payout for all this spending."

An outside observer responded by saying, "Wall Street stubbornly ignores the success of Japanese industrial enterprises—success achieved in long-term planning for market penetration, in lieu of a consuming emphasis on short-term results. If the financial community would lay off the hounding of public-company managements [like Cummins], allowing them to run their businesses instead of wasting valuable time reacting to the ill-conceived criticisms of these Wall Street gurus, domestic enterprises would be all the better for it." A former chairman of the company summed up his own view: "Cummins has a fantastic future because it isn't just factories, machines and cash. It's outstanding people who take intense pride in their work and their community."

Demonstrating that his social skills were matched by an equal financial ability, Cummins's CEO in mid-1990 sold a 27 percent stake of the company to Ford Motor, Tenneco, and Kubota, a Japanese firm. The deal gave Cummins needed new business for its diesel engines and $250 million to reduce debt and invest in modernization. Cummins's continued international expansion and diversification from the mid-1980s into the 1990s proved its worth in 1996. While the heavy-duty truck market in North America had a cyclical downturn, Cummins's annual sales increased by $12 million to $5.257 billion. This marked the second year in a row that Cummins had exceeded the $5 billion mark in total revenue. Cummins Engine Company appears to provide an example that profits and social responsibility can coexist.

Sources: All quotations are from Robert Johnson, "Survivor's Story: With Its Spirit Shaken but Unbeaten, Cummins Shows Decade's Scars," *The Wall Street Journal,* December 13, 1989, pp. A1, A6; and "Letters to the Editor," *The Wall Street Journal,* January 15, 1990, p. A11. Current financial data are from the 1996 Cummins Engine Company annual report.

Discussion Questions

1. Is Cummins's commitment to social responsibility fair to the company's stockholders? If you were Cummins's CEO, would you cut back on social expenditures so you could pay higher dividends to the company's owners?

2. Which principle of social responsibility—the charity principle or the stewardship principle—is the basis of Cummins's approach to social responsibility? Give some examples from the case.

3. Of the four major limits to social responsibility discussed in this chapter, which ones seem to apply to Cummins?

4. Is Cummins an example of what this chapter calls "enlightened self-interest?" Explain your answer.

4

Socially Responsive Management

Socially responsive corporations consider and carefully seek to foster mutually beneficial relationships with their stakeholders. This chapter discusses how businesses must assess environmental forces before attempting to implement a successful social strategy. Once implemented, the social strategy must be evaluated to determine if the firm is acting in a socially responsive manner.

This chapter focuses on these key questions and objectives:

- What groups and social forces changed the way management responds to the social environment?

- What influences and forces should be monitored by managers when developing a socially responsive program?

- What are the stages in the model of social responsiveness?

- What elements are critical for a business to effectively manage the corporate social environment?

- Can a firm's management of the social environment be assessed?

S trategic alliances became common in the 1990s as leading corporations faced an increasing number of social issues. To respond to the complex social problems affecting business, companies joined together and with their key stakeholders (government agencies, community or special interest groups, schools, etc.) to form **collaborative partnerships** (see Exhibit 4–A). By pooling their financial and human resources, a network of organizations could better address the challenges presented by the various social concerns and more effectively achieve their mutual goals.

A collaborative partnership was formed when businesses in Milwaukee, Wisconsin, realized that dramatic changes required dramatic responses. Gangs, drug dealers, and prostitutes became familiar residents of the Avenues West area, a 100-square-block section of the city on the fringe of the downtown business district. Crime in the Milwaukee area was up 22 percent; residential housing was decaying. By 1990, 60 percent of the buildings in the Avenues West area contained 20 or more rental units. Only a small percentage of the housing units were owner-occupied. Absentee landlords frequently let dwellings fall into disrepair or be taken over by drug dealers to become crack houses where drugs are easily purchased. These and other factors led to a collaborative partnership involving business and its stakeholders to seriously address these social challenges. The plan was called the Campus Circle Project.[1]

Announced in November 1991, the project created a partnership with numerous organizations and community groups to redevelop the Avenues West neighborhood. Four local corporations—Wisconsin Energy Corporation, Wisconsin Bell, Catholic Knights Insurance Company, and Aurora Health Care—pledged nearly $15 million. Marquette University, a Jesuit Catholic college located in the Avenues West area, joined the partnership and committed cash, land, and in-kind contributions worth $9 million. The City of Milwaukee created a special tax structure to help pay for public improvements. Finally, a $20 million, five-year federal grant was received to provide further support for the project.

The multiphase project of crime prevention, community planning, housing rehabilitation and construction, and economic development for the Avenues West neighborhood continued throughout the 1990s. Minority- and women-owned businesses and laborers completed more than 30 percent of the work. Green spaces were created in neighborhoods in response to the children, who make up one-third of the community's population. Initial assessments indicate that this type of cooperative partnership between corporate, academic, and governmental institutions may be one way to combat high crime and declining housing in neighborhoods.

But what gave rise to the change in corporate social responsiveness of the 1980s and 1990s? What events or social movements triggered these changes in stakeholder management analysis and the programs developed from the analysis?

The Corporate Social Climate

Decades of challenges by corporate stakeholders seeking social control of business, most evident during the 1960s and 1970s in the United States, created a corporate social environment filled with opportunities for socially responsive strategies. Challenges by corporate stakeholders came from many diverse groups.

---

[1]"Marquette University Leads Urban Revival of Blighted Environs," *The Wall Street Journal,* February 1, 1994, pp. A1, A6.

EXHIBIT
4–A

Business and Government Partnering to Create Jobs

A partnership among businesses and government to address various social issues was reflected in the actions taken by a group of companies in support of a national service program, AmeriCorps. AmeriCorps was run by the Corporation for National Services, a nonprofit organization that selected proposals submitted by thousands of communities seeking to employ local youths or the unemployed. At a time when conservative business interests often attack government-sponsored social programs, the AmeriCorps partnership between business and government has been overwhelmingly supported.

For example, U.S. Health pledged over $150,000 over three years to City Year, a nonprofit organization that sent AmeriCorps members to work with community projects. An executive at the firm pointed out that AmeriCorps recouped more than $376 million of its costs in one year by giving youths skills to become productive adults in the economy. Other corporate support included the following: General Electric contributed $250,000 to 11 United Way chapters for literacy training and food pantries; Tenneco Gas gave $35,000 and provided printing and accounting services to Serve Houston Youth Corps, an AmeriCorps affiliate; Nike promised $150,000 for programs designed to set up fitness-oriented sports leagues and for the renovation of playgrounds; and Fanny May contributed $100,000 to three housing groups to train AmeriCorps members to counsel low-income renters on homeownership.

Since the creation of AmeriCorps in 1993, businesses contributed cash, equipment, and employee volunteers to help 20,000 youths to perform services that range from rehabilitating low-income housing to cleaning up rivers.

Source: "A Social Program CEOs Want to Save," *Business Week,* June 19, 1995, pp. 120–21.

- Consumer advocates, spearheaded by Ralph Nader's fight against the U.S. automobile industry for safer vehicles, demanded safe products, accurate information, and competitive pricing of products.
- Environmentalists held the first Earth Days in the 1970s, calling for businesses to be accountable for air and water quality.
- Anti–Vietnam War activists demanded that businesses participating in what they termed the military industrial complex abandon conventional and chemical weapons production and convert to the manufacture of peacetime goods.
- African-American groups, organized under the civil rights movement, pressed for an end to discriminatory practices in the hiring, promotion, and training of employees.
- Women's groups accused businesses of gender bias and discrimination.
- Workers, of all races and both genders, pushed for safer working conditions.
- Communities protested both the use and transportation of toxic materials by businesses and the construction and operation of nuclear energy plants.

These and other corporate stakeholders dramatically altered the business environment within which managers attempted to perform their tasks. Most of the groups mentioned will be discussed in greater detail in the following chapters of the book. The overall contribution of these groups to the collective social movements demanded a different response from businesses in addition to those embodied in the notions of *corporate social responsibility*. Firms are now required to develop a sense of *corporate social responsiveness*.

As discussed in the previous chapter, corporate social responsibility is based on the principles of charity and stewardship. Expressions of these concepts are seen in corporate philanthropy and the care of the public's resources. However, the basis for **corporate social responsiveness** does not rely on the generosity of a firm's senior management or their awareness of their role as trustees of the public's interests. Corporate social responsiveness is seen in the *processes* a firm establishes to address social demands initiated by corporate stakeholders or in the *social actions* taken by the firm that affect its stakeholders. The contrast between corporate social responsibility and what has been labeled corporate social responsiveness is highlighted in Figure 4–1.

Formulating Socially Responsive Strategies

Before it can form a social strategy, a corporation must skillfully analyze various influences and forces and then weigh the information collected. This section discusses the multiple environments that affect business and the techniques available to analyze them.

The Macroenvironment of Business

To begin formulating a socially responsive strategy, a firm needs a framework of environmental information. Managers must understand what is occurring in many sectors of the external world. According to two authorities, the environment that is relevant for businesses and their managers consists of four distinct segments: social, economic, political, and tech-

Figure 4–1

Contrast between corporate social responsibility and corporate social responsiveness.

	Corporate Social Responsibility	Corporate Social Responsiveness
Origin	1920s	1960s
Basis	Principles of charity and stewardship	Demands made by numerous social stakeholder groups
Focus	Moral obligations to society at large	Practical reponses by businesses to corporate stakeholders
Action	Philanthropy, trustee of the public's interests	Social programs

nological.[2] This **macroenvironment of business** consists of an almost unlimited amount of information, including facts, trends, issues, and ideas; and each of these segments represents a focused area of information, some of it important and relevant to the business. Figure 4–2 illustrates each of the four segments of the macroenvironment of business.

As shown in the figure, the *social segment* focuses on information about (1) demographics, (2) lifestyles, and (3) social values of a society. Managers have a need to understand changes in population patterns, characteristics of the population, emergence of new lifestyles, and social values that seem to be in or out of favor with the majority of the population.

The information from the social segment in the case of the Campus Circle Project, described earlier, was a critical motivation in the formulation of a socially responsive strategy. The Avenues West neighborhood was quickly deteriorating. Housing decay and increases in drug traffic, prostitution, and violent crimes began to challenge the business community's lack of social involvement in the neighborhood. These social conditions had a direct impact on the viability of business and its stakeholders (local community, customers, employees).

The *economic segment* focuses on the general set of economic factors and conditions confronting industries in a society. For example, information about interest rates, unemployment, foreign imports, and many other such factors is relevant to virtually all businesses. The economic segment obviously has a large impact on all business organizations.

Figure 4–2

The macroenvironments of business.

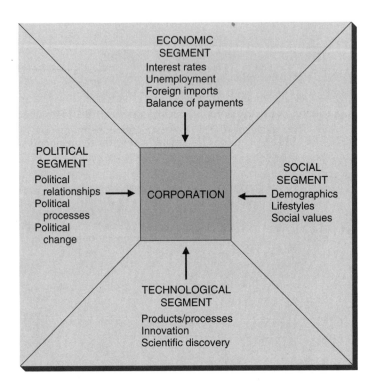

[2]Liam Fahey and V.K. Narayanan, *Macroenvironmental Analysis for Strategic Management* (St. Paul, MN: West, 1986), pp. 28–29.

This impact was also central to the Campus Circle Project. The conditions in the neighborhood contributed to the overall economic decline in the area. Businesses were considering relocating to a safer, more prosperous suburban Milwaukee industrial park. The costs of doing business near the Avenues West area increased as safety programs were created to protect employees as they walked from the parking lot to work. The economic segment of the macroenvironment of business was central to the project's strategic focus. The socially responsive strategy had to deal with the economic objectives and needs of those involved in the partnership, as well as the social ones.

The *political segment* deals with specific political relationships in society, changes in them, and the processes by which society makes political decisions. Changes in the tax code, for example, redistribute income and tax burdens. This involves political relationships between various segments of society. The creation and dissolution of regulatory institutions that set standards for business behavior are examples of changes in the political process.

A critical participant in the Campus Circle Project was the City of Milwaukee. The partnership relied on a special tax structure to help pay for numerous public improvements to the Avenues West area. Another political relationship was evident on the federal level, as the Campus Circle Project secured a $20 million, five-year grant to supplement the private funding for the project.

The *technological segment* is concerned with the technological progress and potential hazards that are taking place in society. New products, processes, or materials, including any negative social impacts; the general level of scientific activity; and advances in fundamental science (e.g., biology) are the key concerns in this area.

Although the technological segment is often understood in terms of manufacturing development or processes, the Campus Circle Project utilized a somewhat unique technology: urban planning. Extensive drafting and revisions were made to plans calling for housing demolition, construction, or rehabilitation. The relocation of numerous businesses into a centrally located mall was carefully planned and coordinated with the business owners. The city was petitioned to close a stretch of a major avenue that cut through the Avenues West area to ensure greater safety for the residents and to create a buffer between the residential neighborhood and the downtown business district.

The macroenvironment, as presented in Figure 4–2, is a system of interrelated segments, each one connected to and influencing the others. In the Campus Circle Project, social decay had economic consequences for businesses and other organizations in the neighborhood. To turn around the Avenues West area, a collaborative partnership of business, government, and educational organizations was formed. This group had to integrate the social, economic, political, and technological segments of their macroenvironment to formulate a socially responsive strategy to address the challenge facing them.

A manager must understand each of these segments, their interrelationships, and those facts that are of direct importance to the corporation. This knowledge will improve his or her understanding of the relevant environment in which strategies must be formulated.

Scanning and Environmental Analysis

To effectively formulate socially responsive strategies, managers must learn about the company's external environment. **Environmental scanning** is a managerial process of analyzing the external social, economic, political, and technological environments. Scanning can be done informally or formally by individual managers or teams. It is largely an information collection, analysis, and processing activity, and it is a valuable first step in building a socially responsive strategy for an organization.

Generally, scanning can be done by focusing on one or more of the following: trends that are occurring in government, society, or segments of each; issues that are emerging in the company's industry or sector of the economy or in nations where it conducts business; and stakeholders that are currently important to the organization or appear to be potentially important in the future.

Trend analysis attempts to understand and project the implications and consequences of current trends into the future. Companies whose products or services have particularly long life spans have a special need for understanding long-term trends. The life insurance industry, for example, regularly enters into individual contracts that have a life span of 20, 30, or even 50 years. A policyholder may pay premiums on life insurance for decades before the insurer is required to pay a benefit. Trends such as increasing life spans and more active lifestyles also can alter the calculation of how many years an insurer may have to pay out on a pension plan or annuity. The failure to understand such trends and their implications can result in poor financial planning that injures the company and the insurance beneficiary or pension recipient.

Issues analysis, described in greater detail in Chapter 2, involves a careful assessment of specific concerns that are having, or may have, an impact on the company. In many companies, public affairs managers do detailed tracking and monitoring of numerous social issues, seeking opportunities for economic and social benefit. Warner-Lambert, for example, believes that responding to critical social issues enhances the company's image, builds company pride among its employees, and helps those in need. The firm addresses various social issues such as hospice care for the terminally ill and the problem of domestic violence. The company has created educational and community outreach programs in response to these emerging social issues.[3]

Introduced in Chapter 1, *stakeholder analysis* places the scanner's focus on the people, groups, and organizations that populate the external environment. By trying to understand the issues that are of concern to the company's primary and secondary stakeholders, managers are better able to predict what types of demands are going to be made in the months ahead. There are many ways to collect such information, ranging from professional reporting services that track leaders of activist groups to direct contacts and discussions with stakeholder representatives. Informal discussions with union leaders or local environmentalists can go a long way toward providing managers with an understanding of what is critical to these groups and why.

Implementing Social Responsiveness

Companies do not become socially responsive overnight. The process takes time. New attitudes have to be developed, new routines learned, and new policies and action programs designed. Once a company is prepared to implement a social strategy, it must follow specific guidelines to achieve its social objectives. Many obstacles must be overcome in implementing socially responsive strategies. Some are structural, such as the reporting relationships between groups of managers; others are cultural, such as a historical pattern of only men or women in a particular job category.

---

[3]"Warner-Lambert's World, Social Responsibility," http://www.warner-lambert.com/info/social.html (July 9, 1997).

A Model of Corporate Social Responsiveness

An early model of how large corporations effectively implement socially responsive policies is illustrated in Figure 4–3. There are three stages to the responsiveness process depicted in this model. Each is discussed below.

The Policy Stage

In the first stage of social responsiveness, the company becomes aware of those parts of the surrounding environment to which it needs to respond and act on. Awareness may occur after stakeholder expectations change, or it may result from a systematic environmental analysis. Whether or not stakeholder pressure exists, a company's management may think, based on environmental analysis, that it should respond to emerging issues, concerns, or social trends.

> *For example, a group of Boston businesses announced a $6 million program designed to guarantee financial aid to all graduates of the city's public high schools who get into college and to provide jobs for those who complete their education. This effort was taken in reaction to a dramatic increase in the dropout rate among Boston-area high school students. In addition to the funds provided, 350 Boston-area companies pledged to help provide jobs to high school graduates, and many offered to help pay for guidance counselors in the schools. This commitment served two purposes: The students and schools were helped, and the companies ensured themselves a future pool of applicants for entry-level jobs. By 1997, businesses managed about 10 percent of the 750 charter schools in the United States, educational institutions owned and operated by for-profit companies.[4]*

A company's social responses need to be guided by policies that are carefully and deliberately developed by its top management and board of directors. Those policies provide a framework for shaping other aspects of the organization's response. New production policies, for example, may result in better quality control for consumer products, may remove job hazards, and may reduce water pollution all at the same time.

The Learning Stage

Once it has identified a social problem—for example, excessive numbers of high school dropouts—and adopted a general policy—an educational opportunity policy—the company must learn how to tackle the problem and make the new policy work. Two kinds of learning are needed: specialized learning and administrative learning.

Specialized learning occurs when a sociotechnical expert—for example, an inner-city educator who is thoroughly familiar with the culture, lifestyles, motivations, and special problems of high school youth—is employed to advise company officers and managers. The kind of specialized knowledge that the sociotechnical expert can provide is particularly helpful in the early stages of social responsiveness when the company is deal-

---

[4]Fox Butterfield, "Funds and Jobs Pledged to Boston Graduates," *New York Times,* September 10, 1986, p. D25; and Steve Stecklow, "Businesses Scramble to Run Charter Schools," *Wall Street Journal,* August 21, 1997, p. B1. Business involvement in public school education is discussed in detail in "Breaking the Mold: The Private Sector's Accelerating Role in Public Education," *Business Week,* October 17, 1994, pp. 122–53.

Figure 4–3

A three-stage model of corporate social responsiveness.

Source: Adapted from Robert W. Ackerman and Raymond A. Bauer, Corporate Social Responsiveness: The Modern Dilemma. (Reston, VA: Reston, 1976).

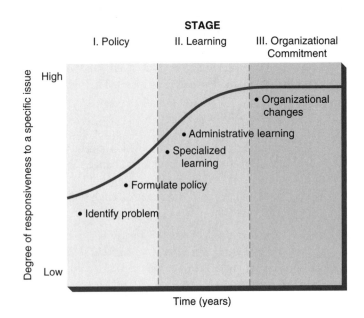

ing with an unfamiliar social problem, whether it is high school dropouts, prejudice against minorities in hiring practices, excessive pollution, or toxic chemical hazards.

Administrative learning occurs when a company's supervisors and managers—those who administer the organization's daily affairs—become familiar with new routines that are necessary to cope with a social problem. A technical expert can assist the company in taking its first steps to solve a problem but cannot do the whole job alone. Social responsiveness requires the full cooperation and knowledge of line managers and staff experts. Personal involvement is essential.

> *The AT&T Learning Network is a $150 million, five-year program designed to assist America's youth in electronic communication. AT&T provides three months of free voice-messaging service and free voice mailboxes to thousands of students, who the company sees as potential customers. To fully implement this program, on-line mentoring is essential. The mentoring aspect of the program involves AT&T managers, technical experts, and other employees across the corporate organization.*[5]

The Organizational Commitment Stage

A final step is needed to achieve full social responsiveness: An organization must *institutionalize* its new social policy.[6] The new policies and routines learned in the first two stages should become so well accepted throughout the entire company that they are considered to be a normal part of doing business. In other words, they should be a part of the

---

[5]Gautan Naik, "AT&T to Give 110,000 Schools Free Services," *The Wall Street Journal*, November 1, 1995, pp. A3, A12.
[6]Robert Ackerman, "How Companies Respond to Social Demands," *Harvard Business Review*, July–August 1973, pp. 88–98.

company and its standard operating procedures. For example, when managers respond to the needs of the local education system or to the students without having to rely on special directives from top management, the socially responsive policy can be considered to be institutionalized.

The normal organizational pressures to resist change mean that both effort and time are needed to improve a corporation's responsiveness. In the past, it took large corporations an average of six to eight years to progress from the first stage to the third stage on any given social issue or problem such as equal employment opportunity or pollution control. Yet some firms are more flexible than others, and some social problems are easier to handle than others, so the time involved may vary considerably. It is clear, however, that a combination of internal factors, especially management willpower, and external factors, especially continued stakeholder action on the problem, is necessary for effective change to occur.

Framework for Social Policy

After reaching the organizational commitment stage, the company must develop specific guidelines to direct the strategic social policy. Two scholars in the strategic management field have created a set of guidelines to enhance the success of a business's social policy.[7] They believe that social policies should:

- *Concentrate action programs on limited objectives.* No company can take significant action in every area of social responsibility. It can achieve more if it selects areas in which to concentrate its efforts. Vermont National Bank targets socially responsible investing that has community impact. The Socially Responsible Banking Fund has attracted more than $85 million in investments. As a result, thousands of loans are made to affordable housing projects, organic farms, small businesses, environmental and conservation projects, and education.

- *Concentrate action programs related to the firm's products or services.* The program should focus on areas strategically related to the present and prospective economic functions of the business. Mario J. Antoci, chairman and CEO of American Savings Bank, initiated a community outreach and urban lending program for California's low-income and minority populations. This initiative gives thousands of Californians the opportunity to purchase homes and has helped American Savings become one of the most stable and profitable thrifts in the country.

- *Begin action programs close to home.* The program should address local issues or social needs before spreading out or acting in far-distant regions. Rachel's Bus Company, a Chicago-based school transportation company, targets inner-city Chicago and its economic devastation when developing its social program guidelines. Rachel Hubka, the company's president, located the company headquarters in the inner-city and hires qualified applicants from the local community. These guidelines foster a stronger pride in the inner-city area that the company serves.

---

[7]Archie B. Carroll and Frank Hoy, "Integrating Corporate Social Policy into Strategic Management," *Journal of Business Strategy,* Winter 1984, pp. 48–57; also see Craig Smith, "The New Corporate Philanthropy," *Harvard Business Review,* May–June 1994, pp. 105–16.

- *Facilitate employee action.* Programs in which employees can become involved as individuals rather than as representatives of the company encourage future participation and commitment. As part of its ongoing commitment to Habitat for Humanity, Coldwell Banker selects sales employees to travel to various sites to help build homes for deserving families. In 1997, four Coldwell Banker employees were flown to Godollo, Hungary, for the project. In past years, employees assisted Habitat for Humanity in various cites located in the United States.

Becoming a Socially Responsive Firm

How does a firm become more socially responsive? Robert Miles, American scholar and consultant, observed that:

Executive leaders of America's largest corporations have been confronted . . . during the last two decades with an unprecedented increase in the social issues impinging upon their business policies and practices. Not only have a variety of social regulations been developed that apply universally to all industries, but each industry has also experienced to varying degrees a proliferation of industry-specific challenges for the corporate social environment.[8]

In response to these pressures, businesses have increased their efforts to manage the corporate social environment. The social environment encompasses business activities influenced by various community and government groups. Many chief executives spend more time on the external affairs of the business than any other activity. Most executives allocate significant personnel, time, and budget to the creation of elaborate staff groups to help them understand and manage this environment and its challenges.

Some firms may be more vulnerable to social group pressure and social regulation than others. A number of factors have been identified as contributing to this vulnerability. A firm may be more vulnerable to social forces if the firm is:

- A large-sized or well-known company thus presenting a big target.
- Located in an urban area and under increased scrutiny by the media and social groups.
- Producing a consumer-oriented product viewed as a necessity by the public.
- Providing a product or service that may cause harm or injury to the user.
- Part of a heavily regulated industry that is expected to meet high public expectations.

Top Management Philosophy

How a firm addresses its exposure to the corporate social environment heavily depends on the values and beliefs of the company managers—the philosophy they hold about the role of the corporation in society. This is called the **top management philosophy.**

Managers sensitive to the impact of social forces and seeking to strategically manage their stakeholders will adopt the view that the firm is a social as well as an economic institution. They embrace the view that the firm has a duty to adapt to a changing social

---

[8]Robert H. Miles, *Managing the Corporate Social Environment* (Englewood Cliffs, NJ: Prentice Hall, 1987). Miles develops a corporate social strategy similar to the one presented here.

environment. In response to emerging social issues, these managers are more likely to modify their business policies and practices than managers who understand their responsibilities to the firm only in an economic context. Managers in socially responsive firms recognize and consider not only the interests of their immediate, core stakeholders but the interests of all of the firm's stakeholders. They see corporate social performance in broad terms extending over the long term and having an impact on their industry. Most important, these managers merge the economic and social goals of their company into the firm's planning, measurement, and reward systems developed to guide and monitor business operations and managers' performance.

Socially Responsive Strategy

Using a socially responsive top management philosophy as a foundation, a firm must develop a **socially responsive strategy.** This strategic orientation tends to emphasize a collaborative and problem-solving approach, as opposed to one that emphasizes only the firm's interests and is adversarial in nature.

Collaborative, problem-solving strategies are distinguished by their emphasis on maintaining long-term relationships based on trust and open communication with all of the company's stakeholders. Managers demonstrate this collaborative characteristic by participating in regulatory advisory committees and trade associations that seek mutually beneficial compromises. However, these managers are quick to explain that their strategy is not purely altruistic. They acknowledge that maintaining ongoing relationships with their stakeholders and seeking mutually beneficial problem-solving strategies will ensure the company's long-term survival. This is an expression of enlightened self-interest as described in Chapter 3.

> *An example of a collaborative strategy is IBM Corporation's "Reinventing Education" grants program. With education as the primary focus of IBM's social strategy, the firm has created partnerships with other businesses, foundations, and educational groups. IBM's involvement includes financial pledges, donations of technology, and expert assistance to participating schools. In cooperation with other institutions, IBM seeks economic profit as well as attempting to manage various forces in the corporate social environment.*[9]

Socially Responsive Structure

The next step in becoming a socially responsive organization is to change the organizational structure to be more responsive to external social challenges and better able to implement socially responsive strategies. This structure evolves from the values and beliefs held by the company's top managers and is expressed through socially responsive business strategies. There are four basic design dimensions that help to distinguish a **socially responsive structure** in an organization. They are breadth, depth, influence, and integration.[10]

Breadth is the number of different staff units that specialize in the socially responsive strategies undertaken by the company. The breadth of the design must be sufficient to enable the firm to adequately monitor and respond to the demands made by social forces.

[9]"IBM Corporate Contributions Program," http://www.technogrants.com/4.html (June 27, 1997).

[10]See Miles, *Managing the Corporate Social Environment,* for his observations of these characteristics in his study of the insurance industry.

Depth is the intensity of the organizational learning process in response to the potential for social challenges and is addressed by the socially responsive strategy process. Companies more vulnerable to social challenges require more developed social response functions, which provide a wide range of perspectives and responses.

Influence and *integration* are the final two dimensions of the socially responsive organizational structure. They refer to the quality of relationships that exist among the company's staff units. The absence of this influence and integration could undermine or bias the corporation's socially responsive strategy process since it could lead to one staff unit, or a few, dominating the process at the sake of other units. The ultimate effectiveness often is due to the degree of integration achieved among the staff units.

Line Manager Involvement

The final element in becoming a socially responsive firm is the extent to which line managers are involved in the strategic process. The degree of **line manager involvement** depends on the sophistication of the company's socially responsive strategy process. The more elaborate the process, the more essential is involvement by line managers.

A high degree of line manager involvement often is difficult to achieve. Initially the strategic process is developed by staff units, but line managers must quickly become involved and assume responsibility for the implementation of the company's socially responsive strategies. For example, if a firm develops a strategy that includes a highly integrated philanthropic contribution and employee volunteerism program with local charities, line managers often are in the best position to screen worthy recipients, determine appropriate levels of contributions, and assign employee volunteers.

In contrast, corporations that rely on staff personnel and do not foster line manager involvement will tend to exhibit a narrow, defensive, and protective socially responsive posture. This approach will buffer the company's line managers and line operations from corporate social environment influences. The degree of line manager involvement is heavily influenced by top management philosophy and generally is consistent with the socially responsive strategy and structure adopted by the company.

Corporate Social Audits

In 1953, Howard Bowen introduced the idea of bringing social impacts to the attention of managers. He proposed a specialized group of social auditors to work within the organization and present their audit findings to managers. A recent definition of **social auditing** challenges businesses to be socially responsive:

> *Today, a social audit examines the social and ethical impact of the business from two perspectives: from the inside, assessing performance against the company's mission statement of objectives; and from the outside, using comparisons with other organizations' behavior and social norms.*[11]

Since the 1960s, the demand for social auditing has gained momentum in Europe, as well as in the United States. A British scholar, George Goyder, made the following passionate plea:

[11]Howard R. Bowen, *Social Responsibilities of the Businessman* (New York: Harper, 1953).

Has the time come for the country which led the first industrial revolution to lead the industrialized nations a second time, by returning to those mutual aid principles which are also the principles of the natural law? For Britain, time is running out. We need the responsible company now.[12]

Modern Day Social Assessment

Throughout the 1970s, managers remained unconvinced that financial measures involved in social auditing could be used in business decision making. They believed that social costs and benefits were too removed from the firm's mainstream functions, especially from its profits. As a result, they argued that financial accounting for social impacts was not helpful in the quest for developing socially responsible strategies or in the assessment of such strategies.[13]

In response to this skepticism, researchers have tried to develop a **social performance audit** or corporate ratings approach. This type of audit involves measuring a firm's corporate activities on an ideal socially responsible scale or comparing the resulting rating of a firm's actions against those of other, similar organizations.[14] For example, if a company supports a tutorial program at a local school, the performance audit might look at not only the number of hours of employee volunteerism but also assess the change in student test scores as an indicator of the program's social impact.

Organizations concerned about stakeholder issues use performance audits to evaluate the impact of corporate social efforts. Examples include universities, churches, charitable groups, and socially responsible mutual funds who invest their money in companies that behave like good neighbors.[15]

As businesses approach the twenty-first century, interest in social auditing is once again rising. Many corporate stakeholders—community groups, employee unions and consumer activists—expect businesses to act responsibly and be contributing members to the society to which the firms and the stakeholder groups belong. One such example of a social audit involves the Body Shop. A social audit was commissioned by Body Shop executives to provide an independent assessment of the company's social and ethical achievements. In the report, high marks were given to the Body Shop in areas such as the quality of its mission statement, corporate philanthropy, and environmental and animal welfare. But, according to Stanford professor Kirk Hanson, who conducted the audit, the company was weak in accepting outside criticism and had a poor relationship with the public and the media.[16] Another example of a corporate social audit is shown in Exhibit 4-B.

---

[12]George Goyder, *The Just Enterprise—A Blueprint for the Responsible Company* (London: Adamantine Press, 1993).

[13]William C. Frederick, "Auditing Corporate Social Performance: The Anatomy of a Social Research Project," in Lee E. Preston, ed., *Research in Corporate Social Performance and Policy* (Greenwich, CT: JAI Press), vol. 1 (1978), pp. 123–37.

[14]See Carolyn Kay Brancato, "New Corporate Performance Measures," Report No. 1118-95-RR, The Conference Board, New York, 1995, for examples of corporate performance measure models from many countries.

[15]Kim Davenport, "Social Auditing: The Quest for Corporate Social Responsibility," in Jim Weber and Kathleen Rehbein, eds., *IABS 1997 Proceedings 8th Annual Conference* (1997), pp. 196–201. Davenport's paper also provides a very complete historical review of corporate social auditing.

[16]Matthew Rose, "Body Shop Gets Taken to Task in 'Social Audit,'" *The Wall Street Journal,* April 19, 1996, p. B9B.

EXHIBIT
4–B

The Citizen's Bank Social Audit

The social audit developed at Citizens Bank, a Canadian financial institution, reported the firm's corporate social performance score. This score measured a number of key issues such as employee relations, the environment, the community, and ethical business practices.

For example, employee relations emphasized workplace safety, occupational stress, employment equity, and other variables that contributed to the firm's overall performance. The audit was performed on a regular basis—every 12 to 18 months. Like a financial audit, the social audit intended to allow the bank's customers and local communities to assess the social performance over time, to see whether or not the firm was living up to its commitment to being a team leader in corporate social responsibility in Canada.

Source: http://www.citizensbank.ca/difference/reportcard.html (August 6, 1997).

Summary Points of this Chapter

- In response to the numerous social challenges facing businesses, managers have recognized the need to develop formal social response strategies and programs.
- Business should monitor the multiple segments within the macroenvironment of business and conduct rigorous environmental scanning before developing a socially responsive program.
- The model of social responsiveness includes the policy stage, the learning stage, and the organizational commitment stage.
- A framework for managing the corporate social environment includes four critical elements: top management philosophy, socially responsive strategy, socially responsive structure, and line manager involvement.
- Corporate social auditing and performance audits are used to assess a firm's management of the corporate social environment.

Key Terms and Concepts Used in this Chapter

- Collaborative partnerships
- Corporate social responsiveness
- Macroenvironment of business
- Environmental scanning
- Top management philosophy

- Socially responsive strategy
- Socially responsive structure
- Line manager involvement
- Social auditing
- Social performance audit

Internet Resources

- http://www.charitynet.org/caf/cafcompanies   Corporate Community Involvement Resource Center
- http://www.hbsp.harvard.edu   Business Enterprise Trust teaching material
- http://www.mcs.net/~commnews   Community News Project

Discussion Case: Aaron Feuerstein—A Socially Responsive Owner

The evening of December 11, 1995, was a special time for Aaron Feuerstein, CEO of Malden Mills. A small surprise 70th birthday party quietly was held in his honor at a local Boston restaurant. But Feuerstein's life took a dramatic turn that evening for a different reason: A boiler at his company's plant exploded, setting off a fire that injured 33 employees and destroyed three of the factory's century-old buildings. Malden Mills was a privately owned firm, with Feuerstein owning a majority share. The firm was located in a small Massachusetts town, Methuen, and employed nearly 3,000 people in the economically depressed area. The fire was a devastating blow for the community. According to Paul Coorey, local union president, "I was standing there seeing the mill burn with my son, who also works there, and he looked at me and said, 'Dad, we just lost our jobs.' Years of our lives seemed gone."

Unexpected tragedies happen all too often, and the aftermath is frequently devastating to the owners, employees, suppliers, local community, and customers of the firm. But the December 1995 tragedy at Malden Mills had a different outcome than most, primarily due to the owner of the factory—Aaron Feuerstein—and the deep sense of corporate social responsiveness he showed through his actions following the tragedy at Malden Mills.

Aaron Feuerstein typically awoke at 5:30 A.M. and began each day by memorizing passages from the scriptures and Shakespeare. He firmly believed in loyalty and fairness to his workers. He often said that the average American wanted businesses and their owners to treat workers as human beings, with consideration and thoughtfulness. Feuerstein tried to meet these expectations. "I have to be worthy," he told his wife over and over again. "Too many people depend on me." He simply could not let anyone down—even after the unexpected and devastating tragedy of the December 1995 fire at his plant.

Aaron Feuerstein knew he had many options after the fire. He could close the factory and walk away with tens of millions of dollars in fire insurance. He could turn over to his industry rivals his profitable, flagship product, Polartec. This synthetic fiber was in great demand by the sport outerwear industry. Its production required a highly skilled, experienced workforce, and Malden Mills basically held a market monopoly. Many of the company's competitors would have paid a high price for the rights to produce Polartec.

Yet, Feuerstein's commitment to his employees led him to a different strategy. "I was telling myself I have to be creative. Maybe there's some way out of this." In an announcement to his employees at a local high school gymnasium four days after the tragic fire, Feuerstein explained that he would keep all the nearly 3,000 employees on the payroll for a month while he started to rebuild the family business. One month later, as the rebuilding process continued at a slow pace, Feuerstein extended the salary offer to his employees for another month; a month later, he extended it for yet a third month. "What I did was merely the decent thing to do," he insisted. "The worker is not just a cuttable expense, a pair of hands. I consider the employees the most valuable asset Malden Mills has."

With the first announcement of guaranteed salaries just days before Christmas, the reactions from employees were understandably positive. "When he did it the first time, I was surprised," said Bill Cotter, a 49-year-old Malden Mills employee. "The second time was a shock. The third . . . well, it was unrealistic to think he would do it again." Nancy Cotter finished her husband's thought: "It was the third time that brought tears to everyone's eyes." By March 1996, most of the company's employees were back to work. Those who were not were offered assistance in making other arrangements or finding other employment in the area.

Another surprising twist to this story of social responsiveness was shown by the outpouring of support by Malden Mills' customers and other local organizations. An apparel company, Dakotah, sent Feuerstein a $30,000 check after the fire. The Bank of Boston donated $50,000, the company's union sent $100,000, and the Chamber of Commerce in nearby Lawrence, Massachusetts, contributed $150,000. Many of Malden Mills' customers promised to stick with the company and wait for them to rebuild and regain their production capacity rather than switch to a competitor.

Just eight months after the fire, three of the four production lines at Malden Mills were fully operational and all but 500 of the nearly 3,000 employees were back to work in the factory. In December 1996, a year after the tragic fire, the company projected sales revenue of $358 million, compared to $400 million in 1995. Malden Mills apparently had weathered the storm following the destructive fire. One of the strongest factors contributing to the firm's reemergence was Aaron Feuerstein's commitment to *both the company's economic and social mission and goals.*

Sources: Tom Mitkowski, "A Glow from a Fire," *Time,* January 8, 1996; Mitchell Owens, "A Mill Community Comes Back to Life," *New York Times,* December 26, 1996, p. B12; Louis Uchitelle, "The Risks of Keeping a Promise," *New York Times,* July 4, 1996, p. C1, C3; Bruce D. Butterfield, "What Flames Could Not Destroy," *Boston Globe,* September 8, 1996, p. A28; Michael Ryan, "They Call Their Boss a Hero," *Parade Magazine,* September 8, 1996, pp. 4–5; Alison S. Lebwohl, "Rising from the Ashes," http://www.afscme.org/afscme/press/peso9614.htm (July 11, 1997); and Bruce D. Butterfield, "More Than a Factory," *Boston Globe,* December 8, 1996, p. E1.

Discussion Questions

1. Conduct a corporate social audit of Malden Mills. What social factors appear to economically benefit the company? What score or grade would you give Malden Mills for its social performance after the December 1995 fire?

2. What factors do you believe influenced Aaron Feuerstein's choice of a socially responsive strategy in reaction to the tragic fire at his factory?

3. Could Feuerstein's actions be a model of corporate social responsiveness for other corporate managers?

PART THREE

Business and the Ethical Environment

5

Ethical Dilemmas in Business

People who work in business—managers and employees alike—frequently encounter and must deal with on-the-job ethical issues. Learning how to recognize the different kinds of ethical dilemmas and knowing why they occur is an important business skill. The costs to business and to society of unethical and illegal behavior are very large. A business firm is more likely to gain public approval and social legitimacy if it adheres to basic ethical principles and society's laws.

This chapter focuses on these key questions and objectives:

- What is ethics? What is business ethics?
- Why should business be ethical?
- Why do ethics problems occur in business?
- What efforts are being made to curtail unethical practices around the world?
- Are ethical behavior and legal behavior the same?

R oger Worsham had just graduated as an accounting major with a business degree and had landed a job with a small regional accounting firm in northern Michigan. Working there would give him the experience he needed to qualify as a certified public accountant (CPA). He, his wife, and their two small children settled in to enjoy small-town life. Roger's employer was experiencing tough competition from large accounting firms that were able to offer more varied services, including management consulting, computerized data processing services, and financial advice. Losing a big client could mean the difference between staying open or closing down one of the local offices.[1]

During one of his first audit assignments of a local savings and loan (S&L) company, Roger uncovered evidence of fraud. Law restricted the S&L at that time to mortgages based on residential property, but it had loaned money to a manufacturing company. To conceal this illegal loan from Roger, someone had removed the file before he began the audit. Roger suspected that the guilty party might have been the S&L president, who, in addition to being the largest owner of the manufacturing firm, was also a very influential lawyer in town.

Roger took the evidence of wrongdoing to his boss, expecting to hear that the accounting firm would include it in the audit report, as required by standard accounting practices. Instead, he was told to put the evidence and all of his notes through a shredder. His boss said, "I will take care of this privately. We simply cannot afford to lose this client." When Roger hesitated, he was told, "You put those papers through the shredder or I'll guarantee that you'll never get a CPA in Michigan, or work in an accounting office in this state for the rest of your life."

Question: If you were Roger, what would you do? If you were Roger's boss, would you have acted differently? What is the ethical thing to do?

Ethical puzzles like this occur frequently in business. They are troubling to the people involved. Sometimes, a person's most basic ideas of fairness, honesty, and integrity are at stake. This chapter explores the meaning of ethics, identifies the different types of ethical problems that occur in business, and tells why these dilemmas arise. A discussion of corporate crime illustrates the relationship of law and ethics. Chapter 6 then tells how ethical performance in business can be improved by providing some tools for grappling with on-the-job ethical dilemmas.

The Meaning of Ethics

Ethics is a conception of right and wrong conduct. It tells us whether our behavior is moral or immoral and deals with fundamental human relationships—how we think and behave toward others and how we want them to think and behave toward us. **Ethical principles** are guides to moral behavior. For example, in most societies lying, stealing, deceiving, and harming others are considered to be unethical and immoral. Honesty, keeping promises, helping others, and respecting the rights of others are considered to be ethically and morally desirable behavior. Such basic rules of behavior are essential for the preservation and continuation of organized life everywhere.

These notions of right and wrong come from many sources. Religious beliefs are a major source of ethical guidance for many. The family institution—whether two parents, a single parent, or a large family with brothers and sisters, grandparents, aunts, cousins,

---

[1]More details about this episode are in LaRue Tone Hosmer, *The Ethics of Management,* 3d. ed. (Homewood, IL: Irwin, 1991), pp. 164–68.

and other kin—imparts a sense of right and wrong to children as they grow up. Schools and schoolteachers, neighbors and neighborhoods, friends, admired role models, ethnic groups—and of course, the ever-present electronic media —influence what we believe to be right and wrong in life. The totality of these learning experiences creates in each person a concept of ethics, morality, and socially acceptable behavior. This core of ethical beliefs then acts as a moral compass that helps to guide a person when ethical puzzles arise.

Ethical ideas are present in all societies, organizations, and individual persons, although they may vary greatly from one to another. Your ethics may not be the same as your neighbor's; one particular religion's notion of morality may not be identical to another's; or what is considered ethical in one society may be forbidden in another society. These differences raise the important and controversial issue of **ethical relativism,** which holds that ethical principles should be defined by various periods of time in history, a society's traditions, the special circumstances of the moment, or personal opinion. In this view, the meaning given to ethics would be relative to time, place, circumstance, and the person involved. In that case, there would be no universal ethical standards on which people around the globe could agree. For companies conducting business in several societies at one time, whether or not ethics is relevant can be vitally important, and we discuss those issues in more detail later in this chapter.

For the moment, however, we can say that in spite of the diverse systems of ethics that exist within our own society and throughout the world, all people everywhere do depend on ethical systems to tell them whether their actions are right or wrong, moral or immoral, approved or disapproved. Ethics, in this sense, is a universal human trait, found everywhere.

What Is Business Ethics?

Business ethics is the application of general ethical ideas to business behavior. Business ethics is not a special set of ethical ideas different from ethics in general and applicable only to business. If dishonesty is considered to be unethical and immoral, then anyone in business who is dishonest with its stakeholders—employees, customers, stockholders, or competitors—is acting unethically and immorally. If protecting others from harm is considered to be ethical, then a company that recalls a dangerously defective product is acting in an ethical way. To be considered ethical, business must draw its ideas about what is proper behavior from the same sources as everyone else. Business should not try to make up its own definitions of what is right and wrong. Employees and managers may believe at times that they are permitted or even encouraged to apply special or weaker ethical rules to business situations, but society does not condone or permit such an exception. People who work in business are bound by the same ethical principles that apply to others.

Employees often admit that they feel pressure at work, which may lead to unethical behavior. A national study released by the Ethics Officers Association and two professional groups claimed that over half of the workers felt some pressure to act unethically on the job. Nearly half of the workers, 48 percent, reported that they had engaged in unethical or illegal actions during the past year and attributed their actions to workplace pressure. Figure 5–1 shows the breakdown of factors that contributed to pressure to act unethically, as reported by the employees in the study.

Figure 5–1

Factors contributing
to pressure in the
workplace.

Source: Ethics Officer
Association and
American Society of
Chartered Life
Underwriters and
Chartered Financial
Consultants, April
1997.

Responses by employees to a national study showed the following factors contributed to pressure to act unethically on the job:			
Balancing work and family	52%	Need to meet goals (e.g., sales)	46%
Poor leadership	51%	Company politics	44%
Poor internal communications	51%	Insufficient resources	40%
Work hours/workload	51%	Incompetent subordinates	39%
Lack of management support	48%	Downsizing effects	33%
Little or no recognition of achievements	46%		

Figure 5–2

Why should business
be ethical?

- Fulfill public expectation for business.
- Prevent harming others.
- Improve business relations and employee productivity.
- Reduce penalties under the U.S. Corporate Sentencing Guidelines.
- Protect business from others.
- Protect employees from their employers.
- Promote personal morality.

Why Should Business Be Ethical?

Why should business be ethical? What prevents a business firm from piling up as many profits as it can, in any way it can, regardless of ethical considerations? For example, what is wrong with Roger Worsham's boss telling him to destroy evidence of a client's fraudulent conduct? Why not just shred the papers, thereby keeping a good customer happy (and saving Roger's job, too)? Figure 5–2 lists the major reasons business firms should promote a high level of ethical behavior.

We mentioned one reason when discussing social responsibility in Chapter 3. Corporate stakeholders, described in Chapter 1, expect business to exhibit high levels of ethical performance and social responsibility. Companies that fail to fulfill this public demand can expect to be spotlighted, criticized, curbed, and punished.

> *For example, Gtech Holding Corporation was one of the largest on-line betting companies in the United States. But during the past year, Gtech's management and security analysts pointed to the firm's recent ethical investigations and allegations of bribery as an explanation for the firm's marginal revenue decrease. Consistently Gtech's clients switched to competitor firms when contracts with Gtech expired. Allegations of shady business dealings prompted numerous federal grand jury investigations and may have contributed to Gtech's former clients' wariness of doing business with the firm. Although*

Gtech stressed it had never been found guilty of corporate wrongdoing, the impression of ethical impropriety seemed to affect the firm's business relations and its profitability.[2]

A second reason businesses and their employees should act ethically is to prevent harm to the general public and the corporation's many stakeholders. One of the strongest ethical principles is stated very simply: Do no harm. A company that is careless in disposing of toxic chemical wastes that cause disease and death is breaking this ethical injunction. Many ethical rules operate to protect society against various types of harm, and businesses are expected to observe these commonsensical ethical principles.

Some people argue that another reason for businesses to be ethical is that it pays. In a recent study, scholars concluded that organizations that promote ethics by adopting a code of conduct to guide their operations were "more effective in managing their ethical activities and were more successful and profitable—both in the short term and the long term."[3] Further support for the relationship between being ethical and being profitable was found in a study conducted by Rutgers University. Researchers found that investors in firms that fostered an ethical work environment realized an annual shareholder rate of return that was about 45 percent higher than firms that ignored ethics.[4]

Being ethical imparts a sense of trust, which promotes positive alliances among business partners. If this trust is broken, the unethical party may be shunned and ignored. This situation occurred when Malaysian government officials gave the cold shoulder to executives of a French company. When asked why they were being unfriendly, a Malaysian dignitary replied: "Your chairman is in jail!"[5] The nurturing of an ethical environment and the development of ethical safeguards, discussed in the next chapter, can be critical incentives for improving business relations and employee and organizational productivity.

The **U.S. Corporate Sentencing Guidelines** provide a strong incentive for businesses to promote ethics at work.[6] The sentencing guidelines come into play when an employee of a firm has been found guilty of a criminal wrongdoing. To determine sentencing, a federal judge computes a culpability (degree of blame) score using the equations contained in the guidelines. The score is significantly affected if a firm's ethics program monitors and aggressively responds to reported criminal violations at work. Under the sentencing guidelines, corporate executives found guilty of criminal activity could receive lighter penalties if their firm has developed a strong ethics program. According to a U.S. Sentencing Commission report, the most frequent target of the sentencing guidelines have been firms that are relatively young (less than 10 years old) and small (fewer than 50 em-

[2]William M. Bulkeley and Steve Stecklow, "Long a Winner, Gtech Faces Resistance Based on Ethical Concerns," *The Wall Street Journal,* January 16, 1996, pp. A1, A6.

[3]Michael K. McCuddy, Karl E. Reichardt, and David L. Schoeder, "Exploring the Relationships between Ethical Business Practices and Organizational Success and Profitability," paper presented at the 1996 national annual Academy of Management meeting, Cincinnati, OH.

[4]Dale Kurschner, "5 Ways Ethical Busine$$ Creates Fatter Profit$," *Business Ethics,* March–April 1996, pp. 20–23.

[5]"Scandals Crimp Business for French Firms," *The Wall Street Journal,* October 20, 1994, p. A20.

[6]For a thorough discussion of the U.S. Corporate Sentencing Guidelines, see Jeffrey M. Kaplan and William K. Perry, "The High Cost of Corporate Crime," *Management Accounting,* December 1991, pp. 43–46; and Dan R. Dalton, Michael B. Metzger, and John W. Hill, "The 'New' U.S. Sentencing Commission Guidelines: A Wake-Up Call for Corporate America," *Academy of Management Executive* 8 (1994), pp. 7–13.

ployees). The commission report said that "97 percent of the 280 firms sentenced under the guidelines since they took effect have been privately held or controlled by only a small group of shareholders."[7] However, it is believed that within the next decade older and larger firms will feel the effect of the U.S. Sentencing Commission guidelines.

A fifth reason for promoting ethical behavior is to protect business firms from abuse by unethical employees and unethical competitors. Security experts estimate that employee pilferage (stealing) has caused more businesses to go into bankruptcy than any other crime. Stealing by employees accounts for 60 to 75 percent of all business losses, according to a U.S. government survey. A study by the U.S. Department of Commerce showed that employee theft in manufacturing plants alone amounted to $8 million a day nationwide.[8] For the retail industry, it is a larger cost to store owners than customer shoplifting. One of the reasons for the magnitude of the problem is the difficulty of detecting the crime. Store owners admit that they are often at the mercy of the employees to act honestly.

A startling example of employee theft was discovered in 1994 involving an MCI Communications employee. U.S. Secret Service agents arrested the employee after it was alleged that he stole more than 60,000 telephone-card numbers, which were sold on the international black market. The four major telephone carriers lost more than $50 million in revenues.[9]

High ethical performance also protects people who work in business. Employees resent invasions of privacy (such as obtrusive video surveillance in workplace restrooms) or being ordered to do something against their personal convictions (such as falsifying an accounting report) or being forced to work in hazardous conditions (such as entering unventilated coal mines or being exposed to dangerous agricultural pesticides in the fields). Businesses that treat their employees with dignity and integrity reap many rewards in the form of high morale and improved productivity. It is a win-win-win situation for the firm, its employees, and society.

A final reason for promoting ethics in business is a personal one. Most people want to act in ways that are consistent with their own sense of right and wrong. Being pressured to contradict their personal values creates much emotional stress. Knowing that one works in a supportive ethical climate contributes to one's sense of psychological security. People feel good about working for an ethical company because they know they are protected along with the general public.

Business Ethics across Organizational Functions

Not all ethics issues in business are the same. Because business operations are highly specialized, ethics issues can appear in any of the major functional areas of a business firm. **Functional-area ethics** tends to have its own particular brand of ethical dilemmas, as discussed next.

---

[7]Joe Davidson, "Corporate Sentencing Guidelines Have Snagged Mostly Small Firms," *The Wall Street Journal,* August 28, 1995, p. B5.

[8]Landmark Investigators, http://www2.thecia.net/users/landmark/employee.html (October 30, 1997).

[9]"MCI Worker Charged in U.S. Investigation of Phone-Card Fraud," *The Wall Street Journal,* October 4, 1994, p. B7.

Accounting Ethics

The accounting function is a critically important component of every business firm. Accounting reports tell owners and managers whether the firm is doing well or poorly. Company managers, external investors, government regulators, tax collectors, and labor unions rely on accounting data to make key decisions. Honesty, integrity, and accuracy are absolute requirements of the accounting function. No other single issue is of greater concern to accountants in industry and public accountancy than ethics. Roger Worsham's dilemma, discussed at the beginning of this chapter, highlights the importance of honest accounting.

Professional accounting organizations—such as the American Institute of Certified Public Accountants and the Financial Accounting Standards Board—have developed generally accepted accounting principles whose purpose is to establish uniform standards for reporting accounting and auditing data. In 1993, the American Institute for Certified Public Accountants dramatically changed its professional code by requiring CPAs to act as whistle-blowers when detecting "materially misstated" financial statements or face losing their license to practice accounting. Examples of this profession's efforts toward promoting ethics are shown in Exhibit 5–A. Spurred by the increasing threat of liability suits filed against accounting firms and the desire to reaffirm professional integrity, these standards go far toward ensuring a high level of honest and ethical accounting behavior.

EXHIBIT 5–A

Professional Codes of Conduct in Accounting and Finance
American Institute of Certified Public Accountants (AICPA)
Code of Professional Conduct

Membership in the American Institute of Certified Public Accountants is voluntary. By accepting membership, a certified public accountant assumes an obligation of self-discipline above and beyond the requirements of laws and regulations.

These Principles of the Code of Professional Conduct of the American Institute of Certified Public Accountants express the profession's recognition of its responsibilities to the public, to clients, and to colleagues. They guide members in the performance of their professional responsibilities and express the basic tenets of ethical and professional conduct. The Principles call for an unswerving commitment to honorable behavior, even at the sacrifice of personal advantage. . . .

- Responsibilities—In carrying out their responsibilities as professionals, members should exercise sensitive professional and moral judgments in all their activities. . . .

- The Public Interest—Members should accept the obligation to act in a way that will serve the public interest, honor the public interest, and demonstrate commitment to professionalism. . . .

- Integrity—To maintain and broaden public confidence, members should perform all professional responsibilities with the highest sense of integrity. . . .

- Objectivity and Independence—A member should maintain objectivity and be free of conflicts of interest in discharging professional responsibilities. A member in public practice should be independent in fact and appearance when providing auditing and other attestation services. . . .

- Due Care—A member should observe the profession's technical and ethical standards, strive continually to improve competence and the quality of services, and discharge professional responsibility to the best of the member's ability. . . .

- Scope and Nature of Services—A member in public practice should observe the Principles of the Code of Professional Conduct in determining the scope and nature of services to be provided.

"Reprinted with permission from the AICPA Code of Professional Conduct, copyright © 1997 by the American Institute of Certified Public Accountants, Inc."

Chartered Financial Analyst (CFA)

Code of Ethics and Standards of Professional Conduct

The financial analyst shall inform his* employer, through his direct supervisor, that the analyst is obligated to comply with the Code of Ethics and Standards of Professional Conduct, and is subject to disciplinary sanctions for violations thereof. He shall deliver a copy of the Code and Standards to his employer if the employer does not have a copy.

The financial analyst shall maintain knowledge of and shall comply with all applicable laws, rules and regulations . . . shall not knowingly participate in, or assist, any acts in violation of any applicable law, rule or regulation . . . [and] shall exercise reasonable supervision over subordinate employees . . . to prevent violations.

Areas of ethical concern for the financial analyst include reasonable basis for investment recommendations and representations, accuracy of research reports, suitability of portfolio recommendations for the client, avoidance of plagiarism, avoidance of misrepresentation of services, fair dealing with customers and clients, disclosure of conflicts of interest, reporting of compensation, preservation of confidentiality, objectivity, and fiduciary duties.

*Masculine personal pronouns, used throughout the Code and Standards to simplify sentence structure, shall apply to all persons, regardless of sex.
Source: Excerpted with permission from *Standards of Practice Handbook, Seventh Edition,* Copyright 1996, Association for Investment Management and Research, Charlottesville, VA. All rights reserved.

Failure to observe these professional ethical standards can produce ethics problems that also occur in other nations; and member-nations of the European Union have discussed the desirability of adopting uniform accounting rules that would apply to all members.[10] The **U.S. Foreign Corrupt Practices Act,** also discussed in Chapter 7, requires U.S. companies with foreign operations to adopt accounting procedures that ensure a full disclosure of the company's relations with sales agents and government officials; the purpose is to prevent bribery and other legally questionable payments.

[10]Andrew Likierman, "Ethical Dilemmas for Accountants: A United Kingdom Perspective," *Journal of Business Ethics* 8 (1989), pp. 617–29. For several excellent examples of ethical dilemmas in accounting, see Leonard J. Brooks, *Professional Ethics for Accountants: Text, Readings and Cases* (St. Paul, MN: West Publishing, 1995).

Financial Ethics

Finance produced some of the most spectacular ethics scandals of recent times. Wall Street financiers were found guilty of insider trading, illegal stock transactions, and various other financial abuses. Three examples of ethical abuses within the financial community follow.

> *Officers at the Bank of Credit and Commerce International fraudulently spent over $20 billion of its investors' deposits to support the financing of illegal arms sales, nuclear weapon production, and laundering of drug-trade profits. Executives involved in the fraud were sentenced to as many as 14 years in prison and fined $9.13 billion.*
>
> *Prudential Insurance improperly sold partnerships without appropriate licenses through a commission-sharing scheme with its subsidiary, Prudential-Bache Securities. From 1983 to 1990, Prudential received $777 million in partnership fees while ignoring warning signs that partnerships may be a highly risky venture.*
>
> *Hundreds of savings and loan associations failed after their managers misused their depositors' funds, rewarded themselves and family members with lavish salaries and perks, misled bank examiners, published false accounting reports, and left U.S. taxpayers to pay the cost of the largest corporate bailout in the nation's history. These lapses in ethical conduct were evident despite efforts by the finance professions to foster an ethical environment, as shown in Exhibit 5–A.*

Several other kinds of financial transactions are potential ethical minefields: investment banks that finance hostile corporate takeovers that threaten employees' jobs and local communities; trust departments that are charged with safely investing funds entrusted to them; money market managers who must vote on shareholder resolutions dealing with controversial ethical issues; banks that must decide whether to side with a corporation's management team that has been a good customer even though management's policies cause damage to the company's stockholders; and stockbrokers' relationships with clients who seek sound investment advice.[11]

Marketing Ethics

Relations with customers tend to generate many ethical problems. Pricing, promotions, advertising, product information, relations between advertising agencies and their clients, marketing research—all of these are potential problem areas. To improve the marketing profession, the American Marketing Association (AMA) adopted a code of ethics for its members (see Exhibit 5–B). The AMA code advocates professional conduct guided by ethics, adherence to applicable laws, and honesty and fairness in all marketing activities. The code also recognizes the ethical responsibility of marketing professionals to the consuming public and specifically opposes such unethical practices as misleading product information, false and misleading advertising claims, high-pressure sales tactics, bribery and

---

[11]For several good examples of these and other areas, see John L. Casey, *Ethics in the Financial Marketplace* (New York: Scudder, Stevens & Clark, 1988); James B. Stewart, *Den of Thieves* (New York: Simon and Schuster, 1991); and Larry Alan Bear and Rita Maldonado-Bear, *Free Markets, Finance, Ethics, and Law* (Englewood Cliffs, NJ: Prentice Hall, 1994).

EXHIBIT
5–B

Professional Codes of Conduct in Marketing and Information Systems

American Marketing Association (AMA)

Code of Ethics

Members of the American Marketing Association (AMA) are committed to ethical professional conduct. They have joined together in subscribing to this Code of Ethics embracing the following topics: . . .

- Responsibilities . . . —Marketers must accept responsibility for the consequences of their activities and make every effort to ensure that their decisions, recommendations, and actions function to identify, serve, and satisfy all relevant publics: customers, organizations, and society. . . .

- "Honesty and Fairness—Marketers shall uphold and advance the integrity, honor, and dignity of the marketing profession . . .

- "Rights and Duties of Parties . . . —Participants in the marketing exchange process should be able to expect that: (1) products and services offered are safe and fit for their intended uses; (2) communications about offered products and services are not deceptive; (3) all parties intend to discharge their obligations, financial and otherwise, in good faith; and, (4) appropriate internal methods exist for equitable adjustment and/or redress of grievances concerning purchases. . . .

- Organizational Relationships—Marketers should be aware of how their behavior may influence or impact on the behavior of others in organizational relationships. They should not demand, encourage or apply coercion to obtain unethical behavior in their relationships with others. . . .

Any AMA members found to be in violation of any provision of this Code of Ethics may have his or her Association membership suspended or revoked.

"Reprinted with permission from the American Marketing Association's Code of Ethics, published by the American Marketing Association.

Association for Computing Machinery (ACM)

Code of Ethics and Professional Conduct

Preamble. Commitment to ethical professional conduct is expected of every member (voting members, associate members, and student members) of the Association for Computing Machinery (ACM).

This Code, consisting of 24 imperatives formulated as statements of personal responsibility, identifies the elements of such a commitment. It contains many, but not all, issues professionals are likely to face. . . . The code and its supplemented Guidelines are intended to serve as a basis for ethical decision making in the conduct of professional work. Secondarily, they may serve as a basis for judging the merit of a formal complaint pertaining to violation of professional ethical standards.

The general imperatives for ACM members include contribute to society and human well-being, avoid harm to others, be honest and trustworthy, be fair and take

Continued

action not to discriminate, honor property rights, including copyrights and patents, give proper credit for intellectual property, respect the privacy of others, and honor confidentiality.

Adherence of professionals to a code of ethics is largely a voluntary matter. However, if a member does not follow this code by engaging in gross misconduct, membership in ACM may be terminated.

Courtesy of the Association for Computing Machinery, Inc.

kickbacks, and unfair and predatory pricing. These code provisions have the potential for helping marketing professionals translate general ethical principles into specific working rules.[12]

Information Systems Ethics

One of the fastest-growing areas of business ethics is in the field of information systems. Exploding in the 1990s were ethical challenges involving invasions of privacy; the collection, storage, and access of personal and business information; confidentiality of communications over the telephone, electronic mail, and facsimile machine; copyright protection regarding software copying; and numerous other related issues. As discussed in Chapter 18, the explosion of information technology raised serious questions of trust between individuals and businesses. Questions centering on who should monitor and possibly control access to information were also raised as important ethical concerns in the field of information systems. In response to calls by businesspeople and academics for an increase in ethical responsibility in the information system field, professional organizations have developed or revised professional codes of ethics, as shown in Exhibit 5–B.[13]

Other Functional Areas

Production and maintenance functions, which may seem to be remote from ethics considerations, can be at the center of some ethics storms. Dangerously defective products can injure or kill innocent persons, and toxic production processes may threaten the health of workers and the general public. Flawed manufacturing and lack of inspection of aircraft fuse pins, which hold the engines to the wing on Boeing 747 jet airplanes, were suspected in some accidents, endangering the lives of passengers as well as innocent bystanders. Union Carbide's pesticide plant in Bhopal, India, was allegedly not properly

---

[12]The AMA Code for Market Researchers and a discussion of numerous marketing ethics issues can be found in Gene R. Laczniak and Patrick E. Murphy, *Ethical Marketing Decisions* (Boston: Allyn and Bacon, 1993); and Lawrence B. Chonko, *Ethical Decision Making in Marketing* (Thousand Oaks, CA: SAGE Publications, 1995).

[13]For further discussion of ethics in information systems see Richard O. Mason, Florence M. Mason, and Mary J. Culnan, *Ethics of Information Management* (Thousand Oaks, CA: SAGE Publications, 1995); M. David Ermann, Mary B. Williams, and Michele S. Shauf, *Computers, Ethics, and Society,* 2d ed. (New York: Oxford University Press, 1997); and Effy Oz, "Ethical Standards for Computer Professionals: A Comparative Analysis of Four Major Codes," *Journal of Business Ethics* 12 (1993), pp. 709–26.

maintained, and this failure was believed to be a contributing cause of the tragic leak that killed over 2,000 people.

Ethics issues also arise in purchasing departments. Kmart Corporation launched a formal investigation involving many of its real estate purchasing officials after allegations of corruption and bribery. This investigation followed a federal grand jury indictment of a former Kmart real estate executive on taking more than $750,000 in bribes.[14]

A survey by the National Association of Purchasing Management reported common ethics problems: exaggerating a problem to receive a better price from a supplier; providing preferential treatment to a supplier who is also a good customer; allowing personal friendships to enter into selection decisions; providing information to a competing supplier; accepting promotional prizes or purchase volume incentives; accepting trips, meals, or entertainment; and giving special treatment to vendors preferred by higher management.[15]

These examples make one point crystal clear: All areas of business, all people in business, and all levels of authority in business encounter ethics dilemmas from time to time. Ethics issues are a common thread running through the business world.

Why Ethical Problems Occur in Business

Obviously, ethics problems in business appear in many different forms. Although not common or universal, they occur frequently. Finding out just what is responsible for causing them is one step that can be taken toward minimizing their impact on business operations and on the people affected. Some of the main reasons are summarized in Figure 5–3 and are discussed next.

Figure 5–3

Why ethical problems occur in business.

Reason	Nature of Ethical Problem	Typical Approach	Attitude
Personal gain and selfish interest	Selfish interest vs. others' interests	Egoistical mentality	"I want it!"
Competitive Pressures on Profits	Firm's interest vs. others' interests	Bottom–line mentality	"We have to beat the others at all costs!"
Business Goals vs. Personal Values	Boss's interests vs. subordinates' values	Authoritarian mentality	"Do as I say, or else!"
Cross-Cultural Contradictions	Company's interests vs. diverse cultural traditions and values	Ethnocentric mentality	"Foreigners have a funny notion of what's right and wrong"

[14]"Kmart Is Dismissing 12 Managers from Its Purchasing Department," *The Wall Street Journal,* July 30, 1996, p. B4.

[15]Renee Florsheim and Eduardo S. Paderon, "Purchasing Practices in a Hospital Environment: An Ethical Analysis," *Hospital Material Management Quarterly* 13, no. 4 (1992), pp. 1–10.

Personal Gain and Selfish Interest

Personal gain, or even greed, causes some ethics problems. Businesses sometimes employ people whose personal values are less than desirable. They will put their own welfare ahead of all others, regardless of the harm done to other employees, the company, or society. In the process of hiring employees, managers make efforts to weed out ethically undesirable applicants, but ethical qualities are difficult to anticipate and measure. The embezzler, the expense-account padder, the bribe taker, and other unethical persons can slip through. Lacking a perfect screening system, businesses are not likely to eliminate this kind of unethical behavior entirely. Moreover, firms have to proceed carefully when screening applicants, taking care not to trample on individuals' rights in the search for potentially unethical employees.

A manager or an employee who puts his or her own self-interest above all other considerations is called an **ethical egoist.** Self-promotion, a focus on self-interest to the point of selfishness, and greed are traits commonly observed in an ethical egoist. The ethical egoist tends to ignore ethical principles accepted by others, believing that ethical rules are made for others. **Altruism**—acting for the benefit of others when self-interest is sacrificed—is seen to be sentimental or even irrational. "Looking Out for Number One" is the ethical egoist's motto.[16]

Competitive Pressures on Profits

When companies are squeezed by tough competition, they sometimes engage in unethical activities to protect their profits. This may be especially true in companies whose financial performance is already substandard. Research has shown that poor financial performers and companies with lower profits are more prone to commit illegal acts.[17] However, a precarious financial position is only one reason for illegal and unethical business behavior, because profitable companies also can act contrary to ethical principles. In fact, it may be simply a single-minded drive for profits, regardless of the company's financial condition, that creates a climate for unethical activity.

Price-fixing is a practice that often occurs when companies vigorously engage in a market with limited growth potential. Besides being illegal, price-fixing is unethical behavior toward customers, who pay higher prices than they would if free competition set the prices. Companies fix prices to avoid fair competition and to protect their profits, as happened in the following cases.

> *One of the most sensational and costly incidences of price-fixing involved companies in the citric acid and lysine industries. Archer-Daniels Midland Company, whose role in this ethics scandal is presented in the discussion case at the end of Chapter 13, was at the forefront. But other firms have been indicted or pleaded guilty, leading to the realization of a global price-fixing conspiracy*

---

[16]For a compact discussion of ethical egoism, see Tom L. Beauchamp and Norman E. Bowie, *Ethical Theory and Business,* 5th ed. (Englewood Cliffs, NJ: Prentice Hall, 1997), pp. 14–19.

[17]For a discussion, see Peter C. Yeager, "Analyzing Corporate Offenses: Progress and Prospects," in William C. Frederick, ed., *Business Ethics: Research Issues and Empirical Studies* (Greenwich, CT: JAI Press, 1990), pp. 168–71; and Michael K. McCuddy, Karl E. Reichardt, and David L. Schroeder, "Ethical Pressures: Fact or Fiction?" *Management Accounting* 74, no. 10 (1993), pp. 57–61.

occurred involving Switzerland's F. Hoffmann–La Roche and Jungbunzlauer International and German-based Bayer Corporation.[18]

In another case, Japan's Fair Trade Commission demonstrated its aggressiveness toward uncovering unfair trade practices in two separate incidents. In May 1993, eight Japanese plastic food-wrapping companies were fined between $54,225 and $72,300, and several executives were suspended for conducting an elaborate price-fixing cartel. Later that year, the commission raided the nation's largest electronic companies to uncover evidence of bid-rigging. Close ties between Japanese businesses and government officials had effectively shut out foreign competition in bidding for public works projects.[19]

Price-fixing among competing companies is not the only kind of unethical behavior that can occur.

Senior Honda executives pleaded guilty in 1995 to accepting bribes and expensive gifts from U.S. dealers as a condition of providing them with an adequate supply of the most popular cars. The former Honda executives could face up to 35 years in prison and fines up to $5 million. Dozens of dealers contend that the corruption began in the 1970s and dramatically escalated later when Honda automobiles were in great demand but import quotas limited supply.[20]

Other kinds of unethical behavior also occur under competitive pressures. Companies can coerce suppliers into lowering their prices through nonmarket pressures, thereby receiving less than a fair price. When company officials have a strict bottom-line mentality shaped almost exclusively by market competition, they may overlook the ethical claims of their stakeholders. Doing so has the unfortunate and needless effect of pitting business against society.

Business Goals versus Personal Values

Ethical conflicts in business sometimes occur when a company pursues goals or uses methods that are unacceptable to some of its employees. *Whistle-blowing* may be one outcome, if an employee goes public with a complaint after failing to convince the company to correct an alleged abuse. (This employee behavior is also discussed in Chapter 16.) Another recourse for employees caught in these situations is a lawsuit. This option has become less of a financial and professional risk for employees in recent years as a result of various governmental protection acts.

Paul Blanch blew the whistle on his employer, Connecticut's Northeast Utilities. Blanch identified safety lapses in plant operations. Shortly after his complaints, Blanch was subjected to negative job evaluations and harassing inter-

---

[18]"Investigators Suspect a Global Conspiracy in Archer-Daniels Case," *The Wall Street Journal,* July 28, 1995, pp. A1, A5; and Scott Kilman, "Two Swiss Chemical Firms Will Plead Guilty, Pay Fines in Price-Fixing Case," *The Wall Street Journal,* March 27, 1997, p. B5.

[19]"Japan's Court Fines Eight Firms," *The Wall Street Journal,* May 24, 1993, p. A6; and Jathon Sapsford, "Japanese Electronics Firms Are Raided by Agency on Suspicion of Bid-Rigging," *The Wall Street Journal,* November 16, 1993, p. A15.

[20]Angelo B. Henderson, "Two Former Honda Officials Convicted of Accepting Bribes From Auto Dealers," *The Wall Street Journal,* June 2, 1995, p. B2; and "Former Honda Officials Sentenced for Kickbacks," *The Wall Street Journal,* August 22, 1995, p. B16.

nal audits. After Blanch sought government protection, the Nuclear Regulatory Commission imposed a $100,000 fine on Northeast Utilities for its actions against him.

Former GE employee Chester Walsh sued General Electric for over-charging the government on aircraft parts destined for Israel. After GE agreed to settle the suit for $39.5 million, a federal judge ordered the firm to pay $11.5 million to Walsh.[21]

The protesting employees in these companies were not troublemakers. They tried to work through internal company procedures to get the problems corrected. The ethical dilemmas arose because the companys' goals and methods required the employees to follow orders that they believed would harm themselves, other employees, customers, the company, and the general public. As far as they were concerned, they were being asked or ordered to do something unethical. Their own internal ethical compass was at odds with the goals and methods of their company.

Cross-Cultural Contradictions

Some of the knottiest ethical problems occur as corporations do business in other societies where ethical standards differ from those at home. Today, the policymakers and strategic planners in all multinational corporations, regardless of the nation where they are headquartered, face this kind of ethical dilemma. Consider the following situations:

U.S. sleepwear manufacturers discovered that the chemicals used to flameproof children's pajamas might cause cancer if absorbed through the child's skin. When these pajamas were banned from sale in the United States, some manufacturers sold the pajama material to distributors in other nations where there were no legal restrictions against its use.

Question: Although the foreign sales were legal, were they ethical? Is dumping unsafe products ethical if it is not forbidden by the receiving nation?

When Honda began building automobile plants in Ohio, it located them in two mostly white rural areas and then favored job applicants who lived within a 30-mile radius of the plant. This policy excluded African-Americans who lived in Columbus, the nearest big city. Earlier, Honda also had agreed to pay nearly half a million dollars to settle an age-discrimination suit brought by older job applicants who had been refused work there.

Question: Were Honda's job-hiring policies, which would have caused few problems in Japan, unethical in Ohio?

These episodes raise the issue of ethical relativism, which was defined earlier in this chapter. Should ethical principles—the ones that help chart right and wrong conduct—take their meaning strictly from the way each society defines ethics? Are Japanese attitudes toward job opportunities for minorities, older workers, and women as ethically valid as U.S. attitudes? Were the children's pajama makers on solid or shaky ethical ground

---

[21]Matthew L. Ward, "Regulator Says Connecticut's Largest Power Company Harassed Worker," *The New York Times,* May 5, 1993, p. B6; and Amal Kumar Naj, "Whistle-Blower at GE to Get $11.5 Million," *The Wall Street Journal,* April 26, 1993, p. A3, A4.

when they sold the cancer-risky pajama cloth in countries where government officials did not warn parents about this possible health risk? Who should assume the ethical responsibility? What or whose ethical standards should be the guide?

As business becomes increasingly global, with more and more corporations penetrating overseas markets where cultures and ethical traditions vary, these questions will occur more frequently. Employees and managers need ethical guidance from clearly stated company policy if they are to avoid the psychological stresses mentioned earlier. One U.S. corporate executive emphasized this point by saying that he and his company recognize that the world consists of a wide array of races, religions, languages, cultures, political systems, and economic resources: "We accept these differences as legitimate and desirable; we recognize that each country must determine its own way. . . . However, we must not use local custom as an excuse for violating applicable laws or corporate policies. We regard observing local law to be the minimum acceptable level of conduct; PPG's own standards frequently oblige us to go beyond that legal minimum and to conduct our affairs according to a higher standard."[22]

Ethics in a Global Economy

Examples of unethical conduct by business employees are reported from nearly every country. One example of unethical activity is **bribery,** a questionable or unjust payment to ensure or facilitate a business transaction. It is found in nearly every sector of the global marketplace.

A Berlin-based watchdog agency, Transparency International, published a survey that ranked corruption by country according to perceptions of executives and the public. Countries where having to pay a bribe is least likely included New Zealand, Denmark, Sweden, Finland, and Canada. At the other end of the index—countries most likely to demand or accept bribes—were Nigeria, Pakistan, Kenya, Bangladesh, and China. The United States ranked as the 15th least corrupt nation out of 54 countries. Other rankings included: Germany, 13; Japan, 17; and Russia, 47.

Examples of bribery and corruption in business have been frequently reported. Payoff scandals plagued Japan throughout the 1990s, involving some of the nation's largest firms: Ito-Yokado, Kirin Brewery, Fuji Photo Film, Takashimaya, Nomura Securities, Ajinomoto, and Dai-Ichi Kangyo Bank. Companies operating in South Korea considered bribery to be a part of business. Executives seeking to conduct business in South Korea believed they were obligated to pay each cabinet minister *ttuk kab,* or "rice-cake expenses," ranging from $6,500 to $19,500 to honor the major holidays of the year. Two IBM executives were indicted in 1997 on bribery charges in connection with a $249 million contract to modernize an information technology system at a state-owned Argentine bank.[23]

Executives representing U.S.-based companies are prohibited by the U.S. Foreign Corrupt Practices Act from paying bribes. According to a U.S. Department of Commerce study, United States competitors lose out on $36 billion of international business deals since they are banned from paying bribes. Some American firms try unusual approaches to comply with the law while conducting business in countries that expect special payments.

---

[22]Vincent A. Sarni, chairman, PPG Industries, Inc., Worldwide Code of Ethics, Pittsburgh, PA, n.d.

[23]For a comprehensive look at the state of ethics around the globe, see "Special Issue: Region- and Country-Related Reports on Business Ethics," *Journal of Business Ethics,* October 1997.

Chubb Corporation, a New Jersey–based insurance company, wanted to tap the vast Chinese insurance market. Rather than illegally paying a bribe to Chinese officials, the company set up a $1 million program to teach insurance at a Shanghai university. Through this philanthropic gift, the Chubb Company attempted to circumvent the typical approach of bribing officials to gain entrance into a new market in this country. According to a Chubb spokesperson, the company spent millions of dollars on similar projects to improve its prospects overseas.[24]

Efforts to Curtail Unethical Practices

Numerous efforts are underway to curb unethical business practices throughout the world. The most common control is through government intervention and regulation. Efforts to address unethical business behavior often begin with national governments, which can enact stiff legislative controls or empower government agencies with more authority. Many governments are attempting to establish a moral minimum as a guide for proper behavior or to draw the line to control unethical action.

Various international organizations, such as the International Labor Organization or the United Nations, have attempted to develop an international code of conduct for multinational corporations. These efforts have emphasized the need for companies to adhere to universal ethical guidelines when conducting business throughout the world. These codes and the ethical issues they address are shown in Figure 5–4.

In addition, a transnational effort toward minimizing corruption in the global marketplace was launched in 1996. This anticorruption campaign was evident

Figure 5–4

International ethics codes and ethics issues addressed in these codes.

Source: This chart is adapted from William C. Frederick, "The Moral Authority of Transnational Corporate Codes," *Journal of Business Ethics* 10 (1991), pp. 165–77, particularly table 1, p. 168; and Kathleen A. Getz, "International Codes of Conduct: An Analysis of Ethical Reasoning," *Journal of Business Ethics* 9 (1990), pp. 567–77.

Ethics Issues Addressed	International Ethics Codes*			
	ICC	OECD	ILO	UN/CTC
Economic Development	X	X	X	X
Technology Transfer	X	X	X	X
Regulatory Action	X	X		X
Employment	X	X	X	
Human Rights			X	X
Environmental Protection	X	X		X
Consumer Protection		X		X
Political Action		X		X

*Key for the international codes of conduct:

ICC   = International Chamber of Commerce code (1972)
OECD   = Organization for Economic Cooperation and Development code (1976)
ILO   = International Labor Organization code (1977)
UN/CTC = United Nations Commision on Transnational Corporations code (1984)

[24]"How U.S. Concerns Compete in Countries Where Bribes Flourish," *The Wall Street Journal*, September 29, 1995, pp. A1, A14.

from many fronts, and organizations appeared to draw energy from each other. In November 1997, members of the Organization for Economic Cooperation and Development agreed to an accord that banned international bribery by criminalizing overseas bribes and eliminating the tax deductibility of these payoffs. The Organization of American States approached its members to approve similar rules. For the first time in its history, the World Bank vowed to revoke loans to governments that let bribes influence business transactions. "The trend line is very positive," said Tony Imler, policy director at Merck & Company, a multinational pharmaceutical company. "This is the issue for the next 10 years [in world trade]."[25]

Some businesses have joined their governments in efforts to control unethical employee behavior. As discussed in the next chapter, corporate codes of ethics have been drafted or recently revised to cover instances of undesired practices in the global marketplace. An example of corporate policy addressing global ethical challenges is shown in Exhibit 5–C. In addition, a consortium of European, Asian, and North American business leaders formed the Caux Roundtable. This group drafted the Caux Principles, an international standard for ethical conduct emphasizing *kyosei* (that is, working for the common good) and a respect for human rights. (Portions of the Caux Principles are presented in Chapter 3.)

Some people question the effectiveness of governmental legislation or corporate policies. Rather than establishing rules, some businesses are trying to educate and motivate their employees worldwide to both respect the customs of other nations and adhere to basic ethical principles of fairness, honesty, and respect for human rights. Some who study international business ethics say that such higher standards of ethics already exist. Thomas Donaldson, a leading ethics scholar, has outlined a set of fundamental human rights—including the right to security, to freedom of movement, to subsistence income, and other rights—that should be respected by all multinational corporations. These standards and other ethical values are at the core of the development of transnational codes of conduct promoted by the United Nations and other international organizations.[26]

Ethics, Law, and Illegal Corporate Behavior

Before discussing specific ways to improve business's ethical performance (in the next chapter), we want to consider the relationship of law and ethics. Some people have argued that the best way to assure ethical business conduct is to insist that business firms obey society's laws. However, this approach is not as simple as it seems.

Law and ethics are not quite the same. Laws are similar to ethics because both define proper and improper behavior. In general, laws are a society's attempt to formalize—that is, to reduce to written rules—the general public's ideas about what constitutes right and wrong conduct in various spheres of life. However, it is rarely possible for written laws to capture all of the subtle shadings that people give to ethics. Ethical concepts—like the people who believe in them—are more complex than written rules of law. Ethics

---

[25]"Anticorruption Drive Starts to Show Results," *The Wall Street Journal,* January 27, 1997, p. A1; and "Bribery Ban Is Approved by OECD," *The Wall Street Journal,* November 24, 1997, p. A14.

[26]For a complete list of fundamental human rights, see Thomas Donaldson, *The Ethics of International Business* (New York: Oxford University Press, 1989).

EXHIBIT
5-C

Levi Strauss & Co. Global Sourcing & Operating Guidelines

Introduction

Levi Strauss & Company developed the following policy to guide the firm through the maze of international business and maintain its high standard of ethical integrity. Levi Strauss & Co. has a heritage of conducting business in a manner that reflects its values. Because we source in many countries with diverse cultures, we must take special care in selecting business partners and countries whose practices are not incompatible with our values. Otherwise, our sourcing decisions have the potential of undermining this heritage, damaging the image of our brands and threatening our commercial success.

Business Partner Terms of Engagement

Terms of Engagement address issues that are substantially controllable by our individual business partners.

We have defined business partners as contractors and subcontractors who manufacture or finish our products and suppliers who provide material (including fabric, sundries, chemicals and/or stones) utilized in the manufacturing and finishing of our products.

1. **Environmental Requirements** We will only do business with partners who share our commitment to the environment and who conduct their business in a way that is consistent with Levi Strauss & Co.'s Environmental Philosophy and Guiding Principles.

2. **Ethical Standards** We will seek to identify and utilize business partners who aspire as individuals and in the conduct of all their businesses to a set of ethical standards not incompatible with our own.

3. **Legal Requirements** We expect our business partners to be law abiding as individuals and to comply with legal requirements relevant to the conduct of all their businesses.

4. **Employment Practices** We will only do business with partners whose workers are in all cases present voluntarily, not put at risk of physical harm, fairly compensated, allowed the right of free association and not exploited in any way. In addition, . . . specific guidelines [are provided in the areas of]: wages and benefits, . . . working hours, . . . child labor, . . . prison labor/forced labor, . . . health and safety, . . . discrimination, [and] . . . disciplinary practices.

5. **Community Involvement** We will favor business partners who share our commitment to contribute to the betterment of community conditions.

Source: Levi Strauss & Co.

deals with human dilemmas that frequently go beyond the formal language of law and the meanings given to legal rules. The following situation demonstrates that there is not always a perfect match between the law and important ethical principles.

> *In 1994, educators and parents voiced their concern over the significant increase in sexually explicit language and violence depicted in video games and computer software. Congress joined in the criticism and called for a system of warnings for consumers. The Interactive Digital Software Association, which represents video game makers, established a five-category system that was voluntarily adopted by the industry. The labeling system informed consumers of the intended target audience: early childhood (3 years old and up), children to adults (ages 6 and up), teenagers (13 and over), mature audience (17 and up), and adults only. The video game industry also agreed to provide content warnings, such as "mild profanity," and to use warning symbols: a hand grenade means violence, a hand partly covering an eye indicates sexual scenes, and an exclamation point warns of foul language.*[27]

This example suggests that legality cannot always define when something is believed to be ethical or unethical. Although laws attempt to codify a society's notions of right and wrong, they are not always able to do so completely. Obeying the law is usually one way of acting ethically, and the public generally expects business to be law-abiding. But at times, the public expects business to recognize that ethical principles are broader than the law. Because of the imperfect match between law and ethics, business managers who try to improve their company's ethical performance need to do more than comply with the law. Society will generally insist that they heed ethical principles and the law.

Corporate Lawbreaking and Its Costs

Although estimates vary, lawbreaking in business may cause serious financial losses. A Department of Justice estimate puts the total annual loss from reported and unreported violations of federal regulations by corporations at $10 to $20 billion. The Chamber of Commerce of the United States, a conservative probusiness organization, has estimated that various white-collar crimes cost the public some $41 billion a year. Ten percent of the $1 trillion spent on U.S. health care is believed lost due to fraud every year. One of the most thorough attempts to calculate the financial loss to the country from corporate crimes was that of a U.S. Senate subcommittee, which put the cost of corporate crime at between $174 and $231 billion a year. Compared with even the lesser of these estimates, the $3 to $4 billion annual loss to street crime—robbery, burglary, assault, and so forth—represents only a small proportion of the economic cost of crime. The United States is not the only nation suffering losses from illegal acts. German officials believed that over 50 billion marks ($29.07 billion) a year was lost from the German economy as a result of inflated accounting, tax evasion, and illegal kickbacks.[28]

---

[27]"Games Industries Introduce Voluntary Ratings System," *The Wall Street Journal,* July, 29, 1994, p. B3.
[28]See Jeffrey S. Hornsby, Donald F. Kuratko, and William Honey, "Emerging Growth Companies and the At-Risk Employee: The Viability of Pre-Employment Honesty Testing," *SAM Advanced Management Journal* 54, no. 4 (1992), pp. 24–29; and Brandon Mitchener, "Germany Says Business Bribes on the Rise," *The Wall Street Journal,* April 14, 1997, p. A12.

Beyond these dollar costs of illegal behavior are the physical and social costs. Over 100,000 deaths each year are attributed to occupational diseases, and many of these result from violations of health and safety laws. Annually over 6,000 workers die from on-the-job injuries. This amounts to an average of nearly 17 workplace deaths each day. Tragically, many of these deaths might have been avoided if employers and workers were informed about the risks and complied with established safety and health regulations.[29]

Summary Points of This Chapter

- Ethics is a conception of right and wrong behavior, defining for us when our actions are moral and when they are immoral. Business ethics is the application of general ethical ideas to business behavior.

- Ethical business behavior is expected by the public, prevents harm to society, fosters business relations and employee productivity, reduces criminal penalties, protects business against unscrupulous employees and competitors, protects business employees from harmful actions by their employer, and allows people in business to act consistently with their personal ethical beliefs.

- Ethics problems occur in business for many reasons, including the selfishness of a few, competitive pressures on profits, the clash of personal values and business goals, and cross-cultural contradictions in global business operations.

- Similar ethical issues, such as bribery, are evident throughout the world, and many international agencies and national governments are actively attempting to minimize such actions through economic sanctions and international codes.

- Although law and ethics are closely related, they are not the same; ethical principles tend to be broader than legal principles. Illegal behavior by business and its employees imposes great costs on business and the general public.

Key Terms and Concepts Used in This Chapter

- Ethics
- Ethical principles
- Ethical relativism
- Business ethics
- U.S. Corporate Sentencing Guidelines
- Functional-area ethics
- U.S./Foreign Corrupt Practices Act
- Ethical egoist
- Altruism
- Bribery
- Law

Internet Resources

- http://www.dii.org   Defense Industry Initiative on Business Ethics and Conduct

[29]An extensive analysis of the U.S. census data on workplace fatalities is in Guy Toscano and Janice Windau, "Fatal Work Injuries: Results from the 1992 National Census," *Monthly Labor Review,* October 1993, pp. 39–48.

- http://www.per2per.com   Gaia Friends: Ethics Information Center
- http://www.depaul.edu/ethics/ethg1.html   The On-Line Journal of Ethics
- http://www.us.kpmg.com/ethics   KPMG Business Ethics Practice

---

Discussion Case   ## Unethical Practices at Daiwa Bank

In November 1995, Daiwa Bank, Japan's 10th-largest financial institution, was rocked by allegations of questionable bank practices and criminal actions by bank employees at their New York–based U.S. operations. As the situation unfolded in the international press, the bank was accused by U.S. banking regulators of

- Not recording more than $1 billion of trading loss between 1983 and 1995 and falsifying records to conceal these losses.
- Concealing this information from U.S. regulators for almost two months under direct orders by Daiwa's senior management.
- Deceiving U.S. federal bank regulators in 1992 and 1993 when Daiwa told the government in writing that custody and trading operations were separated when they had not been.
- Knowingly concealing another $97 million in losses between 1984 and 1987.

In addition, Toshihide Iguchi, a New York–based bond trader for Daiwa Bank, pleaded guilty in a U.S. federal court to six counts of fraud, including money laundering, falsifying bank documents, embezzling $500,000 for personal use, and misappropriating $1.1 billion in Daiwa funds. In defense of his actions, Iguchi filed a letter with the U.S. court claiming that "he suffered years of anguish as he wrestled with whether to confess about the losses." He claimed that "he would have divulged the losses seven years earlier, when they were only $200 million, but the Daiwa executive he intended to tell died unexpectedly." A federal judge sentenced Iguchi to four years in prison and ordered him to pay nearly $2.6 million in fines and restitution for concealing trading losses at Daiwa Bank.

Daiwa Bank was one of Japan's most profitable and fastest-growing financial institutions at the time of the incident. The bank employed over 9,000 people, with 200 Japanese branches and an expanding international network overseas. As of September 1996, Daiwa's assets were more than 18 trillion yen ($162 billion in U.S. currency). The bank reported a quarterly income in September 1996 of nearly 12 billion yen ($108 million).

The U.S. position was one of outrage. On November 3, 1995, the Federal Reserve gave Daiwa Bank 90 days to get out of the country. "It's unprecedented," said Peter Wallison, an international banking expert and former Treasury general counsel. U.S. Senator Alfonse D'Amato, head of the Senate Banking Committee, said that this action sent an important message to the Japanese government that the United States would not tolerate this type of action, since it was evident that the Japanese government knew of the illegality but kept it quiet.

The severity of the punishment to this financial institution that had previously held the respect of the international banking community sent shock waves around the world. Since Daiwa's U.S. operations accounted for 15 percent of its global profits, it was predicted that the impact of the U.S. directive would be a takeover of Daiwa's U.S. operations by another Japanese bank. Threats of a merger circulated for months after the incident, but a year later, Daiwa appeared to have avoided this outcome. Other experts predicted that the bank's unethical behavior might have a profound impact on U.S.–Japan trade relations. Representative Jim Leach, head of the House Banking Committee, felt that the Daiwa incident highlighted the growing lack of international cooperation on bank regulation and the increasing risk of inadequate oversight of financial institutions.

In the aftermath of this ethics scandal, Daiwa attempted to right itself. Takashi Kaiho, the new president of Daiwa, announced a new medium-term management plan aimed at renewing growth in the bank's operations and restoring confidence in the bank's practices. Kaiho stated, "We apologize sincerely for any inconvenience that might have arisen in the wake of this [the November 1995] incident and express our warmest gratitude to a number of people who stood by and supported us during [this] trying period." He continued to say that the bank would treat the incident as a learning experience and outlined a three-step program that emphasized increasing bank controls of overseas management, inspection of overseas offices, and a reorganization of oversight duties to strengthen overseas compliance with regulations. He concluded by saying, "we aim to build a solid internal control system so that customers can deal with the Bank in full confidence."

Yet, some pointed to other actions taken by Daiwa Bank after the guilty plea as less than adequate. For example, former Daiwa president Tetsuya Horie resigned on October 9, 1995, in the midst of the scandal. Yet a month later, Horie was given the title of bank adviser at Daiwa Bank and received a salary, office, and chauffeured limousine. The bank defended these actions by saying that Horie's resignation was intended to defend the honor of the bank and that no one ever suggested that he had any culpability in the incident.

Sources: Information and quotations for this discussion case were taken from Norihiko Shirouzu, "Daiwa Confirms It Told Trader to Hide Losses," *The Wall Street Journal,* October 23, 1995, p. A16; "In a Signal to Japan, U.S. Bars Daiwa Bank and Indicts Institution," *The Wall Street Journal,* November 3, 1995, pp. A1, A5; Frances A. McMorris and Michael Rapoport, "Former Daiwa Bank Trader Gets Four Years in Jail, Fines for Losses," *The Wall Street Journal,* December 17, 1995, p. B10; and Daiwa Bank, http://www.infoweb.or. jp/daiwabank (November 6, 1997).

Discussion Questions

1. Why did these ethical problems occur at Daiwa Bank? Use Figure 5–3 to help you in your analysis.
2. Assess the position and actions taken by Daiwa Bank and the U.S. Federal Reserve. Were these positions and actions unethical or ethically necessary given the competitive world of international finance?
3. Was the punishment by the U.S. federal court just?
4. Was Daiwa Bank's new medium-term management plan a sufficient response to the firm's unethical practices?

6

Ethical Reasoning and Corporate Programs

Businesses can take tangible steps to improve their ethical performance. The most important elements of ethical reform are corporate values and the personal character of the employees, especially managers. Corporate ethical action can be improved by creating or revising various organizational safeguards, such as codes of ethics, ethics committees, and employee ethics training. These programs enable employees to improve their ethical reasoning by emphasizing a concern for achieving the greatest good for all those affected by an action while respecting peoples' rights and striving for a just and fair solution.

This chapter focuses on these key questions and objectives:

- What are managers' major goals and values?
- What roles do personal character and spirituality play in business ethics?
- How do a company's culture and work climate influence the ethical views of managers and employees?
- In analyses of ethics issues, how much weight should be given to harms and benefits, to human rights, and to social justice?
- What are the strengths and weaknesses of ethics codes, ethics training programs, ethics hot lines, and similar reform efforts?

During the 1980s and 1990s, Bausch & Lomb's Hong Kong division was the super-star of the firm's international business operations. This division boasted of 25 percent annual growth, and its revenues rocketed to $100 million by 1993. Unfortunately, it was discovered that some of this division's reported sales were fake. Under heavy pressure from corporate headquarters to maintain its phenomenal success, the Hong Kong unit had pretended to book big sales of Ray-Ban sunglasses to distributors in Southeast Asia. But the goods had never been shipped. Instead, secret, phony invoices, which executives at the Bausch & Lomb headquarters never saw, had instructed employees to send the goods to a nearby warehouse in Hong Kong.[1]

Meanwhile, in late 1994, the Securities and Exchange Commission started reviewing Bausch & Lomb's records at its U.S. contact lens division. This investigation revealed that the lens division improperly had inflated sales and profits by shipping huge quantities of unwanted lenses at the end of the year to distributors. These distributors were assured that they would not have to pay for the lenses until they were sold.

Driven by Bausch & Lomb's CEO, Daniel E. Gill, and his insistence on achieving double-digit annual profit growth, managers at Bausch & Lomb in the 1990s increasingly resorted to what was expedient—often at the expense of what constituted sound business practices or ethical behavior. They gave customers extraordinarily long payment terms, knowingly fed "gray markets" (where products were illegally sold for below market price), and threatened to cut off distributors unless they accepted huge quantities of unwanted products.

In November 1997, Bausch & Lomb agreed to pay $42 million to settle a shareholder class-action suit related to the 1993 overstatement of earnings and revenues from improperly recording contact lens and sunglass sales.

This episode raises some disturbing questions: Can pressure from senior management corrupt a firm's employees around the world, causing them to create dishonest record-keeping procedures to meet high expectations? Can this happen even when those who feel the pressure are of good personal character? More important, what can companies do to guard against such ethical abuses?

In this chapter, we examine ways to improve a business's ethical performance. The keys to success are a blend of managers' values, personal character and spirituality, a company's culture and ethical climate, the tools available for analyzing moral dilemmas, and practical changes in company procedures that permit high ethical performance along with profitable operations.

The Core Elements of Ethical Reform

Whether a company improves its ethical performance depends on three core components: the goals and values of its managers; the personal character and spirituality of its managers and other employees; and the traditions, attitudes, and business practices built into the company's culture. Good ethical practices not only are possible, but they become normal with the right combination of these three components.

Managers' Goals and Values

Managers are one of the keys to whether a company will act ethically or unethically. As major decision makers, they have more opportunities than others to create an ethical tone

---

[1]Mark Maremont, "Blind Ambition," *Business Week,* October 23, 1995, pp. 78–92.

for their company. The values held by these managers, especially the top-level managers, will serve as models for others who work there.

Figure 6–1 shows that U.S. managers' value orientations in the 1990s are pretty much what one would expect. Most managers emphasize a self-focus and a concern for being competent, placing importance on values such as having a comfortable life, living an exciting life, and being capable, intellectual, and responsible. Some managers show a strong concern for values that include others, evident in the values of living in a world at peace or seeking equality among people. One out of four managers emphasize the other set of values—moral values. These managers place greater importance on the value of forgiving others, being helpful, and acting honestly.

What about future managers? A survey of over 2,100 graduate business students across the United States found that 79 percent of them felt that a company must weigh its impact on society. This impact could be seen in the company's environmental responsibility, practices of equal opportunity, treatment of workers' families, and other issues with ethical values. Half of the students surveyed said they would accept lower pay to work for a company they found "very socially responsible." Nearly half (43 percent) said they would not work for an employer that did not demonstrate ethical responsibility, possibly indicating a shift toward a greater moral value focus.[2]

Current discussions about effective organizational leadership often center on individuals' values. For example, an **ethical charismatic leader** exhibiting strong moral character is capable of positively influencing an entire department or organization. Although there are risks associated with assuming this higher moral ground, ethical charismatic leaders, described in Figure 6–2, are seen as other-centered visionaries who bring out the best in their followers. Although varying from the predominant value orientations of managers in the 1990s, the moral standards of the ethical manager may enable business leaders to better address the difficult moral decisions encountered at work. This ethical leadership also may change the negative perception of managers by the general public. In a 1997 *Business Week* poll, businesspersons ranked near the bottom of professions in terms of perceived reputation, along with bankers, journalists, and union leaders.

Figure 6–1

Percentage of U.S. managers emphasizing a value focus in 1990 (*N* = 413).

Source: Adapted from James Weber, "Managerial Value Orientations: A Typology and Assessment." *International Journal of Value-Based Management* 3, no. 2 (1990), pp. 37–54, particularly table 5, p. 49. Reprinted by permission of Kluwer Academic Publishers.

Means-Oriented Values	Goal-Oriented Values		
	Self-focus	vs. Other-focus	Totals
Competency focus vs.	53.5%	21.8%	75.3%
Moral focus	18.4	6.3	24.7
Totals	71.9	28.1	

[2]Keith Hamkonds, "Bleeding Hearts at B-School?," *Business Week,* April 7, 1997, p. 8.

Figure 6–2

Qualities of an ethical charismatic leader.

Source: Adapted from Jane M. Howell and Bruce J. Avolio, "The Ethics of Charismatic Leadership: Submission or Liberation?" *Academy of Management Executive* 6, no. 2 (1992), p. 45.

The ethical charismatic leader
- Uses power to serve others
- Aligns vision with followers' needs and aspirations
- Considers and learns from criticisms
- Stimulates followers to think independently and to question the leader's view
- Fosters open, two-way communication
- Coaches, develops, and supports followers
- Shares recognition with others
- Relies on internal moral standards to satisfy organizational and societal interests

How Managers' Values Can Promote Ethics Reform

Managers are authority figures and role models in their companies. By setting a personal example of high ethical behavior, they can influence others around them. Repeated studies over the years have arrived at the same conclusion: The behavior and ethical attitudes of an employee's boss are seen as the most important factors determining whether the employee will behave unethically on the job.[3]

Personal Character, Spirituality, and Moral Development

Clarence Walton, a seasoned observer of managerial behavior, says that personal character is one of the keys to higher ethical standards in business. "People of integrity produce organizations with integrity. When they do, they become moral managers—those special people who make organizations and societies better."[4] Others agree, including one longtime business executive who did an in-depth study of 24 business managers noted for high-quality ethical standards in their companies. He emphasizes the close connection between ethical leadership and a person's belief system or values.

> *Virtuous leaders are persons of honesty, integrity and trust. As popularly defined in business literature today, they are concerned about excellence. Facing the rough-and-tumble of competition, and its ancillary temptations, they must exhibit moral courage. But virtue requires more than techniques and personal integrity. Virtue requires the acceptance of equity in human relationships and a commitment to act accordingly. It involves that core element, the belief system of a person.[5]*

---

[3]However, a recent study looked at the influence on managers by functional area. It reported that influences may differ depending on whether managers are in the personnel, marketing, manufacturing, or finance departments of the company. See Barry Z. Posner, W. Alan Randolph, and Warren H. Schmidt, "Managerial Values in Personnel, Marketing, Manufacturing, and Finance: Similarities and Differences," *International Journal of Value-Based Management* 6, no. 2 (1993), pp. 19–30.

[4]Clarence C. Walton, *The Moral Manager* (Cambridge, MA: Ballinger, 1988), p. 33 and Part III, "The 'Ethic' of Character."

[5]James E. Liebig, *Business Ethics: Profiles in Civic Virtue* (Golden, CO: Fulcrum, 1990), p. 5.

Personal Spirituality

Personal spirituality, that is, a personal belief in a supreme being, religious organization, or the power of nature or some other external, life-guiding force, has always been a part of the human makeup. Recently, efforts appear to be on the rise to integrate people's work with their spirituality. The influence of personal spirituality on workplace decisions and actions is mentioned more frequently in business literature. Juggling two sets of values—religious principles and business practices—can lead to challenging dilemmas, as shown in the following examples.

- An ambitious summer associate in a large law firm happens to be an Orthodox Jew. What does the associate order for lunch at a posh club when even the house salad is sprinkled with bacon bits?

- How does a Mormon who runs a television-network department avoid violating a moral code when the station produces a promotional campaign using steamy pictures of television stars?

- Can a young Muslim student take out a loan for graduate school even though the Islamic law technically prohibits the paying and collecting of interest?

A person's spirituality or religious beliefs can change corporate practices. At a Dallas Interstate Batteries warehouse, drivers and salespeople gather at 7:00 A.M. Monday morning for their weekly, voluntary Bible study group. Interstate's full-time corporate chaplain leads the employees in prayer. The Bible study is held with the support of Interstate chairman Norman Miller, a devout Christian who believes that religion belongs in the workplace and is an essential part of business success. "I need to be faithful to Jesus 100 percent of the time. And that includes my business."[6] However, others disagree with the trend toward a stronger presence of religion in the workplace. They hold the traditional belief that business is a secular, that is, nonspiritual, institution. They believe that business is business and spirituality is best left for the churches, synagogues, and meditation rooms, not the corporate boardrooms or shop floors. This, of course, reflects the United States' separation of church and state.

Nonetheless, religion has emerged as a consumer-purchasing factor. *Shepherd's Guide,* available in several, large U.S. cities, is a religious yellow pages. It lists Christian accountants, plumbers, real-estate agents, and other businesspeople who have signed statements of faith declaring Jesus as their personal savior.

On the basis of personal spirituality, wealthy top executives have contributed to various social and political causes. Robert Pamplin, Jr., gave 10 percent of R.B. Pamplin Corporation's pretax income, about $8 million in 1994, toward establishing a church program to distribute food to the hungry in Portland, Oregon, and other charities. The DeVos family, cofounders of Amway Company, gave $2.5 million to the Republican political party to build a television studio to promote conservative, fundamental Christian views. Norman Miller of Interstate Batteries supported the Free Market Foundation, an organization that helped voters identify socially and religiously conservative political candidates in Texas.

---

[6]Janny Scott, "In the Maelstrom of New York, Faith Perseveres," *New York Times,* March 5, 1995, pp. 1, 14; and Dan McGraw, "The Christian Capitalists," *U.S. News & World Report,* March 13, 1995, pp. 53–62.

Just as personal values and character are strong influences on employee decision making and behavior in the workplace, personal spirituality and religious values, from all points of the value spectrum, are having an impact on how businesses are operated and where corporate revenues are spent.

Managers' Moral Development

Taken together, personal values, character, and spirituality exert a powerful influence on the way ethical work issues are treated. Since people have different personal histories and have developed their values, character, and spirituality in different ways, they are going to think differently about ethical problems. This is as true of corporate managers as it is of other people. In other words, the managers in a company are liable to be at various **stages of moral development.** Some will reason at a high level, others at a lower level.

A summary of the way people grow and develop morally is diagrammed in Figure 6–3. From childhood to mature adulthood, most people move steadily upward in their moral reasoning capabilities from stage 1. Over time, they become more developed and are capable of more advanced moral reasoning. At first, they are limited to an ego-centered focus (stage 1), fixed on avoiding punishment and obediently following the di-

Figure 6–3

Stages of moral development and ethical reasoning.

Source: Adapted from Lawrence Kohlberg, *The Philosophy of Moral Development* (New York: Harper & Row, 1981).

Age Group	Development Stage and Major Ethics Referent	Basis of Ethics Reasoning
Mature adulthood	**Stage 6** Universal principles: Justice, fairness, universal human rights	Principle-centered reasoning
Mature adulthood	**Stage 5** Moral beliefs above and beyond specific social custom: Human rights, social contract, broad constitutional principles	Principle-centered reasoning
Adulthood	**Stage 4** Society at large: Customs, traditions, laws	Society-and-law centered reasoning
Early adulthood, adolescence	**Stage 3** Social groups: Friends, school, coworkers	Group-centered reasoning
Adolescence, youth	**Stage 2** Reward seeking: Self-interest, own needs, reciprocity	Ego-centered reasoning
Childhood	**Stage 1** Punishment avoidance: Punishment avoidance, obedience to power	Ego-centered reasoning

Direction of Moral Development →

rections of those in authority. Slowly and sometimes painfully, the child learns that what is considered to be right and wrong is pretty much a matter of reciprocity: "I'll scratch your back, if you'll scratch mine" (stage 2).

In adolescence the individual enters a wider world, learning the give-and-take of group life among small circles of friends, schoolmates, and similar close-knit groups (stage 3). Studies have reported that interaction within groups can provide an environment that improves the level of moral reasoning. This process continues into early adulthood. At this point, pleasing others and being admired by them are important clues to proper behavior. Most people are now capable of focusing on other-directed rather than me-directed perspectives.[7]

On reaching full adulthood—the late teens to early 20s in the United States—most people are able to focus their reasoning according to society's customs, traditions, and laws as the proper way to define what is right and wrong (stage 4). Stages 5 and 6 lead to a special kind of moral reasoning, because people often can get above and beyond the specific rules, customs, and laws of their own societies. They are capable of basing their ethical reasoning on broad principles and relationships, such as human rights and constitutional guarantees of human dignity, equal treatment, and freedom of expression. In the highest stage of moral development, the meaning of right and wrong is defined by universal principles of justice, fairness, and the common rights of all humanity.[8]

Research has demonstrated that most people, including managers, typically reason at stages 3 and 4. Although they may be capable of more advanced moral reasoning that goes beyond society or law, their ethical horizons most often are defined by their family, close friends, neighborhood groups, and society's laws and customs. For managers who reason at stages 3 and 4, the company's rules and customary ways of doing things become their main ethical compass. While at work, the company is their ethical reference group. For them, the right way to do business depends on what the boss and their coworkers accept as right and wrong (stage 3 reasoning), as long as everyone also shows a respect for society's laws (stage 4 reasoning).[9]

Another way to think about the development of moral character has been developed by Carol Gilligan. She suggests that men's and women's personal characters are distinct because boys and girls are raised differently. Boys and young men learn that fairness and justice result from obeying rules and principles. For them, being ethical means adhering to rules laid down by parents, teachers, friends, and society's customs and laws. Girls and young women follow a somewhat different path in their moral development. Their ethical orientation is toward responsibility to others, caring for others' well-being, being involved in and wanting to preserve close relationships, and valuing direct actions over

---

[7]Janet M. Dukerich, Mary Lippitt Nichols, Dawn R. Elm, and David A. Vollrath, "Moral Reasoning in Groups: Leaders Make a Difference," *Human Relations* 43, no. 5 (1990), pp. 473–93; and Donald Nelson and Tom E. Obremski, "Promoting Moral Growth through Intra-Group Participation," *Journal of Business Ethics* 9 (1990), pp. 731–39.

[8]For details and research findings, see Lawrence Kohlberg, *The Philosophy of Moral Development* (San Francisco: Harper & Row, 1981); and Anne Colby and Lawrence Kohlberg, *The Measurement of Moral Judgment, Volume I: Theoretical Foundations and Research Validations* (Cambridge, MA: Cambridge University Press, 1987).

[9]James Weber, "Managers' Moral Reasoning: Assessing Their Responses to Three Moral Dilemmas," *Human Relations* 43 (1990), pp. 687–702. See also, Robert Jackall, *Moral Mazes: The World of Corporate Managers* (New York: Oxford University Press, 1988).

dependence on rules when facing an ethical dilemma. Corporate managers with this more caring attitude about others would have an important impact on the way companies cope with on-the-job ethical issues.[10]

The development of a manager's moral character, regardless of whether it arises from a rule-based ethics or a caring-based ethics, can be crucial to a company. Some ethics issues require managers to move beyond selfish interest (stages 1 and 2), beyond company interest (stage 3 reasoning), and even beyond sole reliance on society's customs and laws (stage 4 reasoning). Needed is a manager whose personal character is built on a caring attitude toward others, recognizing others' rights and their essential humanity (a combination of stage 5 and 6 reasoning and care-based reasoning). The moral reasoning of upper-level managers, whose decisions affect companywide policies, can have a powerful and far-reaching impact both inside and outside the company.

Corporate Culture and Ethical Climates

Personal values and moral character play key roles in improving a company's ethical performance. However, they do not stand alone, because personal values and character can be affected by a company's culture.

Corporate culture is a blend of ideas, customs, traditional practices, company values, and shared meanings that help define normal behavior for everyone who works in a company. Culture is "the way we do things around here." Two experts testify to its overwhelming influence:

> *Every business—in fact every organization—has a culture . . . [and it]*
> *has a powerful influence throughout an organization; it affects practically*
> *everything—from who gets promoted and what decisions are made, to how em-*
> *ployees dress and what sports they play. . . . When [new employees] choose a*
> *company, they often choose a way of life. The culture shapes their responses in*
> *a strong, but subtle way. Culture can make them fast or slow workers, tough or*
> *friendly managers, team players or individuals. By the time they've worked for*
> *several years, they may be so well conditioned by the culture they may not*
> *even recognize it.*[11]

Hewlett-Packard, the California-based electronics manufacturer, is well known for a culture that stresses values and ethics. Called the HP Way by employees, the most important values of the culture are confidence in and respect for people, open communication, sharing of benefits and responsibilities, concern for the individual employee, and honesty and integrity. "These values have been integrated into and are central to the company's strategy, its objectives, and its self-image."[12] The impact of this ethics-oriented

---

[10]The *ethic of care* was first presented by Carol Gilligan, *In a Different Voice* (Cambridge, MA: Harvard University Press, 1982). This theme continues in her more recent work, Carol Gilligan, Janie V. Ward, Jill M. Taylor, and Betty Bardige, eds., *Mapping the Moral Domain* (Cambridge, MA: Harvard University Press, 1990).

[11]Terrence E. Deal and Allan A. Kennedy, *Corporate Cultures: The Rites and Rituals of Corporate Life* (Reading, MA: Addison-Wesley, 1982), pp. 4, 16.

[12]Kirk O. Hanson and Manuel Velasquez, "Hewlett-Packard Company: Managing Ethics and Values," *Corporate Ethics: A Prime Business Asset* (New York: The Business Roundtable, February 1988), p. 75.

culture is evident to managers and employees alike. A Hewlett-Packard manager commented that "It is not easy to get fired around HP, but you are gone before you know it if it is an ethics issue." Another manager said, "Somehow, the manipulative person, the person who is less open and candid, who shaves the truth or the corners of policies, doesn't last. They either get passed over for promotion or they just don't find this a comfortable environment."

Ethical Climates

In most companies, a moral atmosphere can be detected. People can feel the way the ethical winds are blowing. They pick up subtle hints and clues that tell them what behavior is approved and what is forbidden.

The unspoken understanding among employees of what is and is not acceptable behavior is called an **ethical climate.** It is the part of corporate culture that sets the ethical tone in a company.[13] One way to view ethical climates is diagrammed in Figure 6–4. Three different types of ethical yardsticks are egoism (self-centeredness), benevolence (concern for others), and principle (respect for one's own integrity, for group norms, and for society's laws). These ethical yardsticks can be applied to dilemmas concerning individuals, a company, or society at large.

For example, if a manager approaches ethics issues with benevolence in mind, he or she would stress friendly relations with an employee, emphasize the importance of team play and cooperation for the company's benefit, and recommend socially responsible courses of action. However, if the manager used egoism to think about ethical problems, he or she would be more likely to think first of self-interest, promoting the company's profit, and striving for efficient operations at all costs. A company's ethical climate depends on which combination it has of the nine climate types shown in Figure 6–4.

Figure 6–4

The components of ethical climates.

Source: Adapted from Bart Victor and John B. Cullen, "The Organizational Bases of Ethical Work Climates," *Administrative Science Quarterly* 33 (1988), p. 104.

	Focus of Ethical Concern		
Ethical Criteria	**Individual Person**	**Company**	**Society**
Egoism (self-centered approach)	Self-interest	Company interest	Economic efficiency
Benevolence (concern-for-others approach	Friendship	Team interest	Social responsibility
Principle (integrity approach)	Personal morality	Company rules and procedures	Laws and professional codes

[13]Karen N. Gaertner, "The Effect of Ethical Climate on Managers' Decisions," in Richard M. Coughlin, ed., *Socio-Economic Perspectives 1990* (Armonk, NY: M. E. Sharpe, 1990), pp. 169–83; and Mary E. Guy, *Ethical Decision Making in Everyday Work Situations* (New York: Quorum Books, 1990), chap. 5.

Research has demonstrated that different companies have different ethical climates. The pioneering study on which Figure 6–4 is based discovered five types of corporate ethical climates.[14]

- *A caring climate*. A benevolence yardstick was predominant here. Employees said such things as, "The most important concern is the good of all the people in the company as a whole."

- *A law-and-code climate*. A principles yardstick produced a positive attitude toward society's laws and professional codes. A typical employee statement here was, "People are expected to comply with the law and professional standards over and above other considerations."

- *A rules climate*. Company rules and regulations were the principles emphasized here. In this climate, employees agreed that "Successful people in this company go by the book."

- *An instrumental climate*. An egoism yardstick was typical in this climate, and it was focused on the self-interest of the company and of employees. Employees agreed that "People are expected to do anything to further the company's interests, regardless of the consequences." They also said, "In this company, people are mostly out for themselves."

- *An independence climate*. People in this climate preferred a yardstick that put the emphasis on personal beliefs. A typical attitude was "In this company, people are guided by their own personal ethics."

The researchers concluded, "Employees were more satisfied with the ethics of their company when they observed greater levels of caring . . . and lower levels of instrumentalism."[15]

Corporate cultures can also signal to employees that ethical transgressions are acceptable. One observer's list of warning signs of such an ethically dysfunctional culture is shown in Exhibit 6–A. By signaling what is considered to be right and wrong, corporate cultures and ethical climates can put much pressure on people to channel their actions in certain directions desired by the company. This kind of pressure can work both for and against good ethical practices. In a caring ethical climate, the interests of the company's employees and external stakeholders most likely would be given high priority. But in an instrumental ethical climate, employees and managers might be encouraged to disregard any interests other than their own.

Analyzing Ethical Problems in Business

Business managers and employees need a set of guidelines that will shape their thinking when on-the-job ethics issues occur. The guidelines should help them (1) identify and analyze the nature of an ethical problem, and (2) decide which course of action is likely to produce an ethical result. The following three methods of ethical reasoning can be used for these analytical purposes, as summarized in Figure 6–5.

---

[14]Bart Victor and John B. Cullen, "The Organizational Bases of Ethical Work Climates," *Administrative Science Quarterly* 33 (1988), pp. 101–25.
[15]Ibid., p. 117.

EXHIBIT 6–A	Five Warning Signs of Ethical Collapse

1. Surround yourself with subordinates who are young, inexperienced, enthralled with power, and deep in debt.
2. Send a clear message that you expect results at any cost.
3. Be certain the CEO and chairman are tyrannical and prone to anger.
4. When an employee's public statements bring criticism of the company, cut the employee loose.
5. When an ethical lapse is discovered, never admit anything.

Source: Marianne M. Jennings, "Five Warning Signs of Ethical Collapse," *The Wall Street Journal,* November 4, 1996, p. A16.

Figure 6–5

Three methods of ethical reasoning.

Method	Critical Determining Factor	An Action Is Ethical When . . .	Limitations
Utilitarian	Comparing benefits and costs	Net benefits exceed net costs	Difficult to measure some human and social costs Majority may disregard rights of minority
Rights	Respecting rights	Basic human rights are respected	Difficult to balance conflicting rights
Justice	Distributing fair shares	Benefits and costs are fairly distributed	Difficult to measure benefits and costs Lack of agreement on fair shares

Utility: Comparing Benefits and Costs

One approach to ethics emphasizes the utility, the overall amount of good, that can be produced by an action or a decision. Should a company close one of its older plants and move production to its modern facility in another part of the country or world? The answer would depend on how much good is produced by the move compared with the harm that could result. If those affected were better off after the move than before, then they would claim that the move was ethical because more good than harm resulted.

This ethical approach is called **utilitarian reasoning.** It is often referred to as cost-benefit analysis because it compares the costs and benefits of a decision, a policy, or an action. These costs and benefits can be economic (expressed in dollar amounts), social (the effect on society at large), or human (usually a psychological or emotional impact). After business managers add up all the costs and benefits and compare them with one another, the net cost or the net benefit should be apparent. If the benefits outweigh the costs, then the action is ethical because it produces the greatest good for the greatest number of people in society. If the net costs are larger than the net benefits, then it is probably unethical because more harm than good is produced.

The main drawback to utilitarian reasoning is the difficulty of accurately measuring both costs and benefits. Some things can be measured in monetary terms—goods produced, sales, payrolls, and profits—but other items are trickier, such as employee morale, psychological satisfactions, and the worth of a human life. Human and social costs are particularly difficult to measure with precision. But unless they can be measured, the cost-benefit calculations will be incomplete, and it will be difficult to know whether the overall result is good or bad, ethical or unethical.

Another limitation of utilitarian reasoning is that the majority may override the rights of those in the minority. Since utilitarian reasoning is primarily concerned with the end results of an action, managers using this reasoning process often fail to consider the means taken to reach the end. Closing an outmoded plant may produce the greatest good for the greatest number, but this good outcome will not change the fact that some workers left behind may be unable to find decent jobs. This problem might be especially difficult for older workers, employees who are not well educated, or members of minority groups.

In spite of these drawbacks, cost-benefit analysis is widely used in business. Because this method works well when used to measure economic and financial outcomes, business managers sometimes are tempted to rely on it to decide important ethical questions without being fully aware of its limitations or the availability of still other methods that may improve the ethical quality of their decisions. One of these other methods is to consider the impact of business decisions on human rights.

Rights: Determining and Protecting Entitlements

Human rights are another basis for making ethical judgments. A right means that a person or group is entitled to something or is entitled to be treated in a certain way. The most basic human rights are those entitlements that enable a person to survive, to make free choices, and to realize his or her potential as a human being. Denying those rights or failing to protect them for other persons and groups is normally considered to be unethical. Respecting others, even those with whom we disagree or dislike, is the essence of human rights, provided that others do the same for us. This approach to ethical reasoning holds that individuals are to be treated as valuable ends in themselves just because they are human beings. Using others for your own purposes is unethical if, at the same time, you deny them their goals and purposes. For example, a union that denies a group of women employees an opportunity to bid for all jobs for which they are qualified is depriving them of some of their rights. Or a company that carelessly disposes of hazardous wastes may be guilty of ignoring the rights of others and simply using the environment for its own selfish purposes.

The main limitation of using rights as a basis of ethical reasoning is the difficulty of balancing conflicting rights. For example, an employee's right to privacy may be at odds with an employer's right to protect the firm's cash by testing the employee's honesty. Some of the most difficult balancing acts have occurred when minorities and women have competed with white males for the right to hold jobs in business and government. Rights also clash when U.S. multinational corporations move production to a foreign nation, causing job losses at home but creating new jobs abroad. In such cases, whose job rights should be respected?[16]

In spite of this kind of problem, the protection and promotion of human rights is an important ethical benchmark for judging the behavior of individuals and organizations. Surely most people would agree that it is unethical to deny a person's fundamental right to life, freedom, privacy, growth, and human dignity. By defining the human condition and pointing the way to a realization of human potentialities, such rights become a kind of common denominator of ethical reasoning, setting forth the essential conditions for ethical actions and decisions.

Justice: Is It Fair?

A third method of ethical reasoning concerns **justice.** Is it fair or just? is a common question in human affairs. Employees want to know if pay scales are fair. Consumers are interested in fair prices when they shop. When new tax laws are proposed, there is much debate about their fairness—where will the burden fall, and who will escape paying their fair share?

Justice, or fairness, exists when benefits and burdens are distributed equitably and according to some accepted rule. For society as a whole, social justice means that a society's income and wealth are distributed among the people in fair proportions. A fair distribution does not necessarily mean an equal distribution. The shares received by people depend on the society's approved rules for getting and keeping income and wealth. These rules will vary from society to society. Most societies try to consider people's needs, abilities, efforts, and the contributions they make to society's welfare. Since these factors are seldom equal, fair shares will vary from person to person and group to group.

Determining what is just and unjust is often a very explosive issue because the stakes are so high. Since distributive rules usually grant privileges to some groups based on tradition and custom, sharp inequalities between groups can generate social tensions and demands for a fairer system. An equal opportunity rule—that is, a rule that gives everyone the same starting advantages in life to health, to education, and to career choices—can lead to a fairer distribution of society's benefits and burdens.

Justice reasoning is not the same as utilitarian reasoning. A person using utilitarian reasoning adds up costs and benefits to see if one is greater than the other; if benefits exceed costs, then the action would probably be considered ethical. A person using justice reasoning considers who pays the costs and who gets the benefits; if the shares seem fair (according to society's rules), then the action is probably just. Is it ethical to move a factory from Boston to Houston? The utilitarian would say yes if the net benefits to all parties were greater than the costs incurred by everyone. A person using justice reasoning would say yes if the benefits and costs caused by the move were fairly borne by all parties affected by the move. The utilitarian reasoner is interested in the net sum. The justice reasoner is interested in fair shares.

[16]For a discussion of ethical rights, see John R. Boatright, *Ethics and the Conduct of Business,* 2d ed. (Upper Saddle River, NJ: Prentice Hall, 1997), pp. 59–65; and Manuel G. Velasquez, *Business Ethics: Concepts and Cases,* 4th ed. (Upper Saddle River, NJ: Prentice Hall, 1998), pp. 85–102.

Applying Ethical Reasoning to Business Activities

Anyone in the business world can use these three methods of ethical reasoning to gain a better understanding of ethical issues that arise at work. More often than not, all three can be applied at the same time. Using only one of the three methods is risky and may lead to an incomplete understanding of all the ethical complexities that may be present. It also may produce a lopsided ethical result that will be unacceptable to others.

Figure 6–6 diagrams the kind of analytical procedure that is useful to employ when one is confronted with an ethical problem or issue. Two general rules can be used in making such an analysis.

The Unanimity Rule

If you want to know whether a decision, a policy, or an activity is ethical or unethical, you first ask the three questions listed in Figure 6–6. As shown in step 2 of the figure, if the answers to all three questions are yes, then the decision or policy or activity is probably ethical. If answers to all three are no, then you probably are looking at an unethical decision, policy, or activity. The reason you cannot be absolutely certain is that different people and groups (1) may honestly and genuinely use different sources of information, (2) may measure costs and benefits differently, (3) may not share the same meaning of justice, or (4) may rank various rights in different ways. Nevertheless, any time an analyst obtains unanimous answers to these three questions—all yeses or all noes—it is an indication that a strong case can be made for either an ethical or an unethical conclusion.

The Priority Rule

What happens when the unanimity rule does not apply? What if there are two yeses and one no, or another combination of the various possibilities? In that case, a choice is necessary. As shown in step 3 of Figure 6–6, a corporate manager or employee then has to assign priorities to the three methods of ethical reasoning. What is most important to the manager, to the employee, or to the organization—utility, rights, or justice? What ranking should they be given? A judgment must be made, and priorities must be determined.

These judgments and priorities will be strongly influenced by a company's culture and ethical climate. A company with an instrumental ethical climate or a rules ethical climate would probably assign high value to a utilitarian approach that calculates the costs and benefits to the company. A caring ethical climate will bring forth a greater respect for the rights of employees and the just treatment of all stakeholders. Obeying the law would be a top priority in a law-and-code ethical climate.

The type of ethical reasoning chosen also depends heavily on managers' values, especially those held by top management, and on the personal character of all decision makers in the company. Some will be sensitive to people's needs and rights; others will put themselves or their company ahead of all other considerations.

Making Ethics Work in Corporations
Any business firm that wishes to do so can improve the quality of its ethical performance. Doing so requires a company to build ethical safeguards into its everyday routines.

Figure 6–6

An analytical approach to ethical problems.

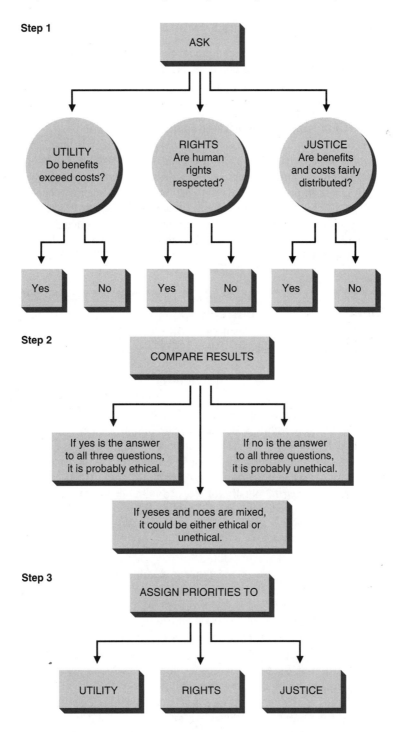

Building Ethical Safeguards into the Company

Managers and employees need guidance on how to handle day-to-day ethical situations; their own personal ethical compass may be working well, but they need to receive directional signals from the company. Several organizational steps can be taken to provide this kind of ethical awareness and direction.

Top Management Commitment and Involvement

When senior-level managers signal employees that they believe ethics should receive high priority in all business decisions, a giant step is taken toward improving ethical performance throughout the company. By personal example, through policy statements, and by willingness to back up words with actions, top management can get its message across. Johnson & Johnson's famous credo, shown in Exhibit 6–B, is a 24-point statement of the company's basic beliefs and is used in just this way. Managers are expected to be familiar with the credo and to use it in decision making. Failure to follow it can lead to reprimand or dismissal.

EXHIBIT 6–B

Johnson & Johnson's Credo

We believe our first responsibility is to the doctors, nurses, and patients, to mothers and fathers and all others who use our products and services. In meeting their needs everything we do must be of high quality. We must constantly strive to reduce our costs in order to maintain reasonable prices. Customers' orders must be serviced promptly and accurately. Our suppliers and distributors must have an opportunity to make a fair profit.

We are responsible to our employees, the men and women who work with us throughout the world. Everyone must be considered as an individual. We must respect their dignity and recognize their merit. They must have a sense of security in their jobs. Compensation must be fair and adequate, and working conditions clean, orderly, and safe. We must be mindful of ways to help our employees fulfill their family responsibilities. Employees must feel free to make suggestions and complaints. There must be equal opportunity for employment, development, and advancement for those qualified. We must provide competent management, and their actions must be just and ethical.

We are responsible to the communities in which we live and work and to the world community as well. We must be good citizens—support good work and charities and bear our fair share of taxes. We must encourage civic improvements and better health and education. We must maintain in good order the property we are privileged to use, protecting the environment and natural resources.

Our final responsibility is to our stockholders. Business must make a sound profit. We must experiment with new ideas. Research must be carried on, innovative programs developed and mistakes paid for. New equipment must be purchased, new facilities provided, and new products launched. Reserves must be created to provide for adverse times. When we operate according to these principles, the stockholders should realize a fair return.

Source: Johnson & Johnson. Reprinted with permission.

Codes of Ethics

Surveys show over 90 percent of all large U.S. corporations have **ethics codes.** Their purpose is to provide guidance to managers and employees when they encounter an ethical dilemma. A typical code discusses conflicts of interest that can harm the company; for example, it might include guidelines for accepting or refusing gifts from suppliers, hiring relatives, or having an interest in a competitor's firm. Rules for complying with various laws, such as antitrust, environmental, and consumer protection laws, also are popular code provisions. The most effective codes are those drawn up with the cooperation and widespread participation of employees. An internal enforcement mechanism, including penalties for violation, puts teeth into a code. A shortcoming of many codes is that they tend to provide more protection for the company than for employees and the general public. They do so by emphasizing narrow legal compliance—rather than taking a positive and broad view of ethical responsibility toward all company stakeholders—and by focusing on conflicts of interest that will harm the company.[17]

Ethics codes are more common in U.S. corporations than in foreign-based companies. About 90 percent of U.S. companies have such codes, compared with only 41 percent of those in England, France, and Germany, according to one survey. But the situation is changing. More and more Japanese firms have begun drafting corporate codes of ethics, prompted by a series of ethical scandals involving the country's securities and banking industries. By 1997, approximately 20 to 30 percent of major Japanese corporations had adopted ethical guidelines for their employees.[18] The New York–based Conference Board has developed guidelines and criteria for ethics standards to be used by business professionals and organizations around the globe.

One comparative study found that corporate ethics codes vary considerably from country to country, reflecting differences in political, governmental, and social approaches to business ethics issues. Employee conduct was included in all of the European business codes but in only 55 percent of U.S. company codes, for example, and local community and environmental affairs were more frequently mentioned in European codes (65 percent) than in U.S. codes (42 percent). However, U.S. companies seemed to be more attentive to customers, suppliers, and contractors than the Europeans.[19]

Ethics Committees

Nearly half of all companies surveyed from the Fortune 1,000 list of companies have created ethics committees to give guidance on ethics matters. It can be a high-level committee of the board of directors, usually chaired by an outside board member to create an arm's-length relationship with top management. In other cases, the committee's members are drawn from the ranks of top management. For example, Boeing's Ethics and Business

---

[17]Patrick E. Murphy, "Corporate Ethics Statements: Current Status and Future Prospects," *Journal of Business Ethics* 14 (1995), pp. 727–40; Center for Business Ethics, "Instilling Ethical Values in Large Corporations," *Journal of Business Ethics* 11 (1992), p. 864; and M. Cash Mathews, *Strategic Intervention in Organizations: Resolving Ethical Dilemmas* (Newbury Park, CA: Sage Publications, 1988), chaps. 4 and 5.

[18]"Japan Is Taking Business Ethics 'More Seriously,'" *Ethikos,* September–October 1997, pp. 12, 15.

[19]Ronald E. Berenbeim, *Corporate Ethics* (New York: The Conference Board, 1987), chap. 3; Leonard J. Brooks, "Corporate Codes of Ethics" [in Canadian companies], *Journal of Business Ethics* 8 (1989), pp. 117–29; Bodo B. Schlegelmilch and Jane E. Houston, "Corporate Codes of Ethics in Large UK Companies," *European Journal of Marketing* 23, no. 6 (1989), pp. 7–24; and Catherine C. Langlois and Bodo B. Schlegelmilch, "Do Corporate Codes of Ethics Reflect National Character? Evidence from Europe and the United States," *Journal of International Business Studies* 21, no. 4 (1990), pp. 519–39.

Conduct Committee is chaired by a senior vice president. It also includes staff vice presidents for finance and human resources and the heads of the company's three operating divisions—commercial, computers, and military.[20]

These committees field ethics questions from employees, help a company establish policy in new or uncertain areas, advise the board of directors on ethics issues, and sometimes oversee ethics training programs.

Ethics Officers

Continued ethical lapses in large corporations throughout the 1980s and 1990s prompted many firms to create a new position: the **ethics officer.** "Ten years ago [1986] they were practically nonexistent," said W. Michael Hoffman, founder and executive director of the Center for Business Ethics at Bentley College. By 1996, he noted, between 35 and 40 percent of major U.S. companies had an ethics officer.[21]

Many of the earliest companies to establish ethics offices, under the direction of an ethics officer, were recipients of U.S. government defense contracts, for example, General Dynamics and Martin Marietta. Since 1991, ethics officers have expanded into many industries, particularly heavily regulated enterprises such as telecommunication and utility companies. The Ethics Officers Association claimed over 500 corporate members by 1998. The more developed corporate ethics offices were led by an ethics officer and staff, who utilized many of the ethical safeguards discussed in this chapter to promote ethics at work: codes of ethics, ethics hot lines, ethics training, and ethics audits.

Ethics Ombudspersons

Pacific Bell, once part of American Telephone and Telegraph, sailed into rough ethical waters when on its own. Critics charged the company with using abusive, high-pressure sales tactics, allowing dial-a-porn companies to use its telephone lines, and violating consumers' privacy by selling lists of their names to telemarketers and direct-mail firms. As part of its response, the company established an ombudsman office. Its function is to give a private and confidential hearing to ethics complaints of employees who might be reluctant to report their concerns to their immediate supervisor. The staff then investigates and acts as a go-between. "We're trying to create an environment where employees feel safe raising [ethics] issues, trying to create a support system within the company," said the company's director of external affairs.[22]

Ethics Hot Lines

In some companies, when employees are troubled about some ethical issue but may be reluctant to raise it with their immediate supervisor, they can place a call on the company's **ethics hot line.** These hot lines have become more common, estimated to be in over 100 companies, since the passage of the U.S. Corporate Sentencing Guidelines in 1991. The Guidelines require a firm to establish an "effective program to detect and de-

---

[20]"The Ethics Committee: 'A Vehicle to Keep the Process Moving,'" *Ethikos,* September–October 1990, p. 6. For a discussion of ethics officers, see Rorie Sherman, "Ethicists: Gurus of the 90s," *National Law Journal,* January 24, 1994, pp. 1, 30–31.

[21]Kim Campbell, "Ethics Officers Roam Hall in More U.S. Workplaces," *Christian Science Monitor,* June 21, 1996, p. 8; and Lynette Khalfani, "Business Tries to Keep the Wolves out of the Flock," *Washington Post,* August 11, 1996, p. H4.

[22]"Pacific Bell: Dial E for Ethics," *Ethikos,* May–June 1990, p. 5.

ter violations of the law." In many cases, this is interpreted as creating a reporting system that employees can use without fear of retribution.

Digital Equipment Corporation made a distinction between their hot line—a device for reporting criminal conduct—and a help line—used in assisting employees who face troubling ethical quandaries. According to the firm's ethics officer, hot-line calls were exceptionally rare; however, help-line calls averaged two or three a week. The opportunity for employees to use the help line was consistent with Digital's open-door corporate culture.

Daniel Kile, former director of ethics at Bell Helicopter Textron, noted that hot lines typically have three uses: (1) to provide *interpretations* of proper ethical behavior involving conflicts of interest and the appropriateness of gift giving, (2) to create an avenue to make known to the proper authorities *allegations* of unethical conduct, and (3) to give employees and other corporate stakeholders a way to discover *general information* about a wide range of work-related topics.[23] An ethics hot line may work with other ethics safeguards, such as at Raytheon where the hot line served as an early warning system for the need to develop a new ethics training program for the firm's supervisors.

Ethics Training Programs

Over 60 percent of all companies responding to an Ethics Resource Center survey reported that they provided ethics training for their managers and employees.[24] After all, firms frequently train their employees in accounting methods, marketing techniques, safety procedures, and technical systems, so why not also give them training in ethics? For example, Union Pacific Railroad, Dunn and Bradstreet, Donnelly Corporation, NYNEX, and Levi Strauss all developed extensive training programs in ethics for their employees in the early 1980s. Other firms, such as Honeywell, Northrup, Hughes Aircraft, and Harris Corporation, made significant revisions to update their existing ethics training programs during this time. Two corporate ethics training programs are featured in Exhibit 6–C.

Numerous approaches are used to promote ethical awareness and decision making: case studies, corporate rules or guidelines, decision frameworks (such as the Golden Rule or ethical principles), and approaches that attempt to develop higher stages of moral reasoning. Most of the corporate ethics training programs are permanent modules in the employee-training curriculum, with a majority offered to all managerial employees.[25]

Ethics Audits

Some firms assess the effectiveness of their ethical safeguards or want evidence of increased ethical employee behavior. One technique used is an **ethics audit**. For example, ethics audit procedures were instituted at Dow Corning, discussed in a case study at the end of the book. A different assessment was initiated at Hewlett-Packard. The ethics audit system at HP emphasized accountability and communications.

---

[23]"Operating an Ethics Hotline: Some Practical Advice," *Ethikos,* March–April 1996, pp. 11–13. Also see Laura Sperry, *Business Conduct and Ethics: How to Set Up a Self-Governance Program* (Chesterland, OH: Business Laws, Inc., 1995).

[24]*Ethics in American Business: Policies, Programs, and Perceptions* (Washington, D.C.: Ethics Resource Center, 1994).

[25]Adapted from Susan J. Harrington, "What Corporate America Is Teaching about Ethics," *Academy of Management Executive* 5, no. 1 (1991), pp. 21–30. See also John Kohls, Christi Chapman, and Casey Mathieu, "Ethics Training Programs in the Fortune 500," *Business and Professional Ethics Journal* 8, no. 2 (n.d.), pp. 55–72.

EXHIBIT
6–C
Two Corporate Ethics Training Programs

Cummins Engine Company

Cummins Engine Company has established a model for ethical business management, similar to efforts taken by other companies such as Allied, Chase Manhattan, Citibank, and General Electric. The company conducts a two-day workshop, divided into three phrases: (1) discussion of the social context of management ethics, (2) introduction of conceptual models for ordering and analyzing ethical issues, and (3) analyses of cases and situations brought to the workshop by the participants.

GTE Telephone

GTE developed a new 44-page Standards of Business Conduct but was not content just to mail the booklet to its 60,000 employees. The company wanted to articulate its standards through companywide training sessions. What made GTE's training unique was that it was conducted by GTE managers, not training specialists or outside consultants. GTE discovered three main benefits in having regular managers conduct the ethics training. First, the managers had to learn the material themselves before they could teach the sessions. Second, managers were exposed to ethical problems confronting employees in their departments through the training discussions. Third, the company's overall commitment to ethics was highlighted by the hands-on approach taken through involving managers in every department. GTE planned to extend its ethics training to the Internet so that training could occur across significant distances and at any time.

Sources: Ronald Nelson, "Training on Ethics: Cummins Engine Company," *Journal of Management Development* 11, no. 4 (1992), pp. 21–33; and Andrew W. Singer, "GTE Telephone Rings Up 'Standards' Training for 60,000," *Ethikos*, March–April 1997, pp. 1–3, 16.

The auditor was required to note any deviations from HP's ethics standards that became evident during the audit and bring them to the attention of the audit supervisor. In addition, the managers of each operating entity made a report to the auditor on the corrective action they took to deal with any deviations from the standards that emerged in the prior year's audit. Managers also reported on the written procedures they established for informing new employees of the standards and for providing ongoing review of the standards with other employees. If a manager was deficient in either of these areas, an appropriate comment was placed on the manager's letter of evaluation.

In addition, the auditing team interviewed the top managers in marketing and manufacturing. During the interviews, each manager was asked both general and detailed questions. On completion of the audit, the auditor was required to sign the following statement: "As a result of the audit tests and procedures performed during the audit of the entity, I did not detect any violations of HP Standards of Business conduct policies, except for those referenced above."[26]

[26]Hanson and Velasquez, "Hewlett-Packard Company," pp. 72–73.

Comprehensive Ethics Programs

The critical component in creating an effective ethics design is the integration of various appropriate ethics safeguards into a comprehensive program. In an Ethics Resource Center survey of U.S. employees, only 20 percent of the employees reported that their employer had developed a *comprehensive ethics program,* that is, a program integrating a code of ethics, ethics employee training, and an ethics officer or ombudsperson. The startling discovery, however, was the dramatic impact a comprehensive ethics program had in creating an ethical work environment for employees. People working at a firm with such a program were more likely to:

- View their firm as responsible in fulfilling its ethical obligations to various stakeholder groups.
- Have better perceptions of their fellow employees' commitment to ethical business conduct.
- Report ethical misconduct in the workplace to the appropriate company authority.
- Be satisfied with the company's investigation of and response to charges of ethical misconduct.

In contrast, firms with only a code of ethics were often perceived as less ethically responsible and less able to address ethical misconduct in the workplace than firms without any ethical safeguards.[27]

Corporate Ethics Awards

Firms have been honored for their efforts to create an ethical climate and improve ethical performance. Business Ethics Awards, sponsored by *Business Ethics* magazine, have been awarded since 1989. The criteria for the award include:

- Be a leader in the field, showing the way ethically.
- Have programs or initiatives that demonstrate sincerity and ongoing vibrancy that reaches deep into the company.
- Have a significant national presence whose ethical behavior sends a loud signal.
- Be a stand-out in at least one area of ethical performance.
- Have recently faced a challenging situation and overcame it with integrity.[28]

Companies receiving this award for ethical leadership include Herman Miller, Johnson & Johnson, H. B. Fuller, Polaroid, Life USA, and Medtronic. These companies and others were honored for their commitment to environmental excellence, employee ownership, general ethical excellence, and exemplary ethics programs.

In March 1994, *Forbes* published the first annual American Business Ethics Awards (ABEA). Merck and Company was one of the four recipients of the ABEA, in recognition of its commitment to provide life-saving medicine to those in need regardless of their ability to pay. Texas Instruments also received an ABEA for its maintenance of an ethics office, ethics training program, ethics hot line, and other efforts aimed at enabling its

---

[27]*Ethics in American Business,* pp. 29–41.
[28]Joel Makower, "The 9th Annual Business Ethics Awards," *Business Ethics,* November–December 1997, pp. 7–9.

employees to act ethically. Hanna Andersson, a childrenswear firm, was another ABEA recipient; it annually donated 5 percent of its profits to charity and created a program to provide clothing to needy children.

These and other award-winning firms provide the foundation for a collection of corporate ethics role models. Their commitment to ethical values and efforts to establish effective ethics programs demonstrate that firms can be financially successful *and* ethically focused.

Summary Points of This Chapter

- Managers' on-the-job values tend to be company-oriented, assigning high priority to company goals. Managers often value being competent and place importance on having a comfortable or exciting life, among other values.

- Personal character and spirituality can greatly assist managers when coping with ethical dilemmas. Personal spirituality has changed business practices and influences business decision making and charitable and political contributions.

- A company's culture and ethical climate tend to shape the attitudes and actions of all who work there, sometimes resulting in high levels of ethical behavior and at other times contributing to less desirable ethical performance.

- People in business can analyze ethics dilemmas by using three major types of ethical reasoning: utilitarian reasoning, rights reasoning, and justice reasoning.

- Companies can improve their ethical performance when top management leads the way and when organizational safeguards are adopted, such as ethics codes, ethics committees, ethics officers, ethics training programs, and ethics audits.

Key Terms and Concepts Used in This Chapter

- Ethical charismatic leader
- Personal spirituality
- Stages of moral development
- Corporate culture
- Ethical climate
- Utilitarian reasoning

- Human rights
- Justice
- Ethics codes
- Ethics officer
- Ethics hot line
- Ethics audit

Internet Resources

- http://snycorva.cortland.edu/
  ~ANDERMD/KOHL/kidmoral.html
- http://csep.iit.edu/codes/codes.html

- http://www.doi.gov/ethics/ethics.html

- http://www.ita.doc.gov/bgp

Kohlberg's ideas on moral reasoning

Illinois Institute of Technology,
   Codes of Ethics Online
U.S. Department of the Interior
   Ethics Office
Best Global Business Practices Program

Discussion Case   # Levi Strauss & Co. in China

The People's Republic of China offered more than one billion consumers and low production costs, but international bodies had long condemned its human rights violations. In 1993, Levi Strauss & Co. faced one of the more difficult decisions in its long corporate history. Would it continue to conduct business in this enormously promising market or honor its high ethical standards and withdraw?

Levi Strauss: History and Ethical Stance

Founded in the United States in 1873, Levi Strauss became the world's largest clothing manufacturer in 1977 and achieved $2 billion in sales by the end of that decade. By 1993, Levi Strauss produced merchandise in 24 countries and sold its products in 60 nations.

Levi Strauss had been a leader among U.S.-based corporations in recognizing the importance of business ethics and community relationships. Levi Strauss's CEO Robert Haas frequently explained to his employees and other company stakeholders the importance of the company's two ethics codes, the Mission Statement and the Aspirations Statement. These documents summarized the core company values and were intended to guide employee and corporate decisions. Efforts to take the values seriously led to specific changes in human resource policies and practices. For instance, Levi Strauss extended liberal domestic partner benefits, offered flexible-work programs, and established child-care voucher programs. It was one of the first companies to establish programs to support AIDS victims.

In 1990, the company closed a Docker's plant in Texas, transferring production to private contractors in Latin America where wages were more competitive. Levi Strauss provided a generous severance package for the laid-off workers that included 90-day notice of the plant's closing and extended medical insurance benefits. Levi Strauss also contributed $100,000 to local support agencies and $340,000 to the city for extra services to the laid-off workers. Despite these efforts, the company received serious criticisms for relocating the plant. (Subsequent layoffs at Levi Strauss drew additional challenges from the company's critics regarding the firm's responsibility to its workers.)

Ethical Standards for International Business

In 1992, Levi Strauss established a set of global sourcing guidelines (shown in Chapter 5) to help ensure that its worldwide contractors' standards meshed with the company values. These guidelines covered numerous environmental, worker health and safety, and community betterment issues. In addition, the company established Guidelines for Country Selection. These guidelines covered issues beyond the control of one particular business partner. Challenges such as worker health and safety, human rights, and political or social stability were considered on a national basis. The company would not source in countries failing to meet these guidelines. The question would soon be raised: Did China meet these guidelines?

Human Rights and Labor Practices in China

China was ranked among the world's gravest violators of human rights, although Chinese officials did not regard their actions as such. The U.S. State Department said that China's human rights record fell "far short of internationally accepted norms." Two specific violations included arbitrary arrest and detention, with torture that sometimes resulted in death. Telephone conversations were monitored, mail was often opened and examined, and people and premises were frequently subjected to search without the necessary warrants. Official rights to free speech and assembly were extremely restricted, as the world witnessed during the Tiananmen Square massacre in 1989. Although China had regulations prohibiting the employment of children, child labor was widespread, especially in rural areas.

Levi Strauss in China

This combination of government practices and labor conditions increased pressure within Levi Strauss to rethink its decision to operate in China. In 1992, the firm's operations in China generated 10 percent of the company's total Asian contracting and 2 percent of its worldwide contracting. Its Chinese operations produced approximately one million pants and shirts.

In assessing the objectionable conditions in China, Levi Strauss management felt it could not improve the situation because the violations went well beyond what could be remedied strictly through company communication and cooperation with contractors. Leaving the country, however, would expose Levi Strauss to the high costs of losing business in a large emerging market. Some managers and employees felt that the company would be supporting a repressive regime if it remained in China, whereas others argued that Levi Strauss was a profit-making business enterprise, not a human rights agency. This latter group saw management's acknowledged responsibility to society as positive, but it felt the company also needed to consider its responsibilities to shareholders and employees. Some employees argued that staying in China would enable Levi Strauss to improve conditions for Chinese citizens. But other stakeholders countered that remaining in China would violate the company's own guidelines about where it would and would not conduct business.

Important issues that complicated the decision included the possibility that China might not accept Levi Strauss back if the company left until conditions improved. If the company ceased production in China, it might have difficulty selling product there because of high tariffs imposed on imported apparel. But, some argued, continuing to manufacture in China would have a damaging impact on Levi Strauss's reputation, possibly putting at risk its valuable brand image.

Levi Strauss's Decision

To address the many issues regarding Levi Strauss's continued operations in China, the company organized a China Policy Group. After approximately 2,000 hours of deliberation, the senior management group remained undecided over what to do. Confronted by the indecision of the group, Levi Strauss's CEO and chairman, Robert Haas, ended the stalemate by recommending the company forgo direct investment in China and end existing contracts over a period of three years due to "pervasive violations of basic human rights." He maintained that the company had more to gain by remaining true to its ideals than by continuing to produce in China.

Reactions to the Decision

Many people were highly skeptical of the company's decision. Some asserted it was only a public relations ploy engineered to make the company look good. These criticisms were fueled by the fact that the company did not directly invest in China; it produced its merchandise through Chinese contractors. However, moving production contracts to other countries in Asia raised costs between 4 and 10 percent. Levi Strauss recognized this cost but considered it the price it had to pay to uphold its integrity and protect its corporate and brand images.

China's leadership showed no interest in the company's decision. One Chinese foreign ministry official was quoted: "At present there are tens of thousands of foreign companies investing in China. If one or two want to withdraw, please do." Coincidentally, the Levi Strauss decision-making process occurred as the United States considered extending China's most favored nation trade status. U.S. trade representative Mickey Kantor voiced his support for Levi Strauss by stating, "As far as what Levi Strauss has done, we can only applaud it; we encourage American companies to be the leader in protecting worker rights and worker safety and human rights wherever they operate."

More recently, President Clinton renewed China's most favored nation trading status without requiring steps to improve human rights. The position of the Clinton administration was that the United States should continue trading with China and hope that economic involvement would contribute to improvement in the conditions of Chinese citizens. Clearly, Levi Strauss took a different position.

Source: Adapted from a case prepared by Timothy Perkins, Colleen O'Connell, Carin Orosco, Mark Rickey, and Matthew Scoble of Saint Mary's College of California for the Second International Conference on Building the Ethics of Business in a Global Economy, November 1995, sponsored by the Council for Ethics in Economics. The core of the case is used with permission from the Council for Ethics in Economics.

Discussion Questions

1. What personal and organizational forces influenced the decisions made by Robert Haas?
2. Should Levi Strauss have stayed in China or was it more ethically responsible to leave? Use the theories of utilitarianism, rights, and justice in justifying your choice.
3. Was the Levi Strauss decision to cease manufacturing operations but continue its sales contracts based on ethical or economic criteria?

7

Global Challenges to Corporate Responsibility

The globalization of business poses new social, ethical, and political challenges for managers and corporations. Diverse cultural values and the differing ways in which political systems treat economic activity challenge managers to develop a sophisticated and global concept of corporate responsibility. Today's managers regularly interact with people from other cultures and socioeconomic systems. The global business environment of the twenty-first century will reflect more change and present more complex problems for corporations and their managers.

This chapter focuses on these key questions and objectives:

- What are the leading factors encouraging the globalization of business?

- What are the critical differences among systems of free enterprise, central state control, and mixed state and private enterprise?

- Why does global economic activity conflict with national sovereignty?

- What do host countries do to encourage or discourage multinational companies from doing business?

- What political and social pressures do companies and their managers face as they engage in international business transactions?

The twenty-first century, according to some experts, is likely to be China's century.[1] For much of the twentieth century, China has been a nation facing war, internal strife, political revolution, and an ancient system of social and economic relationships that reminded many of feudalism. But in the 1990s, China's fortune improved as powerful economic and political changes occurred. The country's size and promise have led some to believe that the twenty-first century will be a time for China to become a dominant power.

The drive to improve life for China's two billion people has produced many political conflicts. Chinese leaders have sometimes desired that the country remain closed to foreign influence and foreign trade. More recently, they have sought foreign trade to help unlock China's vast economic potential. China's role in the global economy is clearly linked to trade and to its political relations with the rest of the world. Normal political relations rest, in turn, on the belief that China's political repression has ended. To many who remember events of a decade ago, that will take some further convincing.

In June 1989, tens of thousands of students demonstrated in Beijing's Tiananmen Square and generated worldwide media coverage of China's democracy movement. When the Chinese military intervened after weeks of protests, television showed the world the raw power of soldiers, tanks, and armored personnel vehicles killing and arresting hundreds of student protesters. People in democratic nations were outraged at the brutality of the Chinese government's response and pressured their governments to condemn China's actions and force release of protestors. Chinese leaders refused to buckle to the pressure and a war of political wills began. A number of countries retaliated by imposing trade sanctions that banned companies from doing business with China. The U.S. government condemned the massacre but refused to impose trade sanctions.

When Bill Clinton won the 1992 presidential election, he promised that human rights would guide U.S. policy toward China and that trade restrictions would follow unless China improved its human rights record. The point of leverage would be the renewal of China's most favored nation (MFN) trading status in 1994. The congressional debate would coincide with the fifth anniversary of events in Tiananmen Square.

Under international law, designation as a most favored nation, would give China special rights to import technology from and export finished products to the United States without any tariffs, duties, and other trade restrictions. President Clinton's willingness to consider China's human rights record during the MFN debate was applauded by human rights groups but criticized by business groups that believed it was a diplomatic mistake to connect commerce and human rights.

Direct and indirect pressures grew as the decision neared. China refused to make concessions; human rights groups lobbied Congress, the White House, and businesses with commercial investments in China. One full-page advertisement in national newspapers named individual business leaders and called on them to ask the president to support human rights in China. Pressures mounted on all sides until Clinton finally announced that MFN status would be renewed despite China's disappointing record on human rights. The president said:

> *Our relationship with China is important to all Americans. We have significant interests in what happens there and what happens between us. China has an*

---

[1]"Can China Reform Its Economy?" *Business Week,* September 29, 1997, pp. 116–24.

atomic arsenal and a vote and veto in the U.N. Security Council. . . . We share important interests, such as in a nuclear-free Korean peninsula and in sustaining the global environment. China is also the world's fastest growing economy. Over $8 billion of United States exports to China last year supported over 150,000 American jobs. . . . Extending M.F.N. will avoid isolating China and instead will permit us to engage the Chinese with not only economic contacts but with cultural, educational and other contacts, and, with a continuing aggressive effort in human rights—an approach that I believe will make it more likely that China will play a responsible role, both at home and abroad.[2]

Many political and business leaders praised the decision as the best possible under difficult circumstances. But some newspapers ran headlines that implied the United States was backing away from democratic principles (e.g., "Profit Motive Gets the Nod," "Back to Business on China Trade," and "Clinton Eats Some Crow over China"). Foreign policy experts pointed to the U.S. need for China's assistance in dealing with the threat of North Korea's nuclear arms as a factor that ultimately influenced the decision. Others argued the view that trade with China is a form of constructive engagement that supports and encourages political and economic freedom.

The decision regarding China's MFN status demonstrates how entwined economic, political, and social interests are in the modern global economy. Commercial and political interdependencies are intricate, and governments and businesses both need to manage this complicated web of relations with great skill. This can only be done when the people involved understand the workings of different socioeconomic systems. As the twenty-first century unfolds, we are certain to encounter difficult situations involving human rights, turbulence in national economies, and social policy problems. Sound business and governmental decisions will depend on managers who understand the dynamics of a global economy and the ethical challenges inherent in such a business environment.

Globalization of Business

Nearly all businesses, large and small, are drawn to doing business across national borders today. This may involve purchasing raw materials from foreign suppliers, assembling products from components made in several nations, or selling finished goods or services to customers in other countries. One of most important trends in the late twentieth century has been the lowering of barriers to such international trade. The list of firms affected by international competitive forces grows longer each day, and even small retailers—such as those that surround college campuses—are affected by the global production and the sales practices of companies that manufacture, import, and sell clothing, CDs, snack foods, books, and computers. Many U.S. companies have subsidiaries, affiliates, and joint venture partners in other countries. In some instances, the number of foreign employees exceeds those from the company's home nation.

Drivers of Globalization

Only a few decades ago, the opportunities for global business were limited. Communication was much slower, travel and shipping took longer, and international commerce was

---

[2]The decision was announced on May 26, 1994, at a White House press conference. This excerpt is from President Clinton's statement. See "Clinton's Call: Avoid Isolating China," *New York Times,* May 27, 1994, pp. A1, A8.

expensive. Today, people can get to virtually any place on the globe in one day and international communication is instantaneous.[3] Federal Express, the international package-shipping company, claims to provide one-day delivery service to destinations representing 96 percent of the world's gross domestic product. Business operations can be managed effectively and profitably in many countries simultaneously. Resources are sometimes more plentiful and less costly in other countries; labor may be cheaper; taxes may be lower. In some cases, it may even be beneficial if the weather is better. Leading factors encouraging the globalization of business include the following:

- *Trade barriers are falling.* Western Europe's democratic nations have agreed to move toward integration of their economies. Liberalization of trade through the North American Free Trade Agreement and expansion of the General Agreement on Tariffs and Trade are also producing new opportunities for doing business with more of the world's populations.

- *Social and political reforms have opened nations once closed to international business.* The former Communist nations of Eastern Europe are now open to doing business around the world. Millions of people in these countries are now able to take advantage of goods and services that global commerce provides in an open and free marketplace. The reunification of East and West Germany and integration of their economies is also creating a powerful global competitor.

- *New regions of the world are becoming dynamic competitors in global markets.* A great wave of change has occurred in the Pacific region. Japan became a leading global economic power in the 1970s and 1980s, producing competitive, high-quality products. During the 1990s, Asian nations such as Taiwan, South Korea, Malaysia, Thailand, and Indonesia grew rapidly and China blossomed as the world's fastest-growing economy. China, India, and Brazil are among the emerging nations that are likely to contribute new markets, new products, and new technologies to the global economy of the twenty-first century. These are among the "must" locations for companies seeking to be where the economic action is in the years ahead.

Doing Business in a Diverse World

Doing business in other nations is much more than a step across a geographical boundary; it is a step into different social, political, cultural, and economic realities. As shown in Chapter 1, even businesses operating in one community or one nation cannot function successfully without taking into account a wide variety of stakeholder needs and interests. When companies do business in several countries, the number of stakeholders to be considered in decision making increases dramatically. And companies such as Coca Cola, McDonald's, and Microsoft, which operate in most of the 200 sovereign nations that exist today, have had no choice but to address this great diversity in building their organizations.

Historically, companies that operated internationally often had an **ethnocentric perspective.** This perspective views the home nation as the major source of the company's capital, revenues, and human resource talent. The home country's laws are viewed as dominant, and the company flies the flag of its home nation. Today's businesses have discov-

---

[3]Comments of Allen Grau, chief financial officer of Federal Express, in an interview on CNBC, September 16, 1997.

ered that they must consider the world, not just one nation, as their home. Companies that have such a **geocentric perspective** adapt their practices to different cultures and environments while maintaining their worldwide identity and policies. They develop managers at all levels from a worldwide pool of talent and seek to use the best people for all jobs regardless of their country of origin.

> Companies such as IBM, General Electric, and Exxon have long histories of bringing their managers from around the world to meetings and workshops for the purpose of broadening everyone's understanding of the world in which their company operates. At Dow Chemical, technical specialists from plants around the world are connected by information technology and physically meet several times each year to discuss advances in science and technology. European firms, such as Nestlé (Switzerland), ABB (Asea, Brown, Boveri, a Swedish-Swiss company), and Unilever (Great Britain–Netherlands) have led the way toward internationally diverse corporate board membership.

Small companies also develop a geocentric perspective when they do business across borders and among different cultures. Managers throughout the southwestern United States, for example, speak Spanish, understand Mexican culture, and engage in cross-border commerce. Citizens of Maine, New York, Michigan, and Washington State know the importance of business with Canadians and are likely to understand such issues as Quebec's movement for independence from Canada. It is not the size of the business that accounts for a geocentric outlook. Geographic location and awareness of the social and cultural features of the firm's stakeholders reinforce the importance of an open approach to cultural differences. To be a global company in the modern economy is to build a geocentric perspective into the very fiber of the business organization.

A World of Diversity

Business opportunities depend greatly on the size and wealth of a population. The population is growing around the world but at quite different rates. Birthrates in Africa, Latin America, and South Asia, for example, are two or three times greater than those in Europe and North America. Companies that sell consumer products such as packaged food, clothing, and even automobiles need to go where the people are. Eventually, fast-food restaurants, entertainment, telecommunications, and other consumer products will find their way to all of the world. To do business in world markets, a company must design a business plan that fits with the cultural, competitive, and political realities of diverse societies defined by features such as language, customs, religion, and traditions.[4]

Basic Types of Socioeconomic Systems

Ideas about the way political power should be held and exercised in society ultimately affect the way economic activity is conducted. Societies differ greatly in their preferences for cooperation versus competition. They also differ in their views about who owns property,

---

[4]Lee A. Tavis, *Power and Responsibility: Multinational Managers and Developing Country Concerns* (South Bend, IN: University of Notre Dame Press, 1997).

who sets the rules for using common resources (e.g., water), and who must approve social investments in technology, public works projects, and care for people. Because these societal arrangements involve decisions about social, political, and economic matters, they are called **socioeconomic systems.**

Four types of socioeconomic systems dominate the modern world. Each system entails some combination of private efforts and government controls, although the balance differs quite greatly. As shown in Figure 7–1, varying amounts of freedom and coercion are present in each system. Some systems are democratic and open; others are dominated by one political party that controls the government and centralizes economic and social decisions.

The socioeconomic system of any nation depends on that nation's history and culture. But history and culture are not the whole story. Socioeconomic systems can and do change. This may occur with dramatic speed, as in the collapse of the Soviet Union and demise of Communist regimes in Eastern Europe in the late 1980s or the rapid change in South Africa, where, following decades of conflict, the system of racial separatism called *apartheid* gave way in the 1990s to a more integrated and democratic way of life.

Business leaders know that the grounds on which they do business are constantly shifting. As commerce becomes more global, with customers, suppliers, and competitors from other nations and cultures, it is important that managers understand how diverse socioeconomic systems affect the markets and the social-political environment for business. Businesses of all sizes have a stake in understanding these issues.

Figure 7–1

Basic types of socioeconomic systems.

Degree of government coercion increases →		
FREE ENTERPRISE	MIXED STATE AND PRIVATE ENTERPRISE	CENTRAL STATE CONTROL
← Degree of political, social, and market freedom increases		
■ Private ownership ■ Free market ■ Multiple-party politics ■ Pluralistic social sytem	■ Both state and private ■ Free market and controlled market ■ Multiple-party politics ■ Pluralistic social system	■ State ownership ■ Controlled market ■ One-party politics ■ Militarized non-democratic regime
Examples United States Singapore Canada Australia	**Examples** France Japan Mexico Argentina India Israel	**Examples** China North Korea Cuba Vietnam

The small business in Michigan that sells machine parts to customers in Canada, or the insurance agency in San Antonio, whose customers speak Spanish and have relatives and relationships in Mexico, are also part of the international business community. Under current trade laws, small businesses are expected to greatly expand the number and value of international transactions.

Free Enterprise

A **free enterprise economy** is based on the principle of voluntary association and exchange. People with goods and services to sell take them voluntarily to the marketplace, seeking to exchange them for money or other goods or services. Other people with wants to satisfy go to the marketplace voluntarily hoping to find the things they want to buy. No one forces anybody to buy or to sell. Producers are drawn voluntarily to the market by their desire to make a profit. Consumers likewise go willingly to the marketplace in order to satisfy their many wants. The producer and the consumer then make an economic exchange in which normally both of them receive an economic benefit. The producer earns a profit, and the consumer has a new good or service that satisfies some want or desire.

In this system, members of society satisfy most of their economic wants through voluntary market transactions. Business firms (like supermarkets) that sell goods and services to consumers for a profit are also fulfilling a social or public need. Usually there is a very large overlap between society's needs and business's efforts to meet those needs through profit-making activities.

Very few economic systems conform strictly to the ideal conception of a free enterprise system. The United States comes the closest of any of the major industrial powers, partly because its historical traditions have favored free markets and partly because the American public has urged leaders to favor less centralized government. All socioeconomic systems have an *ideology*—a guiding philosophy—that explains and justifies the way economic activities are organized. This philosophy shapes the attitudes of people and influences their thinking about how economic problems should be addressed.

Free enterprise ideology originated over 200 years ago in Great Britain. Adam Smith, the Scottish philosopher, first outlined the main components of this capitalist philosophy in 1776 when he wrote *An Inquiry into the Nature and Causes of the Wealth of Nations.* This book has guided business thinking in free market nations ever since. A resurgence of interest in Smith's ideas was sparked when Eastern European nations broke away from the domination of the Soviet Union and struggled to build democratic societies characterized by the core elements of free enterprise ideology (see Exhibit 7–A).

The attraction of a system built on principles of individualism, freedom, private property, competition, and profit remains very powerful. Free enterprise systems have incorporated other principles into their ideology. Foremost among these is the belief in limited government. Beyond protecting private property, enforcing contracts, and providing for public security, the government is expected to do little. A hands-off policy toward business, often called *laissez faire*, is a preferred ideal of free enterprise theory, although many things have changed since that theory was first advanced.

Central State Control

Corporations doing business under a system of **central state control** encounter entirely different rules. In such a system, economic and political power is concentrated in the hands

**EXHIBIT
7–A**

Free Enterprise Philosophy/Ideology

Advocates of the free enterprise system build their case on several basic ideas. The following ideas are the core of this free enterprise ideology.

- *Individualism.* The individual person is considered to be more important than society or its institutions. Social institutions exist to protect and promote the interests of individuals. The opposite is true in a collectivist state, where individuals are subordinate to the powers of government, the military, or organized religion.

- *Freedom.* All individuals must be free to promote and protect their own personal interests. This means that they must have freedom to own property, to choose a job and career, to move freely within a society and to other societies, and to make all of life's basic decisions — where to live, whom to marry, personal life-style — without being coerced by others. In business affairs, it means that companies should be free to pursue profits, and markets should be free of government intervention.

- *Private property.* The bedrock institution on which free enterprise is founded is private property. Unlike socialist states, where government owns the productive system, private property is held by individuals or companies in a free enterprise system. The ownership and use of property allows one to control one's own destiny, rather than to have important decisions made by others.

- *Competition.* Competition is an indispensable part of free enterprise thinking. It encourages the most skilled, the most ambitious, and the most efficient to succeed. Competition is society's way of encouraging high levels of economic performance from all of its citizens. The behavior of firms and individuals is regulated in a system of competition by what Adam Smith called an "invisible hand," rather than the "visible hand" of government regulation. In this way, competition signals business to do its best, or else a competitor will win customers away with a better product or service.

- *Profit.* Profit is a gain made by owners who use their property for productive purposes. Although profits are sometimes made by using property inappropriately (e.g., illegal drug sales), or by not using property at all (e.g., subsidies for not using farmland), a free enterprise economy tends to draw all property into productive uses because that is the way to make profits. Profits are a reward for making a productive contribution to society. They act as a powerful incentive to produce goods and services that are of value to a society.

of government officials and political authorities. The central government owns property used to produce goods and services. Private ownership may be forbidden or greatly restricted, and most private markets are illegal. People need government permission to move from one job to another. Wages and prices are strictly controlled by government planners and bureaucrats. Foreign corporations, if permitted to operate at all, may find it difficult or impossible to take their profits out of the country.

The political system is usually organized around one political party. Not all citizens are permitted to join this one party, so the party's members may form a privileged elite of powerful people. With no political opposition, elections are a formality used by the nation's leaders to reinforce their control over politics, government, and other spheres of society. These leaders also set the terms and conditions under which any businesses, including foreign corporations, are permitted to operate. This means that the business owners, or the corporation's managers, must be skilled in political negotiations with government officials. Moreover, since the decision-making process in government bureaucracies is often slow, business owners or managers must exercise patience.

In this type of socioeconomic system, government is the central actor, making decisions about meeting social and economic needs. Governments in state-controlled systems typically resort to elaborate five-year plans that spell out what goods are to be produced by state-managed factories, in what volume, and what services (e.g., health care) will be available through what institutions (e.g., hospitals, clinics). Government bureaucrats then allocate budget resources to those factories, hospitals, and other organizations and oversee the way in which they meet their goals. All of the key functions performed by individual companies and managers in a free enterprise system—determining what to produce, allocating resources, setting wages and prices—are performed by government officials in a centrally controlled state system.

Under such circumstances, government planners and party leaders may decide economic production is more important than safe factories, clean air and water, and healthy workers. Central state control, exercised through the party or other means, gives them the power to make such decisions. Coercion is the dominant feature of this type of system. There are fewer such regimes in the late 1990s than in earlier times, but Cuba, North Korea, and Nigeria are among nations that still reflect key features of central state control.

Mixed State and Private Enterprise

Standing between the extremes of free enterprise and central state control is another type of socioeconomic system that combines some elements of both of those systems. In a **mixed state and private enterprise** system, a portion (but not all) of a nation's industrial and financial sectors is owned and operated by the government. This may include the central bank through which the country's overall monetary policies are determined; the railroads, bus lines, and airline companies; public utilities such as telephone, water, electric, and gas companies; and basic industries such as steel, auto manufacturing, coal mining, nuclear power, and health care.

Mixed systems provide opportunities for private sector business activity. Private businesses may compete alongside the state enterprises and transact business according to free market principles; they make profits for owners or stockholders, serve consumers, and face the risk of business failure if the market does not value their products and services. This type of socioeconomic system is popular, and many countries have built economies with a mixture of private and state-owned businesses. These countries often provide more economic and political freedom than the central state control systems but with a significant role for the public sector. Political elections are open and free, and the social system tends to be pluralistic and diverse. The amount of market freedom is considerably less than in purely free enterprise economies.

Mexico's government has committed itself to a program of change that will expand private sector activities in an increasingly free enterprise environment. But the government has refused to allow competition to challenge its state-

owned petroleum industry. The state-owned oil industry is a traditional source of Mexico's wealth and a matter of national pride. Fears that competition would damage this national treasure have led political leaders to insist on maintaining the state enterprise. It is noteworthy that this industry is among Mexico's worst environmental offenders.

Eastern European economies evolved from communism toward a form of mixed state and private enterprise in the 1990s. Poland, Hungary, Czechoslovakia (which became two nations, the Czech Republic and Slovakia), and East Germany (which joined with West Germany to form a single German nation) opened their economies to market competition while trying to protect government-run health plans, retirements, housing, and other social services. Some resisted abandoning price controls and state assistance in the form of subsidies to farmers and other groups. Railroads, airlines, and public utilities continued under state-enterprise management for a time, although many are now privatized.

Militarized Nondemocratic Systems

Militarized nondemocratic systems operate in many countries of the world. Central America, for example, has been the scene of powerful military rulers and attempted takeovers in nations such as Panama, Nicaragua, Guatemala, and El Salvador. A small, wealthy class is sometimes allied with the military government, with its members serving in high-level government posts. Human rights and democratic freedoms may be severely curtailed by the government. The press and media are normally government controlled and used for propaganda purposes. Labor unions, religious organizations, and some professional groups (e.g., artists, teachers, writers) are watched carefully by government authorities to keep them from becoming vocal political opponents.

Outwardly, the socioeconomic system may appear to be a mixed system of private and state enterprise. Private markets may be tolerated and many privately owned businesses may exist. The government may welcome foreign investment and foreign corporations. There may be opposition political parties, although the opposition is unlikely to win in elections, which are usually controlled by the government and military. These regimes have sometimes been pawns of the superpowers as they engaged in skirmishes in different parts of the world. (Iran's military rulers were long supported by the United States and its allies as a way of keeping Iran's oil resources away from the Soviet Union.) Sometimes they have been the result of the ambition of local military officers, impatient with other forms of democratic self-government (e.g., Nigeria, North Korea, and Myanmar—formerly Burma—are among the current restrictive military regimes).

Military-political regimes present serious ethical and strategic problems for business leaders. In an effort to generate economic activity, such regimes may make attractive deals with foreign companies. Low taxes, low wages, freedom from criticism in the press, and weak environmental rules and regulations are among the attractions that a military regime can create through its power. Still, if a company knows that human rights are suppressed, that military leaders are lining their own pockets with money that should go to the country, and that corruption and abuse of power are part of the standard operating procedure, business leaders must pause and think about long-term consequences. The strategic business question *is* an ethical question: Do the benefits of doing business in such a system outweigh the economic, human, and social costs?

The New World Economic Order

Political leaders refer to the *new world order* to describe relations among countries no longer facing threats of the cold war. From the 1940s to the 1990s, the world's nations organized into Communist and non-Communist political blocs. The Warsaw Pact and the North Atlantic Treaty Organization (NATO) were alliances created to deter nations from military actions and geopolitical threats. Today, we are witnessing a world order organized around economic interests more than ideology or politics.

Economic relationships are redrawing world maps. As illustrated in Figure 7–2, the European Union provides a framework for trade and commerce on the European continent. In North America, the North American Free Trade Agreement is encouraging integration of the economies of Canada, the United States, and Mexico. Steps are underway to link NAFTA with other Latin American countries, including members of Mercosur, the Latin American trade group that includes Argentina, Brazil, and Chile. In the Asia-Pacific region, trade arrangements are creating links between Australia, China, Indonesia, Taiwan, Thailand, Singapore, Malaysia, and South Korea. Figure 7–3 shows the nations of Southeast Asia that are creating a powerful regional economy. Southeast Asia, in the view of many experts, will remain one of the world's most-promising economic regions despite the serious financial problems facing the region in the late 1990s. The members of the Association of Southeast Asia Nations (ASEAN)—Brunei, Indonesia, Malaysia, Philippines, Singapore, and Thailand—have lowered trade barriers and are creating an integrated market of 330 million people.

The socioeconomic systems of nations in the EU, NAFTA, and ASEAN are quite diverse. These nations do not see the world the same way, and each nation's policies and political systems reflect its unique culture and history. In the end, these features will affect the willingness of people to do business with a foreign company and will shape the way in which that business is done.

The Global Business Enterprise

Much of the world's commerce is done through corporations that operate beyond the borders of any single country. It is estimated that 37,000 multinational corporations do business around the world. United Nations agencies refer to *transnational corporations* (TNCs); other experts prefer the terms *multinational corporation* (MNC), *multinational enterprise* (MNE), or *global corporation* (see Exhibit 7–B on page 157). There is no common agreement as to which of these terms is best.

Corporations that do business across national borders are sometimes so large that their annual revenues from worldwide operations exceed the value of goods and services (gross domestic product) of entire nations. For example, General Motors had revenues of $164 billion in 1996, more than the entire GDP of Norway ($114 billion) or Thailand ($130 billion) and nearly equal to the GDP of Indonesia ($167 billion). Other companies of comparable size in 1996 included Toyota, with worldwide revenues of $108 billion, General Electric ($79 billion), IBM ($75 billion), and Exxon ($116 billion).[5]

In this context, the chief executives of General Motors, Toyota, IBM, and Exxon are responsible for economic activities equal to or greater than those managed by the political leaders of some of the world's most significant economies.

---

[5]"The International 500" and "The World Super Fifty," *Forbes*, July 28, 1997, pp. 178–80.

Figure 7–2

European Union and
NAFTA and Mercosur
countries.

(*a*) Countries of the European Union (EU).

(b) Countries of the North American Free Trade
    Agreement (NAFTA) shown in light cranberry
    and Mercosur in dark cranberry.

Figure 7–3

Southeast Asian
countries.

Size, Power, and Accountability

Years ago, Keith Davis defined the iron law of responsibility as a way of pointing out the relationship between corporate size, power, and responsibility. As he stated, "In the long run, those who do not use power in a way that society considers responsible will tend to lose it"[6] (see Chapter 3). As modern corporations become larger and more global, they affect more people in more nations. Responsibility grows with size. Business is the powerful engine that drives economic growth; it is an incomparable creator of wealth. The creation of wealth is only part of the story; the impact and effect of wealth-creating activities on employees, communities, and nations must also be considered. Business leaders must recognize their accountability to society and the importance of harmonizing business goals with other responsibilities everywhere they operate.

Three ideas guide much of modern understanding about a corporation's private and public roles and responsibilities, whether it is operating at home or in foreign countries. First, it is generally accepted that a company is responsible for the direct consequences that flow from its business activities. Thus, a chemical firm is accountable for its discharges into local rivers, for the quality of products it sells, and for the safety of its op-

[6]The iron law of responsibility was first presented in Keith Davis and Robert L. Blomstrom, *Business and Its Environment* (New York: McGraw-Hill, 1966), pp. 174–75.

EXHIBIT
7–B

What's in a Name?

There is a debate about what to call a company whose business ranges across national borders, tying together home and host countries through corporate policies and practices. Here are some of the terms used to describe these companies:

Transnational Corporation (TNC)
Because companies "transcend" or operate across national borders, some experts prefer the term *transnational corporation,* or TNC. The United Nations favors this term and has created a Research Center for the Study of Transnational Corporations.

Multinational Corporation (MNC)
The fact that companies operate in multiple countries has led some experts to adopt the term *multinational corporation,* or MNC. This term is very popular in the business press and in textbooks. It seems to be the most generic name to describe corporations operating around the world.

Multinational Enterprise (MNE)
Because some of the international giants are state-owned enterprises, rather than corporations, the term *multinational enterprise,* or MNE, has entered the vocabulary of international trade.

Global Corporation
This term became very popular in the 1990s. The term seems to have first been used to describe a small number of companies whose business was conducted in dozens of—perhaps more than 100—nations. Hence, Nestlé has long been described as truly global because the scope of its operations extends to more than 150 nations around the globe. The term is often applied to companies doing business in several areas of the world (e.g., Europe, Latin America, Asia-Pacific, and North America).

erations. When a company fails to meet these expectations—as Union Carbide did at its Bhopal, India, plant, where leaking chemical vapors killed more than 2,000 residents in 1984—government is entitled to take action to hold the corporation accountable for the consequences.

Second, a company's responsibilities are not unlimited. The chemicals discharged by a local plant, for example, cannot be distinguished from those discharged by dozens of other facilities. At that point, government is required to correct the collective problem and allocate the costs among all businesses. In Bhopal, Union Carbide was the only company involved. When dealing with air pollution in Mexico City, for example, there are so many contributors to the pollution that government must find a fair way to set standards and allocate pollution costs.

Third, businesses should reconcile and integrate their private, profit-seeking activities with their public responsibilities. No society holds the view that human beings are accountable only for themselves. Societies cannot function when such ideas prevail. Thus, when a corporation or a business enterprise is part of a community, the leaders of that business are expected to assume responsibility for the community's well-being. Managers must find ways to harmonize the drive for profits with its public responsibilities.

National Sovereignty and Corporate Power

Multinational corporations present real challenges to a nation's sovereignty and independence. The **national sovereignty principle** holds that a nation is a sovereign state whose laws, customs, and regulations must be respected. It means that a national government has the right, power, and authority to create laws, rules, and regulations regarding business conducted within its borders.

The second principle that shapes business-government relations in most countries is the **business legitimacy principle.** This principle holds that a company's behavior is legitimate if it complies with the laws of the nation and responds to the expectations of its stakeholders. In theory, the principles of national sovereignty and business legitimacy are not in conflict. There may be times, however, when conflicts arise.

> *India has had a long and difficult struggle with foreign corporations. In 1977, Coca Cola was forced to leave India for refusing to disclose its secret product formula. Coca Cola was finally able to renegotiate entry into India in 1989 by setting up a bottling plant in one of the country's export processing zones (free trade zone). The plant was to ship 75 percent of its production to markets outside India, thereby helping India's foreign trade balance.*

As multinational corporations reach across national borders, their global operations may exceed the regulatory influence of national governments. This has raised concerns about the emergence of a **stateless corporation.** These corporations have facilities, shareholders, and customers everywhere. Therefore, they seem to owe loyalty to no single nation and are able to organize and reorganize around the globe. There are economic and political advantages to being, or appearing to be, stateless.

For example, when countries impose trade bans on products from another nation, a company may be able to continue its business if it operates through a subsidiary that is incorporated in a nation that is not the target of a ban. Taiwan and South Korea have banned Japanese automobiles as part of their national trade policy. But because Honda Motor Co., another Japanese automaker, had U.S. operations in Marysville, Ohio, it was able to circumvent the restrictions by shipping Honda automobiles from the United States to Taiwan and South Korea. For the purpose of such trade, Honda was considered a U.S. corporation.

Political and Social Challenges of Doing Business Abroad

The multinational firm, the host nation, and the company's home country have important stakes in harmonizing one another's goals and objectives. Conflicts do occur, however, especially when other stakeholders become involved.[7] This forces managers to adjust business activity in light of challenges to economic and ethical decision making.

Political Challenges

International business is affected by political and governmental factors on two levels. First, business operates in an environment shaped by the relationships between governments

---

[7]See, for example, "The Explosive Trade Deal You've Never Heard Of," *Business Week,* February 9, 1998, p. 51, on the Clinton administration's negotiations of the Multilateral Agreement on Investment (MAI), which has been called "NAFTA on steroids" because of its limitations on labor and environmental rules.

(home country and host country), which may range from friendly to hostile. Second, even in an atmosphere of normal relations between governments, companies must recognize that the host government is a powerful political actor that sets the rules of the game by which businesses will operate in the foreign country.

Intergovernmental Relations

Relations between national governments have influence on international business. If two countries are at war, for example, there will be no trade between them.

> *When Great Britain and Argentina went to war over ownership of the Falkland Islands, for example, British companies, such as Unilever, a large consumer products company, found themselves in a serious dilemma. Unilever subsidiaries conducted business in Argentina but were barred by the government from doing business with the "enemy" (i.e., Great Britain). Similarly, Great Britain ordered all British companies to cease commercial transactions with the "enemy" (i.e., Argentina). Unilever was therefore under orders from the warring governments not to send or receive messages between its headquarters and its Argentinean businesses. The dilemma facing Unilever's managers was resolved when it was determined that the headquarters and business units could both report to Unilever's office in a neutral country (e.g., Brazil) without violating the dealing-with-the-enemy rules of the two warring nations.*

Business transactions may be influenced by the political relations of home and host country governments even when there is no war. Japan and the United States have had an important, but difficult, relationship since the end of World War II. The United States helped rebuild Japan's steel, shipbuilding, and auto industries, and by the 1970s Japan had become an industrial giant. It used its efficiencies to export steel, automobiles, and semiconductors to the huge U.S. market. At first, the United States did not object, but as the market share of U.S. firms in these industries declined, business leaders urged Washington to act. Charges of Japanese dumping—selling below real costs—became familiar. Congress threatened to retaliate if Japan did not stop anticompetitive dumping; companies filed lawsuits; government agencies flexed their muscles. The result was a war of words as the U.S. and Japanese governments engaged in trade negotiations while maintaining an uneasy peace. Progress has been uneven: In 1998, for example, Japan agreed to allow U.S. airlines more access to Japanese airports. Only a few months earlier, the United States refused to allow Japanese ships to enter U.S. ports because of a dispute surrounding Japan's refusal to pay unpaid import taxes.[8]

The United States has shifting political relations with Russia, China, Brazil, Great Britain, and many other nations. Economic relations are affected, for better or worse, by political change, and national political priorities shape commercial relations. The United States, for example, banned U.S. companies from selling military products to countries that government agencies believe may threaten U.S. security; it restricts high-technology exports; and it has banned U.S. companies from doing business in Cuba.

Export-oriented industries, like agriculture and high-technology equipment, are especially vulnerable to such policy changes. Sometimes the changes can be positive for businesses, and business and government have often become partners in achieving

---

[8]"Tax Dispute Threatens US–Japan Trade," *New York Times,* October 17, 1997, p. A14.

economic and political goals. When the United States reestablished economic relations with Nicaragua, for example, it removed sanctions and pledged $500 million to help rebuild that country's stagnant economy. Much of the aid was in the form of credits to buy products and services from U.S. companies.

Host Government Influence

Multinational firms are subject to the regulations, controls, licenses, and rules imposed by the host government. Host countries use a variety of sanctions and incentives ("sticks and carrots") to shape and regulate foreign investment, attempting to lure investors but also trying to prevent excessive manipulation by them. The host government must weigh the benefits of technology, jobs, and tax revenues that foreign investment can bring versus the costs of power that the foreign investor will acquire.

National governments use laws, rules, and regulations to ensure that companies do not engage in certain types of conduct. These standards usually apply to all companies in a nation or in a specific industry. In some countries, however, national governments may wish to single out multinational businesses for special treatment. To prevent such discrimination, a *principle of national treatment* has been adopted that guarantees that all companies operating in a country are treated the same as home companies.

Interference becomes extreme when the host government insists on becoming a partial owner of the foreign business. This has happened in basic or natural resources industries such as petroleum and mining. Resource-rich countries such as Brazil, Chile, Papua New Guinea, Saudi Arabia, and Indonesia have often insisted that foreign mining and oil exploration firms share ownership with the government. (See the case study of Shell in Nigeria at the end of the book.) For many years, state-owned enterprises—such as Mexico's national petroleum company—were the rule; then, shared ownership followed. In recent times, some of these countries have allowed foreign ownership of resources that are deemed national assets.

Changes in government control can lead a country to *expropriate,* or seize, a foreign company's assets. The government takes ownership of the property, and it may or may not pay for what it takes. In 1960, Fidel Castro nationalized billions of dollars of assets from U.S. firms in Cuba; in 1990, Iraq seized all of Kuwait's assets, including its oil fields. Such expropriations are relatively rare and are estimated at no more than 5 percent of all foreign-owned assets. More common, by far, is the taking of assets from local owners—especially the political opposition—when a government changes hands or an ethnic war or a revolution occurs.

Social Challenges

The social and cultural differences among nations present challenges for managers, businesses, and families. Language, physical surroundings, and values of the population can create important business and human conflicts. Concepts of human rights, equality among sexes, races, and ethnic groups, and business responsibilities differ around the world. The amount of difference between two social systems, or *cultural distance,* can be very significant.

> *Southern China is industrializing and developing at an explosive rate. In Guangzhu province, change is staggering: Construction sites are everywhere, with companies racing to get their businesses under way. There are many*

problems, but the one most often identified by managers was "people." Procter & Gamble, Motorola, and Johnson & Johnson are companies whose human resources practices are admired. But they cannot get enough people to staff their Chinese operations. U.S. managers face family pressures since housing, schools, and amenities seem very limited. Chinese managers with the proper skills are so scarce that they are regularly recruited away from one employer to another for much more money and responsibility. What is the answer? Managers who were interviewed from many different firms agreed: There are no easy answers.[9]

Inadequate facilities may require a company to build housing, establish schools, and create transportation systems to ease the difficulties for employees. International business needs not only a proper physical infrastructure of airports, telephones, and fax machines but a social infrastructure as well. Whether the project is in the remote highlands of Papua New Guinea, the deep jungle of the Republic of Congo, or the desert city of Amman, Jordan, there are certain requirements that the host country must provide for the business to be successful. There must be a system of law that ensures that contracts will be honored; essential civil services, such as fire and police protection; and a social tolerance for people from different nations and cultures. If the government is unable to provide these, the company may have to do so or conclude that it cannot do business in the host country.

Adherence to a host country's cultural norms may be complicated by a company's home country values. Cultural conflicts can pose serious issues. Stakeholders in the home nation will be watching the company's conduct abroad; if they discover policy violations or unacceptable behavior, there will be pressure on management to change.

When U.S. companies conducted business in South Africa during the 1970s and 1980s, the nation's apartheid system of racial separation offended many U.S. citizens. A campaign was organized to force individual companies to practice racial integration in South Africa, despite the country's public policy, or to withdraw and stop doing business in that setting. Pressures grew, and Congress passed a law imposing economic sanctions on South Africa in 1986 that pressured some U.S. companies to close their South African operations.[10]

Conflicts between the home country and the host country arise for many different reasons. Often, the cultural and political practices of the home country simply are not applied in the host nation. Two examples are familiar to virtually any company doing business around the world: questionable payments and labor standards.

Questionable Payments

Questionable payments are those that raise significant questions of ethical right or wrong in the host or home nation. Some people condemn all questionable payments as bribes, but real situations are not that simple. Managers of a foreign subsidiary may find themselves forced to choose between the host country's laws or customs and the policies of corporate headquarters (see Chapter 5).

---

[9]Interviews conducted by researchers at the Human Resources Policy Institute at Boston University.
[10]Robert Kinloch Massie, *Loosing the Bonds* (New York: Doubleday, 1998).

The Foreign Corrupt Practices Act regulates questionable payments of all U.S. firms operating in other nations. Passed in 1977 in response to disclosure of questionable foreign payments by U.S. corporations, the law has two purposes: (1) to establish a worldwide code of conduct for any kind of payment by U.S. businesses to foreign government officials, political parties, and political candidates, and (2) to require proper accounting controls for full disclosure of the firm's transactions. The law applies even if a payment is legal in the nation where it is made. The intention is to assure that U.S. firms meet U.S. standards wherever they operate. The law has the following major provisions:

- It is a criminal offense for a firm to make payments to a foreign government official, political party, or candidate for political office to secure or retain business in another nation.
- Sales commissions to independent agents are illegal if the business has knowledge that any part of the commission is being passed to foreign officials.
- Government employees "whose duties are essentially ministerial or clerical" are excluded; expediting payments to customs agents and bureaucrats are permitted.
- Payments made in genuine situations of extortion are permitted.
- Companies whose securities are regulated by the Securities Exchange Act must establish internal accounting controls to assure that all payments abroad are authorized and properly recorded.

Many business leaders criticized the U.S. Congress for imposing such regulations. They complained that companies from other nations did not have to operate in similar ways and were permitted to make payments that ultimately tipped the competitive scales against U.S. firms. Proponents of the standards argued that the United States should not slip to the lowest competitive level and should prove its superiority in product quality, service, and other factors, not questionable payments. The latter position seems to have prevailed. In 1997, the 29 leading industrial countries that make up the Organization for Economic Cooperation and Development adopted a code of conduct that bars companies from engaging in corruption and bribery. Twenty years after the U.S. law was written, the concept of business without bribery is becoming a world standard.[11]

Labor Standards

Labor standards refer to those conditions that affect a company's employees or the employees of its suppliers, subcontractors, or others in the commercial chain. For example, in some countries, sweatshop conditions exist in which women and children labor long hours in extreme heat for very little money and with virtually no safety protection.

Levi Strauss, a U.S. company with a reputation for progressive social programs, was accused of using an unethical contractor in Saipan. The contractor was accused of keeping some workers as virtual slaves. Wages were below the legal minimum, and conditions were wretched and unsafe. Levi fired the con-

---

[11]Kathleen A. Getz, "International Instruments on Bribery and Corruption," paper presented at the Conference on Global Codes of Conduct: An Idea Whose Time Has Come? University of Notre Dame, October 6–8, 1997. Also, see Transparency International, "Global Corruption Index," http://www. transparency.de.

tractor and formed a committee of managers to review procedures for hiring contractors. The company became the first multinational to adopt a wide-ranging set of guidelines for its hired factories. The guidelines cover treatment of workers and environmental impacts of production. Levi Strauss now sends inspectors to conduct audits of work and safety conditions at all of its contractors. Deficiencies must be corrected or the company will cancel the contract. The company also led the effort to create industrywide standards.[12]

There is growing pressure to ensure that workers who are willing to work for low wages in developing countries are not exploited by unscrupulous businesses.[13] When the North American Free Trade Agreement was being debated in the United States, labor unions focused on the abuses that could occur as high-paying jobs in the United States became low-paying jobs in Mexico. The creation of labor standards and business commitments to honor them could ease some of this concern. But as the following example suggests, implementation of such commitments has been uneven in recent years.

Sony Corporation, Honeywell, and General Electric were among the first companies alleged to have broken U.S. labor laws under NAFTA. In 1994, Sony (Japanese) and the two U.S. companies were accused of actions to stifle union organizing campaigns at plants in Mexico. Activist organizations filed a complaint with the National Administrative Office, a U.S. agency established to enforce the terms of the agreement. The group claimed that Sony and Mexican authorities failed to enforce laws that give workers in Sony's plant in Nuevo Laredo, along the U.S. border, rights to hold union elections. The company was charged with forcing workers to work beyond the 48-hour maximum under Mexican law, harassing employees who favored unions, and creating dangerous working conditions. Although Sony denied the charges, the complaints foretell a continuing battle to create standards that all stakeholders will support.[14]

Human Rights

Human rights codes of conduct are the newest development in this area of concern. Companies such as Reebok International have created codes of conduct that will be applied to all of its suppliers (see Exhibit 7–C). Some business leaders doubt that company codes can stop labor abuses in other nations, in part because foreign competitors may not abide by similar standards. This has led to calls on the U.S. Congress to create a labor standards law similar to the Foreign Corrupt Practices Act that would set the global labor standards for all U.S. companies wherever they operate. Despite some interest in such action, the Congress has so far failed to develop such legislation.

---

[12]G. Pascal Zachary, "Exporting Rights: Levi Tries to Make Sure Contract Plants in Asia Treat Workers Well," *The Wall Street Journal*, July 28, 1994, pp. A1, A9.

[13]Martin J. Levine, *Worker Rights and Labor Standards in Asia's Four New Tigers: A Comparative Perspective* (New York: Plenum Press, 1997). The author compares the state of worker rights in China, Indonesia, Thailand, and Malaysia.

[14]Asra Q. Nomani, "Sony Is Targeted in Rights Action Based on NAFTA," *The Wall Street Journal*, August 18, 1994, p. A2.

**EXHIBIT
7–C**

Reebok's Human Rights Code (circa 1998)

Reebok has adopted the following human rights production standards in seven specific areas:

Non-discrimination—Reebok will seek business partners that do not discriminate in hiring and employment practices on grounds of race, color, national origin, gender, religion, or political or other opinion.

Working hours/overtime—Reebok will seek business partners who do not require more than 60 hour work weeks on a regularly scheduled basis, except for appropriately compensated overtime in compliance with local laws, and we will favor business partners who use 48 hour work weeks as their maximum normal requirement.

Forced or compulsory labor—Reebok will not work with business partners that use forced or other compulsory labor, including labor that is required as a means of political coercion or as punishment for holding or for peacefully expressing political views, in the manufacture of its products. Reebok will not purchase materials that were produced by forced prison or other compulsory labor and will terminate business relationships with any sources found to utilize such labor.

Fair wages—Reebok will seek business partners who share our commitment to the betterment of wage and benefit levels that address the basic needs of workers and their families so far as possible and appropriate in light of national practices and conditions. Reebok will not select business partners that pay less than the minimum wage required by local law or that pay less than prevailing local industry practices (whichever is higher).

Child Labor—Reebok will not work with business partners that use child labor. The term "child" generally refers to a person who is less than 14 years of age, or younger than the age for completing compulsory education if that age is higher than 14. In countries where the law defines "child" to include individuals who are older than 14, Reebok will apply that definition.

Freedom of association—Reebok will seek business partners that share its commitment to the right of employees to establish and join organizations of their own choosing. Reebok will seek to assure that no employee is penalized because of his or her non-violent exercise of this right. Reebok recognizes and respects the right of all employees to organize and bargain collectively.

Safe and healthy work environment—Reebok will seek business partners that strive to assure employees a safe and healthy workplace and that do not expose workers to hazardous conditions.

Source: Reebok International, Ltd., *Human Rights Productions Standards,* (Stoughton, MA: Reebok International. Ltd., 1998). Also available at http://www.reebok.com/humanrights

Human rights codes have an impact when individual companies take actions based on their codes. For example, Reebok acted on the code principles in Exhibit 7–C when it threatened one of its Chinese contractors, Yue Yuen International (Holdings), Ltd., with cancellation of orders if workers were not moved out of unsafe dormitories and into safer housing. A story in the *Asian Wall Street Journal* described hundreds of women working in conditions that were unsafe and violated labor regulations in Guangdong province. After Reebok's protests, Yue Yuen relocated 800 workers from the unsafe dormitories to newer, safer facilities.[15]

Corporate Social Strategy

Doing business in international settings presents many challenges to managers. There is no magic solution to meeting these issues as they arise. Companies can prepare for the types of challenges discussed in this chapter, however, by designing a **corporate social strategy** that matches and balances the company's economic strategy.[16] These questions are a good place to start the process:

- Are we being socially responsible in what we do? Do we meet the expectations of our host country as well as our home country? Would stakeholders in either country question our behavior?

- Are we responsive to the stakeholders in each country where we do business? Do we treat employees, customers, suppliers, local communities, and others in a fair and just way?

- Do we recognize emerging issues, as well as immediate social issues, in the countries and communities where we operate? Are we anticipating change rather than just reacting to it?

- Do we abide by the host government's regulations and policies? Do we have good systems for ensuring that our employees and the agents who represent us follow our corporate policies?

- Do we conduct business in ways that respect the values, customs, and moral principles of each society? Do we recognize that there may be times when they conflict with principles of other societies? Are we ready to address these conflicts in thoughtful, positive ways?

Companies that address these questions before trouble strikes are better prepared to meet global challenges to corporate responsibility. They are better prepared to prevent crises, anticipate change, and avoid situations that compromise the values and principles for which the company stands. A corporate social strategy helps managers achieve both the economic and the social goals of the company.

Summary Points of This Chapter

- The globalization of business is driven by many factors. The demand for many goods and services is global, and modern transportation and communication systems enable companies to meet consumer demand around the world. The decline of trade barriers,

---

[15]"Reebok Compels Chinese Contractors to Improve Conditions for Workers," *The Wall Street Journal*, August 16, 1994, p. A9; also, Pamela Varley, ed., *The Sweatshop Quandry: Corporate Responsibility on the Global Frontier* (Washington, D.C.: Investor Responsibility Research Center, 1998).

[16]Lee A. Tavis, *Power and Responsibility: Multinational Managers and Developing Country Concerns* (South Bend, IN: University of Notre Dame Press, 1997). See especially, pp. 124–25, where the author draws together stakeholder analysis and the reality of managerial discretion.

opening of markets in economies that were once closed to trade, and dynamic growth in developing nations all contribute to worldwide economic activity.

- Free enterprise, central state control, and mixed state and private enterprise differ from one another in the amount of freedom permitted for making economic choices, including how much government coercion and regulation is present. Militarized nondemocratic regimes present special ethical challenges for global businesses.

- Global business enterprises, or multinational corporations, are powerful actors in the world economy. The size and wealth of the largest of these companies rivals those of nations. National sovereignty is thereby challenged in a world where economic power, global communications, and human mobility are increasing while political barriers are more difficult for nations to enforce. Because they are able to span national boundaries, MNCs are sometimes referred to as stateless corporations.

- Home countries and host countries encourage international business but try to structure the rules of the game in ways that benefit their citizens. Laws and regulations are created to protect national interests as global business expands.

- Businesses face the challenge of maintaining ethical norms and standards when operating in other nations. Host country customs, traditions, and business norms may conflict with home country standards in the workplace and in dealing with government officials.

Key Terms and Concepts Used in This Chapter

- Ethnocentric perspective
- Geocentric perspective
- Socioeconomic systems
- Free enterprise economy
- Central state control
- Mixed state and private enterprise
- Militarized nondemocratic regime

- National sovereignty principle
- Business legitimacy principle
- Stateless corporation
- Questionable payments
- Human rights codes
- Corporate social strategy

Internet Resources

- http://www.census.gov   Census data on global population
- http://www.esd.worldbank.org   World Bank
- http://www.citizen.org/pctrade/   Public Citizen Global Trade Watch
  tradehome.html

Discussion Case   **General Electric in Hungary**

The iron curtain came down in Europe a decade ago. Countries living under Soviet Union domination since World War II celebrated freedom and began to chart a new economic direction. The collapse of communism and its central state control created new opportunities but many uncertainties as well. How would businesses that had lived under central planning do when exposed to the forces of the marketplace? One answer came from Hungary, where Tungsram, an old and well-known lighting company, joined the General Electric Company. This is Tungsram's report card.

In 1989, after the iron curtain fell, the General Electric Company, a U.S.-based multinational company with operations around the world, made a major investment in Hungary when it purchased Tungsram, a maker of lighting products. Tungsram was one of Hungary's leading state-owned companies under Communist rule. Under Hungary's new democratic government, however, state-owned companies were to be privatized. Foreign investment and management experience were sought for companies that would have to operate in competitive market environments. The Hungarians wanted to learn how to compete, and General Electric was eager to have Tungsram as a part of its global business.

Things quickly turned unpleasant. Tungsram was losing large amounts of money on its operations. The equipment was old, work practices were inefficient, communication was poor, and the workforce had a lackadaisical attitude. GE's business strategy was to use Tungsram as an entry point into the Eastern European markets that had been closed to its products. It intended to bring product quality, customer service, and aggressive pricing to the marketplace. By using GE management principles, manufacturing quality could be improved; by using the company's marketing experience, customers could be satisfied and profits could be made. However, nearly every aspect of the strategy ran into problems.

GE managers saw that costs had to be reduced and quality improved if Tungsram's products were to be competitive. When markets were controlled under Communist regimes, neither cost nor quality seemed very important. If plants ran at an operating deficit, the government subsidized the operation. With GE, that was to change. GE's analysis showed that Tungsram had far too many workers for the volume of production. The workforce would have to be cut. GE designed a plan to lay off those who were nearest retirement. Employees received nine months of wages, considerably more than Hungarian law required. But many women who were on leave under Hungary's generous three-year maternity leave were not rehired. In 1992 and 1993, GE's productivity goals became more ambitious and more employees were dismissed. Between 1989 and 1996, Tungsram's employee headcount went from 17,640 to 10,500.

Workers who remained had to undergo a changed mind-set about their work. GE used its American system of *action workouts* at Tungsram to improve productivity. Teams of workers are formed to tackle specific problems. Problems are solved by changing work routines, altering the mix of people and machines, and finding better ways to achieve goals. Communication requires a common language and employee commitment to the company's goals. At Tungsram, workers had to attend English classes and read a book containing many of GE chairman Jack Welch's favorite sayings, including "If we're not No. 1 or No. 2 in a business, improve it, close it or sell it!" A culture change was underway, but progress was slow and difficult to achieve.

In 1993, GE announced that it lost all of the $150 million it had invested when it bought 50.1 percent of Tungsram in 1989. Much more money was required to achieve results. GE would invest more than $550 million in Tungsram by 1995. The strategy that had looked so appealing in 1989 looked very costly after five years.

By 1994, however, progress began to show. Tungsram was successfully competing in the European lighting business. Costs were brought in line with the best lighting manufacturers in the world, and Hungarian scientific expertise helped produce innovative new products. Innovative new processes were making Tungsram's plants more efficient. Sales were approximately $288 million in 1989; they dipped sharply in 1992 and 1993, then began to rise slowly. By 1994 the trajectory was up; and in 1996, Tungsram's total sales exceeded $376 million. GE had invested $700 million, according to observers.

Some problems remain. Workers' pay has not kept pace with Hungary's inflation rate and about one-third of Tungsram's workers live close to the poverty line. Still, GE claims that Tungsram's wages average more than $300 per month, an amount that is in the top 25 percent in each of the eight towns where the company has plants. Peter Wohl, Tungsram's vice president and managing director, says that Tungsram has helped make GE's lighting division run neck and neck with leading competitors Philips and Osram Sylvania. GE, he said, has made a profit on the deal. "Sure they have made [a profit]," he said, "but the problem for the foreign investors looking at the Tungsram acquisition is that they cannot compare it. An almost-100-year-old, relatively good working company like Tungsram, having a good reputation, high technological standards and a huge product range and export markets and a good brand name, that's something [special, compared] . . . to what other Hungarian companies can offer for investors."

Source: "GEL Tungsram—Hungary: Interview—GE Hungary Light Unit Turns Corner," October 26, 1997, Reuters Limited, 1997, DIALOG(R) File, 799, Reuters Info, Services.

Discussion Questions

1. What business objectives led General Electric to invest in Hungary in 1989? What challenges confronted General Electric when it started the process of changing Tungsram into a competitive enterprise?

2. Assess General Electric's decision to lay off workers. Why would they pay more than Hungarian law required to departing employees?

3. In the United States, its home country, GE would be required to rehire women on maternity leave. In Hungary, however, it has not done so. Is it proper for GE to operate with different standards in different countries?

4. Did GE have a corporate social strategy for its business in Hungary? Using the questions on page 165, explain what GE could have done to anticipate the problems it encountered.

PART FOUR

Business and Government in a Global Society

8

The Corporation and Public Policy

Business decision making and political decision making are closely connected. Business decisions affect politics; political decisions affect business. Government actions are an expression of a nation's public policy and shape the business environment in important ways. Managers must understand the public policy process in every nation in which their company operates and be prepared to participate in that process in an ethical and legal manner.

This chapter focuses on these key questions and objectives:

- What are the key elements of the public policy process?

- What major areas of economic policy affect business in every nation?

- How do social welfare policies affect business?

- What are the major forms of government regulation of business?

- What factors have driven the growth of regulation in industrial nations, such as the United States?

- Why is international regulation emerging? How does it work?

William Clay Ford is the fourth generation of Mr. Ford to hold a leadership position at the Ford Motor Company. The board of directors of the Ford Motor Co. named him chairman of the management committee in 1994; by 1997, industry observers and the business press were speculating that he would succeed Alex Trotman as Ford's chief executive officer. As a new century begins, William Clay Ford will have critical responsibilities for leading the company his great-grandfather founded in the early 1900s. And like each of the earlier Mr. Fords, he will face great challenges as he tries to improve the company's position as a world-class automobile manufacturer. Not the least of those challenges has involved dealing with the changing role of government in the national and international economy.

In 1903, when he organized the Ford Motor Co., Henry Ford's relationship with government was relatively simple. There was only one antitrust law on the books, and his business was too small to be bothered by it. There was no federal income tax. Although there were rival carmakers in this country, Ford faced no foreign competition. No unions were permitted in Ford plants, and government regulations about wages, hours, working conditions, and safety and health were unheard of. The government exacted no payments for employee retirement and pension plans because none existed. The company faced no problems of a polluted environment, energy shortages, or consumer complaints about auto safety, all of which in later years would bring the wrath of government down on Ford and the auto industry. Mr. Ford's main worry in those days was a patent infringement suit brought against him by competitors. (He eventually won the lawsuit in the courts.)

In the 1970s, Henry Ford II, the founder's grandson, became chief executive officer of the company in a very different world. He could scarcely make a move without government taking an active hand or peering over his shoulder. That single antitrust law known to his grandfather had grown into a tangle of laws and court rulings regulating competition, pricing practices, mergers, and acquisitions. Labor laws legalized unions and controlled wages, hours, working conditions, safety and health, and employee discrimination. Federal, state, local, and foreign governments levied taxes on company income, plants and equipment, capital gains, auto and truck sales, and salaries.

As the Ford Motor Co. crosses the threshold into the twenty-first century, William Clay Ford faces another major set of changes. Foreign competition has increased in the United States, and U.S. companies no longer dominate the automobile marketplace. Ford also competes in dozens of countries around the world against numerous global competitors. The company's workforce operates across the globe and includes people of many races and nationalities. In many countries, national governments are cooperating with local automobile companies and jointly planning how to compete in the global economy. In a little more than 100 years, the leaders of Ford Motor Co. have seen their relationships with all levels of government become much more complex and change from being adversarial to potential partnerships.

As the newest Mr. Ford looks ahead, the Ford Motor Co. is designing automobiles that will be powered by cleaner fuel sources and controlled by computers in traffic networks that help drivers avoid accidents and traffic congestion. In all of this, government policy—public policy—plays an increasingly important role in the success and operation of the company. This chapter focuses on government as an important stakeholder and influence on all businesses. In no country in the world do businesses have the absolute right to exist and pursue profits; those rights are always conditioned on compliance with appropriate laws and public policy. Government's role is to create and enforce those laws that balance the relationship between business and society.

Governments create the conditions that make it possible for businesses to compete in the modern economy. They set the rules of the game so that competition in the market can generate benefits for society. Governments also impose major costs on businesses through taxes and regulations and hold the power to grant or refuse permission for many types of business activity. Even the largest multinational companies, like Ford Motor Co., which operate in dozens of countries, must obey the laws and public policies of national governments if they are to retain their societal license to operate.

The topics in this chapter are closely related to some of the major ideas in earlier chapters, including the interactive model of business and society (Chapter 1), corporate stakeholders (Chapter 2), the relationship of business strategy to social strategy (Chapters 3 and 4), and how changing public values and ethical expectations influence governments to define business responsibilities (Chapters 5, 6, and 7).

One of the main features of the modern economy is the involvement of business with government. Stakeholders have persuaded governments to regulate business activities to promote or protect social interests. Public policy is also used to encourage businesses to meet social challenges such as drug use, education, and job creation. Global competition has sharpened the understanding of business and government leaders about alternative ways that they can relate to one another. As a result, business firms and governments are interacting more often and in new ways. The relationship between corporations and governments, like that between business and all of society, is a dynamic one.[1]

Public Policy   What Is Public Policy?

Public policy is a plan of action undertaken by government officials to achieve some broad purpose affecting a substantial segment of a nation's citizens. Or, as U.S. Senator Patrick Moynihan is reported to have said, "Public policy is what a government chooses to do or not to do." In general, these ideas are consistent. Governments generally do not choose to act unless a substantial segment of the public is affected and some public purpose is to be achieved. This is the essence of the concept of governments acting in the public interest.

The role of government is extensive in most modern economies. Although there are vigorous debates about the size and specific actions of government, there is broad agreement that government has some appropriate role to play in modern life. As the world's population increases, individual nations have more citizens whose needs have to be met and whose interests and concerns have to be reconciled into reasonable plans of action. These are the roles that government, whatever its specific form, plays in the modern world. Public policy, while differing in each nation, is the basic set of goals, plans, and actions that each national government follows in achieving its purposes.

Powers of Government

The power to make public policy comes from a nation's political system. In democratic societies, citizens elect political leaders who in turn can appoint others to fulfill defined public functions ranging from municipal services (e.g., water supplies, fire protection) to

---

[1] A very readable treatment of this theme in American business history is Louis Galambos and Joseph Pratt, *The Rise of the Corporate Commonwealth: United States Business and Public Policy in the Twentieth Century* (New York: Basic Books, 1988). See also George Lodge, *Comparative Business–Government Relations* (Englewood Cliffs, NJ: Prentice Hall, 1990).

national services, such as public education or national defense. Democratic nations typically spell out the powers of government in the country's constitution. The U.S. Constitution is one of only two sources of governmental power in the United States. The other source is *common law,* the original basis of the American legal system, which gives government the right to regulate human affairs to achieve fairness and justice. The U.S. Constitution embodies such principles and is now the ultimate legal foundation for governmental power.

In nondemocratic societies, the power of government may derive from a monarchy (e.g., Saudi Arabia), a military dictatorship (e.g., Saddam Hussein's Iraq), or religious authority (e.g., the mullahs in Iran). These sources of power may interact, creating a mixture of civilian and military authority. As discussed in Chapter 7, the political systems of China, Russia, and South Africa have undergone profound changes in the past decade. And democratic nations can face the pressures of regions that seek to become independent nations exercising the powers of a sovereign state, as does Canada with Quebec.

Political power shifts and changes in every nation. In the United States, for example, disagreements about state sovereignty and governmental powers prompted the Revolutionary War in the 1700s, the Civil War in the 1800s, and major battles in the Congress in the 1990s. Public policy ultimately reflects all of these forces and influences.

Elements of Public Policy

The governmental action of any nation can be understood in terms of several basic elements of public policy. Many factors, or *inputs,* influence the development of public policy. Government may determine its course of action on the basis of economic or foreign policy concerns, domestic political pressure from constituents and interest groups, technical information, and ideas that have emerged in national politics. Public policy also may be influenced by technical studies of complex issues such as taxation or the development of new technologies such as fiber-optic electronics. All of these inputs can help shape what the government chooses to do and how it chooses to do it.

Public policy *goals* can be noble and high-minded or narrow and self-serving. National values, such as freedom, democracy, and equal opportunity for citizens to share in economic prosperity—that is, high-minded public policy goals—have led to the adoption of civil rights laws and assistance programs for those in need. Narrow, self-serving goals are more evident when nations decide how tax legislation will allocate the burden of taxes among various interests and income groups. Public policy goals may vary widely, but it is always important to inquire, What public goals are being served by this action?

Governments use different public policy tools, or *instruments,* to achieve their policy goals. In budget negotiations, for example, much discussion is likely to focus on alternative ways to raise revenue—higher tax rates for individuals and businesses, reduced deductions, new sales taxes on selected items (e.g., luxury automobiles, tobacco, gasoline, alcohol). In general, the instruments of public policy are those combinations of incentives and penalties that government uses to prompt citizens, including businesses, to act in ways that achieve policy goals. Governmental regulatory powers are broad and constitute one of the most formidable instruments for accomplishing public purposes.

Public policy actions always have *effects.* Some are intended; others are unintended. Because public policies affect many people, organizations, and other interests, it is almost inevitable that such actions will please some and displease others. Regulations may cause businesses to improve the way toxic substances are used in the workplace, thus reducing health risks to employees. Yet it is possible that other goals may be obstructed as an unintended effect of compliance with such regulations. For example, when health risks to pregnant women were associated with exposure to lead in the workplace, some companies removed women from those jobs. This action was seen as a form of discrimination against women that conflicted with the goal of equal employment opportunity. The unintended effect (discrimination) of one policy action (protecting employees) conflicted head-on with the public policy goal of equal opportunity.

In assessing any public policy, it is important for managers to develop answers to four questions:

- What inputs will affect the public policy?
- What goals are to be achieved?
- What instruments are being used to achieve goals?
- What effects, intended and unintended, are likely to occur?

The answers to these questions provide a foundation for understanding how any nation's public policy actions will affect the economy and business sector.

Public Policy and Business

Governments significantly influence business activities. National governments attempt to manage economic growth, using fiscal and monetary policy; state governments shape the business environment through a variety of regional economic policies; and local governments affect business through policies that involve operating permits, licenses, and zoning requirements. As illustrated in Figure 8–1, a nation's well-being is entwined with its economic and social policies. Public policy has direct or indirect impacts on business by shaping the climate in which companies do business in the nation and across national borders.

National Economic Growth

The role of government as manager of the modern economy is widely accepted today. Political and business leaders recognize that government can create, or destroy, the basic conditions necessary for business to compete and citizens to prosper. This is not a new idea. Historically, Spain, France, England, and other European nations during the seventeenth, eighteenth, and nineteenth centuries tried to build strong domestic economies through the colonization of distant lands (North America, Africa, East Indies). Raw materials were brought back to Europe, manufactured goods were sold to settlers in the colonies, and the wealth of the colonies became the wealth of the home country.

Today, the role of government in the national economy is executed through macroeconomic policies. Just as the social environment of the colonial era was tied to the underlying economic conditions and the actions of business and government, so too is today's social environment tied to the effectiveness of government in creating conditions for growth of the modern economy.

National governments generally accept the view that a key role of government is to create public policy that promotes economic growth. After World War II, for example, the U.S. Congress created the Full Employment Act, which established targets for economic growth and unemployment. But as experience proved, healthy economic growth is affected by many factors, thereby requiring continuing efforts by government to manage the macro-

Figure 8–1

Public policies
affecting business.

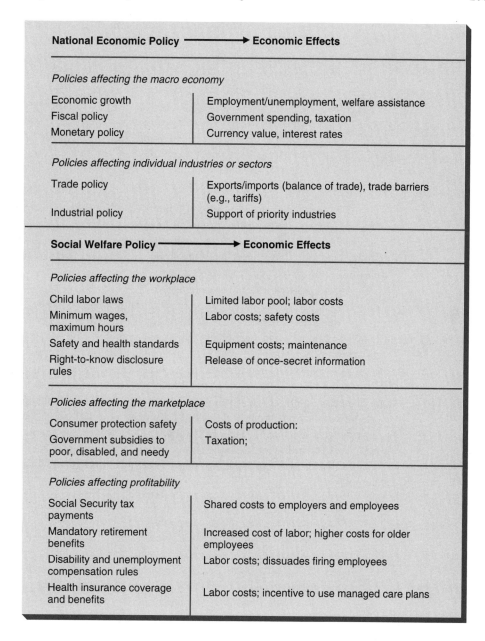

National Economic Policy ⟶ Economic Effects	
Policies affecting the macro economy	
Economic growth	Employment/unemployment, welfare assistance
Fiscal policy	Government spending, taxation
Monetary policy	Currency value, interest rates
Policies affecting individual industries or sectors	
Trade policy	Exports/imports (balance of trade), trade barriers (e.g., tariffs)
Industrial policy	Support of priority industries
Social Welfare Policy ⟶ Economic Effects	
Policies affecting the workplace	
Child labor laws	Limited labor pool; labor costs
Minimum wages, maximum hours	Labor costs; safety costs
Safety and health standards	Equipment costs; maintenance
Right-to-know disclosure rules	Release of once-secret information
Policies affecting the marketplace	
Consumer protection safety	Costs of production:
Government subsidies to poor, disabled, and needy	Taxation;
Policies affecting profitability	
Social Security tax payments	Shared costs to employers and employees
Mandatory retirement benefits	Increased cost of labor; higher costs for older employees
Disability and unemployment compensation rules	Labor costs; dissuades firing employees
Health insurance coverage and benefits	Labor costs; incentive to use managed care plans

economy. Economic growth is stimulated by government policies that encourage investment (e.g., inviting foreign investors to locate facilities in the country); foster technology
development (e.g., patent protection); provide key services (e.g., roads, sanitation, and police protection); and create a capable workforce through education. Each year, dozens of
laws are proposed by legislators to improve the nation's business climate and promote
economic growth.

*The United States is the world's largest economy at the end of the twentieth
century, but it is not among the world's fastest-growing economies. This means
that new opportunities are not being created as rapidly in the United States as
in other, faster-growing nations. Economists generally suggest that a mature
economy like that of the United States should have about a 3 percent growth
rate to meet the needs of population growth. In contrast, the economic growth
rate of developing countries is significantly higher (e.g., People's Republic
of China grew at close to 10 percent per year for most of the 1990s;
Malaysia's growth was more than 6 percent per year). Ultimately, economic
growth affects a nation's capacity to direct resources to social needs and the
environment in which businesses operate.*

Low economic growth can contribute to a nation's social problems, including high
unemployment, costly welfare programs, and pressures to raise taxes. An expanding economy means job opportunities for trained workers but also higher labor costs for businesses.
On balance, political leaders favor economic growth because it creates increased national
wealth.

Fiscal policy refers to those patterns of government spending and taxing in an economy that are intended to stimulate or support the macroeconomy. Governments spend
money on many different types of activities. Local governments employ teachers, trash
collectors, police, and firefighters. State governments typically spend large amounts of
money on roads, social services, and park lands. National governments spend large sums
on military defense, international relationships, and hundreds of public works projects.
During the Great Depression of the 1930s, governments learned that public works projects were an effective way to employ large numbers of people, put money into their hands,
and stimulate consumption of goods and services through such "pump priming." Today,
governments use fiscal policy as the primary way to achieve economic growth and prosperity. As the following example shows, public works projects such as roads and airports
remain among the most popular means of creating employment while achieving other public goals.

*The largest public works project in the United States in the 1990s is Big Dig.
It is a decade-long construction project, employing more than 15,000 people,
to create a tunnel beneath the Boston harbor that will connect the city with its
airport. The project also involves tearing down an elevated roadway known as
the Central Artery that passes through the downtown area and replacing it
with an underground roadway. The project will ease traffic congestion and add
acres of usable land for development in Boston's high-priced financial district.
The benefits do not come cheaply, however. Cost estimates for the Central
Artery/Third Harbor Tunnel project are in excess of $7 billion, an amount be-
ing shared by the federal and state governments. User fees and general tax
revenues will pay for the project. Some critics believe costs of the project will
exceed $10 billion by 2002. All agree that at a cost of more than $1 billion per
mile for each of the seven miles of roadway that will be built, the Big Dig will
be the most expensive roadway per mile ever built in the United States.[2]*

---

[2]"U.S. to Conduct New Audit of Big Dig Costs," *Boston Globe,* August 28, 1997; and "The Big Dig," *Boston
Globe,* three-part series, September 11, 12, and 13, 1994, pp. 1ff.

Taxation Policy

Government actions to raise or reduce taxes on business directly affect how much money firms have to invest in new plants, equipment, and people. The same is true of taxes on individuals: After-tax household income affects spending for food, housing, automobiles, and entertainment. Tax rates also affect the money available for savings and reinvestment in the economy. Even minor rules can have large effects: Rules about the tax deductibility of at-home offices affect 20 million at-home businesses in the United States.

Tax policies are often a consequence of other goals that governments seek to achieve. Governments may be forced to raise taxes because other needs or commitments are great and the pressures of stakeholders exceed the pressures of taxpayers. When nations are at war, for example, taxes are raised; the collection of taxes becomes more aggressive because of the need to pay the costs of waging war. Peacetime spending priorities also affect tax policies. Large social welfare programs can involve major governmental spending requirements that need tax support.

> *One of the largest domestic spending plans of the 1990s was President Clinton's proposal to create a national health-care system. The program was designed to provide health-care coverage for all Americans, but it encountered heavy opposition because of the costs such a plan might create. Estimates of the new taxes needed to finance such a plan ranged from $10 billion to more than $100 billion. Opposition to increased taxes was one of the key reasons the Clinton health-care proposal was defeated.*

A nation's **monetary policy** affects the supply, demand, and value of the country's currency. The value of the currency is affected by the strength of the nation's economy relative to the economies of other countries. The amount of money in circulation and the level of demand for loans, credit, and currency influence inflation, deflation, and government objectives.

In the United States, the Federal Reserve Bank, an independent agency whose members are appointed by the president but whose policies are set by the bank's board of governors, plays the role of other countries' central banks. By raising and lowering the interest rates at which private sector banks borrow money from "The Fed," the board of governors is able to influence the size of the nation's money supply and the value of the dollar relative to other national currencies.

Managing a nation's monetary policy is exceedingly difficult. A healthy economy requires a supply of money and credit that is sufficient to enable people and businesses to maintain economic growth but not so great as to stimulate overbidding for economic resources (i.e., *inflation*). Too small a supply of money produces *deflation,* which involves too few dollars chasing available goods and services.

> *In 1997, Thailand's government was forced to devalue its national currency, the baht, because of inflationary pressures and an overheating of the economy. The decision to devaluate the baht was forced on the government by international currency trading, in which experts continuously look for imbalances in the relationship of one nation's currencies to all others. When the traders concluded that Thailand was overvalued, they sold their bahts in favor of other currencies. Thailand's problems were similar to those of Mexico, which in late 1994 was forced to devalue the peso, creating a huge loss of assets for people*

who owned pesos and for businesses that had to repay loans in other currencies such as U.S. dollars.[3]

The worth, or worthlessness, of a nation's currency has serious effects on business and society. It affects the buying power of money in people's hands, the stability and value of savings, and the confidence of citizens and international investors about the nation's future. This affects the ability of the country to borrow money from other nations and to attract private capital. Businesses are directly affected by the strength or weakness of the national currency as they conduct trade with other nations.

> *When Mexico devalued the peso in December 1994, the government gave no prior warning of its decision. Mattel Inc., a U.S. toy manufacturer, was caught by surprise and was hard hit because the devaluation made its products much more expensive in Mexico. Prior to the devaluation, Mattel's Mexican manufacturing plant had been under repair following a destructive fire. Mexico is Mattel's fifth-largest foreign market, and the company sent toys from its U.S. plants to meet the Christmas-season demand of its Mexican customers. It billed its customers in 1994 pesos but was paid in early 1995 with postdevaluation pesos. Mattel's Mexican customers paid off their obligation to Mattel in pesos that were worth much less than before the government's action. Mattel's toys cost nearly twice as many pesos after the devaluation, leaving the company with a $20 million loss.*[4]

Trade Policy

Trade policy refers to those government actions that are taken to encourage or discourage commerce with other countries. Many countries favor trade with others. Nations with large amounts of natural resources such as oil, timber, coal, minerals, and agricultural products tend to favor trade because it creates markets for their goods and helps them achieve economic growth. Nations that are cost-efficient producers of clothing, electronic equipment, computers, and automobiles also tend to favor international trade because they can offer better prices to customers than their less efficient competitors. But there are social consequences for a nation that opens its borders to trade.

Countries without abundant natural resources or highly efficient manufacturing industries may find trade to be less beneficial for their citizens. Trade may enable wealthy citizens to spend money on foreign-produced goods and services, but citizens who are unemployed will not find jobs if local businesses cannot match the cost efficiencies of foreign firms. The results can be socially explosive, with relatively few people controlling a large percentage of the national wealth while a large number of people suffer in poverty.

Wealthy nations may also find international trade to be a mixed blessing. When the North American Free Trade Agreement was adopted, U.S. labor leaders feared that jobs would be lost to lower-priced labor in Mexico, creating unemployment and causing social damage to American communities. Environmentalists were concerned that Mexico's more permissive laws would encourage U.S. companies to lower their environmental costs

---

[3]"Chavalit Decides to Devalue Baht," *Business Day,* July 3, 1997; "Causes of Economic Problems Cited," *Business Day,* July 28, 1997; and "Thanong Shows His Mettle in Effort to Revitalize Economy," *Business Day,* July 30, 1997; all in archives at http:/bday.net.
[4]"Peso Reduces Mattel's Profit," *New York Times,* January 5, 1995, p. D10.

by operating in Mexico rather than the United States. Such considerations lead some countries to favor open markets and free trade; others favor protected markets and restricted trade.

> *Japan has favored free trade in industries where it has a competitive advantage based on cost or innovative technology. Japanese leaders have pressed other nations to open their economies to imports of steel, consumer electronics, and computers. But Japan has resisted opening its economy to trade with nations whose goods and services are less expensive or technologically advanced. U.S. computer companies, construction firms, and automobile manufacturers have had great difficulty getting permission to sell their products in Japan, while producers of fast food, cigarettes, and designer clothing have had a much easier time getting permission to do business in Japan. But the most difficult U.S. product to get into Japan was one that affected millions of Japanese farmers: rice. For years, the government refused to permit imported rice into Japan. Only an acute shortage of domestic rice, plus intense pressure from the U.S. government on Japanese officials, succeeded in creating an opportunity for U.S. rice imports in Japan.[5]*

Nations often seek to be self-sufficient in some areas of economic activity, such as farming, to preserve traditions and national values, or in industries that employ many people and are therefore vital to the social fabric of the economy. For example, France and Italy are among the nations that have sought to protect their traditional family-based agricultural industry from highly efficient foreign competitors. And many nations have sought to protect declining industries that could not meet world-class production efficiencies but employed many thousands of employees. These pressures may force governments to create trade barriers by imposing extra charges *(tariffs)* on imported goods or strict quality requirements that force the seller to raise the price of the products if they can be sold at all.

Industrial Policy

Many national governments have attempted to direct economic resources toward the development of specific industries within the country. This is known as **industrial policy.** A nation that has oil resources, for example, may structure tax and other policies to encourage exploration and production of oil fields. Many nations have also encouraged industries such as steel, automobiles, textiles, and other large employers through public policy. In the widest application of industrial policy, governments can invest in new technologies (e.g., fiber optics) directly by creating a state-owned enterprise or indirectly by creating rules and conditions that encourage others to invest in new businesses (e.g., casino gambling). Beginning in the 1980s, a vigorous debate occurred in the United States as to whether government should pick winners and losers through industrial policy.[6] U.S. political leaders have generally favored using the power of government to create the conditions for new businesses to grow rather than picking specific industries for growth.

---

[5]S. Lenway, K. Rehbein, and L. Starks, "The Impact of Protectionism on Firm Wealth: The Experience of the Steel Industry," *Southern Economic Journal,* 1990, pp. 1079–93.

[6]The most important version of this argument in recent times is M. Dertouzos, R. Lester, and R. Solow, *Made in America: Regaining the Productivity Edge,* Report of the MIT Commission on Industrial Productivity, (Cambridge, MA: MIT Press, 1989).

Social Welfare Policies

The twentieth century produced many advances in the well-being of people across the globe. The advanced industrial nations have typically developed elaborate systems of social services for their citizens. Developing economies have improved key areas of social welfare (e.g., public health) and will continue to do so as their economies grow. International standards and best practices have supported these trends.

Health Policy

Health care is among the most essential of social services, in part because public health problems can affect all of a nation's population. Advanced industrial nations (e.g., Japan, Britain, the United States) tend to devote significant resources to providing basic health care to the population. Developing countries also recognize the importance of public health as a moral obligation and an investment in human resources.

> *When doctors in the Indian city of Surat discovered that they were dealing with an outbreak of pneumonic plague, a deadly communicable disease, the Indian government mobilized its resources to fight the epidemic. More than 40 people died within two weeks, and hundreds, perhaps thousands, of others were infected. The worst problem, however, was the prospect of the epidemic spreading to other cities in India and, potentially, to other countries around the world. The World Health Organization worked with the Indian government to organize public health resources to deal with the plague in Surat, Bombay, and New Delhi, hundreds of miles away. Thousands of health workers—doctors, nurses, and paramedics—were organized to deal with plague victims.*

Advanced industrial societies rely heavily on hospitals, medical technology, and sophisticated pharmaceutical products to improve health. Many other nations emphasize meeting basic health-care needs through local clinics, community education, and reliance on locally available medicines. Investment in such primary health care tends to produce significant improvement in indicators such as infant mortality, illness rates of small children, and vaccination of the population against disease.

The relationship between health-care expenditures and benefits has been hotly debated for years in many nations. According to a survey of national health-care systems conducted by the World Bank, the United States has a technologically advanced health-care system that produces the largest number of sophisticated procedures, such as heart transplants, but it ranks below the other nations in ensuring primary health care through programs such as child vaccinations.[7] As shown in Figure 8–2, industrial nations vary in their expenditures on health care and in the outcomes, or indicators of success, resulting from that spending. The United States, for example, spends more of its gross domestic product on health care than any other nation, yet people in other countries live longer than Americans. In general, the prevailing view among experts is that by viewing a population as a national resource, health expenditures represent important investments in human capital.

Health policy has become more important as health-care costs have grown. In the early 1990s, economic experts said that U.S. health-care costs would rise from approximately 13 percent of GDP to as much as 20 percent by 2010. This sparked fear of runaway costs that would do much damage to the rest of the American economy. Government officials were pressed to control health-care costs. This type of pressure eventually

[7]World Bank, *World Development Report, 1997: The State in a Changing World* (New York: Oxford University Press, 1997). Available at http://www.worldbank.org/html/extpb/wdr97pa.htm.

Figure 8–2

Comparative health-care costs and benefits.

Source: United Nations, *Human Development Report, 1996* (New York: United Nations Development Program and Oxford University Press, 1996), various tables in Appendix A.

Countries in Order of Life Expectancy	Life Expectancy at Birth (in Years, 1993)	Population (in millions, 1993)	Real GDP (per capita, 1993)	Total Expenditures on Health (percent of GDP)
1. Japan	79.6	126.5	$20,660	6.8%
2. Sweden	78.3	8.7	17,900	8.8
3. Spain	77.7	39.5	13,660	6.5
4. Greece	77.7	10.4	5,825	4.8
5. Canada	77.5	28.8	20,950	9.9
6. Netherlands	77.5	15.3	17,340	8.7
7. Australia	77.8	17.6	18,530	8.6
8. France	77.0	57.5	19,140	9.1
9. Israel	76.6	5.3	15,130	4.2
10. United Kingdom	76.3	57.9	17,230	6.6
11. Germany	76.1	80.9	18,840	9.1
12. United States	76.1	257.9	24,680	13.3
13. Ireland	74.5	3.5	15,120	8.0

led to new legislation to control costs and promoted the rise of health maintenance organizations (HMOs) and the merger of hospitals and health-care companies.

Health issues are entwined with other important areas of public policy. For example, environmental policy is often shaped by the need to protect human health from harmful pollutants. This has been influential in the creation of clean water and clean air legislation and in the development of toxic dumping regulations.[8] A study of death rates attributable to pollution showed that developing countries suffered especially heavy loss of life because of pollution-related diseases (see Exhibit 8–A).

Education has also been influenced by health considerations, such as the need to teach children and teens about sexually transmitted diseases, including AIDS. But the costs of such policies sometimes provoke criticism and calls for change.

> *The Committee for Economic Development (CED), a business organization of about 250 large corporations, has called for an end to efforts to incorporate mentally and physically handicapped children in regular classrooms and has urged that schools move away from providing social services like pregnancy counseling and AIDS education. In their view, these programs deter from educational quality and do not serve the business community's needs for well-trained employees.[9] But educators strongly disagree, arguing that such programs are crucial to helping all students become adults who understand how to function in communities that are filled with risks, challenges, and diversity.*

[8]Nicholas D. Kristof, "Asian Pollution Is Widening Its Deadly Reach," *New York Times,* November 29, 1997, pp. A1, A7.

[9]For a critique of these requirements, see Committee for Economic Development, *Putting Learning First* (New York: Committee for Economic Development, 1994). See also Catherine S. Manegold, "Study Says Schools Must Stress Academics," *New York Times,* September 23, 1994, p. A22.

EXHIBIT 8–A

Death Rates Caused by Pollution in Asian Countries

According to the World Health Organization, at least 2.7 million people die each year from illnesses caused by pollution. WHO distinguishes between indoor pollution (especially smoke from indoor and cooking fires) and outdoor pollution (attributed to industrial and automobile emissions).

Region	Total Deaths	Indoor Pollution		Outdoor Pollution
		Rural	Urban	Urban
India	673,000	496,000	93,000	84,000
Sub-Saharan Africa	522,000	490,000	32,000	*
China	443,000	320,000	53,000	70,000
Other Asian and Pacific countries	443,000	363,300	40,000	40,000
Latin American and Caribbean	406,000	180,000	113,000	113,000
Former socialist economies of Europe	100,000	*	*	100,000
Established market economies	79,000	0	32,000	47,000
Middle East	57,000	*	*	57,000
Total deaths	2,723,000	1,849,000	363,000	511,000

*Not available.

Source: Data are reported in Nicholas D. Kristof, "Asian Pollution Is Widening Its Deadly Reach," *New York Times,* November 29, 1997, pp. A1, A7. See also, Nicholas D. Kristof, "Across Asia, a Pollution Disaster Hovers," *New York Times,* November 28, 1997, pp. A1, A14.

As such examples suggest, the business community has a large stake in the extent to which public health objectives and costs are imposed on economic activity. Businesses must monitor such developments for their immediate and longer-term consequences. These consequences may be positive or negative, depending on the nature of the proposal, the costs involved, and the benefits to business and to society. And, while companies in some industries may suffer higher costs, others (e.g., medical equipment and pharmaceutical firms) will benefit from expanded social investment in health.

Social Security

National governments have traditionally developed various mechanisms for meeting the needs of special segments of the population. In the 1800s, orphan children and poor families often required such assistance; in modern times, children, the elderly, the disabled, and homeless members of society make up a large and needy population. In response, many countries have created government-run social security systems that provide guaranteed economic assistance to needy segments of the population.

In the United States, Social Security has been a national commitment since the 1930s, when the Social Security Act was passed (1934). The legislation created a fund into which working Americans paid a small amount of money from each paycheck. The fund grew as worker contributions grew, and the proceeds were used to make monthly Social Security payments to retirees. For decades the system was very successful.

The Social Security system has suffered from two problems in recent times. First, the population has aged and people are living longer. Retirement payments are rising and draining increasing amounts from the Social Security fund, and reserves decline as the payout exceeds the annual amount paid in. Second, the base of younger workers contributing to the Social Security fund is not rising as fast as the payouts to retirees. Social Security taxes have risen and pressures have grown to reduce benefits. Despite several attempts by the U.S. Congress to balancing revenue inflows with benefit outflows, the Social Security system remains troubled. The financial service industry has urged Congress to privatize the system and give individuals options to invest Social Security payments in personal retirement accounts.

Entitlements

As nations expand social welfare programs, pressures may grow to increase levels of support and assistance. Once programs are in place, citizens may begin to expect that benefits of such programs will rise. This creates an **entitlement mentality,** in which there is the widespread belief that the political system (government) will deliver more social assistance.

Entitlements create dilemmas for political leaders. Pressures arise to expand the number of beneficiaries of social welfare programs and to ensure that benefits are spread generously among the population. Costs rise under such pressures, which creates the dilemma of balancing the interests of taxpayers against those of recipients. Resentment can occur when the public learns of incidents in which people or businesses that do not really need social or economic benefits receive them. The media may portray these as examples of waste, fraud, and abuse.[10] Few nations have developed lasting solutions to the dilemma of providing benefits to the truly needy at a reasonable cost to taxpayers.

Government Regulation of Business

Goals and Objectives

Societies rely on government to establish rules of conduct for citizens and organizations. Because government operates at so many levels (federal, state, local), modern businesses face complex webs of regulations. Companies often require staffs of lawyers, public affairs specialists, and government relations managers to monitor and manage the interaction with government (see Chapter 2). Why do societies turn to more regulation as a way to solve problems? There are a variety of reasons.

---

[10]See William Julius Wilson, *When Work Disappears: The World of the New Urban Poor* (New York: Random House, 1996; Vintage Books ed., 1997). In 1996, the U.S. Congress passed the Welfare Reform Act. This placed new responsibility with the states to administer welfare programs, including a work-fare requirement. For background, see Mickey Kaus, "The Welfare Mess—How It Got That Way," *The Wall Street Journal,* September 12, 1994, p. A16; and "Entitlement Politics, R.I.P.," *The Wall Street Journal,* September 28, 1994, p. A18. The cost of entitlements is discussed in Robert Eisner, *The Misunderstood Economy: What Counts and How to Count It* (Boston, MA: Harvard Business School Press, 1994).

Economic Objectives

Economic objectives characterize some government regulations, but social goals are paramount in others. One economic argument that supports government regulation is the **market failure** argument—that is, the marketplace fails to adjust the product price for the true costs of a firm's behavior. For example, there is no market incentive for a company to spend money on pollution control equipment if customers do not demand it. The market fails to incorporate the social cost (the environmental harm) of pollution into the economic equation. Government can use regulation to force all the competitors in the industry to adopt an antipollution standard. The companies will incorporate the extra cost of compliance with the standard into the product price. In this way, the social cost that is imposed on the environment is passed on to the consumers who actually use the environmental resource.

Ethical Arguments

There is often an ethical rationale for regulation as well. As discussed in Chapter 6, for example, there is a utilitarian ethical argument in support of safe working conditions: It is costly to train and educate employees only to lose their services because of accidents that are preventable. There are also fairness and justice arguments for government to set standards and develop regulations to protect employees, consumers, and other stakeholders. In debates about regulation, advocates for and against regulatory proposals often use both economic and ethical arguments to support their views.

> As Internet technology and applications have become more sophisticated, concerns about peoples' privacy have been raised. It is unethical, in the view of critics, for companies to sell private information without customer approval. Faced with public pressure, companies such as Dell Computer, Compaq Computer, Intel, and Motorola working through the Information Technology Industry Council (a trade association) agreed to a set of principles intended to give consumers confidence and trust that privacy rights will be respected when they engage in electronic commerce. (See Chapter 18 for additional information about computer privacy issues.)[11]

Political Advocacy

Another reason for the expansion of business regulation is the number of advocates who speak for other interests. Environmental groups urge government officials to halt pollution; organizations representing minorities and women seek expansion of equal employment opportunity rules in the workplace; consumer groups advocate government regulations that ensure product quality and safety; and labor unions lobby regulators to set rules that will protect employees from workplace hazards and health risks.

Media Attention

Media attention to disasters and confrontations between business and the public help convince government officials that action is necessary. Throughout history, protests have helped pressure governments into action; in the late twentieth century, as the news media literally connect communities around the globe so that events are seen as they happen, the public and government officials see social needs that should be met. It is hard to resist pressures to act under such conditions.

[11]"Privacy Code Unveiled by High-Tech Firms," *Boston Globe,* December 9, 1997, p. C7.

Types of Regulation

Government regulations come in different forms. Some are directly imposed; others are more indirect. Some are aimed at a specific industry (e.g., banking); others, such as those dealing with job discrimination or pollution, apply to all industries. Some have been in existence for a long time—the Interstate Commerce Commission (ICC) was created in 1887—whereas others, such as those governing state lotteries and other forms of legalized gambling, are of recent vintage in many states.[12]

Industry-Specific Economic Regulations

Our oldest form of regulation by government agency is directed at specific industries such as the railroads, telephone companies, and banks. Regulations of this type are primarily economic in nature and are deliberately intended to modify the normal operation of the free market and the forces of supply and demand. Such modification may come about because the free market is distorted by the size or monopoly power of companies or because the social side effects or consequences of actions in the marketplace are thought to be undesirable. Under such conditions, government regulators substitute their judgment for that of the marketplace in such matters as price-setting, capital expansion, quality of services, and the entry of new competitors. For example, railroads were not permitted to raise most rates to shippers without permission from the ICC, nor could they abandon costly service to a community as a free market firm could do. Nor could telephone companies increase their charges to customers, expand into related lines of business, or deny service to customers without first getting the approval of various local, state, and federal agencies.

Many industries have evolved through various stages of government regulation during the past century. Airlines, natural gas, telecommunications, and banking, for example, have gone through periods of rising regulation designed to correct abuses and problems, followed by periods of consolidation and implementation of regulation. When regulatory programs become ineffective, as command-type regulations often do, pressures to deregulate or otherwise reform the industry arise. Views change regarding how much regulation, and of what type, is required. For example, petroleum was regulated during the 1930s to stabilize a volatile oil marketplace that suffered from gluts and excesses of oil. Regulations were followed until the 1970s, when oil prices rose sharply. New regulatory controls were tried, but reformers concluded that oil prices should be deregulated to encourage exploration and development of oil supplies. Regulation always faces problems of staying current with changes that shape the underlying dynamics of an industry.

All-Industry Social Regulations

All-industry social regulations are aimed at such important social goals as protecting consumers and the environment and providing workers with safe and healthy working conditions. Equal employment opportunity, protection of pension benefits, and health care for employees are other important areas of social regulation. Unlike the economic regulations mentioned above, social regulations are not limited to one type of business or industry. Laws concerning pollution, safety and health, and job discrimination apply to all businesses; consumer protection laws apply to all relevant businesses producing and selling consumer goods.

---

[12]Richard McGowan, *Government Regulation of the Alcohol Industry: The Search for Revenue and The Common Good* (Westport, CT: Praeger/Quorum Books, 1997); and Richard McGowan, *State Lotteries and Legalized Gambling: Painless Revenue or Painful Mirage* (Westport, CT: Praeger/Quorum Books, 1994), chap. 6.

Social regulations typically benefit large segments of society. Critics argue that costs are shared by a narrow segment of society, business and its customers. If the agencies that enforce social regulations do not consider the overall financial impact of their actions, businesses may experience losses and even be forced to close, leaving workers without jobs, communities without tax revenues, and customers without products. This argument does not excuse socially irresponsible conduct. In recent years, more political leaders have recognized that the effect of regulations on an industry's economic health is connected to the public interest.[13]

Functional Regulations

Certain operations or functions of business have been singled out for special attention by government regulators. Labor practices, for example, are no longer left to the operation of free market forces. Government agencies set minimum wages, regulate overtime pay, establish the rules for labor union campaigns, and mediate serious and troublesome labor—management disputes, including, in recent years, strikes by airline pilots, flight attendants, school teachers, and even professional baseball players. Competition is another business function strongly affected by regulation. Antitrust laws and rules (see Chapter 10) attempt to prevent monopolies, preserve competitive pricing, and protect consumers against unfair practices.

Functional regulations, like social regulations, may cut across industry lines and apply generally to all enterprises, as they do in the case of antitrust and labor practices. Or they may, as in the case of regulations governing stock exchanges and the issuance of corporate securities, be confined to specific institutions such as the stock markets or the companies whose stocks are listed on those exchanges. Figure 8–3 depicts these three types of regulation—economic, social, and functional—along with the major regulatory agencies responsible for enforcing the rules at the federal level in the United States. Only the most prominent federal agencies are included in the chart. Individual states, some cities, and other national governments have their own array of agencies to implement regulatory policy.

Problems of Regulation

There is a legitimate need for government regulation in modern economies, but regulation is not without its problems. Businesses feel these problems first-hand, often because the regulations directly affect the cost of products and the freedom of managers to design their business operations. In the modern economy, there are serious issues of regulatory cost and effectiveness that cannot be overlooked. Each is discussed below.

The Costs of Regulation

The call for regulation may seem irresistible to government leaders and officials, but there are always costs to regulation. In recent years, more attention has been given to the costs of government regulation. An old economic adage says, There is no free lunch. Someone eventually has to pay for the benefits created. This is the **rule of cost,** and it applies in all socioeconomic systems, whether free market or central state control.

An industrial society such as that of the United States can afford almost anything, including social regulations, if it is willing to pay the price. Sometimes the benefits are

---

[13]Murray Weidenbaum, *Business, Government, and the Public,* 3d ed. (Englewood Cliffs, NJ: Prentice Hall, 1997).

Figure 8–3

Three types of regulation: Industry-specific economic regulation, all-industry social regulation, and functional regulation.

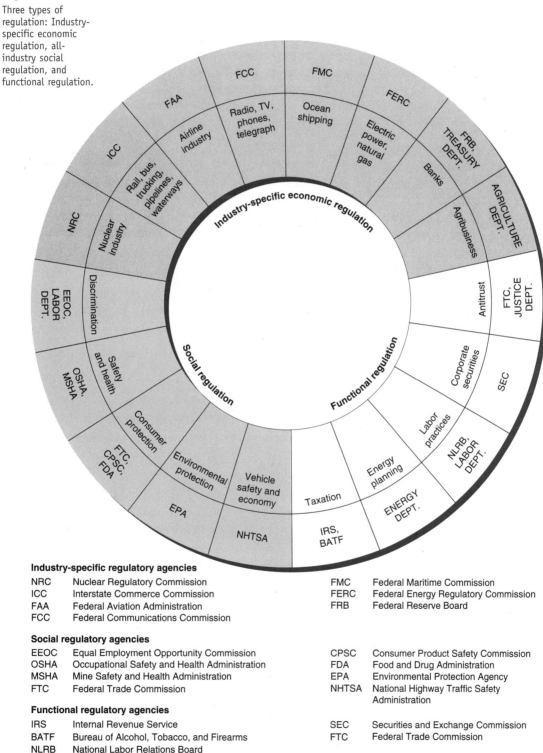

Industry-specific regulatory agencies

NRC	Nuclear Regulatory Commission
ICC	Interstate Commerce Commission
FAA	Federal Aviation Administration
FCC	Federal Communications Commission

FMC	Federal Maritime Commission
FERC	Federal Energy Regulatory Commission
FRB	Federal Reserve Board

Social regulatory agencies

EEOC	Equal Employment Opportunity Commission
OSHA	Occupational Safety and Health Administration
MSHA	Mine Safety and Health Administration
FTC	Federal Trade Commission

CPSC	Consumer Product Safety Commission
FDA	Food and Drug Administration
EPA	Environmental Protection Agency
NHTSA	National Highway Traffic Safety Administration

Functional regulatory agencies

IRS	Internal Revenue Service
BATF	Bureau of Alcohol, Tobacco, and Firearms
NLRB	National Labor Relations Board

SEC	Securities and Exchange Commission
FTC	Federal Trade Commission

worth the costs; sometimes the costs exceed the benefits. The test of **cost-benefit analysis** helps the public understand what is at stake when new regulation is sought. For example, when the U.S. Congress debated the Clinton administration's national health-care proposals, strong opposition arose when it was determined that the plan would impose large regulatory costs. Although the exact cost was in dispute, and debated vigorously, Congress realized that the American public did not want the benefits of a national health-care plan at just any cost; they wanted them at little or no cost.

Figure 8–4a illustrates the increase in costs of federal regulation in the United States over the past three decades. The cost of economic regulation has grown more slowly (about 100 percent over 28 years) than social regulation (about 300 percent over 28 years). This reflects an emphasis on expanding such areas of social regulation as environmental health, occupational safety, and consumer protection. In addition to federal regulatory costs, the costs of regulation by state and local government agencies have also risen greatly over this period.

The growth in federal regulatory programs is not a new phenomenon. As scholars at the Center for the Study of American Business have documented, the growth pattern has been interrupted only briefly during the past three decades. In the early 1980s, President Ronald Reagan led a campaign to cut government regulation. In 1980, 122,000 people staffed federal regulatory agencies; budget cuts reduced the number to 102,000 in 1985. But under President George Bush, staff increases began to push the numbers higher. By 1992, regulatory personnel equaled the 1980 number. By the mid-1990s, federal regulatory personnel grew to 128,000 (see Figure 8–4b).[14] It remains close to that number today.

Effectiveness of Regulation

The need for government regulation must be balanced against both costs of that regulation and assessments of whether the regulation will accomplish its intended purpose. The United States has experimented with different forms of government regulation for more than 200 years, and experts have learned that not all government programs are effective in meeting their intended goals. Thus, government may be called on from time to time to regulate certain types of business behavior and, at other times, to deregulate that behavior if it is believed that the industry no longer needs that regulation or that other, better, means exist to exercise control (e.g., market pressures from competitors).

Deregulation is the removal or scaling down of regulatory authority and regulatory activities of government. Deregulation has been called for by many politicians during the 1990s, but deregulation pressures have existed for many years. President Ronald Reagan symbolized this theme in the early 1980s, when he campaigned on the promise to "get government off the back of people." Major deregulatory laws were enacted beginning in

---

[14]Thomas D. Hopkins, *Regulatory Costs in Profile,* Policy Study Number 132 (St. Louis, MO: Center for the Study of American Business, August 1996). See also, Melinda Warren, *Reforming the Federal Regulatory Process: Rhetoric or Reality?* Occasional Paper 138 (St. Louis: Washington University, Center for the Study of American Business, 1994), p. 5.

Figure 8–4

The costs of regulation, 1970–1998.

Source: Based on publicly available data reprinted in Christopher Douglass, Michael Orlando, and Melinda Warren, Regulatory Changes and Trends: An Analysis of the 1998 Budget of the U.S. Government, Policy Brief 182 (St. Louis: Washington University, Center for the Study of American Business, 1997).

(*a*) The costs of federal regulation have been rising.

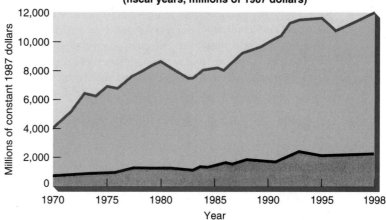

Federal Regulatory Trends in Spending, 1970–1998
(fiscal years, millions of 1987 dollars)

(*b*) Staffing trends at federal regulatory agencies have leveled.

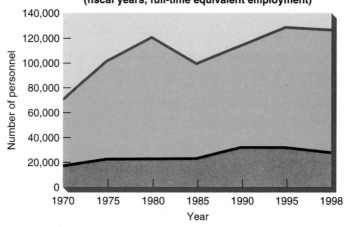

Federal Regulatory Staffing Trends, 1970–1998
(fiscal years, full-time equivalent employment)

ECONOMIC REGULATION

SOCIAL REGULATION

1975 when Gerald Ford was president and continued through the administrations of Jimmy Carter, Ronald Reagan, and George Bush. These laws loosened the grip of the federal government on a number of industries and markets in the following ways.

In the petroleum industry, all price controls on domestic oil were abolished in 1981. Prices of natural gas were gradually decontrolled until all controls ended in 1987. A phased deregulation of commercial airlines removed govern-ment supervision of rates and allowed domestic airlines to enter domestic routes more easily and to make mergers and acquisitions with less delay and oversight. The Civil Aeronautics Board (CAB), the chief airline regulatory agency since the 1930s, was abolished in 1985. Intercity trucking companies were permitted to charge lower prices and provide wider services. More competitors entered the industry. Railroads, which were tightly regulated for a century, were deregulated and given the freedom to set rates in some parts of their business and to compete in new ways. Financial institutions were allowed to be more flexible in setting interest rates on loans and to compete across state lines (interstate banking).

But deregulation does not always succeed. Commercial radio broadcasting was deregulated in the early 1980s, and Congress relaxed the licensing process for radio and television stations. Steps were planned to promote more competition in the entire telecommunications industry—telephone service, electronic information transfer, and cable television broadcasting. But as the development of new technologies advanced, restrictions on the businesses in which regional telephone companies could compete still existed. In 1994, Congress made a major effort to enact a comprehensive communications law that would set the rules for future competition in the telecommunications industry. The complexity of the problems and the lobbying of various special interests, however, proved too much of an obstacle to overcome. A new telecommunications law was not passed until 1996, many years after the original proposals had been presented. Some critics think the Telecommunications Act of 1996 has failed to move the telecommunications industry toward necessary reforms.[15]

Proponents of deregulation always contend with the public's desire to see government solve problems. This produces cross-currents in which government is trying both to deregulate in some areas and to introduce new regulation in others. **Reregulation** is the increase or expansion of government regulation, especially in areas where the regulatory activities had previously been reduced. In the United States, the Clinton administration moved toward reregulation in areas where too little government regulation may be dangerous. Since the early 1990s, the federal government has taken action to toughen worker safety standards, establish new environmental protection standards, set curbs on insider trading of corporate securities, fix requirements for airline collision avoidance equipment, and impose drug testing of train engineers, airline pilots, and others.

Reregulation has occurred in areas such as securities and stock market oversight to prevent scandals such as those involving well-known Wall Street figures Ivan Boesky, Michael Milken, and Dennis Levine, all of whom were convicted of securities law violations. Deregulation in banking led to cutbacks in financial inspection by government officials during the 1980s. Cuts in enforcement budgets have been associated with bank collapses and the savings and loan scandals of the 1980s. More recently, studies of the U.S. financial markets indicate that securities fraud rises as the stock market rises. Securities fraud cost investors more than $6 billion in 1996.[16]

[15]Edmund L. Andrews, "Bill to Revamp Communications Dies in Congress," *New York Times,* September 24, 1994, pp. 1, 43. See http://thomas.loc.gov//cgi-bin/bdquery for a discussion of the 1996 Telecommunications Act (P.L. 104–104). Also, see *Business Wire,* November 21, 1997, for telecommunications articles.
[16]Leslie Eaton, "Investment Fraud Is Soaring Along with Stock Market," *New York Times,* November 30, 1997, pp. 1, 46.

Reinventing Government

The trend toward streamlining government, making its operations more efficient, is called **reinventing government.**[17] This idea draws on business success in reengineering corporations and instituting total quality management systems. It operates on the principle that greater efficiency can be achieved if programs are reengineered to eliminate unnecessary procedures, processes, and people—that is, it is possible to do more with less resources. In 1994, Vice President Al Gore headed a federal government effort to reinvent government in this way. The government report detailed a lengthy list of ways in which federal agencies, including regulatory agencies, could do more with less and save taxpayers' dollars while meeting important needs. Annual reports on the results of these efforts are provided by the government and available to citizens.[18]

International Regulation

International commerce is linking people and businesses in new and complicated ways. U.S. consumers regularly buy food, automobiles, VCRs, and clothing from companies located in Europe, Canada, Latin America, Australia, Africa, and Asia. Citizens of other nations do the same. As these patterns of international commerce grow more complicated, governments see the need to establish rules that protect and serve the interest of their own citizens. No nation wants to accept dangerous products manufactured elsewhere that will injure local citizens. No national government wants to see its economy damaged by unfair competition from foreign competitors. These concerns are the reasons for a rapidly growing set of international regulatory agreements and actions. Three types of such regulation are discussed below and illustrated in Figure 8–5.

Regulation of Imported Products

Every nation has the power to set standards for products to be sold in the country. When a child in Chicago receives a Christmas toy made in Taiwan, for example, that toy has met the product safety standards set by the U.S. Consumer Product Safety Commission. This use of government authority is legitimate. But policymakers may also be tempted to set higher standards for foreign products that are more difficult to meet than those for locally produced goods. If the Consumer Product Safety Commission were to set one standard for U.S. companies and a more demanding standard for foreign toy companies, the result would help U.S. companies and hurt foreign competitors. The standard would discriminate against foreign manufacturers, and the practice would likely be deemed a trade barrier in violation of international trade agreements. This could make the United States liable for damages to the foreign toy producers. Governments, however, are under pressure from other interests, including local companies, labor organizations, and communities, not to open local markets to foreign sellers. These stakeholders may feel threatened by foreign competitors and seek to block them from selling to a "safe" market of cus-

---

[17]David Osborne and Peter Plastrik, *Banishing Bureaucracy: The Five Strategies for Reinventing Government* (Reading, MA: Addison-Wesley, 1997). See also David Osborne and Ted Gaebler, *Reinventing Government: How the Entrepreneurial Spirit Is Transforming the Public Sector* (Reading, MA: Addison-Wesley, 1992).

[18]The current status of the National Performance Review initiative is available at http://www.npr.gov/initiati/ index.html. For the original report, see Al Gore, *From Red Tape to Results: Creating a Government That Works Better and Costs Less: Report of the National Performance Review* (Washington, D.C.: Government Printing Office, 1993).

Figure 8–5

Forms of
international
regulation.

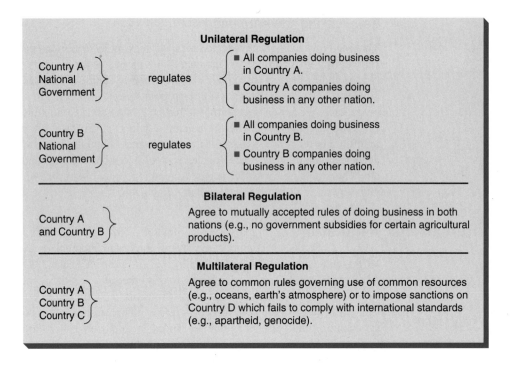

tomers. As discussed in Chapter 7, cooperative political and economic arrangements, such as the European Union, favor free trade and discourage protective regulation. Free trade is not easy to achieve, however, because pressures are put on governments to use regulation to promote and protect various stakeholders.

Regulation of Exported Products

Governments have an interest in knowing what types of products their businesses are exporting to the rest of the world. The federal government is understandably concerned that products that say "Made in America" are of good quality. U.S. companies have sometimes exported products to other nations that were banned from sale at home because of safety concerns. In addition, the government is concerned that U.S. companies not sell military technology to unfriendly nations. In recent years, a number of cases arose in which U.S. businesses illegally sold sophisticated technology with potential military applications to Libya, Iran, and Iraq. These transactions violated U.S. laws that restrict the sale of classified military technology to only those customers approved by the Defense Department.

For example, EG&G, a U.S. manufacturer of specialized electronic equipment for military use, discovered that some of the triggering devices it manufactured for nuclear weapons were being sold to Iraq. In collaboration with U.S. officials, a shipment of such devices was traced through a series of intermediaries to a destination in Europe from which they were to go to Baghdad. With the cooperation of foreign officials and EG&G, the illegal exporters were caught and arrested.

Regulation of International Business Behavior

Nations have sought to standardize trade practices through various international organizations. United Nations agencies such as the World Health Organization have worked with the pharmaceutical industry to create databases on the side effects of drug product characteristics, establish quality standards, and resolve conflicting manufacturing and marketing practices that might harm the public. Elaborate processes of consultation between leaders of business, governmental, and nongovernmental organizations (e.g., consumer groups) are required to make such changes because of the vast number of stakeholders involved. The World Health Organization's international marketing code for infant formula products, for example, required nearly three years of meetings and consultations before a suitable code was ready for adoption by national governments.[19]

National governments sometimes create special organizations to keep the discussions moving forward. For example, the General Agreement on Tariffs and Trade is a set of international agreements among nations on acceptable trade practices. Periodically, nations agree to another round of negotiations to be hosted in a particular nation. In the early 1990s, the Uruguay Round of talks focused on such issues as government subsidies to agriculture that prevent fair competition from occurring. Lengthy and complex negotiations produced a new international body—the World Trade Organization—to enforce the new international trade laws.

Nations also cooperate to establish standards for the use of global resources not owned by any nation. Multilateral international agreements govern ocean fishing, protection of sea mammals such as dolphins and whales, the earth's ozone layer, and dumping of hazardous chemical waste in oceans. In each case, governments acknowledge the problem cannot be solved through one nation's actions. The result is a framework of international agreements, standards, and understandings that attempts to harmonize business activity and the public interest.[20]

The Future

Government interaction with business is a basic feature of all socioeconomic systems. Whether operating in a system of extensive state control of industry or in an environment of free markets, managers will have to deal with government regulations that affect their activities.

In the United States, macroeconomic policy has shaped the business environment and government regulation has influenced how companies compete. The pendulum of regulation has swung back and forth for nearly a century, sometimes favoring more control, sometimes less. Pressures to reduce the role of government contend with pressures for more government effort to solve problems in more cost-efficient ways. Every nation faces these choices and seeks ways to create balanced policies that meet the challenge of harmonizing economic growth with the social welfare of citizens. It is for these reasons that the changing role of government is one of the basic driving forces of change in the modern world.

---

[19]James E. Post, "Codes of Conduct: An Idea Whose Time Has Come," in Oliver Williams, ed., *Global Codes of Conduct: An Idea Whose Time Has Come?* (South Bend, IN: University of Notre Dame Press, forthcoming). See also, S. Prakash Sethi, *Multinational Corporations and the Impact of Public Advocacy on Corporate Strategy* (Hingham, MA: Kluwer, 1994).

[20]William C. Frederick, "The Moral Authority of Transnational Corporate Codes," *Journal of Business Ethics* 10 (1991), pp. 165–77. Also, Kathleen A. Getz, "International Instruments on Bribery and Corruption," paper presented at Conference on Global Codes of Conduct: An Idea Whose Time Has Come? University of Notre Dame, October 6–8, 1997. To be published in Oliver Williams, ed., *Global Codes of Conduct.*

Summary Points of This Chapter

- The key elements of public policy are inputs, goals, instruments to achieve those goals, and effects—both intended and unintended.

- Key national policies affecting business in every nation include economic growth, taxation, government spending, the value of money, international trade, and industrial policy.

- Social welfare policies affect business both directly (e.g., workplace rules) and indirectly (e.g., government spending) and express the social priorities of a nation. Health care, social security, and education are among a nation's most important social welfare policies.

- Government regulation of business is a mechanism for implementing public choices. Economic, social, and functional regulation of business exists in most countries.

- The role of government regulation has grown because society demands and expects more of government. Public exposure to risk creates powerful pressures on government to regulate business.

- International regulation is emerging because global business activity creates problems that cannot be solved by any one nation's government. As nations recognize their needs to cooperate in controlling business activities that cross national borders, international regulations are focusing on imports, exports, and business practices.

Key Terms and Concepts Used in This Chapter

- Fiscal policy
- Monetary policy
- Trade policy
- Industrial policy
- Entitlement mentality
- Market failure
- Rule of cost
- Cost-benefit analysis
- Deregulation
- Reregulation
- Reinventing government

Internet Resources

- http://www.whitehouse.gov/fsbr/ssbr.html   Executive Office of the President of the United States
- http://www.bea.doc.gov   Bureau of Economic Analysis, U.S. Department of Commerce
- http://www.census.gov   Bureau of the Census, U.S. Department of Commerce
- http://www.sec.gov   U.S. Securities and Exchange Commission
- http://www.npr.gov   National Performance Review ("Reinventing Government: Creating a Government That Works Better and Costs Less")

Discussion Case   # Food Safety in the United States

American consumers concerned about food safety have had much to worry about in recent years. Episodes of human illness traced to contaminated food have challenged the confidence of U.S. consumers who buy millions of dollars of fresh and packaged food in American supermarkets and restaurants daily.

According to food experts, the rate of salmonella illness has doubled over the past 20 years. In the past, most cases originated in restaurants or events like church suppers where mistakes were made by food preparers. Today, experts say, food is often tainted during processing at the growing number of huge food factories and is distributed to millions of people before anyone gets sick. A single day's production at a modern ground beef plant can turn out hundreds of thousands of pounds of hamburger, which are then quickly trucked all over the country. According to the Centers for Disease Control and Prevention, more than 9,000 people die every year from food poisoning in the United States.

Concerns about the safety of red meat, especially cooked hamburger meat, soared in 1997 when a rash of food-poisoning cases were reported in Denver, Colorado. The illness was traced to the presence of E. coli bacteria in hamburger patties eaten by the victims. All of the meat, investigators found, came from the same meat-packing plant in Nebraska.

Investigators eventually discovered the likely source of the E. coli bacteria. E. coli is a human bacteria and is introduced into the food supply by workers who may unknowingly spread it to others directly or indirectly. By failing to wash their hands, for example, workers could spread the E. coli bacteria to any food they handled. Thus, it was hypothesized that the contaminated hamburger was infected by an unknown worker at the Nebraska plant.

The U.S. Department of Agriculture oversees meat packing operations and issues inspection permits that allow the packing company to stamp its meat, "USDA Inspected." USDA officials found, however, that they were without authority to close the Nebraska plant. All they could do was threaten the company with loss of permission to use the USDA stamp and publicize the action through the media. Although the company finally agreed to close, the USDA went to the Congress and asked for legal authority to close plants in the future.

Later in the same year, consumers got another severe scare. In May 1997, more than 1,300 cases of cyclospora were reported to the Center for Disease Control. The disease produces severe reactions in humans, including dehydration and diarrhea. Most cases were tied to Guatemalan raspberries that had been processed in the United States and distributed to restaurants and stores. In December 1997, the U.S. Food and Drug Administration announced that it was banning Guatemalan raspberries from March 15 to August 15, 1998, the normal Guatemala raspberry export season. The ban occurred as concerns about food-borne illnesses had risen. Outbreaks of food-borne illnesses have been traced to strawberries, lettuce, alfalfa sprouts, melons, and other kinds of fresh produce, both imported and domestic. The ban will remain in effect "until the problem is worked out" said Robert Lake, director of policy for the FDA's Center for Food Safety. "Our objective is not to create trade barriers but make our food safer" said Lake. The Guatemalan government said it was cooperating with U.S. officials.

Food safety problems also arose when numerous cases of illness were traced to consumption of unpasteurized apple juice. Local farmers throughout the country have developed low-cost ways to make apple cider and apple juice at harvest time. These processes press the apples and mix the juice but do not cook or heat the juice to a temperature that would kill natural bacteria. This unpasteurized juice is often labeled "natural" and sold at local stores and farm stands and promoted for its tasty and fresh qualities. Most large national sellers of apple juice pasteurize their apple juice, in part to create a longer shelf-life for bottled juices that do not need to be refrigerated.

Unpasteurized apple juice must be kept under refrigeration, however. E. coli bacteria will grow in warm temperatures and produce illness for those who consume the juice. Babies and young children are often given apple juice and are especially susceptible to E. coli infection because their digestive systems are not fully developed. Among national food companies, Odwalla, a California-based company, was one of the few that sold unpasteurized apple juice. Odwalla juice was the juice that was consumed by many consumers who became ill (several died) in 1996 and 1997. The events created a near-panic regarding the consumption of apple juice. Sales dropped: In many areas, apple juice consumption was down by 50 to 80 percent. In the months that followed, apple juice producers in some states organized themselves into associations to voluntarily monitor product quality and respond to public concerns. In Massachusetts, for example, producers of about 80 percent of the locally produced apple juice and cider agreed to industry-sponsored quality-control standards. Similar actions took place in other states, and apple producers spent extra money on advertising and product promotion campaigns. Many wondered whether they would be able to continue selling unpasteurized "natural" apple juice.

Sources: "Guatemalan Raspberries Barred from U.S.," *Boston Globe,* December 9, 1997, p. A13; and "Change Cited in Onset of Food-Borne Illnesses," *Boston Globe,* December 10, 1997, p. A20.

Discussion Questions

1. Using the ideas discussed in this chapter, analyze the public policy issues raised by these food safety examples. Compare the stakeholders in each of the three examples cited in the case.
2. Which stakeholders are in common? Which are different? Compare the power and influence of stakeholders in the three situations. Which are more powerful? Which are less powerful?
3. What is the case for regulation in each situation? Should regulation be done by the federal government? By state government? By industry through self-regulation? Why do you favor your choice?
4. What can consumers do to protect themselves against E. coli infections? What should a company selling apple juice do to inform consumers?

9

Managing Business–Government Relations

Businesses face complex challenges in managing their relationships with government and the public policy process. Managers must recognize public issues as they emerge and know how to respond. The dynamics of the public policy process demand an understanding of the political environment and a strategic view of how stakeholders are acting on specific issues. In most nations, businesses have rights to urge governments to act in desired ways. Managers need to ensure that their company is seen as an important stakeholder when government officials make public policy decisions. But political pressures produce ethical dilemmas for companies and managers. The world of politics operates by different rules than the world of business. Sound decisions depend on careful judgment.

This chapter focuses on these key questions and objectives:

- What forms does corporate political activity take?
- What role does business play in electoral politics?
- What does strategic management of business–government relations mean?
- Why is it important for business to be involved in public policy decision making?
- How do the problems of the American political system affect business?

T he Dow Chemical Company is one of the world's largest chemical companies. Dow was founded by Herbert Dow in the early 1900s and still has its headquarters in Midland, Michigan, a small city north of Detroit. Throughout its history, Dow has grown by supplying chemical products to Detroit's booming automobile industry and by creating chemical products for other manufacturing and consumer product industries. The company has invested heavily in research and development to develop such new products as Saran Wrap, the popular plastic wrap. Dow produces many different types of plastic in manufacturing plants located around the world. Chemistry has been Dow's core technology for nearly 100 years.

The chemical industry has produced many products for use by the military. In the 1970s, Dow became embroiled in a controversy surrounding Agent Orange, a chemical defoliant containing dioxin that was used in Vietnam. Dioxin has been called the most toxic substance ever created by humans, and researchers have linked dioxin to cancer in people. Dow was criticized for supplying dioxin to the U.S. government during the Vietnam War, but the company argued that it had an obligation to assist the government when asked to do so.

The Agent Orange controversy took years to subside, and Dow continued to have its critics. Then, as public concern for the environment rose, scientific attention turned to dioxin and its effects on the environment and human beings. Officials in the United States and other advanced industrial nations were pressured by environmental groups to set more stringent regulations on dioxin exposure. This was difficult to do, however, because of the extensive industrial use of chlorine, which contains dioxin. In the paper industry, for example, chlorine is used to bleach colored wood pulp into white paper. A residue of dioxin is typically discharged into the water from local rivers and streams used by paper and pulp mills. When returned to the rivers from which it was taken, the water contains small amounts of dioxin. Fish and other aquatic life ingest the dioxin, and human beings are exposed when they drink the water or eat contaminated fish.

Dow Chemical has been a major producer of chlorine. Its scientists have actively studied many of the issues surrounding chlorine, including the effects of dioxin exposure. Some Dow researchers have argued that the public does not fully understand the facts about chlorine and dioxin. Environmental activists have focused on the many risks presented to humans, livestock, and crops by chemical exposures. This has produced a public fear of chemicals, or *chemophobia,* as industry spokespersons call it. The result has been many new laws, public pressures, and scientific research to better understand the truth about risks. So intense is public concern that industry officials feel the entire future of the industry is at stake when government acts.

The challenge of public concern has grown more complex as scientific evidence has mounted about the effect of industrial emissions on the warming of the earth's atmosphere. This condition, known as *global warming,* can only be addressed by limiting the amount and type of industrial gases emitted into the atmosphere. For industries such as chemical manufacturing, the implications are staggering. To make the situation more complicated, action to address global warming almost certainly requires the cooperation of national governments from many of the world's largest and most-polluting countries.

These issues present Dow Chemical's managers with a huge strategic challenge. There is no way to avoid the public policy debates surrounding chemicals and their risks. Emerging global issues such as atmospheric warming are certain to involve new government deliberations and proposals. And the chemical industry, its operations, and its products are sure to be at the center of these debates.

Dow's senior management decided to take a high-profile approach to the challenge. Its 1990 annual report published an unusual message: *"One issue more than any other will affect our company's prospects in the 1990s and beyond. That issue is the environment."* Every Dow investor and employee and most of the company's customers saw the report. The company took other actions as well: It appointed David Buzzeli, president of Dow Canada, the Canadian subsidiary, vice president and corporate director of environment, health, and safety for Dow's worldwide businesses; it also launched an aggressive effort to improve its environmental performance; and it began to shape a political issues management program with extensive employee participation, became involved in industry associations, created a strong presence in Washington, and strengthened its commitment to actively participate in the public policy process.

This chapter focuses on managing government relations and political issues. Business firms do not have an absolute right to exist and pursue profits. The right to conduct commerce and make profits depends on compliance with appropriate laws and public policy. As discussed in Chapter 8, public policy is shaped by many factors and influences. Public issues, such as dioxin risk, chlorine exposure, and global warming force companies to monitor public concerns, respond to government proposals, and participate in the political process. This chapter discusses, therefore, how managers and their businesses can meet the challenge of managing business–government relations.

Strategic Management of Government Relations

There is a serious debate between those who favor and those who oppose business involvement in government. This debate involves the question of whether, and to what extent, business should legitimately participate in the political process. As shown in Figure 9–1, some people believe business should stay out of politics, whereas others argue that business must be involved.

Figure 9–1

The case for and against political involvement by business.

Reasons business *should* be involved

- A pluralistic system invites many participants
- Economic stakes are high
- Business counterbalances other social interests
- Business is a vital stakeholder of government

Reasons business *should not* be involved

- Executives are not qualified
- Business is naive about politics
- Business is too big, too powerful
- Business risks its credibility in partisan politics

Business and politics are increasingly entwined in the modern world in ways that make it impossible for managers to ignore what is going on in political life. Gradually, business leaders have come to recognize that the survival and prosperity of their businesses are connected to political decisions. Although this trend is clear and visible in all nations, critics worry about the amount of influence corporations can wield on specific governmental decisions.[1] The dilemma for managers is quite clear: *How can a company participate in the political process on issues that matter to it and to its industry but do so in ways that are consistent with the ethical norms and standards of the society that grants business its legitimacy?*

Techniques of Political Action

The techniques used by businesses to participate in governmental politics are similar to those of other interest groups. Three techniques are widely used: direct representation, trade associations, and ad hoc coalitions.

Direct Representation

Many large corporations, such as Dow Chemical, place full-time representatives and staff in Washington, D.C. (or the national capital in other countries) to keep abreast of developments that may affect the company and to communicate with government officials. This enables the company's Washington office staff to directly represent the business before the people and agencies involved in determining legislative and regulatory activity. **Lobbying** is the process of communicating with and trying to persuade others to support an organization's interest or stake as they consider a particular law, policy, or regulation. Company lobbyists may be active in city halls and state capitals as well.

Trade Associations

Many companies also join *trade associations* such as the National Realtors Association (real estate brokers), National Federation of Independent Businesses (small businesses), the National Association of Manufacturers (manufacturers only), or the U.S. Chamber of Commerce (broad, diverse membership), where they count on strength of numbers and a centralized staff to promote their interests with government officials.[2]

> *The U.S. Chamber of Commerce has a membership of 200,000 companies. The Chamber has a multimillion-dollar budget, publishes a widely circulated magazine, and operates a satellite television network to broadcast its political messages. The Chamber takes positions on a wide range of political, economic, and regulatory questions and actively works to promote its members' views of what conditions are necessary for them to compete successfully in a free marketplace.*

Ad Hoc Coalitions

A third commonly used technique involves the creation of *ad hoc coalitions*. Ad hoc coalitions are used to bring diverse business groups together to lobby for or against particular

---

[1]The classic discussion of corporate political action is Edwin Epstein, *The Corporation in American Politics* (Englewood Cliffs, NJ: Prentice Hall, 1969).
[2]Patricia C. Kelley, "Factors That Influence the Development of Trade Associations' Political Behavior," in J. E. Post, ed., *Research in Corporate Social Performance and Policy,* vol. 12 (Greenwich, CT: JAI Press, 1994), pp. 63–142.

legislation or regulation. Businesses will sometimes find themselves working with competitors, companies from other industries, and nonbusiness organizations that share a concern about specific laws, regulations, tax proposals, or other issues. Politics can create unusual alliances and curious conflicts, as the following example illustrates.

> *Several years ago, the U.S. Congress was asked to consider passing a law that would extend daylight saving time. Daylight saving involves setting clocks forward (or backward) in specific areas of the country to lengthen the amount of daylight hours for residents in that area of the country. The original daylight saving time change occurred during World War II as a way of adjusting Americans' daytime activities to conform with maximum amount of daylight. This would help conserve fuel for winter heating and electricity consumption. Over the intervening years, adjustments have been made from time to time by the Congress in response to specific needs. The proposal to lengthen the period of daylight saving came from California, where proponents sought to change the fall-back date from late October to a date in November. Among the proponents were two conflicting businesses, the barbecue grill industry and candy manufacturers. The barbecue industry felt an extra few weeks of daylight saving would help boost the sale of grills, charcoal, and utensils. The candy industry had a different view: If daylight saving was extended past Halloween, candy sales would decline as fewer children went out trick or treating.*

The legislative battle eventually drew in police departments, child welfare agencies, television stations, and many other advocates of one or another position. Advocates and opponents of various proposals rearranged themselves many times as different proposals were discussed. In the end, no action was taken because coalitions effectively blocked every proposal.

Political Involvement

Business executives must decide on the appropriate level of political involvement for their company. As shown in Figure 9–2, there are multiple levels of involvement and many ways to participate. To be successful, a business must think strategically about objectives and how specific political issues and opportunities relate to those objectives.

> *A software company that designs and manufacturers products for use in computer systems around the world has a long-term strategic interest in strong copyright laws and other intellectual property protection (IPP) to prevent piracy of ideas and products. The time to start lobbying for such laws is not when the company's hot new product is introduced—that is much too late. Years in advance, the company must be working with others in the political process to secure the intellectual property laws that will protect future generations of ideas and products from piracy. It may need strong domestic laws to protect it at home and the commitment of its government to negotiate and enforce IPP agreements with foreign governments.*

Strategic interests may be indirect as well as direct. Many businesses have sought to persuade state, local, and national governments to improve public education. Some do

Figure 9–2

Levels of business
political involvement.

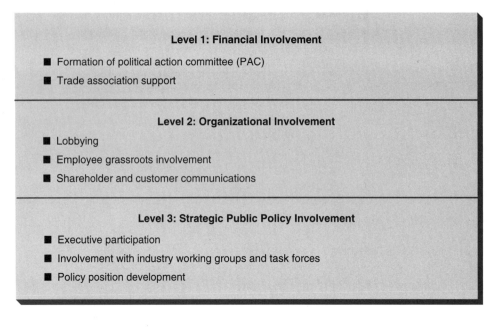

Level 1: Financial Involvement

- Formation of political action committee (PAC)
- Trade association support

Level 2: Organizational Involvement

- Lobbying
- Employee grassroots involvement
- Shareholder and customer communications

Level 3: Strategic Public Policy Involvement

- Executive participation
- Involvement with industry working groups and task forces
- Policy position development

so out of the belief that it is immoral for students to leave schools without the skills needed to get jobs and survive in the modern economy. Others have a longer-term and more self-interested point of view: Future workers who do not have sound education will create a shortage of critical skills and, hence, a problem for the companies that will want those skills in their own employees.

Managing the Political Agenda

Political life reflects the larger trends and complexities of modern society. The political process is an *arena* in which substance and symbols are often intertwined. Since the 1960s, scholars such as E. E. Schattschneider and Murray Edelman have seen political issues as a dynamic conflict.[3] This view places the *conflict process* at the center of analysis rather than individuals, leaders, agencies, institutions (e.g., Congress), or political parties. As Roger Cobb and Marc Howard Ross, two current advocates of the view, argue,

> *Most of politics revolves around the development and expansion of conflict surrounding evolving political issues. People with grievances need to gain the attention of additional individuals and do this by redefining their most intense concerns to draw others into the battle. A growing maelstrom of concern could catapult an issue to the top of the political heap.*[4]

Cobb and Ross focus on events that are expected to occur, but which do not. Why does this happen? How does it happen? Their book looks at a series of situations in seven areas, including federal regulatory agencies (e.g., Securities and Exchange Commission,

[3]E. E. Schattschneider, *The Semi-Sovereign People: A Realist's Guide to Democracy in America* (New York: Holt, 1960); and Murray Edelman, *The Symbolic Uses of Politics* (Urbana, IL: University of Illinois Press, 1964).

[4]Roger Cobb and Marc Howard Ross, eds., *Cultural Strategies of Agenda Denial: Avoidance, Attack, and Redefinition* (Lawrence, KS: University Press of Kansas, 1997) p. ix.

Food and Drug Administration), and such public health issues as the national health insurance debates of both the 1940s and 1990s. They write,

> *In a variation on Edelman's view that politics is about the distribution of tangible and symbolic benefits, we suggest that agenda conflicts are about both the concrete decision whether government will or will not consider a particular issue and the competing interpretations of political issues to which people attach great emotional significance. Politics, from this point of view, not only determines who gets what, when, and how but also provides a forum for choosing among competing views concerning how we should live, what government ought to do, how we relate to the environment, and who the enemies are.*[5]

Such ideas are the foundation on which much of the current thinking about corporate political action is based.

Corporate Political Strategy

Business has a complex relationship with society. One of government's roles is to mediate the interests of many diverse people, organizations, and interests in society. John Mahon and Richard McGowan have drawn this relationship as a triangle of interests as shown in Figure 9–3. Business must participate in politics, according to Mahon and McGowan, because there are too many issues of too great an importance to a business that govern-

Figure 9–3

The Triangle of Business–Government–Society Relationships.

Source: John F. Mahon and Richard A. McGowan, *Industry as a Player in The Political and Social Arena* (Westport, CT: Quorum, 1996), p. 29. Used with permission.

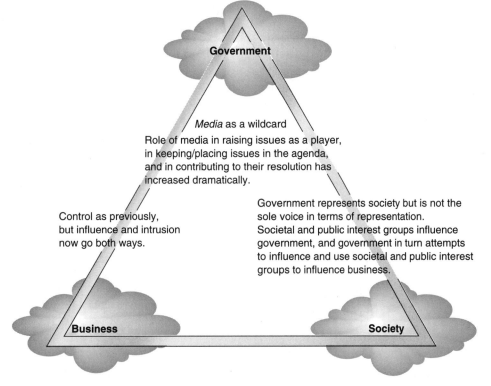

Government

Media as a wildcard
Role of media in raising issues as a player, in keeping/placing issues in the agenda, and in contributing to their resolution has increased dramatically.

Control as previously, but influence and intrusion now go both ways.

Government represents society but is not the sole voice in terms of representation. Societal and public interest groups influence government, and government in turn attempts to influence and use societal and public interest groups to influence business.

Business

Society

[5]Ibid., p. 29.

Figure 9-4

Motorola's public policy agenda.

Source: Author's archival research and articles published in *The Wall Street Journal, Business Week,* and other business media, 1995–1998.

	Example
Product level (Motorola business unit only)	Standards for cellular telephones
Business unit level (Motorola corporate level)	Foreign competitors' dumping practices
Industry level (Motorola and competitors)	Encryption standards/regulations
Multi-industry level (Motorola and noncompetitors)	
■ Specific proposals	U.S. trade policy (e.g., sanctions); tying China's MFN trade designation to its human rights record
■ General proposals	Free trade policies (GATT, NAFTA); government macroeconomic policies

ment must and will act upon. Without a corporate political strategy, the company's interests can not be adequately represented and protected.[6]

What is corporate political strategy? Mahon and McGowan define **corporate political strategy** as "those activities taken by organizations to acquire, develop, and use power to obtain an advantage (a particular allocation of resources or no change in the allocation) in a situation of conflict."[7] This definition assumes that the many interests in a society will produce conflict about what to do and how to do it. Whether the issue is as broad as global warming or as specific as the risk posed by dioxin in a particular neighborhood, government is the place where such conflicts are resolved. A corporate political strategy is an approach to such relationships in a way that will enable the company to acquire power, use it, and obtain an advantage from it whenever such conflicts affect the firm or its business activities.

The importance of a corporate political strategy can be understood by looking more closely at the public policy agenda of one large and reasonably typical company. The variety of issues around which Motorola, a manufacturer of electronic equipment and related products, has actual or potential conflicts with others in society is shown in Figure 9-4. Notice that the company has a clear and vital *business* interest in a wide range of political issues. Some are quite specific, involving an individual product (e.g., cellular telephones); others are quite broad, such as the opening of foreign markets to American electronic products. Motorola or companies like it are likely to be engaged in trying to influence what government does in such areas because of their stake in the outcome. They are, in other words, *stakeholders* of the public policy process and the political system.

American Politics at the Turn of a New Century

American business and American government have alternated between conflict and cooperation throughout most of the nation's history. In the colonial era, businesses were oppressed by high taxes and supported independence from England. During the twentieth century, business has often had periods of intense conflict with government. Since the 1930s, the federal government has been an activist in efforts to guide the economy

[6]John F. Mahon and Richard McGowan, *Industry as a Player in the Political and Social Arena* (Westport, CT: Quorum Press, 1996).
[7]Ibid., p. 29.

toward growth, full employment, and social well-being. Activist government emerged during the Great Depression, when most people agreed that government should do all that it could to restore economic prosperity. But 50 years of activist government produced a powerful backlash by the 1980s, when President Reagan argued "government is the problem, not the solution" to America's needs. During the 1980s and 1990s, efforts were made to shrink the size of government, narrow its focus, and limit its activities. Still, with the passage of time, people have tended to rethink old ideas of how government and business should relate to one another. Business leaders agree that there is a need for strong and effective government to do certain things in a modern society. And government leaders recognize the need for a strong and efficient business sector. Still, the debate about precisely where to draw the lines between business and government is underway as we move into a new century.

Many Americans believe that the nation's economic and social problems require government to set the course and create the framework for prosperity. But many others believe that high taxes deprive them of income necessary to make private choices while feeding a big government that is frequently out of touch with its citizens. **Political cynicism** refers to a social climate of distrust about politics and politicians. America suffered from serious political cynicism in the 1990s. Voters have been angry with a system that seemed unable to deliver on its promises. Voter turnout has been low in most elections, and even presidential races barely drew 50 percent of registered voters in most states. Candidates for political office often used negative campaigning, in which one candidate attacks the positions and personal qualities (e.g., truthfulness) of his or her opponent.[8] Attack ads have been used to damage the image of opponents because the public responds to them; political advertising has become a highly specialized world of polling, focus groups, and audience responses. As a result, public respect for politicians is declining. The public has come to distrust long-serving incumbents, media-slick new candidates who advocate change, and political campaigns in general. Such negative attitudes ultimately affect how public policy is made and what ideas become law.

There is a long-standing debate among political experts about how politics and public policy interrelate. Marxists believe that those who control the economic system also will find ways to control the political system. Pluralists, on the other hand, think that many different interests compete for influence in the political system. Still others believe that the bureaucracy of government itself dominates the political system and that other interests are secondary to the influence of civil servants and career bureaucrats.[9] A fourth view holds that a social elite, which includes business leaders and others, makes key decisions without much regard to popular wishes. The American political scene at the turn of a new century seems to offer some evidence, and some counterevidence, for each of these views. The United States remains a mostly pluralistic political system. Interest groups abound and they have a powerful effect on political life. Because there are so many different interests in modern America, coalitions have to be formed to advance certain ideas, specific legislation, or regulations.

According to some experts, all areas of modern political life reflect coalition politics, which means that no special interest is ever powerful enough, by itself, to determine

---

[8]See, for example, Tim Curran, "Late, Outside Money Begins to Flow through Independent Expenditures," *Roll Call* 40, no. 30 (October 24, 1994), pp. 1, 12.

[9]Kevin Phillips, *Arrogant Capital: Washington, Wall Street, and the Frustration of American Politics* (Boston: Little, Brown & Company, 1994). See also Jeffrey Birnbaum, *The Lobbyists: How Influence Peddlers Get Their Way in Washington* (New York: Random House/Times Books, 1992).

how an issue should be resolved.[10] Other experts argue that coalitions are formed so rapidly and with such resources as to create a type of political gridlock in which action cannot occur. Still others disagree, citing the extent to which a few special interests—especially Wall Street and Washington insiders (named the Beltway Bandits because they tend to be located within the road that circles the nation's capital)—dominate the political agenda.[11]

Political parties are a vital part of a pluralistic society, representing grand coalitions of individuals and interest groups seeking to promote their own welfare through political action. Although political parties are not mentioned in the U.S. Constitution, they have long been an important part of the system of representative government. Not only do they make the electoral process possible by providing a means for proposing candidates for public office, they serve as a rallying point for individuals and groups to work with others who hold similar ideas about how to run the government.[12]

However, political parties have steadily lost their power to hold together diverse political interests and to keep government running. Third-party presidential campaigns in 1980 (when John Anderson ran against Jimmy Carter and Ronald Reagan) and 1992 (when Ross Perot ran against George Bush and Bill Clinton) have symbolized the inability of the traditional political parties to speak for all voters at the federal level. Between 1992 and 1994, when the Democratic party still had majority control of the House of Representatives and the Senate, President Bill Clinton failed to achieve much of his legislative agenda because the some Democratic members would not vote with their leaders. Newt Gingrich, who became Republican Speaker of the House of Representatives in 1995, had some success holding his majority, but experts doubted that the unity would last. By 1998, the experts were proven correct. Political parties seem to command more loyalty at the state and local levels, although there is considerable variation, with large numbers of voters registered as independents and more candidates running outside conventional party designations.

Critical Problems

Business operates within a political system that is rife with conflicts, issues, and problems. Political scientists disagree whether the system has ever been more embattled, but at a time when other nations look to the United States as a democratic model, pressures are building for major reforms of the American system. As a participant in the political process, business has a large stake in ensuring that the system operates in a manner that is consistent with the ideals of democracy. Several central problems are discussed below.

Money and Campaign Financing

American politics is very expensive. Candidates for public office at every level of government—from local government officials to the president of the United States—are forced to spend money to get elected. Costs range from a few thousand dollars in local

---

[10]Haynes Johnson and David S. Broder, *The System: The American Way of Politics at the Breaking Point* (Boston: Little, Brown, 1996).

[11]Johnson and Broder, *The System;* and Phillips, *Arrogant Capital.*

[12]Johnson and Broder, *The System.* The authors document the failed efforts of the Clinton administration to create a national health insurance plan. The roles of political parties, pressure groups, and coalitions is told in an interesting and lively style. For a historical view of political parties, see Arthur M. Schlesinger, Jr., *The Cycles of American History* (Boston: Houghton Mifflin, 1986).

elections to tens of millions of dollars for high federal government positions. More than $20 billion was spent by candidates trying to get elected at every level of government in 1994; in 1996, spending in federal campaigns grew by 33 percent over 1992 spending. It is estimated that political spending on campaigns will continue to rise and probably pass the $40 billion level by the year 2000.[13]

This dependence on money for campaigns forces candidates to raise funds from potential donors. Many elected officials, such as representatives to Congress, face campaigns every two years and begin campaigning for their next term of office on virtually the day they start their current term. This has been called the problem of the **perpetual political campaign.** At the heart of this problem is the need of candidates to raise funds (Discussion case on page 216).

Business is involved in campaign financing in several ways. Direct contributions by corporations to political candidates for federal offices are forbidden by federal law; some, but not all, states also place restrictions on corporate contributions to candidates in state elections. Since the mid-1970s, companies have been permitted to spend company funds to organize and administer **political action committees (PACs).** PACs are independently incorporated organizations that can solicit contributions from stockholders and employees and then channel the funds to those seeking political office. Companies that have organized PACs are not permitted to donate corporate funds to the PAC or to any political candidate; all donations to company-organized PACs must come from individuals. Labor union and other interest group PACs also raise money and support candidates.

As Figure 9–5 shows, PACs have proved to be very popular with business as well as with other groups. Corporate PACs are the most numerous, accounting for over 40 per-

Figure 9–5

Profile of political action committees (PACs), 1975–1994.

Source: Federal Election Commission. Reported in *Almanac of Federal PACs, 1996–97* (Washington, D.C.: Congressional Research Service, 1997), pp. 427–43.

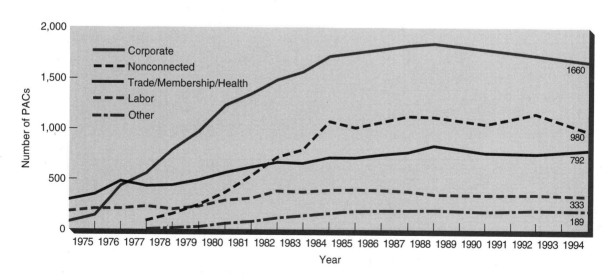

[13]Based on data reported in *The National Journal* in 1992, 1994, and 1997. See also the Web site of the Federal Election Commission, http://www.fec.gov.

cent of nearly 4,000 PACs, and are among the biggest money raisers and spenders. But as illustrated in Figure 9–6, trade and membership organizations (e.g., National Rifle Association, American Medical Association), labor groups, and nonconnected organizations (e.g., National Association of Realtors) also ranked high in money raised and spent. Labor unions are among the biggest contributors, although as a whole they represent less than 10 percent of all PACs. Interestingly, the number of PACs seems to have peaked in the late 1980s, although the amount of money raised continued to reach new heights throughout the 1990s. By 1997, a crescendo of criticism produced congressional investigations of the entire campaign finance system.[14]

The Federal Election Commission has established rules to regulate PAC activities. For example, PACs are not allowed to give more than $5,000 to a single candidate for each election, although the winner of a primary election may be given another $5,000 for the general election. These limits were imposed on all PACs to reduce the role of concentrated wealth in determining the outcome of elections to public office. One consequence is that candidates and donors constantly seek new ways to get around the rules.

For example, many wealthy donors are looking for loopholes that will allow them to spend money to support candidates they favor. One popular method has been the payment of **soft money.** Soft money refers to funds donated directly to political parties to support party-building activities such as televised campaign commercials that do not support a specific candidate, get-out-the-vote drives, and other activities in conjunction with presidential and congressional races. In contrast to the hard money that is closely regulated by FEC rules, contributors are allowed to make donations of unlimited amount to political parties for party-building activities. In the 1996 presidential election, both

Figure 9–6

Financial activity of political action commitees (PACs).

Source: Federal Election Commission. Reported in *Almanac of Federal PACs,* 1996–97 (Washington, D.C.: Congressional Research Service, 1997), pp. 427–43.

	1993–4 *n*	Money Spent On		Money Donated To	
		Senate Races	House Races	Democratic Candidates	Republican Candidates
All PACs	3,954	$54.1 million	$136.2 million	$117.6 million	$71.4 million
Corporate PACs	1,660	24.2	45.2	34.0	35.4
Labor	333	7.7	34.0	39.9	1.7
Trade/ membership/ health organizations	792	12.9	39.9	28.3	24.4
Non-connected	980	6.1	11.9	10.8	7.2
Other	189	2.0	5.0	4.5	2.6

Note: Numbers have been rounded.

[14]*1996 Almanac of Federal PACs, 1996–97* (Washington, D.C.: Congressional Research Service, 1997), pp. 427–43.

the Democratic and Republican parties ran ads featuring their candidates (Clinton and Dole) and stressing the "vote Democrat or Republican" theme. These qualified as party-building activities even though they indirectly boosted political candidates. In 1996, soft money contributions to the two major political parties exceeded $260 million, up more than 200 percent from the $86 million raised in the 1992 presidential race.[15]

One consequence of this money game is the candidacy of extremely wealthy individuals (e.g., presidential candidates Steve Forbes and Ross Perot, and Michael Huffington, who spent more than $100 million in a failed bid to become U.S. Senator from California). Personal fortunes can be used without restriction in support of their political campaigns as long as a candidate refuses to accept public campaign funds.

Lobbying and the Power of Special Interests

For 50 years, since the end of World War II, the U.S. federal government has been the focus of both social policy and economic management of the national economy. One consequence is tremendous growth in the number of special interests that are connected to the many decisions made by government. Most important, these interests—groups as diverse as gun owners represented by the National Rifle Association, business interests represented by trade associations such as the National Association of Manufacturers, and poor and needy children represented by the Children's Defense Fund—have learned to use the tools of political influence. They are insiders in the high stakes game of public policy making.

Business firms and other interests use many tools to directly influence the development of public policy. Most involve efforts to transmit information, express a point of view, or communicate a message to an official or regulator.[16] Lobbying involves direct contact with a government official to influence the thinking or actions of that person on an issue or public policy. It is usually done through face-to-face contact, sometimes in lengthy discussions or in meetings that may last only minutes. **Grassroots programs** are organized efforts to get voters to influence government officials to vote or act in a favorable way. Many companies have asked their shareholders to participate in grassroots efforts to persuade their congressional representatives to reduce capital gains taxes and thereby make stock purchases and other investments more lucrative. These programs send strong messages to elected officials that the desired action is supported by voters.

Direct forms of political action also include letter-writing, fax, telegram, telephone, and Internet campaigns to register approval or disapproval of a government official's position on an important issue. Businesses often invite government officials to make visits to local plant facilities, give speeches to employees, attend awards ceremonies, and participate in activities that will improve that official's understanding of management and employee concerns. These activities help to humanize the distant relationship that can

[15]This theme runs throughout the 1990s. See, for example, Michael Oreskes, "The Trouble with Politics," *New York Times,* March 18, 1990, p. 11; "GOP 'Soft Money' Topped $16 Million in Two Months," *The Wall Street Journal,* January 11, 1995, p. A6; and "Campaign Finance Scandals Unfold," *New York Times,* January 24, 1998, pp. A1ff.

[16]John Mahon, "Shaping Issues/Manufacturing Agents: Corporate Political Sculpting," and Kathleen Getz, "Selecting Corporate Political Tactics," both in Barry M. Mitnick, ed., *Corporate Political Agency: The Construction of Competition in Public Affairs* (Newbury Park, CA: Sage, 1993). See also Robert L. Heath and Richard Alan Nelson, *Issues Management: Corporate Public Policymaking in an Information Society,* 2d ed. (Beverly Hills, CA: Sage, 1997).

LIVERPOOL JOHN MOORES UNIVERSITY
Aldham Roberts L.R.C.

otherwise develop between government officials and the public. Democracy requires citizen access and communication with political leaders. In the United States, with 260 million individuals and millions of businesses, the challenge of maintaining open, balanced communications between officials and the public is complicated and very expensive.

Role of the Media

The 1990s produced an explosion of new media outlets, including television and radio talk shows, public affairs programming (e.g., C-Span), including live coverage of congressional debates, and Internet services. Cable television stations often provide live coverage of hearings, debates, and votes. Critics claim that the growth of these media outlets has resulted in more attention to personalities of government officials than to the content of their ideas. This may be an exaggeration, but there is no doubt that media is very influential in shaping public opinion. Consider, for example, these media stars of the late 1990s.

> *Ted Koppel is the founding host of the popular ABC network late night program, "Nightline." Since the late 1970s, this program has focused on the major news stories of each day, often bringing together opponents on major political issues. Koppel's interviewing is direct and challenging, featuring a form of traditional journalism.*
>
> *Larry King became a media star by broadcasting his talk show from Washington, DC, five nights a week on Cable News Network (CNN). An aggressive style has won him a loyal following of viewers who expect tough questions and clever talk. King's own positions are not disguised, and he has become a voice that sometimes advocates as well as reports.*
>
> *Rush Limbaugh, whose radio and television personality leave no doubt about his biases, prejudices, and points of view, doesn't even try to be balanced in his role as a conservative spokesperson. Articulate and persuasive, Limbaugh became one of the most powerful media voices in the new politics of the 1990s. When the Clinton administration's national health-care proposals were being debated, for example, Limbaugh staged a vigorous assault against President and Mrs. Clinton. Supporters credit Limbaugh as an influential force that helped Republicans win control of the House of Representatives and Senate in the 1994 elections.*
>
> *Matt Druge created an Internet service called the Druge Report. It became a familiar and well-known name in January 1998 when it broke the story about President Clinton's alleged involvement with Monica Lewinsky. The Web site carried the news that* Newsweek *magazine had suppressed the story of the alleged affair at the request of independent prosecutor Kenneth Starr. Druge changed news events by outing a story that other news organizations refrained from publishing or broadcasting. Once the story was out, however, other news organizations raced to publish their stories.*

People's tastes vary, and different segments of the television viewing audience—that is, the public—favor each of these stars and their programs. These media stars have a powerful effect on how Americans understand the public policy issues facing government and make decisions about whom to believe and whom to trust. Defenders of the media claim this is precisely what democracy was envisioned to be, a contest among a multitude of views and opinions. To these analysts, the solution is to present even more views in more ways. They consider 500-channel cable television stations, interactive media, the Internet, and a public that is more involved in talk-show democracy as positive developments. In California, a Democracy Network was created as a multimedia, on-line service for voters who wanted to compare the views, finances, and positions of the candidates for governorship.[17]

Critics point to excesses and poor taste as reasons to place restraints or limitations on the way media treat political issues. Many nations limit the media's freedom to report on political issues and the political process. But the U.S. Constitution protects citizens' freedom of speech and freedom of the press. Courts, including the U.S. Supreme Court, have interpreted these constitutional rights in ways that minimize what can be done to control the content of media programs, although it seems certain that the Constitution's drafters never foresaw television, the Internet, or the information superhighway. Excesses are unlikely to stop unless the public changes its listening and viewing habits.

Transparency of the Political Process

Transparency refers to the degree of openness or visibility of a government's decision-making processes. The openness of America's political system is one of its strengths: It creates opportunities for people to closely observe what decisions are being made and in what way. "Washington is a giant fishbowl," according to one veteran lobbyist, and the result is too much accountability, not too little. As another lobbyist said, "These representatives can't blow their noses without having to answer to someone."[18] Some scholars argue that government officials are agents acting on behalf of people who elected or appointed them (the principals). This view, called **corporate political agency theory,** holds that conditions that enable citizens to observe how elected officials behave will promote action that serves those that put them in office.[19]

Another view is that although elected officials are sent to office to represent their constituents, they are also sent to act in the broad public interest. Sometimes elected officials have to look beyond the interests of voters in their districts and take action—such as approval of new taxes—that will be unpopular but are in the broad public interest. The problem in the current political climate, according to this view, is that officials are unwilling to do so when this occurs in the glaring spotlight of attention to each vote, issue, and constituency. "Vote against your constituents on an important issue," said one 20-year veteran of the House of Representatives, "and you will pay the price of never being able to vote against them again!"[20]

One remedy is to have more closed-door sessions in which votes can be taken without being recorded or reported.[21] However, such a view feeds the mood of public distrust:

---

[17]Virtually every congressional office was on-line by 1998; most congressmen also have Web pages that describe the officeholder's positions on key legislative issues.

[18]Author's interviews during the national health-care debate, Washington, D.C., July 1994. See also Johnson and Broder, *The System.*

[19]Mitnick, *Corporate Political Agency.*

[20]Author's interview, see note 18.

[21]Katharine Q. Seelye, "Americans Take a Dim View of the Government, Survey Finds," *New York Times,* March 10, 1998, p. A15; and, "More Power to Speaker," *Roll Call,* October 24, 1994, p. 4.

Legislators might do in private what they dare not do in public. It is doubtful that this approach will solve problems of transparency without adding to public cynicism. When Republicans took power in Congress after the 1994 elections, the new leaders of the Senate and House of Representatives promised to open the process. They soon discovered the need to work behind closed doors to get things done.

Incumbents and Appointed Officials

Public disgust with politics is often fueled by the people involved. Incumbent politicians and officials who seem to be appointed for life sometimes act in crude, arrogant, and self-serving ways designed to perpetuate power.[22] This may include doing favors for constituents, directing public works money to local communities, and acting on behalf of local companies caught in regulatory snarls and problems. The greater the seniority of elected officials, the more likely they are to exercise real power in government affairs. This makes them targets of political influence, which, in turn, helps them as fund-raisers and facilitates their reelection and continuation in positions of power.

Experts have offered a number of proposals to minimize abuses of power. One of the most popular ideas is **term limits,** which would permit elected officials to serve for a maximum number of years. This would weaken the power of long-serving members of Congress, for example, some of whom have served for more than 35 years. It would open committee assignments, create opportunities for new members, and still provide a broad base of experience in the legislature. Opponents argue that term limits will deprive voters and communities of electoral choice and the benefits of experience, including the knowledge, contacts, and credibility that are won with experience.

Although there are signs that voters are dissatisfied with the political system, there are contradictions in public attitudes. Voters often reelect officials for many terms, despite campaigns that focus on the virtues of change. Business faces such dilemmas too. Many business leaders favor term limits in principle, but then seek the favor of elected officials and provide campaign support to reelection campaigns. Why? The concept of limited terms may seem attractive, but businesses, like other special interests, recognize that incumbents can be very helpful in meeting their needs and solving their problems. This is one reason that PAC spending so often favors incumbents rather than challengers.

Referendum Politics

The complexity of government decision-making processes can frustrate efforts to transform a popular idea into law. Government committees, procedures, and compromises often stop, delay, or deflect proposals that seem to have broad public support. To counter these bureaucratic obstacles, advocates of change sometimes use a **public referendum,** or popular vote, to force a public ballot on a particular issue.

Many states have adopted laws permitting citizens' initiatives to be placed on the ballot of a general election. The initiative process usually requires that a number of citizens (usually 1 to 5 percent of registered voters) sign a petition asking that the initiative resolution or question be placed on the ballot. If the resolution is adopted by a majority of voters, the legislature is obligated to turn the resolution into law.

---

[22]Birnbaum, *The Lobbyists.* See also Johnson and Broder, *The System.*

California has produced many public referenda, including landmark proposals dealing with taxes, discrimination, affirmative action, and immigration. In 1996, for example, voters adopted Proposition 209, which banned affirmative action in state hiring and public university admissions in California. These proposals often led the way for national political movements. One scholar who studied all of the initiatives placed on California's ballot from 1976 to 1988 concluded that it is one of the most important policy arenas in that state.[23] In 1988 alone, for example, Californians faced 18 ballot questions in their general election. Californians have used the citizens' initiative process to establish tax limits on property taxes (Proposition 3) in the early 1980s, environmental protections and warnings (the Big Green Proposition) in the 1990s, and restrictions on education and welfare benefits for the state's large population of illegal immigrants (Proposition 187 in 1994). Each initiative generated hot political debate, but gained broad support by tapping into public concerns in California and other states.

Research shows that the initiatives often propose actions that business interests oppose. A 1992 California ballot initiative sought to change the pricing of automobile insurance rates. Industry claimed it would be badly hurt by such a law and vigorously opposed the proposition. In Massachusetts, a 1994 ballot proposition launched by a tax reform coalition sought to change the state's 5.95 percent flat tax on earned income into a graduated tax that would set higher rates for higher levels of income. The governor, a former U.S. senator, and business leaders opposed it, saying it was poisonous to impose such taxes on small businesses that are the source of new jobs.[24]

Politics is the art of the possible. It involves working together, compromising in order that everyone's interests are taken into account and recognizing that no interest can win—or should win—all the time. Referendum politics appeals to people frustrated at losing in the political process; it is a way of fighting the system.

Citizens' initiatives are expensive to launch and sustain, however. Tom Thomas, who studied California's initiative history, concluded that campaign spending affected voting results in the California initiative process, especially in cases where nonbusiness groups sought to impose new regulations or costs on business. By heavily outspending proponents of the initiative, business was often successful in defeating ballot initiatives.

Responsible Business Politics in a Global World

Political action by business—whether to influence government policy or the outcome of elections—is natural in a democratic, pluralistic society. In the United States, business has a legitimate right to participate in the political process, just as consumers, labor unions, environmentalists, and others do. The rules differ in other nations where restrictions may affect business political activities. Exhibit 9–A shows that lobbying is extensive in the European Union.

This is not true in Japan, however. American companies have not had a high political profile in Japan. Japanese companies long ago learned how to organize special interests, employ lobbyists, and leverage high-level contacts into coherent and successful political strategies in Washington. U.S. companies did not even have a significant trade

[23]Tom Thomas, "Campaign Spending and Corporate Involvement in the California Initiative Process, 1976–1988," in J. E. Post, ed., *Research in Corporate Social Performance and Policy,* vol. 12 (Greenwich, CT: JAI Press, 1991), pp. 37–61.

[24]Chris Reidy, "Grad Tax Foes Muster 'All-Star' Support," *Boston Globe,* October 25, 1994, pp. 39, 41.

**EXHIBIT
9–A**

Ten Thousand Lobbyists in Brussels

Lobbying is not just an American practice. Companies all around the world are learning new ways to connect with government officials. In short, whenever a government body controls a resource that business needs—permits, licenses, subsidies—or sets rules that affect what business can do, lobbying is bound to follow.

The European Union is composed of 15 nations that are integrated in economic and political ways. The European Commission is the legislative and administrative body for the EU and has its headquarters in Brussels. According to a 1994 study, there are more than 3,000 groups in Brussels employing more than 10,000 lobbyists to communicate with the commission's officers and staff.

The lobbyists speak for many interests. Nearly all big European corporations, trade groups, and labor unions have lobbyists; so too do Japanese trade associations and companies. American companies are represented by the U.S. Chamber of Commerce, and some companies also have their own lobbyists in Brussels. Because the European Commission is setting rules for the way competition will be conducted in Europe's big marketplace, the stakes are very high.

Lobbyists operate differently in Brussels than in the United States. They can, for example, provide technical help to commission bureaucrats and collaborate more openly with insiders. Learning to Euro-lobby effectively takes time, money, and people. By 1999, the number of lobbyists in Brussels is expected to grow to as many as 20,000.

Source: Based on Ronald Facchinetti, "Viewpoint: Why Brussels Has 10,000 Lobbyists," *New York Times,* August 21, 1994, sec. 3, p. 9.

association working on their behalf until late 1994 when the U.S. Chamber of Commerce organized meetings with Japanese party leaders and cabinet ministers, including Japan's prime minister. "This is an attempt to go directly to people at the political level who make policy," said a chamber official. American companies will not be making campaign contributions, however; the Foreign Corrupt Practices Act forbids U.S. companies from making donations to foreign politicians (see Chapter 7).

One danger arising from corporate political activity is that corporations may wield too much power. As businesses operate in different local communities and in different global communities, it is important that ethical norms and standards guide managers as they deal with political factors. If corporate power tips the scales against other interests in a society, both business and society may lose. This is also true of union power, religious power, consumer power, or any concentrated power that may exist in a democratic society.

Political reform spawns many proposals. Some involve absolute limitations on lobbying, political spending, and fund-raising by businesses. Others involve a system of public financing (total or matching funds) that would serve to level the campaign playing field. A number of political leaders have offered proposals to require television networks and stations to provide free time for candidates' advertising. As shown in Figure 9–7,

Figure 9–7

What other countries do to control money in politics.

Source: Michael Oreskes, "The Trouble with Politics: Running versus Governing," *New York Times*, March 21, 1990, pp. A1, A22.

	Public Financing	Limits on Fund Raising or Spending	Television
U.K.	No	Yes	Free time based on party's strength in previous election
France	Reimburse candidates based on votes received	Yes	Free and equal time to candidates
Japan	No	Yes	Candidates given some free time for speeches; no negative advertising
Germany	Reimbursement to parties according to votes received	No	Free time to candidates on public stations

other democratic nations utilize a combination of such ideas to reduce the impact of money on electoral politics. In Japan, for example, the U.S. Chamber of Commerce initiative is not expected to have immediate results because, as one analyst commented, "This isn't an American-lobbyist straightforward type of relationship. It isn't so easy to get fruits out of this kind of meeting."[25]

Whether in electoral politics or more traditional lobbying, business leaders must address the issues of how to manage relationships with government and special interests in society in ethically sound ways. Ultimately, business has an important long-term stake in a healthy, honest political system.

Summary Points of This Chapter

- Corporate political activity is focused on governmental policies and decision making and on electoral politics. Political action committees, lobbying, and grassroots programs are among the most popular types of corporate political activities.

- Businesses play a role in electoral politics by providing campaign funds and other forms of support to candidates. Firms take positions on campaign issues, lending support to ideas that support business interests and opposing ideas they believe are harmful.

- Strategic management of government relations involves understanding how a business's long-term economic and social interests are entwined with government policy and then acting to support that relationship.

[25]Michael Williams, "U.S. Business Lobby in Japan Launches First Campaign Aimed at Policy Makers," *The Wall Street Journal*, October 19, 1994, p. A17.

- Businesses need to be involved in public policy decision making for several reasons: They have a large stake in government actions and provide a voice that should be heard on many economic and social policy issues.

- Businesses have a stake in the critical issues facing the nation's political system. Campaign financing, the power of special interests, the media's role, incumbency, and referendum politics are among the issues prompting calls for political reform. The way managers conduct their companies' governmental relations will be influenced by changes in these areas.

Key Terms and Concepts Used in This Chapter

- Lobbying
- Corporate political strategy
- Political cynicism
- Perpetual political campaign
- Political action committees (PACs)
- Soft money

- Grassroots programs
- Transparency
- Corporate political agency theory
- Term limits
- Public referendum

Internet Resources

- http://www.fec.gov   Federal Election Commission
- http://www.allpolitics.com   CNN/Time Allpolitics news service
- http://www.cq.com   World Wide Washington Congressional Quarterly

- http://www.citizen.org/congress/ reform/cfr/public_speaking/facts.html   Campaign facts and financial information

Discussion Case   **Business, Politics, and Money**

The 1990s have been a decade of expensive and corrupting political campaigns. The cost of campaigning grew at an explosive rate, with average costs skyrocketing for virtually every local, state, and federal elected office. The high costs created several phenomena that now characterize unsavory campaign practices in American politics. These trends have significant implications for businesses that are often called on to contribute funds to candidates and political parties.

First, politicians now engage in continuous fund-raising. There was a time when fund-raising was done just before a scheduled election. Then, it was discovered that a large war chest of funds could dissuade challengers. Not surprisingly, incumbents now hold fund-raising events from the day they are elected. The rise in contributions by political action committees (see Figure 9–6) is accounted for, in part, by the shift to continuous fund-raising. A business lobbyist in Washington, DC, can literally attend fund-raising events every night of the year, with plenty of invitations left over. Many lobbyists now make two or three stops per evening, with their companies making contributions to the candidate hosting each event.

The high cost of campaigning has been driven by the rising cost of, and need for, media exposure. This has led many candidates to cheat on the election finance laws. The list of campaign finance violations is long and has tainted the presidencies of Ronald Reagan, George Bush, and Bill Clinton in recent years. President Clinton and Vice President Gore were investigated for various violations, including use of federal property for campaign fund-raising; solicitation of contributions on federal premises; solicitation of funds from foreign citizens; and selling nights at the White House, especially the Lincoln bedroom. Republican politicians repeatedly called on Attorney General Janet Reno to appoint an independent prosecutor to investigate these incidents.

The influence of foreign money was especially notable during the Clinton presidency. Testimony at Senate investigatory hearings—the Thompson Hearings, chaired by Senator Fred Thompson (R, TN)—showed that China, Indonesia, and other countries employed a variety of agents and intermediaries (individuals and companies) to funnel money to the Clinton reelection campaign. Democrats on the committee tried to counter the charges by showing that Republican fund-raisers, especially GOP chairman Haley Barbour, also courted foreign donations that would have been illegal. Both parties were forced to return some contributions to donors, leaving their party coffers with serious deficits.

To eliminate an estimated $10 million Democratic party debt, for example, President Clinton hit the road in 1997 and 1998 with a series of fund-raising events. Ironically, at many of these dinners, the president's speech included a call for campaign finance reform. Meanwhile, Congress was considering a major piece of reform legislation known as the McCain-Feingold bill. Despite the public call for reform, the bill was killed in committee, making it unlikely that any reform would occur before the presidential election in the year 2000.

Sources: Based on articles appearing in *New York Times, Washington Post,* and *The Wall Street Journal* from June 1997 to April 1998.

Discussion Questions

1. Who are the stakeholders in the campaign reform issue? What stake does a large company such as Boeing or Coca Cola have in campaign reform?
2. What are the arguments for and against a company establishing a political action committee? What benefits can a PAC produce for a company?
3. Assume you are the branch manager of a national retail store. Your local Congressman is holding a fund-raising dinner in two weeks, and you have just received an invitation. A contribution of $250 is requested. Would you go to the dinner? Would you contribute the $250? More? Less?

10

Antitrust, Mergers, and Global Competition

All socioeconomic systems face the problem of deciding how much power should be held by leading enterprises, whether they are privately owned or controlled by the state. In the United States, antitrust laws have long been used to curb corporate power, preserve competition, and achieve various social goals. As the economy has changed, however, new factors have raised policy issues concerning business competitiveness. These trends have presented public policymakers and corporate leaders with a need to reconcile corporate power, shareholders' interests, and social responsibility with new realities.

This chapter focuses on these key questions and objectives:

- What dilemma does corporate power present in a democratic society?
- What are the objectives of the antitrust laws, and how are they enforced?
- What are some recent key issues in antitrust policy?
- How have the mergers of the 1990s affected business-society relations?
- How has the rise of global competition affected the enforcement of antitrust policy?
- Why are intellectual property issues so important to competition policy?

W hen Staples, the office-supply superstore, announced its intention to acquire its competitor, Office Depot, in 1997 for $3.4 billion, it promised to create a huge chain of over a thousand stores nationwide. But just days after the announcement, the Federal Trade Commission (FTC) stepped in to block the proposed merger, saying it would lead to higher everyday prices for paper, pens, and pocket calculators. "In communities where Staples faces competition from Office Depot, prices are considerably lower than where it does not," commented an FTC official. Staples executives expressed disappointment, citing their long record of price discounting, and vowed to fight the government agency in court.

In 1993, a judge in Arkansas ruled that Wal-Mart, the largest chain of discount stores in the United States, had illegally sold merchandise below cost to drive its competitors out of business. Wal-Mart had been sued by three small drugstores, who argued that the discounter's predatory pricing had hurt their sales of everyday products like toothpaste, mouthwash, and nonprescription medicines. Predatory pricing is illegal in the United States under both federal and state antitrust laws. Wal-Mart's spokesperson called the decision anticonsumer, saying that it would result in higher prices. Others believed, however, that the decision would help consumers in the long run by preventing Wal-Mart from gaining a monopoly in local markets.

When Guardian Industries, a glassmaker based in Michigan, tried to sell its products in Japan, the company "ran into a wall of exclusionary business practices," one of their executives claimed. Guardian Industries went to the Justice Department, complaining that a group of leading Japanese glass companies had shut them out by threatening retaliation against allied firms that did business with the Americans—a charge the Japanese vigorously denied. U.S. regulators were uncertain how to proceed in this and other similar cases. Should the government bring suit against foreign companies that violated U.S. antitrust laws, hurting American exporters? Or should these issues better be addressed through trade negotiations?[1]

These examples of competitive conflicts—involving private businesses, the government, and the courts, in the United States and abroad—illustrate how anticompetitive practices can arise in the free market system. This chapter looks at how the United States and other countries have traditionally sought to preserve and enhance competition through antitrust and related policies. As business becomes increasingly global, as services outgrow manufacturing, and as research and development become more vital to industry, antitrust and other competition policies are being reexamined.

The Dilemma of Corporate Power

By almost any measure used, the world's largest business enterprises are impressively big, as shown in Figure 10–1. Size can be measured in several ways—by annual sales, profits, and shareholders' equity—and a company's rank will vary depending on the measurement used. As measured by sales, the big five in 1996 were General Motors and Ford (U.S. automakers), Mitsui and Mitsubishi (Japanese conglomerates), and Royal Dutch/Shell (a Dutch-

---

[1]"Office Depot, Staples Blocked in Merger Bid; Antitrust Showdown on Superstores Looms," *Washington Post,* March 11, 1997, p. A1; "Superstore Merger Stalled," *Washington Times,* March 11, 1997, p. B7; "Wal-Mart's Pricing on Drugstore Items Is Held to Be Illegal," *New York Times,* October 13, 1993, pp. A1, C5; "Wal-Mart Loses a Case on Pricing," *The Wall Street Journal,* October 13, 1993, pp. A3, A8; and "Commerce Cops: Can Justice Open Up Foreign Markets?" *Business Week,* December 13, 1993, pp. 69–70.

Figure 10–1

The ten largest
global corporations,
1996–1997.

Source: "The Business
Week Global 1,000,"
Business Week, July 7,
1997, pp. 52–92. Used
by permission.
Copyright © by
McGraw-Hill
Companies.

Note: Data for sales
and profits are for
1996 fiscal years. Data
for market value is as
of May 30, 1997.

Rank	By Sales (billions of U.S. $)	By Profits (billions of U.S. $)	By Market Value (billions of U.S. $)
1	General Motors 164.1	Royal Dutch/Shell 9.3	General Electric 198.1
2	Ford Motor 147.0	Exxon 7.5	Coca-Cola 169.0
3	Mitsui Corp. 135.5	General Electric 7.3	Royal Dutch/Shell 169.0
4	Mitsubishi Corp. 135.5	Philip Morris 6.3	NTT 151.6
5	Royal Dutch/Shell 134.3	General Motors 5.9	Microsoft 148.6
6	Itachi 131.0	IBM 5.9	Exxon 147.2
7	Maruberi 120.0	AT&T 5.6	Intel 124.1
8	Exxon 116.7	Intel 5.2	Toyota Motor 108.7
9	Sumitomi Corp 115.3	HSBC Holdings 5.1	Merck 108.5
10	Toyota Motor 105.0	Ford Motor 4.5	Philip Morris 106.6

British oil company). Two oil companies, Royal Dutch/Shell and Exxon, were the most profitable. General Electric and Coca-Cola, both U.S. consumer products firms, topped the world's firms in market value. The world's largest tobacco company, Philip Morris, placed in the top 10 in both profits and market value. Microsoft and Intel, both U.S.-based high-technology companies, placed in the top 10 as measured by shareholder's value.

These giant enterprises are not completely representative of business in the United States or other nations. The overwhelming majority of business firms are owned by individual proprietors or by small groups of partners. Only one of every five business firms in the United States is a corporation, and many of these corporations are small. The largest firms at the top of the business pyramid are the focus of so much attention because of their size, power, and influence, not because they represent the entire business community.

Neither size nor power alone is bad when it comes to corporate performance. A big company may have definite advantages over a small one. It can command more resources, often produce at a lower cost, plan further into the future, and weather business fluctuations somewhat better. Big companies make tougher competitors against foreign firms. Many communities have benefited from the social initiatives and influence of large firms.

The dilemma of **corporate power** concerns how business uses its influence, not whether it should have power in the first place. Most people want to know if business power is being used to affirm broad public-purpose goals, values, and principles considered to be important. If so, then corporate power is considered to be legitimate, and the public accepts large size as just another normal characteristic of modern business. On the other hand, when corporate power is misused—for example, to gain an unfair advantage over competitors—then public policy may be required to check abuses.[2]

U.S. antitrust laws, highly controversial and far from perfect, stand as a monument to our society's efforts to cope with the dilemma of corporate power. For more than a century, since the first federal antitrust law was enacted, U.S. public policy has sought to balance economic power with social control. As antitrust policy enters its second century, the new realities of global competition and global economic power are forcing a reexamination of how power and social control are best balanced. We examine those issues after outlining the goals of antitrust regulation and major U.S. antitrust federal laws.

Antitrust Regulation

Someone once remarked that antitrust is as American as apple pie. Certainly it is an article of faith deeply embedded in the minds of many people. U.S. **antitrust laws** originated in the late nineteenth century in the wake of some spectacular competitive abuses by leaders of big business and their companies. An aroused public feared the uncontrolled growth of big business. The first antitrust laws were passed in this climate of fear and mistrust of big business. Since those early years, other antitrust laws have been enacted, and the first laws have been amended. The result is a formidable tangle of laws, regulations, guidelines, and judicial interpretations that present business with a need to carefully manage relationships with competitors and government antitrust officials.

Objectives of Antitrust

Antitrust laws serve multiple goals. Some of these goals—such as preserving competition or protecting consumers against deceptive advertising—are primarily economic in character. As one authoritative source states, "The U.S. antitrust laws are the legal embodiment of our nation's commitment to a free market economy."[3] Other goals, though, are more concerned with social and philosophical matters, such as a desire to curb the power of large corporations or even a nostalgic wish to return to the old Jeffersonian ideal of a nation of small-scale farmers and businesses. The result is multiple, overlapping, changing, and sometimes contradictory goals.

The most important economic objectives of antitrust laws are the following:

First, *the protection and preservation of competition* is the central objective. This is done by outlawing monopolies, prohibiting unfair competition, and eliminating price discrimination and collusion. The reasoning is that customers will be best and most economically served if business firms compete vigorously for the consumers' dollars. Prices should fluctuate according to supply and demand, with no collusion between competitors,

[2]For two classic analyses of corporate power, see Alfred C. Neal, *Business Power and Public Policy* (New York: Praeger, 1981); and Edwin M. Epstein and Dow Votaw, eds., *Rationality, Legitimacy, Responsibility: Search for New Directions in Business and Society* (Santa Monica, CA: Goodyear, 1978).
[3]Bureau of National Affairs, *Antitrust and Trade Regulation Report,* vol. 55 (Washington, D.C.: Bureau of National Affairs, 1988), p. 5–4.

whether behind the scenes or out in the open. An important 1994 case illustrates this feature of antitrust regulation.

> *Six of the largest airlines in the United States were charged by the Justice Department with violating antitrust laws for colluding to set ticket prices between 1988 and 1992. The government said that the airlines used a sophisticated computerized fare information system, called ATP, to carry on a "detailed electronic dialogue" that allowed them to "signal" each other about changes in ticket prices. For example, an airline would post a proposed fare on a particular route, and then receive counterproposals from other airlines electronically until a consensus was reached. A Justice Department official said, "Although [the airlines'] method was novel, the conduct amounted to price fixing, plain and simple." The six companies—American, Delta, Northwest, Continental, TWA, and Alaska Airlines—agreed in 1994 to stop using the ATP system to exchange information about scheduled fare changes.*[4]

A second objective of antitrust policy is *to protect the consumer's welfare by prohibiting deceptive and unfair business practices.* The original antitrust laws were aimed primarily at preserving competition, assuming that consumers would be safeguarded as long as competition was strong. Later, though, it was realized that some business methods could be used to exploit or mislead consumers, regardless of the amount of competition. Consider the following hypothetical situations:

> *A company supplying plastic parts for electrical appliances bribed the purchasing agent for the appliance maker to buy the company's parts, even though they were priced higher than those made by a competitor. As a result, the consumer paid more for the appliances. This type of commercial bribery would be forbidden by the antitrust laws because it takes unfair advantage of innocent consumers.*
>
> *A distributor of compact discs sent purchasing club members more CDs than they had ordered and then demanded payment, substituted one CD for another in some orders, and delayed prepaid orders of some customers for several months. Such practices would be considered to be unfair by antitrust authorities.*

A third objective of antitrust regulation is *to protect small, independent business firms from the economic pressures exerted by big business competition.* As shown in the Wal-Mart example at the beginning of this chapter, antitrust laws prohibit predatory pricing—the practice of selling below cost to drive rivals out of business. The objective of these laws is to protect small companies from unfair competition. In other cases, small businesses may be undersold by larger ones because manufacturers are willing to give price discounts to large-volume buyers. For example, a tire maker wanted to sell automobile and truck tires to a large retail chain at a lower price than it offered to a small gasoline station. The antitrust laws prohibit such discounts to be given exclusively to large buyers unless it can be proved that there is a genuine economic saving in dealing with the larger firm.

---

[4]"Six Airlines Settle Price Fixing Charges," *Corporate Crime Reporter,* March 21, 1994, p. 7.

In promoting the interests of small business over large business in these ways, antitrust regulations disregard both competition—because big businesses are not permitted to compete freely—and consumer welfare—because big firms could sell at a lower price than small firms. This inconsistency occurs because these laws serve the multiple and sometimes contradictory goals of many different groups. A recent case that involved possible unfair methods of competition, as well as economic pressure exerted by big business, is profiled in Exhibit 10–A.

A fourth objective of antitrust policy is *to preserve the values and customs of small-town America.* A strong populist philosophy has been part of the antitrust movement from its beginning. Populists favored small town life, neighborly relations among people, a democratic political system, family-operated farms, and small business firms. They believed that concentrated wealth poses a threat to democracy, that big business would drive small local companies out of business, and that hometown merchants and neighboring farmers might be replaced by large impersonal corporations headquartered in distant cities. Antitrust restrictions on big business, populists believed, might further these social and political goals. One hundred years later, however, these populist goals often conflict with business views of what is required in a world of global competition.[5]

EXHIBIT 10–A

Chipping Away at the Competition

The owner of a small snack-food distribution business in Cleveland's east side neighborhood was surprised when several mom-and-pop store owners told him they no longer wanted to carry his products. The potato chips, pork rinds, and onion rings the man delivered sold well, and the store owners had no complaints about his service. "They told me Frito-Lay supervisors had offered them free merchandise, if they stopped carrying my product," the distributor reported. The owner of the small business consulted an attorney, who told him that Frito-Lay, the country's largest salty-snack corporation and a unit of PepsiCo, might be guilty of antitrust violations. "What is unfair is that they are paying stores not to carry (my client's) product," the attorney said.

After several similar complaints, the Justice Department launched a probe of the snack-food giant, concerned that it might have illegally pressured retailers to squeeze out rival products. For its part, Frito-Lay denied any wrongdoing, saying that the Cleveland small distributor simply could not hold his own in the intensely competitive salty-snack business. "We've never done anything illegal," a Frito-Lay spokesperson said.

Sources: "Chipping Away at Competition: Frito Lay Accused of Unfair Tactics against Small Company," *Cleveland Plain Dealer,* March 30, 1997, pp. 1B; and "The Cops Are Coming: A New Generation of Trustbusters Is Reshaping National Policy," *Business Week,* June 10, 1996, pp. 32–33.

---

[5]A lucid historical account may be found in Louis Galambos and Joseph Pratt, *The Rise of the Corporate Commonwealth: Business and Public Policy in the Twentieth Century* (New York: Basic Books, 1988).

The Major Antitrust Laws

Today's antitrust laws are the outcome of many years of attempting to make American business fit the model of free market competition. Many people have pointed out how unrealistic it is to expect a modern, high-technology, diversified, worldwide corporation to conform to conditions that may have been considered ideal a century ago when both business and society were simpler. The challenge of applying existing antitrust legislation to the technological, financial, political, and social environment of the late twentieth century begins with an understanding of the major antitrust laws.

Rather than trying to present all of the many detailed provisions of these laws and the history of each one, we concentrate here on the four main federal antitrust statutes and give a brief summary of each. Figure 10–2 identifies the purpose of these four laws and the major components of the enforcement process. States also have antitrust laws with similar goals and purposes.

The Sherman Act

Although several states enacted antitrust laws before the federal government did, the Sherman Act of 1890 is considered to be the foundation of antitrust regulation in the United States. This law

- Prohibits contracts, combinations, or conspiracies that restrain trade and commerce (for example, collusion among a group of producers to fix prices).

Figure 10–2

Antitrust laws and enforcement at the federal level.

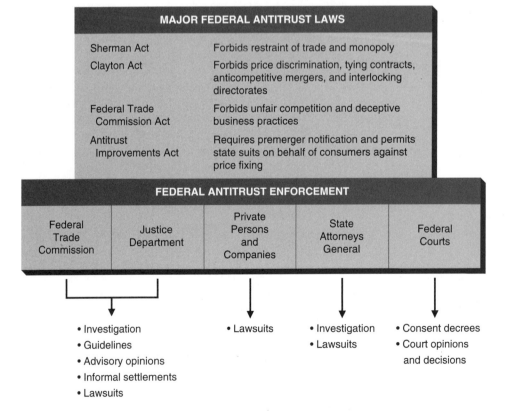

MAJOR FEDERAL ANTITRUST LAWS	
Sherman Act	Forbids restraint of trade and monopoly
Clayton Act	Forbids price discrimination, tying contracts, anticompetitive mergers, and interlocking directorates
Federal Trade Commission Act	Forbids unfair competition and deceptive business practices
Antitrust Improvements Act	Requires premerger notification and permits state suits on behalf of consumers against price fixing

FEDERAL ANTITRUST ENFORCEMENT				
Federal Trade Commission	Justice Department	Private Persons and Companies	State Attorneys General	Federal Courts

- Investigation
- Guidelines
- Advisory opinions
- Informal settlements
- Lawsuits

- Lawsuits

- Investigation
- Lawsuits

- Consent decrees
- Court opinions and decisions

- Prohibits monopolies and all attempts to monopolize trade and commerce.
- Provides for enforcement by the Justice Department, and authorizes penalties, including fines and jail terms, for violations.

The Clayton Act

Originally passed in 1914 to clarify some of the ambiguities and uncertainties of the Sherman Act, the Clayton Act, as amended, now

- Prohibits price discrimination by sellers (as illustrated by the tire maker who was forbidden to sell lower-priced tires to a chain store while selling at a higher price to a smaller independent store).
- Forbids tying contracts that require someone to buy a related and perhaps unwanted product in order to get another one produced by the same company (for example, it would be illegal for a computer company to force hardware purchasers to accept an unwanted maintenance contract as a condition of sale).
- Prohibits companies from merging through purchase of shares or assets if competition is lessened or a monopoly is created (as illustrated by the FTC's review of the proposed merger between Staples and Office Depot).
- Outlaws interlocking directorates in large competing corporations (for example, Chevron and Mobil Oil would not be permitted to have a single person serve as a member of the board of directors of both companies at the same time).

The Federal Trade Commission Act

This act, too, became law in 1914 during a period when populist sentiment against big business was very strong. In addition to creating the Federal Trade Commission to help enforce the antitrust laws, it prohibited all unfair methods of competition (without defining them in specific terms). In later years, the act was amended to give more protection to consumers by forbidding unfair and deceptive business practices, such as misleading advertising, bait-and-switch merchandising, and other consumer abuses.

The Antitrust Improvements Act

All of the important additions made to the antitrust laws during the 1930s and 1950s were incorporated into the three major laws as summarized above. But in 1976, Congress put a new and separate law on the books. The Antitrust Improvements Act strengthens government's hand in enforcing the other three laws. This law

- Requires large corporations to notify the Justice Department and the FTC about impending mergers and acquisitions so that the regulators can study any possible violations of the law that may be caused by the merger (for example, to preserve competition the Justice Department delayed the merger of two large steel companies until two of the steel mills were sold).
- Expands the Justice Department's antitrust investigatory powers.
- Authorizes the attorneys general of all 50 states to bring suits against companies that fix prices and to recover damages for consumers.

Exemptions

Not all organizations are subject to these four antitrust laws. Major League Baseball, for example, has been exempt from antitrust regulation since 1922. This exemption has been criticized for permitting baseball owners to collude to restrict the number of teams, drive up ticket prices, and force concessions from cities eager to attract or keep a major league team.[6] Also not covered by U.S. antitrust laws are labor unions that attempt to monopolize the supply of labor; agricultural cooperatives that sometimes engage in anticompetitive behavior; insurance companies, which are regulated by state, not federal, laws; and some business transactions related to national defense. The exemption of cooperative research and development efforts is discussed later in this chapter.

Enforcing the Antitrust Laws

The two main antitrust enforcement agencies shown in Figure 10–2 are the Antitrust Division of the U.S. Department of Justice and the Federal Trade Commission. Both agencies may bring suits against companies they believe to be guilty of violating antitrust laws. They also may investigate possible violations, issue guidelines and advisory opinions for firms planning mergers or acquisitions, identify specific practices considered to be illegal, and negotiate informal settlements out of court. Under the Clinton administration, antitrust regulators have become more activist, especially in prosecuting price-fixing, blocking anticompetitive mergers, and dealing with foreign companies that violate U.S. laws on fair competition.[7] At the same time, regulators have tried to be sensitive to the impact of antitrust policy on the competitiveness of U.S. firms internationally, as described in a later section of this chapter.

Antitrust suits also can be initiated by private persons or companies who believe themselves to have been damaged by the anticompetitive actions of a business firm and seek compensation for their losses. Nearly 95 percent of all antitrust enforcement actions are initiated by private parties, not government officials, as illustrated by the following example.

> *In 1993, Nestlé USA Inc. initiated an antitrust lawsuit against two infant formula manufacturers—Abbott Laboratories (makers of Similac) and Bristol-Myers Squibb (makers of Enfamil)—and the American Academy of Pediatrics. Nestlé charged that the three organizations had conspired to prevent Nestlé's Carnation brand product from entering the lucrative infant formula market. The pediatrics group had long advocated a ban on advertising of infant formula, arguing that it could discourage mothers from breast-feeding. But Nestlé claimed that the real point of the advertising ban was to give an unfair advantage to infant formula products, like Enfamil and Similac, already established in the market. During the 1980s, the pediatrics group received millions of dollars in contributions from Abbott and Bristol-Myers. In 1996, Abbott Labs settled with Nestlé for $32 million.[8]*

---

[6]For a critique of baseball's antitrust exemption, see Andrew Zimbalist, *Baseball and Billions: A Probing Look Inside the Big Business of Our National Pastime,* (New York: Basic Books, 1992); and Frank Dell'Apa, "Do Pro Sports Take Advantage of Their Fans?" *Public Citizen,* May–June 1993.

[7]"Annie Gets Her Antitrust Gun," *Business Week,* August 23, 1993, p. 23; and "The Game of Anti-Monopoly," *San Francisco Examiner,* July 29, 1994, pp. B1, B4.

[8]"Battle for Baby Formula Market," *New York Times,* June 15, 1993, pp. C1, C15; and "Abbott Agrees to Pay $32.5 Million to Settle Infant Formula Case," *The Wall Street Journal,* May 26, 1996, p. A26.

Attorneys general of the various states also may take action against antitrust violators, not only to protect consumers from price-fixing (under the Antitrust Improvements Act) but also to enforce the antitrust laws of their own states. The National Association of Attorneys General has a special section on antitrust laws, and state officials often cooperate in the investigation and prosecution of cases. In 1993, for example, the New York state attorney general sued to block Kraft's acquisition of RJR Nabisco's cold cereals, saying that the move would lessen competition and contribute to "soaring [cold cereal] price increases, far out of line with other food products."[9]

Finally, the courts usually have the last word in enforcement, and the outcome is never certain. Cases may be tried before a jury, a panel of judges, or a single judge. The U.S. Supreme Court is the court of final appeal, and its opinions carry great weight. Antitrust regulators and businesses alike often appeal their cases to this final forum because the stakes are so high and the judicial precedents created by the high court are so important in the long-run development of antitrust regulation.

Key Antitrust Issues

The business community, government policymakers, and the general public have to seek answers to several key issues if the nation's antitrust laws and regulations are to serve both business and society well. Some of the most important ones are briefly discussed.

Corporate Size

The key question here is, Is large size evidence of monopoly or a threat to competition? In general, the courts have said that absolute size by itself is not a violation of the antitrust laws. If, however, a firm uses its larger size to take advantage of rivals through price discrimination, collusion with others, or other specific actions banned by the antitrust laws, then it may be found guilty. For example, in evaluating recent strategic alliances and joint ventures, regulators have held that it is not the size of the arrangement that matters, but its competitive effects.

Economic Concentration

The key question here is, Does domination of an industry or a market by a few large corporations violate the antitrust laws? Or, as some ask, Should the biggest firms in each industry be broken up? Many major industries and markets are dominated by a handful of mammoth companies—examples are automobiles, tires, computers, computer operating systems, chemicals, insurance, steel, some food and beverage products, paper, and others. Where this kind of concentration exists, competition changes. Companies tend to compete less by underpricing their rivals and more by making their products appear distinctive, by servicing their customers, by building reliability into products and parts, by developing brand-name loyalty in customers, and by advertising.

Critics claim that economic concentration eliminates effective price competition, reduces consumer choices, causes firms to grow too large to be efficient, inhibits innovation, and concentrates profits in too few hands. The best solution, they say, is to break up the giants into smaller units. Others counter by claiming that big firms have become dominant because they are more efficient; that price competition still occurs along with other types men-

---

[9]"Waking Up to Higher Cereal Prices," *New York Times,* August 10, 1993, pp. C1, C5.

tioned above; that today's firms give consumers more, not fewer, choices of goods and services; that large companies can finance more innovation than small business; and that profits are distributed widely to an increasing number of stockholders. Breaking up large corporations would deprive society of these benefits, say the defenders, and should not be done.

Efficiency versus Competition

Another antitrust issue is efficiency versus competition. The key question here is, Is big business efficiency more important than preserving competition? Many big companies claim that their large size makes possible many operating economies. Today's complex technology, far-flung markets, complicated financial systems, and transnational competition make bigness essential for survival and efficient operation. Placing restrictions on today's corporate growth just to preserve a competitive ideal formed during the eighteenth and nineteenth centuries seems to make little economic sense. On the other hand, others point out that competition stands at the heart of private enterprise ideology and that small businesses, consumers, and workers should be protected against big business expansion even though it may mean a loss of efficiency.[10]

Two other issues in antitrust policy, the impact of global competition and intellectual property rights, are discussed at the end of this chapter.

Corporate Mergers

A wave of **corporate mergers** took place in the mid- and late-1990s, echoing in some respects the extended merger boom of the mid-1980s. As Figure 10–3 shows, merger and acquisition activity, after falling dramatically in the early 1990s,

Figure 10–3

Value of mergers and acquisitions, 1982–1996.

Sources: Data for 1982–1983 are from the Bureau of the Census, *Statistical Abstract of the United States, 1990* (Washington, D.C.: U.S. Government Printing Office, 1990), table 883. Data for 1984–1996 are from the "M&A Profile" published annually by *Mergers & Acquisitions.* Used by permission of *Mergers & Acquisitions.*

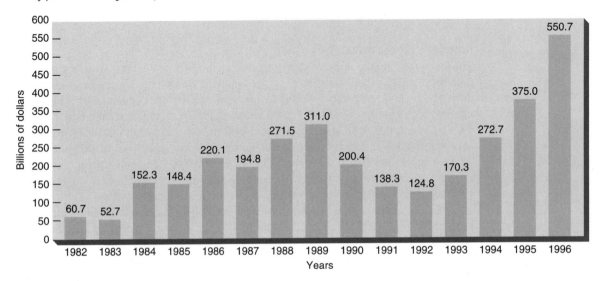

[10]A full discussion of U.S. regulators' current understanding of these issues may be found in *Anticipating the Twenty-First Century: Competition Policy in the New High-Tech Global Marketplace* (Washington, D.C.: Federal Trade Commission, 1996).

was up sharply again beginning in 1994, leading one expert to predict "the start of the next great merger wave."[11] These new mergers raised, once again, important questions about the social and economic impact of such corporate consolidation. Not surprisingly, antitrust officials were deeply involved in deciding which mergers were acceptable and which were not.

Students of corporate mergers usually distinguish between three different types of business combinations, as depicted in Figure 10–4. **Vertical mergers** occur when the combining companies are at different stages of production in the same general line of business. For example, a rubber-tire manufacturer may combine with a company owning rubber plantations and with a chain of auto parts dealers that sells the tires. Production from the ground up is then brought under a single management umbrella, so it is referred to as a vertical combination. **Horizontal mergers** occur when the combining companies are at the same stage or level of production or sales. For example, if two retail grocery chains in an urban market tried to combine, antitrust regulators probably would not permit the merger if the combined firms' resultant market share appeared to lessen competition in that area.

A **conglomerate merger** occurs when firms that are in totally unrelated lines of business are combined. Gulf & Western (G&W), for example, a well-known conglomerate of the 1970s, merged under its corporate umbrella firms that manufactured pipeline equipment, auto and truck parts, cigars, chocolate candy, steel mill equipment, pantyhose, and paperback books; other units ran racetracks, distributed educational films, and staged the Miss Universe and Miss USA beauty pageants. Proponents argue that a conglomerate

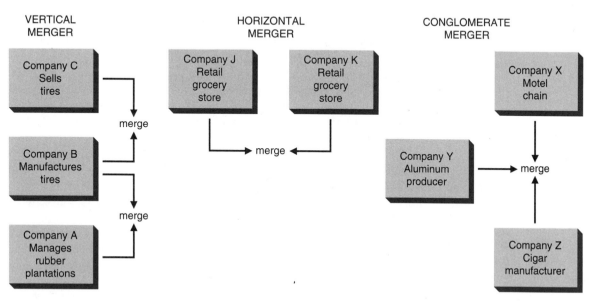

Figure 10–4

Three different types of corporate mergers.

---

[11]"Same Old Feeding Frenzy, Different Bait," *Business Week,* August 8, 1994, pp. 22–23.

with pooled resources is more capable of responding to the ups and downs of the business cycle than a firm with a single product or service; pooled resources enable a conglomerate to provide many centralized managerial, technical, and financial services to small business units that otherwise would be unable to afford them.

Corporate mergers seem to occur in waves at different periods of history, each with its own distinctive characteristics. The 1950s and 1960s saw much activity, culminating in 6,000 mergers during 1969. Many of these mergers produced conglomerates and may have been motivated in part by strict antitrust enforcement that made vertical and horizontal mergers more difficult. Most observers seem to agree that one factor stimulating the 1980s surge, by contrast, was the government's general philosophy of deregulation and a more relaxed attitude toward enforcement of the nation's antitrust laws. This philosophy and approach placed a greater degree of faith in the private enterprise system to preserve competition, protect consumers, and ensure high levels of productivity than the opposite philosophy of curbing corporate power by strong antitrust regulations. In this general climate of greater permissiveness, the number of corporate mergers ballooned.

The 1980s brought large numbers of all types of mergers. Some were designed to improve a company's share of the market in particular industries, whereas others emphasized vertical integration or financial diversity. Much of the activity in the 1980s and 1990s has emphasized breaking up conglomerates created in the past that did not achieve hoped-for results. Many business leaders concluded that it was important for a company to be more carefully focused on those activities it performs well. Then by selling parts of the business that are performing poorly or not related to its core capability, a firm could raise money to invest in the core business.

In the most recent wave, many mergers of the 1990s have been driven by technological or regulatory changes. Disney's $19 billion buyout of Capital Cities/ABC was just one of several blockbuster mergers in telecommunications and media, where major companies jockeyed for a favorable position on the information superhighway. Telecommunications deregulation led to a spate of mergers among long-distance phone companies, regional carriers, and cable operators. In health care, several big mergers—including Columbia/HCA Healthcare Corp.'s acquisition of Value Health Inc. and Merck's acquisition of Medco Containment Services—were spurred by anticipated regulatory changes in the delivery of health care.

Other deals have been prompted by a rapidly globalizing economy in which many companies have found they must be big to compete effectively on the world stage. "We are moving toward a period of the megacorporate state in which there will be a few global firms within particular economic sectors," commented one investment banker.[12]

Similar to what occurred in the United States, a new wave of mergers swept Europe in the late 1990s. Many of these mergers crossed national borders to create new, multinational companies. In just one of many transactions in 1997, for example, Assicurazioni Generali, an Italian insurer, acquired Assurances Generales de France, a French insurer,

---

[12]"Corporations' Dreams Converge in One Idea: It's Time to Do a Deal," *The Wall Street Journal,* February 26, 1997, pp. A1, A12; "A Pack of 800-Lb. Gorillas," *Business Week,* February 3, 1997, pp. 34–35; and "Land of the Giants," *Business Week,* September 11, 1995, pp. 34–35.

the biggest takeover in French history. The European merger wave was driven, in part, by an effort to remain competitive with U.S.-based firms that had recently grown through their own acquisitions. But it was also driven by the European Union's plans to create a common currency, the *euro,* reducing foreign exchange risk and making cross-border investments more attractive within the continent.[13]

The Consequences of Corporate Mergers

In the wake of the most recent wave of corporate mergers in the United States, what will the results be? What stakeholders were helped, and what stakeholders were hurt? No one knows the final story, but some results are already observable.

The megamergers of the 1990s created enormously larger corporations, thus continuing a trend toward bigger and bigger business units. In many cases, this led to greater efficiencies and market clout. When Chemical Banking and Chase Manhattan merged in 1996, the combination of branches and functional areas, like the loan department, led to a leaner and more competitive business. Gillette's purchase of Duracell allowed it to use its global distribution network to sell batteries alongside shaving gear. On the other hand, employees often lost their jobs when companies merged, as duplicate staffs were combined, and local communities suffered when a large company moved out or shifted its activities to other regions.

The results of mergers are mixed for stockholders. Share values often rise when a merger or acquisition is announced, if shareholders perceive benefits from synergies between the two firms. The share prices of Boeing, Gillette, and Tosco all shot up after they announced merger plans. But shareholders can also be hurt, particularly when an acquisition is overpriced or not well thought out. A 1995 study found that about half of large mergers (those valued at more than $500 million) had led to at least some decline in shareholder returns.[14]

There will remain a need for economic restructuring in the decades ahead, so mergers and acquisitions will continue. They can serve as a dynamic stimulus, producing gains for shareholders and the entire economy from improved efficiency and market pressure. Experience has shown, however, that when carried to excess such business combinations can be costly in economic and social terms for some stakeholders.[15] Social control, expressed through antitrust policy, will continue to seek the best balance between competition and other social goals.

Global Competition and Antitrust Policy

The first antitrust laws were passed in the United States in the late nineteenth century, when most commerce was regional or national in scope. This is no longer the case. Today, as discussed in Chapter 7, business has greatly expanded its global reach. Foreign

---

[13]"A Day of Mega-Mergers Wakes Up Europe," *The Wall Street Journal,* October 14, 1997, pp. A16, A19.
[14]"The Case against Mergers," *Business Week,* October 30, 1995, pp. 122–130.
[15]J. Fred Weston and Kwang S. Chung, "Takeovers and Corporate Restructuring: An Overview," *Business Economics,* April 1990, pp. 6–11. See also J. Fred Weston et al., *Mergers, Restructuring and Corporate Control* (Englewood Cliffs, NJ: Prentice Hall, 1990).

sales are a critical part of the revenues of many U.S.-based firms. An increasing proportion of products and services purchased by American consumers are made abroad. Trade barriers are falling, and new regions of the world are rapidly entering the world marketplace.

The rapid globalization of business has created many new challenges for antitrust enforcement. Federal regulators, policymakers, and the courts must now address difficult and complex questions, often not anticipated by the framers of antitrust law, such as the following:

- Should the government permit mergers, joint ventures, or other cooperative arrangements among companies, even if they reduce competition *within* the United States, if they enhance the ability of American businesses to compete internationally?

- Should the government move to break up monopolies *within* the United States, if the global marketplace for the products or services offered by these companies is highly competitive? What if these companies help the United States become more competitive internationally?

- Should federal regulators and the courts try to enforce U.S. antitrust laws against foreign companies, if these companies operate subsidiaries in the United States? What if these companies simply sell their products or services in the United States?

- What steps can the government take to create a level playing field for U.S. corporations, so that U.S. and foreign firms operate under a common set of antitrust rules and regulations?

The sections following will discuss how government, business, and society have tried to answer these questions in recent years, concluding with an examination of the special problem of protecting intellectual property in the global marketplace.

Antitrust Enforcement and National Competitiveness

Antitrust regulators have become increasingly sensitive to the impact of enforcement on the ability of U.S. firms to compete effectively in the global economy. They have been reluctant to block mergers, break up monopolies, or prevent joint research efforts where these would strengthen the **national competitiveness** of the United States. This sometimes creates dilemmas for regulators, when the goal of a free, competitive market nationally conflicts with that of a strong U.S. economy, relative to other countries.

Since the mid-1980s, the U.S. government has generally permitted cooperative activities among U.S. firms that enhance their competitiveness in the global economy. The National Cooperative Research Act (NCRA), passed in 1984, clarified the application of U.S. antitrust laws to joint research and development (R&D) activities. This law sought to balance the positive effects of cooperative R&D with the preservation of competition by instructing the courts to use a "rule of reason" in assessing individual cases. Companies wishing to form joint R&D activities that may have anticompetitive effects are required to submit notice of their plans to the U.S. attorney general and Federal Trade Commission. If approved, the companies may share information and cooperate in ways that would otherwise violate antitrust standards.

An example of an R&D consortium permitted under the NCRA is SEMATECH. Founded in 1987, SEMATECH is a group of 14 semiconductor manufacturers that came together, with support from the Department of Defense, to rebuild the U.S. chip industry in the face of intense Japanese competition. SEMATECH played a significant role in developing several new generations of chip-making technology. By the mid-1990s, the U.S. semiconductor industry had achieved a dramatic turnaround in its global market share.[16]

The U.S. Justice Department has also loosened the rules governing joint production agreements that create important economies of scale.[17] Joint manufacturing and marketing deals between U.S. and foreign firms are becoming more frequent, often without serious antitrust objections from government. Hewlett-Packard, for example, has formed strategic alliances with Samsung (Korea), Northern Telecom (Canada), and Sony, Hitachi, Canon, and Yokogawa (Japan). Antitrust authorities also approved the joint manufacturing plant set up by General Motors and Toyota in California. Such a joint venture between GM and either Ford or Chrysler surely would have drawn antitrust objections on traditional grounds.[18]

The United States has also been reluctant to move against some companies that dominate their industries if they are effective global competitors. The efforts of regulators to balance the sometimes conflicting goals of promoting U.S. national competitiveness and assuring fair competition domestically are described in the discussion case on Microsoft Corporation at the end of this chapter.

Enforcing Antitrust Laws against Foreign Firms

In recent years, the government has become increasingly concerned about possible violations of antitrust law by foreign companies. In the Guardian Industries example at the beginning of this chapter, antitrust regulators considered how best to protect U.S. glassmakers from the anticompetitive practices of Japanese firms. In a similar incident, the Justice Department in 1994 settled a case against a British firm, Pilkington, also a glassmaker, for monopolizing the technology for making sheet glass. The Justice Department said it had jurisdiction in the case because Pilkington is part owner of an American glass company. Since many international companies do business in the United States by setting up operations or buying a subsidiary, this case signaled a new strategy by regulators to prosecute foreign firms under U.S. antitrust laws.[19]

In other cases, U.S. authorities have gone even further, going after foreign companies that violate antitrust law within their own borders. When Swiss drug companies Sandoz and Ciba-Geigy merged, the FTC required the firms to divest some product lines to avoid a monopoly, even though neither company was based in the United States. In 1997, several Japanese fax-paper makers were prosecuted for price-fixing after they had

---

[16]Henry H. Beam, "Technology Fountainheads: The Management Challenge of R&D Consortia," *Academy of Management Executive* 11 (February 1997), pp. 123–24.

[17]Robert B. Reich, "Who Is Us?" *Harvard Business Review,* January–February 1990, pp. 53–64.

[18]"Trust the Trust, or Bust the Trust?" *The Economist,* September 2, 1989, pp. 63–64.

[19]"U.S. Sues British in Antitrust Case," *New York Times,* May 27, 1994, pp. A1, D2.

shared information on pricing, products, and customers. "We'll attack these cartels whether the conspirators are in the United States or beyond our borders," said one Justice Department official. But some legal observers felt that prosecutors had gone too far. In this view, antitrust laws should not extend to the actions of foreign firms acting in their own countries.[20]

Harmonizing International Antitrust Policies

Although in many instances antitrust policies in the United States are more stringent than those of its global competitors, other nations have their own versions of antitrust laws, often referred to as *competition policies.* Japan has an antimonopoly law, first implemented during the Allied occupation after World War II, although the Japanese cartels known as *keiretsu* in many cases would probably be illegal under U.S. antitrust laws. The European Union recently adopted a set of competition policies that reflect the newly integrated European economy. In 1994, the European Commission, the EU's executive branch, fined a group of carton-board manufacturers about $165 million for fixing prices, the EU's largest fine ever. U.S. antitrust regulators have worked with officials in developing countries, like Zimbabwe and Kazakhstan, to develop their own domestic antitrust policies.

Some efforts have been made to coordinate antitrust enforcement among nations. Several bilateral (two-country) treaties are in place, and the Organization for Economic Cooperation and Development, a 28-nation group, has worked to coordinate antitrust enforcement. Their goal is to create a level playing field among their members' competing national economies. The issues of antitrust and competition policy have also been taken up in international trade negotiations, such as those over the General Agreement on Tariffs and Trade. But the explosion of international commerce has far outstripped the pace of international negotiations, and global business still lacks a common, enforceable set of competition policies.

Antitrust policymakers are wrestling with the new realities of global business competition. The days of the self-contained U.S. economy are gone. Virtually all businesses are touched, directly or indirectly, by the world marketplace. Cooperation among U.S. firms and foreign competitors often makes economic sense. But the need for some form of social control on the excesses of anticompetitive business behavior has not disappeared, both in the United States and abroad. The optimal fit between antitrust protection and the global marketplace is not easily achieved.

Intellectual Property

The foundations of U.S. antitrust policy were created in the late nineteenth century when railroads were the leading technology of the day and control of natural resources—land, oil, minerals—was the surest way to wealth. More than 100 years later, the economic foundations of the United States and other advanced, industrialized countries are quite different. Some researchers now refer to these countries as **knowledge economies.** Services now equal or exceed manufacturing of consumer and industrial goods as an employer of workers and as a source of economic growth. Manufacturing itself is highly dependent on new technologies and innovation to remain competitive in world markets. The contribu-

---

[20]"U.S. Trust Busters Increasingly Target International Business," *The Wall Street Journal,* February 5, 1997, pp. A1, A10.

tions of most workers are based not on their physical skill, strength, or dexterity, but on their knowledge. According to one observer, "The most valuable resource in the modern economy is the human mind."

The ideas, concepts, and other symbolic creations of the human mind are often referred to as **intellectual property.** In the United States, intellectual property is protected through a number of special laws and public policies including copyright, patent, and trademark laws. These laws rest on two central premises:

- The creator, be it a person or an organization, of an idea or invention should be entitled to the benefits that flow from that original creation if it can be proved that the creation came from that person or organization. For example, a company that develops a new medicine to treat AIDS should be able to patent its invention and to benefit from its efforts.

- However, the right to get special economic advantage from such inventions should not exist forever. At some point, ideas enter the public domain and can be used by others. Thomas Edison was entitled to make money from inventing the electric light bulb, but this should not require everyone who has ever used a light bulb to pay something to Edison or his heirs forever.

Not all nations have similar policies, however. In China, for example, the traditional Communist view was that intellectual property belonged to all the people, not to individuals or companies. Some other countries' laws governing intellectual property also differ significantly from those of the United States.[21]

In today's global economy, many temptations can arise for businesses and individuals to use other people's ideas without permission. Patents, copyrights, and other intellectual property are sometimes infringed, or wrongfully used, by those who see an opportunity for quick profit, a practice known as **commercial piracy.** For example, Levi Strauss discovered that many imitation Levi's jeans were being manufactured in the Far East, imported into the United States, and sold to unsuspecting buyers. Of course, the buyers were paying for the Levi's name and the quality it represents. To protect its reputation for quality, Levi Strauss had to aggressively pursue the pirate businesses that wrongfully used the Levi's name. Many lawsuits and governmental actions were required before the pirates halted their practice.

A great deal of pirating occurs in industries such as computer software and hardware, industrial machinery, printing and publishing, and designer clothing. Because some governments do not curb such practices, businesses that create ideas are injured. One estimate is that U.S. companies lose more than $60 billion of sales each year because of infringement by non-U.S. competitors. The U.S. government has made such intellectual property issues part of its international trade negotiating position. One nation in which the pirating of U.S. intellectual property has posed an especially severe problem is China, as described in Exhibit 10–B.

In coming decades, many new ideas will be developed and commercially exploited in such fields as bioengineering, computer software, fiber optics, and medicine, to name a few. In a global economy, these forms of intellectual property are economically valuable. A society that is scientifically and artistically creative has a big stake in laws that

---

[21]"U.S. China Copyright Rift Easing?" *Christian Science Monitor,* November 25, 1996, Business Section, p. 8.

EXHIBIT
10–B

Intellectual Piracy in China

In dozens of factories in China's southern provinces in the mid-1990s, counterfeiters churned out illegal copies of computer software, movie videocassettes, and compact discs made and copyrighted in the United States. In one incident, Microsoft discovered that a plant in the city of Guilin was illegally producing thousands of CD-ROMs of its Windows and Word software programs for sale in Russia. Microsoft had not received a penny. Officials estimated that commercial piracy in China cost U.S. firms more than $2 billion a year.

In February 1995, the United States and China, after hard negotiations, signed an agreement on intellectual property rights. In its wake, China took steps to crack down on piracy. It posted government watchdogs in renegade factories and required plants to stamp CDs and other products with a special code, so royalties could be charged. Bootleg CDs and videos were seized, and repeat violators were shut down. But the process was difficult. Directives issued by the central government often were simply ignored, and new factories would spring up almost as fast as others could be closed.

Many in the United States were concerned that China had not done enough. In February 1996, U.S. trade officials threatened to slap stiff tariffs on Chinese imports to the United States if the Chinese government did not do a better job of cracking down on counterfeiters. Some executives in Hollywood and the Silicon Valley applauded the action.

But others thought that threatening a trade war was not an effective way to approach the problem. China might retaliate by blocking U.S. exports into its huge and growing market. Increasing tariffs on Chinese goods sold in the United States would raise prices for American consumers.

What else could be done? One idea was to recruit potential pirates as joint partners, giving them a stake in protecting intellectual property rights. Others favored the use of sophisticated encryption technologies to protect items from copying or Internet transmission. Some argued that entertainment and software companies needed to lower their prices, to cut the financial incentive for overseas consumers to seek bootleg products.

At the last moment, both sides backed down and signed a new, tougher agreement on intellectual property rights. In 1997, China passed a domestic copyright law, and some observers thought the rate of piracy had dropped. But one trade expert commented, "it is naive to think this problem is over."

Sources: "China Faces Trade Sanctions over Copyright Piracy," *USA Today,* May 1, 1996, p. 1B; "Once More to the Brink: The China-U.S. Copyright Tiff Goes into Overtime," *Asia Week,* May 24, 1996, p. 34; "The Diminishing Returns of Slapping China for Piracy of U.S. Copyrights," *Los Angeles Times,* May 26, 1996, p. M2; "China: Tough Laws to Guard Copyrights," *China Daily,* January 21, 1997, p. 1. Software piracy in Eastern Europe is also discussed in Chapter 18.

protect the companies that create new ideas. The employees who work for those companies have an important stake in the fair use of intellectual property, as do customers who license the technology or buy the products. A growing challenge for public policy and international trade negotiations is how to coordinate national laws protecting intellectual property rights.

Summary Points of This Chapter

- The world's largest corporations are capable of wielding much influence because of the central functions they perform in their respective societies and throughout the world. Corporate power is legitimate when used to affirm broad public purposes, but it may also be abused.

- In the United States, antitrust laws have been used to curb the influence of corporations and to protect consumers, small business competitors, and others affected unfairly by noncompetitive practices.

- Courts and regulators have generally maintained in recent years that large size and domination of an industry by a few firms do not in themselves constitute a violation of antitrust laws. Also important are the actual impacts of size and market dominance on efficiency and competitiveness.

- The mid- and late-1990s witnessed a fresh wave of mergers and acquisitions. Some believed that it was good for stockholders; others expressed concern about the long-run effects such mergers would have on both business and society.

- The emergence of global competition in many industries has led business and political leaders to adjust antitrust rules to help the United States better compete in the world economy, for example, by permitting joint R&D efforts where appropriate and by blocking anticompetitive practices by foreign firms.

- As services and knowledge-based manufacturing have grown in economic importance, efforts have expanded to protect the intellectual property rights of U.S. firms doing business abroad, through trade negotiations and other means.

Key Terms and Concepts Used in This Chapter

- Corporate power
- Antitrust laws
- Corporate mergers
- Vertical, horizontal, and conglomerate mergers

- National competitiveness
- Knowledge economies
- Intellectual property
- Commercial piracy

Internet Resources

- http://www.usdoj.gov   U.S. Department of Justice
- http://www.ftc.gov   U.S. Federal Trade Commission
- http://www.207.49.1.6/antitrust   American Bar Association, antitrust section
- http://www.yahoo.com/   Information on current antitrust cases
  Government/Law/Cases

Discussion Case   **The Antitrust Case against Microsoft**

In March 1998, Bill Gates, chairman of Microsoft Corporation, went to Congress to answer charges that Microsoft had become a high tech monopolist, stifling its competitors in the market for applications software. In dramatic testimony before the Senate Judiciary Committee, Gates vigorously asserted that Microsoft's success was not the result of anti-competitive practices, but of its ability to innovate. "At the end of the day," he concluded, "what really counts is building great software."

Microsoft's adversaries would have none of it. James Barksdale, CEO of Netscape Communications, Gates's main competitor in the Internet browser market, turned to the Senate audience and asked how many of them used personal computers. Most members raised their hands. "How many of you have a computer with Internet Explorer?" he added, referring to Microsoft's browser. Most of the same hands went up. "That is a monopoly," Barksdale stated.

The background to this confrontation was an ongoing antitrust investigation of Microsoft by federal regulators. Just four months earlier, the Justice Department had charged that the company violated an earlier agreement by requiring computer makers to install Internet Explorer (IE) on their computers as a condition of licensing Microsoft's popular Windows 95 operating system. In response, Microsoft argued that IE was simply an enhancement of Windows, not a separate product, so no antitrust laws had been broken.

The Senate hearing and the Justice Department's actions were just the latest salvos in a long series of government antitrust skirmishes with Microsoft, dating back to the early 1990s. Many believed this ongoing dispute was an important test of antitrust laws in the new knowledge economy, where dominance of cyberspace was as important as dominance of oil supplies or rail lines had been a century earlier.

Microsoft Corporation is one of the success stories of the information age. Founded in 1975 by Gates, a computer whiz who dropped out of Harvard, the company first made its mark by developing MS-DOS, an operating system that directs a computer's inner workings. When IBM adopted MS-DOS for use in its personal computers (PCs), the program quickly became the industry standard. Microsoft later introduced an improved operating system, Windows, and branched out into applications software, developing word processing, spreadsheet, and other desktop programs, as well as Internet Explorer. By the late 1990s, Microsoft controlled 85 percent of the market for all PC operating systems and was pulling in revenues of $5 billion a year. Gates himself was the wealthiest person in the country.

Government regulators and some of Gates's competitors believed that Microsoft used its dominance in operating systems to hurt its rivals in the applications business. For example, Microsoft could use its advance knowledge of upcoming changes in Windows to get a head start on developing compatible word processing or spreadsheet software. Or Microsoft could deliberately design features into its operating systems that would make them incompatible with competitors' products. Adobe Systems, a maker of typefaces, for example, complained that Windows had been designed so that Microsoft's own typefaces would run at twice the speed of Adobe's products.

The government was also concerned about Microsoft's purchase of competing companies. In 1995, Microsoft abandoned a plan to buy Intuit, a maker of personal finance software programs, after the government threatened an antitrust suit. Two years later, the government launched investigations of Microsoft's acquisition of WebTV, a company that made equipment allowing viewers to cruise the Internet using a television, and of its investment in Apple Computer, a longtime rival.

In response to its critics, Microsoft insisted that it did not fit the monopolist mold. High-tech industry differed from old-line manufacturing industry, transportation, and utilities because there were few barriers to entry. All that was needed to compete in software was brains, entrepreneurial zeal, and a good idea. "In the computer software industry," Gates noted, "rapid and unpredictable changes constantly create new market opportunities and threaten the position of existing competitors."

Moreover, the company argued, government efforts to restrict the company would be poor public policy. The software industry was a major provider of jobs, growing two-and-a-half times faster than the U.S. economy overall in the 1990s. Microsoft's dominance of operating system software had helped the United States balance of trade and contributed to the emergence of the United States as a world technology leader.

The outcome of the ongoing dispute between Microsoft and its government critics would be critical to antitrust enforcement into the new century, many believed. "Justice is taking a stand here," said one industry analyst. "It will be a watershed event no matter which way it goes." Commented Senator Orrin Hatch (R-Utah): "I think the current antitrust laws are adequate. But understanding how these crucial high-technology markets work [and] whether competition and innovation are being fostered or inhibited is a very important issue for our economy and our society."

Sources: "Statement of Bill Gates, chairman and CEO, Microsoft Corporation," U.S. Senate Judiciary Committee, March 3, 1998, available at http://www.microsoft.com/corpinfo/3-2billtest.htm; "Mr. Gates Goes to Washington," *Time,* March 16, 1998, pp. 58–59; "Microsoft vs. The World," *Newsweek,* March 9, 1998, pp. 36–43; and "An Icon of Technology Encounters Some Rude Political Realities," *New York Times,* March 4, 1998, p. D4.

Discussion Questions

1. In what ways have Microsoft's actions promoted the public interest? In what ways have they harmed the public interest?

2. Why did the Department of Justice believe that Microsoft had violated U.S. antitrust law? Do you agree with government antitrust regulators, or not?

3. What is the best solution to Microsoft's market dominance: (*a*) breakup into smaller companies, (*b*) strict legal enforcement of applicable antitrust laws, or (*c*) increased competition from innovative rivals?

4. The basic antitrust laws were written in the late nineteenth or early twentieth century, an era when the economy was dominated by manufacturing firms, and business competition was primarily national or regional in scope. Do you think these laws are relevant to the situation of Microsoft and other high-technology companies that emerged in the late twentieth century? If not, in what ways should antitrust policy be changed to better fit today's society?

PART FIVE

The Corporation and the Natural Environment

11

Ecology, Sustainable Development, and Global Business

The world community faces unprecedented ecological challenges in the twenty-first century. Many political and business leaders have embraced the idea of *sustainable development*, calling for economic growth without destroying the natural environment or depleting the resources on which future generations depend. Yet the concept has remained controversial, and implementation has been difficult. The task for policymakers and corporate leaders will be to find ways to meet both economic and environmental goals in the coming decades, without sacrificing either.

This chapter focuses on these key questions and objectives:

- What is sustainable development? What are the obstacles to developing the world's economy to meet the needs of the present without hurting future generations?

- What are the major threats to the earth's ecosystem?

- In what ways have population growth, poverty, and industrialization accelerated the world's ecological crisis?

- What environmental issues are shared globally by all nations?

- What steps has the world business community taken to reduce ecological damage and promote sustainable development?

I n June 1997, representatives of 170 nations gathered in New York on the fifth anniversary of the United Nations–sponsored Conference on Environment and Development, popularly known as the Earth Summit. At the original gathering in Rio de Janeiro, world political and business leaders had considered, on one hand, the growing dangers of environmental degradation. On the other, they also examined the urgent need for economic development in the world's poorer nations. Would it be possible, they had asked, to foster economic growth sufficient to lift the majority of the world's people out of poverty, without compromising the ability of future generations to meet their own needs?

Now, five years later, some evidence did not look encouraging to the delegates to the Earth Summit Plus Five. Consider that at the 1992 gathering

- Delegates had pledged to attack the problem of global warming—increases in the earth's temperature caused in part by carbon dioxide from the world's factories, utilities, and vehicles. The conference had called on developed countries to cut back to 1990 levels by the year 2000. But only half the developed countries had met this target, and annual emissions of carbon dioxide had reached new highs, threatening disruption of the world's climate. The Department of Energy estimated that by the year 2000, the United States would exceed the target by a full 11 percent.

- Delegates had committed to a framework Convention on Biological Diversity, dedicated to conserving the earth's biological resources, particularly in species-rich tropical forests. But by 1997, the United States had still not signed the treaty, and many species remained endangered. Vast stretches of rain forest had been cut down. In Indonesia, for example, home to large numbers of endangered birds, mammals, and reptiles, tropical forest was being logged for timber and burned to clear land at an astonishing rate, destroying habitat and, not incidentally, causing serious air pollution throughout Southeast Asia.

- Many developed nations had pledged to increase foreign aid to 0.7 percent of their gross national product (GNP) to help poorer countries develop their economies in an environmentally sustainable way. But during the intervening years, aid had actually fallen to just 0.3 percent of GNP, the lowest level since the early 1970s. Now the question was just as urgent as it had been before: Who would pay for the costs of clean development in the poorer countries?

On the other hand, the delegates to the Earth Summit Plus Five noted important evidence of progress. Although the world population was still growing, the rate of growth had dropped somewhat. The World Bank, an important lender to developing countries, had instituted a strict environmental review process, refusing to fund ecologically destructive projects. Important gains had been made in efforts to restore the health of the ozone layer. And possibly most promisingly, many segments of the global business community had become increasingly active in promoting environmentally sound management practices. Could the world's governments, businesses, nongovernmental organizations, and individuals, working together, meet the ecological challenges of the twenty-first century and put the global economy on a more sustainable course?[1]

[1]"Five Years after Environmental Summit in Rio, Little Progress," *New York Times,* June 17, 1997, p. B14; "Five Years after Rio, U.N. to Review Eco-Agenda," *Daily Yomiuri,* February 8, 1997, p.10; and Christopher Flavin, "The Legacy of Rio," in Lester R. Brown et al., eds., *State of the World 1997: A Worldwatch Institute Report on Progress toward a Sustainable Society* (New York: W.W. Norton, 1997), pp. 3–22. See also the United Nations' Web site for Earth Summit 5, at http://www.un.org/dpcsd/earthsummit.

Ecological Challenges

Humankind is now altering the face of the planet, rivaling the forces of nature—glaciers, volcanoes, asteroids, and earthquakes—in impact. Human beings have literally rerouted rivers, moved mountains, and burned forests. By the last decade of the twentieth century, human society had transformed about half of the earth's ice-free surface and made a major impact on most of the rest. In many areas, as much land was used by transportation systems as by agriculture. Although significant natural resources—fossil fuels, fresh water, fertile land, and forest—remained, exploding populations and rapid industrialization threatened a day when the demands of human society would exceed the carrying capacity of the earth's ecosystem.

Ecology is the study of how living things—plants and animals—interact with one another in such a unified natural system, or ecosystem. Damage to the ecosystem in one part of the world often affects people in other locations. Depletion of the ozone layer, destruction of the rain forests, and species extinctions have an impact on all of society, not just particular regions or nations.

The Global Commons

Throughout history, communities of people have created *commons*. A commons is a shared resource, such as land, air, or water, that a group of people uses collectively. The paradox of the commons is that if all individuals attempt to maximize their own private advantage in the short term, the commons may be destroyed, and all users—present and future—lose. The only solution is restraint, either voluntary or through mutual agreement.[2] The tragedy of the commons—that freedom in a commons brings ruin to all—is illustrated by the following parable.

> *There was once a village on the shore of a great ocean. Its people made a good living from the rich fishing grounds that lay offshore, the bounty of which seemed inexhaustible. Some of the cleverest fishermen began to experiment with new ways to catch more fish, borrowing money to buy bigger and better equipped boats. Since it was hard to argue with success, others copied their new techniques. Soon fish began to be harder to find, and their average size began to decline. Eventually, the fishery collapsed altogether, bringing economic calamity to the village. A wise elder commented, "You see, the fish were not free after all. It was our folly to act as if they were."*[3]

We live on a **global commons,** in which many natural resources, like the fishing grounds in this parable, are used collectively. The image of the earth as seen from space—a blue and green globe, girdled by white clouds, floating in blackness—shows that we share a single, unified ecosystem. Preserving the global commons and assuring its continued use is a new imperative for governments, business, and society. As we move into the twenty-first century, to quote Maurice Strong, secretary general of the original Earth Summit, "We now face the ultimate management challenge, that of managing our own future as a species."

---

[2]Garrett Hardin, "Tragedy of the Commons," *Science,* 162 (December 1968), pp. 1243–48.
[3]Abridgment of "The Story of a Fishing Village," from *1994 Information Please Environmental Almanac.* Copyright © 1993 by World Resources Institute. Reprinted by permission of Houghton Mifflin Co. All rights reserved.

Sustainable Development

The World Commission on Environment and Development, which includes leaders from many industrialized and developing nations, described the need for balance between economic and environmental considerations as **sustainable development.** This term refers to development that "meets the needs of the present without compromising the ability of future generations to meet their own needs."[4] The concept includes two core ideas:

- *Protecting the environment will require economic development.* Poverty is an underlying cause of environmental degradation. People who lack food, shelter, and basic amenities misuse resources just to survive. For this reason, environmental protection will require providing a decent standard of living for all the world's citizens.

- *But economic development must be accomplished sustainably,* that is, in a way that conserves the earth's resources for future generations. Growth cannot occur at the expense of degrading the forests, farmland, water, and air that must continue to support life on this planet.

In short, the idea of sustainable development encompasses a kind of puzzle. It challenges government and business leaders to eradicate poverty and develop the world economy but to do so in a way that does not degrade the environment or plunder natural resources.

Sustainable development is an appealing idea but also a very controversial one. For sustainable development to work, rich nations like the United States and Japan would have to consume fewer resources and dramatically cut pollution, without simply exporting environmental stresses to other countries. Some less developed nations, such as China or Pakistan, for their part, would have to use less destructive agricultural practices, cut birthrates, and industrialize more cleanly. This would only be possible with the aid of money, technology, and skills from the developed nations.

What would the idea of sustainable development mean for business? One attempt to apply this concept to business operations has been made by an initiative in Sweden called The Natural Step, described in Exhibit 11–A. Other voluntary efforts by the business community to operate with less harm to the environment are addressed in the last section of this chapter.

Threats to the Earth's Ecosystem

Sustainable development requires that human society use natural resources at a rate that can be continued over an indefinite period. Human activity affects three major forms of natural resources: water, air, and land. Biologists distinguish between renewable resources, such as fresh water or forests, that can be naturally replenished and nonrenewable resources, such as fossil fuels (oil, gas, and coal), that once used are gone forever. Many natural resources, renewable and nonrenewable, are now being depleted or polluted at well above sustainable rates. Consider the following examples.

---

[4]World Commission on Environment and Development, *Our Common Future* (Oxford: Oxford University Press, 1987), p. 8. For an account of the origins of the concept of sustainable development, see W. Adams, *Green Development: Environment and Sustainability in the Third World* (London: Routledge, 1990).

Water Resources

Only 3 percent of the water on the earth is fresh, and most of this is underground or locked up in ice and snow. Only about one-tenth of 1 percent of the earth's water is in lakes, rivers, and accessible underground supplies, and thus available for human use. Water is, of course, renewable: Moisture evaporates from the oceans and returns to earth as fresh-water precipitation, replenishing used stocks. But in many areas, humans are using up or polluting water faster than it can be replaced or naturally purified, threatening people and businesses that depend on it.

> *One of the most important aquifers (underground water sources) in the United States is the Ogallala formation, stretching from South Dakota to Texas. The Ogallala is the source of almost a third of all groundwater used for irrigation in the United States. In some areas, as much as a quarter of the aquifer has been depleted by unsustainable pumping, threatening local businesses such as farms and cattle ranches.[5]*

**EXHIBIT
11–A**

The Natural Step

The Natural Step (TNS) was founded in 1989 by a prominent Swedish physician, Karl-Henrik Robert. Dr. Robert joined other leading scientists in Sweden to develop a consensus document on how businesses, governments, and individuals could act in a way that was consistent with the principle of sustainable development. Their report was endorsed by the King of Sweden, and a summary was distributed to all households in the country.

The Natural Step encouraged businesses to act voluntarily to cut back on the use of synthetics and nonrenewable resources, minimize their consumption of energy, and preserve natural diversity and ecosystems. By 1997, over 300 companies and half the cities in Sweden had adopted TNS principles, and the movement was spreading to other countries, including the United States, the Netherlands, and Australia.

An example of a company that has followed The Natural Step is IKEA, the Swedish-based global home-furnishings retailer. IKEA signed on, committing itself to the use of materials, technologies, and transportation methods that had the "least possible damaging effect on the environment." For example, the company switched from truck to rail shipping where possible to conserve fuel and introduced a new line of furnishings, called the Eco-Line, that used only recycled materials or wood and fibers that had been sustainably harvested. The company said that the initiative not only had enabled them to protect the environment and attract "green" customers, it had actually helped the bottom line by avoiding waste and saving on energy and materials.

Sources: "Green Principles Growing Worldwide," *Minneapolis Star Tribune,* June 5, 1997, p. 26A; Andrea Larson and Joel E. Reichart, "IKEA and the Natural Step," Darden School of Management, University of Virginia, 1996; "Is This Man a Natural?" *The Guardian,* October 18, 1995, p. 4; Karl-Henrik Robert, "Educating a Nation: The Natural Step," *In Context,* Spring 1991, p. 10. IKEA's Web site, including material on the company's environmental policies, is available at http://www.ikea.com.

---

[5]Lester R. Brown, "Facing the Prospect of Food Scarcity," in Brown et al., *State of the World 1997,* pp. 23–41; and Sandra Postel, "Carrying Capacity: Earth's Bottom Line," in Lester R. Brown, ed., *State of the World 1994* (New York: W. W. Norton, 1994), pp. 3–21.

By one estimate, if society were able to eliminate all pollution, capture all available fresh water, and distribute it equitably—all of which are unlikely—demand would exceed the supply within a hundred years. In the 1990s, regional shortages had already caused the decline of local economies and in some cases had contributed to regional conflicts.[6]

Fossil Fuels

Fossil fuels, unlike water, are nonrenewable. Human society used 60 times as much energy in 1985 as it did in 1860. Most of this came from the burning of fossil fuels; 80 percent of all commercial energy in the 1980s came from the combustion of coal, oil, and natural gas. The amount of fossil fuel burned by the world economy in one year took about a million years to form. No one knows how long present supplies will last, because many reserves remain to be discovered. However, some estimates suggest that oil and gas will begin to run out in about 40 and 60 years, respectively. Coal reserves are more plentiful and could last three to four more centuries, although coal is more polluting than either oil or natural gas. Eventually, however, many fossil fuel reserves will be depleted, and the world economy will need to become much more energy efficient and switch to renewable energy sources, such as those based on water, wind, and sunshine.

Arable Land

Arable (fertile) land is necessary to grow crops to feed the world's peoples. Land, if properly cared for, is a renewable resource. Although the productivity of land increased through much of the twentieth century, by the 1990s much of the world's arable land was threatened with decline. About half of irrigated farmland in developing countries required reclamation because of salinization (excess salt) or poor drainage. In other areas, poor farming practices had caused previously arable land to turn into desert. Other areas had become contaminated by agricultural chemicals or ruined by overly intensive farming practices. In all, nearly 30 percent of the world's vegetated surface had been degraded to some degree by the late 1990s, according to the United Nations.[7]

Forces of Change

Pressure on the earth's resource base is becoming increasingly severe. Three critical factors have combined to accelerate the ecological crisis facing the world community and to make sustainable development more difficult. These are population growth, world poverty, and the rapid industrialization of many developing nations.

The Population Explosion

A major driver of environmental degradation is the exponential growth of the world's population. (A population that doubled every 50 years, for example, would be said to be growing exponentially. Many more people would be added during the second 50 years than during the first, even though the rate of growth would stay the same.) Just 10,000 years ago, the earth was home to no more than 10 million humans, scattered in small settlements. For many thousands of years, population growth was gradual. Around 1950, as

---

[6]"For Third World, Water Is Still a Deadly Drink," *New York Times;* January 9, 1997, pp. A1, A6; and Donella H. Meadows, Dennis L. Meadows, and Jorgen Randers, *Beyond the Limits: Confronting Global Collapse, Envisioning a Sustainable Future* (Post Mills, VT: Chelsea Green Publishing Co., 1992), p. 56.
[7]"Five Years after Environmental Summit in Rio," *New York Times*; World Resources Institute with the United Nations, *World Resources 1992–93* (New York: Oxford University Press, 1992), chap. 8.

shown in Figure 11–1, the world population reached 2.5 billion. World population is expected to cross the six billion mark around the turn of the century. The United Nations estimates that the population will eventually level out at a bit under 11 billion around 2150. To gain some perspective on these figures, consider that in the course of a single human lifetime—for example, someone born in 1950 who lived to be 75 years old—the world population will increase by more than five billion people.

This growth will not be distributed equally. In the industrialized countries, especially in Europe, population growth has already slowed down. About 95 percent of the world's population growth over the next 30 years is predicted to be in less developed countries, especially in Africa, Latin America, and Asia.

The world's burgeoning population will put increasing strain on the earth's resources. Each additional person uses raw materials and adds pollutants to the land, air, and water. The world's total industrial production would have to quintuple over the next 40 years just to maintain the same standard of living that people have now. Protecting the environment in the face of rapid population growth is very difficult. For example, in some parts of western Africa, population growth has put great pressure on available farmland, which is not allowed to lie fallow. Because much of the available firewood has already been cut, people use livestock dung for fuel instead of fertilizer. The result has been a deepening cycle of poverty, as more and more people try to live off less and less productive land.[8]

World Poverty

A second important cause of environmental degradation is poverty and the inequality between rich and poor countries. Although economic development has raised living standards for many, large numbers of the world's people continue to live in severe poverty. According to 1997 estimates by the United Nations, around 1.3 billion people had in-

Figure 11–1

World population growth.

Source: United Nations Population Fund estimates.

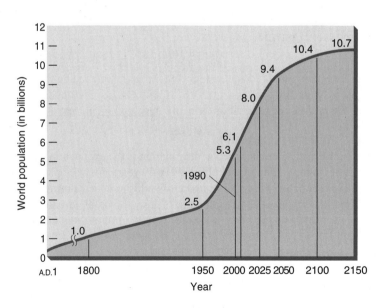

---

[8]Postel, "Carrying Capacity," p. 7.

comes below $1 a day, well below the level needed for a nutritionally adequate diet and other basic necessities of life. These people—most of them in sub-Saharan Africa, East and Southeast Asia, on the Indian subcontinent, and in Haiti—lived very near the margin of subsistence. They had only a tiny fraction of the goods and services enjoyed by those in the industrialized nations. Many suffered from hunger, including 158 million malnourished children under the age of five.[9]

> *Some of the most extreme poverty is found on the outskirts of rapidly growing cities in developing countries. In many parts of the world, people have moved to urban areas in search of work. Often, they must live in slums, in makeshift dwellings without sanitation or running water. In Bangkok, Thailand, a sprawling city of eight million, 35 percent of the population now lives in such areas. In Manila in the Philippines, thousands live in a garbage dump called Smokey Mountain.*[10]

The world's income is not distributed equally among nations. As Figure 11–2 shows, in 1994 the richest fifth of the world's nations received about 86 percent of all income, while the poorest fifth received little more than 1 percent. Japan's national income, to cite one example, was roughly on a par with that of the entire developing world, which had about 35 times as many people. Inequality is an environmental problem because countries (and people) at either extreme of income tend to behave in more environmentally destructive ways than those in the middle. People in the richest countries consume far more fossil fuels, wood, and meat, for example. People in the poorest countries, for their part, often misuse natural resources just to survive, for example, cutting down trees for fuel to cook food and keep themselves warm.

Industrialization

Parts of the third world are industrializing at a rapid pace. This is a positive development because it holds out the promise of reducing poverty and slowing population growth. But industrialization has also contributed to the growing ecological crisis. Industry requires energy, much of which is secured from combustion that releases pollutants of various types. The complex chemical processes of industry produce undesirable by-products and

Figure 11–2

Global income distribution, 1960–1994.

Source: United Nations Development Program, *Human Development Report 1992, 1994, and 1997* (New York: Oxford University Press).

Year	Share of Global Income (%)		Ratio of Richest to Poorest
	Richest 20 Percent	Poorest 20 Percent	
1960	70.2%	2.3%	30 to 1
1970	73.9	2.3	32 to 1
1980	76.3	1.7	45 to 1
1991	84.7	1.4	61 to 1
1994	85.8	1.1	78 to 1

[9]United Nations Development Program, *Human Development Report 1997* (New York: Oxford University Press, 1997), pp. 2–12, and table 1, pp. 146–148.
[10]"Warning: All Roads Lead to Asian Cities," *Los Angeles Times,* November 30, 1993, pp. 1, 4.

wastes that pollute land, water, and air. Its mechanical processes often create dust, grime, and unsightly refuse. More recently, the agricultural "green" revolution—although it has greatly increased crop yields in many parts of the world—has produced overkill with pesticides, herbicides, chemical fertilizers, and refuse from cattle-feeding factories.

The Limits to Growth

Some observers believe that the earth's rapid population growth, peoples' rising expectations, and the rapid industrialization of less developed countries are heading for a collision with a fixed barrier: the limited carrying capacity of the earth's ecosystem. According to *Beyond the Limits* by Donella Meadows and her colleagues, human society is now overshooting the carrying capacity of the earth's ecosystem.[11] Just as it is possible to eat or drink too much before your body sends you a signal to stop, so too are people and businesses using up resources and emitting pollution at an unsustainable rate. But because of delays in feedback, society does not understand the consequences of its actions until the damage is done.

If human society does not make a correction, a collapse may occur, possibly within the lifetimes of many who are alive today. What kind of collapse? Meadows and her colleagues developed several computer models to predict what would happen under different scenarios. If the world continued on its present course, with no major technical or policy changes, they predicted that by the year 2015, food production would begin to fall, as pollution degraded the fertility of the land. Around 2020, nonrenewable resources such as oil would begin to run out, and more and more resources would be needed to find, extract, and refine what remained. By midcentury, industrial production would begin to collapse, pulling down with it the service and agricultural sectors. Life expectancy and population would fall soon after, as death rates were driven up by lack of food and health care.

Critics of the **limits to growth hypothesis** suggest that these doomsday predictions are unnecessarily bleak, because there are important offsets to these limits. Market forces are one such offset. For example, as natural resources such as oil and gas become more scarce, their prices will rise, and people and businesses may be motivated to use natural resources more efficiently or to find substitutes. Another offset is technology. Technological advances may slow environmental degradation by developing more reliable birth control, more productive crops through genetic engineering, or nonpolluting sources of energy such as solar-powered engines. The authors of *Beyond the Limits* acknowledge these offsets but stick to their conclusion that if human society does not adopt sustainable development, economic and social catastrophe is just a matter of time.[12]

Global Environmental Issues

Some environmental problems are inherently global in scope and require international cooperation. Typically these are issues pertaining to the global commons, that is, resources shared by all nations. Three global problems that will have major consequences for business and society—all of which

---

[11]Meadows, Meadows, and Randers, *Beyond the Limits.*
[12]For a classic critique of an earlier version of the limits to growth hypothesis, see Robert M. Solow, "Is the End of the World at Hand?" *Challenge,* March–April 1973, pp. 39–50.

were extensively discussed at the Earth Summit and its follow-up conferences—are ozone depletion, global warming, and biodiversity.

Ozone Depletion

Ozone is a bluish gas, composed of three bonded oxygen atoms, that floats in a thin layer in the stratosphere between 8 and 25 miles above the planet. Although poisonous to humans in the lower atmosphere, ozone in the stratosphere is critical to life on earth by absorbing dangerous ultraviolet light from the sun. Too much ultraviolet light can cause skin cancer and damage the eyes and immune systems of humans and other species.

In 1974, scientists first hypothesized that chlorofluorocarbons (CFCs)—manufactured chemicals widely used as refrigerants, insulation, solvents, and propellants in spray cans—could react with and destroy ozone. Little evidence existed of actual ozone depletion, however, until 1985, when scientists discovered a thin spot, or hole, in the ozone layer over Antarctica. Studies showed that the hole was indeed the work of CFCs. In the upper atmosphere, intense solar rays had split CFC molecules, releasing chlorine atoms that had reacted with and destroyed ozone. In the early 1990s, scientists for the first time reported evidence of ozone depletion in the northern latitudes over Europe and North America during the summer, when the sun's ultraviolet rays are the strongest and pose the greatest danger.

World political leaders moved quickly in response to scientific evidence that CFCs posed a threat to the earth's protective ozone shield. In 1987, a group of nations negotiated the **Montreal Protocol,** agreeing to cut CFC production and use by 50 percent by 1999. In 1992, the deadline for phasing out manufacture of CFCs completely was moved up to 1996, in view of evidence that the ozone layer was being depleted even faster than feared earlier. Developing countries were given until 2010 to phase out the chemicals completely.

By the late 1990s, most businesses in the developed world had completed the transition to CFC substitutes, and many had made money by doing so. DuPont, Allied Signal, Elf Altochem, and several other chemical companies had developed profitable substitutes for banned ozone-depleting chemicals. All the major appliance manufacturers, such as Electrolux in Sweden and Whirlpool in the United States, had brought out successful new lines of CFC-free refrigerators and freezers, and carmakers had developed air conditioners that operated without the dangerous coolant.

Although CFCs are now illegal in the United States, unfortunately large quantities of the chemical are still being smuggled into the country from Mexico and other developing countries where it is still manufactured. In 1997, U.S. officials reported that 1.5 million pounds of illegal CFCs had been seized in the past three years alone.[13]

Unfortunately, even the complete phaseout of CFC use by signatories of the Montreal Protocol will not solve the problem for many years to come. CFCs are remarkably stable and can persist in the atmosphere for as long as 50 years, so those released in the early 1990s may still be reaching the upper atmosphere as late as the 2040s. CFCs will

---

[13]"Freon Smugglers Face Charges in Four States as Part of Crackdown," *The Wall Street Journal,* January 10, 1997, p. B3A.

also continue to be released from products made before the ban took effect and from countries where they are still manufactured. A number of other ozone-depleting chemicals, including some used as substitutes for CFCs, are not yet fully regulated by treaty. Ironically, even though world leaders and businesses have moved aggressively to eliminate CFCs, ozone depletion will likely get worse before it gets better.

Global Warming

Another difficult problem facing the world community is the gradual warming of the earth's atmosphere. Although uncertainty remains about the rate and causes of **global warming,** business and governments have begun to respond to the issue.

The earth's atmosphere contains carbon dioxide and other trace gases that, like the glass panels in a greenhouse, prevent heat reflected from the earth's surface from escaping into space, as illustrated in Figure 11–3. Without this so-called greenhouse effect, the earth would be too cold to support life. Since the Industrial Revolution, which began in the late 1700s, the amount of greenhouse gases in the atmosphere has increased by as much as 25 percent, largely due to the burning of fossil fuels such as oil and natural gas. According to the Intergovernmental Panel on Climate Change (IPCC), a group of 2,500 of the world's leading atmospheric scientists, the earth has already warmed by between 0.3 and 0.6 degrees Celsius over the past century (1 degree Celsius equals 1.8 degrees Fahrenheit, the unit commonly used in the United States). If societal emissions of greenhouse gases continue to grow unchecked, the IPCC predicted, the earth could warm by as much as 3.5 degrees Celsius more in the next century.

Figure 11–3

Global warming.

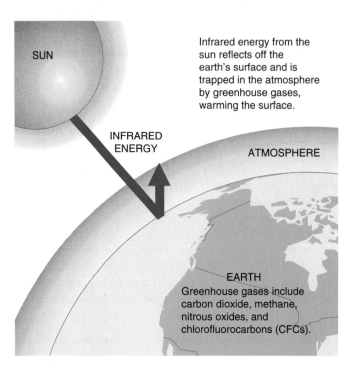

SUN

Infrared energy from the sun reflects off the earth's surface and is trapped in the atmosphere by greenhouse gases, warming the surface.

INFRARED ENERGY

ATMOSPHERE

EARTH
Greenhouse gases include carbon dioxide, methane, nitrous oxides, and chlorofluorocarbons (CFCs).

There are many possible causes of global warming. The burning of fossil fuels, which releases carbon dioxide, is the leading contributor. But consider the following additional causes.[14]

- *Deforestation.* Trees and other plants absorb carbon dioxide, removing it from the atmosphere. Deforestation—cutting down and not replacing trees—thus contributes to global warming. Burning forests to clear land for grazing or agriculture also releases carbon directly into the atmosphere as a component of smoke. Large-scale deforestation thus contributes in two ways to global warming.

- *Beef production.* Methane, a potent greenhouse gas, is produced as a by-product of the digestion of some animals, including cows. Large-scale cattle ranching releases significant amounts of methane.

- *Population growth.* Human beings produce carbon dioxide every time they breathe. More people mean more greenhouse gases.

- *CFCs.* In addition to destroying the ozone, these are also greenhouse gases. The Montreal Protocol will have the unintended beneficial consequence of slowing global warming.

If global warming continues, the world may experience extreme heat waves, air pollution crises, and damaging wildfires in the twenty-first century. The polar ice caps may partially melt, raising sea levels and causing flooding in low-lying coastal areas like Florida, Bangladesh, and the Netherlands. It may become as difficult to grow wheat in Iowa as it is now in arid Utah. Such climate change could devastate many of the world's economies and destroy the habitats of many species.

In late 1997, many of the world's nations gathered in Kyoto, Japan, to consider amendments to the Convention on Climate Change, an international treaty on global warming first negotiated at the 1992 Earth Summit. In difficult negotiations, the parties hammered out an agreement that would require industrial countries, such as the United States, to reduce greenhouse gas emissions more than 5 percent *below* 1990 levels, over a period of several years. But the group postponed consideration of controversial proposals, supported by the United States, that would give each nation *allowances* for a certain quota of carbon emissions. Countries that reduced their emissions below their quotas would be able to sell allowances to others; those that exceeded their quotas would have to buy allowances on the open market. The Kyoto Protocol, as the agreement was known, would have to be ratified by each nation.[15]

What did world business leaders think about global warming and the proposed solutions, including those debated in Kyoto? Some of the widely divergent perspectives within the business community on this issue are presented in Exhibit 11–B.

---

[14]For a collection of diverse views on global warming, see Andrew J. Hoffman, ed., *Global Climate Change: A Senior Level Debate at the Intersection of Economics, Strategy, Technology, Science, Politics, and International Negotiations* (San Francisco: New Lexington Press, 1997). For an analysis of the science of global warming, see Stephen H. Schneider, *Global Warming: Are We Entering the Greenhouse Century?* (San Francisco: Sierra Club Books, 1989). An argument cautioning against the global warming alarm may be found in Patrick J. Michaels, *Sound and Fury: The Science and Politics of Global Warming* (Washington, D.C.: CATO Institute, 1992).

[15]"Agreement Is Reached in Kyoto on Greenhouse Gases," *New York Times,* December 11, 1997, pp. A1, A10; and "Clear Skies Are Goal as Pollution Is Turned into a Commodity," *The Wall Street Journal,* October 3, 1997, pp. A1, A5.

EXHIBIT 11–B

Global Warming: The Many Perspectives of Business

In the late 1990s, different segments of the world business community held widely divergent views on global warming and what, if anything, should be done about it.

On one end of the spectrum stood the Global Climate Coalition (GCC), representing many companies in the *oil, coal, chemical,* and *auto* industries. The GCC downplayed the threat of climate change and argued that any government controls on the emission of greenhouse gases would be costly and premature. When asked by a reporter what she hoped would be accomplished at the global climate change talks in Kyoto, Japan, in 1997, the president of the coalition held up her fingers to form a zero.

Although most of the big oil companies subscribed to the GCC's view, a few did not. In 1996, British Petroleum (BP) quit the group. The following May, the chief executive of BP America gave a widely publicized speech to an audience at Stanford University in which he said, "The time to consider the policy dimensions of climate change is not when the link between greenhouse gases and climate change is conclusively proven . . . but when the possibility cannot be discounted. . . . We in BP have reached that point."

One of the industries most worried about climate change was, perhaps not surprisingly, *insurance.* In the early 1990s, the insurance industry was walloped by a series of huge payouts for major floods, hurricanes, and severe storms. Although no one could pin the blame for sure on global warming, many saw a connection. "There is a significant body of scientific evidence indicating that the [recent] record insured losses from natural catastrophes was not a random occurrence," commented the general manager of Swiss Re, a large European insurer. "Failure to act," he added, "would leave the industry and its policyholders vulnerable to truly disastrous consequences."

A moderate position was staked out by the International Climate Change Partnership (ICCP), representing many big *manufacturers* and *service firms,* including AT&T, Du Pont, General Electric, and 3M. This group accepted the evidence for climate change but argued that corporations, not government, should take the lead by identifying profitable opportunities to reduce emissions. AT&T, for example, was interested in promoting telecommuting as an alternative to driving to work.

The *electric utility* industry seemed unwilling to commit itself unequivocally. "We sell electricity and we do not care where it comes from," said a spokesperson for the Edison Electric Institute, a trade group. "The power lines do not know [whether] it comes from coal, wind, or solar cells. We are with the future." The Business Council for Sustainable Energy, representing producers of *solar power, wind power,* and *natural gas*—along with some utilities promoting energy conservation—called for stabilization, and then reductions of greenhouse gas emissions.

Said one lobbyist for alternative energy producers, "[The oil and coal companies] want you to believe that the science [on global warming] is divided, while business is united. In fact, the reverse is true."

Sources: David L. Levy and Aundrea Kelley, "The International Climate Change Partnership: An Industry Association Faces the Climate Change Issue," Management Institute for Environment and Business, 1996; Ross Gelbspan, *The Heat Is On: The High Stakes Battle over Earth's Threatened Climate* (Reading, MA: Addison-Wesley, 1997); "Industries Revisit Global Warming: Some Producers Now Support Curbing Greenhouse Gases," *New York Times,* August 5, 1997, p. A1, A4; and "Green Warrior in Gray Flannel," *Business Week,* May 6, 1996, p. 96. The speech of John Browne, chief executive of BP America, on his company's position on global warming, is available at http://dns.wbcsd.ch/speeches.

Biodiversity

Biodiversity refers to the number and variety of species and the range of their genetic makeup. To date, approximately 1.7 million species of plants and animals have been named and described. Many scientists believe these are but a fraction of the total. The earth contains at least 10 million species and possibly more than 100 million. Scientists estimate that species extinction is now occurring at 100 to 1,000 times the normal, background rate, mainly because of pollution and the destruction of habitat by human society.[16] Biological diversity is now at its lowest level since the disappearance of the dinosaurs some 65 million years ago. The eminent biologist Edward O. Wilson has eloquently stated the costs of this loss:

> *Every species extinction diminishes humanity. Every micro-organism, animal and plant contains on the order of from one million to 10 billion bits of information in its genetic code, hammered into existence by an astronomical number of mutations and episodes of natural selection over the course of thousands or even millions of years of evolution. . . . Species diversity—the world's available gene pool—is one of our planet's most important and irreplaceable resources. . . . As species are exterminated, largely as the result of habitat destruction, the capacity for natural genetic regeneration is greatly reduced. In Norman Myers' phrase, we are causing the death of birth.[17]*

Genetic diversity is vital to each species' ability to adapt and survive and has many benefits for human society as well. By destroying this biological diversity, we are actually undermining our survivability as a species.

Ethicists have recently given greater attention to the responsibilities of humans to conserve the natural environment and to prevent the extinction of other species of plants and animals. This emerging philosophical perspective is profiled in Exhibit 11–C.

A major reason for the decline in the earth's biodiversity is the destruction of rain forests, particularly in the tropics. Rain forests are woodlands that receive at least 100 inches of rain a year. They are the planet's richest areas in terms of biological diversity. In the 1990s, rain forests covered only around 7 percent of the earth's surface but accounted for somewhere between 50 to 90 percent of the earth's species. Only about half of the original tropical rain forests still stand, and at the rate they are currently being cut, all will be gone or severely depleted within 30 years. The reasons for destruction of rain forests include commercial logging, cattle-ranching, and conversion of forest to plantations to produce cash crops for export. Overpopulation also plays a part, as landless people clear forest to grow crops and cut trees for firewood.

The destruction is ironic, because rain forests may have more economic value standing than cut. Rain forests are the source of many valuable products, including foods, medicines, and fibers. The pharmaceutical industry, for example, each year develops new medicines based on newly discovered plants from tropical areas. The U.S. National Cancer Institute has identified 1,400 tropical forest plants with cancer-fighting properties. As rain forests are destroyed, so too is this potential for new medicines.

---

[16]Kal Raustiala and David G. Victor, "Biodiversity since Rio: The Future of the Convention on Biological Diversity," *Environment,* 38, no. 4 (May 1996), pp. 16ff.

[17]Edward O. Wilson, "Threats to Biodiversity," in *Managing Planet Earth: Readings from Scientific American Magazine* (New York: W. H. Freeman and Co., 1990), pp. 57–58. This article originally appeared in *Scientific American*, September 1989. Used by permission.

EXHIBIT 11–C   **The Emergence of Environmental Ethics**

Environmental ethics is concerned with the ethical responsibilities of human beings toward the natural environment. In much of Western philosophy, there exists a fundamental dualism, or separation, between humans and nature. Some Western philosophers have believed that the purpose of civilization was to dominate and control the environment (or nature) and other living things. This perspective may be contrasted with an emerging philosophical view that human society is part of an integrated ecosystem and that humans have ethical obligations toward nature. The following quotations are drawn from proponents of the latter view.

A thing is right when it tends to preserve the integrity, stability, and beauty of the biotic community [of living things]. It is wrong when it tends otherwise.

Aldo Leopold

The well-being and flourishing of human and non-human Life on Earth have value in themselves. . . . These values are independent of the usefulness of the non-human world for human purposes.

Arne Naess

What is proposed here is a broadening of value, so that nature will cease to be merely "property" and become a commonwealth. . . . If we now universalize "person," consider how slowly the circle has enlarged . . . to include aliens, strangers, infants, children, Negroes, Jews, slaves, women, Indians, prisoners, the elderly, the insane, the deformed, and even now we ponder the status of fetuses. Ecological ethics queries whether we ought to again universalize, recognizing the intrinsic value of every ecobiotic [living] component.

Holmes Rolston

Source: The first two quotations are from Susan J. Armstrong and Richard G. Botzler, eds., *Environmental Ethics: Divergence and Convergence* (New York: McGraw-Hill, 1993), pp. 382 and 412; the third quotation is from Roderick Nash, *The Rights of Nature* (Madison: University of Wisconsin Press, 1989), pp. 3–4.

Madagascar, the fourth-largest island in the world, located off the eastern coast of Africa, is widely regarded as a biological treasure trove. Researchers discovered, for example, that the rosy periwinkle plant, found in the island's tropical rain forest, contained a unique genetic trait that was useful in the treatment of Hodgkin's disease, childhood leukemia, and other cancers. Over 90 percent of Madagascar's rain forest has been cleared, destroying perhaps half of the 200,000 species of plants and animals found there.[18]

One of the issues discussed at the Earth Summit was the right of nations, such as Madagascar, to a fair share of profits from the commercialization of genetic material for which they are the source. Until a few years ago, drug companies, for example, often col-

[18]Jeremy Rifkin, *Biosphere Politics: A New Consciousness for a New Century* (New York: Crown Publishers, 1991), p. 67; and *1994 Information Please Environmental Almanac* (Boston: Houghton Mifflin, 1994), p. 356.

lected genetic samples from foreign countries without compensation. In most cases, source countries are now more aware of the commercial value of their biological resources and have required the payment of royalties when genetic material is developed commercially. Partnerships have also developed between business firms and source nations that respect the unique contribution of each.

> *Shaman Pharmaceuticals, founded in 1990 by Lisa Conte, a biochemist with a graduate degree in business and a strong commitment to the environment, is a small U.S.-based company that specializes in developing medicines from rain forest plants. The company employs a group of field researchers who live and work alongside traditional healers, known as* shamans, *in the rain forests of Central America, identifying plants for possible medicinal use. In 1997, Shaman Pharmaceuticals was conducting tests on two promising drugs derived from the tropical croton tree—one a treatment for genital herpes, the other for diarrhea—and planned to apply soon for FDA approval to market them. Conte's goal is to donate a portion of the company's profits to an organization dedicated to preserving tropical folk medicine.*[19]

As noted in the introductory section of this chapter, the Earth Summit produced a treaty, the Convention on Biological Diversity, which by the end of 1996 had been ratified by 162 countries. (The United States was not among them.) The treaty commits these countries to draw up national strategies for conservation, protect ecosystems and individual species, and take steps to restore degraded areas. It also allows countries to share in the profits from sales of products derived from their biological resources.

Response of the International Business Community

The international business community has undertaken many initiatives to put the principle of sustainable development into practice.

World Business Council for Sustainable Development

One of the leaders in the global effort to promote sustainable business practices is the World Business Council for Sustainable Development (WBCSD). The Council was formed in 1995 through a merger of the Business Council for Sustainable Development, a group of corporate executives who had supported the original Earth Summit, and the World Industry Council for the Environment, a project of the International Chamber of Commerce. In 1997, the Council was made up of about 125 companies, drawn from over 30 countries and 20 industries. The WBCSD's goals were to encourage high standards of environmental management and to promote closer cooperation among businesses, governments, and other organizations concerned with sustainable development.

The WBCSD called for businesses to manufacture and distribute products more efficiently, consider their lifelong impact, and recycle components. In a series of publica-

---

[19]Elaine Pofeldt, "The Self-Made Woman," *Success* 44, no. 5 (June 1997), p. 37ff; Mark Jenkins and Tom McGrath, "The Secret Garden: Amazon Rain Forests and Their Medicinal Plants," *Men's Health* 8, no. 12 (October 1997); and David Riggle, "Pharmaceuticals from the Rainforest," *In Business,* January–February 1992. Another promising partnership between an American pharmaceutical company and a country rich in biological resources is described in Michele Zebich-Knos, "Preserving Biodiversity in Costa Rica: The Case of the Merck-INBio Agreement," *Journal of Environment and Development,* June 1997, pp. 180–86.

tions, the group set forth the view that the most eco-efficient companies—those that added the most value with the least use of resources and pollution—were more competitive and more environmentally sound. **Eco-efficiency** was only possible, the Council concluded, in the presence of open, competitive markets in which prices reflected the true cost of environmental and other resources. In the past, environmental costs have not been fully accounted, for example, in calculating measures of production such as the gross domestic product. One study showed, for example, that when the true costs of depletion of timber, oil, and topsoil were included, the economic growth rate of Indonesia from 1971 to 1984 was not 7 percent, as officially calculated, but only 4 percent.[20] The WBCSD recommended revising systems of national accounting to include the costs of environmental damage, and pricing products to reflect their full environmental costs.[21]

Several other groups, in addition to the WBCSD, have given serious attention to the idea of sustainable development and its implications for business. Exhibit 11–D profiles the efforts of several important national and international organizations to develop codes of environmental conduct, including the new 14000 certification program of the International Organization for Standardization (ISO).

Many individual businesses and industry groups have also undertaken voluntary initiatives to improve their environmental performance. These are the subject of the next section.

Voluntary Business Initiatives

Many firms around the world have tried to determine how sustainable development translates into actual business practice. Some of the more important voluntary initiatives undertaken by businesses include the following:

Life-cycle analysis involves collecting information on the lifelong environmental impact of a product, all the way from extraction of raw material to manufacturing to its distribution, use, and ultimate disposal. The aim of life-cycle analysis is to minimize the adverse impact of a particular product at all stages. One of the initial pioneers of life-cycle analysis was Procter & Gamble, the U.S.-based consumer products maker. After conducting a life-cycle analysis of a liquid fabric softener, for example, the company introduced a triple-strength version, refillable plastic containers made with recycled material, and paperboard refill cartons. The result was greatly reduced packaging waste.

Industrial ecology refers to designing factories and distribution systems as if they were self-contained ecosystems. For example, businesses can save materials through closed-loop recycling, use wastes from one process as raw material for others, and make use of energy generated as a by-product of production.

> *An example of industrial ecology may be found in the town of Kalundborg, Denmark, where several companies have formed a cooperative relationship*

[20]Robert C. Repetto et al., *Wasting Assets: Natural Resources in the National Income Accounts* (Washington D.C.: World Resources Institute, 1989).

[21]The WBCSD's publications include two books: Stephan Schmidheiny and Federico J. L. Zorraquin, *Financing Change: The Financial Community, Eco-Efficiency, and Sustainable Development* (Cambridge, MA: MIT Press, 1997); and Stephan Schmidheiny, *Changing Course: A Global Business Perspective on Development and the Environment* (Cambridge, MA: MIT Press, 1992); and several reports on sustainable production and consumption, trade and the environment, environmental impact assessment, and eco-efficiency. See a list of WBCSD's publications at http://dns.wbcsd.ch/prodoc. Many practical actions that business can take are discussed in Claude Fussler, *Driving Eco-Innovation* (London and New York: Pittman Publishing, 1996).

EXHIBIT 11–D

International Codes of Environmental Conduct

A number of national and international business organizations have developed codes of environmental conduct. Among the most important ones are the following.

International Chamber of Commerce (ICC)

The ICC developed the Business Charter for Sustainable Development, 16 principles that identify key elements of environmental leadership and call on companies to recognize environmental management as among their highest corporate priorities.

Global Environmental Management Initiative (GEMI)

A group of over 20 companies dedicated to fostering environmental excellence, GEMI developed several environmental self-assessment programs, including one that helps firms assess their progress in meeting the goals of the Business Charter for Sustainable Development.

Keidanren

This major Japanese industry association has published a Global Environmental Charter that sets out a code of environmental behavior that calls on its members to be "good global corporate citizens."

Chemical Manufacturers Association (CMA)

This U.S.-based industry association developed Responsible Care: A Public Commitment, which commits its member-companies to a code of management practices, focusing on process safety, community awareness, pollution prevention, safe distribution, employee health and safety, and product stewardship. The group is working for the international adoption of these principles.

CERES Principles

These are 10 voluntary principles developed by the Coalition for Environmentally Responsible Economies that commit signatory firms to protection of the biosphere, sustainable use of natural resources, energy conservation, risk reduction, and other environmental goals.

International Organization for Standardization (ISO)

ISO 14000 is a series of voluntary standards introduced in 1996 by the ISO, an international group based in Geneva, Switzerland, that permit companies to be certified as meeting global environmental performance standards.

Sources: For further information on these organizations and their codes, see http://www.iccwbo.org/charter (International Chamber of Commerce); http://www.gemi.org (Global Environmental Management Initiative); http://www.keidanren or jp/english/profile (Keidanren); http://cmahq.com/rescare.html (Chemical Manufacturers Association); http://ceres.org (Coalition for Environmentally Responsible Economies); and http://iso.ch (International Organization for Standardization).

that produces both economic and environmental benefits. The local utility company sells excess process steam, which had previously been released into a local fjord (waterway), to a local pharmaceutical plant and oil refinery. Excess fly ash (fine particles produced when fuel is burned) is sold to nearby businesses for use in cement making and road building. Meanwhile, the oil refinery removes sulfur in the natural gas it produces, to make it cleaner burning, and sells the sulfur to a sulfuric acid plant. Calcium sulfate, produced as a residue of a process to cut smoke emissions, is sold to a gypsum manufacturer for making wallboard. The entire cycle both saves money and reduces pollution.[22]

Design for disassembly means that products are designed so that at the end of their useful life they can be disassembled and recycled. At Volkswagen, the German carmaker, engineers design cars for eventual disassembly and reuse. At the company's specialized auto recycling plant in Leer, built in 1990, old cars can be completely taken apart in just three minutes. Plastics, steel, precious metals, oil, acid, and glass are separated and processed. Many materials are used again in new Volkswagens.[23]

Sustainable development will require **technology cooperation** through long-term partnerships between companies in developed and developing countries to transfer environmental technologies, as shown in the following two examples.

Since the mid-1960s, Nippon Steel, a major Japanese steel producer, has had a partnership with Usiminas, a Brazilian firm, to develop and run a basic steel industry in the state of Minas Gerais in southeastern Brazil. Modern environmental technology has been part of the project from the start. For example, the Japanese helped introduce energy-efficient continuous casting and a system to clean and recover basic oxygen furnace emissions. The result is a third-world steel industry as clean as the most advanced in the world.

The leather tanning industry traditionally generates large amounts of noxious waste. In Kenya, a major leather producer, a Leather Development Centre has been established with funds from the United Nations and Germany. The Centre has developed a model tannery that uses the most environmentally advanced methods and trains Kenyan tanners in their application.[24]

Although many companies around the world have undertaken valuable experiments, the idea of sustainable development remains controversial in the business community. Nevertheless, one study showed that the proportion of senior executives who believe environmental issues are "extremely important" increased threefold in a two-year period in the early 1990s, and many were taking action to improve the ways their firms managed environmental risk.[25]

Protecting the environment and the well-being of future generations is, as the founder of the Business Council on Sustainable Development put it, "fast becoming a business necessity and even an opportunity."[26] Environmental regulations are getting tougher, consumers want cleaner products, and employees want to work for environmentally conscious companies. Finding ways to reduce or recycle waste saves money. Many executives are championing the importance of corporations' moral obligations to future generations. The

---

[22]Arthur D. Little, "Industrial Ecology: An Environmental Agenda for Industry," (Cambridge, MA: Arthur D. Little, Center for Environmental Assurance, 1991); "Growth vs. Environment," *Business Week,* May 5, 1992, p. 75. For a full discussion, see R. H. Socolow et al., *Industrial Ecology and Global Change,* (New York, NY: Cambridge University Press, 1994).

[23]Schmidheiny, *Changing Course,* pp. 305–8.

[24]Ibid., pp. 206–9, 224–28.

[25]Study by Booz, Allen, and Hamilton, cited in "Hope for the Future," Special Advertising Section, *Business Week,* December 30, 1991, p. 83.

[26]Stephan Schmidheiny, "The Business Logic of Sustainable Development," *Columbia Journal of World Business,* 27, no. 3–4 (1992), pp. 19–23.

most successful global businesses in coming years may be those, like the ones profiled in this chapter, that recognize the imperative for sustainable development as an opportunity both for competitive advantage and ethical action.

Summary Points of This Chapter

- Many world leaders have supported the idea of sustainable development—economic growth without depleting the resources on which future generations will depend. But achieving sustainable development remains a challenge, and the community of nations has not yet worked out who will pay.

- Major threats to the earth's ecosystem include depletion of nonrenewable resources such as oil and coal, air and water pollution, and the degradation of arable land.

- Population growth, poverty, and rapid industrialization in many parts of the world have contributed to these ecological problems. The limits to growth hypothesis maintains that human society will soon exceed the carrying capacity of the earth's ecosystem, unless changes are made now.

- Three environmental issues—ozone depletion, global warming, and biodiversity—are shared by all nations. International agreements have been negotiated addressing all three issues, although more remains to be done.

- Global businesses have begun to put the principles of sustainable development into action through such innovative actions as life-cycle analysis, industrial ecology, design for disassembly, and technology cooperation. But many believe that voluntary actions by business cannot solve environmental problems without supportive public policies.

Key Terms and Concepts Used in this Chapter

- Ecology
- Global commons
- Sustainable development
- Limits to growth hypothesis
- Ozone
- Montreal Protocol
- Global warming

- Biodiversity
- Eco-efficiency
- Life-cycle analysis
- Industrial ecology
- Design for disassembly
- Technology cooperation

Internet Resources

- http://www.epa.gov/globalwarming   Environmental Protection Agency global warming site
- http://www.epa.gov/docs/ozone   Environmental Protection Agency ozone site
- http://www.unep.org   United Nations Environmental Program
- http://dns.wbcsd.ch   World Business Council on Sustainable Development

Discussion Case   **Damming the Yangtze River**

Along the banks of the Yangtze River in central China in the late-1990s, a massive project was underway to construct the largest hydroelectric dam in the world. A visiting journalist described the scene:

From horizon to horizon, the ancient landscape here has been sundered, scored, and stripped by the big steel blades of countless front-end loaders. Dust storms rise from monster caravans hauling a million boulders across a riven plain . . . . Mountains are disappearing and a new concrete topography is rising in their place, connected in a manmade design whose foundations are being laid across a dust bowl so broad that it seems almost planetary in scale.

When completed in 2009, the Three Gorges Dam was expected to be over a mile across and to have the capacity to generate 18,200 megawatts of electricity, 18 times as much as a standard nuclear power plant. This energy would be crucial to the fast-developing Chinese economy, where demand for electricity was projected to double every 15 years. "The dam will make life better for our children," said one construction worker. "They'll have electric lights, TV, be able to study their lessons. With luck they'll go to the university."

The 400-mile-long reservoir and locks that would be created behind the dam would be deep enough to bring oceangoing ships 1,500 miles inland to the city of Chongqing, opening markets in the vast interior of China. The government also hoped that the dam would end the disastrous floods that had inundated the region every five or so years throughout history. In the twentieth century alone, 300,000 lives had been lost and millions of homes destroyed. The construction effort itself employed 40,000 people and pumped billions of dollars into the local economy.

But the project had its share of critics, both inside and outside China. Before the waters could be unleashed, 1.9 million Chinese, mostly in rural towns and villages along the river, would have to be resettled to higher ground. Homes and jobs would need to be found for them. A quarter-million acres of fertile farmland would be flooded, as would many unexcavated archaeological sites.

The project would inundate the Three Gorges, thought by many to be among the most starkly beautiful scenery in the world. At this point in its course, the Yangtze passes through a narrow passage, with dramatic limestone walls towering as high as 3,000 feet above the river. In addition to destroying this landscape, the dam would radically transform the ecology of the river. Environmentalists pointed out that fish migrations would be blocked and plants and animals adapted to the river habitat would die out.

Moreover, no provisions had been made to treat the billions of tons of industrial and municipal sewage expected to flow into the reservoir. In the past, the fast-moving river had carried untreated waste to the sea. No provisions had been made, either, to relocate existing landfills and dumps, many containing toxic waste, that lay in the area that would be flooded.

But other environmentalists thought that the project had merit. Hydroelectric power, of the sort to be generated by the Three Gorges Dam, was nonpolluting. The main practical alternative to the dam was to build more coal-fired power plants, which in the late-1990s supplied over three-quarters of China's energy. Coal combustion produces sulfur dioxide, a cause of acid rain, and carbon dioxide, a major contributor to global warming. China was already the second-biggest emitter of carbon in the world (after the United States); it was responsible for 13 percent of the world's emissions, even though its economy accounted for only 2 percent of the world's GDP. The air in much of China is fouled by coal dust and smoke, and a quarter of all deaths are caused by lung disease.

Sources: Arthur Zich, "China's Three Gorges: Before the Flood," *National Geographic* 92, no. 3 (September 1997), pp. 2–33; and "Cracks Show Early in China's Big Dam Project," *New York Times,* January 15, 1996, pp. A1, A4.

Discussion Questions

1. What stakeholders will be helped by the Three Gorges Dam? What stakeholders will be hurt by it?
2. How does construction of a dam on the Yangtze River relate to the issues of global warming, biodiversity, and water pollution discussed in this chapter?
3. Do you agree with the decision of the Chinese government to construct the Three Gorges Dam? Why or why not?
4. What strategies do you believe would best promote economic development in China without destroying the environmental resources on which future generations depend?

12

Managing Environmental Issues

Growing public interest in protecting the environment has prompted political and corporate leaders to become increasingly responsive to environmental issues. In the United States, policymakers have moved toward greater reliance on market-based mechanisms, rather than command and control regulations, to achieve environmental goals. At the same time, many businesses have become increasingly proactive and have pioneered new approaches to effective environmental management.

This chapter focuses on these key questions and objectives:

- What are the main features of U.S. environmental laws, and what are the advantages and disadvantages of different regulatory approaches?

- What are the costs and benefits of environmental regulation?

- What is an ecologically sustainable organization, and through what stages do firms pass as they become more sustainable?

- How can businesses best manage environmental issues?

- Does effective environmental management make firms more competitive?

L os Angeles, California, is one of the most smog-ridden cities in the United States. On many days, the city is covered by a dense blanket of orange haze, and residents cannot catch even a glimpse of the lovely San Gabriel mountains just a few miles to the east. In 1993, southern California air-quality regulators, frustrated with old approaches, tried something new—a market-driven plan called *RECLAIM*. This plan required major overall reductions in smog-producing chemical emissions but permitted individual businesses to buy and sell pollution credits. Hailed by business as a less burdensome and less costly way to reduce urban smog, the *RECLAIM* program was expected to reduce targeted emissions by 70 percent over 10 years. By the late 1990s, an active market had emerged, and companies were even trading pollution credits on-line.[1]

The Environmental Defense Fund (EDF), a leading environmental advocacy organization, believed that its old strategy of suing companies and lobbying legislators was not working well enough. Instead, the group tried a cooperative approach, joining McDonald's Corporation to study the issue of fast-food packaging waste. After just a few months, McDonald's agreed to abandon its clamshell, foam hamburger box, replacing it with a paper wrapper. Encouraged by this and other successes, EDF joined in an ambitious partnership with a group of major companies, including Time Warner, Johnson & Johnson, and Prudential Insurance, to promote the manufacture of ecologically safe paper. The companies in the group used their combined purchasing power of over $1 billion to encourage the paper industry to use cleaner production methods and recycled materials.[2]

Dow Chemical Corporation initiated a wide-ranging program called Waste Reduction Always Pays, WRAP for short. The idea was that it would be more efficient, and less expensive, for the company to prevent pollution in the first place than to treat and dispose of pollutants at the "end of the pipe." The company reduced the use of hazardous chemicals in production, to cut down on waste. Where this was not possible, the company tried to recycle waste by-products. By the late-1990s, the company reported that WRAP was saving the company over $20 million annually. The company's president concluded that "the most compelling actions industry can take with respect to environmental protection are voluntary."[3]

As the turn of the century approached, many political leaders, corporate executives, and environmental advocates—like those profiled in these examples—became increasingly concerned that old strategies for promoting environmental protection were failing and new approaches were necessary. In the United States, policymakers moved toward greater reliance on market-based mechanisms, rather than command and control regulations, to achieve environmental goals. Environmentalists engaged in greater dialogue with industry leaders. Many businesses pioneered new approaches to effective environmental management, such as pollution prevention programs.

The challenge facing government, industry, and environmental advocacy organizations alike, as they tried out new approaches and improved on old ones, was how to further economic growth in an increasingly competitive and integrated world economy while promoting sustainable and ecologically sound business practices.

---

[1]"This Commodity's Smokin': Companies Trade Smog Credits on Online Exchange," *Los Angeles Times,* April 30, 1997, p. D2.

[2]Information on environmental alliances in which the Environmental Defense Fund has participated is available at http://www.edf.org.

[3]Information on Dow Chemical Corporation's environmental, health, and safety programs, including the WRAP initiative, is available at http://www.dow.com/eh_s.

Role of Government

The U.S. government has been involved in regulating business activities in order to protect the environment at least since the late nineteenth century, when the first federal laws were passed protecting navigable waterways. The government's role in environmental protection began to increase dramatically, however, around 1970, which marks the beginning of the modern environmental era.

Government has a major role to play in environmental regulation. Business firms have few incentives to minimize pollution if their competitors do not. A single firm acting on its own to reduce discharges into a river, for example, would incur extra costs. If its competitors did not do the same, the firm might not be able to compete effectively and could go out of business. Government, by setting a common standard for all firms, can take the cost of pollution control out of competition. It also can provide economic incentives to encourage businesses, communities, and regions to reduce pollution, and it can offer legal and administrative systems for resolving disputes.

Figure 12–1 summarizes the major federal environmental laws enacted by Congress since 1969. In adopting these laws, Congress was responding to strong public concerns and pressures to save the environment from further damage.

Figure 12–1

Leading U.S. environmental protection laws.

1969	National Environmental Policy Act	Created Council on Environmental Quality to oversee quality of the nation's environment.
1970	Clean Air Act	Established national air quality standards and timetables.
1972	Water Pollution Control Act	Established national goals and timetables for clean waterways.
1972	Pesticide Control Act	Required registration of and restrictions on pesticide use.
1973	Endangered Species Act	Conserved species of animals and plants whose survival was threatened or endangered.
1974 & 1996	Safe Drinking Water Act	Authorized national standards for drinking water.
1974	Hazardous Materials Transport Act	Regulated shipment of hazardous materials.
1976	Resource Conservation and Recovery Act	Regulated hazardous materials from production to disposal.
1976	Toxic Substances Control Act	Established national policy to regulate, restrict, and, if necessary, ban toxic chemicals.
1977	Clean Air Act amendments	Revised air standards.
1980 & 1986	Comprehensive Environmental Response Compensation and Liability Act (Superfund)	Established superfund and procedures to clean up hazardous waste sites.
1987	Clean Water Act amendments	Authorized funds for sewage treatment plants and waterways cleanup.
1990	Clean Air Act	Required cuts in urban smog, acid rain, greenhouse gas emissions; promoted alternative fuels.
1990	Pollution Prevention Act	Provided guidelines, training, and incentives to prevent or reduce pollution at the source.

The nation's main pollution control agency is the **Environmental Protection Agency (EPA).** It was created in 1970 to coordinate most of the government's efforts to protect the environment. Other government agencies involved in enforcing the nation's environmental laws include the Nuclear Regulatory Commission (NRC), the Occupational Safety and Health Administration (OSHA), and various regional, state, and local agencies.

Major Areas of Environmental Regulation

The federal government regulates in three major areas of environmental protection: air pollution, water pollution, and land pollution (solid and hazardous waste). This section will review the major issues and the laws in each and briefly consider the special problem of cross-media pollution that cuts across all three areas.

Air Pollution

Air pollution occurs when more pollutants are emitted into the atmosphere than can be safely absorbed and diluted by natural processes. Some pollution occurs naturally, such as smoke and ash from volcanoes and forest fires. But most air pollution today results from human activity, especially industrial processes and motor vehicle emissions. Air pollution degrades buildings, reduces crop yields, mars the beauty of natural landscapes, and harms people's health.

The American Lung Association estimated that two-thirds of the people in the United States were breathing unsafe air for at least part of each year. According to one study, air pollution caused by particulate matter, such as soot and dirt from cars, trucks, smokestacks, mining, and construction activity, was responsible for as many as 60,000 premature or unnecessary deaths annually.[4]

The EPA has identified six criteria pollutants, relatively common harmful substances that serve as indicators of overall levels of air pollution. These are lead, carbon monoxide, particulate matter, sulfur dioxide, nitrogen dioxide, and ozone. (Ozone at ground level is a dangerous component of smog.) In 1997, the agency strengthened its standards for *fine particles,* tiny motes of dust from industrial sources and automobiles thought to be especially harmful to health. In addition, the agency also has identified a list of toxic air pollutants that are considered hazardous even in relatively small concentrations. These include asbestos, benzene, chloroform, dioxin, vinyl chloride, and radioactive materials. Emissions of toxic pollutants are strictly controlled.

A special problem of air pollution is **acid rain.** Acid rain is formed when emissions of sulfur dioxide and nitrogen oxides, by-products of the burning of fossil fuels by utilities, manufacturers, and motor vehicles, combine with natural water vapor in the air and fall to earth as rain or snow that is more acidic than normal. Acid rain can damage the ecosystems of lakes and rivers, reduce crop yields, and degrade forests. Structures, such as buildings and monuments, are also harmed. Within North America, acid rain is most prevalent in New England and eastern Canada, regions that are downwind of coal-burning utilities in the midwestern states. Acid rain is especially difficult to regulate, because adverse consequences often occur far—often, hundreds of miles—from the source of the

---

[4]American Lung Association, *Health Effects of Outdoor Air Pollution* (Washington, D.C.: American Lung Association, 1996); and "Studies Say Soot Kills up to 60,000 in U.S. Each Year," *New York Times,* July 19, 1993, pp. A1, A16.

pollution, sometimes across international borders. The major law governing air pollution is the Clean Air Act, first passed in 1970 and most recently amended in 1990. The 1990 Clean Air Act toughened standards in a number of areas, including stricter restrictions on emissions of acid rain–causing chemicals.

The efforts of the U.S. government to reduce acid rain illustrate some of the difficult trade-offs involved in environmental policy. These are described in Exhibit 12–A.

Water Pollution

Water pollution, like air pollution, occurs when more wastes are dumped into waterways than can be naturally diluted and carried away. Water can be polluted by organic wastes (untreated sewage), by the chemical by-products of industrial processes, and by the disposal of nonbiodegradable products (which do not naturally decay). Heavy metals and toxic chemicals, including some used as pesticides and herbicides, can be particularly persistent. Like poor air, poor water quality can decrease crop yields, threaten human health, and degrade the quality of life.

EXHIBIT 12–A

Moving Mountains to Fight Acid Rain

As part of its efforts to control acid rain, the U.S. government in 1990 initiated stricter new restrictions on the emission of sulfur dioxide by utilities. Many electric companies complied with the law by switching from high-sulfur coal, which produces more sulfur dioxide when burned, to low-sulfur coal, which produces less. This action had the beneficial effect of reducing acid rain.

But the law had some environmentally destructive results that had been unintended by regulators. Much of the highest-quality low-sulfur coal in the United States is in southern and central West Virginia, in horizontal layers near the tops of rugged mountains. Some coal companies discovered that the most efficient way to extract this coal was through what came to be known as *mountaintop removal*. Explosives were used to blast away up to 500 feet of mountaintop. Massive machines called draglines, 20 stories tall and costing $100 million each, were then used to remove the debris to get at buried seams of coal. In the late 1990s, by some estimates, 15 to 25 percent of the mountains in the affected regions of West Virginia were being leveled.

Although coal operators were required to reclaim the land afterwards—by filling in adjacent valleys with debris and planting grass and shrubs—many environmentalists believed the damage caused by mountaintop removal was severe. Many rivers and creeks were contaminated and habitat destroyed. Aquifers dried up, and the entire region became vulnerable to devastating floods. Many felt it was deeply ironic that a law that had benefited the environment in one way had indirectly harmed it in another.

Source: "Sheer Madness," *U.S. News and World Report,* August 11, 1997, p. 26 ff. For an account of EPA's acid rain program, see http://www.epa.gov/acidrain.

In 1993, around 370,000 people in Milwaukee, Wisconsin, contracted diarrhea. The cause of the mass outbreak was discovered to be a parasite that had contaminated the municipal water supply, and residents were told to boil their water until the problem could be corrected. Health authorities suspected the source of the parasites might have been runoff of water from upstream farms with infected cattle.[5]

In the United States, regulations address both the pollution of rivers, lakes, and other surface bodies of water and the quality of the drinking water.

The nation's main law governing water pollution is the Water Pollution Control Act, also known as the Clean Water Act. This law aims to restore or maintain the integrity of all surface water in the United States. It requires permits for most *point* sources of pollution, such as industrial emissions, and mandates that local and state governments develop plans for *nonpoint* sources, such as agricultural runoff or urban storm water. The Pesticide Control Act specifically restricts the use of dangerous pesticides, which can pollute groundwater.

The quality of drinking water is regulated by another law, the Safe Drinking Water Act of 1974, most recently amended in 1996. This law sets minimum standards for various contaminants in both public water systems and aquifers that supply drinking wells.

Land Pollution

The third major focus of environmental regulation is the contamination of land by both solid and hazardous waste. The United States produces an astonishing amount of solid waste each year, most of which is disposed of in municipal landfills. About 279 million tons of this waste is considered hazardous and requires special treatment. Improperly disposed waste can leach into groundwater or evaporate into the air, posing a danger to public health. Many businesses and communities have established programs to recycle certain kinds of solid waste. Some of these programs are described in Exhibit 12–B.

Several federal laws address the problem of land contamination. The Toxic Substances Control Act of 1976 requires EPA to inventory the thousands of chemicals in commercial use, identify which are most dangerous, and, if necessary, ban them or restrict their use. For example, polychlorinated biphenyls (PCBs), dangerous chemicals formerly used in electrical transformers, were banned under this law. The Resource Conservation and Recovery Act of 1976 (amended in 1984) regulates hazardous materials from "cradle to grave." Toxic waste generators must have permits, transporters must maintain careful records, and disposal facilities must conform to detailed regulations. All hazardous waste must be treated before disposal in landfills.

Some studies have suggested that hazardous waste sites are most often located near economically disadvantaged African-American and Hispanic communities. Since 1994, EPA has investigated whether state permits for hazardous waste sites violate civil rights laws and has blocked permits that appear to discriminate against minorities. Efforts to prevent inequitable exposure to risk, such as from hazardous waste, is sometimes referred to as the movement for **environmental justice.**[6]

---

[5]World Resources Institute, *1994 Information Please Environmental Almanac* (Boston: Houghton Mifflin, 1994), pp. 67–70.

[6]Bunyan Bryant, ed., *Environmental Justice: Issues, Policies, and Solutions* (Washington, D.C.: Island Press, 1995).

**EXHIBIT
12–B**

Recycling: How Successful?

Recycling paper, steel and aluminum cans, and plastic and glass containers is becoming increasingly popular. In 1997, more than 7,000 U.S. communities had curbside recycling programs, up from just 1,000 a decade earlier. At many college campuses, businesses, and government offices across the country, people are asked to separate their trash for disposal in brightly marked containers. But what happens to all this carefully sorted trash? Unfortunately, the demand for recycled materials has not kept up with the supply. A 1997 study found that it cost waste management companies—such as industry leaders WMX Technologies Inc. and Browning-Ferris Industries—$142 a ton, on average, to collect and sort recyclables. Prices for recycled materials, however, were wildly volatile. The price of old newspapers, for example, in some years soared to $150 a ton; in other years, it dropped to nothing. As a result, the big waste management companies were losing money on recycling most of the time. Solutions to this problem will involve a combination of new technologies, government incentives, and private initiatives to stabilize prices and develop new markets for used paper, glass, plastic, and metals. A promising development is the Buy Recycled Business Alliance, a group of more than 3,000 companies, including American Airlines, Coca-Cola, and Rubbermaid, that has committed to increasing purchases of recycled materials.

Sources: Frank Ackerman, "Recycling: Looking beyond the Bottom Line," *BioCycle,* May 1997, pp. 67–70; "Recycling: Higher Price, Lower Priority?" *Washington Post,* March 30, 1997, p. A1; "Rethinking Recycling," *Scholastic Update* 29, no. 12, (March 21, 1997), p. 10; and "Recycling Business Stinks," *Arizona Business Gazette,* November 21, 1996, p. 8. For an example of an ambitious state effort to promote business procurement of recycled products, see http://www.recycleiowa.org.

A promising new regulatory approach to waste management, sometimes called **source reduction,** was taken in the Pollution Prevention Act of 1990. This law aims to reduce pollution at the source, rather than treat and dispose of waste at the end of the pipe. Pollution can be prevented, for example, by using less chemically intensive manufacturing processes, recycling, and better housekeeping and maintenance. Source reduction often saves money, protects worker health, and requires less abatement and disposal technology. The 1990 law provides guidelines, training, and incentives for companies to reduce waste.

The major U.S. law governing the cleanup of existing hazardous waste sites is the **Comprehensive Environmental Response, Compensation, and Liability Act (CER-CLA),** popularly known as **Superfund,** passed in 1980. This law established a fund, supported primarily by a tax on petroleum and chemical companies that were presumed to have created a disproportionate share of toxic wastes. EPA was charged with establishing a National Priority List of the most dangerous toxic sites. Where the original polluters could be identified, they would be required to pay for the cleanup; where they could not be identified or had gone out of business, the Superfund would pay.

An example of a hazardous waste site on EPA's list is the Brio Superfund site, two former waste disposal plants located near the Southbend subdivision outside Houston, Texas. Local wells have been polluted by dangerous chemicals like xylene, and a black tar-like substance has bubbled into driveways and garages. Air pollution is suspected as a possible cause of a rash of birth defects, and children have contracted leukemia and other serious illnesses. The once-thriving community of 2,800 is now largely boarded up, and the cleanup is expected to drag on past the year 2000.[7]

Remarkably, one in four U.S. residents now lives within four miles of a Superfund site. The 1,200 or so sites originally placed on the National Priority List may be just the tip of the iceberg. Congressional researchers have said that as many as 10,000 other sites may need to be cleaned up.

Although Superfund's goals were laudable, it has been widely regarded as a public policy failure. Slightly under 500 listed waste sites—only 40 percent or so of the total— had been cleaned up by 1997, almost two decades after the program had been established. Some analysts estimated that the entire cleanup could cost as much as $1 trillion and take half a century to complete. In a debate on possible Superfund reforms, some policymakers argued that companies should be required to pay only for cleaning up the proportion of a waste site they were actually responsible for, with shares determined by a neutral arbitrator. Others called for clearer priorities for cleanup efforts, focusing attention first on sites posing the greatest risk to public health and those most amenable to remediation with currently available technology. The opinions of one small business owner about possible reforms of Superfund are described in Exhibit 12–C.

Cross-Media Pollution

Cross-media pollution refers to pollution that cannot easily be blamed on any specific source, or medium. For example, hazardous wastes disposed in a landfill might leach out, contaminating groundwater, or evaporate, causing air pollution. The migration of pollutants has apparently become more frequent and severe in recent years. Unfortunately, cross-

---

EXHIBIT 12–C

Superfund: A Small Business View

The owner of a small restaurant in Gettysburg, Pennsylvania, was shocked when she was sued for $76,000 under the Superfund law. The U.S. Environmental Protection Agency had originally sued the owner of a dangerous landfill that had been designated as a Superfund site, to force its cleanup. The landfill owner, in turn, had sued hundreds of small businesses, boroughs, and school districts that had contributed waste to the site over the years. Among them was the restaurant owner, who had hired a commercial waste hauler to carry away her trash, mainly food scraps. "I am here to tell you," the restaurant owner later told a congressional hearing, "that your wonderful idea [the Superfund law]. . . does not work in the real world."

One of the provisions considered as Congress once again debated reauthorization of the law in 1997 would exempt small businesses, such as this restaurant, from liability for Superfund cleanup.

Source: "Superfund and a Tale of a $76,000 Trash Bill," *Christian Science Monitor,* March 12, 1997, p. 3.

---

[7]"Brio Superfund Cleanup May Drag on Past 2000," *Chemical Marketing Reporter,* January 15, 1996, p. 7; and "Toxic Dumps," *Time,* September 13, 1993, pp. 63–64.

media pollution (also called *multimedia pollution*) is especially difficult to control, because laws and regulatory agencies tend to focus on particular kinds of pollution, such as air or water. Several states have experimented with an integrated approach designed to better control pollution from multiple sources. One place this approach has been tried is the Great Lakes region.

> *Pollution in the Great Lakes comes from many sources, including discharge of waste into the lakes, airborne toxics, pesticide runoff from farmland, and landfill leaching. In the late 1980s and 1990s, regulators experimented with new approaches. For example, agencies responsible for these different pollutants have developed joint remedial plans for several contaminated hot spots.*[8]

New institutional arrangements like these will be needed to achieve integrated regulation of cross-media pollution.

Alternative Policy Approaches

Government can use a variety of policy approaches to control air, water, and land pollution. The most widely used method of regulation historically has been to impose environmental standards. Increasingly, however, government policymakers have relied more on market-based and voluntary approaches, rather than command and control regulations, to achieve environmental goals.

Environmental Standards

The traditional method of pollution control is through **environmental standards.** Standard allowable levels of various pollutants are established by legislation or regulatory action and applied by administrative agencies and courts. This approach is also called **command and control regulation,** because the government commands business firms to comply with certain standards and often directly controls their choice of technology.

One type of standard is an environmental-quality standard. In this approach a given geographical area is permitted to have no more than a certain amount or proportion of a pollutant, such as sulfur dioxide, in the air. Polluters are required to control their emissions to maintain the area's standard of air quality. A second type is an emission standard. For example, the law might specify that manufacturers could release into the air no more than 1 percent of the ash (a pollutant) they generated. Emission standards, with some exceptions, are usually set by state and local regulators who are familiar with local industry and special problems caused by local topography and weather conditions.

Some people believe that businesses should be given more flexibility in how they meet government environmental standards. A new initiative by EPA to provide greater flexibility, involving one of Intel Corporation's semiconductor plants, is described in the discussion case at the end of this chapter.

Market-Based Mechanisms

In recent years, regulators have begun to move away from command and control regulation, favoring increased use of market-based mechanisms. This approach is based on the idea that the market is a better control than extensive standards that specify precisely what companies must do.

---

[8]Barry G. Rabe, "An Empirical Examination of Innovations in Integrated Environmental Management: The Case of the Great Lakes Basin," *Public Administration Review,* July–August, 1997, pp. 372–81.

One approach that has become more widely used is to allow businesses to buy and sell the right to pollute, as shown in the opening example of this chapter. The Clean Air Act of 1990 incorporated the concept of **tradable allowances** as a key part of its approach to pollution reduction. The law established emission levels and permitted companies that achieved emissions below the standard to sell their rights to the remaining permissible amount to firms that faced penalties because their emissions were above the standard. Over time, the government would reduce permissible emission levels. The system would therefore gradually reduce overall emissions, even though individual companies might continue to pollute above the standard. Companies would be able to choose whether to reduce their emissions—for example, by installing pollution abatement equipment—or to buy allowances from others.

> *For example, the Tennessee Valley Association (TVA), an electric utility, purchased the right to emit 10,000 tons of sulfur dioxide, a chemical that causes acid rain, from Wisconsin Power and Light. The price was around $3 million. The transaction gave the TVA additional time to comply with the 1990 Clean Air Act. Wisconsin Power and Light, for its part, was able to profit from "overcomplying" with federal regulations.*

One study showed that the tradable permit program for acid rain may have saved companies as much as $3 billion per year, by allowing them the flexibility to choose the most cost-effective methods of complying with the law.[9]

Another market-based type of pollution control is establishment of emissions charges or fees. Each business is charged for the undesirable waste that it emits, with the fee varying according to the amount of waste released. The result is, "The more you pollute, the more you pay." In recent years, both federal and state governments have experimented with a variety of so-called green taxes or ecotaxes that levy a fee on various kinds of environmentally destructive behavior. In some cases, the revenue from these taxes is specifically earmarked to support environmental improvement efforts. In addition to taxing bad behavior, the government may also offer various types of positive incentives to firms that improve their environmental performance. For example, the government may decide to purchase only from those firms that meet a certain pollution standard, or it may offer aid to those that install pollution control equipment. Tax incentives, such as faster depreciation for pollution control equipment, also may be used.

In short, as the turn of the century drew near the trend was to use more flexible, market-oriented approaches—tradable allowances, pollution fees and taxes, and incentives—to achieve environmental objectives where possible.

Information Disclosure

Another approach to reducing pollution that became more widely used in the late 1980s and 1990s is popularly known as *regulation by publicity,* or *regulation by embarrassment.* The government encourages companies to pollute less by publishing information about the amount of pollutants individual companies emit each year. In many cases, companies take steps voluntarily to reduce their emissions, to avoid public embarrassment.

The major experiment in regulation by publicity has occurred in the area of toxic gas and liquid emissions. The 1986 amendments to the Superfund law, called SARA, included a provision called the Community Right-to-Know Law, which required manufac-

---

[9]http://www.epa.gov/acidrain/overview.

turing firms to report, for about 300 toxic chemicals, the amount on site, the number of pounds released, and how (if at all) these chemicals were treated or disposed of. EPA makes this information available to the public in the *Toxics Release Inventory,* or *TRI,* published annually and posted on the Internet.

From 1988 to 1995, reporting manufacturers in the United States cut their emissions of hazardous chemicals by 46 percent, according to *TRI* data. Some of the biggest cuts were made by the worst polluters. These dramatic results were especially surprising to regulators, because many of the hazardous chemicals were not covered under clean air and water regulations at the time. The improvements, in many instances, had been completely voluntary. Apparently, fear of negative publicity had compelled many companies to act. "We knew the numbers were high, and we knew the public wasn't going to like it," one chemical industry executive explained.

The apparent success of this law prompted EPA several times in the 1990s to expand the toxics release reporting program to include utilities, mines, and large recyclers as well as manufacturers and to expand the list of chemicals that must be reported. EPA tried a similar approach in its risk management program rule, requiring many businesses to publish worst case scenarios and their plans to minimize risk. The agency's intention was to use public concern to force businesses to be more proactive in managing environmental risk.[10]

The advantages and disadvantages of alternative policy approaches to reducing pollution are summarized in Figure 12–2.

Civil and Criminal Enforcement

Traditionally, companies that violate environmental laws have been subject to civil penalties and fines. Increasingly, however, regulators have turned to the use of criminal statutes to prosecute companies and their executives who break these laws. Proponents of this approach argue that the threat of prison can be an effective deterrent to corporate outlaws who would otherwise degrade the air, water, or land. Since 1989, about 100 individuals and companies have been found guilty of environmental crimes each year. For example, the owner of a Chicago metal-plating factory was sentenced to 15 months in prison. His crime was ordering a worker to pour 4,000 gallons of cyanide and cadmium waste down a floor drain. The toxic chemicals had killed 20,000 fish in the Chicago River and forced authorities to temporarily shut down a branch of the city sewer system.

The U.S. Sentencing Commission, a government agency responsible for setting uniform penalties for violations of federal law, has established guidelines for sentencing environmental wrongdoers. Under these rules, penalties would reflect not only the severity of the offense but also a company's demonstrated environmental commitment. Businesses that have an active compliance program, cooperate with government investigators, and promptly assist any victims would receive lighter sentences than others with no environmental programs or that knowingly violate the law. These guidelines provide an incentive for businesses to develop active compliance programs to protect themselves and their officers from high fines or even prison if a violation should occur.[11]

[10]*Toxics Release Inventory* data may be found on-line at http://www.rtk.net.
[11]"A Warning Shot to Scare Polluters Straight," *Business Week,* November 22, 1993, p. 60; *Final Report of the Advisory Working Group on Environmental Offenses* (Washington, D.C.: United States Sentencing Commission, November 1993); and World Resources Institute, *1994 Information Please Environmental Almanac,* p. 26.

Figure 12-2

Advantages and disadvantages of alternative policy approaches to reducing pollution.

Policy Approach	Advantages	Disadvantages
Environmental standards	• Enforceable in the courts • Compliance mandatory	• Across-the-board standards not equally relevant to all businesses • Requires large regulatory apparatus • Older, less efficient plants may be forced to close
Market-based mechanisms		
Tradable allowances	• Gives businesses more flexibility • Achieves goals at lower overall cost • Saves jobs by allowing some less efficient plants to stay open • Permits the government and private private organizations to buy allowances to take them off the market	• Gives business a license to pollute • Allowances are hard to set • May cause regional imbalances in pollution levels • Enforcement is difficult
Emissions fees and taxes	• Taxes bad behavior (pollution) rather than good behavior (profits)	• Fees are hard to set • Taxes may be too low to curb pollution
Government incentives	• Rewards environmentally responsible behavior • Encourages companies to exceed minimum standards	• Incentives may not be strong enough to curb pollution
Information disclosure	• Government spends little on enforcement • Companies able to reduce pollution in the most cost-effective way	• Does not motivate all companies

Costs and Benefits of Environmental Regulation

One of the central issues of environmental protection is how costs are balanced by benefits. In the quarter century or so since the modern environmental era began, the nation has spent a great deal to clean up the environment and keep it clean. Some have questioned the value choices underlying these expenditures, suggesting that the costs—lost jobs, reduced capital investment, and lowered productivity—exceeded the benefits. Others, in contrast, point to significant gains in the quality of life and to the economic payoff of a cleaner environment.

As a nation, the United States has invested heavily in environmental clean up. Figure 12–3 shows U.S. pollution control spending in recent years and how much will be spent in the year 2000. According to a study by EPA, by 1990 environmental spending exceeded $100 billion a year, about 2 percent of the nation's gross national product. Pollution control expenditures were predicted to reach around $160 billion annually by the year 2000. Business spending to comply with environmental regulation has diverted funds that might otherwise have been invested in new plants and equipment or in research and development. Sometimes, strict rules have led to plant shutdowns and loss of jobs.

Figure 12–3

How much has been spent on pollution control in the United States and how much will be spent in the year 2000.

Source: EPA, *Environmental Investments: The Cost of a Clean Environment* (Washington D.C.: EPA, 1990).

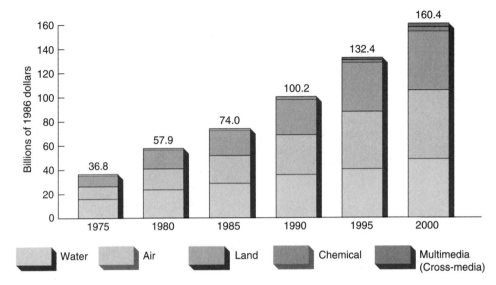

Some regions and industries, in particular, have been hard hit by environmental regulation, especially those with high abatement costs, such as paper and wood products, chemicals, petroleum and coal, and primary metals. Economists often find it difficult, however, to sort out what proportion of job loss in an industry is attributable to environmental regulation and what proportion is attributable to other causes. For example, the oil industry witnessed a net loss of tens of thousands of jobs in the 1980s. Some economists blamed environmental regulations, such as restrictions on drilling off-shore and in the Alaskan wilderness. But others pointed to declining oil prices on the world market and increased drilling costs as more important factors. No one knew for sure.

The costs of environmental regulation must be balanced against the benefits. In many areas, the United States has made great progress in cleaning up the environment, as these figures show.

- Emissions of nearly all major pollutants in the United States have dropped substantially since 1970, when the Environmental Protection Act was passed. On its twenty-fifth anniversary in 1995, EPA estimated that total emissions of the criteria air pollutants had declined by 24 percent. Levels of particulates in the air were less than a quarter of what they would have been without controls; lead in the air was just 2 percent of what it would have been. The citizens of Los Angeles experienced one-third fewer days of unhealthy air than they had just a decade earlier, despite huge increases in population and vehicle traffic. These gains in air quality translate into significant reductions in medical costs.

- Water quality had also improved. More than one billion tons of toxic pollutants had been prevented from being discharged into the nation's waterways since the Water Pollution Control Act had gone into effect. Many lakes and riverways had been restored to ecological health. The Cuyahoga River in Ohio, for example,

Figure 12–4

Costs and benefits of environmental regulations.

Costs	Benefits
• $160 billion a year spent by business and individuals in the United States by 2000. • Job loss in some particularly polluting industries. • Competitiveness of some capital-intensive, "dirty" industries impaired.	• Emissions of nearly all pollutants have dropped since 1970. • Air and water quality improved, some toxic waste sites cleaned; improved health; natural beauty preserved or enhanced. • Growth of other industries, such as environmental products and services, tourism, and fishing.

which at one time was badly polluted by industrial waste, had been restored to the point where residents could fish and even swim in the river.[12]

Environmental regulations also stimulate some sectors of the economy. The environmental services and products industry, for example, has grown dramatically since the mid-1980s. While jobs are being lost in industries like forest products and high-sulfur coal mining, others are being created in areas like environmental consulting, asbestos abatement, instrument manufacturing, waste management equipment, and air pollution control. Other jobs are saved or created in industries like fishing and tourism when natural areas are protected or restored. Moreover, environmental regulations can stimulate the economy by compelling businesses to become more efficient by conserving energy, and less money is spent on treating health problems caused by pollution.

Because of the complexity of these issues, economists differ on the *net* costs and benefits of environmental regulation. In some respects, government controls hurt the economy, and in other ways they help, as summarized in Figure 12–4. An analysis of data from several studies found that, on balance, U.S. environmental regulations did not have a large overall effect on economic competitiveness, because losses in one area tended to balance gains in another.[13] What is clear is that choices in the area of environmental regulation reflect underlying values, expressed in a democratic society through an open political process. Just how much a society is prepared to pay—and how "clean" it wants to be—are political choices, reflecting the give and take of diverse interests in a pluralistic society.

The Greening of Management

Environmental regulations—such as the laws governing clean air, water, and land described in this chapter—establish minimum legal standards that businesses must meet. Most companies try to comply with these regulations, if only to avoid litigation, fines, and, in the most extreme cases,

[12]For an analysis of the benefits of clean air for the nation's medical costs, see American Lung Association, *The Value of Clean Air: A Survey of Economic Benefit Studies from 1990–1996* (Washington, D.C.: American Lung Association, 1997). The EPA's twenty-fifth anniversary self-assessment is available at http://www.epa.gov/25year.

[13]Adam B. Jaffe, Steven R. Peterson, Paul R. Portney, and Robert N. Stavins, "Environmental Regulations and the Competitiveness of U.S. Industry," prepared for the U.S. Department of Commerce, July 1993. For another summary of the evidence that comes to a similar conclusion, see Steven Peterson, Barry Galef, and Kenneth Grant, "Do Environmental Regulations Impair Competitiveness?" prepared for the U.S. EPA, September 1995.

criminal penalties. But many firms are now voluntarily moving *beyond compliance* to improve their environmental performance in all areas of their operations. Researchers have sometimes referred to the process of moving toward more proactive environmental management as the **greening of management.** This section describes the greening process and discusses what organizational approaches companies have used to manage environmental issues effectively. It also explains why green management can improve a company's strategic competitiveness.

Stages of Corporate Environmental Responsibility

Although environmental issues are forcing all businesses to manage in new ways, not all companies are equally green, meaning proactive in their response to environmental issues. Researchers have identified five stages of environmental responsibility, depicted in Figure 12–5.

According to this model, companies pass through five distinct stages in the development of green management practices. At the *beginner* level, managers ignore potential liability and dismiss the need for specialized environmental programs. Environmental responsibility, if addressed at all, is added onto other programs and positions. Beginners might include older firms established before the modern environmental era, small firms that feel they cannot afford specialized programs, or simply companies in industries where regulatory oversight is perceived to be minimal. *Firefighters,* companies at the next developmental stage, address environmental issues only when they pose an immediate threat, such as when an unexpected accident or spill occurs. Environmental management is seen as an exception to business as usual. Companies as *concerned citizens,* at the third stage, believe environmental protection is worthwhile and may even have specialized staff but devote few resources and little top management attention to green issues. *Pragmatists* actively manage environmental issues, have well-funded programs, and evaluate risk as well as immediate problems. In addition to having all the programmatic elements of pragmatists, *proactivists*—companies in the final stage of development—also have senior executives who champion environmental responsibility, extensive training, and strong links between environmental staff and other parts of the organization.

Figure 12–5

A five-stage model of corporate environmental responsibility.

Source: Adapted from Christopher B. Hunt and Ellen R. Auster, "Proactive Environmental Management: Avoiding the Toxic Trap," *Sloan Management Review,* Winter 1990, pp. 7–18. Used by permission of the publisher. Copyright 1990 by the Sloan Management Review Association. All rights reserved.

Commitment of Organization			
Developmental Stage	General Mindset of Corporate Managers	Resource Commitment	Support and Involvement of Top Management
Beginner	Environmental management is unnecessary	Minimal resource commitment	No involvement
Firefighter	Environmental issues should be addressed only as necessary	Budgets for problems as they occur	Piecemeal involvement
Concerned citizen	Environmental management is a worthwhile function	Consistent, yet minimal budget	Commitment in theory
Pragmatist	Environmental management is an important business function	Generally sufficient funding	Aware and moderately involved
Proactivist	Environmental management is a priority item	Open-ended funding	Actively involved

Research shows that most firms are still in the early stages in their development of green management practices, with no more than 10 to 25 percent of all companies in the United States now at the proactivist stage. A majority of corporations are now in transition, with many moving from lower to higher stages in the developmental sequence.[14]

The Ecologically Sustainable Organization

An **ecologically sustainable organization (ESO)** is a business that operates in a way that is consistent with the principle of sustainable development, as presented in Chapter 11. In other words, an ESO could continue its activities indefinitely, without altering the carrying capacity of the earth's ecosystem. An ecologically sustainable organization would have moved beyond even the proactivist level in the stage model described earlier. Such businesses would not use up natural resources any faster than they could be replenished or substitutes found. They would make and transport products efficiently, with minimal use of energy. They would design products that would last a long time and that, when worn out, could be disassembled and recycled. They would not produce waste any faster than natural systems could absorb and disperse it. They would work with other businesses, governments, and organizations to meet these goals.[15]

Of course, no existing business completely fits the definition of an ecologically sustainable organization. The concept is what social scientists call an *ideal type,* that is, a kind of absolute standard against which real organizations can be measured. A few visionary businesses, however, have embraced the concept and begun to try to live up to this ideal.

> *One such business is Interface, a $1 billion company based in Atlanta, Georgia, that makes 40 percent of the world's commercial carpet tiles. In 1994, CEO Ray C. Anderson announced, to many peoples' surprise, that Interface would seek to become "the first sustainable corporation in the world," and he even set a date by which to accomplish this goal—the year 2000. Anderson and his managers undertook hundreds of initiatives. For example, the company started a program by which customers could lease, rather than purchase, carpet tile. When tile wore out in high-traffic areas, Interface technicians would replace just the worn units, reducing waste. Old tiles would be recycled, creating a closed loop.*
>
> *In 1997, Interface reported a 20 percent growth in revenue, a 30 percent growth in profits, and zero increase in physical throughput. But Anderson said it was "just a start. It's daunting, trying to climb a mountain taller than Everest."*[16]

---

[14]Kurt Fischer and Johan Schot, *Environmental Strategies for Industry: International Perspectives on Research Needs and Policy Implications* (Washington, DC: Island Press, 1993); and James E. Post and Barbara W. Altman, "Models of Corporate Greening: How Corporate Social Policy and Organizational Learning Inform Leading-Edge Environmental Management," *Research in Corporate Social Performance and Policy,* 23, (1992), pp. 3–29.

[15]Mark Starik and Gordon P. Rands, "Weaving an Integrated Web: Multilevel and Multisystem Perspectives of Ecologically Sustainable Organizations," *Academy of Management Review* (October 1995), pp. 908–35. For a related discussion, see Paul Shrivastava, *Greening Business* (Cincinnati, OH: Thomson Executive Press, 1996), chap. 2, "Sustainable Development and Sustainable Corporations," pp. 21–50.

[16]Interface Corporation, "Sustainability Report," 1997; "The Front Lines; Business Achieves Greatest Efficiencies When at Its Greenest," *The Wall Street Journal,* July 11, 1997, p. B1; and "Facing the Facts at Interface," *The New Bottom Line,* October 7, 1997, http://www.eco-ops.com.

No companies, including Interface, have yet become truly sustainable businesses, and indeed it will probably be impossible for any single firm to become an ESO in the absence of supportive government policies and a widespread movement among many businesses and other social institutions.

Elements of Effective Environmental Management

Companies that have begun to move toward environmental sustainability have learned that new structures, processes, and incentives are often needed. Some of the organizational elements that many proactive green companies share are the following.[17]

Top Managers with Environmental Responsibilities

One step many companies have taken is to give environmental managers greater authority and access to top levels of the corporation. Many leading firms now have a vice president for environmental affairs with a direct reporting relationship with the CEO. These individuals often supervise extensive staffs of specialists and coordinate the work of managers in many areas, including research and development, marketing, and operations.

Dialogue with Stakeholders

Environmentally proactive companies also engage in dialogue with external stakeholders, such as environmental organizations. Dow Chemical Corporation, for example, has set up a Corporate Environmental Advisory Council, a group of outside environmental advocates who are regularly invited to the company's headquarters for discussions with top executives and board members about environmental issues facing the company. Many local Dow Chemical facilities have established community advisory panels.

Line Manager Involvement

Environmental staff experts and specialized departments are most effective when they work closely with the people who carry out the company's daily operations. For this reason, many green companies involve line managers and workers directly in the process of change. At the Park Plaza Hotel in Boston, green teams of employees make suggestions ranging from energy-efficient windows to refillable bottles of soap and shampoo.

Codes of Environmental Conduct

Environmentally proactive companies put their commitment in writing, often in the form of a code of conduct or charter that spells out the firm's environmental goals. Over 80 percent of Fortune 500 firms now have such a code.

Cross-Functional Teams

Another organizational element is the use of ad hoc, cross-functional teams to solve environmental problems, including individuals from different departments. These teams pull together key players with the skills and resources to get the job done, wherever they are

[17]Anne T. Lawrence and David Morell, "Leading-Edge Environmental Management: Motivation, Opportunity, Resources, and Processes," *Research in Corporate Social Performance and Policy,* supp. 1 (1995), pp. 99–127; Patricia S. Dillon and Kurt Fischer, *Environmental Management in Corporations: Methods and Motivations* (Medford, MA: Tufts University Center for Environmental Management, 1992); and James Maxwell, Sandra Rothenberg, Forrest Briscoe, and Alfred Marcus, "Green Schemes: Corporate Environmental Strategies and Their Implementation," *California Management Review* 39, no. 3, (March 22, 1997), p. 118 ff.

located in the corporate structure. At Lockheed Missiles and Space Corporation's facility in Sunnyvale, California, a Pollution Prevention Committee includes representatives from each of the five major business areas within the company. Each year, the committee selects about a dozen projects from among many proposed from each area. Interdivisional, cross-functional teams are set up to work on approved projects, such as one to recycle wastewater.

Rewards and Incentives

Businesspeople are most likely to consider the environmental impacts of their actions when their organizations acknowledge and reward this behavior. The greenest organizations tie the compensation of their managers, including line managers, to environmental achievement and take steps to recognize these achievements publicly.

Environmental Audits

Green companies closely track their progress toward environmental goals. Some have full-blown environmental audits (comparable to the social audits discussed in Chapter 4) that periodically review environmental initiatives. National Semiconductor Corporation, for example, initiated a new audit protocol that scored company facilities in such areas as air pollution control, water pollution control, hazardous waste management, and groundwater protection. Audits can assess progress and also help spread good ideas across a company. At least two dozen major U.S. firms now publish annual environmental progress reports.

Interorganizational Alliances

Many firms have formed alliances with others to promote mutual environmental goals. For example, the Chemical Manufacturers Association started a program called Responsible Care, committing its member-companies to work together to respond to public concerns about chemicals.

Environmental Partnerships

Another approach, described in one of the examples at the beginning of this chapter, is for businesses to form voluntary, collaborative partnerships with environmental organizations and regulators to achieve specific objectives. These collaborations, called **environmental partnerships,** draw on the unique strengths of the different partners to improve environmental quality or conserve resources.[18]

> *An example of an environmental partnership involves Starbucks Coffee, the gourmet coffee retailer. In 1996, Starbucks formed a partnership with the Alliance for Environmental Innovation, a group sponsored by the Environmental Defense Fund. The company's goal was to work with the Alliance to reduce adverse environmental impacts, for example, by encouraging the use of reusable cups.[19]*

[18]Frederick J. Long and Matthew B. Arnold, *The Power of Environmental Partnerships* (Forth Worth, TX: Dryden Press, 1995).

[19]"Starbucks Coffee Company—Alliance for Environmental Innovation Task Force: Project Summary" (Cambridge, MA: Alliance for Environmental Innovation, January 1997) and "Starbucks Tests Cups to Help Environment," *Boston Globe,* July 29, 1997, p. B2. The Environmental Defense Fund's Web site, which includes information on environmental partnerships it is involved in, is at http://www.edf.org.

Many of these programmatic elements represent specific applications of the general model of corporate social responsiveness presented in Chapter 4. This model describes how companies identify a social problem (in this case, environmental degradation), learn how to tackle it, and finally institutionalize procedures to address the problem on an ongoing, routine basis.

Environmental Management as a Competitive Advantage

Some researchers believe that by moving toward ecological sustainability, business firms gain a *competitive advantage.* That is, relative to other firms in the same industry, companies that proactively manage environmental issues will tend to be more successful than those that do not. One top business executive who has embraced this view is Robert Shapiro, CEO of Monsanto. Under his direction, Monsanto sold its chemicals division and refocused on the more earth-friendly goal of harnessing biotechnology to improve human health and nutrition. Said Shapiro, "I don't think it ultimately matters whether my soul is pure or I want to make a lot of money for shareholders; we come out at the same place. If Monsanto and other companies can get environmentally better products that people want [and get them] to market faster at lower costs, we will kick butt in the marketplace."[20]

Effective environmental management confers a competitive advantage in four different ways.

Cost Savings

Companies that reduce pollution and hazardous waste, reuse or recycle materials, and operate with greater energy efficiency can reap significant cost savings, as shown in the example of Dow Chemical's WRAP program at the beginning of this chapter. Another example is Herman Miller, the office furniture company.

> *Herman Miller goes to great lengths to avoid wasting materials. The company sells fabric scraps to the auto industry for use as car linings; leather trim to luggage makers for attaché cases; and vinyl to stereo makers for sound-deadening material. Herman Miller also buys back its used furniture from businesses, so it can refurbish and resell it. The result is that the company actually makes money from materials that, in the past, it would have had to pay to have hauled away and dumped.*[21]

Product Differentiation

Companies that develop a reputation for environmental excellence and that produce and deliver products and services with concern for their sustainability can attract environmentally aware customers. This approach is sometimes called **green marketing.** The size of the green market was estimated to account for 16 percent of all consumer product sales by 1996. For example, when Procter & Gamble introduced its concentrated Downy fabric softener in a refillable pouch, rather than a throwaway container, it attracted new customers and increased its market share.

Technological Innovation

Environmentally proactive companies are often technological leaders, as they seek out imaginative new methods for reducing pollution and increasing efficiency. In many cases,

---

[20]"Monsanto's Bet: There's Gold in Going Green," *Fortune,* April 14, 1997, p. 116.
[21]"Who Scores Best on the Environment," *Fortune,* July 26, 1993, pp. 114–22.

they produce innovations that can then be marketed to others, as new regulations spur their adoption in broader markets, as illustrated by the following example.

> *At its huge copper smelter outside of Salt Lake City, Utah, Kennecott Corp. engineers devised an ingenious method to capture sulfur in processed ore, cutting emissions of acid-rain–producing sulfur dioxide by a dramatic 96 percent. Kennecott managers hoped to sell the innovative process to other companies, particularly in Latin America, where governments had begun to toughen environmental regulations.*[22]

Strategic Planning

Companies that cultivate a vision of sustainability must adopt sophisticated strategic planning techniques, to allow their top managers to assess the full range of the firm's effects on the environment. The complex auditing and forecasting techniques used by these firms help them anticipate a wide range of external influences on the firm, not just ecological influences. Wide-angle planning helps these companies foresee new markets, materials, technologies, and products.

In short, proactive environmental management may help businesses not only promote sustainability but also become more competitive in the global marketplace.[23]

Summary Points of This Chapter

- The United States regulates in three major areas of environmental protection: air pollution, water pollution, and land pollution. Environmental laws have traditionally been of the command and control type, specifying standards and results. New laws have added market incentives to induce environmentally sound behavior and have encouraged companies to reduce pollution at the source.

- Environmental laws have brought many benefits. Air, water, and land pollution levels are in many cases lower than in 1970. But some improvements have come at a high cost. A continuing challenge is to find ways to promote a clean environment and sustainable business practices without impairing the competitiveness of the U.S. economy.

- Companies pass through five distinct stages in the development of green management practices. Many businesses are now moving from lower to higher stages. An ecologically sustainable organization is one that operates in a way that is consistent with the principle of sustainable development.

- Effective environmental management requires an integrated approach that involves all parts of the business organization, including top leadership, line managers, and production teams, as well as strong partnerships with stakeholders.

[22]"Escape from Dante's Inferno," *Business Week,* December 21, 1992, p. 86A.

[23]For a general statement of the argument that environmental management confers a competitive advantage, see Michael E. Porter and Claas van der Linde, "Green and Competitive: Beyond the Stalemate," *Harvard Business Review,* September–October 1995, p. 120 ff; and Stuart L. Hart, "Beyond Greening: Strategies for a Sustainable World," *Harvard Business Review,* January–February, 1997, pp. 66–76. The discussion of the competitive advantages of environmental management is adapted, in part, from Anthony Saponara, "Competitive Advantage in the Environment," *Corporate Environmental Strategy: The Journal of Environmental Leadership* 3, no. 1 (Summer 1995).

- Many companies have found that proactive environmental management can confer a competitive advantage by saving money, attracting green customers, promoting innovation, and developing skills in strategic planning.

Key Terms and Concepts Used in This Chapter

- Environmental Protection Agency (EPA)
- Acid rain
- Environmental justice
- Source reduction
- Superfund (CERCLA)
- Cross-media pollution
- Environmental standards
- Command and control regulation
- Tradable allowances
- Greening of management
- Ecologically sustainable organization
- Environmental partnerships
- Green marketing

Internet Resources

- http://www.epa.gov   Environmental Protection Agency
- http://www.envirolink.org   Environmental organizations
- http://www.igc.apc.org/greenmarket   Green marketing
- http://www.enviroindustry.com Environmental industry
- http://www.lungusa.org   American Lung Association

Discussion Case   Common Sense in Arizona

In November 1996, the Environmental Protection Agency signed a historic agreement with Intel Corporation, the nation's largest maker of computer chips. Under the deal, Intel would be given almost unlimited flexibility in operating its new factory in Chandler, Arizona, in exchange for reducing pollution even more than the law required. EPA administrator Carol Browner hailed the agreement as a "common sense solution" for both industry and regulators.

"This is an attempt to move away from the regulatory battle and make things performance-related," said an Intel spokesperson. "What we get is flexibility and the ability to run our business as efficiently and effectively as possible, as long as we stay under the limits."

The site of this bold experiment, Intel's $2.5 billion Chandler plant, was expected when completed to become the second-largest chip making factory in the world, employing 1,500 workers and with a central clean room spanning a full eight acres.

EPA's deal with Intel was one of the first negotiated under a new federal program called Project XL (for *excellence* and *leadership*). In 1995, the EPA began a major effort, called its *reinvention initiative*. The idea was to create innovative alternatives to current regulatory approaches that would improve environmental quality while making it simpler and less expensive for businesses to comply with environmental rules. Under Project XL, a key part of the initiative, companies could negotiate agreements with EPA to simplify their permitting requirements, as long as they achieved certain overall goals. These agreements would have to be approved not only by EPA but also by affected stakeholders, such as local and state governments, environmentalists, and community organizations.

The five-year agreement with Intel required the company to cap overall air pollution at Chandler at 50 tons a year, below existing EPA limits, and to recycle much of the water used and nonhazardous waste generated at the plant. It also required Intel to monitor its own emissions on an ongoing basis and to report complete and current information on the Internet as well as with the government. In exchange, the company was given a facilitywide permit instead of having to obtain a separate permit for each process.

Intel was pleased, citing the speed with which it could implement changes. "We are the epitome of a quick-to-market company," said the company's government affairs manager for environment, health, and safety. "So we're constantly having to change our processes to keep up with technological progress. . . . Every time we make a change, we have to go back for a permit revision, and by the time we get it, the technology is outdated. Project XL enables us to solve that problem."

But some activists criticized the agreement. A group called the Coalition for Responsible Technology (CRT), comprised of over 100 community, environmental, and health and safety organizations, blasted it as a "sweetheart deal" that "turn[ed] back the clock on hard-won laws that protect the environment." The coalition was concerned that the agreement would permit higher emissions of *particular* toxic chemicals than allowed under existing standards, threatening the health of those working in or living near the factory. CRT was also worried that emissions from the plant would not be routinely monitored by regulators.

In addition, the coalition criticized the stakeholder board established by EPA, charging that it did not include enough community and labor representatives and did not give its members the resources and technical assistance they needed to do their job properly. The result of the deal, CRT charged, would be a "race to the bottom" as other high-tech facilities would insist on similar regulatory leniency.

Sources: "EPA Innovates at Big Arizona Factory," *New York Times,* November 20, 1996, p. A10; "Intel to Be Its Own Pollution Watchdog," *San Jose Mercury News,* November 20, 1996, pp. A1, A10; "Intel Gets Multimedia Project XL Permit," Bureau of National Affairs *Daily Environment Reporter,* November 20, 1996, p. AA1; "Intel Defends Environmental Deal with U.S," *San Francisco Chronicle,* November 21, 1996, p. D1; "Intel to Put Environmental Data Online," *Arizona Republic,* November 20, 1996, p. B1; and "Washington Wreck," *Industry Week,* August 18, 1997, p. 116. The Web site for the Campaign for Responsible Technology is http://www.igc.apc.org/svtc/crt.

Discussion Questions

1. Of the alternative policy approaches discussed in this chapter, of which is Project XL an example? If Project XL includes features of more than one regulatory approach, please list these features and state how they have been combined.

2. What are the benefits and costs of the regulatory approach taken by the EPA in this case? Please answer this question from the perspective of the following stakeholders: Intel managers, Intel employees, the Chandler, Arizona, community, environmental organizations, and federal environmental regulators.

3. Do you support Project XL? Why or why not? How might the approach illustrated in this case be modified to address the concerns of various stakeholders in the process?

PART SIX

Responding to Stakeholders

13

Stockholders and Corporate Governance

Stockholders occupy a position of central importance in a corporation because they are its legal owners and they expect high levels of economic performance. But the corporation is not always run solely for their benefit, so they contend with management and the board of directors for control of company policies. Recent changes in corporate governance have strengthened the influence of stockholders and increased the attention given to this stakeholder group by managers and boards of directors.

This chapter focuses on these key questions and objectives:

- Who are stockholders and what are their goals and legal rights?

- Who controls the corporation, and how has the power of stockholders, relative to that of boards of directors and managers, shifted in recent years?

- What have social activist investors done to change corporate policies?

- What are the pros and cons of employee ownership of corporations?

- Are top corporate executives paid too much?

- How are stockholders affected by insider trading, and how does the government protect against stock market abuses?

I n 1996, John G. Smale stepped down as chairman of the board of directors of General Motors, ending a critical period in the company's history. GM's president and chief executive, John F. Smith, Jr., assumed the additional role of chairman. Three years earlier, Smale, formerly the head of Procter & Gamble and an outside member of GM's board, had led a coup that deposed then-chairman and chief executive Robert C. Stempel. Many members of the board at that time were concerned that Stempel was not moving quickly enough to turn around the sagging behemoth. Smith's promotion suggested that the board approved the job he was doing. But some institutional investors, including the California Public Employees Retirement System (CalPERS), expressed disappointment, saying that separating the jobs of board chairman and chief executive had led managers to be more accountable to shareholders.

Sisters of the Blessed Sacrament, a small Catholic religious order based in Philadelphia, placed a resolution on the 1997 shareholder ballot of Walt Disney, opposing the entertainment company's executive compensation practices. That year, the board of directors had recommended a pay package for CEO Michael Eisner, linking his compensation to the performance of the company's stock, which could be worth hundreds of millions of dollars over the next decade. Despite support from some institutional investors, including a teachers' pension fund and a union representing Disney's own workers, the nuns' proposal received less than 10 percent of the vote. Eisner defended his pay to stockholders, saying, "Compensation is a very complicated matter. If the stock doesn't go up, I will not benefit."

In France, a mining company called Eramet took an action that angered some of its foreign investors. The company, which was partly owned by the French government, offered to swap one of its nickel mines for another, owned by separatists, that was worth less. The motive was political. The government wanted to appease the separatists, who were organizing for independence for the French territory of New Caledonia. But foreign investors, including the College Retirement Equity Fund and Fidelity Investments, objected vigorously, saying that the action would reduce the value of the company's stock. After the foreign investors threatened to put the matter to a vote by all shareholders, the company backed down and agreed to reforms of its decision-making process. This incident was part of what many observers saw as a spread of shareholder activism from the United States to other countries, following the growing globalization of stock trading.[1]

What motivates a major institutional investor like a state pension fund or union to challenge the top management of companies like General Motors or Walt Disney? Should managers of big firms pay attention to the wishes of investors such as the Sisters of the Blessed Sacrament? How have foreign companies, like Eramet, responded to challenges from stockholders from both the United States and other countries? Each of these examples and the questions they raise involve the complex relationship between the corporation and its legal owners, the stockholders. Managements and boards of directors face very difficult issues in responding to corporate owners and balancing their demands with other company goals. This chapter addresses this important set of issues and relationships.

---

[1]"Chairman to Step Down in G.M. Shift," *New York Times,* December 5, 1995, p. D1; "Eisner's New Pay Plan Could Top $200 Million," *Chicago Tribune,* February 26, 1997, Business section, p.1; "Investors to Lobby Disney on Pay Disparities," *Financial Times,* February 7, 1997, p. 24; "Big Pension Fund Joins Disney Board Foes," *Orange County Register,* February 22, 1997, p. C1; and "Eramet Minority Investors Force France to Back Down on Shareholder Rights," *The Wall Street Journal,* August 1, 1997, p. A10.

Stockholders

Stockholders—or shareholders, as they also are called—are the legal owners of business corporations. By purchasing a *share* of the company's stock, they become part owners of the company. For this reason, stockholder-owners have a big stake in how well their company performs. The firm's managers must pay close attention to their needs and assign a high priority to their interests in the company.

Who Are Stockholders?

Two types of stockholders own shares of stock in U.S. corporations: individual and institutional.

Individuals may own stock directly, by purchasing shares in companies, usually through stockbrokers. Or they may own shares indirectly, for example, by purchasing shares of mutual funds, buying insurance policies, or joining pension funds. Since the 1960s, growth in the numbers of such **institutional investors** has been phenomenal. Studies by the securities industry showed that in 1996, institutions accounted for 53 percent of the value of all equities (stocks) owned in the United States, worth a total of $5.3 *trillion*, more than four times the value of institutional holdings a decade earlier.[2]

By 1997, 43 percent of all U.S. adults owned shares of stock, either directly as individuals or indirectly through institutions. Stockholders are a diverse group. People from practically every occupational group own stock: professionals, managers, clerks, craft workers, farmers, retired persons, and even unemployed adults. Although older people are more likely to own stock, young people (aged 18 to 34) now own about a fifth of all shares. Women make up almost half of all investors.[3]

Figure 13–1 shows the relative stock holdings of individual and institutional investors from the 1960s to the late-1990s. It shows the growing influence of the institutional sector on the market over the past three decades.

Objectives of Stock Ownership

Individuals and institutions own corporate stock for a number of reasons.

Economic Objective

Foremost among these reasons is the goal of receiving an economic gain, or a return on investment. Rather than placing such money in banks to earn interest with relatively little risk, investors choose stocks because they believe equities will produce greater gains. Different types of corporate ownership produce varying levels of return through dividends and increases in stock price. A company that pays a relatively high dividend (6 to 7 percent) is not likely to have rapid price appreciation. Conversely, a company with good growth prospects and whose stock is likely to appreciate in price can choose to pay a lower dividend, if any at all, and still attract investors. Investors are thereby free to choose companies that are less speculative (high dividends) or more speculative, depending on their personal goals and willingness to assume risk.

---

[2]Securities Industry Association, "Holdings of U.S. Equities Outstanding," *Securities Industry Factbook* (New York: Securities Industry Association, 1997), p. 56. These data are based on analysis of the Federal Reserve Bank's flow of funds accounts.

[3]New York Stock Exchange, "Shareownership, 1995"; and Peter D. Hart Research Associates, "A National Survey among Stock Investors" (New York: Nasdaq, February 1997).

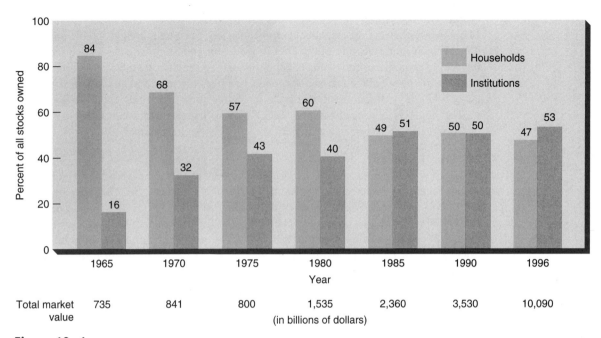

Figure 13–1

Individual household versus institutional ownership of stock in the United States, 1965–1996.

Source: Securities Industry Association, *Securities Industry Factbook* (New York: Securities Industry Association, 1997). Based on Federal Reserve flow of funds accounts (revised). Used by permission.

Social Objective

Some investors use stock ownership to achieve a social or ethical objective. A growing number of mutual funds and pension funds screen companies in which they invest, weeding out ones that pollute the environment, discriminate against their employees, or make dangerous products like tobacco or weapons. In 1995, according to the Social Investment Forum, $639 billion in the United States was invested in mutual funds or pensions using social responsibility as an investment criterion, up from $65 billion just a decade earlier. This accounted for almost one in every ten investment dollars.[4] Social criteria may also be used when selling stocks. In the 1970s and 1980s, many individuals and institutions sold stocks of companies that did business in South Africa because of that country's discriminatory racial policies. With South Africa's transition to multiracial democracy in 1994, many bans on investment there were lifted, and the attention of social investors shifted to other countries. Some called for *divestment* (sale of stock) from companies that had operations in China, where some products were made by forced labor, and in Nigeria and Burma, where repressive military regimes had been accused of human rights abuses.[5]

---

[4]"Do-Good Investing Grabs Market Share in U.S.," *Christian Science Monitor,* June 5, 1996, p. 8.
[5]Simon Billenness, "Beyond South Africa: New Frontiers in Corporate Responsibility," *Business and Society Review,* Summer 1993, pp. 28–31.

Mixed Objectives

Many investors, whether individuals or institutions, invest with both economic and social objectives in mind. They are interested in receiving good returns but also want to invest in socially responsible companies. Such investors require their stockbrokers or investment advisers to apply both social and economic criteria they regard as important to the purchase and sale of stock. Some managers of mutual funds that apply social criteria in selecting stocks have argued that this approach may increase economic returns, since socially responsible companies may perform better in the long term.

Corporate Control

There are other reasons for investing in corporate stock. Some investors, including corporate raiders, are interested in gaining control of the corporation. This may be for the purpose of merging it with another firm or selling its assets to buyers who will pay more for the parts than for the whole company. Many of the takeovers of the 1980s were of this type. Such investments also may have a long-term economic purpose, but the immediate objective is to take control of the company and its assets. Other investors may purchase stock to influence management strategy, perhaps by gaining a seat on the board of directors.

Stockholders' Legal Rights and Safeguards

To protect their financial stake in the companies whose stocks they hold, stockholders have several legal safeguards. Specific rights of stockholders are established by law. Stockholders have the following legal rights, and these vary somewhat among states: They have the right to share in the profits of the enterprise if dividends are declared by directors. They have the right to receive annual reports of company earnings and company activities, and they have the right to inspect the corporate books, provided they have a legitimate business purpose for doing so and that it will not be disruptive of business operations. They have the right to elect directors and to hold those directors and the officers of the corporation responsible for their acts, by lawsuit if they want to go that far. Furthermore, they usually have the right to vote on mergers, some acquisitions, and changes in the charter and bylaws and to bring other business-related proposals before the stockholders. And finally, they have the right to sell their stock. Figure 13–2 summarizes the major legal rights of stockholders.

Many of these rights are exercised at the annual stockholders' meeting, where directors and managers present an annual report and shareholders have an opportunity to

Figure 13–2

Major legal rights of stockholders.

- To receive dividends, if declared
- To vote on
    Members of board of directors
    Major mergers and acquisitions
    Charter and bylaw changes
    Proposals by stockholders
- To receive annual reports on the company's financial condition
- To bring shareholder suits against the company and officers
- To sell their own shares of stock to others

approve or disapprove of management's plans. Approval is generally expressed by re-electing incumbent directors, and disapproval may be shown by attempting to replace them with new ones. Because most corporations today are large, typically only a small portion of stockholders attend to vote in person. Those not attending are given an opportunity to vote by absentee ballot, called a *proxy*. The use of proxy elections by stockholders to influence corporate policy is discussed later in this chapter.

Stockholder Lawsuits

If stockholders think that they or their company have been damaged by actions of company officers or directors, they have the right to bring lawsuits in the courts. Lawsuits may be brought either by individual shareholders or by a group of individuals in a class action. **Shareholder lawsuits** may be initiated to check many abuses, including insider trading, an inadequate price obtained for the company's stock in a buyout or takeover, lush executive pension benefits, or fraud committed by company officials. For example, the shareholders of a computer graphics company in California sued, saying that management had made optimistic projections of its future prospects that it knew to be false.[6]

In the 1990s, many companies, especially in high-technology industries, complained that they were the target of frivolous shareholder lawsuits. In 1995, in response to these concerns, Congress passed legislation that made it harder for investors to sue companies for fraud. But some executives felt that the legislation had not gone far enough, because many shareholder suits disallowed under federal law could still be filed in state courts, and they called on Congress for a uniform national standard for securities lawsuits. Some investor groups, consumer activists, and trial lawyers opposed such a move. A citizens' initiative in California called Proposition 211, which would have made it *easier* for investors to sue companies for fraud, was defeated after many businesses rallied against it.

Corporate Disclosures

Giving stockholders more and better company information is one of the best ways to safeguard their interests. The theory behind the move for greater disclosure of company information is that a stockholder, as an investor, should be as fully informed as possible to make sound investments. By law, stockholders have a right to know about the affairs of the corporations in which they hold ownership shares. Those who attend annual meetings learn about past performance and future goals through speeches made by corporate officers and documents such as the company's annual report. Those who do not attend meetings must depend primarily on annual reports issued by the company and the opinions of independent financial analysts.

Historically, management has tended to provide stockholders with minimum information. But prompted by the Securities and Exchange Commission and by professional accounting groups, companies now disclose more about their affairs, in spite of the complicated nature of some information. A few corporations go further than required and publish financial information from the detailed 10-K section of their official reports to the SEC. Stockholders therefore can learn about sales and earnings, assets, capital expenditures and depreciation by line of business, and details of foreign operations.

---

[6]"Will Congress Build a Safer Harbor against Investor Lawsuits?" *Business Week,* June 16, 1997, p. 47.

Corporations also are required to disclose detailed information about directors, how they are chosen, their compensation, conflicts of interest, and their reasons for resigning in policy disputes with management. New rules, discussed later in this chapter, also require companies to publish information about the compensation of their executives.

Corporate Governance

The term **corporate governance** refers to the overall control of a company's actions. Several key stakeholder groups are involved in governing the corporation.

- *Managers* occupy a strategic position because of their knowledge and day-to-day decision making.
- The *board of directors* exercises formal legal authority over company policy.
- *Stockholders*, whether individuals or institutions, have a vital stake in the company.
- *Employees,* particularly those represented by unions or who own stock in the company, can affect some policies.
- *Government* is involved through its laws and regulations.
- *Creditors* who hold corporate debt may also influence a company's policies.

The following discussion concentrates on the roles of three groups that traditionally govern the corporation in addition to stockholders: the board of directors, top management, and creditors.

The Board of Directors

The board of directors is a central factor in corporate governance because corporation laws place legal responsibility for the affairs of a company on the directors. The board of directors is legally responsible for establishing corporate objectives, developing broad policies, and selecting top-level personnel to carry out these objectives and policies. The board also reviews management's performance to be sure that the company is well run and stockholders' interests are protected.

Corporate boards are legally permitted to vary in size, composition, and structure so as to best serve the interests of the corporation and the shareholders. A number of patterns do exist, however. Corporate boards average 11 members, with the largest boards in banks and financial institutions and the smallest in small and midsized firms. Of these members, it is likely that about 80 percent will be *outside* directors (not managers of the company), including chief executives of other companies, retired executives of other firms, investment bankers, major shareholders, former government officials, academics, and representatives of the community. Over two-thirds of all companies have at least one woman on the board, and a third have at least one African-American board member.

Most corporate boards perform their work through committees. The executive committee (present in 65 percent of corporate boards) works closely with top managers on important business matters. The audit committee (present in virtually all boards) is normally composed entirely of outside directors; it reviews the company's financial reports, recommends the appointment of outside auditors, and oversees the integrity of internal financial controls. The compensation committee (99 percent), also staffed by outside directors, administers and approves salaries and other benefits of high-level managers in the company. The nominating committee (73 percent) is charged with finding and recommending candidates for officers and directors, especially those to be elected at the annual stockholders' meeting. A significant number of corporations (19 percent) now have a special committee devoted to issues of corporate responsibility. Compensation for board members averages over $30,000 a year.[7]

These committees, which may meet several times each year, give an active board of directors very important powers in controlling the company's affairs. In addition, when the entire board meets, it hears directly from top-level managers and has an opportunity to influence their decisions and policies.

What kind of boards work the best? A recent study by *Business Week* identified the characteristics of the most effective boards of directors of U.S. companies. The study's conclusions are summarized in Figure 13–3.

Top Management

Professional managers generally take the leading role in large corporations. These managers might have backgrounds in marketing and sales, in engineering design and production, or in various aspects of financial analysis. The expanding scale and complexity of national and international business calls for management specialists to guide the affairs of most big companies. The source of their power is a combination of their managerial expertise and the organizational responsibility, given to them by their firms, for carrying out the needed work.

Figure 13–3

The best boards of directors.

Source: "The Best and Worst Boards: Our New Report Card on Corporate Governance," *Business Week*, November 25, 1996, p. 86. Based on a survey of large pension fund and money managers and experts in corporate governance. Used by permission. Copyright © By McGraw-Hill Companies.

The best boards:

- Evaluate performance of the CEO annually in meetings of independent directors.
- Link the CEO's pay to specific performance goals.
- Review and approve long-range strategy and one-year operating plans.
- Have a governance committee that regularly assesses the performance of the board and individual directors.
- Pay retainer fees to directors in company stock.
- Require each director to own a significant amount of company stock.
- Have no more than two or three inside directors.
- Require directors to retire at 70 years of age.
- Place the entire board up for election every year.
- Place limits on the number of other boards on which its directors can serve.
- Ensure that the audit, compensation, and nominating committees are composed entirely of independent directors.
- Ban directors who directly or indirectly draw consulting, legal, or other fees from the company.
- Ban interlocking directorships: "I'm on your board, you're on mine."

[7]The figures in the preceding two paragraphs are based on data presented in Korn/Ferry International, *Board Meeting in Session: 23rd Annual Board of Directors Study* (New York: Korn/Ferry International, 1996). All data are for 1995.

Managers increasingly tend to consider their responsibilities as being primarily to the company rather than just to the stockholders. They perceive themselves to be responsible for (1) the economic survival of the firm; (2) extending its life into the future through product innovation, management development, market expansion, and other means; and (3) balancing the demands of all groups in such a way that the company can achieve its objectives. This viewpoint considers shareholders to be just one of several stakeholder groups that must be given attention. Concerning their specific responsibilities to owners, managers today often express the belief that "what is good for the company in the long run is good for the stockholder." Some observers believe that the power of top managers has declined somewhat in recent years, as boards of directors, institutional stockholders, and other stakeholders have grown more assertive.[8]

Creditors

Since the mid-1980s, creditors have become a powerful influence in the governance of corporations. Traditionally, creditors have lent money to businesses to help them finance the purchase of new buildings, equipment, or the expansion of a business into new areas of activity. In the 1980s, a number of financiers persuaded corporate executives that issuing high-risk, high-yield bonds, known as *junk bonds,* could enable them to acquire other firms, reorganize them, sell off unwanted portions, and both meet the debt payments and improve total corporate financial performance.

The idea was appealing, and dozens of companies used such financing to build larger and larger corporate empires. The threat of unwanted takeover bids became so serious that many managers sought to find ways of making their companies private, that is, eliminating the public stockholders. This led, in turn, to further use of debt in a series of **leveraged buyouts (LBOs).** An LBO uses debt financing (bonds or borrowed money) to purchase the outstanding shares of stock from public shareholders. For management, this arrangement replaces impatient shareholders, who are ready to sell their stock to the highest bidder, with a creditor whose view is longer term. As long as the company can continue to pay the high yield on the bonds, management is relatively well protected from hostile takeover action. During the recession of the early 1990s, however, many users of debt financing found that revenues were insufficient to pay bond interest. The result was often bankruptcy or even complete dissolution of the company. This course of action was forced by the creditors, who wanted some return—albeit less than full value—on the money they had loaned. Dealing with creditors has therefore become a major corporate governance issue for companies.[9]

The Process of Corporate Governance

Who will govern the corporation internally is a central issue facing business. There is no easy answer to the question, Who's in charge? The current system of corporate governance is the product of a long historical process, dating back to the emergence of the

---

[8]For a classic argument for management's expanded obligations to a variety of stakeholders, see James O'Toole, *Vanguard Management: Redesigning the Corporation,* (New York: Doubleday, 1985).

[9]Michael C. Jensen, "Eclipse of the Public Corporation," *Harvard Business Review,* September–October 1989, pp. 61–74.

modern, publicly held corporation in the late 1800s. This section presents two contrasting models of corporate governance, against which recent developments may be compared.

According to the traditional, legal model of corporate governance, stockholders hold the ultimate authority in the firm. In this view, stockholders exercise control through their legal right to elect the board of directors. The directors, in turn, hire top management, set overall strategy, and are responsible for making sure stockholders earn a fair return from a well-managed operation. These principles of governance are embodied in corporate law and in the legal rights stockholders enjoy, presented earlier in Figure 13–2. In the traditional model, stockholders are the group at the top of the chain of command within the firm, as shown in Figure 13–4.

Many analysts of the modern corporation, however, have long maintained that the traditional model is not a very realistic picture of how companies really work. In this revisionist view, several forces counteract the legal power of stockholders. Historically, most shareholders in the United States have been individuals who owned a small number of shares. Typically, shareholders as a group were (and still are) geographically dispersed, and government rules made it difficult for them to contact each other or to organize on behalf of their collective interests. Most owners of stock who disapproved of management were more likely to do the "Wall Street walk"—simply selling their shares and walking away—than they were likely to try to change corporate policy.

Moreover, according to the revisionist model, a firm's top managers were more likely to control the board of directors rather than vice versa as in the traditional model. Members of the board, in practice, were (and still are in many companies) nominated by top managers and served at their pleasure. Contested elections for board seats were rare. Board members, who usually served on a part-time basis, often lacked the information or expertise to challenge full-time managers and were likely to rubber-stamp decisions placed before them. In the revisionist view, then, corporate governance was

Figure 13–4

Traditional and revisionist models of corporate governance.

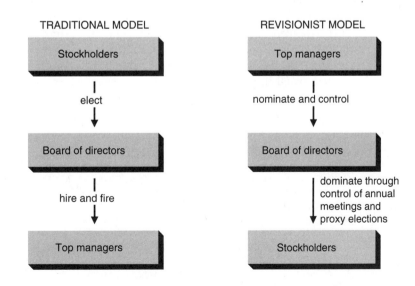

turned on its head, with top managers having the ultimate authority and stockholders at the bottom.[10] The traditional and revisionist models are contrasted in Figure 13–4.

Recent trends in corporate governance suggest that neither model may any longer be an accurate description of how corporations are run. The relative power of stakeholder groups within the firm, both in the United States and other countries, has changed significantly. Stockholders, particularly large institutions, and boards of directors have became more assertive relative to top management. Social activist shareholders have exerted influence through the proxy (absentee ballot) election process, and in some cases workers have exercised control through new forms of stock ownership. These important developments are profiled in the next section.

Current Trends in Corporate Governance

The Rise of Institutional Investors

As shown earlier, institutional investors—pensions, mutual funds, endowment funds, and the like—have enlarged their stockholdings and since the mid-1980s have become more assertive in promoting the interests of their members. This trend has had important implications for corporate governance.

One reason institutions have become more active is that it is more difficult for them to sell their holdings if they become dissatisfied with management performance. Large institutions have less flexibility than individual shareholders, because selling a large bloc of stock could seriously depress its value. Accordingly, institutional investors have a strong incentive to hold their shares and organize to change management policy. One example of such activism by institutional investors, at Archer Daniels Midland, is presented in the discussion case at the end of this chapter.

In 1985, the Council of Institutional Investors was formed. Since then, the Council has grown to almost 100 members and represents institutions and pension funds with investments totaling more than $900 billion. The Council developed a Shareholder Bill of Rights and urged its members to view their proxies as assets, voting them on behalf of shareholders rather than automatically with management. The activism of the Council's institutional members was facilitated in the early 1990s by new Securities and Exchange Commission (SEC) rules that made it easier for shareholders to communicate with one another, get access to lists of other shareholders, and circulate proxy campaign material.[11]

---

[10] A discussion of the legal basis for the roles of stockholders, boards, and managers in the modern corporation may be found in the American Law Institute, *Principles of Corporate Governance* (Philadelphia: 1994). Early statements of the revisionist argument appear in Robert A. Gordon, *Business Leadership in the Large Corporation* (Berkeley: University of California Press, 1948); and Myles Mace, *Directors: Myth and Reality* (Boston: Harvard Business School Press, 1971). For more recent discussions of corporate governance, see Jay W. Lorsch with Elizabeth MacIver, *Pawns or Potentates: The Reality of America's Corporate Boards* (Boston: Harvard Business School Press, 1989); Robert A. G. Monks and Nell Minow, *Power and Accountability* (New York: Harper Business, 1991); Murray Weidenbaum, *The Evolving Corporate Board* (St. Louis: Center for the Study of American Business, 1994); Michael Useem, *Executive Defense: Shareholder Power and Corporate Reorganization* (Boston: Harvard University Press, 1993); and Michael Useem, *Investor Capitalism: How Money Managers Are Changing the Face of Corporate America* (New York: Basic Books, 1996).

[11] "A Lethal Weapon for Shareholders" *Business Week,* June 15, 1992, p. 40.

The 1990s witnessed a movement toward **relationship investing.** This occurs when large shareholders—pensions, mutual funds, or a group of private investors—form a long-term, committed link with a company. Often, institutional owners buy a significant stake in a company and acquire a seat on the board; at the least, they meet frequently with management. The benefits of relationship investing are that companies gain long-term commitments from key shareholders, who in turn get more say in management. At Sears, for example, a leading advocate of relationship investing, Robert Monks, bought a major share in the company and then convinced managers to spin off its financial units and make other major changes. Monks's partner stated, "Corporate governance is our tool for making money. We are talking about non-takeover takeovers. Like the raiders, we hope to realize value that's buried. We've found a better, earlier way to do it."[12] Some observers maintained that the movement for shareholder rights had matured, as many corporations increasingly accepted an enlarged role in corporate governance for institutional owners.

The activism of institutional investors has begun to spread to other countries. These efforts in many cases have been spearheaded by U.S.-based pension and mutual funds that in recent years acquired large stakes in foreign companies. By 1997, about one in every eight dollars controlled by American pension funds and endowments was invested in overseas stocks or bonds.[13] To protect their globalized investments, fund managers have become active in proxy battles in Japan, Britain, Hong Kong, and many other countries. Although these efforts have usually been unsuccessful, in the long run they may influence corporate governance abroad, as the following example shows.

> *In Germany, a representative of CalPERS, the California state employees' pension fund, stood up at the annual meeting of a major utility company and denounced shareholder voting restrictions, calling them "an embarrassing anachronism which pulls Germany out of step with international norms." The restrictions were not changed, but the German press gave the incident wide coverage, calling the confrontation "unprecedented."*

A 1994 study of 13 nations found that nearly half of the companies surveyed reported growing contact with institutional investors over the past three years.[14]

Movements for shareholder rights often confront formidable obstacles abroad, where stock markets may be smaller and corporate governance is often dominated by networks of allied businesses, creditors, and managers, to the exclusion of stockholders. Many countries do not share the U.S. principle of one share, one vote or traditions of open debate at shareholder meetings. Even so, stockholders have successfully ousted top executives in Britain, organized for higher dividends in Japan, and blocked antitakeover provisions in the Netherlands. The movement for the rights of shareholders, like the investments they hold, is becoming increasingly globalized.[15]

---

[12]"Relationship Investing: A New Shareholder Is Emerging—Patient and Involved," *Business Week,* March 15, 1993, pp. 68–75.

[13]"Investment Management 1996/97 Greenwich Report (Greenwich, CT: Greenwich Associates, 1997).

[14]Ronald E. Berenbeim, "Company Relations with Institutional Investors" (New York: The Conference Board, 1994).

[15]An excellent comparative analysis of corporate governance in different countries may be found in "Corporate Governance: A Survey," *The Economist,* January 29, 1994, pp. 3–18.

Changing Role of the Board of Directors

Like institutional investors, some boards of directors have also become more assertive. At both ailing and healthy companies, boards have stopped rubber-stamping management policies and have begun thinking more independently. As the General Motors example that opened this chapter illustrated, some boards have fired their chief executives. Others have redirected, reorganized, and generally rethought their companies. One CEO commented, "[Boards] are thinking through the whole process of corporate governance—what they're responsible for—and going into more detail about it."

The new assertiveness of some boards has several sources. Directors have found themselves pressured by institutional investors anxious to protect their shareholders' interests. Another factor has been an increase in lawsuits against board members. Since the mid-1980s, a number of court decisions have held directors personally liable for poor management decisions, making them more sensitive to their responsibilities to stockholders. Organizational reforms of the board have also led to increased independence from management. Growing representation by outside directors is one such trend; outsiders now make up over 80 percent of board members, on average. Another such reform is separation of the duties of the chief executive and the board chairman, rather than combining the two in one person as is done in many corporations. With this split in responsibilities, a board has an improved chance of receiving completely candid reports about a company's affairs. Nineteen percent of boards now have a nonexecutive chairman.[16]

Social Responsibility Shareholder Resolutions

Another important current trend in corporate governance is the rise of **social responsibility shareholder resolutions,** such as the resolution offered by the Sisters of the Blessed Sacrament, illustrated in one of the opening examples of this chapter.[17]

The Securities and Exchange Commission allows stockholders to place resolutions concerning appropriate social issues, such as environmental responsibility or alcohol and tobacco advertising, in proxy statements sent out by companies. These SEC rules reflect a belief that stockholders should be allowed to vote on social as well as economic questions that are related to the business of the corporation. The SEC has tried to minimize harassment by requiring that a resolution must receive minimum support in order to be resubmitted in subsequent years—5 percent of votes cast the first year, 8 percent the second year, and 10 percent the third year. Resolutions cannot deal with a company's ordinary business, since that would constitute unjustified interference with management's decisions in running the company. In 1997, the SEC proposed new rules that would further limit the rights of investors to place such issues before other stockholders for a vote. Social activists have vigorously opposed these proposals.[18] Despite continuing controversy, in recent years the number and variety of social responsibility shareholder resolutions has continued to increase markedly.

---

[16]Korn/Ferry International, *Board Meeting in Session.*

[17]For general historical background on the rise of investor social activism, see Lauren Talner, *The Origins of Shareholder Activism* (Washington, DC: Investor Responsibility Research Center, 1983); and David Vogel, *Lobbying the Corporation: Citizen Challenges to Business Authority* (New York: Basic Books, 1978).

[18]Further information about this debate appears at the Web site of the Social Investment Forum, http://www.socialinvest.org.

Shareholder activists in 1997 sponsored 226 resolutions dealing with major social issues at meetings of more than 100 corporations. Over 100 church groups were joined by individual shareholders, unions, environmental groups, and a growing number of pension funds. Many of these groups were members of a coalition, the Interfaith Center on Corporate Responsibility (ICCR), that coordinated the activities of the social responsibility shareholder movement. Some of the key issues raised in these resolutions included executive compensation, environmental responsibility, alcohol and tobacco advertising, equal employment opportunity, and investments in countries with human rights problems.[19]

Since shareholder resolutions not favored by management rarely garner enough votes to be adopted, what is their point? There are several answers. The annual meetings provide a forum for debating social issues. Stockholders have a legal right to raise such issues and to ask questions about how their company is responding. Management is questioned about controversial issues and has to justify its policies in public. To avoid the glare of publicity, an increasing number of corporations have met with dissident groups prior to the annual meeting and have agreed to take action on an issue voluntarily. For example, in 1994 General Motors agreed to endorse the CERES Principles, a code of environmental conduct described in Chapter 11, after three years of discussion between the company and religious investors who had backed shareholder resolutions in support of the code. The coordinator of the CERES negotiating team said that GM's voluntary agreement "demonstrates the new power of shareholders in corporate America. Shareholders can bring companies and public interest groups together to produce environmental commitments that are both local and global in scope."[20]

Employee Stock Ownership

A final trend, one that affects a small but growing number of U.S. corporations, is the form of stock ownership known as an **employee stock ownership plan (ESOP).** An ESOP is a kind of benefit plan in which a company purchases shares of its own stock and places them in trust for its employees. The idea is to give employees direct profit-sharing interest in addition to their wage and salary income. ESOP advocates claim that this kind of share ownership benefits the company by increasing worker productivity, reducing job absenteeism, and drawing management and employees closer together into a common effort to make the company a success. Not only do ESOP participants receive regular dividends on the stock they own, but workers who quit or retire can either take their stock from the fund or sell their shares back to the company. A major financial benefit to an ESOP company is that its contributions to the plan are tax deductible.

Beginning in the mid-1970s, ESOPs grew at an explosive pace, mainly because of new federal and state laws that encouraged their formation. From less than 500 in 1975, ESOPs grew to about 10,000 by 1997, covering over 10 million employees and controlling $300 billion in corporate stock. Most ESOPs are in private companies, but they have become popular in public firms as well, where employees typically own less than 30 percent of the company's stock.[21]

[19]"Corporate Responsibility Challenges 1997," *The Corporate Examiner* 25, no. 7–8, p. 1.

[20]"General Motors Endorses CERES Principles," *The Corporate Examiner* 12, no. 10, p. 1.

[21]National Center for Employee Ownership, "Statistical Profile of Employee Ownership," May 1997.

An example of an employee-owned company is United Airlines. In 1994, the airline set up an ESOP, and employees traded a 15 percent cut in pay for 55 percent of the stock. United workers not only owned a majority of the airline, they also participated in management directly—from brainstorming teams at the lowest levels up to the board of directors, where they held 3 out of 12 seats. Productivity at the airline surged, and United began taking market share from its two biggest rivals, American and Delta.[22]

Studies have shown that where employee ownership is linked with participative management practices, as at United, companies experience significant gains in performance.[23]

In sum, the past decade has been a period of fluidity and flux in corporate governance. The answer to the question, Who governs the corporation? is becoming, Many people and groups. The authority of top managers has been increasingly checked by powerful groups of institutional investors, newly assertive boards of directors, and, in a smaller number of cases, activist shareholders and worker owners. It is clear that the process of corporate governance is undergoing significant change, much of it leading to a greater dispersion of power within the firm and a greater emphasis on enhancing shareholder value.

Executive Compensation: A Special Issue

An issue of increasing controversy is **executive compensation.** Even as the authority of top managers has diminished, in some respects their salaries have soared. Are top managers paid too much, or are their high salaries and bonuses well-deserved rewards for their contributions to the companies they lead? This debate has been the focus of much recent attention by boards of directors, shareholders, and government regulators seeking to increase the accountability of top managers.

Executive compensation in the United States, by international standards, is very high. In 1996, the chief executives of the largest corporations in the United States earned, on average, $5.8 million, including salaries, bonuses, and the present value of retirement benefits, incentive plans, and stock options, according to *Business Week.* This was a 54 percent increase over the previous year's total compensation.[24] By contrast, top managers in other countries earned much less. A 1996 survey found that although the pay of top executives in Western Europe was catching up, it was still in most cases less than half of what comparable managers in the United States earned.[25]

---

[22]"United We Own," *Business Week,* March 18, 1996, p. 96.

[23]Michael Quarrey and Corey M. Rosen, *Employee Ownership and Corporate Performance* (Oakland, CA: National Center for Employee Ownership, 1996). For further analysis of the impact of ESOPs, see Joseph Blasi and Douglas Kruse, *The New Owners: The Mass Emergence of Employee Ownership in Public Companies and What It Means to American Business* (New York: HarperCollins, 1991); and Corey M. Rosen, Katherine J. Klein, and Karen M. Young, *Employee Ownership in America: The Equity Solution* (Lexington, MA: Lexington Press, 1986).

[24]"Executive Pay: Special Report," *Business Week,* April 21, 1997, pp. 58–66. By contrast, chief executives at small and midsize companies make much less. One survey of companies with annual revenues below $400 million found median annual compensation of CEOs to be $312,000; see "Pay Gap Grows for Chiefs of Big Firms and Small Ones," *The Wall Street Journal,* October 25, 1994, p. B2.

[25]"So Far Away," *The Wall Street Journal,* April 11, 1996, p. R12.

Another way to look at executive compensation is to compare the pay of top managers with that of average employees. In the United States, CEOs in 1996 made about 209 times what the average worker did.

Why are American executives paid so much? Corporate politics play an important role. Graef S. Crystal, a compensation expert and critic of inflated executive pay, argued in his book *In Search of Excess* that one reason salaries are so high is that they are set by compensation committees of boards of directors. These committees are usually made up of individuals handpicked by the CEO; often, they are CEOs themselves and sensitive to the indirect impact of their decisions on their own salaries. Moreover, compensation committees rely heavily on the advice of consultants who conduct surveys of salaries in similar firms. Graef argued that since boards usually want to pay their own executives above the median for comparable firms, "it doesn't take a Ph.D. in statistics to figure out that under those circumstances, the median is going to keep going up."[26]

Some observers say that the comparatively high compensation of top U.S. executives is justified. In this view, well-paid managers are simply being rewarded for outstanding performance. For example, Stephen J. Ross, the former CEO of Time Warner and for many years one of the top-paid U.S. executives, delivered a compound return of almost 24 percent annually between 1973 and 1990. To many shareholders, his pay ($78 million in 1991, his last full year in office) was clearly worth it. Much of the increase in executive compensation in the 1980s and 1990s can be accounted for by the exercise of stock options (a benefit whose value typically rises with stock prices). Of course, the bull market in stocks during many of those years benefited shareholders as well as executives.

Supporters also argue that high salaries provide an incentive for innovation and risk taking. In an era of intense global competition, restructuring, and downsizing, the job of CEO of a large U.S. corporation has never been more challenging, and tenure in the top job has become shorter. Another argument for high compensation is a shortage of labor. In this view, not many individuals are capable of running today's large, complex organizations, so the few that have the necessary skills and experience can command a premium. Today's high salaries are necessary for companies to attract top talent. Why shouldn't the most successful business executives make as much as top athletes and entertainers?[27]

On the other hand, critics argue that inflated executive pay hurts the ability of U.S. firms to compete with foreign rivals. High executive compensation diverts financial resources that could be used to invest in the business, increase stockholder dividends, or pay average workers more. Multimillion dollar salaries cause resentment and sap the commitment of hardworking lower-level employees who feel they are not receiving their fair share. As for the performance issue, critics suggest that as many extravagantly compensated executives preside over failure as they do over success. A study published in the *Harvard Business Review* concluded that "in most publicly held companies, the compensation of top executives is virtually independent of performance."[28]

[26]Graef S. Crysal, *In Search of Excess: The Overcompensation of American Executives* (New York: W. W. Norton, 1991). For a further discussion of executive pay and its impact on society, see Derek Bok, *The Cost of Talent: How Executives and Professionals Are Paid and How It Affects America* (New York: Free Press, 1993).
[27]A defense of high executive pay may be found in Andrew Brownstein and Morris J. Panner, "Who Should Set CEO Pay? The Press? Congress? Shareholders?" *Harvard Business Review,* May–June 1992, pp. 28–38.
[28]Michael C. Jensen and Kevin J. Murphy, "CEO Incentives—It's Not How Much You Pay, but How," *Harvard Business Review,* May–June 1990, pp. 138–49.

Some shareholder activists have tried to rein in excessive executive compensation, as illustrated in the opening example involving Walt Disney. Executive compensation has also been the subject of new government regulations. Under SEC rules introduced in 1992, companies must clearly disclose what their five top executives are paid and lay out a rationale for their compensation. A separate chart must report the company's stock and dividend performance. These rules expand stockholders' rights by making it easier for them to determine a manager's total compensation and whether it is justified by the firm's record. The SEC also for the first time allowed nonbinding shareholder votes on executive and director compensation. Congress passed a rule that would prevent companies from taking tax deductions on executive salaries in excess of $1 million annually, although many compensation experts said it would make little difference in how much top managers were paid.

Some companies have responded to these stakeholder pressures by changing the process by which they set executive pay. Most now staff compensation committees of the board of directors exclusively with outside directors and permit them to hire their own consultants. At American Exploration Co., an oil and gas company, the board voted against extra compensation for top executives after an independent consultant told them it was not necessary to remain competitive. Other companies have sought to restructure compensation to tie top executives' pay more closely to performance. A few top managers have even taken pay cuts or refused compensation altogether—like Netscape's CEO James Barksdale, who accepted no salary or bonus in 1997 after his company's stock price plummeted. Some firms, including Du Pont and Tandem Computers, have made stock options available to all employees, giving everyone, not just the top executives, a stake in the company's performance. A handful of companies have ruled that top executives cannot earn more than a certain multiple of others' pay.[29]

The active debate over excessive executive compensation is part of the larger issue of the relative power within the corporation of managers, directors, and stockholders and of governmental regulation of their roles.

Governmental Protection of Stockholder Interests

Securities and Exchange Commission

The major government agency protecting stockholders' interests is the Securities and Exchange Commission. Established in 1934 in the wake of the stock market crash and the Great Depression, its mission is to protect stockholders' rights by making sure that stock markets are run fairly and that investment information is fully disclosed. The agency, unlike most in government, generates revenue to pay for its own operations.

Governmental regulation is needed because stockholders can be damaged at times by abusive practices. One area calling for special efforts to protect and promote stockholder interests is insider trading.

Insider Trading
Insider trading occurs when a person gains access to confidential information about a company's financial condition and then uses that information, before it becomes public knowledge, to buy or sell the company's stock. Since others do not know what an inside

---

[29]For some recommendations on how companies can better structure executive compensation, see Ira T. Kay, *Value at the Top: Solutions to the Executive Compensation Crisis* (New York: Harper Business, 1992).

trader knows, it is possible for the insider to make advantageous investments or sell stock well in advance of other stockholders.

Insider trading is illegal under the Securities and Exchange Act of 1934, which outlaws "any manipulative or deceptive device." The courts have generally interpreted this to mean that it is against the law to:

- Misappropriate (steal) nonpublic information and use it to trade a stock.

- Trade a stock on the basis of a tip from someone who had an obligation to keep quiet; for example, a man would be guilty of insider trading if he bought stock after his sister, who was on the board of directors, told him of a pending offer to buy the company.

- Pass information to others with an expectation of direct or indirect gain, even if the individual did not trade the stock for his or her own account.

In an important 1997 case, *U.S.* vs. *O'Hagen,* the Supreme Court clarified insider trading law. The court ruled that someone who traded on the basis of inside information when he or she *knew* the information was supposed to remain confidential was guilty of misappropriation, whether or not the trader was directly connected to the company whose shares were purchased. In the 1997 case, the court upheld the conviction of a Minneapolis lawyer who had made millions trading stock options after he learned of a pending takeover involving a client of his firm. Under the new court interpretation, insider trading rules would cover a wide range of people—from lawyers, to secretaries, to printers—who learned of and traded on information they knew was confidential. They would not, however, cover people who came across information by chance, for example, by overhearing a conversation in a bar. In this situation, the trader would not necessarily know the information was confidential.[30]

The most spectacular insider-trading scandal in Wall Street history occurred in 1986 when several individual investors and a few officers of investment banking firms were revealed to have made millions of dollars illegally through insider trading. By sharing confidential information about forthcoming mergers of large corporations, they were able to buy and sell stocks before the mergers were announced to the public. Although this scandal temporarily put a damper on insider trading, within a year the rate of trading based on inside information was as high as ever. More recently, the merger wave of the mid- and late-1990s, described in Chapter 10, apparently contributed to a new surge in insider trading, as investors with knowledge of pending deals bought or sold in advance of public information. The number of insider trader cases brought by the SEC in 1994, 1995, and 1996 were well ahead of earlier years. Many of these cases involved not big-time investment bankers, as in the 1980s, but lower-level corporate employees and their friends and family members.[31]

Many instances of insider trading have emerged in the former Communist countries of Eastern Europe. The transition there to a market economy was generally not accompanied by adoption of the same kinds of governmental controls that exist in the United States. The result was, in many instances, stock price manipulation and insider trading. The president of one mutual fund

---

[30]"Supreme Court Upholds S.E.C.'s Theory of Insider Trading," *New York Times,* June 26, 1997, pp. C1, C23.
[31]"The Boeskys of Main Street: Suspect Trading Rises, with New Kinds of Insiders Seen," *New York Times,* April 16, 1997, p. D1.

*with investments in Eastern Europe, speaking of the Czech Republic, com-
plained, "Like most post-Communist countries, there was an ingrained
system—never tell the truth and always help your buddies."*[32]

Insider trading, whether in new market economies or established ones, is contrary
to the logic underlying stock markets: all stockholders ought to have access to the same
information about companies. None should have special privileges or gain unfair advantages over others. Only in that way can investors have full confidence in the fairness of
the stock markets. If they think that some investors can use inside knowledge for their
own personal gain while others are excluded from such information, the system of stock
buying might break down because of lack of trust.

Stockholders and the Corporation

Stockholders have become an increasingly powerful
and vocal stakeholder group in corporations. Manage-
ment dominance of boards of directors has weakened, and shareholders, especially institutional investors, are pressing directors and management more forcefully to serve stockholder interests. Institutional investors also have acquired new power as creditors, using
their purchases of corporate bonds as an additional form of leverage on corporate management. Shareholder activists and worker owners have also changed the contours of corporate governance.

Clearly, stockholders are a critically important stakeholder group. By providing capital, monitoring corporate performance, assuring the effective operation of stock markets,
and bringing new issues to the attention of management, stockholders play a very important role in making the business system work. Corporate leaders have an obligation to
manage their companies in ways that promote and protect a variety of stakeholders. Balancing these various interests is a prime requirement of modern management. Although
stockholders are no longer considered to be the only important stakeholder group, their
interests and needs remain central to the successful operation of corporate business.

Summary Points of This Chapter

- Individuals and institutions own shares of corporations as a means of economic gain.
  Social purposes sometimes guide investors, as when certain businesses are avoided
  because of their negative social impacts. Shareholders are entitled to vote, receive information, select directors, and attempt to shape corporate policies and action.

- The corporate governance system is the relationship among directors, managers,
  shareholders, and sometimes creditors. It determines who has legitimate power and
  how this power can be exercised. Corporate governance has changed during the
  1990s. Newly assertive institutional investors and boards of directors have challenged
  the authority of top management.

- Activists have influenced corporate actions in some cases through social responsibility shareholder proposals, although such proposals rarely gain enough votes to pass.

[32]"A U.S. Fund Manager in Prague Has Found Privatization Corrupt," *New York Times,* December 3, 1997,
p. D8.

- Employee stock ownership programs give employees a stake in the financial success of a company and may enhance worker commitment and productivity, although they also leave employees vulnerable to declining stock prices.

- Some observers argue that the compensation of top U.S. executives is justified by performance and that high salaries provide a necessary incentive for innovation and risk taking in a demanding position. Critics, however, believe that executive compensation is too high. In this view, high pay hurts firm competitiveness and undermines employee commitment.

- Insider trading is illegal and unethical. It benefits those with access to information at the expense of those who do not have it. Ultimately, it undermines fairness in the marketplace.

Key Terms and Concepts Used in This Chapter

- Stockholders
- Institutional investors
- Shareholder lawsuits
- Corporate governance
- Leveraged buyouts (LBOs)
- Relationship investing

- Social responsibility shareholder resolutions
- Employee stock ownership plan (ESOP)
- Executive compensation
- Insider trading

Internet Resources

- http://www.nyse.com   New York Stock Exchange
- http://www.irrc.org   Investor Responsibility Research Center
- http://www.ciicentral.com   Council of Institutional Investors
- http://www.socialinvest.org   Social Investment Forum

Discussion Case   Shareholders Demand Reforms at Archer Daniels Midland

In October 1996, a group of irate institutional investors converged on the annual stockholders meeting of Archer Daniel Midlands (ADM) demanding reform. The Decatur, Illinois–based company, which called itself the "supermarket to the world," was a global producer of agricultural goods such as corn syrup, vegetable oil, and ethanol. Since 1970, the company, under the leadership of CEO Dwayne Andreas, had seen its market value soar from $78 million to almost $12 billion.

The agribusiness giant was reeling from bad news. Just days earlier, the company had pled guilty to federal charges that it had conspired to fix the prices of lysine and citric acid, two widely used ingredients in food products. It had agreed to pay a $100 million criminal fine, the largest in the history of antitrust enforcement. ADM's first quarter fiscal year profits, $174 million, were more than wiped out by the cost of the fines and $90 million in related civil settlements.

Many institutional shareholders blamed the company's troubles, in part, on the unusually cozy relationship between ADM's management and its board of directors.

The *New York Times* called ADM "a virtual family fief under Mr. Andreas's iron-fisted control." Of the 17-person board of directors, 10 were current or former executives or relatives of Andreas; several others were considered personally loyal to him. Some shareholders believed that, because of its lack of independence, the board had failed to exercise strict oversight over the company's operations.

"The $100 million fine is shareholder assets that are being squandered to pay for criminal activity that never should have occurred," said a representative of CalPERS, the California public pension fund. "Where was the board of directors?"

One group of institutional investors, led by the California and Florida pensions, proposed that a majority of the board be comprised of outsiders. Another proposal, by the pension fund for New York City firefighters, called for secret shareholder voting. These proposals received 42 and 46 percent of the votes cast, unusually high for ones opposed by an incumbent board. Some investors also called for Andreas's resignation.

Although the shareholder proposals failed, the company took steps voluntarily to reform its governance process. Four managers, all with close ties to Andreas, stepped down from the board, and several other members were replaced. Two executives implicated in the price-fixing scandal, including Andreas's son and heir apparent, left the company. And the board approved a new governance structure, in which Andreas would share power as part of a four-person executive committee.

But big shareholders were not mollified. "We do support companies that distribute power when there are signs of trouble," said a representative of the Council of Institutional Investors in November 1996. "But this is shocking . . . instead of bring[ing] in a new CEO, they do this." In April 1997, Dwayne Andreas finally retired as CEO at the age of 79, although he retained the title of chairman of the board. The company announced that he would be succeeded by G. Allen Andreas, Dwayne's nephew and former head of the company's European operations.

Sources: "The Tale of the Secret Tapes," *New York Times,* November 16, 1997, pp. B1, B10; "ADM's New CEO: Allen Andreas," *Chicago Tribune,* April 18, 1997, Business Section p. 1; "It Isn't Dwayne's World Anymore" *Business Week,* November 18, 1996, p. 82; "Andreas Creates Executive Team," *Washington Post,* November 1, 1996, p. F3; "Archer Daniels Midland Agrees to Big Fine for Price Fixing," *New York Times,* October 15, 1996, pp. A1, C3; "ADM Governance Committee Urges Broad Changes in Board Makeup," *Milling and Baking News,* January 23, 1996, p. 10; and additional news reports appearing in the *New York Times, Chicago Tribune, Washington Post,* and *The Wall Street Journal.*

Discussion Questions

1. Why were some institutional investors dissatisfied with actions of Archer Daniels Midland's management and board of directors?
2. Do you believe that the composition of the board of directors was a factor in the company's involvement in the price-fixing scandal? Why or why not?
3. As an individual shareholder of Archer Daniels Midland, would you have been satisfied with the company's managers and board of directors? With the subsequent actions of the institutional investors? If not, what could you do about it?
4. Do you believe that the actions of top management, the board of directors, and shareholders in this case are consistent with the trends in corporate governance discussed in this chapter? Why or why not?

14

Consumer Protection

Safeguarding consumers while continuing to supply them with the goods and services they want is a prime social responsibility of business. Many companies recognize that providing customers with excellent service and product quality is an effective, as well as ethical, business strategy. Consumers, for their part, have become increasingly aware of their rights to safety, to be informed, to choose, and to be heard—and, increasingly, of their right to privacy. Government agencies serve as watchdogs for consumers, supplementing the actions taken by consumers to protect themselves and the actions of socially responsible corporations.

This chapter focuses on these key questions and objectives:

- Why did a consumer movement develop in the United States?

- What are the major rights of consumers?

- In what ways do government regulatory agencies protect consumers? To what extent *should* government protect consumers?

- Why has advertising become a target of consumer activists and government regulators?

- Is there a product liability crisis, and what reforms, if any, should be made?

- How have socially responsible corporations responded to consumer needs?

I n 1997, the Food and Drug Administration (FDA) ordered two of the nation's most popular diet drugs off the market after they were linked to serious heart problems in some users. The drugs, *dexfenfluramine* and *fenfluramine,* had been used with another medicine called *phentermine* in a combination popularly known as fen-phen. Fen-phen had enabled many obese people to lose weight, and many patients and doctors were enthusiastic. The two diet drugs had been big moneymakers for their manufacturer, Wyeth-Ayerst Laboratories, producing over $300 million in sales in 1996. But doctors found that some patients developed potentially fatal heart-valve problems while taking the medication, and several previously healthy dieters died. When the government showed Wyeth-Ayerst officials the clinical data, the company readily agreed to withdraw the drugs. "Our first commitment is to our patients and their doctors," said a representative of Wyeth-Ayerst. "Even though this new information . . . is difficult to evaluate, the company is taking the most prudent course of action." Wyeth-Ayerst placed full-page advertisements in newspapers announcing the drugs' withdrawal and established a toll-free number for patients.[1]

A Texas man had to have his foot amputated after a hunting rifle he was unloading, the Remington Model 700, accidentally discharged, seriously wounding him. Five years later, in 1994, a jury returned a verdict of $17 million against Remington, including $15 million in punitive damages. The company called the rifle "a safe and reliable sporting firearm" and disputed that it was in any way defective. But the Texan's attorney introduced internal documents showing that Remington had received complaints about the rifle dating back to 1982 and that the company had designed a safer firing mechanism but had decided not to use it. Guns are among the few consumer products for which the government has no authority to regulate safety. Although firearm accidents cause as many as 1,400 deaths a year, the National Rifle Association and gun manufacturers have vigorously opposed federal oversight.[2]

In 1993, after nearly a decade of controversy, the U.S. government approved bovine somatropin (BST), a genetically engineered hormone to boost milk production in cows. Years of testing by the FDA and health organizations showed that milk produced with BST was indistinguishable from milk that was not. But the day before the hormone was released for use, several of the country's largest food companies—including Kroger, Pathmark, and Southland, operator of 7-Eleven convenience stores—announced that they would not buy milk produced by cows given the drug. "Food is an emotional issue," a spokesperson for Southland said. "We felt a responsibility to take this action because of concern expressed by our customers."[3]

These three episodes demonstrate some of the complexities of serving consumers today. New standards of business performance are being demanded. Today's consumers are increasingly aware of the broad impact that consumption can have not only on themselves but on society generally. This chapter examines these issues and the various ways that consumers, government regulators, and business firms have dealt with them.

---

[1]"How Fen-Phen, a Diet 'Miracle,' Rose and Fell," *New York Times,* September 23, 1997, p. F1; and "Two Top Diet Drugs Are Recalled Amid Reports of Heart Defects," *New York Times,* September 16, 1997, p. A1.
[2]"Remington Faces a Misfiring Squad," *Business Week,* May 23, 1994, pp. 90–91.
[3]"Crying over Unnatural Milk," *Business Week,* November 22, 1993, p. 48; and "Grocers Challenge Use of New Drug for Milk Output," *New York Times,* February 4, 1994, pp. A1, A8.

Pressures to Promote Consumer Interests

As long as business has existed—since the ancient beginnings of commerce and trade—consumers have tried to protect their interests when they go to the marketplace to buy goods and services. They have haggled over prices, taken a careful look at the goods they are buying, compared the quality and prices of products offered by other sellers, and complained loudly when they felt cheated by shoddy products. So, consumer self-reliance has always been one form of consumer protection. The Latin phrase, *caveat emptor*—meaning "let the buyer beware"—has put consumers on the alert to look after their own interests. This form of individual self-reliance is still very much in existence today.

However, the increasing complexity of economic life in the twentieth century, especially in the more advanced industrial nations, has led to organized, collective efforts to safeguard consumers. These organized activities are usually called consumerism or the **consumer movement.**

The Anatomy of Consumerism

At the heart of consumerism in the United States is an attempt to expand the rights and powers of consumers. The goal of the consumer movement, which began in the 1960s as part of a broader movement for social change (discussed in Chapter 3), is to make consumer power an effective counterbalance to the rights and powers of business firms that sell goods and services.

Within an advanced, industrialized, private-enterprise nation, business firms tend to grow to a very large size. They acquire much power and influence. Frequently, they can dictate prices. Typically, their advertisements sway consumers to buy one product or service rather than another. If large enough, they may share the market with only a few equally large competitors, thereby weakening some of the competitive protections enjoyed by consumers where business firms are smaller and more numerous. The economic influence and power of business firms may therefore become a problem for consumers unless ways can be found to promote an equal amount of consumer power.

Most consumers would feel well protected if their fundamental rights to fair play in the marketplace could be guaranteed. In the early 1960s, when the consumer movement in the United States was in its early stages, President John F. Kennedy told Congress that consumers were entitled to four different kinds of protection:

1. *The right to safety*—to be protected against the marketing of goods that are hazardous to health or life.
2. *The right to be informed*—to be protected against fraudulent, deceitful, or grossly misleading information, advertising, labeling, or other practices, and to be given the facts to make an informed choice.
3. *The right to choose*—to be assured, wherever possible, access to a variety of products and services at competitive prices, and in those industries in which competition is not workable and government regulation is substituted, to be assured satisfactory quality and service at fair prices.
4. *The right to be heard*—to be assured that consumer interests will receive full and sympathetic consideration in the formulation of government policy and fair and expeditious treatment in its administrative tribunals.

The **consumer bill of rights,** as it was called, became the guiding philosophy of the consumer movement. If those rights could be guaranteed, consumers would feel more confident in dealing with well-organized and influential corporations in the marketplace. In the mid-1990s, some activists and government regulators began to call for laws protecting a fifth consumer right, the *right to privacy*. This issue is discussed in the case at the end of this chapter.

Reasons for the Consumer Movement

This consumer movement exists because consumers want to be treated fairly and honestly in the marketplace. Some business practices do not meet this standard. Consumers may be harmed by abuses such as unfairly high prices, unreliable and unsafe products, excessive or deceptive advertising claims, and the promotion of some products known to be harmful to human health, such as cigarettes or farm products contaminated with pesticides.

Additional reasons for the existence of the consumer movement are the following: .

- *Complex products have enormously complicated the choices consumers need to make when they go shopping.* For this reason, consumers today are more dependent on business for product quality than ever before. Because many products are so complex—a personal computer or an automobile, for example—most consumers have no way to judge at the time of purchase whether their quality is satisfactory. Many of the component parts of such products are not visible to consumers, who, therefore, cannot inspect them even if they have the technical competence to do so. Consumers find that they are almost entirely dependent on business to deliver the quality promised. In these circumstances, unscrupulous business firms can take advantage of uninformed consumers.

- *Services, as well as products, have become more specialized and difficult to judge.* When choosing lawyers, dentists, colleges, or hospitals, most consumers do not have adequate guides for evaluating whether they are good or bad. They can rely on word-of-mouth experiences of others, but this information may not be entirely reliable. Or, when purchasing expensive items such as refrigerators, consumers have to judge how well the items will perform and know what to do when they break down. The consumer faces a two-tier judgment problem in making purchases: First, is the product a good one? Then, what will good service cost? The uninformed or badly informed consumer is frequently no match for the seller who is in the superior position.

- *When business tries to sell both products and services through advertising, claims may be inflated or they may appeal to emotions having little to do with how the product is expected to perform.* An example was an ad for a stereo that declared, "She's terrific in bed, she's witty and intelligent and makes her own pasta." But, the ad continued, "she didn't own [the advertised sound system], so he married a woman who did." The ad was withdrawn after numerous complaints poured in to the manufacturer.[4] A survey by *American Demographics* magazine found that nearly a third of adults found sexual references or images in advertising offensive.[5] Ad-industry critics have also frequently found fault with advertise-

---

[4]"Does Sex Sell? Yes, But . . . ," *The Detroit News,* June 12, 1994.
[5]Doris Walsh, "Safe Sex in Advertising," *American Demographics,* April 1994, pp. 24–30.

ments that air during children's television programs and feature violence, sell sweetened cereals, or promote toys—for example, the Ninja Turtle or G.I. Joe characters—by building program plots around these products, thus taking advantage of young children unable to differentiate between a fictional program and a commercial advertisement.[6] Beer commercials that feature "good old boys" relaxing after work and auto advertisements that link male virility with horsepower and speed have come under attack for ignoring the negative impacts of alcohol abuse and high-speed automobile deaths and injuries.

- *Product safety has often been ignored.* The symbolic beginning of consumerism in the United States was Ralph Nader's well-publicized charges in the early 1970s about the hazards of driving the Corvair.[7] As public interest in health and nutrition grew, many consumers worried about food additives, preservatives, pesticide residues left on fruits and vegetables, diet patterns that contributed to obesity, and the devastating health effects of long-term tobacco use. If the public could not count on business to screen out these possible dangers to consumers, to whom could they turn for help? This question was raised more and more often, which led eventually to corrective actions by business, government, and consumer advocacy groups.

Consumer Advocacy Groups

One of the impressive features of the consumer movement in the United States is the many organized groups that actively promote and speak for the interests of millions of consumers. One organization alone, the Consumer Federation of America, brings together over 240 nonprofit groups to espouse the consumer viewpoint; they represent some 50 million Americans. A nonprofit organization, Consumers Union, conducts extensive tests on selected consumer products and services and publishes the results, with ratings on a brand-name basis, in *Consumer Reports* magazine. Consumer cooperatives, credit unions, Web sites catering to consumers, and consumer education programs in schools and universities and on television and radio round out a very extensive network of activities aimed at promoting consumer interests.

The most-publicized consumer advocate is Ralph Nader, who with his associates formed a network of affiliated organizations. Public Citizen, founded in 1971, became the umbrella organization for specialized units, the main fund-raising organization, and a publishing arm for consumer publications. The Health Research Group has taken the lead in urging a ban on harmful color dyes used in various foods, putting warning labels on dangerous products, setting exposure limits on hazardous substances, and alerting the public to possibly dangerous medical products on the market, such as silicone breast implants. Other organizations under the Public Citizen umbrella include the Litigation Group, which gives legal assistance to people who have difficulty in gaining adequate access to the court system; Congress Watch, which monitors Congress; and Global Trade Watch, which ed-

[6]"Watch What Your Kids Watch," *Business Week,* January 8, 1990, pp. 50–52.
[7]Ralph Nader, *Unsafe at Any Speed: The Designed-In Dangers of the American Automobile* (New York: Grossman, 1972).

ucates consumers about the impact of economic globalization. Nader's organization is also allied with a network of state and local activist groups.[8]

How Government Protects Consumers

The federal government's involvement in protecting consumers' interests is extensive. During the 1960s and 1970s, Congress passed important laws to protect consumers, created new regulatory agencies, and strengthened older consumer protection agencies. These developments meant that consumers, rather than relying solely on free market competition to safeguard their interests, could also turn to government for protection. During most of the 1980s, a deregulatory attitude by the federal government tended to blunt federal initiatives on behalf of consumers. However, state governments became more active, particularly regarding price-fixing, car insurance rates, and corporate takeovers that threatened jobs and consumer incomes. The mid- and late-1990s have witnessed a revival of government regulatory activism in many areas of consumer protection.

Goals of Consumer Laws

Figure 14–1 lists some of the safeguards provided by **consumer protection laws.** Taken together, these safeguards reflect three goals of government policymakers and regulators.

First, some laws are intended to provide consumers with better information when making purchases. Consumers can make more rational choices when they have accurate information about the product, thereby making comparison with competing products easier. For example, the Truth in Lending Act requires lenders to inform borrowers of the annual rate of interest to be charged, plus related fees and service charges. The laws requiring health warnings on cigarettes and alcoholic beverages broaden the information consumers have about these items. Knowing the relative energy efficiency of household appliances, which must be posted by retailers, permits improved choices. Manufacturers, retailers, and importers must specify whether warranties (guarantees or assurances by the seller) are full or limited, must spell them out in clear language, and must give consumers the right to sue if warranties are not honored.

Deceptive advertising is illegal. Manufacturers may not make false or misleading claims about their own product or a competitor's product.

A 1993 law requires food manufacturers to adopt a uniform nutrition label, specifying the amount of calories, fat, salt, and other nutrients contained in packaged, canned, and bottled foods. The same kind of information about fresh fruits and vegetables, as well as fish, must be posted in supermarkets.

A second aim of consumer legislation is to protect consumers against possible hazards from products they may purchase. Required warnings about possible side effects of pharmaceutical drugs, limits placed on flammable fabrics, the banning of lead-based paints, and inspections to eliminate contaminated or spoiled meats are examples of these safeguards. In 1997, following several outbreaks of bacterial poisoning, President Clinton proposed new rules designed to reduce the risk of food-borne illness. One incident of bacterial contamination in food, involving fresh fruit juice made by Odwalla, Inc., is described in a case study at the end of the textbook.

---

[8]Further information about Public Citizen is available at http://www.citizen.org.

Figure 14–1

Major consumer protections specified by consumer laws.

Information protections

Hazardous home appliances must carry a warning label.

Home products must carry a label detailing contents.

Automobiles must carry a label showing detailed breakdown of price and all related costs.

Credit loans require lender to disclose all relevant credit information about rate of interest, penalties, and so forth.

Tobacco advertisements and products must carry a health warning label.

Alcoholic beverages must carry a health warning label.

All costs related to real estate transactions must be disclosed.

Warranties must specify the terms of the guarantee and the buyer's rights.

False and deceptive advertising can be prohibited.

Food and beverage labels must show complete information.

Food advertising must not make false claims about nutrition.

Direct hazard protections

Hazardous toys and games for children are banned from sale.

Safety standards for motor vehicles are required.

National and state speed limits are specified.

Hazardous, defective, and ineffective products can be recalled under pressure from EPA, CPSC, NHTSA, and FDA.

Pesticide residue in food is allowed only if it poses a negligible risk.

Pricing protections

Unfair pricing, monopolistic practices, and noncompetitive acts are regulated by FTC and Justice Department and by states.

Liability protections

When injured by a product, consumers can seek legal redress.

Other protections

No discrimination in the extension of credit.

Congress has also recently addressed the problem of pesticide and herbicide residues left on farm products. Some of these chemicals cause nerve damage if consumed in large quantities; others have produced cancers in test animals. Children are thought to be especially at risk. In 1996, Congress repealed the 1958 Delaney Clause, which had banned all food additives known to cause cancer, and replaced it with a single standard for fresh and processed food. The new standard allowed pesticide residue in food only if it posed a negligible risk, except for some stronger provisions designed to protect children. The goal of the new law was to protect the public's health without causing unnecessary harm to agricultural producers.

A third goal of consumer laws is to encourage competitive pricing. When competitors secretly agree to divide markets among themselves, to rig bidding so that it appears to be competitive, or to fix prices of goods and services at a noncompetitive, artificially high level, they are taking unfair advantage of consumers. Both federal and state laws forbid these practices, as discussed in Chapter 10. Competitive pricing also was promoted by the deregulation of railroads, airlines, intercity bus lines, trucking, telephones, and various financial institutions in the 1970s and 1980s. Prior to deregulation, government agencies frequently held prices artificially high and, by limiting the number of new competitors, shielded existing businesses from competition.

Major Consumer Protection Agencies

Figure 14–2 depicts the principal consumer protection agencies that operate at the federal level, along with their major areas of responsibility. The oldest of the six is the Food and Drug Administration, which, along with the Department of Agriculture's meat and poultry inspection programs, dates back to the first decade of the twentieth century. The Federal Trade Commission was established in 1914 and has been given additional powers to protect consumers over the years. Three of the agencies—the Consumer Product Safety Commission, the National Highway Traffic Safety Administration, and the National Transportation Safety Board—were created during the great wave of consumer regulations in the 1960s and early 1970s. Not listed in Figure 14–2 is the Antitrust Division of the Department of Justice, which indirectly protects consumers by policing monopolistic and anticompetitive practices of business firms. Its functions are described further in Chapter 10.

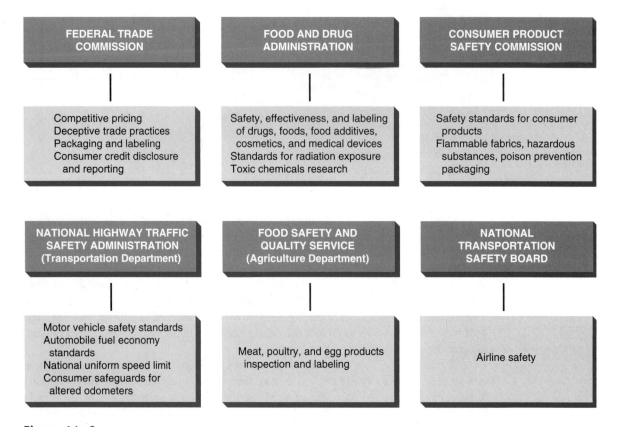

Figure 14–2

Major federal consumer protection agencies and their main responsibilities.

   A recent controversy surrounding rule-making by the National Highway Traffic Safety Administration, concerning air bags, is profiled in Exhibit 14–A.

   Of these agencies, the one with perhaps the greatest impact on the business community is the Food and Drug Administration. The FDA's mission is to assure the safety and effectiveness of a wide range of consumer products, including pharmaceutical drugs, medical devices, foods, and cosmetics. The agency has authority over $960 billion worth of products, about a quarter of all consumer dollars spent each year.

EXHIBIT 14–A

Air Bags: Do They Help or Hurt Safety?

Should consumers have the right to refuse to use safety equipment mandated by the government? Should the government mandate equipment that, while helping many, might hurt a few? Should manufacturers and dealers be held responsible if a consumer did not use safety equipment provided? These questions were raised in connection with automobile air bags.

An air bag is a safety device that works by inflating rapidly during a collision, preventing the occupant from moving forward and striking the steering wheel, dashboard, or other hard object. In 1995, the National Highway Traffic Safety Administration (NHTSA) required automatic seat belts or driver-side air bags in most cars sold in the United States and driver *and* passenger-side air bags were required as standard equipment on most cars by 1998.

But in 1996, concern emerged about possible hazards of the air bags themselves to children and small adults. Although air bags were believed to have saved more than 1,750 lives since their introduction in 1986, they had also apparently killed 52 people, over half of them children, when they deployed forcefully and struck passengers. Many of those killed or injured had not been wearing seat belts, or had not been properly belted, and had been thrown toward the dashboard in emergency braking. As news of these deaths spread, some consumers complained to the safety agency, and some even tried to disable their own air bags.

In 1997, the NHTSA announced new rules. Beginning with the following model year, automakers could offer less powerful bags as an option. Eventually, the government said it would require so-called smart air bags that would adjust the force of deployment according to the weight of the occupant. The government also proposed that consumers be allowed to request that their dealer or mechanic disconnect their vehicle's air bags.

The response of auto dealers and manufacturers was mixed. Some dealers were worried about shutting off air bags at the customer's request. "What if a dealer disables an air bag [and] the owner drives out of the lot and gets into an accident?" asked a representative of the National Automobile Dealers Association. Manufacturers were also worried about liability, but they also saw the new rules as a way to alleviate customers' concerns about possible air bag hazards.

Sources: "New Government Rule Seeks to Stem Danger from Air Bags," *New York Times,* March 15, 1997, p. A11; "U.S. to Propose Air Bag Rule Changes Today to Protect Children, Small Adults," *The Wall Street Journal,* December 30, 1996, p. A14; and the National Highway Traffic Safety Administration, http://www.nhtsa.dot.gov/cars/rules/rulings. In November 1997, the government announced that, effective immediately, consumers would be allowed to install switches to disable passenger-side air bags, if they could demonstrate a good reason, such as the need to place a small child in the front seat.

One of the FDA's jobs is to review many new products prior to their introduction. This job requires regulators to walk a thin line as they attempt to protect consumers. Two types of regulatory errors may occur. On one hand, the agency must not approve products that do not work or are harmful, as illustrated by the example of fen-phen at the beginning of this chapter. On the other hand, the agency must also not delay beneficial new products unnecessarily, as shown by the following example.

> *The Sensor Pad is a simple $7 medical device, consisting of two sealed plastic sheets separated by a layer of lubricant, designed to help women conduct monthly breast self-exams. Many doctors praised the product, and its developer was honored as a finalist in an inventor-of-the-year contest. The Sensor Pad product was readily approved in Canada and many European and Asian countries. But its manufacturer in Decatur, Illinois, Inventive Products, Inc., fought unsuccessfully for almost a decade to win FDA approval. Regulators expressed concern that the device would give women a false sense of security, and they demanded that the company conduct exhaustive clinical trials comparing the number of cancers detected with and without use of the Sensor Pad. In 1994, Inventive Products' president laid off all the company's workers except two and stated, "We're at the point of surrender."*[9]

The FDA has been criticized both for overly zealous regulation and for lax oversight of consumer safety. In the early 1990s, the agency undertook a major internal reorganization aimed at better serving the public and easing the regulatory burden on business.[10]

All six government regulatory agencies shown in Figure 14–2 are authorized by law to intervene directly into the very center of free market activities if that is considered necessary to protect consumers. In other words, consumer protection laws and agencies substitute government-mandated standards and the decisions of government officials for decision making by private buyers and sellers.

The Social Dimension of Advertising

One issue long of concern to both consumer activists and government regulators is the social dimension of advertising. Commercial advertisements, whether on billboards or television, in magazines or newspapers, or in newer media such as on-line services, do more than simply attempt to sell products. Many advertisements carry strong, sometimes controversial social messages as well. Advertising's social influence is seen in the pictures and images of people depicted in ads, in the health claims made for some products, and in the promotion of alcohol and tobacco products—particularly to young people.

Advertising Images

It is natural for all groups in society to want to be fairly and accurately represented in advertisements. Advertising images, because they are sent out to so many viewers, have the

---

[9]"How a Device to Aid in Breast Self-Exams Is Kept off the Market," *The Wall Street Journal,* April 12, 1994, pp. A1, A5.

[10]"Getting the Lead out at the FDA," *Business Week,* October 25, 1993, pp. 96–98; and "Inside FDA: Building New Consensus to Improve Public Safety," *Washington Post,* July 15, 1993, p. A25.

potential to influence the way people think about other people, as well as about the product or service being advertised. Some advertisers have learned this lesson the hard way, as shown in the following illustration.

> *Many people were offended when a county police officers' association in Virginia ran an advertisement promoting its annual dinner-dance in a local newspaper. The drawing used in the ad appeared to portray a white couple dancing, a black bellhop, and a dark-skinned waiter. An organization of black police officers demanded an apology, saying that the ads depicted African-Americans in stereotyped, demeaning roles. "It was really offensive as soon as I saw the faces," commented one African-American captain in the department. The police chief apologized, and said that "In today's society, we need to be more aware of issues like this that can be perceived as insensitive."*[11]

Another controversy over the depiction of groups in the media, concerning the use of sexual images of young people in advertising by the designer Calvin Klein, is profiled in Exhibit 14–B.

Health-Related Claims

Even more serious impacts can occur when companies make excessive health claims for their products.

The Food and Drug Administration pressured U.S. drug firms to stop promoting aspirin as an aid in reducing the risk of a first heart attack. The companies' claims were based on a scientific study that said taking an aspirin every other day had lowered the risk of heart attacks in middle-aged men. The FDA said that the study's findings were preliminary, were restricted to the test group, and could not be recommended for the general population. After meeting with FDA officials, the companies voluntarily stopped their advertising claims.

Five of the country's largest commercial diet programs, including Weight Watchers International, Nutri/System, and Jenny Craig, were sued by the Federal Trade Commission for making unsubstantiated promises of weight loss. The agency wanted the diet programs to back up their advertising claims and to warn consumers that weight loss was often temporary. A FTC representative stated, "The bottom line is that losing weight is hard work—and keeping it off is harder still. . . . Consumers who buy into these programs need to understand that all too often, promises of long-term weight loss raise false hopes of an easy fix for a difficult problem."[12]

Food manufacturers must also be careful not to make exaggerated claims for their products. Under new food-labeling rules, companies must follow strict guidelines when using words such as *healthy, light,* or *low-fat* to describe their products. For example, the FDA ruled that Tang, an orange-flavored drink, could not be called healthy because it did not restore nutrients that were originally in fresh oranges. Since 1994, food advertisers have been required to follow these guidelines.[13]

---

[11]"Blacks' Portrayal in Police Union Ad Draws Complaints," *Washington Post,* February 27, 1996, p. B1.

[12]"Five Diet Firms Charged with Deceptive Ads," *Los Angeles Times,* October 1, 1993, pp. A1, A15.

[13]"U.S. Issues Rules for Labeling Food 'Healthy,'" *New York Times,* May 5, 1994, p. B8; and "FTC to Require Food Ads to Follow FDA Label Guides," *The Wall Street Journal,* May 16, 1994, p. A6.

EXHIBIT **14–B**	## Calvin Klein's "Pornographic" Ads

During the summer of 1995, Calvin Klein, the clothing designer, unveiled a new advertising campaign for CK jeans. A series of print advertisements, bus posters, billboards, and TV spots featured adolescent-looking models in a variety of provocative poses, many with their underwear casually exposed.

In one of the most notorious television spots, a young man was shown leaning against a dingy paneled wall as an off-camera male voice talked to him. "You got a real nice look," the gravelly voice said. "How old are you? Are you strong? You think you could rip that shirt off you? That's a real nice body. You work out? I can tell."

The ad campaign, which was produced by the company's in-house CRK Advertising, generated a storm of protest. Commentators denounced the ads as just a step short of child pornography. The conservative American Family Association threatened a boycott of stores selling the jeans and called for a government investigation. Some magazines, including *Seventeen*, refused to carry the ads. Even President Clinton weighed in with critical remarks.

At the end of August, after the campaign had run for only a few weeks, Klein withdrew the ads voluntarily. He refused to apologize, however, defending the ads as a tribute to the "spirit, independence, and inner worth of today's young people."

The brief ad campaign and flurry of negative publicity that followed had the combined effect of powerfully boosting sales of CK jeans to young people. In September, the editor of *Fashion Network Report* noted that the jeans were "flying out of the stores" and called Klein a "marketing genius" who had cleverly timed the controversy to coincide with the back-to-school buying period.

In response to public protest, the Justice Department launched an investigation. Two months later, however, government regulators backed off after determining that the company had not used underage models or in any other way violated child pornography laws.

In 1997, Calvin Klein changed course, introducing a new ad campaign for perfume showing a wholesome family relaxing at the beach. The company's ad agency described the spots as showing "the eternal love between parents and child." The very conservatism of the new campaign, ironically, prompted some to attack the company for hypocrisy. Once again, Calvin Klein's ads had generated their own publicity.

Source: "Calvin Klein Finds Family Values," *Boston Globe,* February 28, 1997, p. C2; "Calvin Klein Ads Cleared," *Washington Post,* November 16, 1995, p. D7; and "Where Calvin Crossed the Line," *Time,* September 1, 1995, p. 64.

Curbing Alcohol and Tobacco Promotions

Alcoholic beverages and tobacco carry health risks, not just for users but for others as well. For that reason, when liquor and tobacco companies advertise their products, they are having an impact on public health that goes beyond a company's goal of persuading smokers and drinkers to use a particular brand.

Awareness of this public health problem is widespread. Some activists have been particularly concerned with beer ads that are apparently designed to attract young drinkers by featuring popular rock stars or clever cartoon frogs and lizards. A group called Center for Media Education attacked liquor companies for developing slick Web sites to "find and woo the younger generations . . . in the open fields of cyberspace." A survey commissioned by *The Wall Street Journal* found that almost half of U.S. consumers favor banning all television ads for beer and wine.[14]

Cigarette advertising is increasingly restricted, in the United States and other nations. In 1997, cigarette manufacturers negotiated an agreement with a group of state attorneys general and public health officials that would, among other things, ban most cigarette advertising in the United States, including the use of cartoon characters such as Joe Camel to promote tobacco products. (This historic agreement is discussed in more detail in a case study at the end of the textbook.) Several other nations, including Italy, Portugal, Norway, Sweden, Canada, Singapore, China, and Thailand, have already banished tobacco ads from television and the print media. Even the Moscow city council passed a resolution barring most cigarette promotions.[15]

In all of these ways, consumers and their government representatives were sending strong signals to the manufacturers and their advertising agencies that alcohol and tobacco promotions should be strictly curbed. It is another example, among many mentioned in this book, that firms operate within a web of social values and social attitudes that can have a vital impact on how they should conduct business.

Product Liability: A Special Problem

In today's economy, consumers' relationships with products they use and their relationships with producers of those products are complicated and abstract. The burden of responsibility for product performance has been shifted to the producer, under the legal doctrine of **product liability.** Although many businesses have attempted to assume much of the responsibility through money-back guarantees and other similar policies, consumers have thought that this is not enough and have demanded that business assume a larger burden of responsibility. The result has been a strengthening of product liability laws and more favorable court attitudes toward consumer claims. Walls protecting producers from consumer lawsuits have crumbled, and there has been a dramatic increase in product liability suits. These trends have led many business groups to call for reforms of the nation's product liability laws.

Strict Liability

Within the last few years courts have increasingly taken the position that manufacturers are responsible for injuries resulting from use of their products. One result has been a rapid rise in the number of product liability lawsuits—from about 12,437 in 1992 to 27,584 in 1996 in the federal courts.[16] Eighty-three percent of executives in a recent poll felt that their decisions were increasingly affected by the fear of lawsuits, and 62 percent said the

---

[14]"Besieged on Most Fronts, Tobacco Companies and Booze Makers Are Setting Their Sites on the Web, Where They're Running up against–What Else? More Opposition," *Entertainment Weekly,* April 25, 1997, p. 75. For the survey data, see "Rebelling against Alcohol, Tobacco Ads," *The Wall Street Journal,* January 14, 1989, pp. B1, B11.

[15]For regulations in other countries, see "A Red Flag in Moscow on Tobacco and Liquor Ads," *New York Times,* July 20, 1993, p. C1.

[16]John Gibeaut, "At the Crossroads," *American Bar Association Journal,* March, 1998.

civil justice system significantly hampered the ability of U.S. firms to compete with Japanese and European companies.[17] Small companies are especially vulnerable to lawsuits and may be driven out of business by sky-high liability insurance rates.

Under existing court interpretations, it is not necessary for consumers to prove either negligence or breach of warranty by the producer. Nor is the consumer's own negligence an acceptable defense by the manufacturer. If a product is judged to be inherently dangerous, manufacturers can be held liable for injuries caused by use of the product. This doctrine, known as **strict liability,** extends to all who were involved in the final product—suppliers, sellers, contractors, assemblers, and manufacturers of component parts. The following case illustrates the extent to which businesses can be held liable.

> *In 1994, an 81-year-old woman was awarded $2.9 million by a jury in Albuquerque, New Mexico, for burns suffered when she spilled a cup of hot coffee in her lap. The woman, who had purchased the coffee at a McDonald's drive-through window, was burned when she tried to open the lid as she sat in her car. In court, McDonald's argued that customers like their coffee steaming, that their cups warned drinkers that the contents are hot, and that the woman was to blame for spilling the coffee herself. But jurors disagreed, apparently swayed by arguments that the woman's burns were severe—requiring skin grafts and a seven-day hospital stay—and by evidence that McDonald's had not cooled down its coffee even after receiving many earlier complaints. McDonald's appealed the jury's verdict and later settled the case with the elderly woman for an undisclosed amount.[18]*

In this case, McDonald's was held liable for damages even though it provided a warning and the customer's actions contributed to her burns.

Business Efforts to Reform Product Liability Laws

Many businesses have argued that the evolution of strict liability has unfairly burdened them with excess costs. Liability insurance rates have gone up significantly, as have the costs of defending against liability lawsuits and paying large settlements to injured parties.

Businesses have also argued that concerns about liability exposure sometimes slow research and innovation. For example, many pharmaceutical companies halted work on new contraceptive methods because of the risk of being sued. Despite the need for new contraceptives that would be more effective and also provide protection against viral diseases, such as herpes and AIDS, research had virtually come to a halt by the late 1990s, according to some public health groups.[19]

Faced with increasing liability suits and the costs of insuring against them, business has lobbied for changes in laws and court proceedings. In the 1980s and 1990s, bills were

---

[17]"Guilty! Too Many Lawyers and Too Much Litigation: Here's a Better Way," *Business Week,* April 13, 1992, p. 66.

[18]"How a Jury Decided that a Coffee Spill Is Worth $2.9 Million," *The Wall Street Journal,* September 1, 1994, pp. A1, A5; and "McDonald's Settles Lawsuit over Burn from Coffee," *The Wall Street Journal,* December 2, 1994, p. A14.

[19]"Birth Control: Scared to a Standstill," *Business Week,* June 16, 1997, pp. 142–44; and "Fears, Suits, and Regulations Stall Contraceptive Advances," *New York Times,* December 27, 1995, pp. A1, A9.

introduced in Congress that would establish the following principles in product liability suits:

- *Set up uniform federal standards for determining liability.* Companies would not have to go through repeated trials on the same charges in many different states, which would lower legal costs for companies and help them develop a uniform legal strategy for confronting liability charges in court.

- *Shift the burden of proving liability to consumers.* Consumers would have to prove that a manufacturer knew or should have known that a product design was defective before it began producing the item. Under present law and judicial interpretations, a company is considered to be at fault if a product injures the user, whether or not the company was negligent.

- *Eliminate some bases for liability claims.* Products not measuring up to a manufacturer's own specifications—for example, poorly made tires that blow out at normal speeds—could be the basis for a liability claim, but the vast majority of liability cases go further and blame poorly designed products or a failure of the manufacturer to warn of dangers.

- *Require the loser to pay the legal costs of the winner.* If a plaintiff (consumer) refused an out-of-court settlement offer from the company and then received less in trial, he or she would have to pay the company's legal fees, up to the amount of his or her own fees. This would discourage many plaintiffs from proceeding to trial.

- *Limit punitive damages.* Punitive damages punish the manufacturer for wrongdoing rather than compensate the victim for actual losses. Punitive damage awards over the past 25 years have averaged $625,000, and some awards in recent years—like the one in the Remington case, mentioned at the beginning of this chapter—have been for multimillions of dollars.[20] One proposal would limit punitive damages to $250,000 or three times compensatory damages, whichever was greater.

In 1997, Congress once again took up the issue of product liability law reform. Although supported by many business groups, including the Business Roundtable and the National Association of Manufacturers, these reform proposals faced vigorous opposition from consumers' organizations and from the American Trial Lawyers Association, representing plaintiffs' attorneys. These groups defended the existing product liability system, saying that it put needed pressure on companies to make and keep products safe.[21]

One alternative to product liability lawsuits is described in Exhibit 14–C.

Positive Business Responses to Consumerism

The consumer movement has demonstrated to businesses that they must perform at high levels of efficiency, reliability, and fairness to satisfy the consuming public. Because firms have not always responded quickly or fully enough, consumer advo-

---

[20]"Product Suits Yield Few Punitive Awards," *The Wall Street Journal,* January 6, 1992, p. B1.

[21]For a discussion of the consumer viewpoint on product liability reform, see Peter Nye, "The Faces of Product Liability: Keeping the Courthouse Door Open," *Public Citizen,* November–December 1992, pp. 16–21.

**EXHIBIT
14-C**

An Alternative to Product Liability Lawsuits

Product liability lawsuits cost businesses and consumers a lot of money, and many cases are held up for years in backlogged courts. Often, large proportions of any settlement go to attorneys rather than to the people who were injured by defective products. Businesses are unable to predict the extent of their liability exposure. Is there a better way to resolve disputes between businesses and consumers?

Some people think that alternative dispute resolution (ADR) may be an answer. In ADR, a professional mediator works with both sides to negotiate a settlement outside the traditional court system. Generally, if the negotiation fails, the parties can still proceed to trial. The nonprofit American Arbitration Association has developed a panel of experts skilled in resolving liability claims. Several for-profit organizations, such as JAMS/Endispute of Irvine, California, also provide ADR services.

Supporters of ADR say it saves money that would be spent on lawyers' fees, so more can go to plaintiffs in a settlement. Cases can be resolved quickly, rather than waiting for an opening on a busy judge's calendar. Critics, however, worry that ADR deprives plaintiffs of their day in court, and injured consumers may get less than if their cases were heard before a jury.

Eventually, ADR may be widely used to settle individual complaints brought under mass torts, such as those involving injuries from asbestos, tobacco, or defective medical devices. In this situation, a court would set up a procedure and a set of rules by which individuals could negotiate a settlement tailored to the facts of their own case. Some businesses feel that such a process would enable them to better predict, and budget for, future liabilities.

Source: John Gibeaut, "At the Crossroads," *American Bar Association Journal,* March 1998.

---

cates and their organizations have turned to government for protection. On the other hand, much effort has been devoted by individual business firms and by entire industries to encourage voluntary responses to consumer demands. Some of the more prominent positive responses are discussed next.

Total Quality Management

In the 1980s and 1990s, many businesses adopted a philosophy of management known as **total quality management (TQM).** This approach, which borrows from Japanese management techniques, emphasizes achieving high quality and customer satisfaction through teamwork and continuous improvement of a company's product or service. TQM businesses seek to "delight the customer," as shown in the following example.

> *At the Saturn plant in Spring Hill, Tennessee, TQM methods have been used to produce a car of superior quality. Joint labor–management teams designed the car from the start to compete head-on with popular Japanese imports. Workers can stop the assembly line if they see a defect. Saturn keeps in close contact with car buyers, so it can correct any problems that crop up. The result has*

been a vehicle that has been extremely popular with customers. In 1997, Saturn topped all other cars, foreign and domestic, in the J. D. Power survey of customer satisfaction.[22]

Total quality management is a response to pressure from consumer activists and an attempt by business to address its customers' needs. It is an example of the interactive strategy discussed in Chapter 2, where by companies try to anticipate and respond to emerging stakeholder expectations. One of the primary changes created by the TQM movement has been for companies to focus on the customer. This occurs in many different ways.

Consumer Affairs Departments

Many large corporations operate consumer affairs departments, often placing a vice president in charge. These centralized departments normally handle consumer inquiries and complaints about a company's products and services, particularly in cases where a customer has not been able to resolve differences with local retailers. Some companies have installed **consumer hot lines** for dissatisfied customers to place telephone calls directly to the manufacturer.

> *One of the largest hot lines, General Electric's Answer Center, fields three and a half million questions a year on thousands of products. One technician diagnosed a mysterious refrigerator noise by asking the customer to hold the phone to up to the appliance. Another advised a frantic caller on how to extract a pet iguana from the dishwasher. "This isn't a job for the faint of heart," said one consultant who works with company consumer hot lines.*[23]

Many companies now communicate with their customers and other interested persons through Web sites on the Internet. Eighty percent of the 500 biggest companies had Web sites by 1997, according to one survey. Some sites are interactive, allowing customers to post comments or questions that are answered via e-mail by customer relations staff.[24]

Experienced companies are aware that consumer complaints and concerns can be handled more quickly, at lower cost, and with less risk of losing goodwill by a consumer affairs department than if customers take a legal route or if their complaints receive widespread media publicity.

Arbitration

In the 1990s, the use of **arbitration** to handle consumer complaints became much more common. Many companies, especially in the health care and financial services industries, required customers to bring disputes before a private arbitrator rather than sue the company. An arbitrator, a neutral person not related to either party, would make a final decision resolving the dispute.

---

[22]Barry Bluestone and Irving Bluestone, "Reviving American Industry: A Labor–Management Partnership," *Current,* May 1993, pp. 10–16; and "German Cars Follow Saturn in Buyer Satisfaction Ratings," *Seattle Times,* June 7, 1997, p. D1.
[23]"What's This? Confused or Curious, Consumers Know Where to Call," *Newsday,* October 18, 1995, p. B37.
[24]"Simplest E-Mail Queries Confound Companies," *The Wall Street Journal,* October 21, 1996, pp. B1, B9.

Many businesses favored arbitration because it tended to reduce their legal costs and the risk of big jury awards. Some consumers favored the process as well, because their complaints could often be resolved more quickly and cheaply. But some advocates were wary of any action by firms that unilaterally took away customers' rights to sue if they were injured or mistreated.[25]

Product Recalls

Companies also deal with consumer dissatisfaction by recalling faulty products. A **product recall** occurs when a company, either voluntarily or under an agreement with a government agency, takes back all items found to be dangerously defective. Sometimes these products are in the hands of consumers; at other times they may be in the factory, in wholesale warehouses, or on the shelves of retail stores. Wherever they are in the chain of distribution or use, the manufacturer tries to notify consumers or potential users about the defect so that they will return the items. A recalled product may be repaired, replaced, or destroyed, depending on the problem.

> *In 1997, Shimano American Corp., in cooperation with the Consumer Product Safety Commission, announced it would voluntarily recall more than one million cranks installed on bicycles, after it had received numerous complaints that the cranks had broken, injuring riders. (The crank connects the pedal to the front gear.) Shimano offered to have all defective cranks replaced, for free, at authorized repair shops.[26]*

The four major government agencies responsible for most mandatory recalls are the Food and Drug Administration, the National Highway Traffic Safety Administration, the Environmental Protection Agency (which can recall polluting motor vehicles), and the Consumer Product Safety Commission.

Consumerism's Achievements

After 35 years of the consumer movement, its leaders could point to some important gains for U.S. consumers. Consumers today are better informed about the goods and services they purchase, more aware of their rights when something goes wrong, and better protected against inflated advertising claims, hazardous or ineffective products, and unfair pricing. Several consumer organizations serve as watchdogs of buyers' interests, and a network of federal and state regulatory agencies acts for the consuming public.

Some businesses, too, have heard the consumer message and reacted positively. They have learned to assign high priority to the things consumers expect: high-quality goods and services, reliable and effective products, safety in the items they buy, fair prices, and marketing practices, such as advertising, that do not threaten important human and social values.

All of these achievements, in spite of negative episodes that occasionally occur, have brought the U.S. consuming public closer to realizing John F. Kennedy's four consumer rights: to be safe, to be informed, to have choices, and to be heard.

---

[25]"In Fine Print, Customers Lose Ability to Sue; Arbitrators, Not Courts, Rule on Complaints," *New York Times,* March 10, 1997, pp. A1, C7.

[26]"Product Recalls: Kid's Clothing, Bike Parts, and Fans Pulling a Fast One," *Newsday,* July 16, 1997, p. A47.

Summary Points of This Chapter

- The U.S. consumer movement that began in the 1960s represents an attempt to promote the interests of consumers by balancing the amount of market power held by sellers and buyers.

- The four key consumer rights are the rights to safety, to be informed, to choose, and to be heard. Recent discussion has focused on consumers' right to privacy.

- Consumer protection laws and regulatory agencies attempt to assure that consumers are treated fairly, receive adequate information, are protected against potential hazards, have free choices in the market, and have legal recourse when problems develop.

- The general public's growing awareness of the ability of advertising to exert widespread social influence brought new demands for business to be socially responsible in serving consumers.

- Business has complained about the rising number of product liability lawsuits and the high cost of insuring against them. But efforts to reform product liability laws have been opposed by consumer groups and lawyers representing people injured by dangerous or defective products.

- Socially responsible companies have responded to the consumer movement by giving serious consideration to consumer problems, increasing channels of communication with customers, instituting arbitration procedures to resolve complaints, and recalling defective products. They have also pursued total quality management in an effort to meet, and even anticipate, consumers' needs.

Key Terms and Concepts Used in This Chapter

- Consumer movement
- Consumer bill of rights
- Consumer protection laws
- Deceptive advertising
- Product liability

- Strict liability
- Total quality management (TQM)
- Consumer hot lines
- Arbitration
- Product recalls

Internet Resources

- http://www.cpsc.gov   U.S. Consumer Product Safety Commission
- http://www.ftc.gov   U.S. Federal Trade Commission
- http://www.igc.apc.org:80/cbbb   Better Business Bureau

Discussion Case   ## Consumer Privacy in the Information Age

In 1996, Netscape, maker of the widely used Navigator Web browser, generated a storm of controversy over a new technology somewhat whimsically called a *cookie.*

The new release of Netscape's browser was designed so that the software would automatically record which Web sites the user visited and which Web pages had been accessed at each site. This information would then be stored on the user's own computer in a site called a cookie. The user, in many cases, would not even be aware that the cookie had been created.

The problem, from the standpoint of privacy, was that the cookie could be accessed and read by each subsequent Web site visited by the user, without the user's consent. Netscape's software was designed to permit the Web site to learn only about previous visits to that specific site, not other sites the user might have visited. However, the technology could potentially be modified to permit the Web site to read the entire cookie.

Many commercial Web sites welcomed the cookie technology as a valuable way to learn more about the characteristics and preferences of their customers. For example, an operator of cruise lines would be able to learn that most visitors to its site were interested in Caribbean vacations, prompting it to develop more detailed coverage of this subject.

Users were concerned, however, that access to their cookies represented an unauthorized use of personal information and a violation of their privacy. Businesses in turn worried that concerned customers were less likely to use the Internet and to shop there. In response to numerous complaints, Netscape announced that subsequent versions of the software would give users the option of enabling or disabling cookies.

The controversy over Netscape's cookie software highlighted the broader issue of consumer privacy in the information age. New technologies made collection of data about consumer behavior, often without the consumer's knowledge or consent, increasingly possible. Not only could data be collected from a Web user's cookie, but stores, banks, pharmacies, airlines and other businesses often had access to considerable information about consumers that could be collected, used, sold, or even stolen.

Research showed that consumers were increasingly concerned about the potential threat to their privacy in the information age. A 1995 Louis Harris poll, for example, reported that 82 percent of respondents were very concerned about their personal privacy, up from 64 percent in 1978. The dilemma over how best to protect consumer privacy while fostering legitimate Internet commerce generated a wide-ranging debate. Some consumer advocacy organizations and privacy activists favored new government regulations requiring that consumers be notified when information was collected, be allowed to opt out, and have access to their files and a means of correcting errors. Some even called for a new regulatory agency charged with protecting privacy.

Many Internet-related businesses, on the other hand, argued that they should be allowed to regulate themselves. In May 1997, a group of about 60 companies, including Netscape, proposed a new voluntary privacy scheme called an Open Profiling Standard (OPS). Under this system, users would store facts about themselves on a protected file on their own hard drive. When users visited a participating Web site, they would be able to determine what information, if any, the site could access.

Evolving technologies also gave Web surfers new ways to protect themselves. Software like the Cookie Crusher helped manage cookies, and surfing through special intermediary sites provided user anonymity. "We have to develop mechanisms that allow consumers to control information about themselves," commented a representative of the Center for Democracy and Technology, a civil liberties group.

In June 1997, the Federal Trade Commission convened public hearings on Internet privacy issues. "Three things must exist for electronic commerce to prosper," commented the FTC commissioner. "Ease, ubiquity, and trust. Technology can take care of the first two. But how can consumers be sure that their transactions are secure and private? . . . The question we're grappling with is whether government has a role in creating that trust."

Sources: "Exposed Online," *U.S. News & World Report,* June 23, 1997, pp. 59 ff.; Andrew L. Shapiro, "Privacy for Sale: Peddling Data on the Internet," *The Nation,* June 23, 1997, pp. 11–16; "Making America Safe for Electronic Commerce," *New York Times Week in Review,* June 22, 1997, p. 4; "Fear of Prying," *Marketing Tools,* June, 1997, pp. 46 ff.; "Privacy Watch: Is Your Computer Spying on You?" *Consumer Reports,* May, 1997, p. 6; John Hagel III and Jeffrey F. Rayport, "The Coming Battle for Consumer Information," *Harvard Business Review,* January–February 1997, pp. 53 ff.; "They're Watching You Online," *Business Week,* November 11, 1996, p. 19; "How to Practice Safe Surfing," *Business Week,* September 9, 1996, p. 120.

Discussion Questions

1. In his consumer bill of rights, President Kennedy outlined four basic consumer rights. Do you believe consumers have an additional right to privacy? Why or why not?
2. In the case Netscape's cookie technology, do you believe Netscape acted in a socially responsible way? Identify all the stakeholders in this situation, and tell how each would answer this question.
3. Who do you believe should be mainly responsible for protecting consumer privacy on the Internet? Should it be the individual consumer, the companies that make Internet-related technology, the companies that gather or use information, or the consumer-protection agencies of government? Why do you think so?

15

The Community and the Corporation

When a business has a good relationship with its community, it can make an important difference in the quality of that community's life and in the successful operation of the company. Communities look to businesses for civic leadership and for help in coping with local problems, while firms expect to be treated in fair and supportive ways by the local community. Corporate restructuring can create special problems that require cooperation between business and community groups.

This chapter focuses on these key questions and objectives:

- What critical links exist between the community and business?

- How do businesses respond to community problems and needs?

- What goals and objectives are achieved when businesses contribute to the community?

- How does volunteerism contribute to building strong relationships between businesses and communities?

- What are the community impacts of corporate restructuring, and what strategies do companies and communities use in responding?

- How are social partnerships between businesses and the communities used to address today's pressing social problems?

T he Walt Disney Company is one of America's leading entertainment corporations. Founded by Walt Disney, and best known for animated movies such as *Fantasia, The Little Mermaid,* and *The Lion King,* and characters such as Mickey Mouse and Donald Duck, Disney has also created the famous theme parks Disneyland and Disney World in the United States and international theme parks in France and Japan. The company has had unparalleled success integrating its movies, theme parks, and related products into a commercial colossus. Imagination, creativity, and dedicated people have enabled Disney to become a leader in the multibillion dollar entertainment industry.

Disney began planning a new generation of theme parks in the early 1990s. In November 1993, the company announced that it had purchased an option on a 3,000-acre tract of land in Haymarket, Virginia, on which it intended to build an American history theme park called Disney's America. The land, located in Prince William County about 35 miles southwest of Washington, DC, is near the Manassas National Battlefield Park, site of the battles of Bull Run, two of the Civil War's bloodiest battles. Plans called for building a theme park, as many as 2,281 homes, 1,340 hotel rooms, and about 1.96 million square feet of retail and commercial space.

Critics immediately argued that the thousands of visitors expected at such a theme park would overwhelm the ability of local communities to absorb and manage side effects. A group calling itself Protecting Prince William County was quickly formed to provide organized opposition to the Disney plan. But local and county officials, working with Disney staff, concluded that the negative effects were being exaggerated and would, in any event, be outweighed by benefits the region would reap, including 19,000 jobs and nearly $50 million in new tax revenues. Both the jobs and the tax revenues were seen as vital to the long-term well-being of the county's communities and residents.

For nearly a year, hearings were held by local, state, and federal government legislatures and agencies. Repeatedly, local opponents presented arguments against the project while Disney executives and local government officials tried to argue the benefits of the project. According to participants, Disney representatives were always cordial, evidenced a willingness to compromise, and sought to find win-win solutions to the concerns being raised. But opponents had no interest in compromise. A group of historians, including several famous Civil War experts, campaigned against the Disney project through an organization called Project Historic America. They argued that Disney's proposed virtual reality battles would trivialize and sanitize the true battles that had occurred at the site. The Piedmont Environmental Council, a coalition of 70 organizations and more than 5,000 families from northern Virginia, took a different approach: they sued Disney, alleging violations of state and federal environmental laws. Lobbying occurred at all levels of government, and it was estimated that hundreds of lawyers, lobbyists, and political advisers were employed on behalf of Disney, its opponents, and interested parties.

By 1995, Disney was forced to announce plans to drop the project. Its option on the land was about to expire, forcing it to either renew the option or buy the land outright. Either would be costly, and in the face of opposition generated since the announcement, it was unlikely that the company could complete the project by its intended completion date in 1998. In announcing the decision, John Cooke, chairman of Disney's America, said, "We are starting afresh and are reaching out to historians who have opposed us to make sure our portrayal of the American experience is responsible." Recognizing that his community would get neither jobs nor new tax revenues, Mayor Jack Kapp of Haymarket, Virginia, spoke more directly: "People around here are devastated. It's an economic blow to Prince William County. I feel like I've been to a funeral today."[1]

Disney's America illustrates some of the complex issues that can arise between a company and the community in which it operates. What did the company do wrong? Why didn't others see the benefits of the proposal as Mayor Kapp did? What could Disney have done differently? This chapter examines how companies try to integrate community and citizenship concerns with their financial goals and objectives. Although it is not always possible to do so, as Disney's America shows, businesses and communities can often do much together to create win-win solutions to common problems.

Community Relations

The **community** discussed in this chapter involves a company's area of local business influence. It includes many individual stakeholders, and may include more than one geographic or political community, for such boundaries do not necessarily follow economic and social impacts. A bank in a large metropolitan area, for example, has numerous stakeholders (see the stakeholder model in Chapter 1) and may define its community as the central city and the towns and cities in which it does business. A local merchant's community may comprise several surrounding cities or towns. A multinational firm may have a separate community for each of the local areas it serves around the world. In all cases, both company and community have a mutual dependence that is significant in economic and social terms.

The involvement of business with the community is called **community relations.** Community relations today are quite different from those of 50 or 100 years ago. Advances in technology, especially information technology, population shifts in the United States and much of the industrialized world, and the globalization of business operations are putting great pressures on the business-community relationship. Community relationships in the United States and other countries are also entwined with cultural norms. Business decisions have become more complex, and the impact of those decisions has loomed larger in the life of communities. Keeping community ties alive, well, and relevant is a major task for today's businesses.

Many corporations have established community relations offices to coordinate community programs, manage donations of goods and services, work with local governments, and encourage employee volunteerism in nonprofit and civic groups.[2] Companies have increasingly become involved with local communities on diverse issues, including education reform, environmental risk management, local taxes, and improving the lives of the homeless. Their aims are to improve local conditions that produce or attract a workforce qualified to meet the company's needs and to build a positive relationship between the firm and important local groups. Community relations officers work closely with other corporate offices that link the corporation to the external world, such as the employee re-

---

[1]Based on articles in the *New York Times* and *The Wall Street Journal* appearing in 1993–1998. See especially Sallie Hofmeister, "Disney Vows to Seek Another Park Site," *New York Times,* September 30, 1994, p. A12; and Michael Janofsky, "Town 'Devastated' by Loss of Project," *New York Times,* September 30, 1994, p. A12.

[2]James E. Post and Jennifer J. Griffin, *The State of Corporate Public Affairs* (Washington, D.C.: The Foundation for Public Affairs, 1997). Trends in this area are discussed in James E. Post and the Foundation for Public Affairs, "The State of Corporate Public Affairs in the United States: Results of a National Survey," in J. Post, ed., *Research in Corporate Social Performance and Policy,* vol. 14 (Greenwich, CT: JAI Press, 1993), pp. 79–89; and Lee Burke, Jeanne Logsden, and David Vogel "Corporate Community Involvement in the San Francisco Bay Area," *California Management Review,* Spring 1986, pp. 121–41.

lations, public relations, or public affairs offices (see Chapter 2). These links form important bridges between the corporation and community groups.[3]

Limited Resources Face Unlimited Community Needs

Every community has many social needs requiring far more resources than are available. Choices must be made and priorities established. In some instances, the community decides the priorities, but in other instances, business influences community priorities very directly. Further, in all cases, once management has decided to help serve a need, it still must decide how its resources can best be applied to that need. This means that any action management takes will result in some dissatisfaction from those who get no help and from those who do not get as much help as they want.

Figure 15–1 illustrates the variety of expectations that communities have of business. Each year, companies receive requests for artistic, educational, and charitable assistance serving both special groups and the community as a whole. A company may agree

Figure 15–1

What the community and business want from each other.

Requests Made by the Community to Business
• Assistance for less-advantaged people
• Support for air and water pollution control
• Support for artistic and cultural activities
• Employment and advancement of minorities and women
• Assistance in urban planning and development
• Support of local health-care programs
• Donation of equipment to local school system
• Support of local bond issues for public improvements
• Aid to community hospital drive
• Support of local program for recycling
• Executive leadership for United Way fund-raising campaign
Community Services Desired by Business
• A cultural and educational environment that supports a balanced quality of life for employees
• Adequate family recreational activities
• Public services, such as police and fire protection, and sewage, water, and electric services
• Taxes that are equitable and do not discriminate for or against business
• Acceptance of business participation in community affairs
• A fair and open public press
• An adequate transportation system to business and residential areas (e.g., suitable public transportation and well-maintained streets)
• Public officials, customers, and citizens who are fair and honest in their involvement with business
• Cooperative problem-solving approach to addressing community problems

[3]Boston College Center for Corporate Community Relations, "Profile of the Community Relations Profession," *Community Relations Letter,* (Chestnut Hill, MA: Boston College Center for Corporate Community Relations, March 1993).

to support some, but not all, of these requests, and its work with these groups will consume hundreds of days of employee time and thousands of dollars of company resources. Meanwhile, the company must still meet its business objective of serving customers competitively throughout the nation.

Community Involvement and Firm Size

Community involvement has become a part of most business lifestyles. Studies show that both large and small businesses, whether they are local firms or branches of national firms, tend to be active in community affairs.[4] Business leaders bring knowledge and ability to civic and community matters. Much of this activity involves participation in local and regional groups (e.g., business councils, associations, and roundtables); leadership on civic task forces; and personal involvement of executives as directors, trustees, or advisers to schools, community groups, and collaboratives. Through such activities executives become familiar with local needs and issues and involved in finding ways for businesses and communities to cooperate.

Large companies usually have more public visibility in community affairs (see discussion in Chapter 4). These well-known firms are more established and help to characterize their surrounding towns.[5] Executives, often acting as board members and consultants, tend to participate more actively in philanthropy, volunteerism, and community issues when the headquarters is located in the community.[6]

When a company has numerous *branches,* its community involvements extend into those cities and towns, and corporate policy has to be implemented in different local situations. An effective policy has to recognize the unique needs of each community in which the firm is involved. This makes it desirable for corporate headquarters to give local managers broad leeway to make community-related decisions.

> *Target Stores is a retailer with more than 600 stores throughout the United States. Community involvement—which Target calls its Good Neighbor program—is a basic part of every store's business strategy. Local store managers are expected to develop innovative community outreach programs to reinforce the message that Target is a good neighbor whose deeds make the community a better place for all to live. Target Stores are not alone in assigning community relations responsibility to local managers. Research studies have found that nearly 60 percent of firms have delegated local community relations responsibilities, including corporate contributions, to managers in local plants, branch offices, and service branches.[7]*

Foreign-owned companies also participate in community affairs. As shown in Figure 15–2, their profile of activities is quite similar to that of domestic companies. This pattern seems to operate in many countries and suggests that communities in many countries

[4]Center for Corporate Public Involvement, *Helping Families, Strengthening Communities: The Life and Health Insurance Industry Annual Report on Community Involvement* (Washington, DC: American Council of Life Insurance and Health Insurance Association of America, 1995).
[5]Ibid.
[6]See Burke et al., "Corporate Community Involvement," for a discussion of these involvements.
[7]Target Stores data provided by company. The program is dicussed in Molly McKaughan, *Corporate Volunteerism: How Families Make a Difference,* (New York: The Conference Board, 1997). See also, Audris Tillman, *Corporate Contributions in 1995* (New York: The Conference Board, 1996).

Figure 15-2

Community involvement of foreign-owned corporations in the United States.

Source: David Logan, *Community Involvement of Foreign-Owned Companies in the United States,* Research Report 1089-94 (New York: The Conference Board, 1994).

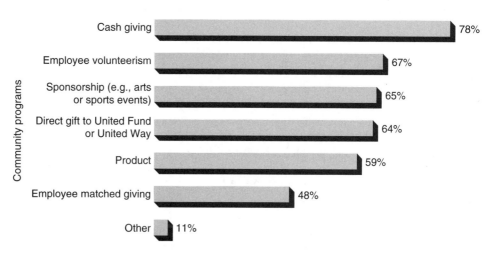

Percent of companies participating (*n* = 108)

tend to develop local norms of business-community relations. When a new company enters a community and begins to do business with local stakeholders, expectations develop as to the proper role and responsibilities of that firm to the new community.

Small business participation in community activities is just as important as large business involvement. Small business representatives, such as automobile dealers, restaurants, real estate brokers, supermarkets, and other retail merchants, significantly influence the quality of community life. They tend to be personally and professionally involved in community affairs, often expressing a deep commitment to the community based on many years of residence. In large urban areas, different ethnic neighborhoods may exist, often with family-operated stores, restaurants, and services. Cultural norms may affect the willingness of such business owners to participate in community development activities. In many cities, Community Development Corporations (CDCs) have been formed to help bring together and focus the energy of local residents and businesses to improve neighborhood life for all.

Local businesses are often part of a community's Chamber of Commerce, Kiwanis, and Rotary clubs. These organizations work on community issues such as parking and traffic, business development, and cooperation with local schools. In one community, for example, a real estate brokerage donated the time of its employees to several local middle schools that needed adult assistance to run a weekly bottle and can recycling collection. Every Friday morning, teams of real estate brokers worked with students at each middle school to receive the bottles and cans dropped off by residents during the morning commuting hours.

Community Support of Business

The relationship of business and community is one of mutual interdependence. Each has responsibilities to the other because each has social power to affect the other. This power-responsibility equation applies to both parties and reminds that success is a matter of mutual support, rather than opposition. The concept of a *social contract* is fundamental to the relationship between business and the community.

Businesses normally expect various types of support from the local communities in which they operate. As previously shown in Figure 15–1, businesses expect fair treatment, and they expect to be accepted as a participant in community affairs because they are an important part of the community. They also expect community services such as a dependable water supply and police protection. Companies are encouraged to remain in the community and grow if there are appropriate cultural, educational, and recreational facilities for their employees and, of course, if taxes remain reasonable. Businesses also have come to recognize that they rely heavily on the public school system and other local services to run their businesses efficiently.

This combination of business-community mutual support is illustrated in Figure 15–3. The diagonal line in the diagram illustrates the situation when a business receives support from the community that is equal to that which it provides to the community. Sometimes, a business will invest more in the community than the community seems to provide to it in return. This is illustrated by the area above the diagonal line. Conversely, a community sometimes provides much more support to a business than the business seems to contribute to the community. This is shown by the area below the diagonal line. Ideally, the business and community provide relatively equal amounts of support to each other and, more important, their interaction moves from the lower left end of the box to the upper right. This signifies a high degree of interaction and relatively equal amounts of support for one another. As a company grows, for example, it provides more jobs, tax revenues, volunteers for community projects, support to local charities, and so forth. But positive relationships between a company and a community are sometimes difficult to develop.

> *Wal-Mart has encountered serious local objection to its plans to build super-stores and distribution centers in a number of local communities. Wal-Mart's founder, Sam Walton, now deceased, was fond of saying that he would never try to force a community to accept a Wal-Mart store. "Better to go where we are wanted," he is reported to have said. In recent years, however, that view is less often endorsed by Wal-Mart management. In a series of high-profile local conflicts, Wal-Mart sparked intense local opposition from several communities*

Figure 15–3

Business and the community need support from each other.

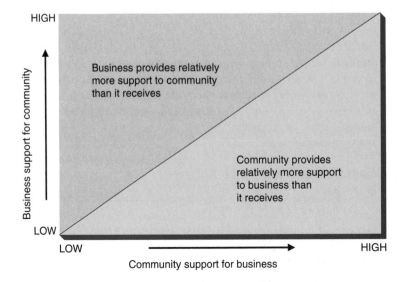

that were worried about traffic patterns, safety, and negative effects on local small businesses from the opening of giant Wal-Mart facilities. The problem seems likely to grow more complex for Wal-Mart as it continues its expansion into international markets.[8]

Strengthening the Community

Business initiatives have helped improve the quality of life in communities in many ways, some of which are listed in Figure 15–4. Although not exhaustive, the list suggests the range of community needs that a corporation's executives are asked to address. These community concerns challenge managers to apply talent, imagination, and resources to develop creative ways to strengthen the community while still managing their businesses as profitable enterprises.

Improving Economic Development

Business leaders and their companies are frequently involved in local or regional economic development, which is intended to bring new businesses into an area or to otherwise improve local conditions.[9] Central business districts, unlike older and often neglected

Figure 15–4

Community projects of 320 insurance companies.

Source: Center for Corporate Public Involvement, *Helping Families, Strengthening Communities: The Life and Health Insurance Industry Annual Report on Community Involvement* (Washington, DC: Center for Corporate Public Involvement and American Council of Life Insurance and Health Insurance Association of America, 1995).

Types of Projects	Percentage of Reporting Companies Involved
Education	87%
Arts and culture	77
Youth activities	76
Local health programs	72
Neighborhood improvement programs	68
Programs for hunger/homeless	61
Minority affairs	47
Programs for the handicapped	45
Drug or alcohol abuse programs	45
AIDS education and treatment	44
Housing programs	42
Activities for senior citizens and retired persons	41
Safety programs	38
Environmental programs	36
Hard-to-employ programs	31
Crime prevention	29
Prenatal and well-baby care	27
Day-care programs	26
Health promotion/low-income and minority	26
Other	32

[8]In a short period of time, Wal-Mart encountered opposition in several Massachusetts and Vermont communities. See "Town Residents Oppose Proposed Wal-Mart Center," *The Wall Street Journal*, August 22, 1994, p. B5.
[9]George Peterson and Dana Sundblad, *Corporations as Partners in Strengthening Urban Communities,* Research Report 1079–94 (New York: The Conference Board, 1994).

poorer residential areas, have benefited from businesses during recent decades. Business has helped transform these business areas in major U.S. cities into a collection of shining office buildings, entertainment facilities, fashionable shopping malls, conference centers, and similar urban amenities. In spite of these developments, many urban areas have become forbidding and inhospitable places, fraught with drugs, violence, and frighteningly high crime rates.[10]

Through extensive cooperative efforts, planners are trying to control development so that the central business districts will again become attractive to all citizens. Some of the ingredients needed are police protection that ensures safety, open spaces devoted to fountains, green grass, and trees, outdoor sitting areas, arcades, a variety of attractive stores, outdoor cafes, theaters, and interesting people.

The rush of business development can present problems, as well as opportunities, for a community.

> *When Toyota announced that it would build an automobile plant in George-town, Kentucky, residents were both pleased and anxious. The plant was expected to add as many as 3,500 jobs, but local people worried about how the community would be able to absorb the influx of outsiders and how their tightly knit community would be affected. Acknowledging its responsibility for the expected changes, Toyota gave Georgetown $1 million to build a community center. By working closely with local government officials, acknowledging their responsibility, and communicating openly about expected problems, Toyota helped the community become a more dynamic place to live while expanding its business presence. In 1998, the company announced another expansion of its facility, adding more than 1,000 jobs to the payroll. Toyota executives cited the positive relationship with the community as a contributing factor in the expansion decision.[11]*

The congestion and other problems that accompany metropolitan growth are not limited to large cities. Office building has mushroomed in many suburban areas; almost two-thirds of new office space built in the late 1980s was in the suburbs, creating in many metropolitan areas what is called **urban sprawl.** Technological changes permit many business operations to be located away from central headquarters, and suburban building and rental costs are usually much less than those of center-city locations. In the San Francisco suburb of Walnut Creek, for example, local citizens voted to bar large-scale office buildings and retail projects until traffic congestion was relieved. The most celebrated case in recent years, however, may have been the failed efforts of the Disney Company to build a history theme park in Virginia near Civil War battle sites (see the opening example in this chapter). Residents were concerned about traffic from the park, but they were also worried about the long-term impact of office and residential construction on their communities.

---

[10]Dennis R. Judd and Todd Swanstrom, *City Politics: Private Power and Public Policy* (New York: Harper-Collins College Publishers, 1994).

[11]The community involvements of foreign-owned companies are discussed in David Logan, *Community Involvement of Foreign-Owned Companies in the United States,* Research Report 1089–94 (New York: The Conference Board, 1994). See also, "Toyota in Bluegrass Country," *Industry Week,* June 5, 1989, pp. 30–33; and "As U.S. Car Makers Cut Back, Toyota Is Expanding Briskly," *New York Times,* January 1, 1991, p. A1.

Housing

Suburban areas appeal to businesses because of generally less crowded conditions. Many people choose to live in suburban communities, which usually feature space and some sense of the small-town atmosphere that is rooted in American culture. Many suburban communities have grown during periods of prosperity, as families sought to move from apartments to houses or from smaller homes to more spacious dwellings. When communities have been battered by layoffs and plant closings, they are often pleased to have any new businesses open. But rarely will communities ignore public concerns about the types of growth and businesses that locate in a town. To avoid community backlash and an anti-growth attitude, business leaders need to work with community groups in balancing business growth with respect for community values. Community planning efforts by municipal governments, done in cooperation with private industry, represent one of the steps that businesses can take to achieve this balance.

Life and health insurance companies have taken the lead in programs to revitalize neighborhood housing through organizations such as Neighborhood Housing Services (NHS) of America. NHS, which is locally controlled, locally funded, nonprofit, and tax-exempt, offers housing rehabilitation and financial services to neighborhood residents. Similar efforts are being made to house the homeless. The New York City Coalition for the Homeless includes corporate, nonprofit, and community members. In Los Angeles, Transamerica Life Companies, a founding partner of the Greater Los Angeles Partnership for the Homeless, has provided money and sent trained people to assist the partnership's efforts. Banks are also involved in meeting the housing needs of low-income residents.

Under the federal Community Reinvestment Act, banks are required to demonstrate their commitment to local communities through low-income lending programs and to provide annual reports to the public. This has led many banks to begin viewing the inner city as a new opportunity for business development. In the late 1990s, leading banks have even created special subsidiaries that have as their mission the development of new lending and development in needy urban neighborhoods.

Education Reform

The aging of the post–World War II baby boom generation and the subsequent decline in the number of entry-level workers have forced businesses to pay attention to the quality of the workforce. In assessing how the available workforce can be improved, many businesses have recognized that local public schools are a critical resource. Amidst the severe criticism of America's public schools, which began with the publication, *A Nation at Risk,*[12] businesses have become significantly involved in education reform.

Thousands of local school-business partnerships were formed during the 1980s and 1990s. Many of these collaborations, or adopt-a-school partnerships, engaged businesses in working with school teachers for the first time. Business leaders began participating on school boards and as advisers to schools and government officials who needed business-specific training. The National Alliance of Business (NAB), for example, developed a social compact project in which local businesses pledged their assistance and support to lo-

[12]National Commission on Excellence in Education, *A Nation at Risk: The Imperative for Educational Reform* (Washington, DC: U.S. Government Printing Office, 1983).

cal schools. Demonstration projects in 12 cities led to an improved understanding of the factors required for successful business-education collaboration.[13]

According to one leading research organization, business involvement in education has passed through four stages, or waves.[14] Beyond business support for programs (first wave) and the application of management principles to school administration (second wave), business has become increasingly committed to public policy initiatives (third wave) and collaboration with all of education's stakeholders to reform of the entire system (fourth wave). An example of systemic reform in Kentucky is described in Exhibit 15–A; also see the end-of-book case about the efforts of Unum Corporation and the State of Maine Education Excellence initiative.

**EXHIBIT
15–A**

Kentucky's Educational Reform Partnership

Kentucky, one of America's five commonwealth states,* has become a leader in the nation's efforts to reform public education. The active involvement of the state's largest business corporations and the personal involvement of chief executives and managers from companies of all sizes have been key factors in Kentucky's commitment to reforming the entire educational system.

Public education faced a crisis in Kentucky when a court decision declared the system unconstitutional because of discrimination among racially divided schools. The decision was a wake-up call for political leaders, many of whom had not been previously involved in education reform. Business leaders recognized that without a functioning school system, Kentucky businesses would not be able to hire new employees with the fundamental skills needed for productive activity in the workplace.

Kentucky has become home to a wide range of manufacturing and service industries. Among the largest and best-known companies headquartered in Kentucky are Ashland Oil, Humana, and United Parcel Service. Financial services have also grown rapidly, including General Electric's credit operations, which are located in Louisville. These each employ many thousands of people whose skills are vital to the productivity and success of the companies. With such a large stake in an educated workforce, Kentucky's business leaders stepped forward and announced the Partnership for Kentucky School Reform in 1990. At an inaugural meeting in 1991, 50 business leaders formally committed their efforts to the passage of the Kentucky Education Reform Act (KERA)—a state law that would radically restructure the schools—thereby joining dozens of other political and education leaders to form a powerful coalition for educational improvement.

(continued next page)

---

[13]Sandra A. Waddock, *Not by Schools Alone: Sharing Responsibility for America's School Reform* (New York: Praeger, 1995); and Sandra Waddock, "Understanding Social Partnership: An Evolutionary Model of Partnership Organizations," *Administration and Society* 21 (May 1989), pp. 78–100. The NAB project is described in National Alliance of Business, *The Compact Project: School-Business Partnerships for Improving Education* (Washington, DC: National Alliance of Business, 1989).

[14]Sandra A. Waddock, *Business and Education Reform: The Fourth Wave,* Research Report 1091–94 (New York: The Conference Board, 1994), p. 13.

The Partnership for Kentucky School Reform set forth three goals: (1) to promote support for the implementation of KERA's provisions and goals; (2) to provide an ongoing forum for discussion of problems and concerns; and (3) to serve as a vehicle for securing the technical assistance and expertise needed to facilitate implementation of school reform. Most important, the companies that agreed to become Partnership members have made a 10-year commitment. As Kent "Oz" Nelson, chairman and chief executive officer of United Parcel Service, said, "KERA has been recognized by many as the most comprehensive education reform legislation in the nation. . . . It is also a vast undertaking, which requires a serious and deep commitment if it is to be implemented successfully." Kentucky businesses have made that commitment and will be engaged in the cause of improving public education well into the twenty-first century.

*The other commonwealth states are Maryland, Massachusetts, Pennsylvania, and Virginia.
Source: Sandra A. Waddock, *Business and Education Reform: The Fourth Wave,* Research Report 1091–94 (New York: The Conference Board, 1994) pp. 26–27.

Efforts at workforce improvement involve direct business participation in worker training and retraining, especially efforts to train the disadvantaged. Much of this participation has come about as a result of federal job legislation, which requires that public sector job-training programs be supervised by private sector managers through private initiative councils (PICs) in every community where federal funds are used. Businesses have generally welcomed this chance to participate as a way to better match school and community efforts with business workforce opportunities and needs.

Jobs, Training, and Welfare Reform

In the late 1990s, government leaders have called on American businesses to help address one of the most vexing and costly social problems—welfare reform. Welfare is a form of public assistance to those who are unable to work and live an independent and self-sufficient life. Most societies have some basic form of public assistance to the needy, and some countries (Germany, France, and the United States) are known for their relatively generous assistance programs. As the costs of such programs have risen, however, many citizens have pressured their governments to curb the cost of welfare-assistance programs.

In the United States, a movement to reform welfare programs included tightened eligibility for assistance, limits on the length of time one can claim welfare benefits, and most important in the views of many, requirement that welfare recipients earn their eligibility by working in an approved public job. These programs—known as *workfare* in many states—depend heavily on businesses to provide job opportunities. President Clinton called on American businesses to come forward with innovative job-training opportunities to help move people from welfare to workfare, and a number of companies, such as Marriott and Pennsylvania Blue Shield, created new job and training programs. George Grode, senior vice president of Pennsylvania Blue Shield, noted:

Training, realistic goal-setting, and steady, constructive feedback are three key elements of any successful program intended to promote movement from the world of welfare to the world of work. Collaboration between the private sector employers and public sector support agencies is also essential. The rewards can be high for the employer, the employee, and all taxpayers, as is shown by our experience. Over a three-year period, 208 former welfare workers were trained, hired, and retained as productive members of our workforce. The government saved 2.4 million (dollars) in welfare benefits, and collected 1.3 million (dollars) in payroll taxes.[15]

Technical Assistance to Government

In a number of cities, businesses have spearheaded programs to upgrade the quality of local government. They provide special advice and technical expertise on budgeting, financial controls, and other management techniques. Many of the techniques of total quality management pioneered in the private sector are now being adapted to the analysis and improvement of government programs. Business know-how in these matters can inject vitality and efficiency into government systems that are often overburdened, obsolete, and underfinanced.[16]

Aid to Minority Enterprise

In addition to programs to hire and train urban minorities for jobs in industry, private enterprise has extended assistance to minority-owned small businesses that must struggle for existence in the inner cities. These businesses are often at a great economic disadvantage: they do business in economic locations where high crime rates, congestion, poor transportation, low-quality public services, and a low-income clientele combine to produce a high rate of business failure. Large corporations, sometimes in cooperation with universities, have provided financial and technical advice to minority entrepreneurs and have helped launch programs to teach managerial, marketing, and financial skills. They also have financed the building of minority-managed inner-city plants and sponsored special programs to purchase services and supplies from minority firms. Still, in the view of many, there is the need, and opportunity, for businesses to do much more.

In January 1998, Reverend Jesse Jackson announced a new campaign by his Rainbow/PUSH coalition to get Wall Street firms and the nation's largest companies to expand diversity programs and extend more economic opportunity to people of color. Reverend Jackson put the issue in these terms: "We'll pay for not investing; we're in one big tent." The view was endorsed by U.S. Treasury Secretary Robert Rubin, a former Wall Street banker himself, who said: "Our economy is going to fall short of its potential unless it is for all of us. . . . Inclusion is critical to the bottom line."

Jackson continued, "Riker's Island [a New York prison] is a more expensive university than NYU [New York University]," referring to the high cost per year of caring for prisoners who do not contribute to the nation's well-being. "What's missing in this dialogue has been corporate America. They must lead

[15]Felice Davidson Perlmutter, *From Welfare to Work* (New York: Oxford University Press, 1997). See C-SPAN, November 26, 1997, comments of Eli Segal, "The Welfare to Work Partnership," speech to the U.S. Chamber of Commerce. Also, John C. Winfrey, *Social Issues: The Ethics and Economics of Taxes and Public Programs* (New York: Oxford University Press, 1998).

[16]Peterson and Sundblad, *Corporations as Partners.*

the way on making the case, as educators and in skills and training. There is this wealth gap here. The biggest since 1929."[17]

Environmental Programs

The positive impacts of business on the community are balanced by a number of negative effects, including environmental problems. As local landfills near capacity, for example, communities have become concerned about the disposal of solid wastes. Citizen groups using slogans like NIMBY ("not in my back yard") or GOOMBY ("get out of my back yard") have resisted development of additional landfills to handle solid-waste disposal, to which businesses contribute in great quantities. So high was public concern about solid-waste disposal in Seattle, for example, that Procter & Gamble began a pilot project there to collect and recycle disposable diapers. Seattle's families provided an enthusiastic test case for Procter & Gamble's experiment in recycling, and P&G learned important lessons about public perceptions of the environmental impact of its products.

Community perceptions of environmental risk can have a powerful effect on the ability of companies to operate existing facilities and to expand their businesses. Chemical companies are among the industrial manufacturers facing such problems. They have created **community advisory panels (CAPs)** to bridge communications between managers of their facilities and residents of local communities. These advisory panels have a continuing dialogue with plant managers and bring issues of public concern to the meetings. The chemical industry formally adopted this approach as part of the Responsible Care Program commitments all its members make to the communities in which they operate.

Disaster Relief

One common form of corporate involvement in the community is disaster relief. Throughout the world, companies, like individuals, tend to provide assistance to local citizens and communities when disaster strikes. When major floods occurred in the midwestern United States in 1994, for example, assistance worth millions of dollars poured into affected communities from companies across the country and overseas. And when eastern Canada, including Montreal and much of the province of Quebec was devastated by ice storms in the winter of 1998, assistance poured in from Canadian and U.S. companies. Hundreds of volunteers from electric companies in the United States rushed to help restore electric power to more than 3 million Canadian residents.[18]

The willingness of companies to provide emergency assistance is an international phenomenon. When an earthquake seriously damaged the Japanese port city of Kobe in 1995, individuals and businesses from all over the world sought to provide assistance.

Abbott Laboratories, a health-care products company headquartered near Chicago, Illinois, joined dozens of other companies to provide needed medical products for Kobe's survivors. Abbott contributed 1,600 cases of sterile water, intravenous solutions, antibiotics, and pharmaceuticals to a coordinated relief effort organized by AmeriCares, a private international relief organization based in New Canaan, Connecticut. A shipment of more than 200,000 pounds

---

[17]Peter Truell, "On Wall St., Fervent Pleas for Minorities," *New York Times,* January 16, 1998, p. C4.
[18]News reports published in *New York Times* and *Boston Globe,* January 11–16, 1998. Also, network news television reports January 11–16, 1998, and http://www.cnn.org.com.

of materials was airlifted to Japan where another organization, the Japan International Rescue Action Committee, distributed the products to earthquake victims in Kobe.

Networks of volunteer agencies, such as the American Red Cross and AmeriCares, are instrumental in aligning resources with needs in such instances. International relief efforts are becoming more important, as communications improve and people around the world are able to witness the horror of disasters. Corporate involvement in such efforts, then, is an extension of the natural tendency of people to help one another when tragedy strikes.

Corporate Giving

America is a generous society. According to information collected by the Internal Revenue Service, individuals and organizations give more than $150 billion each year to churches, charities, and other nonprofit organizations. American businesses are a small, but important, part of this broad cultural tradition of giving. One of the most visible ways in which businesses help communities is through gifts of money, property, and employee service. This **corporate philanthropy,** or **corporate giving,** demonstrates the commitment of businesses to assist the communities by supporting such nonprofit organizations as United Way, Community Chest, and individual hospitals, schools, homeless shelters, and other providers of important community services (see discussion in Chapter 3).

The federal government has encouraged corporate giving for educational, charitable, scientific, and religious purposes since 1936.[19] The current IRS rule permits corporations to deduct from their taxable income all such gifts that do not exceed 10 percent of the company's before-tax income. In other words, a company with a before-tax income of $1 million might contribute up to $100,000 to nonprofit community organizations devoted to education, charity, science, or religion. The $100,000 in contributions would then reduce the income to be taxed from $1 million to $900,000, thus saving the company money on its tax bill while providing a source of income to community agencies. Of course, there is nothing to prevent a corporation from giving more than 10 percent of its income for philanthropic purposes, but it would not be given a tax break above the 10 percent level.

As shown in Figure 15–5, average corporate giving in the United States is far below the 10 percent deduction now permitted. Though it varies from year to year, corporate giving has been closer to 1 percent of pretax income since the early 1960s, with a rise that reached a peak in 1986. Although a few corporations, including a cluster headquartered in the Minneapolis–St. Paul metropolitan area, have pledged 5 percent of their pretax income, most companies average between 1 and 2 percent of pretax income.[20] Even at the national average of 1 percent giving, substantial amounts of money are channeled to education, the arts, and other community organizations. Corporate giving totaled more than $8 billion in 1997, including more than $2.5 billion for education.[21]

---

[19]The evolution of corporate philanthropy is summarized in Mark Sharfman, "Changing Institutional Rules: The Evolution of Corporate Philanthropy, 1883–1953," *Business and Society,* 33, no. 3 December 1994), pp. 236–69; and "Charities Tap Generous Spirit of Hong Kong," *The Wall Street Journal,* November 3, 1994, pp. B1, B8.

[20]Audris Tillman, *Corporate Contributions in 1995* (New York: The Conference Board, 1996).

[21]Useful references include The Conference Board, *Corporate Contributions, annual 1964–1998*; and Ann Kaplan, ed., *Giving USA, 1998* (New York: AAFRC Trust for Philanthropy, 1998).

Figure 15–5

Corporate contributions as a percentage of pretax net income.

Source: Audris Tillman, *Corporate Contributions in 1995* (New York: The Conference Board, 1996). This chart is derived from Internal Revenue Service data presented in an appendix to Tillman's book.

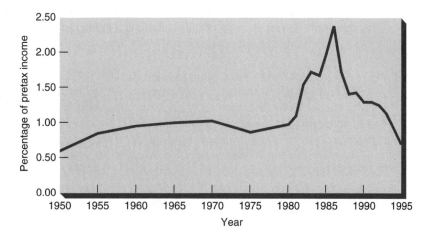

Some critics have argued that corporate managers have no right to give away company money that does not belong to them. According to this line of reasoning, any income earned by the company should be either reinvested in the firm or distributed to the stockholders who are the legal owners. The courts have ruled, however, that charitable contributions fall within the legal and fiduciary powers of the corporation's policymakers. Corporate contributions are one additional way in which companies link themselves to the broader interests of the community, thereby advancing and strengthening the company rather than weakening it.

Companies also help local communities through the substantial number of business donations that are not recorded as philanthropy because they are not pure giving. Routine gifts of products and services for local use often are recorded as advertising expenses; gifts of employee time for charity drives and similar purposes usually are not recorded; and the costs of soliciting and processing employee gifts, such as payroll deductions for the United Way, usually are not recorded as corporate giving. Still, they add value to the local community of which the company is a part.

Many large U.S. corporations have established nonprofit **corporate foundations** to handle their charitable programs. This permits them to administer contributions programs more uniformly and provides a central group of professionals that handles all grant requests. Foreign-owned corporations use foundations less frequently, although firms such as Matsushita (Panasonic) and Hitachi use highly sophisticated corporate foundations to conduct their charitable activities in the United States. As corporations expand to more foreign locations, pressures will grow to expand international corporate giving. Foundations, with their defined mission to benefit the community, can be a useful mechanism to help companies implement philanthropic programs that meet this corporate social responsibility.

Corporate Giving in a Strategic Context

One way to stretch the corporate contributions dollar is to make sure that it is being used strategically to meet the needs of both the recipient and the donor. Creating a strategy of mutual benefits for business and society is one of the major themes of this book, and this type of **strategic philanthropy** is a means of achieving such win-win outcomes. As shown in Figure 15–6, strategic philanthropy blends traditional corporate philanthropy with giving programs that are directly or indirectly linked to business goals and objectives. In the 1990s, more companies have transformed their corporate philanthropic giving to this strategic focus.[22]

One example of linking business goals to charitable giving is **cause marketing,** pioneered by American Express as a way to promote wider use of its credit cards. Today, following the lead of American Express, many companies have created formulas for making contributions to nonprofit organizations based on how many of the particular nonprofit organization's members use the company's credit card or purchase its products. In 1994, Johnson & Johnson broke new ground when it introduced Arthritis Foundation pain-relief medicine. It agreed to make a contribution to the Arthritis Foundation for each package of pain reliever sold under the AF name. Such activities increase corporate giving while enhancing the revenues of the donors.

One group of scholars pointed out that strategic philanthropy occurs in two forms. One, called *strategic process giving,* applies a professional business approach to determine the goals, budgets, and criteria for specific grants. The second approach, called *strategic outcome giving,* emphasizes the links between corporate contributions and business-oriented goals such as introducing a new product, providing needed services to employees (e.g., child-care centers), or maintaining positive contacts with external stakeholder groups

Figure 15–6

Corporate giving and community relations.

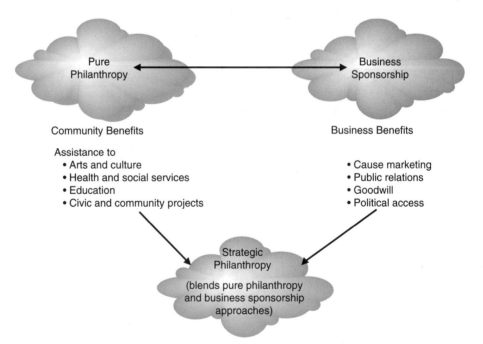

[22]Barbara W. Altman, "*Corporate Community Relations in the 1990s: A Study in Transformation,*" unpublished doctoral dissertation, Boston University, 1997. Abstract published in *Business and Society,* forthcoming, 1998. See also Craig Smith, "The New Corporate Philanthropy," *Harvard Business Review* 72, no. 3 (May–June 1994), pp. 105–112, and Myra Alperson, *New Strategies for Corporate Giving* (New York: The Conference Board, 1995).

(e.g., Asian-Americans).[23] Pressures to justify the use of every corporate dollar are leading managers to think about new ways to tie charitable contributions to business goals.

Priorities in Corporate Giving

The distribution of corporate contributions reflects how the businesses view overall community needs. As shown in Figure 15–7, corporate giving from 1982 to 1995 varied somewhat among categories, but the pie was divided in approximately the same way. These percentages are not identical among different companies and industries, however; some companies tend to favor support for education, whereas others give relatively greater amounts to cultural organizations or community groups.

where do they want to help the most?

good

The actual contributions of an individual company will depend on company goals and priorities. Corporate giving is often justified as a *social investment* that benefits business in the long run by improving the community, its labor force, the climate for business, or other conditions affecting business. An alternative view is that routine local gifts are a *normal expense* of operating a business in the community and should be treated like other public relations expenses. Another view holds that the corporation is a citizen and, as such, has a *citizenship responsibility* to give without regard to self-interest. Some believe that giving should be *linked to business purposes* as exemplified in the cause-related marketing pioneered by American Express. The customer gets the product or service, the charity receives a contribution, and company sales grow.

Another point of view is that some corporate gifts take on the characteristics of taxes. Since it is widely believed that corporations should be good citizens, helpful neighbors, and human institutions, the community's expectations come close to imposing some

Figure 15–7

Distribution of corporate contributions, 1982–1996.

Source: Audris Tillman, *Corporate Contributions in 1995* (New York: The Conference Board, 1996).

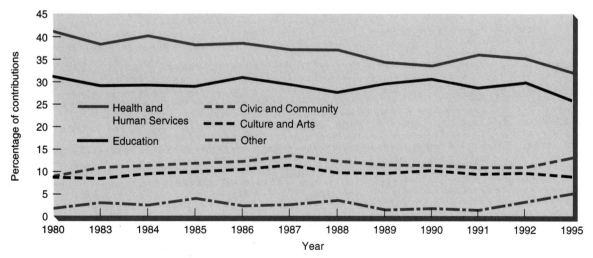

[23]Jeanne M. Logsdon, Martha Reiner, and Lee Burke, "Corporate Philanthropy: Strategic Responses to the Firm's Stakeholders," *Nonprofit and Voluntary Sector Quarterly* 19, no. 2 (Summer 1990), pp. 93–109.

types of gift giving on the corporation as a form of *unofficial tax.* The gifts are given to retain public approval.

Regardless of whether gifts are considered to be an investment, an expense, philanthropy, or a tax, most of their costs are ultimately passed on to consumers, making corporate giving in the long run a cost of doing business. Businesses are then acting partly as agents and trustees for the community, receiving funds and distributing them according to perceived and expressed community needs. In the trusteeship role, businesses respond to various stakeholder claims in the community, and one of these responses is gifts to those whose claims are perceived as being either legitimate or so powerful that they threaten the business if not satisfied. Thus, both the legitimacy of claim and the power of claimants are considered when making a decision concerning corporate giving.

The Role of Volunteerism

Volunteerism involves the efforts of people to assist others in the community through unpaid work. The United States has a long and distinguished tradition of volunteerism, with many examples dating back to the founding of communities as the population moved west across the continent (see discussion in Chapter 3). In the 1980s, the spirit of volunteerism was invoked by presidents Ronald Reagan and George Bush as an alternative to government programs to solve community problems. The business community formed the Council on Private Sector Initiatives as a mechanism to encourage voluntary business-community activities.

Volunteerism received a highly publicized boost in the 1980s when Bush launched his 1,000 Points of Light campaign to celebrate 1,000 voluntary efforts by individuals and organizations to solve problems in American communities. In the 1990s, volunteerism was spurred by the work of the Points of Light Foundation, a catalyst for stimulating voluntary action programs in local communities.[24] Volunteerism received another push in 1997 when former presidents Jimmy Carter, Gerald Ford, and George Bush and President Bill Clinton supported an initiative led by General Colin Powell to tackle the problems of youth, education, and community in a bipartisan call for broad voluntary action. The campaign was high profile, with extensive media coverage of events and General Powell's personal involvement.[25]

Businesses, large and small, are often enlisted as allies in such efforts to improve communities. Managers are asked to announce, publicize, and promote such efforts among staff members, employees, and associates. Some companies may also provide money, supplies, T-shirts, transportation, or other resources to these community efforts. Corporate community relations managers are frequently the executives who are asked to coordinate these efforts.

For example, Coca Cola, Bell South, and other leading companies operating in Atlanta became leaders of that city's campaign to host the 1996 Summer Olympic Games. Corporate volunteer commitments were an important element of the city's bid. By the time the Olympic Games were actually held, the com-

---

[24]Points of Light Foundation, "Special Report: The 1994 National Community Service Conference," *Newsletter* 2, no. 7 (Washington, DC: Points of Light Foundation, July–Aug. 1994).

[25]Jonathan Alter, "Powell's New War," *Newsweek,* April 28, 1997, pp. 28–32. The cover of *Newsweek* showed General Powell pointing toward the reader and saying "I Want You." The tag line read, "Why Colin Powell Is Asking America to Volunteer."

munity relations staffs at Coca Cola, Bell South, and dozens of other Atlanta-based companies had coordinated tens of thousands of employee days of volunteer work in support of the Olympics.

Although most companies and communities are involved in activities that are less visible than the Olympic Games, nearly every city and local community has community needs that require the helping hands of volunteers. This means that in addition to providing jobs, paying taxes, and directing charitable contributions dollars to worthy causes, there is a role for companies as catalysts in encouraging volunteerism that helps build local communities.

Corporate Restructuring and Community Relations

Since the 1980s, and continuing on through the 1990s, American businesses have gone through massive corporate restructuring, reorganization, and reengineering. This change process, which many believe is vital if American firms are to be successful in global competition, has also become a serious and disruptive fact of life for communities.

Corporate restructuring means that companies are reshaping their business activities in some fundamental way so as to become more competitive. Restructured companies often close down older, less productive facilities, improving the firm's ability to produce goods more efficiently. Sometimes they sell off assets to other corporations that may not have the same relationship to the local community as the previous owner. Management may voluntarily restructure the company to avoid being taken over by hostile corporate raiders or simply to meet the forces of global competition by introducing labor-saving technology, moving production facilities to low-wage regions of the world, or using new, substitute materials such as plastic and ceramic auto parts.

Social Costs of Restructuring

Whatever the reasons for the restructuring, the effects on the community are similar: local plants close, workers are laid off, jobs are lost, and individuals are relocated. Studies show that displaced workers seldom have managed to find new jobs as good or as well paying as the ones they lost when a plant closed. Single-income families may be so hard hit that they cannot make home mortgage payments, and some may sell homes to meet back taxes. Sometimes pension benefits and health-care insurance are lost. Older workers, minorities, and women suffer more than other groups of displaced workers, taking longer to find new jobs and receiving lower pay when they do. Family tensions build up; divorce rates increase; depression and mental illness increase; suicides become more frequent; alcoholism and drug abuse grow; child abuse and spouse abuse occur more often. The impact was summed up in a *Time* cover story: "We're #1 and It Hurts."[26]

---

[26]George J. Church, "We're #1 and It Hurts," *Time,* October 24, 1994, pp. 50–56. Job cuts in large companies have become a way of life in American business. In 1997, 434,350 jobs were eliminated; this was the lowest annual total since 1991. The largest 1997 layoffs occurred at Eastman Kodak (19,900) and Boeing (12,000), well below the 40,000 job cuts announced at AT&T in January 1996. Companies may go through several rounds of cuts. In early 1998, for example, AT&T announced a further job cut (15,000). See "The Falling Ax," *Fortune,* March 2, 1998, p. 224, based on data provided by the job outplacement firm, Challenger Gray & Christmas.

Community Responses

Communities may be unable to adjust as corporate restructuring reshapes the local business community. Many cities are dependent on one or a few large employers to anchor the economic base of the community. Rochester, New York, for example, suffered severe effects when Eastman Kodak—known as "Father Yellow" for its high level of community involvement in its headquarters city—announced major job reductions in 1997 (see Chapter 1). The following example illustrates how difficult in can be for communities to deal with such losses.

> *Akron, Ohio, was for many years known as the Rubber Capital. Millions of tires and inner tubes were produced in Akron's massive tire factories until more than 10,000 jobs were lost in the tire industry's intense global competition during the 1980s. Struggling to recover from these devastating losses, Akron's city government worked hard to attract and develop smaller and mid-sized businesses in the city to replace some of the jobs that were lost. Although local supporters boast of the New Akron, economic recovery is slow, requiring many more smaller businesses to provide an equivalent number of jobs to off-set those that were lost. The new industries also require more cooperation between public and private sector officials to create the conditions for business success.*

The human and community problems created by restructuring are not confined to the industrial Rust Belt of the midwestern United States. California's Silicon Valley and Massachusetts's high-technology belt also have been squeezed by foreign competition in the 1990s. Texas, Louisiana, and other oil-producing states have faced falling oil prices since the 1980s, resulting in dramatic and well-publicized failures of savings and loan institutions, a decline in the local housing markets, and in the mid-1990s, a wave of job reductions and downsizings by major oil companies. These job losses have resulted in the same negative impacts on people and communities that have occurred elsewhere.

The end of the cold war also meant the reduced need for large military forces and a defense industry that employed millions of workers. California alone suffered the loss of hundreds of thousands of jobs in the early 1990s because of what were called **defense industry conversion** pressures.

> *Lockheed was one of Southern California's largest employers for more than 30 years from the 1960s to the early 1990s. The company manufactured airplanes and other aerospace equipment, developing a reputation as one of the American defense industry's most reliable contractors. As defense budgets began to shrink in the post–cold war era, Lockheed began to trim its business operations. From a high of more than 100,000 employees, the company reduced its workforce to less than 30,000 by early 1994. Then, in an announcement that shocked many, Lockheed management announced that the company would be merged into Martin Marietta, another defense contractor.[27]*

In the United States, each year during the 1980s plant closings displaced about 500,000 workers who had more than three years on the job; in the 1990s, corporate re-

---

[27]"Aerospace: Swords into Satellites," *The Economist*, September 3, 1994, pp. 60–61.

structurings continued to eliminate jobs at the rate of more than 400,000 jobs per year, including a high of more than 600,000 jobs in 1993. As shown in Figure 15–8, job losses have a cascading effect in the community. Job losses were once primarily felt by lower-wage, hourly workers, including members of minority groups. But in the 1990s, the impact has affected workers at all income levels, including professional staffs and managers.

Many stakeholder groups are affected by these restructuring activities. Local, state, and federal governments, company management, employees, labor unions, local businesses, and community organizations all suffer the impact of restructuring-induced job losses. There is no official estimate of the social costs that have resulted from restructuring during the 1990s, but the cumulative costs of unemployment taxes, social assistance to unemployed workers and their families, and economic-adjustment assistance to affected businesses attributable to corporate restructuring is thought to have surpassed $100 billion from 1990 to 1994. In 1994 alone, corporate America spent more than $10 billion on restructuring while communities spent much more.[28]

As the number of plant closings grew, and their impact became better understood, state and federal governments stepped up their efforts to protect workers and communi-

Figure 15–8

The cascading effects of job losses on a community.

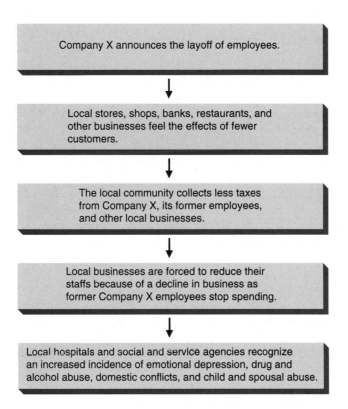

[28]"When Slimming Down Is Not Enough," *The Economist,* September 3, 1994, pp. 59–60; "Downsizing Government," *Business Week,* January 25, 1995, pp. 34–41; and "Defense Improvement," *Business Week,* February 6, 1995, pp. 144–45. See Sylvia Nasar, "Layoff Law Is Having Slim Effect," *New York Times,* August 3, 1993, pp. C1, C2; and Ronald G. Ehrenberg and George H. Jakubson, "Advance Notification of Plant Closing: Does It Matter?" *Industrial Relations,* Winter 1989, pp. 60–71.

ties. State legislatures created **plant closing laws** that required a company to give advance warning before closing a plant. In 1988, the U.S. Congress enacted the Worker Adjustment and Retraining Notification Act (WARN). WARN required employers to give 60 days' advance notice of plant closings and major layoffs that result in permanent job losses. Many state legislatures have also created plant closing laws that require a company to give advance warning before closing a plant. The business community has generally opposed such laws.

Business argued that the need for companies to become more efficient in the face of competition required faster action than these laws would permit. Some research suggests, however, that most of the negative impacts on business were temporary, and there is little evidence that such laws have deterred corporate restructuring in the 1990s. Much of the current U.S. worker legislation is modeled on Western European government requirements that employers provide notice to employees, job training, and job search assistance when layoffs are necessary. European laws often require compensation payments to the community as well. The European Union, for example, tried to create common standards of compensation and provided funds to communities and regions that lost jobs to the new competition of the international marketplace.[29]

Company Responses

Management practices vary from company to company when corporate restructuring occurs. In some cases, management gives advance notice, makes an effort to find new jobs for displaced workers, and works with local citizens' groups and municipal officials to ease the impact of a closing. At other times, only the minimum legal requirements are met by a company that does not want to be pressured to reverse its decision. It may offer little aid to employees, local government, or the community.

Restructuring does not always work as planned; some companies have discovered that employees they wished to retain have taken advantage of early retirement or other voluntary programs. Others have learned that employees who remain with the company are disillusioned, unhappy, and fearful of the next round of layoffs. This can result in lack of loyalty and low morale among remaining employees, making it more difficult for the company to respond effectively to the competitive pressures that forced the restructuring in the first place.[30]

The Age of Anxiety

Employees faced with job loss suffer a variety of fates. Some may move to another job with the same company but in a different location. Some are retrained and enter a new skill or craft. Others hang on to false hopes: one steel mill worker with 20 years of experience with a company simply refused to accept reality, saying, "I think the mill is going to open again." Those who find new jobs often end up with lower pay, have less desirable jobs, and lose their seniority. Former U.S. secretary of labor Robert Reich led a highly visible campaign to convince employees and employers that lifelong learning and continued development of job skills are the only real security that people can have in a

---

[29]See, for example, "Steel Region Wins £36 Million EU Funds," *Financial Times,* October 14, 1994, p. 9. The EU's rules on plant closing are updated in *European Labor Law,* Washington, D.C., BNA Research, 1994–98.
[30]William Bridges, "The End of the Job," *Fortune,* September 19, 1994, pp. 62–74.

world of rapid competitive change. As Secretary Reich delivered his message around the nation, he began referring to the 1990s as "The Age of Anxiety."[31]

The era of corporate restructuring has led some corporations to downsize and reevaluate activities, including corporate giving. As the following example shows, even charitable contributions are no longer a sacred cow in the highly competitive, global business environment.

> *In 1994, the senior management of ARCO, one of the world's largest petroleum companies, informed the senior executive of the ARCO Foundation that a decision had been made to reduce its funding and eventually eliminate the foundation. ARCO had been a highly visible and much-admired corporate citizen in its headquarters community of Los Angeles. The company provided important leadership in Los Angeles in such efforts as education reform, community development, and Rebuild LA, a major attempt to address the city's complex social and racial issues after the 1992 riots. Through the ARCO Foundation, millions of dollars had been focused on meeting community needs. Still, persistently low prices for oil forced petroleum companies to reduce staffs, trim expenses, and reengineer operations. A consulting firm was called in by ARCO's top management and concluded that no lasting damage would be done to ARCO's image or profits by cutting out its contributions program. Despite its record of good works, the cost-cutting ax fell on the ARCO Foundation.*

The Need for Partnership

The need for **public–private partnerships** between business and government are very apparent when dealing with community problems. The idea of such partnering is not new. As one group of business executives said in 1982:

> *Whether growing or contracting, young or old, large or small, in the Frost Belt or Sun Belt, America's urban communities possess the resources of an advanced and affluent society: highly educated and skilled individuals, productive social and economic institutions, sophisticated technology, physical infrastructure, transportation and communications networks, and access to capital. Developing this potential will require cooperation. . . . Public–private partnerships are a source of energy and vitality for America's urban communities.*[32]

Corporate restructuring and refocusing has underscored the importance of this point nearly 15 years later. Many community problems are people problems involving hopes, attitudes, sentiments, and expectations for better human conditions. Neither government nor business can simply impose solutions or be expected to find quick and easy answers to problems so long in the making and so vast in their complications. Moreover, neither government nor business has the financial resources to solve these issues. Grassroots involvement is needed, where people are willing and able to confront their own needs, imagine solutions, and work to fulfill them through cooperative efforts and intelligent planning. In that community-oriented effort, government and business can be partners,

[31]Robert Reich, Address to the National Alliance of Business, September 25, 1994, Washington, D.C. See Catherine S. Manegold, "Reich Urges Executives to Aid Labor," *New York Times,* September 25, 1994, p. 25.
[32]Committee for Economic Development, *Public-Private Partnership: An Opportunity for Urban Communities* (New York: Committee for Economic Development, 1982), p. 1.

contributing aid and assistance where feasible and being socially responsive to legitimately expressed human needs. Exhibit 15–B describes such an effort in communities along the U.S.-Mexico border.

A study by the Conference Board and the Urban Institute identified three distinct strategies that corporations can use to become effective partners with urban communities.[33] One is to become *directly involved* in addressing specific problems in specific neighborhoods or communities. A second approach is to develop *partnerships* with the community wherein the community's needs and priorities guide the form and type of corporate activity. The third strategy is for the corporation to be involved in the community through an *intermediary organization,* such as a citywide umbrella organization that helps to coordinate the efforts of many local businesses and nonprofits.

Communities need jobs, specialized skills, executive talents, and other resources that business can provide. Business needs cooperative attitudes in local government, basic

---

EXHIBIT 15–B	**Business Meets the Maquiladoras***

The South Texas border with Mexico is not the usual hotbed of corporate community affairs. It is, however, a hotbed of commercial expansion as companies from around the world establish manufacturing and assembly operations called *maquiladoras.* Inexpensive Mexican labor and easy access to American markets make the maquiladoras the vehicle for boomtown development.

The boomtowns are growing in areas where social problems—including no schools, no housing, and no social infrastructure to hold together the community—abound. In El Paso, for example, low wages and the prestige of a Made in the USA label have helped keep employment high, with more than 20,000 jobs in the apparel industry in 1994. More than 100 million pairs of jeans are made in El Paso each year. But the stiff competition also helps keep El Paso as the poorest metropolitan region in the United States, with personal incomes only 59 percent of the national average. Patricia Fogerty, a former NYNEX community affairs officer who lives in McAllen, Texas, says, "Some [companies] are finding they have to develop the entire social infrastructure in the towns."

A model for doing so is being developed by the El Paso Community Foundation. It organizes Hispanic wives of workers to do community work and serves as a bridge between employers and social problems in the border communities. Among the leadership companies that have partnered with community groups are Levi Strauss, General Electric, Sierra West, and Alcoa. Yet the maquiladora conditions are so bad that many church groups in the United States are campaigning to press companies to do much more in dealing with these poor and needy communities on both sides of the border.

*There are two accepted spellings for this word. We have chosen to use "maquiladora" rather than "machiladora," which also appears in published materials.
Source: Allen R. Myerson, "Jeans Makers Flourish on Border," *New York Times,* September 29, 1994, pp. D1, D9; and "Machiladora Blues," in Craig Smith, ed., *Corporate Philanthropy Report,* vol. 5, no. 1 (August–September 1989), p. 12. See also, "Doing Business in the Maquiladoras," a case study at the end of this book.

---

[33]Peterson and Sundblad, *Corporations as Partners.*

public services, and a feeling that it is a welcome member of the community. Under these circumstances much can be accomplished to upgrade the quality of community life. The range of specific business-community involvements is extensive, giving business many opportunities to be socially responsible. Corporate restructurings, erratic growth patterns, and an explosion of community needs challenge business involvement with the community. Still, by using management skills, corporate philanthropy, employee volunteerism, and other creative means, companies can have a positive impact on the quality of community life.

Summary Points of This Chapter

- Businesses and the communities have a mutual dependence that is both economically and socially significant. Thus, businesses work to be accepted as participants in community affairs by supporting community interests as well as their own.

- Many corporations have established a community relations office that links their activities to local needs and community groups and develops strategies for creating win-win approaches to solving community problems.

- Corporate contributions to educational, charitable, scientific, and community programs help sustain vital community institutions while benefiting business in a variety of ways. Strategic philanthropy represents a way of linking corporate giving and business goals.

- Corporate volunteerism involves encouraging employees to participate in projects that address a wide range of community needs. Some companies have made volunteerism an explicit part of their strategy.

- Corporate restructuring and layoffs can affect many community groups, including merchants, employees, school systems, local government, and charitable organizations. Successful strategies for coping with the social consequences and pressures that restructuring can place on community life involve cooperation among business, government, employees, labor unions, and community organizations.

- The development of public-private partnerships has proven to be effective in tackling some problems in education, economic development, and social service needs. Partnerships and volunteerism provide models of a shared responsibility in which business and communities address social problems. Many businesses and communities are creating new strategies based on these models.

Key Terms and Concepts Used in This Chapter

- Community
- Community relations
- Urban sprawl
- Community advisory panels (CAPs)
- Corporate philanthropy, corporate giving
- Corporate foundations
- Strategic philanthropy
- Cause marketing
- Volunteerism
- Corporate restructuring
- Defense industry conversion
- Plant closing laws
- Public-private partnerships

Internet Resources

- http:// www.disney.com   Walt Disney Company
- http://www.fdncenter.org   The Foundation Center
- http://www.cof.org   Council on Foundations
- http://www.bs.edu/bc_org/avp/csom/cccr Boston College Center for Corporate
                                          Community Relations
- http:// www.impactonline.org/points Points of Light Foundation

Discussion Case   Abbott Laboratories Helps Habitat for Humanity

Habitat for Humanity is a worldwide organization that builds homes and sells them to low-income families on a no-profit, no-interest basis. Habitat was founded in 1976 and has built more than 30,000 homes throughout the world. It has more than 1,000 affiliates in its worldwide network.

Among Habitat's many affiliates are groups of people who are employed by companies such as Abbott Laboratories, a pharmaceutical and health-care products manufacturer that employs more than 50,000 people. About 15,000 Abbott employees and retirees live in Lake County, Illinois, where Abbott's world headquarters is located. Employees of Abbott Laboratories are involved in many types of volunteer activity in their local communities, so it was no surprise when a group decided to form the Abbott Chapter of Habitat for Humanity. The Abbott Chapter has worked closely with Lake County's Habitat organization to identify needs and plan a construction project. Local government officials have also been instrumental in identifying sites for Habitat projects and for obtaining needed permits. Since its formation, the Abbott Chapter has helped renovate several buildings in North Chicago and Waukegan, Illinois.

Robin Coleman and her four children learned that they had been selected as the family to work with the Abbott Chapter in building a new house in North Chicago. Habitat families are selected on the basis of need, ability to make a low mortgage payment, and a willingness to help construct the homes of others as well as their own. With the help of more than 200 Abbott employee volunteers, a $38,000 grant for materials from the Abbott Laboratories Fund, and more than 500 hours of sweat equity by the Coleman family, Habitat volunteers built the house in less than one year. Cheers and tears of joy were abundant when Coleman and her family received the keys to their new home.

A dedication ceremony was held at the new Coleman family home. Abbott officials, the mayor of North Chicago, Habitat for Humanity officials, and many of the volunteers attended. Jim Donovan, an R&D quality manager in Abbott's diagnostic division and president of the Abbott chapter of Habitat, said, "All the people involved in this project have felt a great sense of pride in contributing to the future of the Coleman family as well as to the community."

Source: Information provided by the corporate communications department, Abbott Laboratories, Abbott Park, Illinois.

Discussion Questions

1. What is the motivation for Abbott employees to participate in the Habitat project? What is the motivation for Abbott to provide charitable contributions to the project?

2. What do you believe the Abbott/Habitat project means to the long-term relationship between the company and the North Chicago community? Use Figure 15–3.

3. What are the elements of community partnership that are essential to the success of this effort?

4. If you were an employee of Abbott Laboratories, what would attract you to participate in such a project?

16

The Employee-Employer Relationship

Employees and employers are engaged in a critical relationship affecting the corporation's performance. There is a basic economic aspect to this relationship. Employees provide labor for the firm; employers compensate workers for their contribution of skill or productivity. Yet, also present in the employee-employer exchange are numerous social, ethical, legal, and public policy issues. Attention to the multiple aspects of this association can benefit the firm, its workers, and society.

This chapter focuses on these key questions and objectives:

- Do employers have a duty or obligation within the employer-employee contract to provide job security and equal opportunities for employment to their workers?

- What rights do workers have to organize and bargain collectively?

- As governmental intervention into employee safety and health issues increases, what are a business's duties in protecting its workers?

- How does greater diversity in the workforce affect a business's obligations to its employees?

- Does a business's acquiring information about its workers violate an employee's right to privacy? For example, do monitoring employee communication, AIDS testing, and honesty tests violate an employee's privacy?

- Do employees have a duty to blow the whistle on corporate misconduct, or should employees always be loyal to their employer?

S anto Alba began working for Raytheon Company in February 1988. Nine years later, on May 15, 1997, he died, decapitated by a circular saw used for cutting sheet metal in one of the shops he supervised. The coroner ruled the death a suicide. Yet the Alba family had a different version of the circumstances that led to Santo's grisly death.

The Alba family alleged that Santo sent several memos to his manager in 1996 that said he felt overwhelmed by increased responsibilities at work. Restructuring had slashed over half the people in his department. According to the Alba family, because of Raytheon's workforce reductions, Santo Alba had been required to work 70 to 80 hour weeks, including weekends.

In March 1994, Alba had sought counseling and was hospitalized for several days. According to his medical records, he was admitted for "severe anxiety/depression related to fear of job loss, stress, [and] working very long hours in highly driven work atmosphere." His family said he told doctors that he had considered suicide because he was so anxiety-ridden. The Albas filed charges, claiming that Raytheon drove Santo to his death by overloading him with work and failing to make accommodations for his depression.[1]

Is Raytheon responsible for Santo Alba's suicide? Legally? Ethically? What obligation does a firm have to attend to the needs of the workers still employed after corporate downsizing? What obligations does a firm have to a worker with a documented mental illness?

The Employee-Employer Contract

Employees and employers are engaged in a stakeholder relationship that includes numerous expectations by both parties. The employer, for example, has assumed various duties and obligations. Some of these responsibilities are economic or legal; others are social or ethical in nature.

The relationship is clearly more than simply paying a worker for the labor provided. Cultural values and traditions also play a role. In Europe, employers feel they have a duty to include workers on the board of directors to assist in forming company policy. For many years, Japanese employers have offered their workers lifelong employment, although this practice has become less widespread in recent years. In the United States, since the late 1800s, the contractual basis for employee labor has been employment-at-will. **Employment-at-will** means that employees are hired and retain their jobs "at the will of," or as decided by, the employer. However, over time, an increase in wrongful discharge claims by employees has dramatically curtailed American employers' freedom to terminate workers.

The New Social Contract

In recent years, basic expectations underlying the employee-employer relationship have changed, both in the United States and in other countries around the globe. Beginning in the late 1980s and continuing through the 1990s, fierce global competition and greater attention to improving the bottom line resulted in significant corporate restructuring and downsizing (termination) of employees. Along with corporate restructuring came a new way of thinking about the employee-employer relationship. As described in Figure 16–1, the new **employer-employee social contract** shifted the focus of employers' obligations

[1]Audrey Choi, "Family Claims Raytheon Caused Suicide," *Wall Street Journal,* November 3, 1995, p. B5.

Figure 16-1

The new employer-employee social contract.

Sources: James E. Post, "The New Social Contract," in Oliver Williams and John Houck, eds., *The Global Challenge to Corporate Social Responsibility* (New York: Oxford University Press, 1995); and Barbara W. Altman and James E. Post, "Challenges in Balancing Corporate Economic and Social Responsibilities," Boston University Working Paper, Boston, MA, 1994.

Emphasizes

- The burden of maintaining employment shifts from the employer to the employee.
- Job security is no longer based on seniority but on job performances.
- Worker employability is enhanced by training and development programs.

Positive Results for Employers	Negative Results for Employers
• Greater ability to move employees job to job	• Lower employee morale
• Greater ease in removing marginal performers	• Reduced productivity
• Greater ability to recruit and retain high performers	• Employee mistrust of the firm
• More flexibility due to temporary workforce	• Temporary workforce more difficult to manage
• More self-directed, independent employees	• Increase in unplanned turnover
• Development of diversity and work/family programs	• Uncertainty of job skills possessed by future workforce
	• Pressure to develop social programs to replace job security

away from long-term job security. The new relationship was aimed at satisfying employees at work by emphasizing interesting and challenging work, performance-based compensation, and training to help workers become more employable within and outside the company. In return, employees were expected to contribute to the employer-employee social contract by providing a strong commitment to the job task and work team. Employees were expected to share in the responsibility of achieving company success. The new message for employees was: *you* are responsible for your lifetime employment. It is not the responsibility of the employer.[2]

Although initially seen in the United States, evidence of this change of contractual employment is appearing in many countries. The International Labor Organization reported that in 1995, 30 percent of the world's labor force, or 750 million people, were either unemployed or underemployed. Throughout the 1990s, U.S. firms continued to restructure their organizations, often leading to a dramatic reduction of the number of employees. In 1994, employers announced more than 3,100 job terminations *per day*. Three years later, 10 of the nation's largest employers—including Eastman Kodak, Woolworth, Citicorp and International Paper—announced layoffs exceeding 4,000 employees per firm, averaging more than 16 percent of the firms' workforces. The dramatic financial tumble of the Asian economies impacted workers there. Experts estimated that layoffs could reach two million employees in Indonesia, Thailand, South Korea, Japan, and Hong Kong alone.[3]

---

[2]See a collection of papers in *Human Resources Briefing: The New Employer-Employee Contract* (New York: The Conference Board, 1994); "Writing a New Social Contract," *Business Week,* March 11, 1996, pp. 60–61; and "Rewriting the Social Contract," *Business Week,* November 20, 1995, pp. 120–ff., 120–123, 126, 130, 134.

[3]"Jobs Shock," *Business Week,* December 22, 1997, pp. 48–49; and G. Pascal Zachary, "Study Predicts Rising Global Joblessness," *The Wall Street Journal,* February 22, 1995, pp. A2, A5; Eric Rolfe Greenberg, "Downsizing AMA Survey Results," *Compensation and Benefits Review,* July–August 1991, pp. 33–38; and "Big Knives of 1997," *Business Week,* December 15, 1997, p. 6.

The Government Role in the Employment Relationship
The relationship between employers and employees in the United States is influenced in important ways by laws and regulations that shape worker rights to organize and bargain collectively and that prescribe standards of equal opportunity and occupational safety and health. Some of the roles that government plays are described in this section.

The Role of Labor Unions

An important voice for employees on the job is a labor union. The influence of labor unions in the United States has waxed and waned over the years. During the New Deal, federal laws were passed that gave many employees the right to organize unions and to bargain collectively with their employers. Many workers, particularly in manufacturing industries such as automobiles and steel, joined unions, and the ranks of organized labor grew rapidly during the 1930s and 1940s. Unions negotiated with employers for better wages, benefits such as pensions and health insurance, and improved working conditions. Since the mid-1950s, however, the proportion of American workers represented by unions has declined. In 1997, only about 14 percent of all employees were union members. (The percentage was somewhat higher in government employment.)

Some observers believe, however, that unions in the United States may be poised for recovery. The AFL-CIO, the major federation of labor unions, elected new leaders in 1995 who vowed to devote more resources to organizing new members. A possible indicator of labor's resurgence was the 1997 Teamsters' strike against the United Parcel Service (UPS). After a several day strike that crippled the ability of many businesses to transport important documents and packages, management agreed to a new contract that included higher wages and more full-time job opportunities for part-time workers. The Teamsters believed that strong support from the public for the rights of part-time workers was an important factor in their victory. Polls showed a 2-to-1 margin of support for striking workers over management. Experts believed that public confidence might encourage other unions to take a harder line against management in future negotiations.

Labor union power was evident in other ways in the late 1990s. Time Warner faced an unexpected foe at the company's 1996 annual stockholder meeting: its labor union. A total of 12 labor unions used shareholder activism (discussed in Chapter 13) to score a number of victories regarding union representation in corporate governance. New alliances were formed between labor unions and diverse activist organizations such as the Sierra Club and the National Association for the Advancement of Colored People.[4]

Some labor unions also sought to work cooperatively with employers for their mutual benefit. At Saturn, AT&T, and Kaiser Permanente (a large health maintenance organization), management and unions forged new partnerships aimed both at giving workers a greater say in the business and improving quality and productivity. However, the adversarial tone that had so often characterized management-union relations could also be found. At Caterpillar, management took a tough stance when the machinists union called a strike. The firm hired replacement workers, used retirees, salaried employees, and clerical staff in plant operation positions, and shifted work to outside contractors. When the United Auto Workers went on strike months later at a McDonnell Douglas plant, the firm followed Caterpillar's strategy.

[4]Joann S. Lublin, "Unions Brandish Stock to Force Change," *Wall Street Journal,* May 17, 1996, pp. B1, B2; and Aaron Bernstein, "Big Labor Invites a Few Friends Over," *Business Week,* April 21, 1997, p. 44.

Equal Job Opportunity

Working to ensure **equal job opportunity** continues to be a socially desirable goal for U.S. businesses. This area of employee relations calls for positive responses and initiatives if businesses are to continue evolving toward social responsiveness and public approval.

Government Policies and Regulations

Government efforts against workplace discrimination began in the United States on a major scale in the 1960s. U.S. presidents issued directives, and Congress enacted laws intended to improve equal treatment of employees. These government rules apply to most businesses in the following ways:

- Discrimination based on race, color, religion, sex, national origin, physical or mental disability, or age is prohibited in all employment practices. This includes hiring, promotion, job classification, and assignment, compensation, and other conditions of work.

- Government contractors must have written affirmative action plans detailing how they are working positively to overcome past and present effects of discrimination in their workforce. However, affirmative action plans must be temporary and flexible, designed to current past discrimination, and cannot result in reverse discrimination against whites or men.

- Women and men must receive equal pay for performing equal work, and employers may not discriminate on the basis of pregnancy.

Governmental efforts to eliminate discrimination in the workplace vary from country to country. As shown in Figure 16–2, more regulatory control exists in the United States, Canada, and France than in Venezuela and Hong Kong.

The major agency charged with enforcing federal equal employment opportunity laws and executive orders in the United States is the **Equal Employment Opportunity**

Figure 16–2

Prohibition of workplace discrimination around the world.

Country	Age	Sex	National Origin	Race	Religion	Marital Status
United States	yes	yes	yes	yes	yes	no
France	some	yes	yes	yes	yes	yes
Greece	no	yes	no	yes	yes	yes
Great Britain	no	yes	yes	yes	no	no
Venezuela	no	no	no	no	no	no
Canada	yes	yes	yes	yes	yes	yes
Hong Kong	no	no	no	no	no	no
Japan	no	yes	yes	yes	yes	no
Italy	yes	yes	some	yes	yes	no
Spain	no	yes	yes	yes	yes	yes
Belgium	some	yes	yes	yes	yes	yes
Netherlands	no	yes	yes	yes	yes	yes

Source: Laura B. Pincus and James A. Belohlav, "Legal Issues in Multinational Business Strategy: To Play the Game, You Have to Know the Rules," *Academy of Management Executive,* 10, no. 3 (1996), pp. 52–61.

Commission (EEOC). The EEOC was created in 1964 and given added enforcement powers in 1972 and 1990. This agency is primarily responsible for enforcing provisions of the Civil Rights Acts of 1964 and 1991, the Equal Opportunity Act, the Equal Pay Act, the Age Discrimination in Employment Act, and the Americans with Disabilities Act.

Regulators and courts first used a results-oriented approach to these laws. In other words, a company would be considered in violation of the law if statistical analysis revealed that its jobs were out of line with the proportions of whites and nonwhites or men and women potentially available for such work. Later, other judicial interpretations were handed down. In the early 1980s, these decisions were seen as gains for business because companies were less vulnerable to discrimination lawsuits and freer to make personnel decisions on their own. In the 1990s, however, government efforts placed additional responsibilities on businesses and overturned the effects of the U.S. Supreme Court decisions from the early 1980s. For example, under the 1990 EEOC guidelines, employers faced greater liability for employee conduct involving sexual harassment. In addition, employers were obligated to demonstrate that alleged discriminatory practices were job related and consistent with practices necessary to operate a business, according to the 1991 Civil Rights Act.

Corporate Responses

Generally, businesses have developed a number of approaches to curb discrimination and equalize employment opportunities. An example of one company that has done a particularly good job at this is the Inland Steel Company, shown in Exhibit 16–A. Companies

---

**EXHIBIT
16–A**

Addressing Discrimination at Inland Steel

In the mid-1980s, four African-American managers at Inland Steel, two men and two women, came forward with a complaint. Although they had been with the company for many years and had excellent performance evaluations, they had not advanced in their careers as far as they felt they should have. They perceived that their way up the corporate ladder was blocked because of race and gender discrimination.

Inland responded proactively. White, male managers were encouraged to attend workshops sponsored by the Urban Crisis Center in Atlanta and directed by the charismatic civil rights activist, Reverend Charles King, Jr. At these workshops, participants were helped to understand what it really felt like to be a minority and to be excluded from contributing to the decision process.

The company increased its number of affirmative action focus groups. Their goal was to ensure that all people at Inland were treated equally and fairly and had the opportunity to achieve their potential. The groups also tried to draw attention to subtle forms of discrimination and to give minorities and women a greater voice in the company.

These efforts paid off. Hiring of minorities and women increased. Many employees who had been passed over for years were promoted to positions commensurate with their years of experience and performance evaluations. Inland Steel had made real progress in incorporating affirmative action practices into its everyday culture.

In 1992, the company won an award from the Business Enterprise Trust for its efforts to reduce discrimination. Other companies that have received this award are profiled in Chapter 3.

that have failed to promote equal opportunity in employment often find themselves facing expensive lawsuits based on charges of employee discrimination.

> *One of the more sensational examples of racial discrimination in the workplace involved Texaco. A number of African-American employees sued the big oil company, charging discrimination. In the course of investigating the case, these employees' attorneys obtained a copy of a tape recording, apparently of top Texaco executives at a meeting to discuss how to respond to the lawsuit. The tape seemed to contain offensive racial epithets as well as some discussion of destroying evidence that would be harmful to Texaco's position. When a transcript of the tape was published, it was very embarrassing for the company.*
>
> > *Texaco settled the lawsuit out of court. The firm agreed to pay $176.1 million over five years, the largest settlement in the history of racial discrimination suits in the United States. The company also created organizational programs promoting racial sensitivity at work. An Equality and Tolerance Task Force was created with committee members appointed by the firm and the plaintiff's lawyers. Willie Stamfield, an African-American Texaco executive, was appointed as an assistant to the task force chairperson to oversee diversity issues at the firm.[5]*

Potentially costly lawsuits can involve other forms of discrimination as well. Age discrimination was the charge made by 239 former First Union Corporation employees. The nation's sixth-largest bank agreed to pay $58.5 million to settle the class-action suits. Charges of age discrimination were also filed against the Adolph Coors brewing company, Schering-Plough pharmaceutical firm, and investment bankers and traders at Kidder, Peabody & Company. Although the cases against the last three firms have not been proven in court, it does illustrate the widespread potential for costly discrimination lawsuits in business.

> *In a survey of 515 trial verdicts involving wrongful termination lawsuits from 1988 to 1992, successful age-bias claims resulted in an average award of more than $300,000, compared with approximately $250,000 awarded for sex discrimination actions. Race bias and disability discrimination claims, on average, received approximately $200,000 per claim.[6]*

Promoting equal opportunity in hiring, promotion, and job assignment is good business, both because it allows firms to use the widest possible range of talent and it avoids expensive lawsuits.

Affirmative Action

One way to promote equal opportunity and remedy past discrimination is through **affirmative action.** Since the mid-1960s, major government contractors have been required by presidential executive order to adopt written affirmative action plans specifying goals, actions, and timetables for promoting greater on-the-job equality. Their purpose is to

---

[5]"Texaco to Pay $176.1 Million in Bias Suit," *Wall Street Journal,* November 187, 1996, pp. A3, A6.
[6]"Age-Bias Cases Found to Bring Big Jury Awards," *Wall Street Journal,* December 17, 1993, pp. B1, B8.

reduce job discrimination by encouraging companies to take positive (that is, affirmative) steps to overcome past employment practices and traditions that may have been discriminatory.

Affirmative action became increasingly controversial in the late 1990s. In some states, new laws (such as Proposition 209 in California) were passed banning or limiting affirmative action programs in public hiring and university admissions, and the issue was debated in Congress and in the courts. Backers of these programs argued that affirmative action was an important tool for achieving equal opportunity. Roger Wilkins, a well-known African-American historian, supported this view: "We believe that minorities and women are still disadvantaged in our highly competitive society and that affirmative action is absolutely necessary to level the playing field." Some large corporations have found that legally required affirmative action programs are helpful in monitoring the company's progress in providing equal job opportunity. General Electric, AT&T, and IBM have said that they would continue to use affirmative action goals and timetables even if they were not required by law.

Critics of affirmative action, however, argued that affirmative action was inconsistent with the principles of fairness and equality. Some pointed to instances of so-called **reverse discrimination,** which occurs when one group is unintentionally discriminated against in an effort to help another group. For example, if a more qualified white man were passed over for a job as a firefighter in favor of a less qualified Hispanic man to remedy past discrimination in the fire department, this might seem unfair to the white candidate. Critics of affirmative action also argued that these programs could actually stigmatize or demoralize the very groups they were designed to help. For example, if a woman were hired for a top management post, other people might *think* she got the job just because of affirmative action preferences, even if she was truly the best qualified. This might undermine her effectiveness on the job or even cause her to question her own abilities. Some women and members of minority groups actually wanted *less* emphasis on affirmative action, preferring to achieve personal success without preferential treatment.[7]

In 1995, the Supreme Court ruled in an important decision that affirmative action plans were legal but only if they were temporary and flexible, designed to correct past discrimination, and did not result in reverse discrimination against men or whites. Under this ruling, *quotas* (e.g., a hard-and-fast rule that 50 percent of all new positions will go to women, say, or African-Americans) would no longer be permitted in most cases. Clearly, affirmative action is an issue that will continue to be debated, not just in the courts but in business, society, and government generally.

Americans with Disabilities Act

The Americans with Disabilities Act (ADA) of 1990 requires employers to make accommodations for disabled workers and job applicants and prohibits employers from discriminating on the basis of a person's disability. A more elaborate description of the provisions in the ADA is shown in Figure 16–3.

---

[7]Peter Coy, "The Best Kind of Affirmative Action," *Business Week,* May 19, 1997, p. 35; and "A 'Race-Neutral' Helping Hand?" *Business Week,* February 27, 1995, pp. 120–121.

Figure 16–3

Provisions of the Americans with Disabilities Act of 1990.

Source: Adapted from The Equal Employment Opportunity Commission, *The Americans with Disabilities Act of 1990* (Washington, DC: 1991. U.S. Government Printing Office, (Washington D.C.: U.S. Government Printing Office, 1991).

Prohibits employers when hiring from inquiring about

- Medical history
- Prior insurance claims
- Work absenteeism due to illness
- Past treatment for alcoholism
- Mental illness

Defines a qualified disabled worker as

- One who can perform the "essential functions" of a job, with or without reasonable accommodations

Requires employers to make reasonable accommodations to disabled workers by

- Modifying work equipment
- Providing readers or interpreters
- Adjusting work schedules
- Making existing facilities accessible

Even before the law was signed, employers complained that the definition of disability was unclear. Nonetheless, the act was passed, and those with disabilities began to exercise their new rights. The EEOC reported it had received over 16,000 ADA-related complaints by the end of 1993. Nearly half of the charges involved the discharge of a disabled employee. Other complaints accused employers of failing to provide reasonable accommodations for the disabled at work, discriminatory hiring practices, or the harassment of disabled workers. By 1995, the EEOC relaxed restrictions on what questions employers could ask job applicants with disabilities.

Corporate responses were generally slow. However, leaders of the country's largest firms and labor unions joined forces to form the National Organization on Disability and the Industry-Labor Council of the National Center for Disability Services. These organizations seek to promote the hiring and advancement of people with disabilities. Many employers have been encouraged to hire people with disabilities, based on the good results others have achieved through this practice.

Courts have interpreted the ADA to cover persons with acquired immunodeficiency syndrome (AIDS). Discrimination against persons with AIDS or infected with the virus that causes AIDS is prohibited under the ADA, so long as the person can perform essential elements of the job. The employment rights of workers with AIDS are discussed later.

Job Safety and Health

Much industrial work is inherently hazardous because of the extensive use of high-speed and noisy machinery, production processes requiring high temperatures, an increasing reliance on sophisticated chemical compounds, and the nature of such work as construction, underground, and undersea tunneling, drilling, and mining. Accidents, injuries, and illnesses are likely to occur under these circumstances.

Over the past decade, new categories of accidents or illnesses have emerged, including the fast-growing job safety problem of office injuries. Stress from rising productivity pressure and escalating job demands can cause cumulative trauma disorders, such as the wrist pain sometimes experienced by supermarket checkers, meatcutters, or keyboard operators. The number of health problems attributed to the use of video display terminals and computer keyboards and to tasks requiring repetitive motion have increased tenfold in the past decade. *Ergonomics* quickly became an office buzzword in the 1990s. **Ergonomics** means adapting work and work conditions and equipment to suit the worker rather than forcing the worker to adapt to the design of the machine, for example. Office furniture that lacks ergonomic features may be partly responsible for poor productivity and lost time due to illness and injury.

Annually, nearly 10,000 workers are killed, 6 million are injured, and 300,000 become ill while on the job, according to union reports. As the workforce continues to get older, workplace injuries are of greater concern. According to the Bureau of Labor Statistics, older workers are nearly four times as likely as younger ones to die from job-related injuries. Despite some decreases in worker fatalities and injuries, "the annual death rate is still radically higher than other industrialized nations," stated Donald Millar, director of the National Institute for Occupational Safety and Health. Corporate liability for on-the-job injuries also is escalating. Employers in 14 states have been sentenced to prison for ignoring warnings to improve safety at work. One plant owner was sentenced to serve 20 years in jail for a workplace fatality.[8]

Occupational Safety and Health Administration

The **Occupational Safety and Health Administration (OSHA),** created by Congress in 1970, has been one of the most controversial of the government agencies established in the great wave of social legislation during the 1970s. Congress gave OSHA important powers over employers, requiring them to provide for each employee a job "free from recognized hazards that are causing or likely to cause death or serious physical harm." Employers found in violation of OSHA safety and health standards can be fined and, in the case of willful violation causing the death of an employee, jailed as well.

Over the years, OSHA has sometimes been more aggressive, sometimes less aggressive, in policing the health and safety of American workplaces. In the late 1980s and early 1990s, the agency vigorously pursued significant safety violations and imposed large fines on violators.

> *In 1988, Chrysler agreed to pay $1.6 million to settle OSHA charges of worker overexposure to lead and arsenic and other alleged health and safety violations. In 1993, OSHA charged the Wyman-Gordon Company with 149 safety violations at its Massachusetts metal forging plant. Over $1 million in penalties was proposed.*[9]

By the mid-1990s, however, OSHA appeared to be more cooperative. From 1995 to 1997, OSHA inspections declined 43 percent, citations for serious safety violations dropped 64 percent, and the agency appeared more open to business concerns in seeking collaborative solutions to workplace hazards.

---

[8]Helen L. Richardson, "Accept Responsibility for Safety," *Transportation and Distribution,* August 1992, pp. 29–32; and Michael Moss, "For Older Employees, On-the-Job Injuries Are More Often Deadly," *The Wall Street Journal,* June 17, 1997, pp. A1, A10.

[9]"Chrysler to Pay Record Penalty in OSHA Case," *The Wall Street Journal,* February 2, 1987, p. 20; and "OSHA Asks Safety Penalties of More than $1 Million," *The Wall Street Journal,* August 13, 1993, p. B2.

Management's Responses

Although some have praised OSHA as an aggressive government watchdog, businesses have generally criticized it as being too costly. Small businesses in particular had a difficult time carrying the paperwork required by OSHA's rules. Other companies objected to the high cost of redesigning machinery and production processes, saying that these expenses far outweighed any tangible or marginal benefit in increased safety and health for workers. Some employees themselves refused to wear required safety goggles, earplugs, respirators, and other special equipment to protect them from harm, but if they were to be injured while not wearing such items, the employer, not the employee, would be subject to penalty.

Some businesses have developed their own systems to reduce the threats of workplace injuries. One of the more popular and widespread methods is **workplace safety teams.** Safety teams are generally made up of equal numbers of workers and managers. In operation, these teams not only reduce employee accidents, they also lower workers' compensation costs. The effect is particularly dramatic at small companies that typically do not have the financial or human resources to develop the more elaborate and costly safety programs and committees found in large corporations.

The experience with employee safety teams has been encouraging. Norfolk Southern reduced its number of injuries by two-thirds while reducing the size of its safety staff by 84 percent. The rise in worker compensation costs at State Fair Foods was reversed after the firm initiated worker-safety teams and gave them the authority to correct problems immediately.[10]

Businesses seem to be responding with cautious cooperation to government regulations designed to protect employees. Some appear to be complying only with the letter of the law; others are exceeding government standards to avoid regulatory investigation. In spite of these mixed results, many firms accept their responsibility to protect their employees' health and safety.

Workplace Violence

Another social issue affecting their employees' safety is challenging employers: violence in the workplace. Stories of angry or distraught employees, ex-employees, or associates of employees attacking workers, coworkers, or superiors at work are becoming more frequent. For example, there is a growing trend for workers who have lost their jobs to seek vengeance against individuals who terminated them, often in calculated and cold-blooded fashion. In a three-year period there were six shootings at a Detroit-area auto plant. In another incident, an employee fired eight years earlier from James River Corporation, a Pennsylvania paper products manufacturer, faked a family emergency to gain access to the company's executive offices. The former employee shot Brenton F. Halsey, Jr., vice president and the son of the company's founder, eight times before turning the gun on himself.

Nearly one-fourth of the 311 companies surveyed reported that at least one of their employees had been attacked or killed on the job since 1990. Another 31 percent claim threats have been made against workers. The Justice Department reported that nearly

---

[10]Michael A. Verespej, "Better Safety through Empowerment," *Industry Week,* November 15, 1993, pp. 56–68.

one million people every year were victims of violent crimes while working, costing 1.75 million days of lost work and over $55 million in lost wages.[11]

Unfortunately, many companies are poorly prepared to deal with these situations. Only 24 percent of employers offer any type of formal training to their employees in coping with workplace violence, and just 10 percent offer this type of training to *all* employees. Government intervention in this area of employee safety is also lacking.

Working Conditions around the World

Recent headlines have turned the public's attention to the problem of sweatshops, factories where employees are forced to work long hours at low wages, under abhorrent working conditions. One of the most publicized scandals involved shoe manufacturer Nike. A study of the work conditions at Nike's factory in Vietnam reported that workers were paid below minimum wages, limited to one trip to the bathroom and two drinks of water per shift, verbally abused, sexually harassed, and commonly subjected to corporal punishment. Similar charges were made against four of the nation's largest retailers—Wal-Mart, Kmart, Nordstroms, and Limited—whose merchandise was made at New York City factories.[12]

In an effort to address the worldwide issue of work conditions, the Council on Economic Priorities introduced Social Accountability 8000, or SA 8000. Modeled after the quality initiative developed by the International Organization for Standardization, ISO 9000 (now used in 80 countries), SA 8000 established criteria for companies to meet in order to receive a "good working condition" certification. The criteria include:

- Do not use child or forced labor.
- Provide a safe working environment.
- Respect workers' rights to unionize.
- Do not regularly require more than 48-hour workweek.
- Pay wages sufficient to meet workers' basic needs.

Workplace Diversity

The sheer diversity of the U.S. workforce spawns many new employee issues and problems. Women, African-Americans, Hispanics, Asians, the physically or mentally challenged, and other entrants are changing the nation's labor pool in dramatic ways. According to the Hudson Institute, 85 percent of the growth expected in the U.S. workforce by the year 2000 will come from white and nonwhite women, nonwhite men, and immigrants of both sexes and various races. As the large group of white men now dominant in the labor force ages and retires, they will occupy a smaller share of the total labor pool, only about 39 percent by the year 2000, according to the U.S. Department of Labor.

Businesses adjusting to these changes in the workforce may be in a position to reap the benefits of a well-integrated yet culturally diverse work population. These advantages

[11]"Disgruntled Workers Intent on Revenge Increasingly Harm Colleagues and Bosses," *The Wall Street Journal,* September 15, 1992, pp. B1, B10; "Waging War in the Workplace," *Newsweek,* July 19, 1993, pp. 30–31, 34; "Companies See More Workplace Violence," *The Wall Street Journal,* April 12, 1994, pp. B1, B6; "Murder in Workplace Is a Major Part of the Latest Death-on-the-Job Statistics," *The Wall Street Journal,* August 11, 1994, p. A4; and Jim McKay, "Worked Over at Work," *Pittsburgh Post-Gazette,* May 28, 1995, p. C1.
[12]"Nike Workers in Vietnam Suffer Abuse, Group Says," *The Wall Street Journal,* March 28, 1997, p. B15.

include attracting applicants from a large potential labor pool, a work environment enriched by multiple cultures, and the ability to meet the needs of a culturally diverse customer base in the United States and abroad.

> *Voice Processing Corporation, which manufactures speech-recognition software, has 11 nationalities represented among its 40 corporate headquarters' staff members. Combined, these employees speak 30 languages, including Mandarin Chinese, Russian, Hindi, Turkish, Thai, and Serbo-Croatian. The multilingual workforce enabled Voice Processing to more easily introduce and market its products in countries all over the world.*[13]

Language in the Workplace

About one of five workers seeking jobs in the 1990s was a recent immigrant. For employers, that often meant relying on employees whose limited knowledge of English could interfere with their work.

> *Motorola confronted the problem by offering to meet employees halfway. English communication classes were provided at the company's expense and, increasingly, on company time. The company spent over $30 million on the program, which included basic literacy for English speakers. Motorola says about 6,000 employees received language training.*

The push for on-the-job language efficiency can lead to problems, however, if a company decides that all of its rules and regulations must be exclusively in English. The U.S. Supreme Court has upheld these English-only rules. In 1994, the Court refused to overturn a lower court ruling that permitted a California company to require its employees to speak English on the job. However, according to the U.S. Equal Employment Opportunity Commission, these practices can be used to discriminate against certain groups at work, thereby heightening ethnic tensions. Where non-English-speaking employees make up a large bulk of a company's workforce, employers need to demonstrate a commitment to fairness by adopting a flexible language policy.

Managing a Diverse Workforce

Managers have many new lessons to learn if they are to be effective in motivating and directing their multicultural employees. One lesson is to listen—to hear the distinct and often subtle ways of speaking and communicating that are routinely used by various ethnic groups, and to hear the often submerged voices of women employees, Hispanics, Native Americans, African-Americans, Asian-Americans, the physically or mentally challenged, and others. Yet, as shown in Exhibit 16–B, it may require a costly lawsuit to become more attentive to workplace diversity issues.

> *A group of regional and national companies have formed the Diversity Council. The purpose of the organization is to help member firms manage diversity issues through cooperative efforts. Through the council, member firms are able to share ideas and participate in group problem solving for workforce diversity management and training. Managing the corporate culture regarding diversity*

[13]"Small Company Goes Global with Diverse Work Force," *Wall Street Journal,* October 12, 1994, p. B2.

EXHIBIT
16–B

Diversity at Shoney's

Raymond Danner, cofounder of Shoney's restaurants, liked to shake up the staffs at his restaurants because some of them "were too dark." Employees claimed that he ordered managers to fire black employees if they seemed too visible to white customers. He would often make racial slurs at work. Now retired, Danner gives heavily to black causes and believes that the restaurant staffs need to be more representative of minorities in America's ever-changing business environment. "We have a policy of zero tolerance [at Shoney's]," said Juanita Presley, a black lawyer and one of two employees investigating discrimination and harassment complaints at the company.

So what took Shoney's from racial insensitivity to a company aggressively pursuing workplace diversity? A costly, attention-grabbing lawsuit, changing times, and, some think, an actual change of heart by Shoney's leadership.

Since 1989, the family-style restaurant chain added 83 black dining-room supervisors. Two of its 24 vice presidents were black, and an African-American was on the company's nine-member board of directors. Black-owned franchises had increased from 2 in 1989 to 13 in 1996. The firm spent $17 million annually to buy goods and services from minority-owned companies in 1996, compared with $2 million in 1989.

The company operated an 800-number, posted in all corporate offices and its 700 restaurants, to field complaints about racial discrimination or harassment. In 1996, it fired an employee who left racial slurs on a tape recording, reinforcing its claim of having a zero tolerance policy on racism.

The firm came a long way since taking a $77.2 million charge to settle the class-action lawsuit, which claimed that Shoney's was a racist enterprise. In total, Shoney employees who filed the lawsuit received $105 million, with Raymond Danner paying over $50 million out of his own pocket.

Source: Dorothy J. Gaiter, "How Shoney's, Belted by a Lawsuit, Found the Path to Diversity," *The Wall Street Journal,* April 16, 1996, pp. A1, A6.

involves providing a work environment that encourages all employees to perform their best and to feel that they are part of the company. To be successful, firms must adopt cultural diversity as a corporate priority and recognize the different ways people think, see, and respond to the world around them.

When employees believe they are respected, rather than ridiculed, for the way they talk, for the way they approach business problems, or for their gender or ethnic background, their morale is higher and a company's productivity tends to be higher.

Corporations in the United States are slowly beginning to acknowledge differences in employee sexual orientation and lifestyles. Gay and lesbian employees are becoming a vocal minority, winning important victories in the courts. Spurred by this mounting pressure, firms are responding.

More than 350 U.S. and Canadian corporations offered domestic-partner benefits, including coverage for the partners of gay employees. Lotus Development was the first major employer to offer spousal benefits to same-sex partners. AT&T, Chase Manhattan, General Motors Canada, and Microsoft are among other firms responding to employee sexual orientation diversity. A few firms also cover heterosexual unmarried couples, including Ben and Jerry's, Levi Strauss, Federal National Mortgage Association, and Borland International.[14]

Addressing issues of cultural or sexual diversity in the workplace is simply another way of saying what other chapters in this book say: business operations always occur within a social and cultural setting, and the best managers are those who make their decisions on that basis. The next chapter in this book focuses on the workplace issues that occur as greater numbers of women seek jobs.

Challenging Employees' Privacy

Privacy rights in the business context refer primarily to protecting a person's private life from intrusive and unwarranted business actions. The employees believe that their religious, political, and social beliefs, as well as personal lifestyles, are private matters and should be safeguarded from snooping or analysis. Exceptions are permitted grudgingly only when job involvement is clearly proved. For example, it may be appropriate to know that an employee is discussing with a competitor, through e-mail messages, the specifications of a newly developed product not yet on the market. Other behaviors are not so clear-cut. For example, should a job applicant who is experiencing severe financial problems be denied employment out of fear that he may be more inclined to steal from the company? Should an employee be terminated after the firm discovers that she has a serious medical problem, although it does not affect her job performance, since the company's health insurance premiums may dramatically increase? At what point do company interests weigh more heavily than an employee's right to freedom and privacy?

Information Technology

As discussed in Chapter 18, the technology age brought many ethical issues to the forefront. A company's need for information, particularly about employees, to conduct business may be at odds with an employee's privacy. Several federal laws govern the dissemination of information: the Fair Credit Reporting Act (1970), Privacy Act (1974), Right to Financial Privacy Act (1978), Video Privacy Protection Act (1988), and Computer Matching and Privacy Protection Act (1988). Each of these laws has loopholes. For example, under the Fair Credit Reporting Act, anyone with a "legitimate business need" can gain access to personal information in credit files. The Right to Financial Privacy Act is intended to forbid access to individuals' bank accounts; however, the act makes exceptions for state agencies, law enforcement officials, and private employers.

Besides the collection and storage of employee information, corporations are actively involved in observing workers' activities. Since employers are exempt from the Electronic Communications Privacy Act (1986), they are free at any time to view employees on closed-circuit televisions, to tap their telephones, e-mail, and network communications, and to rummage through their computer files with or without employee knowledge or consent.

---

[14]"Gay Employees Win Benefits for Partners at More Corporations," *Wall Street Journal,* March 18, 1994, pp. A1, A2.

The ability of employers to monitor employee activities exploded in the 1990s with the greater availability of sophisticated surveillance equipment, the greater affordability of this equipment, and the ease of access to employee activity through technological advances in e-mail and facsimile machines (faxes), as the following example illustrates.

> *Procter & Gamble's (P&G) company practices were exposed in a book,* Soap Opera: The Inside Story of Procter & Gamble, *by Alecia Swasy. In the book, the company's activities of routinely obtaining medical records of employees, watching them with video cameras, monitoring their telephone calls from P&G offices and their homes, and following them on business trips were described. For years, the firm employed former agents from the government's Central Intelligence Agency and Federal Bureau of Investigation, as well as former police officers, as part of a security department that conducted investigations that bordered on harassment and invasions of privacy, according to Swasy.*[15]

Management justifies the increase in employee monitoring for a number of reasons: to achieve greater efficiency at work, to maintain an honest workforce and protect the firm from employee theft, and to reduce health insurance premiums by reducing employee negligence or failure to comply with safety regulations. Yet employees are becoming more aware of corporate monitoring and are challenging it in court as an invasion of privacy. Judges have ruled that workers must prove that their reasonable expectations for privacy outweigh the company's reasons for secretive monitoring. Employers sometimes satisfy the court's demands by simply informing workers of the company's surveillance policies. Others require job applicants to sign a privacy waiver before being hired.

AIDS Testing

AIDS has become a major public health problem. Emerging first among homosexual males and drug users, the AIDS epidemic now affects all segments of the world's population. It was estimated that by the year 2005 approximately 1 in every 250 Americans would be infected with the human immunodeficiency virus (HIV) that causes AIDS. The problem of exposure is far greater in other countries, particularly in Africa and Asia. Education seems to be the key in controlling the spread of AIDS. New drug therapies have also allowed those infected with the disease to live longer. The Center for Disease Control reported in 1996 that for the first time fewer of those infected with AIDS were dying than in the previous year.[16]

In business, employees with AIDS are protected against discrimination. In 1990, the federal government passed the strongest anti-AIDS discrimination legislation embodied in the Americans with Disabilities Act, introduced earlier in this chapter. More than 30 states have laws that bar job discrimination against people with AIDS. Yet the issue of AIDS testing is a highly volatile topic. Opponents of AIDS testing argue that employees should not be tested for the presence of HIV because it would be an invasion of privacy, the available tests are frequently inaccurate, and the tests do not reveal whether a person having AIDS

---

[15]"Is Your Boss Spying on You?" *Business Week,* January 15, 1990, pp. 74–75; "P&G Keeps Tabs on Workers, Others, New Book Asserts," *The Wall Street Journal,* September 7, 1993, pp. A3, A10; and Alecia Swasy, *Soap Opera: The Inside Story of Procter & Gamble* (New York: Times Books, 1993).

[16]"Insurance Industry and the AIDS Epidemic," the Insure Foundation, June 1995; and Oscar Suris, "AIDS Deaths Drop Significantly for First Time," *The Wall Street Journal,* February 28, 1997, pp. B1, B16.

antibodies will ever develop the disease. According to guidelines issued in 1985 by the U.S. Department of Health and Human Services, since AIDS cannot be contracted by casual and normal workplace contacts, employees with the illness should not be segregated from others nor should they be restricted in performing jobs for which they are qualified.

As noted earlier, many firms believe that information is the best defense against AIDS. The benefits of such an information program are listed in Figure 16–4. Even so, AIDS imposes costs on companies, especially through their health benefit programs. Insurance companies favor trying to isolate high-risk applicants by means of AIDS antibody tests, fighting off attempts by some states to ban such blood tests and using substitutes for tests where they are banned. Insurers also favor denying new policies on grounds of the enormous costs to society; they aggressively fight existing policyholders' claims in court. According to the National Commission on AIDS, if this nation is to conquer AIDS then "strong, positive leadership is needed to overcome ignorance and fear, as well as to rectify the serious flaws and deficits in care and prevention strategies."[17]

Smoking in the Workplace

The life-threatening health dangers of tobacco for smokers have been repeatedly proven in medical research studies, as reported in the case study "The Tobacco Deal" at the end of this textbook. In addition, health officials estimate that environmental tobacco smoke—smoke emitted from a lit cigarette, cigar, or pipe, or exhaled by a smoker—causes nearly 50,000 nonsmoker deaths in the United States each year. Concern about the effects of smoking on nonsmokers has led many companies to restrict smoking to designated areas and private offices. Other firms have completely banned smoking on company grounds. A more extreme corporate policy is described in the following example.

> *As you enter the lobby of Kimball Plastics, an electronic manufacturer, receptionist Jennifer Walsh administered the "sniff test." If a whiff of tobacco smoke was detected on your breath, hair or clothes, you were asked to step outside. According to the firm's antismoking policy, to protect its employees' health, no one who has smoked in the previous two hours or smells of smoke is admitted into the company's laboratories. Kimball Plastics' 50 employees were on the honor system, but if any employee complained of a tobacco smell, the offending coworker faced disciplinary charges.*

Figure 16–4

Advantages of an AIDS information program.

- Minimizes disruption in the workplace
- Decreases chances of costly litigation
- Establishes consistent company guidelines
- Reduces health-care costs
- Enhances employee-employer relations
- Provides up-to-date AIDS information to employees
- Promotes a responsible corporate public image

[17]"How Insurers Succeed in Limiting Their Losses Related to the Disease," *The Wall Street Journal,* May 18, 1987, p. 12; and "Who Will Pay the AIDS Bill?" *Business Week,* April 11, 1988, p. 71. Quotation by the National Commission on AIDS is from Romuald A. Stone, "AIDS in the Workplace: An Executive Update," *Academy of Management Executive* 8, no. 3 (1994), pp. 52–64.

Estimates of the cost of smoking in the workplace provide additional support for corporate smoking bans. Over $47 million is lost annually because of productivity loss and disability time related to smoking. A smoker, on average, costs his or her firm $753 annually in medical expenses and misses two more workdays per year than a nonsmoker. Many firms offer their employees smoking-cessation programs, which cost about $165 per person.

Employees who smoke were divided in their reaction to smoking restrictions or bans at work. Some smokers welcomed the opportunity to stop smoking, and many took advantage of company-paid smoking-cessation programs. Others, however, were incensed at what they perceived as a violation of personal rights and freedoms. Some employers have sought government protection from the growing intolerance of workplace smoking and have joined the tobacco industry in appealing to state legislatures. By the mid-1990s, 28 states and the District of Columbia had passed laws making job discrimination against smokers illegal. Although the laws do not affect office smoking bans or smoke-free areas in the workplace, they do prohibit companies from refusing to hire smokers and from firing employees who choose to continue to smoke.

Employees' Rights and Responsibilities

Just as an employer must assume certain duties and obligations in the employee-employer relationship, so must the employee as a corporate stakeholder assume certain responsibilities. Employees have rights that must be protected from violation by the employer, yet workers can lose their privileged rights through irresponsible or illegal activities. It is possible that employees' responsibilities to coworkers, an industry, or society can place the employee at odds with the employer.

Whistle-Blowing

Sometimes the loyal bonds between a company and an employee are strained to the breaking point, especially when a worker thinks the company is doing something wrong or harmful to the public. When an employee reports alleged organizational misconduct to the public or to high-level company officials, **whistle-blowing** has occurred. In the United States, employee whistle-blowers exposed fraud in the country's defense contracting system and in the health-care, municipal bond, and pharmaceutical industries. One of the most publicized whistle-blowers in the 1990s alleged fraud within the tobacco industry.[18]

Government protection for whistle-blowers has increased at federal and state levels. The federal False Claims Act permits employees to sue companies suspected of government fraud and then to share in any financial restitution. Another federal law protects federal employees from retaliation by their supervisors when they expose government waste or fraud. Under the growing possibility of similar legal assistance for employees of private companies, employees are more willing to challenge employers' actions in the courts.

Whistle-blowing has both defenders and detractors. Those defending whistle-blowing point to the millions of dollars of fraudulent activities detected in the defense and health-care industries. Under the False Claims Act, more than $1.2 billion was returned

---

[18]For a sample of articles on whistle-blowers, see Randall Smith, "Whistle-Blower Rattles the Muni Industry," *Wall Street Journal,* July 17, 1995, pp. C1, C14; and Suein L. Hwang, "The Executive Who Told Tobacco's Secrets," *Wall Street Journal,* November 28, 1995, pp. B1, B6.

to the federal government, otherwise lost to fraud. However, opponents of whistle-blowing cite the hundreds of unsubstantiated cases, often used by disgruntled workers seeking to blackmail their employers.[19]

Generally, employees are not free to speak out against their employers because there is a public interest in allowing companies to operate without harassment from insiders. Company information is generally considered to be proprietary and private. If employees, based on their personal points of view, are freely allowed to expose issues to the public and allege misconduct, the company may be thrown into turmoil and be unable to operate effectively. On the other hand, there may be situations in which society's interests override those of the company, so an employee may feel an obligation to blow the whistle. According to one expert, certain conditions must be satisfied to morally justify blowing the whistle to outsiders (e.g., informing the media or government officials):

- The unreported act would do serious and considerable harm to the public.
- Once such an act has been identified, the employee has reported the act to his or her immediate supervisor and has made the moral concern known.
- If the immediate supervisor does nothing, the employee tries other internal pathways for reporting the problem.[20]

Only after each of these conditions has been met should the whistle-blower go public.

Testing to Control Employees' Actions

The issues discussed in this section focus on actions taken by businesses to control particular employee behavior. For example, the rampant increase in employee drug and alcohol use on the job or its affect on job performance prompted companies to institute drug and alcohol testing. Employee theft gave impetus to employers conducting honesty tests of their employees and job applicants.

Employee Drug Use and Testing

Abuse of drugs, particularly hard drugs such as heroin and cocaine, has become an epidemic problem for employers. By the late 1980s, 75 percent of drug users reported that they had used drugs on the job, and 64 percent said that they had sold drugs on the job. Eighteen percent of drug users had drug-related job accidents, and 60 percent reported impaired job performance. Nearly one in five said they stole from their employer to pay for drugs. Drug abuse costs the U.S. industry and taxpayers an estimated $176 billion in health claims, compensation, and lost workdays, including $99 billion in lost productivity.

One way business has dealt with on-the-job drug abuse is through drug testing. Company drug testing increased from 5 percent in 1982 to almost 50 percent in 1988 to 84 percent in 1993. Some of this increase may be attributed to the Drug-Free Workplace Act of 1988, which requires federal contractors to establish and maintain a workplace free of drugs. Tests of job applicants in several different industries revealed that, in 1988, 12 percent of prospective employees tested positive. The SmithKlein Beecham Clinical Labo-

[19]Catherine Yang and Mike France, "Whistle-Blowers On Trial," *Business Week,* March 24, 1997, pp. 172–174, 178.

[20]Richard DeGeorge, *Business Ethics,* 4th ed. (Englewood Cliffs, NJ: Prentice Hall, 1995), pp. 231–38.

ratories, which performed more than 3.6 million workplace drug tests annually, reported a decline in positive tests over seven consecutive years.[21]

Typically, drug testing is used on three different occasions.

- *Preemployment screening.* Some companies test all job applicants or selected applicants before hiring, usually as part of a physical examination, often informing the applicant ahead of time that there will be a drug screening.

- *Random testing of employees.* This type of screening may occur at various times throughout the year. In many companies, a member of a particular job category (e.g., an operator of heavy machinery) or job level (e.g., a supervisor) is eligible for screening at any time.

- *Testing for cause.* This test occurs when an employee is believed to be impaired by drugs and unfit for work. It is commonly used after an accident or some observable change in behavior.

Small businesses are also becoming more involved in employee drug testing. "The word on the street is that people with drug problems are going to small companies because they know that the IBMs and the Xeroxes and the GTEs are drug screening and have been for years," said an operations vice president at Corporate Wellness, a drug consulting firm.[22] So, employers at small businesses see a growing need to protect themselves from drug abusers.

The debate over employee drug testing is summarized in Figure 16–5. In general, proponents of testing emphasize the need to control the potential harm to others and the

Figure 16–5

Pros and cons of employee drug testing.

Arguments favoring employee drug testing
• Business cooperation with U.S. "War on Drugs" campaign
• Improves employee productivity
• Promotes safety in the workplace
• Decreases employee theft and absenteeism
• Reduces health and insurance costs
Arguments opposing employee drug testing
• Invades an employee's privacy
• Violates an employee's right to due process
• May be unrelated to job performance
• May be used as a method of employee discrimination
• Lowers employee morale
• Conflicts with company values of honesty and trust
• May yield unreliable test results
• Ignores effects of prescription drugs, alcohol, and over-the-counter drugs
• Drug use an insignificant problem for some companies

[21]For a presentation of the 1993 American Management Association study of workplace drug testing, see "Fewer People Fail as Workplace Drug Testing Increases," *HR Focus,* June 1993, p. 24. Also see, "Workplace Drug Tests Show Fewer Positives," *The Wall Street Journal,* March 7, 1995, p. B6.

[22]"Small Companies Move to Increase Anti-Drug Programs," *The Wall Street Journal,* November 6, 1990, p. B2.

cost to business and society attributed to drug use on the job. Opponents challenge the benefits of drug testing and its intrusion on individual privacy.

Alcohol Abuse at Work

Another form of employee substance abuse, which causes twice the problems of all illegal drugs combined, also challenges employers: alcohol use and addiction. Studies show that up to 40 percent of all industrial fatalities and 47 percent of industrial injuries are due to alcohol abuse. U.S. businesses lose an estimated $102 billion per year in productivity directly related to alcohol abuse.[23]

Company programs for drug abusers and alcohol abusers are often combined. Since the 1980s, an increasing number of firms recognized that they had a role to play in helping alcoholics control or break their habit. As with drug rehabilitation programs, most alcoholism programs work through employee assistance programs (EAPs) that offer counseling and follow-up. In 1994, 84 percent of companies responding to a survey indicated that they provide EAPs for alcohol and drug abusers. United Airlines' EAP reported dramatic reductions of absenteeism plus excellent recovery rates during a 10-year period, and it is considered a model for other firms.

Employee Theft and Honesty Testing

Employees can irresponsibly damage themselves, their coworkers, and their employer by stealing from the company. Employee theft has emerged as a significant economic, social, and ethical problem in the workplace. It accounts for an estimated 60 percent of all retail losses, and employee-related thefts occur 15 times more often than shoplifting. The U.S. Department of Commerce estimates that employee theft of cash, merchandise, and property costs businesses $40 to $50 billion a year. Employee theft accounts for 20 percent of the nation's business failures. In Canada, employee theft costs firms $20 billion a year.[24]

Many companies in the past used polygraph testing as a preemployment screening procedure or on discovery of employee theft. In 1988, the Employee Polygraph Protection Act became law. This law severely limited polygraph testing by employers and prohibited approximately 85 percent of all such tests previously administered in the United States. In response to the federal ban on polygraphs, many corporations have switched to written psychological tests, or **honesty tests,** that seek to predict employee honesty on the job. These pen-and-paper tests rely on answers to a series of questions that are designed to identify undesirable qualities in the test taker. When a British chain of home improvement centers used such tests to screen more than 4,000 applicants, theft dropped from 4 percent to 2.5 percent, and actual losses from theft were reduced from 3.75 million pounds to 2.62 million pounds.

The use of honesty tests, like polygraphs, is controversial. The American Psychological Association noted that there is a significant potential for these tests to generate false positives, indicating that the employee probably would or did steal from the company even though this is not true. After extensively studying the validity of honesty tests

---

[23]"Alcohol and Other Drugs in the Workplace," National Council on Alcoholism and Drug Dependencies, http://www.ncadd.org/workplace.html (January 12, 1998).

[24]"A Critical Look at Loss Prevention and Employee Theft," *Vito's Private Investigation Newsletter,* http://www.americasbright.com/employer/vito/new961101.html (November 1–15, 1996).

and the behavior they try to predict, Dan Dalton and Michael Metzger, leading academic researchers in this field, concluded that the tests are only 13.6 percent accurate at best and only 1.7 percent accurate at their worst. Critics also argue that the tests intrude on a person's privacy and discriminate disproportionately against minorities.[25]

Employees as Corporate Stakeholders

The issues discussed in this chapter illustrate forcefully that today's business corporation is open to a wide range of social forces. Its borders are very porous, letting in a constant flow of external influences. Many of these social forces are brought inside by employees whose personal values, lifestyles, and social attitudes become a vital part of the workplace.

Managers and other business professionals need to be aware of these employee-imported features of today's workforce. The employee-employer relationship is central to getting a corporation's work done and to helping satisfy the wishes of those who contribute their skills and talents to the company. The task of a corporate manager is to reconcile potential clashes between employees' human needs and the requirements of corporate economic production. Acknowledging the important stake that employees have in the successful pursuit of a corporation's economic mission enables business leaders to cope more effectively with the many issues that concern employees.

Summary Points of This Chapter

- Fierce global competition and other economic factors led to dramatic employee downsizing worldwide. Employers no longer assumed the responsibility of maintaining long-term job security for their employees. Instead, employees were expected to contribute to the firm's success and thus increase their employability.

- U.S. labor laws give most workers the right to organize unions and to bargain collectively with their employers. Some believe that unions are poised for a resurgence after many years of decline.

- Job safety and health concerns have increased as a result of rapidly changing technology in the workplace. Employers must comply with expanding OSHA regulations and respond to the growing trend toward violence at work.

- An increasingly diverse workforce requires corporate managers to respect and be able to deal effectively with a wide range of cultures and social attitudes among today's employees.

- Employees' privacy rights are frequently challenged by employers' needs to have information about their health, their work activities, and even their off-the-job lifestyles.

[25]Support for the reliability of honesty tests can be found in Denis S. Ones, Cockalingam Viswesvaran, and Frank L. Schmidt, "Comprehensive Meta-Analysis of Integrity Test Validities: Findings and Implications for Personnel Selection and Theories of Job Performance," *Journal of Applied Psychology,* August 1993, pp. 679–703; and H. John Bernardin and Donna K. Cooke, "Validity of an Honesty Test in Predicting Theft among Convenience Store Employees," *Academy of Management Journal,* October 1993, pp. 1097–108. The American Psychological Association's challenge to these tests and the opinions noted in this paragraph can be found in Dan R. Dalton and Michael B. Metzger, "'Integrity Testing' for Personnel Selection: An Unsparing Perspective," *Journal of Business Ethics,* February 1993, pp. 147–56.

When these issues arise, management has a responsibility to act ethically toward employees while continuing to work for a high level of economic performance.

- Blowing the whistle on one's employer is often a last resort to protest company actions considered to be harmful to others. It can usually be avoided if corporate managers encourage open communication and show a willingness to listen to their employees.

Key Terms and Concepts Used in This Chapter

- Employment-at-will
- Employer-employee social contract
- Equal job opportunity
- Equal Employment Opportunity Commission (EEOC)
- Affirmative action
- Whistle-blowing
- Reverse discrimination

- Ergonomics
- Occupational Safety and Health Administration (OSHA)
- Workplace safety teams
- Privacy rights
- Honesty tests

Internet Resources

- http:// www.drugfreeworkplace.org   Institute for a Drug-Free Workplace
- http:// www.eeoc.gov   United States Equal Employment Opportunity Commission
- http://www.osha.gov   United States Department of Labor, Occupational Safety and Health Administration
- http://www.whistleblowers.org   National Whistleblowers Center

Discussion Case   Responding to AIDS in the Workplace

Tim, a service-support manager for San Francisco—based Wells Fargo Bank, had been an exemplary employee for several years. A strong leader who had a good reputation, 32-year-old Tim was well liked by upper management and the 15 employees he supervised.

This up-and-coming individual also had a medical condition that was beginning to wear down his body's immune system. Infected with the human immunodeficiency virus, Tim had developed a form of AIDS, which can result in such symptoms as shortness of breath, a lingering dry cough, skin rashes, extreme fatigue, and lightheadedness. Symptoms never surface in many people who are infected, and others develop conditions years after infection.

Extreme fatigue became part of Tim's daily life and was a detriment to his usual top-notch performance. As his health deteriorated, he began to realize his physical limitations. About 15 months earlier, Tim revealed the information about his health to his middle-management supervisor, Sandra. He asked her to keep the news confidential. Tim was aware of his condition several months before he informed his manager. Because HIV is not contagious through casual contact, this individual was not a health risk to other bank employees and therefore was under no obligation to share such personal information with his employer. Because he could not keep up with his workload, however, Tim wanted to inform Sandra that the problem was medical. Knowing that Wells Fargo's policy on HIV ensured his confidentiality, Tim believed that the company would accommodate him by not disclosing his illness.

After her discussion with Tim, Sandra consulted Bryan Lawton, the bank's employee assistance director and a clinical psychologist. She asked how to respond to managers and employees who have questions about workers who have HIV. "Sandra was distressed because she was concerned about Tim's health," said Lawton. Tim was showing signs of fatigue and was missing work. His coworkers began to wonder if he was ill. "Sandra was afraid that Tim was wearing himself down," Lawton added. "She also was concerned about the impact the illness was having on the people he supervised—people who had suspicions about him being infected with the disease, but who didn't know what to say or do."

Sandra was aware of the company's four-point policy:

- Keep confidential all information about the medical condition and medical records of an employee who has AIDS.
- Consult Employee Assistance Services (EAS) immediately after learning that an employee has been diagnosed with AIDS.
- Work with EAS and your personnel officer to arrange job accommodations that are deemed medically necessary for the employee with this condition.
- Help employees learn about AIDS by asking EAS for the AIDS Education Program.

Yet, even though Sandra was aware of the policy, she had never had to implement it or manage its effects. She had several questions and needed assistance in how to implement company policy on Tim's behalf. She also wanted to demonstrate concern and compassion for her fellow employee while staying within the legal boundaries of confidentiality. One particular point of interest for Sandra was possible job-based adjustments that Tim might need in the months ahead. Because Tim was a valued employee, Sandra wanted to minimize his concerns while maximizing his tenure.

Source: Jennifer Laabs, copyright April 1990. Used with permission of ACC Communications Inc./*Personal Journal* (now known as *Workforce*), Costa Mesa, CA. All rights reserved.

Discussion Questions

1. Given the passage of the Americans with Disabilities Act, does the bank's AIDS policy adequately protect the rights of all Wells Fargo employees?
2. Is the protection of Tim's privacy rights more important than, less important than, or equally as important as the bank's need to be efficient in getting its day-to-day work done? Should Tim be removed from his job?
3. If Tim is given special job privileges because of his illness, would other bank employees have a right to complain about unequal and discriminatory treatment?

Part Seven

Social Issues

17

Women, Work, and the Family

Developing opportunities for women who work in business has become a major social challenge for corporations. Barriers to women's equal participation in the workplace are yielding to the forces of economic change, greater need for skilled people in all categories, the demands of women to be treated equally, and equal opportunity laws. Achieving full workplace parity remains a goal to be reached. Women's greater participation in the nation's labor force has brought adjustments in family life and social values, requiring changes in corporate practices and policies.

This chapter focuses on these key questions and objectives:

- Why have women entered the workforce in such large numbers, and what problems have women faced as workers?

- What roles do women play as managers and business owners, and do women manage differently from men?

- What role does the government play in securing women's workplace rights and opportunities?

- What can companies do to develop policies and practices that promote women's workplace opportunities and support both women and men in their efforts to balance work and family responsibilities?

I n 1997, Jill Barad was promoted to the position of chief executive officer of Mattel, Inc., the toy maker. Barad, then 45 years old, had earned her spurs at Mattel by giving the venerable Barbie doll a makeover, transforming her into a doctor, teacher, and businesswoman, quadrupling the doll's revenues in a decade. Barad was the first woman to take leadership of a major U.S. corporation.

The same year, the Equal Employment Opportunity Commission (EEOC) announced that it would join a private lawsuit against Home Depot, Inc. The suit alleged that Home Depot, a retailer of home improvement products, hired women into low-level jobs, such as cashier, with little chance for advancement into sales or management positions. "Home Depot traps its female employees into what amounts to a glass basement," said a lawyer for the EEOC.[1]

These two examples capture some of the contradictions that face women in the business world in the United States. Nearly half of all U.S. workers, and more than 4 of every 10 managers, are women. For a half century, women have been entering the workforce in increasingly larger numbers, finding jobs formerly denied to them. Women have made great strides in the professions, skilled trades, and middle ranks of management. A few, like Jill Barad, have reached the pinnacle of success in corporate America. Yet most women, like those who are alleged to have experienced discrimination at Home Depot, still work in relatively low-paying jobs with poor prospects for upward mobility in traditionally female-dominated occupations.

The enormous transition that has occurred as women have entered the workforce in greater numbers has produced new social challenges. In this chapter, we discuss these changes and their implications for business. Understanding the history of women in society is a key to seeing what business can do today to meet these challenges.

The Status of Women in Society: Historical Background

The status of both women and men in society is largely a product of social custom and tradition. Customs evolve over extremely long periods of time, and they resist change. In all societies it is customary for men to perform certain tasks and for women to perform others. Once established, these distinctions between women's tasks and men's tasks—the **sexual division of labor**—tend to be accepted as proper and are reinforced over time by habit and custom. The sexual division of labor exerts a strong influence on the relative amounts of power and influence possessed by men and women within the family, clan, tribe, and larger society. Societies around the world and throughout history have varied greatly in how they arrange this basic division of labor.

Most societies in human history have been both patriarchal—men serve as head of the family or clan—and patrilineal—family lineage is traced through the father's ancestors. Because these male-centered social customs allocate power and privileges mainly to men, women have generally found themselves with relatively less social standing. Matriarchal societies—where women are politically, economically, and socially dominant—have occasionally existed but not as frequently. Generally it has been men, rather than women, who become chiefs, clan heads, tribal elders, shamans and priests, monarchs, presidents, prime ministers, generals, and corporate executives. Women's social standing

---

[1]"She Reinvented Barbie; Now, Can Jill Barad Do the Same for Mattel?," *The Wall Street Journal,* March 5, 1997, pp. A1, A8; and "U.S. to Intervene in Suit against Home Depot," *Los Angeles Times,* March 25, 1997, p. D3.

in these patriarchal (male-dominated) societies has been tied closely to childbearing and family sustenance.[2]

This general pattern of male-female relations continues in modern societies. Sex segregation based on custom has meant that today's women in general possess less economic and political power than men. Until quite recently, leadership positions in politics, government, business, religion, trade unions, sports, engineering, university teaching, military service, space exploration, science, and other fields have been considered off-limits to women. Although today's research demonstrates that women are as well qualified and capable as men to hold these high-level positions, sex discrimination based on custom, social habit, and gender bias has limited their opportunities.

Exhibit 17–A explains how these persistent, gender-based customs have affected the jobs women hold, even long after explicit sex discrimination was outlawed.

The Women's Movement

The women's movement that began in the 1960s and has continued to the present is the most recent phase of women's efforts to redress the unequal balance that cultural history has left on contemporary society's doorstep. The fight for equal rights for women in modern times began over a century earlier in England as women sought the right to vote. In the United States, women secured that same right in 1920 with the passage of the Nineteenth Amendment to the U.S. Constitution.

The women's movement that renewed itself among American women in the 1960s proved to be a watershed. On one side were customs that cast most women in their traditional roles of homemaker and helpmate to their male companions—loyal sister, dutiful

---

EXHIBIT 17–A

The Long Shadow of Sex Segregation

"The explicit policies to segregate the workplace and to fire married women that I have uncovered in the historical records of hundreds of firms would be clearly illegal today. . . . Many of these discriminatory policies, at least as the written procedures of firms, were abandoned sometime after 1950. Some were changed in the 1950s as a response to tighter labor supply conditions, while others were altered only later when the policies became clearly illegal. *But their impact remained long after.* If few women worked for extensive periods of time, even fewer would remain when jobs were dead end and when women were barred from promotional ladders. When virtually no woman was an accountant, for example, few would train to be accountants. And if women's work was defined in one way and men's in another, few individuals would choose to be the deviant, for deviance might cost one dearly outside the workplace. Thus change in the economic sphere is slowed not only by the necessity for cohorts (age groups) to effect change, but also by the institutionalization of various barriers and by the existence of social norms maintained by strong sanctions."

Source: Claudia Goldin, *Understanding the Gender Gap: An Economic History of American Women.* Copyright © 1990 by Oxford University Press, Inc. Reprinted by permission. Emphasis added.

---

[2]For a discussion of the history of patriarchy, see Gerda Lerner, *The Creation of Patriarchy* (New York: Oxford University Press, 1986).

daughter, faithful wife, nurturing mother. On the other side, events produced a new attitude toward women's place in society. This attitude supported the liberation of women from customary restraints and emphasized the importance of equality, greater choice, and personal control. Without rejecting the vital social contributions women had long made, leaders of the movement nevertheless advocated greater independence for women and a re-examination of long-accepted social habits and attitudes. In this new climate, women began to question their roles, their lives, their relationships, and where it all was leading them.[3]

This questioning ran deeper than had the earlier struggles of women to gain the right to vote, to own and control property, and to regulate family size. None of those earlier campaigns, even when successful, had seriously challenged society's prevailing distribution of power, privileges, and jobs that favored men. Women now were seeking equal rights, equal privileges, and the kind of liberty that would permit them to pursue lives determined largely by options of their own choosing. Their aims were self-determination and social justice, which meant having an equal claim on human rights and an equal standing with others around them.

Some believe that the women's movement lost ground in meeting these goals during the 1980s, a decade characterized by author Susan Faludi as one of backlash against women. A 1995 survey found that 45 percent of women believed that women were still mostly given low- or mid-level jobs, while men held the real power.[4]

Why Women Have Entered the Workplace

Women have always worked, whether paid or not. In farming-based societies, including the United States through the mid-1800s, the family was the primary economic unit. Women's work was essential to the family economy and involved farming, food preparation, the manufacture of household items, and the care of children. In the slave-based system of the southern states prior to the Civil War, the labor of African-American women made essential contributions to the plantation economy. The advent of the industrial revolution in the early and mid-1800s profoundly altered the nature of women's work by bringing females into the wage labor force. During the late 1800s and the first half of the 1900s, with the exception of periods of wartime, women who worked outside the home were mostly young and single, widowed or divorced, or married to men unable for some reason to support their families.

During the post–World War II period, the proportion of women working outside the home rose dramatically, as shown in Figure 17–1. In 1950, about a third of adult women were employed. This proportion has risen almost steadily since, standing at 59 percent in 1996. Participation rates (the proportion of women in the workforce) have risen for all groups of women, but the most dramatic increases have been among married women, mothers of young children, and middle-class women, those who had earlier been most likely to stay at home. Men's participation rates declined somewhat during this period; by the year 2005, the proportions of adult women and men at work are projected to be within 7 percentage points of each other (66 percent and 73 percent, respectively). The expanding participation of women in the workforce has posed many challenges for business.

---

[3]The seminal work that energized the U.S. women's movement is Betty Friedan's *The Feminine Mystique,* first published in 1963. For her views of what the movement had accomplished after 20 years, see the foreword of *The Feminine Mystique,* 20th anniversary ed. (New York: Norton, 1983).
[4]Susan Faludi, *Backlash: The Undeclared War against American Women* (New York: Doubleday, 1991); and "Women More Pessimistic about Work," *New York Times,* September 12, 1995, p. D5.

Figure 17–1

Proportion of women
in the labor force,
1950–1996.

Source: U.S. Bureau of
Labor Statistics.

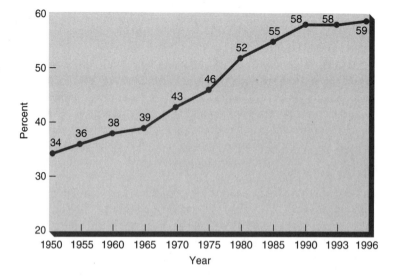

Women have entered the workforce for many of the same reasons men do. They need income to support themselves, their children, their aging, retired, or sick parents or other close relatives, and their marital partner, and to enjoy a satisfying lifestyle. A paycheck is a ticket to economic freedom, a symbol of freeing oneself from having to ask others for money to pursue one's own interests. Having a job with pay also gives a woman psychological independence and security. It can open up new vistas of opportunity, permitting and encouraging higher degrees of self-actualization. Being economically productive and contributing to society through paid work contributes as much to women's as to men's sense of self-esteem.

When marriages terminate, through either divorce or the death of one partner, the remaining person usually needs a paying job. Many women who choose not to work outside the home during their married life confront this necessity when joint savings or life insurance are inadequate for their post-marriage life. Research reveals that most women, even those with jobs, suffer a decline in their living standard following divorce. During the 1980s and 1990s, when many corporate takeovers and mergers, along with increased global competition, resulted in massive job layoffs, working women often found themselves the sole breadwinners in their families.

Inflation also puts financial pressure on families, frequently pushing women into the labor force just to sustain an accustomed standard of living or to put children through college or to care for aging parents. The inadequacies and uncertainties of retirement plans and health-care programs frequently mean that women, as well as men, need to save, invest, and plan for the future.

The rapid rise of female labor force participation also reflects the expansion of segments of the economy that were major employers of women. In 1940, about one-third of all U.S. jobs were white-collar (not requiring manual labor); by 1980, over half were white-collar. Professional, technical, and service jobs also grew relative to the economy. The creation of many new positions in fields traditionally staffed by women produced what economists call a *demand-side* pull of women into the labor force. More "women's jobs" meant more women working.

The widespread entry of women into the labor force has changed the character of many families and some kinds of family life. In 1996, in half of U.S. married households—29 million families in all—both husband and wife worked, far outnumbering the traditional family in which the husband works while the wife remains at home, which comprised only 13 percent of married households. (In 24 percent, neither husband nor wife worked; in 8 percent, only the wife or other family member worked; and in 5 percent, one spouse and another family member worked.) The decline of traditional family arrangements, as more and more women have entered the labor force, has been responsible for much of the criticism directed toward women who work outside the home. It also has focused attention on the numbers and types of jobs actually held by women, which we examine next.

Where Women Work and What They Are Paid

Highlights about working women in the United States include the following:[5]

- Over half (59 percent) of all women are employed.
- Women make up nearly half (46 percent) of the entire labor force.
- Three-quarters of all working women (74 percent) have full-time jobs.
- Women now own nearly 8 million businesses, an increase of 78 percent in the decade ending in 1996.
- Almost two-thirds (63 percent) of married women with children under the age of six hold jobs outside the home.
- The main jobs held by women are administrative support and clerical work (25 percent of all women's jobs), service work (18 percent), and sales (13 percent). About one of every eight working women (13 percent) is a manager.
- Women hold 44 percent of all executive, administrative, and managerial posts, but most of these are at low and middle levels of organizations.
- Women make up 10 percent of *all* corporate officers, but only 2.4 percent of *top* corporate officers (chairman, vice chairman, CEO, president, chief operating officer, or executive vice president) at Fortune 500 companies.

Although women have become major participants in doing the paid work of U.S. society, their distribution among jobs and industries remains lopsided. They have found more places in the service industries than in manufacturing, mining, or agriculture. They serve more as clerks and low-level administrative helpers than as high-level leaders in organizational life, and as staff workers more than as workers in line jobs with central authority over policies and practices.

One persistent feature of the working world is that women on average receive lower pay than men. This **gender pay gap** narrowed during the 1980s and the early 1990s, but as Figure 17–2 shows, it widened again more recently. Women as a group still earned

[5]Bureau of Labor Statistics, Division of Labor Force Statistics, private communication; National Foundation for Women Business Owners, "Women-Owned Businesses in the United States 1996: A Fact Sheet," 1996; and Catalyst, "The 1996 Catalyst Census of Women Corporate Officers and Top Earners of the Fortune 500," New York, 1996. All data are for 1996.

Figure 17–2

The gender pay gap, 1980–1996.

Source: U.S. Bureau of Labor Statistics.

Women's Earnings as Percent of Men's Median Weekly Earnings (Full-time Employees)

Year	
1980	64
1985	68
1990	72
1992	75
1994	76
1996	75

only three-quarters of men's pay in 1996. The gap is narrower in some jobs that call for more education, or among younger workers or where the experience of men and women is more balanced. The gender pay gap is smaller between African-American and Hispanic women and men than between white women and men, reflecting the lower wages of non-white men.

Most observers believe that the pay gap persists because of what is called **occupational segregation,** which concentrates women in traditionally female-dominated jobs. In 1996, over a quarter (29 percent) of all working women were employed in what has been called the *pink-collar ghetto* of jobs dominated by women—clerk, waitress, nurse, child-care worker, cashier, elementary school teacher, secretary, retail salesworker, and health technologist (e.g., dental hygienist). Because so many women hold these relatively low-paying jobs, women's average income is pulled down below the average wages of men. The labor market produces this kind of occupational segregation partly because women find better-paying jobs less accessible to them when they look for work. In some cases, an entire occupational category such as bank teller or clerical worker will shift from employing all men to hiring virtually all women, as men move on to more attractive and high-paying job opportunities. Occupational segregation frequently means that women cannot get the jobs that could break the cycle of relatively low pay.[6]

Women in Management

The most prestigious and highest-paying jobs in a corporation are in top management. Because corporations are organized hierarchically, top management jobs are few in number. For that reason, only a minority of either men

[6]Diana M. Pearce, "Something Old, Something New: Women's Poverty in the 1990s," in Sherri Matteo, ed., *American Women in the Nineties,* (Boston: Northeastern University Press, 1993), pp. 79–97; and U.S. Department of Labor, private communication.

or women can hope to reach the upper levels of management. Men have traditionally filled most of these desirable spots. Business's challenge now is to broaden these high-level leadership opportunities for women.[7]

Where Women Manage

Almost 8 million U.S. women were managers by the mid-1990s, doubling their numbers in one decade. In 1996, as Figure 17–3 reveals, more than 4 out of every 10 managers—and a majority of managers in some categories, such as finance and health care—were women. Clearly, women have broken into management ranks. Women are more likely to be managers, though, in occupational areas where women are more numerous at lower levels, including medicine and health care, personnel, labor relations, and education. They also are concentrated in service industries and in finance, insurance, real estate, and retail businesses. Women managers have also made gains in newer industries, such as biotechnology, where growth has created opportunity.[8]

Where women managers are scarce is in the executive suites of large corporations. Ten percent of all corporate officer positions, but barely more than 2 percent of the very top jobs, are held by women. Women are also scarce on corporate boards; only 10 percent of board members of Fortune 500 firms were women in 1996. Occasional exceptions do occur, as at Student Loan Marketing Association, where women held 57 percent of corporate officer positions in 1995.[9]

Access to management jobs is restricted in most areas of the world, according to a study of women managers in several nations.

> *In country after country, the proportion of women holding managerial positions falls short of men's share. Corporations, it appears, have systematically ignored women as a potential resource. In all countries, the higher the rank within the organization, the fewer the women found there. In some countries, the percentages, though small, have increased over the last decade; but in none have they approached equality. This pattern prevails in oriental and occidental cultures, communist, socialist, and capitalist systems, and [in] both economically developed and developing countries.*[10]

---

[7] For a variety of perspectives on women in corporate management, see the special edition of *Journal of Business Ethics,* vol. 16, no. 9 (June 1997).

[8] "Biotech Industry Is Bonanza for Women," *The Wall Street Journal,* June 6, 1994, pp. B1, B10.

[9] Catalyst, "1996 Catalyst Census of Women Board Members of the Fortune 500," New York, 1996; and Catalyst, "Fact Sheet: 1996 Census of Women Corporate Officers and Top Earners," New York, 1996.

[10] Nancy Adler and Dafna N. Izraeli, eds., *Women in Management Worldwide* (Armonk, NY: Sharpe, 1988), pp. 7–8. For a discussion of international aspects, see also Nancy Adler and Dafna N. Izraeli, eds., *Competitive Frontiers: Women Managers in the Global Economy* (Cambridge, MA: Basil Blackwell, 1994); and Ariane Berthoin Antal and Dafna N. Izraeli, "A Global Comparison of Women in Management: Women Managers in Their Homelands and as Expatriates," in Ellen A. Fagenson, ed., *Women in Management: Trends, Issues, and Challenges in Management Diversity* (Newbury Park, CA: Sage, 1993). A recent account of the status of women managers in Europe may be found in "Out of the Typing Pool, into Career Limbo," *Business Week,* April 15, 1996, pp. 92–94. Profiles of women managers in several countries appear in "Women in Business: A Global Report Card," *The Wall Street Journal,* July 26, 1995, pp. B1, B12.

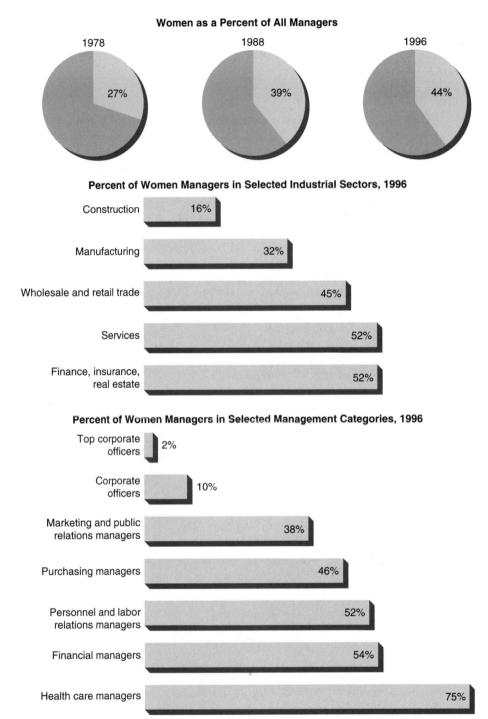

Figure 17–3

Where women manage.

Source: U.S. Bureau of Labor Statistics.

Do Women and Men Manage Differently?

When women do become managers, do they bring a different style and different skills to the job? Are they better, or worse, managers than men? Are women more highly motivated and committed than male managers? Are they accepted by those they manage, or do customary ways of thinking cause both men and women to react negatively to having female managers?

The research evidence strongly suggests that managers of both sexes do not seem to differ in any significant way in performing their tasks. Female managers do not appear to be more people-oriented than men, nor do they tackle task-oriented jobs less effectively than their male counterparts. Male managers and female managers score about the same on motivation tests. Women are sometimes more job-committed than men, at other times less. For both sexes, commitment is always stronger when people have satisfying jobs, when they believe their work is meaningful, and when their skills are used and appreciated. On-the-job sex discrimination can contribute to lowered job commitment by making the workplace less attractive for women.

The amount of time and commitment that anyone brings to a job and career is also affected by the amount of home-based support the individual receives. Women who bear a disproportionately large share of household tasks and family care may be unable to make as full a commitment to job and career as they would prefer.

Reactions of subordinates to female managers vary, but "once subordinates have worked for both female and male managers, the effects of [traditional sex-role] stereotypes disappear and managers are treated as individuals rather than representatives of their sex."[11]

Some research supports the idea that women bring different attitudes and skills to management jobs, such as greater cooperativeness, an emphasis on affiliation and attachment, nurturance, and a willingness to bring emotional factors to bear in making workplace decisions. These differences are seen to carry advantages for companies, because they expand the range of techniques that can be used to help the company manage its workforce effectively.[12]

A study commissioned by the International Women's Forum discovered a management style used by some women, and by some men, that differs from the command-and-control style traditionally used by male managers. Using an "interactive leadership" approach, "women encourage participation, share power and information, enhance other people's self-worth, and get others excited about their work. All these things reflect their belief that allowing employees to contribute and to feel powerful and important is a win-win situation—good for the employees and the organization." The study's director predicted that "interactive leadership may emerge as the management style of choice for many organizations."[13]

[11]Gary N. Powell, "One More Time: Do Female and Male Managers Differ?" *Academy of Management Executive,* August 1990, pp. 68–75. For a discussion of similarities and differences among male and female managers, see Powell's book *Women and Men in Management,* 2d ed. (Newbury Park, CA: Sage, 1993).

[12]Jan Grant, "Women as Managers: What They Can Offer to Organizations," *Organizational Dynamics,* Winter 1988, pp. 56–63.

[13]Judy B. Rosener, "Ways Women Lead," *Harvard Business Review,* November–December 1990, pp. 119–125.

The Glass Ceiling

Although women are as competent as men in managing people and organizations, they very rarely attain the highest positions in corporations. Their ascent seems to be blocked by an invisible barrier, or what is called a **glass ceiling**.

Failure to attain the topmost jobs in some cases is due to lack of experience or inadequate education. Because gender bias has kept women out of management until recent years, most women have not had time to acquire the years of experience that are typical of most high-ranking executives. Also in earlier years, women were discouraged from entering graduate schools of engineering, science, business, and law, which have been pathways to corporate management. Even as those barriers have been lowered, though, women remain underrepresented at executive levels. As a group, they have not yet broken through the glass ceiling to become chief executive officers, presidents, or board chairpersons.

What continues to hold women back? Recent studies by the U.S. Department of Labor and others have identified several reasons for the persistence of the glass ceiling. One barrier women face is **glass walls**: fewer opportunities to move sideways into jobs that lead to the top. Female managers are often found in staff positions, such as finance or public relations, rather than in line positions in such core areas as marketing, sales, or production where they can acquire the broad management skills necessary for promotion. Many women also experience what one sociologist called the "sticky floor." This means that sometimes women do not advance because they are concentrated in low-level jobs that do not lead to well-defined career paths. One study shows that the sticky floor was particularly evident for Hispanic, African-American, and Native-American women.[14]

Another problem women face is reliance on word-of-mouth by recruiters for top positions, the old boys' network from which women are often excluded. Other causes include a company's lack of commitment to diversity and too little accountability at the top management level for equal employment opportunity.[15]

The success of a few women, however, has demonstrated that the glass ceiling can be shattered. A 1994 study of a group of highly successful executive women found that most had been helped by top-level supporters and multiple chances to gain critical skills. Some companies have promoted women's mobility by assigning mentors—more-senior counselors—to promising female managers and by providing opportunities that include wide-ranging line management experience. In 1989, for example, Motorola revamped its career planning process to identify high-potential women and give them the opportunities they needed to merit promotion. By 1997, Motorola had 38 female vice presidents, up from just 2 when the program started.[16]

Women Business Owners

Some women have risen to the top by founding or taking over their own businesses. By 1996, nearly eight million businesses—over one-third of all those in the United States—

[14]"Study Says Women Face Glass Walls as Well as Ceilings," *The Wall Street Journal,* March 3, 1992, pp. B1, B2; and "At Work: And Now the 'Sticky Floor,'" *New York Times,* November 22, 1992, p. F23.

[15]Ann M. Morrison, Randall P. White, and Ellen Van Velsor, *Breaking the Glass Ceiling: Can Women Reach the Top of America's Largest Corporations?* 2nd ed. (Reading, MA: Addison-Wesley, 1992); and U.S. Department of Labor, "Good for Business: Making Full Use of the Nation's Human Capital: A Fact Finding Report of the Federal Glass Ceiling Commission," March 1995.

[16]Lisa A. Mainiero, "Getting Anointed for Advancement: The Case of Executive Women," *Academy of Management Executive,* May 1994, pp. 53–63; and "Breaking Through," *Business Week,* February 17, 1997, p. 64.

were owned or controlled by women, according to the National Foundation for Women Business Owners. Many of these businesses are in services, retail trade, finance, insurance, and real estate. Women are now forming new businesses at roughly twice the rate that men are. Although most female-headed firms are small, collectively they employ over 18 million people in the United States, more than the Fortune 500 firms do worldwide.[17]

> *An example of a successful female entrepreneur is Judy Figge, CEO of In Home Health, a company that provides nursing care to patients in their homes. A registered nurse, Figge bought the company in 1981, when revenues were $300,000 annually. 1993 sales were $104 million, with an annual growth rate of 76 percent over the past five years. "I always wanted to run my own business, and this [nursing] is what I knew," Figge said.*[18]

Contrary to popular belief, female entrepreneurs are just as successful as men, according to a mid-1980s study of over 400 midwestern small firms. The study's researchers reported that "the determinants of survival and success operated in much the same way for men and women. . . . Despite the widely shared assumption that women are less apt than men to innovate, for example, we found no evidence of women's being less likely to do this in their businesses. Moreover, we found no evidence that men were more confident of their business abilities."[19]

Government's Role in Securing Women's Workplace Rights

From early in the twentieth century, government laws and regulations—nearly all of them enacted at the state level—were used to protect women from some of the harsh and risky conditions found in factories, mines, construction sites, and other places of business. These protective laws were adopted on grounds that women were weaker physically than men, that their childbearing powers should be shielded from workplace harms, and that whatever work they performed was generally to supplement family income rather than to provide the main income. However, "protection" often meant being excluded from certain jobs and occupations, thus contributing to occupational segregation and unequal pay. Protective laws, however well intentioned, put women at a competitive disadvantage in the labor market.

Equal Pay and Equal Opportunity

The idea that women should be paid the same as men has been around for a long time. In the 1860s, for example, male printers demanded that female printers should receive equal pay for equal work, mainly so that their own wages would not be depressed by competition from lower-paid women. The same fear that female workers would lower all wage rates was observed during the First and Second World Wars, when women took over jobs formerly held by men who were in the armed forces. It was not until 1945 that an equal

[17]The National Foundation for Women Business Owners, "Women-Owned Businesses in the United States 1996: A Fact Sheet"; and "Women Entrepreneurs: They're Forming Small Businesses at Twice the Rate of Men," *Business Week*, April 18, 1994, pp. 104–10.

[18]"Lessons from America's Fastest Growing Companies," *Fortune*, August 8, 1994, p. 59.

[19]Arne L. Kalleberg and Kevin T. Leicht, "Gender and Organizational Performance: Determinants of Small Business Survival and Success," *Academy of Management Journal*, March 1991, pp. 157–58.

pay bill was introduced in Congress; even then, it was a tactic to defeat or forestall a more comprehensive equal rights amendment to the U.S. Constitution. The Equal Pay Act finally became law almost 20 years later in 1963.

One year after that, Congress adopted the Civil Rights Act, which prohibits employment discrimination on the basis of race, color, religion, sex, or national origin. When the Civil Rights Act was strengthened in 1972 and again in 1991, working women—along with minorities—had additional legal machinery to use in their quest for workplace equality.[20] For more than half a century, an equal rights amendment to the U.S. Constitution has been advocated but never ratified by the necessary number of states. The proposed amendment declares: "Equality of rights under the law shall not be denied or abridged by the United States or any state on account of sex."

Figure 17–4 outlines the major laws and one executive order that are intended to promote women's on-the-job opportunities. These equal opportunity laws and regulations are discussed in more detail in Chapter 16.

Comparable Worth

Equal pay for equal work combats pay discrimination within the same job categories within the same firm—for example, providing equal pay rates for men and women carpenters and equal salaries for men and women managers performing identical work. However, it does little to reduce pay inequities when men and women hold different jobs that require approximately equal skills but are paid at unequal rates. Much of the gender pay gap discussed earlier occurs because many women are employed in jobs and occupational categories that are lower paying than those held predominantly by men. Equalizing pay levels in the same job category does nothing about the unequal rates paid to different jobs or occupations. The problem is especially unfair when these different jobs call for about the same degree of skill, effort, and responsibility. For example, the chief bookkeeper and payroll manager of the city of Princeton, Minnesota—a woman—earned $5,678 a year less than supervisors of road maintenance and sewer repair, typically men. When the state legislature required city governments to equalize the pay of women and

Figure 17–4

Major federal laws and an executive order to protect women's workplace rights.

Equal Pay Act (1963)—Mandates equal pay for equal work.

Civil Rights Act (1964) (amended 1972, 1991)—Forbids sex discrimination in employment.

Executive Order 11246 (1965)—Mandates affirmative action for all federal contractors and subcontractors.

Equal Employment Opportunity Act (1972)—Increased power and Equal Employment Opportunity Commission to combat sex and other types of discrimination.

Pregnancy Discrimination Act (1978)—Forbids employers to discharge, fail to hire, or otherwise discriminate against pregnant women.

Family and Medical Leave Act (1993)—Requires companies with 50 or more employees to provide up to 12 weeks unpaid leave for illness, care of a sick family member, or the birth or adoption of a child.

[20]Claudia Goldin, *Understanding the Gender Gap: An Economic History of American Women* (New York: Oxford University Press, 1990), pp. 201–2. The word *sex* was inserted in the 1964 civil rights bill, just one day before Congress voted on it, by a congressional opponent who was said to believe that its inclusion would help defeat the bill.

men in jobs requiring similar levels of education, skill, and responsibility, the bookkeeper got a raise.[21]

Comparable worth is an attempt to overcome this kind of pay inequity. Jobs are matched with each other in terms of skills, effort, responsibility, and working conditions, and pay is made equal when these factors for the two jobs are about equal or comparable with one another. As of the mid-1990s, pay equity based on comparable worth had been rejected by U.S. federal courts, but some states—like Minnesota, mentioned in the example above—have laws authorizing comparable worth plans for public employees. The European Union now requires that companies assess jobs and pay women and men the same for jobs of comparable value. Canada, Great Britain, and Australia have national comparable worth laws that appear to be effective in lessening pay discrimination.[22]

What Firms Can Do: Policies and Strategies

As women enter the labor force in large numbers, seeking permanent, well-paying, full-time jobs and aspiring to lifelong business careers, and as new laws pass protecting equal workplace rights for women, some changes are bound to take place in the way business firms organize and conduct their affairs. Three types of changes are needed. First, firms must reform their personnel policies to assure equal opportunities. Second, they must provide support programs to make a working life and a family life possible and rewarding for both men and women. Finally, businesses must remove sexist attitudes and behavior toward working women. Gender bias occurs throughout society, not just in the workplace, so these business reforms represent only those steps that firms themselves can take to provide equal workplace opportunities for women.

Reforming Personnel Policies

If women are to be treated equally in the workplace, all jobs and occupations must be open to them so that they may compete on the same terms as all others. A company's recruiters need to seek qualified workers and not assume that women are unqualified. Rates of pay and benefits need to be matched to the work to be done not to the gender of the jobholder. Pay raises for doing a current job well, along with promotions to more attractive jobs, also require equal treatment. Job assignments should be made on the basis of skills, experience, competence, capability, and reliability—in other words, proven ability to get the job done, not whether women have traditionally worked at one task rather than another.

Career ladders, whether short ones going only a few steps or longer ones leading into the higher reaches of corporate authority, should be placed so that both men and women can climb them as high as their abilities can carry them.

Providing Support Programs for Work and Family

No other area of business illustrates the basic theme of this book better than the close connection between work and family life. *Our basic theme is that business and society—in*

---

[21]Naomi Barko, "Equal Pay in Your Pocketbook," *Working Mother,* November 1993, p. 42.

[22]Laura B. Pincus and James A. Belohlav, "Legal Issues in Multinational Business Strategy," *Academy of Management Executive,* August 1996, pp. 52–61; and Kenneth A. Kovach and Peter E. Millspaugh, "Comparable Worth: Canada Legislates Pay Equity," *Academy of Management Executive,* May 1990, pp. 92–101.

this case, the family symbolizes society—are closely and unavoidably intertwined, so that what affects one also has an impact on the other. When large numbers of women began to enter the ranks of business in the 1940s, 1950s, and 1960s, they did not shed their usual roles in society. Women continued to marry and bear children. The customary roles of wife, homemaker, and child-caretaker did not disappear. Women were still expected to be "feminine" even as they filled what had formerly been "masculine" jobs. So when women came to work, they carried more than a lunch pail or a briefcase; they also bundled their customary family roles on their backs.

Study after study has demonstrated that women continue to do more housework than their male partners. Caring for children, preparing meals, cleaning house, shopping, and other household functions are still seen to be the responsibility of the mother more than the father, even when both parents work full-time. Many women thus work what has been called a "second shift" before and after their paying job.[23] In the 1960s and 1970s, women worked a month longer each year in combined job and housework than men did, and later studies show a continuation of the general pattern.

In other words, many women and men work within a surrounding network of social obligations imposed by tradition. For them and for their employers, business and the family are inseparably intertwined. This close relationship between family and work presents business with new kinds of challenges and requires changes in customary routines. Some of these are discussed next.

Child Care and Elder Care

The demand for **child care** is enormous and growing. Millions of children need daily care, especially the nearly 7 out of every 10 children whose mothers hold jobs. A major source of workplace stress for working parents is concern about their children; and problems with child care are a leading cause of absenteeism. Businesses lose an estimated $3 billion a year because of child-related absences.[24]

Business has found that child-care programs, in addition to reducing absenteeism and tardiness, also improve productivity and aid recruiting by improving the company's image and helping to retain talented employees. Eighty-six percent of large U.S. companies provide some type of child-care assistance, including referral services, parent education, dependent-care accounts, and vouchers. Slightly fewer than 1 in 10 large companies provides on-site child-care services. An example is Johnson Wax, a consumer products firm that cares for 400 children in a state-of-the-art center at its Racine, Wisconsin, headquarters. "This isn't a benefit," explained a company spokesperson. "It's a good business decision because we want to attract the best." Fel-Pro, an auto parts manufacturer in Skokie, Illinois, offers a summer day camp for employees' school-aged children.[25]

Other companies have combined child care with **elder care,** since many of today's families must find ways to care for aging parents and other older relatives. This issue will become increasingly important to businesses in the coming decade as baby boomers pass through their 40s and 50s, the prime years for caring for elderly parents. According to

[23]Arlie Hochschild, *The Second Shift: Working Parents and the Revolution at Home* (New York: Viking, 1989); see especially the appendix, "Research on Who Does the Housework and Childcare."

[24]Catalyst, "INFObrief: Childcare," New York, 1994.

[25]"Balancing Act Is Gaining Ground," *Seattle Times,* April 28, 1997, p. E1; and "What Price Child Care?" *Business Week,* February 8, 1993, pp. 104–5.

the consulting firm Work/Family Directions, the proportion of workers with elder-care responsibilities will rise from around 15 percent in 1994 to 37 percent by 2005.[26] Many businesses have found that job flexibility and referrals to services for the elderly can greatly help affected employees.

Parental Leaves

What was once called a maternity leave has become a **parental leave;** or when care of elderly parents is involved, it is called a **family leave.** Both parents may need time off from work when children are born and during the important early months of the child's physical and emotional development, and men and women may need time to care for elderly or ill parents or other family members. Under the Family and Medical Leave Act (FMLA), passed in 1993, companies that employ 50 or more people must grant unpaid, job-protected leaves of up to 12 weeks to employees faced with serious family needs, including the birth or adoption of a baby. Smaller companies, not covered by the FMLA, usually do less for expectant and new parents.

How many fathers actually take leave to care for children? Several studies have demonstrated that men are reluctant to take advantage of parental leave programs. Because a man typically makes more money than his spouse, taking a long unpaid job leave may impose greater financial hardships on the family. Men also fear, as do women, that being away from the job will interfere with their careers. However, there is some evidence that this pattern has begun to shift in the wake of the FMLA. In 1993, for example, 32 fathers at Du Pont Corporation took advantage of the company's parental leave policy, up from 18 the year before.[27]

Work Flexibility

Companies have also accommodated the changing roles of women and men by offering workers more flexibility through such options as flextime, part-time employment, job sharing, and working at home.

Aetna Life & Casualty, one of America's biggest insurance companies, demonstrates the benefits of the many kinds of work flexibility for both company and employees.[28]

> In some departments at Aetna, as many as 40 percent of employees work flextime schedules, beginning and quitting at different times of the day. Others share jobs, with each working half a week. Many jobs are held on a part-time basis, leaving the worker time to be at home with children or elderly parents. Several hundred Aetna employees telecommute—work with computers—from their homes. The company has a Work/Life Strategies unit to assist employees in using these programs to meet family needs without seriously disrupting company routines. Aetna estimates it saves $1 million a year by not having to train new workers.

Aetna is not the only corporation introducing these practices. A 1996 survey of large companies revealed that 72 percent had flexible schedules, 64 percent offered part-time work,

---

[26]"The Aging of America Is Making 'Elder Care' a Big Workplace Issue," *The Wall Street Journal,* February 16, 1994, p. A1, A8.

[27]"More Dads Take Off to Look After Baby," *The Wall Street Journal,* December 17, 1993, p. B1.

[28]"As Aetna Adds Flextime, Bosses Learn to Cope," *The Wall Street Journal,* June 18, 1990, pp. B1, B5; "Work and Family," *Business Week,* June 28, 1993, p. 83; and "The Childless Feel Left Out When Parents Get a Lift," *New York Times,* December 1, 1996, p. C12.

and 36 percent permitted job sharing. Twenty percent allowed employees to work from home.[29]

Reforming Attitudes in the Workplace

The largest obstacle to equity for working women is conventional attitudes about the place of women in society. Both men and women hold these attitudes. Such views contribute to continued occupational segregation, unequal pay and job opportunities, stymied career paths, and the failure of society to draw fully on all of its human resources for greater productivity and higher living standards. A key problem that symbolizes the need for changed workplace attitudes is sexual harassment.

Sexual Harassment

Sexual harassment at work occurs when any employee, woman or man, experiences repeated, unwanted sexual attention or when on-the-job conditions are hostile or threatening in a sexual way. It includes both physical conduct—for example, suggestive touching—as well as verbal harassment, such as sexual innuendoes, jokes, or propositions. Women are the target of most sexual harassment. Guidelines issued by the U.S. Equal Employment Opportunity Commission give limited legal protection to employees.

Harassment can occur whether or not the targeted employee cooperates. Jobs can be lost or gained by sexual conduct; if such behavior is treated as a requirement or strong expectation for holding a job or getting a promotion, it is clearly a case of unlawful sexual harassment. This kind of sex discrimination is not limited to overt acts of individual coworkers or supervisors. If a company's work climate is blatantly and offensively sexual or intimidating to employees—through prevailing attitudes, bantering, manner of addressing coworkers, lewd photographs, or suggestive behavior—then sexual harassment exists.[30]

> *An important legal case decided by the Supreme Court in 1993 made it easier for women to win sexual harassment lawsuits against their employers. In this case,* Harris v. Forklift Systems Inc., *a woman manager at a truck-leasing firm was subjected to repeated offensive comments by the company president. For example, he asked her in front of other employees if she used sex to get a particular account and suggested that the two of them "go to the Holiday Inn to negotiate [her] raise." The manager quit her job and sued.*
>
> *The Supreme Court upheld her charges, saying that the president's behavior would reasonably be perceived as hostile or abusive, even though it had not caused "severe psychological injury" or caused the woman to be unable to do her job. Some employers' attorneys expressed concern that this decision would open the door to frivolous claims of sexual harassment. Others welcomed the ruling and believed it would encourage many employers to develop policies and training to prevent such incidents.[31]*

---

[29]*Work and Family Benefits Provided by Major U.S. Employers in 1996* (Lincolnshire, IL: Hewitt Associates, 1996), cited in "Lies Parents Tell Themselves about Why They Work," *U.S. News and World Report,* May 12, 1997, p. 58.

[30]Catalyst, "INFObrief: Sexual Harassment," New York, 1993. For a discussion of legal issues, see Titus E. Aaron with Judith A. Isaksen, *Sexual Harassment in the Workplace* (Jefferson, NC: McFarland & Co., 1993); for a discussion of workplace strategies for women, see Ellen Bravo and Ellen Cassedy, *The 9 to 5 Guide to Combating Sexual Harassment* (New York: John Wiley, 1992).

[31]"Court, 9-0, Makes Sex Harassment Easier to Prove," *New York Times,* November 10, 1993, pp. A1, A15.

Women employees regularly report that sexual harassment is common. From 38 to 60 percent of working women have told researchers that they have been sexually harassed on the job. Managers and supervisors are the most frequent offenders, and female office workers and clerical workers are the main targets. As many as 90 percent of incidents of harassment are never reported.

Like most other problems that confront women in the workplace, sexual harassment stems from customary attitudes about women's functions in society. One expert explains these attitudes as **sex-role spillover,** meaning that many men continue to think of women mainly as performing their traditionally defined roles of sex partners, homemakers, and childbearers and only secondarily as coworkers and qualified professionals. These attitudes spill over into the workplace, leading to improper behavior that has no relation to the work to be done. This kind of conduct is most likely to occur where jobs and occupations are sex-segregated and where most supervisors and managers are men.[32]

What can companies do to combat sexual harassment? Exhibit 17–B summarizes four major steps recommended by one authority. The twin keys to success are (1) a writ-

---

EXHIBIT 17–B

Controlling Sexual Harassment

Barbara Gutek, an authority on sexual harassment in the workplace, advocates companies adopt a four-point action program to curb sexual harassment.

1. *Adopt a companywide policy forbidding sexual harassment, and communicate it to all employees and others who deal with the company.* Specific actions include orientation of new employees, training films and seminars, posters, a personal statement by top management, and designation of a neutral third party to hear complaints and field questions from employees.

2. *Vigorously investigate all complaints and act on the findings.* Specific actions include giving investigative responsibility to a qualified person who understands the psychological and organizational dimensions of sexual harassment. Follow-up based on the findings is required if the policy is to have meaning for everyone in the company.

3. *Include sexual harassment in performance appraisals of all employees, punishing those who violate company policy.* Treat sexual harassment as a form of unprofessional conduct that lowers the victim's job satisfaction, affects her or his progress and career in the company, and lowers overall company performance and productivity. Promoting or otherwise rewarding a harasser sends the wrong message about sexual harassment.

4. *Create and reinforce a climate of professional behavior that discourages sexual harassment.* Specific steps include frequent reminders of the importance of acting professionally, alerting employees to professional forms of addressing one another (avoiding *girlie, doll,* and *sweetie,* for example), and striving for sex-neutral interchanges when men and women work together.

Source: Adapted from Barbara A. Gutek, *Sex and the Workplace: The Impact of Sexual Behavior and Harassment on Women, Men, and Organizations* (San Francisco: Jossey-Bass, 1985), pp. 173–178.

---

[32]Barbara A. Gutek, *Sex and the Workplace* (San Francisco: Jossey-Bass, 1985), chap. 8.

ten policy, visibly supported by a company's top management, and (2) rewards for sex-neutral behavior and punishments for harassment. Only then is there a chance that the company's culture and work climate will begin to encourage attitudes that welcome women as full and equal workers and professionals.

A recent case involving sexual harassment at Mitsubishi Motors is profiled in the discussion case at the end of this chapter.

The Gender-Neutral, Family-Friendly Corporation
As a desirable goal for both business and society, a gender-neutral, **family-friendly corporation** would be one that has removed sex discrimination from all aspects of its operations and that has supported both men and women in their efforts to balance work and family responsibilities. Job advantages would not be granted or

---

EXHIBIT 17–C

A Family-Friendly Company

The most family-friendly company in the United States, according to a recent survey conducted for *Business Week* by the Center on Work and Family, is First Tennessee National Corp., a midsized regional bank based in Memphis, Tennessee. In 1993, First Tennessee initiated a Family Matters program that integrates family considerations into every aspect of the bank's operations. Some of the program's innovations include:

- On-site child care, or vouchers for employees who prefer to use other providers.
- Flexible scheduling, including condensed workweeks, job sharing, and telecommuting.
- Fitness centers.
- Jobs designed to accommodate family needs.
- A classroom visitation program that allows parents time off to participate in school activities.

The Family Matters program, managers believe, has had important bottom-line benefits. An internal study showed that employees were less likely to leave the bank, and so were customers. First Tennessee's customer retention rate was 95 percent, well above the industry average. Over a three-year period, profits at the bank were up 55 percent.

"We flip-flopped our entire corporate philosophy," said First Tennessee's CEO Ralph Horn. "Here it's employees first versus putting the shareholders first like at other financial institutions. The philosophy is that profit begins with satisfied employees."

Source: "Family Values: Corporations Find Family Programs Increase Employee Motivation as Well as the Bottom Line," *Incentive,* December 1996, pp. 23–27; and "Balancing Work and Family," *Business Week,* September 16, 1996, p. 74.

denied on the basis of gender. People would be hired, paid, evaluated, promoted, and extended benefits on the basis of their qualifications and ability to do the tasks assigned. The route to the top, or to satisfaction in any occupational category, would be open to anyone with the talent to take it. The company's stakeholders, regardless of their gender, would be treated in a bias-free manner. All laws forbidding sex discrimination would be fully obeyed. Programs to provide leaves or financial support for child care, elder care, and other family responsibilities would support both men and women employees and help promote an equitable division of domestic work.

Many companies believe that adopting gender-neutral, family-friendly policies improve business performance by reducing turnover and absenteeism and by increasing employee loyalty and commitment. An example of such a company is given in Exhibit 17–C. Gender-neutral and family-friendly companies, such as First National Tennessee, embody the ethical principles of social justice and respect for human rights and demonstrate the kind of social responsiveness that serves the corporation's stakeholders.

Summary Points of This Chapter

- Women have entered the workforce in large numbers to gain economic security, find satisfying work, and achieve psychological independence. Working women continue to encounter job discrimination, including unequal pay and occupational segregation, but they have registered some gains in the last half of the twentieth century.

- The proportion of women in management has grown, although women continue to face a glass ceiling blocking their access to top executive ranks. The number of women-owned businesses has increased sharply, and women now form businesses at twice the rate men do. Research shows that men and women managers do not differ significantly in their leadership styles.

- Government laws and regulations prohibit employment discrimination on the basis of sex, mandate equal pay for equal work, and require unpaid family and medical leave under some circumstances.

- To provide equal opportunity, corporations need to support the career development of female employees, provide family-friendly programs, and help create positive workplace attitudes about working women. Corporations also need written policies prohibiting sexual harassment.

Key Terms and Concepts Used in This Chapter

- Sexual division of labor
- Gender pay gap
- Occupational segregation
- Glass ceiling
- Glass walls
- Comparable worth
- Child care
- Elder care
- Parental leave (family leave)
- Sexual harassment
- Sex-role spillover
- Family-friendly corporation

Internet Resources

- http://www.dol.gov/dol/wb — Women's Bureau of the U.S. Department of Labor
- http://www.workfamily.com — Work & Family Connection; information about work-life issues and practices
- http://www.hewittassoc.com — Hewitt Associates; information about family-friendly benefits at U.S. Corporations
- http://www.wfd.com — Work/Family Directions, Inc.; consulting firm specializing in workforce commitment
- http://www.now.org — National Organization for Women; advocacy organization

Discussion Case   Sexual Harassment at Mitsubishi

In April 1996, the Equal Employment Opportunity Commission sued Mitsubishi Motor Manufacturing of America, Inc. (MMMA) for sexual harassment. If the charges were upheld, total damages against the company could run as high as $150 million, potentially the biggest sexual harassment case in U.S. history.

The EEOC suit alleged that several hundred female employees at the company's assembly plant in Normal, Illinois, had been subject to "gross discrimination." The EEOC claimed that male workers and managers had propositioned women, grabbed their breasts and genitals, and called them *bitches* and *whores*. In one particularly shocking incident, a man was said to have shoved an air gun between a woman's legs and pulled the trigger. "It's very much a hostile environment," said one woman who had filed a complaint.

MMMA, a subsidiary of Mitsubishi Motors Corp. of Japan—itself part of a large group of affiliated companies all using the Mitsubishi name—operated the firm's only automobile assembly plant in the United States. The Illinois facility employed 4,233 people, about a fifth of them women, and was the second-largest employer in the region.

Mitsubishi's U.S. unit had a written policy forbidding sexual harassment, and 10 people had been fired for violating it since the plant opened in 1988. However, the company's contract with its union did not have specific procedures for dealing with sexual harassment, unlike contracts at the Big Three automakers. Prior to the EEOC suit, 29 women had filed private sexual harassment lawsuits against the company.

Mitsubishi's American subsidiary vigorously denied the EEOC's charges and immediately went on the offensive. The company offered to give its employees the day off and a free lunch to travel by bus to the EEOC's regional headquarters in Chicago to protest the lawsuit. Almost 3,000 workers participated. Management also installed phones in the plant and encouraged employees to call lawmakers, at company expense, to complain about the charges.

Many workers expressed concern that the suit might hurt sales, causing layoffs. "I have only a high school education," commented one welder. "Where else will I make $19 an hour with benefits?" Hundreds of women employees signed a petition supporting the company.

With the crisis on the front pages of U.S. newspapers, Mitsubishi Motors Corp. chairman Minoru Makihara intervened. On May 15, the Japanese company announced that it had hired former U.S. secretary of labor Lynn Martin to review its workplace policies and develop a new master plan to prevent sexual harassment.

As news of Mitsubishi's troubles reached Japan, many Japanese firms began sensitivity training sessions for their executives posted in the United States. Some practices alleged at Mitsubishi "would hardly raise an eyebrow in Japan," commented one reporter. "Businessmen openly thumb through porn at work, drink at hostess bars with clients, and typically know few professional women. Tradition dictates that women belong in the home."

In February 1997, Secretary Martin announced a comprehensive set of recommendations, including a policy of zero tolerance of harassment and a system to investigate and resolve complaints. The lawsuit, however, remained unresolved. Two months later, an exasperated EEOC official commented that Mitsubishi continued to be "extraordinarily aggressive in defending the . . . lawsuit. They have not indicated any interest in resolving it promptly."

Sources: "EEOC Sues Mitsubishi Unit for Harassment," *The Wall Street Journal,* April 10, 1996, pp. B1, B8; "Mitsubishi Plant Reeling over Harassment Lawsuit," *Boston Globe,* May 1, 1996, Metro Section, p. 1; "Fear and Loathing at Mitsubishi," *Business Week,* May 6, 1996, p. 35; "A Mitsubishi Unit Is Taking a Hard Line in Harassment Battle," *The Wall Street Journal,"* April 22, 1996, pp. A1, A12; "Japanese Firms Fight against Sexual Harassment," *Chicago Tribune,* April 27, 1997, Business Section, p. 8; and "Cramming for the Exotic U.S. Workplace," *The Wall Street Journal,* July 9, 1996, p. A14.

Discussion Questions

1. In your opinion, did sexual harassment occur at Mitsubishi? Please review the definition of sexual harassment. Did the alleged incidents meet all elements of the definition?

2. In your opinion, what factors, either internal or external, contributed to sexual harassment at Mitsubishi? What steps should management have taken, or should it take, to prevent sexual harassment from occurring?

3. How did Mitsubishi managers respond to EEOC charges of sexual harassment? Identify at least three actions taken by management. Do you believe these actions were ethical and socially responsible? Why do you think so?

18

Technology as a Social Force

Technology is an unmistakable social force in our lives whether we are at home, in school, or in the workplace. The latest wave of technological innovations has dramatically changed how we live, play, learn, work, and interact with others. Accompanying these marvels of technology are equally powerful social and ethical challenges for business, government, and society. Can we use technology to enhance the quality of our lives and not be controlled by it?

This chapter focuses on these key questions and objectives:

- What are the dominant features of technology?
- How has technology changed our lifestyle at home, our education at school, and our health?
- How has business utilized the advantages of technology in the workplace?
- What are some of the social and ethical threats emerging from rapid technological change?
- How have governments and businesses taken responsibility to monitor and control technological advancements?

"Technology in the home is about to take off. Consumer demand for technology will be the fastest-growing area for technology providers in the next few years," predicted high-tech guru George Forrester Colony.[1] Colony envisioned homes transformed by multimedia personal computers and on-line services. Already "software helpers" have become available to home computer users. These helpers provide access to local weather forecasts, movie reviews, stock quotes, and business news. Others predicted that consumers would soon have access to affordable computers with speech recognition capabilities, 3-D graphic animation, and wearable computers. Another technological revolution is upon us and life looks very good—easier access to information, more information available at affordable prices, and greater opportunities to improve our lives through technological assistance.

But, not so fast, cried a group of technology critics concerned about the impact of technological advancement on the quality of our lives. They extolled traditional values and lifestyles, advocating families gathering together in their homes for singing or storytelling rather than relying on stereos, televisions, or computers for entertainment. Technology was seen as a source of ecological irresponsibility, an inappropriate substitute for family and social group interaction, and a catalyst for automation in the workplace that destroys job satisfaction, creativity, and jobs themselves.

Is technological change happening too fast? Is there too much technological development? Technology has improved the quality of our lives and our ability to communicate with others, yet has it also taken away something from our lives and the way we interact with others?

The Technology Invasion

Throughout history technology has had an enormous effect. It has pressed onward like a glacier, slowly and steadily exerting its influence. It appears virtually impossible to stem the advancement of technology. Though the Industrial Revolution created new and serious human problems for some people in society, it was a great advance in the history of civilization. New jobs and skills replaced older ones, living standards were raised, and economic abundance extended life expectancy for millions of people.

Technology continues to grow because of people themselves. Human beings have sampled and embraced the fruits of knowledge. It seems that people have acquired an insatiable desire for it. They forever seek to expand knowledge of their environment, probably because of the excitement of learning and their belief that more knowledge will help them adapt to their environment.

Features of Technology

The dominant feature of **technology** is *change* and then more change. Technology forces change on people whether they are prepared for it or not. In modern society it has brought so much change that it creates what is called *future shock,* which means that change comes so fast and furiously that it approaches the limits of human tolerance and people lose their ability to cope with it successfully. Although technology is not the only cause of change, it is the primary cause. It is either directly or indirectly involved in most changes that occur in society.

[1]G. Christian Hill, "Talking Technology," *The Wall Street Journal,* June 19, 1995, p. R33.

Some years ago, right after the start of the personal computer revolution, in-dustry experts observed that if automobiles had developed at the same rate as the computer business, a Rolls Royce would cost $2.75 and go 3 million miles on a gallon of gasoline. Today's microcomputers cost less than those of a decade or even a few years ago and offer many times the power and many more times the speed of their predecessors.

Another feature of technology is that its effects are *widespread,* reaching far beyond the immediate point of technological impact. Technology ripples through society until every community is affected by it. For example, **telecommunications,** the transmission of information over great distances via electromagnetic signals, has played a historically significant and positive role in our society's development. This innovation enhanced international commerce, linked relatives living great distances apart, and enabled us to discover many of the mysteries of outer space. Yet, along with these advances came the potential for a greater invasion of privacy through databases and telemarketing practices. The human touch in our communication with others has been diminished through the convenience of electronic voice mail.

The shock waves pushed their way into even the most isolated places. People could not escape it. Even if they traveled to remote places like the Grand Canyon, technology was still represented by vapor trails from airplanes flying overhead, microwave communication signals from satellites moving at the speed of light, and a haze from air pollution often preventing a view of the other side.

An additional feature of technology is that it is *self-reinforcing.* As stated by Alvin Toffler, "Technology feeds on itself. Technology makes more technology possible."[2] This self-reinforcing feature means that technology acts as a multiplier to encourage its own faster development. It acts with other parts of society so that an invention in one place leads to a sequence of inventions in other places. Thus, invention of the microprocessor led rather quickly to successful generations of the modern computer, which led to new banking methods, electronic mail, bar-code systems, and so on.

Phases of Technology in Society

Looking at technology in a very general way, we can see that five broad phases of technology have developed, as shown in Figure 18–1. In history, nations have tended to move sequentially through each phase, beginning with the lowest technology and moving higher with each step, so the five phases roughly represent the progress of civilization throughout history.

The current phase of technology is the **information society.** This phase emphasizes the use and transfer of knowledge and information rather than manual skill. It dominates work and employs the largest proportion of the labor force. Work becomes abstract, the electronic manipulation of symbols. Businesses of all sizes, including the smallest firms, are exploring the benefits of the information age.[3] Examples of people in information jobs are news editors, accountants, computer programmers, and teachers. Even a transplant surgeon, who must use a delicate manual skill, is primarily working from an information or intellectual base. Examples of information industries are newspaper publishing, television, education, book publishing, telecommunications, and consulting.

---

[2]Alvin Toffler, *Future Shock* (New York: Bantam, 1971), p. 26.
[3]Shoshanah Zuboff, *In the Age of the Smart Machine* (New York: Basic Books, 1988); and "Mom and Pop Go High Tech," *Business Week,* November 21, 1994, pp. 82–90.

Figure 18-1

Phases in the development of technology in the United States.

Technology Level	Phases in the Development of Technology	Approximate Period of Dominance in U.S.	Activity	Primary Skill Used
1	Nomadic-agrarian	Until 1650	Harvests	Manual
2	Agrarian	1650 – 1900	Plants and harvests	Manual
3	Industrial	1900 – 1960	Builds material goods	Manual and machine
4	Service	1960 – 1975	Focuses on providing services	Manual and intellectual
5	Information	1975 – 1990s and beyond	Abstract work	Intellectual and electronic

An information society's technology is primarily electronic in nature and is heavily dependent on the computer and the semiconductor silicon chip. The power of these devices rests on their ability to process, store, and retrieve large amounts of information with very great speed. With the arrival of the 1990s, the information age exploded into nearly every aspect of business and society. Civilization had never experienced that much change that fast. The information age radically transformed the way people learn, think, conduct business, and live their lives. These inventions have catapulted societies into **cyberspace,** where information is stored, ideas are described, and communication takes place in and through an electronic network of linked systems. The technology developed in this new age provided the mechanisms for more information to be produced in a decade than in the previous 1,000 years.

Technology in Our Daily Lives

People around the world are acquiring easier access to more technological innovations than ever before. Residents in economically developing countries enjoy energy-powered appliances, entertainment devices, and communication equipment at a rapidly increasing pace. Individuals and businesses in economically developed countries, like the United States and many European and Asian countries, are multiplying their dependence on electronic communication devices, thus increasing access to information needed for decision making and conducting business transactions.

The United States, for example, is spawning a technological-gadget generation. By 1996, 90 percent of all U.S. households had a color television, radio, telephone, and videocassette recorder. Most homes in the United States had a cordless telephone, telephone answering machine, stereo system, and compact disc player. Other technological gadgets, such as personal computers, printers, cellular telephones, and pagers, electric car alarms, and camcorders, had also found their place in American homes.[4] Moreover, the speed in which technological change occurs is rapidly shortening, as shown in Figure 18–2.

The technological invasion also targeted schools. Spending on technology in American public schools, grades kindergarten through 12, doubled in six years in the 1990s.

[4]"The Technology Culture," *The Wall Street Journal,* June 16, 1996, p. R4.

Invention

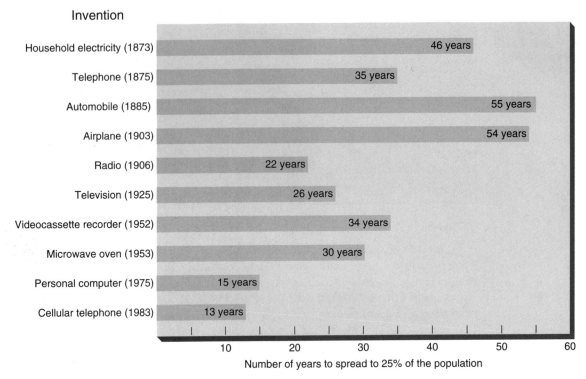

Invention	Number of years to spread to 25% of the population
Household electricity (1873)	46 years
Telephone (1875)	35 years
Automobile (1885)	55 years
Airplane (1903)	54 years
Radio (1906)	22 years
Television (1925)	26 years
Videocassette recorder (1952)	34 years
Microwave oven (1953)	30 years
Personal computer (1975)	15 years
Cellular telephone (1983)	13 years

Number of years to spread to 25% of the population

Figure 18–2

The speed of technological change.
Source: "The Technology Culture," *The Wall Street Journal,* June 16, 1996, p. R4.

Fees levied on business telephone service bills directed $2.25 billion over five years to subsidize access to the Internet for schools and libraries in the United States. In the United States, the ratio of computers to students plummeted from 125 to 1 in the mid-1980s to about 12 to 1 in the mid-1990s.[5]

> *In 1990, as part of a desegregation plan, Dillard High School in Fort Lauderdale, Florida, turned to financial aid from the school district, state and federal governments, and private donations to buy computer equipment. By 1996, it had acquired more than $1 million of computer hardware, software, and peripherals, enabling the establishment of a technology magnet school, a school within a school where students needed a C-grade average for admission.*
>
> *The results by any standard were impressive. Students in the technology program scored higher in test scores and grade-point average than students at Dillard High School not involved in the technology program. Only 3 of the program's 200 students failed Florida's mandatory high school competency test on the first try, compared with a 47 percent failure rate schoolwide. About 60 percent of the program's graduates entered college, nearly double the rate for the rest of Dillard's student body.[6]*

[5]William M. Bulkeley, "Back to School," *The Wall Street Journal,* November 13, 1995, p. R6.
[6]Steve Stecklow, "Magnet Miracle," *The Wall Street Journal,* November 13, 1995, p. R14.

Seemingly, everywhere we turn—whether in our homes, in school, or at work—the technology invasion is all around us and its influence and opportunities seem inescapable.

The Internet

Certainly one of the most visible and widely used technological innovations in the 1990s was the **Internet** or **World Wide Web.** Springing to life in 1994, this conduit of information revolutionized how business was conducted, students learned, and households operated. The *Wall Street Journal* reported in 1996 that "the number of U.S. households with *Internet* access more than doubled to 14.7 million in the past year." Roughly nine million adult Americans log onto the Internet daily, and twice as many sign on weekly.[7] Increased Internet usage was predicted with continued innovations like WebTV networks, new devices that enable users Internet access via their television sets, and technology that allows people to make telephone calls and access the Internet via electric outlets in walls.

As depicted in Figure 18–3, most users of the Internet in 1997 were males between the ages of 30 and 49 with a college degree or some college education and an annual income over $25,000. Besides helping with work-related tasks, the Internet's influence expanded to help people plan their leisure time, as described in Exhibit 18–A. Experts predicted that use of the Internet would continue to expand dramatically over the next few years, especially with the wiring of schools to the World Wide Web.

Technological Medical Breakthroughs

Technological breakthroughs in the medical and health-care fields have also dramatically affected people's lives. How people are examined, diagnosed, and treated, how health-related information is collected and stored, and the time and costs associated with health care have been changed by technological innovations within the past few years.

Figure 18–3

World Wide Web users.

Source: Amy Cortese, "A Census in Cyberspace," *Business Week,* May 5, 1997, p. 84.

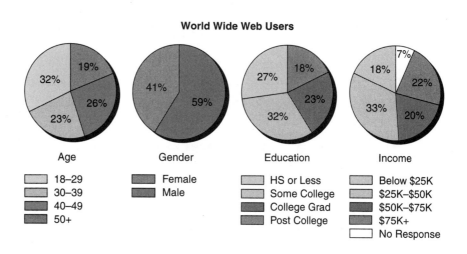

World Wide Web Users

Age: 18–29, 30–39, 40–49, 50+
Gender: Female, Male
Education: HS or Less, Some College, College Grad, Post College
Income: Below $25K, $25K–$50K, $50K–$75K, $75K+, No Response

[7]Jared Sandberg, "U.S. Households with Internet Access Doubled to 14.7 Million in Past Year," *The Wall Street Journal,* October 21, 1996, p. B9.

EXHIBIT
18–A

Vacation Planning on the World Wide Web

Vacation planners discovered a new and exciting source for getaway ideas, exotic locations, and travel information—the World Wide Web. Thousands and thousands of travel-related Web sites cropped up on the Internet, blanketing nearly every corner of the globe and representing airlines, hotels, car-rental agencies, cruise companies, travel agencies, and tourist offices. The Web provides consumers an opportunity to make reservations, research fares, or converse with travelers who had already visited vacation paradises they were considering.

For example, the Subway Navigator site (http://metro.jussieu.fr: 10001/bin/cities/english) allows consumers to download maps and display routes for dozens of cities' public railway systems. Using the U.S. Department of Transportation's Bureau of Transportation Statistics (http://www.bts.gov), an individual can learn about on-time performance of airline carriers for flights between his or her home city and vacation destination. Commercial sites, such as Kroll Travel Watch Advisories (http://www.krollassociates.com/kts), offer safety and security tips, health-care precautions, and much other traveler-friendly advice for people venturing to cities around the world, although this site is only open to subscribing businesses. Individuals could receive this information by fax for a modest fee.

At the Association for Computing Machinery's 1997 conference, 100 people volunteered for a "telepresent" medical exam—their medical information was being diagnosed 3,000 miles away at a medical facility. Fifteen volunteers were found to have serious, previously undiagnosed medical problems.

Technology has revolutionized how people are treated. At Johns Hopkins University, a robotic arm was developed to deliver radioactive therapy to patients with liver cancer. The robotic technology can deliver the treatment faster than previous technology, which is critical since a patient's slightest movement through breathing can reduce the effectiveness of the treatment.[8]

The Integration of Technology into Business

The integration of technological innovation into routine business operations can be observed in nearly every workplace function. Communications and access to information are two of the more visible areas. Firms look to improve internal communication through electronic messages, or **e-mail.** Firms can keep better track of their inventory, orders, or project schedules through technologically enhanced information systems. The corporate Web site emerged as an effective marketing tool, and on-line merchandising helped firms shorten their purchase-to-delivery cycle time. "The integration of database, Internet, and CD-ROM is where the real breakthrough thinking is going on. The beautiful thing is it's equally available to small and large companies," explained marketing consultant Richard Cross.

[8]Bob Metcalfe, "We Do Not Need Science Fiction for Today's Telemedicine Wonders," *InfoWorld,* March 24, 1997, p. 50; and "Robots May Plant Seeds for Recovery," *R&D,* February 1997, pp. 33–34.

*Richard A. Penn, vice president of Puritan Clothing Company, a $20 million
Massachusetts firm, created a database to track store sales and coordinate
customer mailings. Bill Tuszynski, manager at Inolex Chemical, spent hours in
front of his personal computer monitoring cybermarketing tactics of his competitors, scanning bulletin boards for product ideas, and checking out home
pages of emerging businesses for materials or new technologies.*[9]

Information as Corporate Power

The explosion of the general public's use of the Internet or World Wide Web was mirrored by business. In the 1990s, business connections to the Internet increased from 1,000
firms to an estimated 21,000 or more by 1996. Experts predict this growth to increase
rapidly into the year 2000.

The Internet can provide firms with many advantages. For example, developing a
marketing strategy that relies on the Internet can benefit firms by replacing electronic mail
systems, providing a global reach to customers, selling products and services in cyberspace, and creating on-line databases, media lists, and other marketing tools. Firms discovered that customer service was enhanced with the Internet.

*Federal Express Corporation emerged as a World Wide Web success story in
the mid-1990s. The package-delivery company moved 2.4 million pieces every
day in 1994, serving over 12,000 customers. In November 1994, the firm gave
its customers a direct window into the FedEx package-tracking database. By
enabling its customers to click their way through the FedEx Web pages to locate and determine the status of their parcels, rather than having a FedEx employee do it, the firm estimated that it saved up to $2 million a year.*[10]

Use of the Internet became one of the hottest new strategies in the securities trading industry. Brokers had more information available to them to assist their clients since
resources were available electronically. In addition, Internet-based brokers can be reached
anytime from any computer with a secure Web browser, making them more accessible to
their clients.

Paperless libraries dramatically changed the way information was stored and significantly reduced costs to businesses. Rather than printing information on paper, firms
documented information on CD-ROMs, videodiscs, and the Internet, where it was stored
and retrieved at less cost.

Supplementing the Internet as a communication tool are **intranets,** private or limited information network systems cordoned off from public access by software programs
called *firewalls.* The corporate use of intranets exploded as companies found that these
information communication systems were very inexpensive. A survey in 1997 found that
the average time needed to train a typical intranet user was 2.4 hours, costing about $46.
Comparable training for traditional software took 4.4 hours per user and cost $85.[11] Firms
quickly discovered that intranet systems were an inexpensive yet powerful alternative to
other forms of internal communication.

---

[9]Gary McWilliams, "Small Fry Go On-Line," *Business Week,* November 20, 1995, pp. 158–64.
[10]Amy Cortese, "Here Comes the Intranet," *Business Week,* February 26, 1996, pp. 76–84.
[11]"Corporate Use of Intranets Is Taking Off, Study Says," *The Wall Street Journal,* March 28, 1997, p. B3.

From AT&T to Levi Strauss to 3M, hundreds of companies jumped into the intranet arena in the mid-1990s. Employees at Compaq Computer Corporation could reallocate investments in their 401(k) retirement funds. An intranet link at Ford Motor Company helped engineers in Asia, Europe, and the United States work together on projects for the 1996 Taurus. Other managers, engineers, and scientists found that intranet systems enabled them to exchange ideas and information quickly and inexpensively with colleagues around the world.[12]

Satellite imaging was another technological advancement that showed promise for integrating technology into business. For decades, governments used satellite imaging to spy on their enemies. In the 1990s, companies were finding other uses for this technology. Coldwell Banker Corporation offered real-estate shoppers pictures from space of homes, neighborhoods, and traffic patterns rather than maps and ground photographs. Pacific Bell, a telecommunications company, plotted the laying of telephone lines through satellite imaging, bypassing the costly practice of sending out crews to study and map the terrain.

Medical Research Breakthroughs

Experts believed that humankind was poised for a remarkable revolution in medical knowledge, based on advances in biological science. "This was the century of physics and chemistry," proclaimed 1996 Nobel prize–winning chemist Robert F. Curl. "But it is clear that the next century will be the century of biology."[13]

In February 1997, the century of biology predicted by Professor Curl appeared to arrive with the announcement of the first successful **cloning** of an animal. Scottish embryologist Ian Wilmut stunned the medical community and the world with Dolly, a cloned Dorset lamb. Dolly was created when researchers took cells from a sheep's mammary gland, put them into a test tube, and forced the cells into an inactive state by limiting their intake of nutrients. Next, medical researchers took unfertilized eggs from female sheep and mechanically removed the DNA nucleus from each egg. Finally, the DNA cells were inserted into the cells taken from the mammary glands. Of the 277 experiments, only 29 survived for a few days and were surgically implanted into the womb of 13 ewes. One of the 13 sheep became pregnant and gave birth to a lamb who was an exact genetic copy of the adult sheep whose mammary gland was tapped for DNA cells.

Recent advances in biological research may have potential business applications. Agricultural companies believe breaking down the genetic code will enable them to better combat bacteria and other crop-destroying elements. Genetic testing enabled a Canadian scientist to identify Alzheimer's disease patients who might benefit from the only approved drug in the United States. Continued advancements in genetic testing could help companies in the pharmaceutical industry as well as reduce medical costs for businesses in general.

Economic Effects of Technology

Perhaps the most fundamental effect of technology is *greater efficiency* in terms of quality and quantity. Seeking a more efficient method or means of production is the main rea-

---

[12]Cortese, "Here Comes the Intranet."
[13]John Carey, Naomi Freundlich, Julia Flynn, and Neil Gross, "The Biotech Century," March 10, 1997, pp. 78–90.

son that most technology is adopted. Numerous scientific studies support the claim that using computers increases employee productivity.

> *For example, Famous Footware used technology to automate its human re-*
> *source processes to reduce or eliminate paperwork tied to hiring, payroll*
> *changes, attendance reporting, personnel reviews, labor scheduling, and termi-*
> *nations. The company reported that the new-generation technologies integrated*
> *with human resource information systems resulted in markedly greater effi-*
> *ciency for its human resource personnel.*[14]

Technology places more emphasis on *research and development* (R&D). Research concerns the creation of new ideas, and development is their useful application. Growth in R&D expenditures for technological development is seen in both government and private business. The Japanese parliament passed a law in 1996 designed to produce a world-class research system for technological innovation. The law mandated a 12.5 percent annual rise in government R&D spending. When fully implemented, Japanese R&D spending on technology will exceed that of the United States by the year 2002.[15]

> *Thousands of R&D projects have been undertaken by private corporations. For*
> *example, IBM launched a $32 million project to develop holographic data*
> *storage technology. This new technology stores 12 times more data at the same*
> *cost as magnetic data storage. At Bell Laboratories a technique for transmit-*
> *ting data over fiber-optic lines at a rate of one terabit per second—400 times*
> *faster than current technology—was the result of a successful R&D strategy.*

The third economic effect of technology is that it creates an *insatiable demand for capital.* Large capital investments are required to build the enormous production systems that save labor time and provide other benefits of technology. At the turn of the century, an investment of $1,000 for each worker often was adequate in a factory, but modern investments in pipelines and petroleum refining exceed $200,000 for each worker.

Technology is costly but essential for business, thereby creating a problem for managers. The failure to maintain up-to-date technology can mean a loss of competitiveness, as occurred in the U.S. steel industry in the 1980s. Both productivity and product quality can suffer. However, such expenditures do not tell the entire story. New technology requires other expenditures to keep the labor force up to date with the machinery and technological changes. This in turn requires managers to select their technology carefully, train people properly, and encourage the continuous improvement of employees' understanding about the best ways to make use of technological capability. These demands also require businesses to generate large amounts of capital and engage in more long-range planning and budgeting for capital use. Global competitiveness requires each nation to invest heavily in its technological future.[16]

[14]Randall K. Fields, "Leveraging Information Technology Can Increase Professionalism," *Human Resources Professional,* January–February 1996, pp. 29–32.

[15]Wil Lepkowski and Richard Seltzer, "Japan Reinvents Its R&D Effort, Aims to Develop First-Class Universities," *Chemical and Engineering News,* September 9, 1996, pp. 27–28. For an analysis of the R&D policies for technological development created by the five major industrialized countries, see Rolf G. Sternberg, "Government R&D Expenditure and Space: Empirical Evidence form Five Industrialized Countries," *Research Policy,* August 1996, pp. 741–58.

[16]See, for example, Michael L. Dertouzos, Richard K. Lester, and Robert M. Solow, *Made in America* (Cambridge, MA: MIT Press, 1989), which was influential in public discussion of this issue in the early 1990s.

Social and Ethical Concerns

Technological change has brought dramatic enhancements to our lives, work, and health. Few people would argue against the belief that technological advances have improved the quality of life. Yet there are signs that technological change may need to have limits or guidance to best serve business, government, and society.

Too Much, Too Fast?

Despite the explosion of Internet users, medical breakthroughs to enhance the quality of our lives, and numerous other technology advances, there remain people whom the technology invasion has left behind. A 1996 survey of business executives found that 20 percent of the 245 CEOs and senior executives did not have a personal computer on their desk and half of all CEOs surveyed did not use a computer at work.[17] This resistance to computers is often related to age, reflecting a generation gap between those proficient in information technology and those whose business training predates the availability of personal computers.

Technology was developing so fast that **information overload,** the availability of too much information to process or assist in decision making, occurred and more information became useless information.

> *The Direct Marketing Association estimated that a mailing to one million people would cost about $827,000 in 1996. Yet, Internet advertisers could reach the same number of people for the cost of local telephone calls and a few hundred dollars for on-line costs. Software was available that would allow businesses to send thousands of messages to prospective customers for only a few hundred dollars.*[18]

The emergence of junk e-mail and the saturation of the World Wide Web with advertisers quickly inundated businesses and customers with more information than they could handle.

The threat of technological inefficiency was attributed to not only those unskilled in using computers but those highly skilled: **computer hackers.** Computer hackers are individuals who break into company databases or other secure information banks to steal or delete information or cause confusion for those trying to use the information. It is difficult to estimate the cost hackers impose on businesses since most firms do not report hacker trespass, either out of embarrassment or because they do not realize the breach of security. According to a survey by a U.S. Senate subcommittee, major banks and other large corporations incurred an estimated $800 million in losses in 1995 because of hacker intrusions into their computer systems.[19]

Questions of Privacy

With the emergence of mass marketing, consumers gave away their **privacy** piece by piece. Long before the Internet, consumers provided data when applying for credit cards,

---

[17]Joann S. Lublin, "Computer Illiterates Still Roam Executive Suites," *The Wall Street Journal,* June 24, 1996, pp. B1, B8.

[18]Randi Feigenbaum, "Garbage In—And In and In," *Business Week,* September 9, 1996, p. 110.

[19]John J. Fialka, "Intrusions by Computer Hackers Cost Big Business $800 Million in 1995," *The Wall Street Journal,* June 6, 1996, p. B6.

signing up for frequent flier programs, or receiving supermarket discount cards. But the information age dramatically changed the extent that personal information was stored and available to others.

Some Web sites, for example, will provide your name, address, telephone number, driving record, and even your Social Security number to any interested paying party. Embedded in Netscape software are what are called *cookies*. Cookies help merchants using the Internet to track what a particular customer purchases and how long he or she takes in making the selection. In response to consumer objections to cookies as invasions of privacy, Netscape Communications Company informed consumers that it was changing its Internet browser so customers could prevent on-line merchants from tracking their purchasing patterns on the Internet. This situation is discussed more fully in the discussion case at the end of Chapter 14.

Invasions of privacy also occurred at work. An individual's electronic mail to a coworker could be read by his or her boss. An employee's squandering of company time by browsing the World Wide Web, visiting sex-related sites, or sending massive quantities of private e-mail could be detected by the company's monitoring of computer activity. E-mail, whether at work or in a university computer lab, is the property of the company or university, not the private property of the sender. Stored in the company or university databases, these messages are available to authorities at any time.

Monitoring of workplace communication over the Internet or e-mail is seen as warranted when employees use these forms of communication technology in ways viewed as socially unacceptable, for example, sending racist or sexist messages. Three examples of inappropriate e-mail disseminated at work are described in Exhibit 18–B.

Intellectual Property

Ethical issues arise over obtaining copyrighted or patented material without acquiring permission or purchasing the rights. **Intellectual property** was a hotly contested issue in the 1990s, also discussed in Chapter 10. The copying of compact discs, or CD piracy, soared in 1997 as the availability of machines used to copy movies, music, and CD-ROMs flooded the marketplace from Europe, mostly into Asian countries. According to one estimate, nearly 200 million illegal CDs annually were stamped in the mid-1990s, almost 60 percent of them from China. The International Federation of the Phonographic Industry claimed annual losses of $2 billion to intellectual property pirates in 1996.[20]

The U.S. government responded to the intellectual piracy crisis by drafting a hit list of countries known to be the biggest violators. Those with inadequate protection against intellectual piracy included Argentina, Greece, Indonesia, India, Japan, and countries in the European Union.

China was singled out and threatened with economic sanctions because of the magnitude of its participation in illegal copyright violations. In June 1996, China agreed to close entirely or partly factories known to manufacture illegal CDs, shut down six major distribution markets of illegal CDs, and stop more than 5,000 minitheatres from showing pirated videos for a fee. The Chinese Ministry of Public Security added intellectual property violations to its Severe Campaign Against Crime. Chinese custom agents stepped up border surveillance, seizing 80,000 pirated discs in just a few months in 1996. China also

---

[20]Robert S. Greenberger and Craig S. Smith, "CD Piracy Flourishes in China, and West Supplies Equipment," *The Wall Street Journal,* April 24, 1997, pp. A1, A12.

**EXHIBIT
18-B**

Racist E-Mail at Work

In the space of six weeks, employees at three different companies claimed that racist e-mail messages were sent via their company's communications network. The first was at Morgan Stanley & Company. Two African-American employees charged that they should not have been subjected to racist jokes sent via electronic mail at the firm. After the two employees complained about the messages they allegedly were denied promotions. The firm denied discriminating against the two employees and stated that after the employees filed their internal complaints, three managers were found to have spread racist e-mail messages and were placed on probation.

Just four days later, a racial discrimination suit was filed against R.R. Donnelly & Sons Company, a Chicago-based commercial printing company. More than 500 African-American employees joined the racial discrimination charges against the firm and released documents that included a list of 165 racial, ethnic, and sexual jokes that allegedly were sent through the electronic mail system. Donnelly officials said that senior management had no knowledge of the documents, but if these messages did exist it would be a clear violation of company policy.

A month later, two African-American employees of Citibank, a unit of Citicorp, filed a racial discrimination lawsuit after racist jokes were allegedly sent via electronic mail by several bank supervisors. The employees claimed that supervisors, including company vice presidents, spread offensive e-mail to colleagues around the country. According to the employees, the e-mail created a "pervasively abusive, racially hostile work environment." When reported in the press, the company had no comment since officials had not yet had time to review the charges.

Sources: Frances A. McMorris, "Morgan Stanley Employees File Suit, Charging Race Bias over E-Mail Jokes," *The Wall Street Journal,* January 13, 1997, p. B2; Alex Markels, "Racist E-Mail Messages as Donnelly Show Pattern of Bias, Attorneys Claim," *The Wall Street Journal,* January 17, 1997, p. B2; and Frances A. McMorris, "Citibank Workers File Bias Lawsuit over Racist E-Mail," *The Wall Street Journal,* February 19, 1997, p. B5.

established an enforcement verification system to prevent piracy, including inspectors on the job 24 hours a day at every CD factory. Any CD found on the market without a registry number issued by the state was subject to immediate seizure.[21]

Fears of Cloning

The medical breakthrough of cloning an animal, described earlier in this chapter, was received not only as a giant technological advancement but also as the terror of science fiction becoming reality. Whether it is visions of Jurassic Park dinosaurs running loose in a metropolitan downtown area or the eerie absurdity of cloning multiple Adolph Hitlers in the film *The Boys of Brazil,* fears of cloning living tissue have invaded our lives.[22] In February 1997, there were no laws on record that prevented scientists from attempting human cloning.

[21]Kathy Chen and Helene Cooper, "U.S. and China Reach an Agreement, Averting Trade Sanctions by Both Sides," *The Wall Street Journal,* June 18, 1996, pp. A2, A6.

[22]Robert Langreth, "Cloning Has Fascinating, Disturbing Potential," *The Wall Street Journal,* February 24, 1997, pp. B1, B2; and George Johnson, "Ethical Fears Aside, Science Plunges On," New York Times, December 7, 1997, p. 6.

Experts recognized that the technique used in Scotland to clone a sheep was so simple, requiring little high-tech equipment, that it could be attempted by most biology laboratories with a budget of a few hundred thousand dollars. The ease with which this experiment could be attempted using human DNA cells and the lack of governmental control quickly brought the public and the scientific community's fears over cloning to an unprecedented level.

In June 1997, the U.S. National Bioethics Advisory Commission proposed that scientists be barred from implanting a cloned embryo into a woman's uterus. However, this proposal did not ban scientists from cloning embryos used for research but not implanted into a woman. The group of scientists, lawyers, and ethicists based much of their opposition on concerns for a fetus's safety and urged that the ban be respected for at least through the year 2002.[23] This debate will inevitably continue into the next century.

Responsibilities for Technological Advancements

Many technological advancements, including the unprecedented development of cloning living cells, outpaced government regulation, business oversight, and professional standards. As with most issues in society, the public looked to governmental regulation of business or voluntary self-regulation to ensure that societal interests were considered along with corporate economic interests. Businesses joined consumer advocates and employee watchdog groups to impose controls on the fast-growing technological frontier.

The Role of Government

Numerous efforts were taken as governments tried to bring control to cyberspace. Some countries attempted to censor subversive or socially unacceptable material on the Internet by banning access to it or criminalizing its distribution. Since the Internet is a global medium, however, national laws did little to stop the crossnational transmission of information or images. As discussed in the case at the end of this chapter, Internet users themselves or those with authority over the users, such as parents or companies, may need to provide the necessary controls to restrict access to some Internet sites.

> *Five German police officers spent much of their time in 1997 surfing the Internet for pornographic material. They were attempting to build a case against CompuServe's German subsidiary based on allegations that the firm's general manager was an accessory to the dissemination of pornography.*
>
> *In Finland, the courts ordered Johan Helsingius to shut down what was reported to be the world's largest anonymous electronic-mail service after one of his service's users was linked to child pornography. The court made this ruling even though the Finnish police who were directly involved in the investigation reported that Helsingius's service the service was not designed to transmit photographs and there was no reason to believe that pornography was disseminated. Nonetheless, antipornography crusaders said that the service was used to help people find child prostitutes.*[24]

---

[23]Laurie McGinley, "U.S. Bioethics Panel to Recommend Ban on Cloning to Produce a Human Being," *The Wall Street Journal,* June 9, 1997, p. B3.

[24]Silvia Ascarelli and Kimberley A. Strassel, "Two German Cases Show How Europe Still Is Struggling to Regulate Internet," *The Wall Street Journal,* April 21, 1997, p. B7B; and "Finnish E-Mail Service Closed after Charges of Child Pornography," *The Wall Street Journal,* September 4, 1996, p. B8.

In 1996, the U.S. government launched an eight-month investigation aimed at uncovering software piracy in businesses and homes. Primary targets were computer bulletin boards used, according to the FBI, to distribute copyrighted software from some of the industry's most prominent suppliers. According to official reports, software piracy activities spilled over into the theft of telephone calling cards, the distribution of stolen credit cards, the spread of computer viruses, and the unauthorized access into corporate computer networks to steal proprietary information.

Other governments attacked information technology on the grounds of political subversion. Singapore officials blacklisted numerous Web sites, stating that they contained "content which may undermine public morals, political stability and religious harmony of Singapore."[25]

Similar bans of access to Internet information occurred in China. This country blocked over 100 sites on the World Wide Web, according to Chinese and Westerners who monitor the Internet. Chinese officials shut down access to some English-language sites sponsored by such U.S. news media giants as *The Wall Street Journal,* the *Washington Post,* and CNN because of what they perceived to be anti-Beijing messages. Chinese-language sites were not exempt; added to the list of Web sites found to be offensive to the Chinese government were those that presented news and commentaries from Taiwan, which government leaders in Beijing considered to be "a renegade province of China."

Business Responsibility for Technological Change

Although governmental control of technology increased in the 1990s, businesses also served as society's designated agents responsible for monitoring new technology. In light of the economic self-interest involved, corporate control of the use of technology emerged, and society's interests were protected as well.

Electronic games are often useful in education, but they tend to be a temptation for inappropriate behavior for employees in the workplace. In response, many corporations monitor employee use of computers at work and encourage the appropriate use of these productivity tools.

> *The 17,000 employees at Compaq Computer Corporation saw a warning flashing on their computer screen when they logged onto the company network. The warning read: improper and illegal duplication of corporate data will be punished. It also reminded employees that the firm reserved the right to read all e-mail messages sent over the network (see Exhibit 18–B). Twelve workers at Compaq's Houston headquarters were fired when it was discovered that they had visited sexually explicit Web sites while at work.*

SurfWatch developed a software that allowed companies to block employee access to any Internet site. Although it was originally developed for parents to block pornographic Web sites from their children's viewing, companies such as Lockheed Martin Corporation encouraged the software manufacture to develop a version for the corporate market. Other firms, such as IBM, Microsoft, AT&T, and America Online, joined the movement to develop ways that pornography and other offensive material could be blocked from

---

[25]Wayne Arnold, "Internet Censorship in China, Singapore May Affect Law-Abiding Citizens Most," *The Wall Street Journal,* September 13, 1996, p. B11B.

company Internet networks. Business firms identified temptations for employees' abusive use of technology in the workplace and developed or acquired controls to minimize these opportunities.

Summary Points of This Chapter

- One of the dominant features of technology is change and more change. Technology also has widespread effects and tends to be self-reinforcing.

- The current phase of technology—the information society—has changed our lifestyle, our education, and the field of medical research by providing more information with easier access at a quicker pace. One of the most visible technological innovations in the 1990s was the creation of the Internet.

- Businesses seized many opportunities to enjoy the advantages of technology by understanding that information is power. This power can be seen in new corporate communication systems, such as e-mail, intranets, and satellite imaging.

- Technology brought social and ethical challenges along with the advantages of innovation. Information overload, invasions of privacy, violations of intellectual property, and fears of medical research going too far all caused people to question the benefits of technology.

- Governments have attempted to protect the public from technological infringements on social values, such as the dissemination of child pornography, software piracy, or political subversion. Likewise, businesses have tried to ensure the appropriate use of technology in the workplace and aggressively monitored employee use of e-mail and the Internet.

Key Terms and Concepts Used in This Chapter

- Technology
- Telecommunications
- Information society
- Cyberspace
- Internet, or World Wide Web
- E-mail
- Intranets
- Cloning
- Information overload
- Computer hackers
- Privacy
- Intellectual property

Internet Resources

- http://www.bnt.com — BizNet Technologies
- http://www.compinfo.co.uk/index.html — Computer Information Centre
- http://ciber.bus.msu.edu/busres.htm — International Business Resources on the WWW
- http://ds.internic.net/ds/dsdirofdirs.html — InterNIC Directory of Directories

Discussion Case   Pornography on the Internet

Doug Jackson logged onto the Internet nearly every day. It provided Doug with volumes and volumes of information that allowed him to complete educational assignments, explore new worlds, and communicate with people in many countries. One day Doug clicked on a search button and typed in *nude photos*. Within seconds thousands of Web sites were available to him. After randomly selecting one site, Doug was asked: "Are you 18 years of age? If no, click on the EXIT button and leave this adult site. If yes, click on the ENTER button." Doug did not hesitate to click on the ENTER button. There he found hundreds of explicit sexual photographs of women. Also listed on this Web site were directories of stories describing men and women having bizarre sexual encounters, contact information for women waiting to talk to Doug on the telephone for a fee, and telephone numbers for escort services in his hometown.

Social and religious values vary across cultures and countries, but in the United States in the 1990s, Doug—a 26-year-old man—was allowed to view these Web sites. But what if Doug were a 15-year-old high school student who was encouraged by his friends at school to browse these sites, or simply a curious adolescent?

Access to pornographic material or entertainment is controlled by law and enforced by those providing the material or entertainment. For example, a clerk at a convenience store that sells adult magazines is required to ask for identification to verify that buyers are of legal age. A manager of an adult bookstore or nightclub featuring nude or topless dancers is required to check identification of all patrons who enter the establishment. Yet who monitors access to adult Web sites on the Internet and validates that all browsers are of legal age to view the adult-oriented material?

The question of censorship or supervising the Internet was a growing problem in 1997. Who should control access to adult material on the Internet? Should it rest with the user, the provider, parents or other authorities, or the government?

Adult Web sites ask users if they are of legal age to access sexually oriented material. It seems unlikely that this type of regulation would be successful. Most of the larger commercial on-line and Web servers either say they examine advertisements individually or accept all ads but regulate their content or limit their display to specific search words. Only a few of the servers, including America Online and Starwave Corporation (producers of ESPNet Sportszone and other sites), ban adult material advertisers. Yet these companies also admit that they can not keep up with the massive flow of new advertisers on their services and that the cost of this control is enormous.

Parents, school officials, or company supervisors have another option. Numerous censors offer their services to parents or institutions to control what users can see on the Internet, such as WebTrack, SurfWatch, NetNanny, CyberPatrol, CYBERsitter, and SafeSurf. CYBERsitter is a content-intelligent system that identifies and blocks inappropriate Web sites for its subscribers. The firm also offers CYBERtimer, which defines allowable times during the day when on-line access is permitted.

SurfWatch is another popular Web screen. This firm offered software for parents and educators for $49.95 (in 1997) to deal with the flood of sexually explicit material on the Internet. As reported in one of the company's advertisements, "since creating the market for Internet filtering technology in May 1995, SurfWatch has shipped more than 7.2 million copies of the software and has become the industry-standard tool for blocking access to unwanted materials on the Internet."

Traditionally the government has stepped in as the regulator of adult-oriented material or entertainment. This appeared to be the path the United States was taking to censor the Internet in 1996 when the Communications Decency Act was signed into law. The outcry from free-speech advocates and marketers using the Internet was deafening, and in June 1997, the U.S. Supreme Court declared the act unconstitutional. As Justice John Paul Stevens wrote, "We presume that governmental regulation of the content of speech is more likely to interfere with the free exchange of ideas than to encourage it." Thus, the question of who will control access to the Internet bounced back into the free market.

The presence of the Internet and its recent massive growth makes the question of monitoring access to pornography or adult-oriented Web sites critical. Should this material be controlled, and if so, who should say what is inappropriate material for minors and how would monitoring Web access be achieved?

Discussion Questions

1. Since the Internet is a widely used, free-access source of information, should pornographic material be banned from the World Wide Web?
2. Who do you believe should be responsible for monitoring access to adult material on the Internet: the user, the provider, parents, schools, or the government? Why do you think so?
3. Should Web screens, such as SurfWatch, be provided free to all parents, educators, or managers who want them? Should the government pay for this software technology?

Case Studies
in
Corporate Social Policy

Case Study:
ODWALLA, INC., AND THE E. COLI OUTBREAK

October 30, 1996, was a cool, fall day in Half Moon Bay, California, a coastal town an hour's drive south of San Francisco. At the headquarters of Odwalla, Inc., a modest, two-story wooden structure just blocks from the beach, company founder and chairman Greg Steltenpohl was attending a marketing meeting. Odwalla, the largest producer of fresh fruit and vegetable-based beverages in the western United States, had just completed its best-ever fiscal year, with sales of $59 million, up 40 percent over the past 12 months.

The company's CEO, Stephen Williamson, urgently knocked on the glass door and motioned Steltenpohl into the hall. Williamson, 38, a graduate of the University of California at Berkeley and a former investment banker, had served as president of Odwalla from 1992 and 1995, when he became CEO.

It was unlike him to interrupt a meeting, and he looked worried. "I just got a call from the King County Department of Health," Williamson reported. "They've got a dozen cases of E. coli poisoning up there in the Seattle area. A number of the families told health officials they had drunk Odwalla apple juice." E. coli O157:H7 was a virulent bacterium that had been responsible for several earlier outbreaks of food poisoning, including one traced to undercooked Jack-in-the-Box hamburgers in 1993.

Steltenpohl was puzzled. "What do they know for sure?"

"Right now, not a whole lot. It's just epidemiology," Williamson replied. "They don't have any bacteriological match-ups yet. They said it might be a while before they would know anything definitive."

"We'd better see what else we can find out."

Steltenpohl and Williamson returned to their offices, where they began placing calls to food safety experts, scientists at the Food and Drug Administration and the Centers for Disease Control, and the company's lawyers. A while later, Steltenpohl came out to speak to his next appointment, who had been waiting in the lobby for over an hour. "I'm awfully sorry," the chairman said apologetically. "I'm not going to be able to see you today. Something important's happening that I've got to deal with right away."

History of Odwalla, Inc.

Odwalla, Inc., was founded in 1980 by Steltenpohl, his wife Bonnie Bassett, and their friend Gerry Percy. Steltenpohl, then 25, was a jazz musician and Stanford graduate with a degree in environmental science. The group purchased a used hand juicer for $200 and began producing fresh-squeezed orange juice in a backyard shed in Santa Cruz, California. They delivered the juice to local restaurants in a Volkswagen van. Steltenpohl later said that he had gotten the idea from a book, *100 Businesses You Can Start*

Note: This is an abridged version of a longer case: Anne T. Lawrence, "Odwalla, Inc., and the E. Coli Outbreak (A), (B), and (C), presented at the annual meeting of the North American Case Research Association, October 24, 1997. This case was written with the cooperation of management, solely for the purpose of stimulating student discussion. Sources include articles appearing in the *Natural Foods Merchandiser, Nation's Business, San Jose Mercury News, Rocky Mountain News, San Francisco Chronicle, Seattle Times, Fresno Bee, New York Times, The Wall Street Journal,* and *Squeeze* (Odwalla's in-house newsletter); press releases issued by Odwalla and by the American Fresh Juice Council; and Odwalla's annual reports and prospectus. Odwalla's Web site may be found at http://www.odwallazone.com.

for Under $100. His motivation, he reported, was simply to make enough money to support his fledgling career as a musician and producer of educational media presentations. The company's name came from a jazz composition by the Art Ensemble of Chicago, in which Odwalla was a mythical figure who led the "people of the sun" out of the "gray haze," which the friends chose to interpret as a reference to overly processed food.

During the 1980s, Odwalla prospered, gradually extending its market reach by expanding its own distribution and production capabilities and by acquiring other juice companies. In 1983, the company moved into a larger production facility and added carrot juice to its product line. In 1985—the same year Odwalla incorporated—the company purchased a small local apple juice company, Live Juice. With apple added to the line, the company expanded its distribution efforts, moving into San Francisco and further north into Marin County. In 1986, Odwalla purchased Dancing Bear Juice Company in Sacramento and assimilated that company's juice products and distribution network in central California.

The company financed its rapid growth in its early years through bank loans and private stock offerings in 1991, 1992, and 1993. In December 1993, the company went public, offering for sale one million shares of common stock at an initial price of $6.375 a share. The proceeds of the initial public offering were used in part to construct a 65,000 square foot state-of-the-art production facility in Dinuba, in California's agricultural Central Valley.

The company also made additional acquisitions. In June 1994, the company acquired Dharma Juice Company of Bellingham, Washington, to distribute its products in the Pacific Northwest. In January, 1995, Odwalla purchased J.S. Grant's, Inc., the maker of Just Squeezed Juices, which became the distributor for Odwalla products in the Colorado market. The strategy appeared to be successful. By 1996, Odwalla, which already controlled more than half the market for fresh juice in northern California, had made significant inroads in the Pacific Northwest and Colorado and was poised to extend its market dominance into New Mexico, Texas, and southern California.

Product Line

The company considered its market niche to be "fresh, minimally processed juices and juice-based beverages."

The company produced a range of products from fresh juice, some single strength and some blended. Odwalla chose fun, clever names, such as Strawberry C-Monster (a vitamin C-fortified fruit smoothie), Femme Vitale (a product formulated to meet women's special nutritional needs), and Guava Have It (a tropical fruit blend). Packaging graphics were brightly colored and whimsical. Pricing was at the premium level; a half gallon of fresh-squeezed orange juice retailed for around $5.00; a 16-oz. blended smoothie for $2.00 or more.

Odwalla was committed to making a totally fresh product. In the company's 1995 annual report, for example, the letter to shareholders stated:

> Our juice is FRESH! We believe that fruits, vegetables and other botanical nutrients must be treated with respect. As a result, we do not heat-treat our juice, like the heavily processed products made by most other beverage companies.

The company's products were made without preservatives or any artificial ingredients, and the juice was not pasteurized (heat treated to kill microorganisms and to extend shelf life). Unpasteurized juice, the company believed, retained more vitamins, enzymes, and what Steltenpohl referred to as the "flavor notes" of fresh fruits and vegetables.

Although Odwalla did not pasteurize its juice, it took many steps in the manufacturing process to assure the quality and purity of its product. To avoid possible contamination, the company did not accept ground apples, only those picked from the tree. Inspectors checked field bins to see if there was any dirt, grass, or debris; and bins with evidence of ground contact were rejected. The company's manufacturing facility in Dinuba was considered the most advanced in the industry. The plant operated under a strict code of Good Manufacturing Practices. At Dinuba, apples were thoroughly washed with a sanitizing solution of phosphoric acid and scrubbed with whirling brushes. All juice was produced under extremely strict hygienic standards.

Marketing

Odwalla marketed its products through supermarkets, warehouse outlets, specialty stores, natural food stores, and institutions such as restaurants and colleges. Slightly over a quarter of all sales were with two accounts—Safeway, a major grocery chain, and Price/Costco, a discount warehouse.

A distinctive feature of Odwalla's strategy was the company's direct store distribution, or DSD, system. Most sites, from supermarkets to small retailers, were provided with their own stand-alone refrigerated cooler, brightly decorated with Odwalla graphics. Accounts were serviced by route sales people (RSPs), who were responsible for stocking the coolers and removing unsold juice that had passed its "enjoy by" date. RSPs kept careful records of what products were selling well, enabling them to adjust stock to meet local tastes. As an incentive, salespeople received bonuses based on their routes' sales, in addition to their salaries.

Although the DSD system was more expensive than using independent distributors, it allowed the company to maintain tight control over product mix and quality. Moreover, because the company assumed responsibility for ordering, stocking, and merchandising its own products within the store, Odwalla in most cases did not pay "slotting" and other handling fees to the retailer.

Corporate Culture

The fresh juice company was always, as Steltenpohl put it, "values driven." In 1992, around 80 Odwalla employees participated in a nine-month process that led to the creation of the company's vision, mission, and core values statements. These focused on nourishment, ecological sustainability, innovation, and continuous learning.

Concerned that rapid growth might erode common commitment to these values, in 1995 the company initiated annual three-day training sessions, held on site at multiple locations, known as Living Vision Conferences, for employees to talk about the application of the vision to everyday operating issues. An internal process the company called Vision Link sought to link each individual's job to the Odwalla vision. Managers were expected to model the company's values. The company called its values a "touchstone [for employees] in assessing their conduct and in making business decisions."

In addition, Odwalla instituted a "strategic dialogue" process. A group of 30 people, with some fixed seats for top executives and some rotating seats for a wide cross-section of other employees, met quarterly in San Francisco for broad discussions of the company's values and strategic direction.

Social responsibility and environmental awareness were critical to Odwalla's mission. Community service efforts included aid to farm families in the Central Valley, scholarships to study nutrition, and gifts of cash and juice to many local community organizations. The company instituted a recycling program for its plastic bottles. It attempted to divert all organic waste away from landfills—for example, by selling pulp for livestock feed and citrus peel for use in teas and condiments and past-code juice for biofuels. In the mid-1990s, the company began the process of converting its vehicle fleet to alternative fuels. Odwalla's corporate responsibility extended to its employees, who received innovative benefits that included stock options, extensive wellness programs, and an allowance for fresh juice. The company won numerous awards for its environmental practices, and in 1993, *Inc.* magazine honored Odwalla as Employer of the Year.

During these years, the Odwalla brand name became widely identified with a healthful lifestyle, as well as with California's entrepreneurial business climate. In an oft-repeated story, Steve Jobs, founder of Apple Computer, was said to have ordered unlimited quantities of Odwalla juice for all employees working on the original development of the Macintosh Computer.

The E. Coli Bacterium

The virulent strain of bacteria that threatened to bring down this fast-growing company was commonly known in scientific circles as Escherichia coli, or E. coli for short.

The broad class of E. coli bacteria, microscopic rod-shaped organisms, are common in the human intestinal tract, and few pose a danger to health. In fact, most E. coli play a beneficial role by suppressing harmful bacteria and synthesizing vitamins. A small minority of E. coli strains, however, cause illness. One of the most dangerous of these is E. coli O157:H7. In the intestine, this strain produces a potent toxin that attacks the lining of the gut. Symptoms of infection include abdominal pain and cramps, diarrhea, fever, and bloody stools. Most cases are self-limiting, but approximately 6 percent are complicated with hemolytic uremic syndrome, a dangerous condition that can lead to kidney and heart failure. Young children, the elderly, and those with weakened immune systems are most susceptible.

E. coli O157:H7 lives in the intestines of cows, sheep, deer, and other animals. The meat of infected animals may carry the infection. E. coli is also spread to humans through fecal contamination of food. For example, apples may be contaminated when they fall to the ground and come in contact with cow or deer manure. Secondary infection may also occur, for example, when food is handled by infected persons who have failed to wash their hands after using the toilet. Unfortunately, only a small amount of 157—as few as 500 bacteria—is required to cause illness. As one epidemiologist noted, "It does not take a massive contamination or a major breakdown in the system to spread it."

E. coli O157:H7 is known as an emergent pathogen, meaning that its appearance in certain environments is viewed by researchers as a new phenomenon. The organism was first identified in 1982, when it was involved in a several outbreaks involving undercooked meat. Since then, poisoning incidents had increased dramatically. By the mid-1990s, about 20,000 cases of E. coli poisoning occurred every year in the United States; about 250 people died. Most cases were believed to be caused by undercooked meat. Although a serious threat, E. coli is not the most common food-borne illness. In the United States, five million cases of food poisoning are reported annually, with 4,000 of these resulting in death. Most cases are caused by mistakes in food preparation and handling, not by mistakes in food processing or packaging.

E. coli in Fresh Juice

It was widely believed in the juice industry that pathogens like E. coli could not survive in an acidic environment, such as citrus and apple juice. Odwalla apple juice had a pH (acidity) level of 4.3. (On the pH scale, 7 is neutral, and levels below 7 are increasingly acidic.) Odwalla did conduct spot testing of other, more pH-neutral products. The Food and Drug Administration, although it did not have specific guidelines for fresh juice production, indicated in its Retail Food Store Sanitation Code that foods with a pH lower than 4.6 were *not* potentially hazardous.

In the early 1990s, however, scattered scientific evidence emerged that E. coli O157:H7 might have undergone a critical mutation that rendered it more acid-tolerant. In 1991, an outbreak of E. coli poisoning sickened 23 people in Massachusetts who had consumed fresh, unpasteurized apple cider purchased at a roadside stand. A second, similar incident occurred in Connecticut around the same time. In a study of the Massachusetts outbreak published in 1993, the *Journal of the American Medical Association* reported that E. coli O157:H7, apparently introduced by fecal contamination of fresh apples, had unexpectedly survived in acidic cider. The journal concluded that E. coli O157:H7 could survive at a pH below 4.0 at the temperature of refrigerated juice. The journal recommended strict procedures for sanitizing apples used to make fresh juice, all of which Odwalla already followed.

Although the FDA investigated both instances in New England, it did not issue any new regulations requiring pasteurization of fresh juice, nor did it issue any advisories to industry. At the time of the Odwalla outbreak, neither the FDA nor state regulators in California had rules requiring pasteurization of fresh apple juice.

Considering the Options

In the company's second-floor conference room, later in the day of October 30, Steltenpohl and Williamson gathered the company's senior executives to review the situation.

King County officials had identified about a dozen cases of E. coli infection associated with Odwalla apple juice products. But, as Steltenpohl later described the situation, "It was all based on interviews. They didn't yet have bacteriological proof." Washington health officials had not yet made a public announcement, nor had they ordered or even recommended a product recall.

Conversations with federal disease control and food safety specialists throughout the day had turned up troubling information. From them, Odwalla executives had learned of the two earlier outbreaks of E. coli illness associated with unpasteurized cider in New England. And they had been told that 157 could cause illness in very minute amounts, below levels that would reliably show up in tests. The FDA had indicated that it planned to launch an investigation of the incident but did not suggest that Odwalla had broken any rules.

Management understood that they had no *legal* obligation to order an immediate recall, although this was clearly an option. Another possibility was a nonpublic recall. In this approach, the company would quietly pull the suspect product off the shelves and conduct its own investigation. If a problem were found, the company could then choose to go public with the information.

The company carried general liability insurance totaling $27 million. It had little debt and about $12 million in cash on hand. The cost of various options, however, was hard to pin down. No one could be sure precisely how much a full or partial product recall would cost, if they chose that option, or the extent of the company's liability exposure.

Ordering a Recall

At 3 P.M., Steltenpohl and Williamson, about four hours after they had received the first phone call, issued a public statement.

> Odwalla, Inc., the California-based fresh beverage company, issued today a national product recall of fresh apple juice and all products containing fresh apple juice as an ingredient. . . . Our first concern is for the health and safety of those affected. We are working in full cooperation with the FDA and the Seattle/King County Department of Public Health.

The recall involved 13 products, all containing unpasteurized apple juice. At the time, these 13 products accounted for about 70 percent of Odwalla's sales. The company did not recall its citrus juices or geothermal spring water products.

"Stephen and I never batted an eyelash," Steltenpohl later remembered. "We both have kids. What if it had turned out that something was in the juice, and we left it on the shelf an extra two weeks, or week, or even two days, and some little kid gets sick? What are we doing? Why are we in business? We have a corporate culture based on values. Our mission is nourishment. We really never considered *not* recalling the product. Looking back, I suppose the recall was the biggest decision we made. At the time, it seemed the only possible choice."

Once the decision to recall the product had been made, the company mobilized all its resources. On Thursday morning, October 31, 200 empty Odwalla delivery trucks rolled out from distribution centers in seven states and British Columbia with a single mission: to get the possibly tainted product off the shelves as quickly as possible. Organizing the recall was simplified by the facts that Odwalla operated its own fleet of delivery vehicles and that, in most cases, the product was displayed in the company's own coolers. The delivery drivers simply went directly to their own accounts, and removed the recalled juices. In cases where the product was shelved with other products, Odwalla worked with retailers to find and remove it.

A group of employees in San Francisco, one of the company's major distribution centers, later recounted the first day of the recall:

> Every single person who is or was an RSP (route salesperson), express driver, or merchandiser, worked that first full day and the next.
>
> What was amazing was there were a lot of people who we didn't even have to call to come in. It might have been their day off, but they'd call to ask, "What can I do?"
>
> Right. They'd ask, "When should I come in? Where do you need me to be?" . . . It was an amazing effort. . . . We were able to make it to every single account on that first Thursday. That's a thousand accounts.

Within 48 hours, the recall was complete. Odwalla had removed the product from 4,600 retail establishments in seven states and British Columbia. "This is probably as speedy as a product recall gets," a stock analyst commented. "They probably accomplished it in world-record time."

On October 31, as it was launching its recall, the company also took several additional steps.

- The company announced that it would pay all medical expenses for E. coli victims, if it could be demonstrated that Odwalla products had caused their illness.

- The company offered to refund the purchase price of any of the company's products, even those that had not been recalled.

- The company established a crisis communications center at its headquarters and hired a PR firm, Edelman Public Relations Worldwide, to help it handle the crush of media attention. It also set up a Web site and an 800 hot line to keep the public and the media apprised of the most recent developments in the case. Twice-daily media updates were scheduled.

- The company decided to extend the recall to include three products made with carrot juice. Although these products did not contain apple juice, carrot juice was produced on the same line. Until the company had determined the cause of the outbreak it felt it could not guarantee the safety of the carrot juice products.

On October 31, as the company's route sales people were fanning out to retrieve the juice, Odwalla's stock price was plummeting. The company's stock lost 34 percent of its value in one day, falling from $18\frac{3}{8}$ to $12\frac{1}{8}$ on the NASDAQ exchange. Trading volume was 20 times normal, as 1.36 million shares changed hands.

Tracking the Outbreak

Over the next few days, the full extent of the outbreak became clearer. In addition to the cases in Washington, new clusters of E. coli poisoning were reported by health authorities in California and Colorado. As the company received reports about individual cases, Steltenpohl and Williamson attempted to telephone families personally to express their concern. They were able to reach many of them.

On November 8, a 16-month-old toddler from a town near Denver, Colorado, who had developed hemolytic uremic syndrome, died following multiple organ failure. Tests later showed antibodies to O157:H7 in the girl's blood. It was the first, and only, death associated with the E. coli outbreak. Steltenpohl immediately issued a statement that read:

> On behalf of myself and the people at Odwalla, I want to say how deeply saddened and sorry we are to learn of the loss of this child. Our hearts go out to the family, and our primary concern at this moment is to see that we are doing everything we can to help them.

Steltenpohl, who had spoken with the girl's parents several times during her hospitalization, flew to Denver, with the family's permission, to attend the child's funeral. The girl's father later told the press, "We don't blame the Odwalla company at all. They had no bad intentions throughout all this, and they even offered to pay all of [our child's] hospital bills. I told them yesterday that we don't blame them, and we're not going to sue."

By the time the outbreak had run its course, 61 people, most of them children, had become ill in Colorado, California, Washington, and British Columbia. Except for the Colorado youngster, all those who had become ill, including several children who had been hospitalized in critical condition, eventually recovered.

Investigation of the Outbreak

As the outbreak itself was running its course, the investigation by both the company and federal and state health authorities proceeded. On November 4, the FDA reported that it had found E. coli O157:H7 in a bottle of unopened Odwalla apple juice taken from a distribution center in Washington State. As it turned out, this was the only positive identification of the pathogen in any Odwalla product. Eventually, 15 of the 61 reported cases (5 in Colorado and 10 in Washington) were linked by molecular fingerprinting to E. coli found in the Odwalla juice sample. The origin of contamination in the other 46 cases remained unknown.

Meanwhile, federal and state investigators converged on Odwalla's Dinuba manufacturing plant, inspecting it from top to bottom, in an attempt to find the source of the pathogen. On November 18, the FDA announced that it had completed its review of the Dinuba facility and had found no evidence of E. coli O157:H7 anywhere in the plant. The investigators then turned their attention to the growers and packers who supplied apples to the Dinuba plant, on the theory that the company might have processed a batch of juice containing some ground apples contaminated by cow or deer feces. In their interim report, the FDA noted that although no E. coli was found at Dinuba, "microbial monitoring of finished product and raw materials used in processing [was] inadequate." Odwalla sharply challenged this conclusion, noting that the FDA did not have any requirements for microbiological testing.

Searching for a Solution

The recall placed enormous financial pressure on the company, and challenged its executives to decide how and when to reintroduce its products to the market.

As a short-term measure, Odwalla announced on November 7 that it would immediately reintroduce three of its recalled products, all juice blends, that had been reformulated without apple juice. These products would continue to be produced at Dinuba, but not on the apple processing line. In announcing the reformulation, Steltenpohl told the press, "Until we are assured of a completely safe and reliable method of producing apple juice, we will not include it in our juices."

But the reformulation of a few blended juice smoothies was hardly a long-term solution, since apple juice was a core ingredient in many of the company's top-selling products. Odwalla urgently needed to find a way to get apple juice safely back on the market. How to do so, however, was not obvious.

To assist it in finding a solution to the problem, Odwalla assembled a panel of experts, dubbed the Odwalla Nourishment and Food Safety Advisory Council, to recommend ways to improve product safety. In late November, with the help of these experts, Odwalla executives conducted detailed scenario planning, in which they reviewed a series of possible options. Among those they considered were the following:

- **Discontinue all apple juice products.** In this scenario, the company would eliminate all apple juice and blended juice products until it could be fully assured of their safety.

- **Improve manufacturing processes.** In this scenario, the company would take a number of steps to improve hazard control at various points in the production process, for example, through modified product handling procedures, multiple antiseptic washes, routine sample testing, and stricter controls on suppliers.

- **Modify labeling.** Another option was to disclose risk to the consumer through product labeling. For example, an unpasteurized product could be sold with a disclaimer that it was not suitable for consumption by infants, the elderly, or those with compromised immune systems, because of the very rare but still possible chance of bacterial contamination.

- **Use standard pasteurization.** Standard pasteurization involved slowly heating the juice to a point just below boiling and holding it at that temperature for several minutes. The heat killed dangerous microorganisms and also had a side benefit of extending the shelf life of the product. Standard pasteurization, however, also destroyed many of the nutritional benefits of raw juice.

- **Use modified pasteurization.** Modified pasteurization, also known as flash pasteurization, involved quickly heating the juice to a somewhat lower temperature, 160 degrees F., and holding it very briefly at that temperature to kill any harmful bacteria. In tests of this procedure, Odwalla technicians found that it yielded an apple juice that had a "lighter" taste than unpasteurized juice, but with a more "natural" taste than standard pasteurized apple juice. The process destroyed some nutrients, but fewer than standard pasteurization. Flash pasteurization did not, however, extend the shelf life of the product.

- **Use alternative (non–heat-based) technologies for removing pathogens.** The company also examined a number of alternative methods of killing pathogens. These included a high-pressure process in which pressure was used to explode the cell walls of bacteria; a process in which light waves were directed at the juice to destroy pathogens; the use of electricity to disrupt bacteria; and the use of herbal antiseptic products.

A key factor in the decision, of course, was what customers wanted. The company commissioned some market research to gauge consumer sentiment; it also carefully monitored public opinion as revealed in calls and letters to the company and discussions on public electronic bulletin boards, such as America Online.

The company also had to consider its financial situation. Remarkably, despite the recall, sales for the quarter ending November 30, 1996, were actually 14 percent ahead of the same period for 1995 because of excellent sales prior to the outbreak. The E. coli incident, however, had caused significant operating losses. By the end of November, the recall had cost the company about $5 million. Expenses had included the cost of retrieving and destroying product, legal and professional fees, and increased marketing costs. At the end of the fiscal quarter, Odwalla had a cash position of about $9 million, down from $12 million at the time of the outbreak.

On December 5, Odwalla announced that it had decided to flash pasteurize its apple juice. In a statement to the press, Williamson stated:

> Odwalla's first priority is safety. After much consideration and research, we chose the flash pasteurization process as a method to produce apple juice. It is safe, yet largely preserves the great taste and nutritional value allowing Odwalla to remain true to its vision of optimal nourishment. Importantly, we will continue to aggressively pursue the research and development of alternative methods to bring our customers safe, unpasteurized apple juice.

The following day, all apple juice and blended juice products were reintroduced to the market with flash pasteurized juice. The label had been redesigned to indicate that the product had been flash pasteurized, and Odwalla coolers prominently displayed signs so advising customers.

At the same time, the company moved forward with its expert panel to develop a comprehensive Hazard Analysis Critical Control Points (HACCP) (pronounced hassip) plan for fresh juice production. HACCP was not a single step, but a comprehensive safety plan that involved pathogen control at multiple points in the juice production process, including sanitation of the fruit, testing for bacteria, and quality audits at several points in the process. The company also continued to monitor new, alternative technologies for controlling bacterial contamination.

Regulating the Fresh Fruit Juice Industry

In the wake of the E. coli outbreak, public concern about food safety mounted, and federal and state regulators began considering stricter regulation of the fresh fruit juice industry. On December 16, the FDA sponsored a public advisory hearing in Washington, D.C., to review current science and to consider strategies for improving the safety of fresh juice. Debate at the two-day hearings was wide-ranging.

Steltenpohl and Williamson represented Odwalla at the hearing. In their testimony, the Odwalla executives reported that they had decided to adopt flash pasteurization, but argued *against* government rules requiring all juice to be heat-treated. "Mandatory pasteurization would be a premature and unnecessary step in light of the vast new technologies emerging," Steltenpohl told the hearing. He warned the panel that mandates could "lead to widespread public fears about fresh food and beverages."

Steltenpohl and Williamson called on the FDA to continue to explore different methods for producing fresh juice safely. In addition, they called for industry self-regulation aimed at adoption of voluntary standards for safe manufacturing practices and hazard control programs. The Odwalla executives reported that they viewed flash pasteurization as the last line of defense in a comprehensive program to eliminate pathogens.

Some other juice makers and scientists supported Odwalla's position. Several small growers vigorously opposed mandatory pasteurization, saying they could not afford the expensive equipment required. A representative of Orchid Island Juice Company of Florida asked, "What level of safety are you trying to achieve? We don't ban raw oysters and steak tartar, although the risks are much higher. Nor do we mandate that they be cooked, because it changes the flavor." A number of food safety experts testified about emerging technologies able to kill pathogens without heat treatment.

Some scientists and industry representatives, however, were on the other side. Two major firms, Cargill and Nestlé, both major producers of heat-treated juice products, argued vigorously for a government mandate, saying that "other technologies just won't do the job." Dr. Patricia Griffin of the Centers for Disease Control and Prevention noted that "current production practices do not guarantee the safety of apple cider, apple juice, and orange juice." She called for pasteurization of apple juice and cider, as well as product labels warning customers of potential risk. A representative of the Center for Science in the Public Interest called for a label warning the elderly, infants, and persons with suppressed immune systems to avoid fresh, unpasteurized juice.

Several days after the hearing, the advisory panel recommended against mandatory pasteurization, for the moment at least, calling instead for "good hazard control" at juice manufacturing plants and in the orchards that supplied them. However, an FDA spokesman added, "we can never say that forced pasteurization is completely off the boards." The agency indicated that it would continue to study a number of alternative approaches to improving juice safety, including mandatory pasteurization.

Looking to the Future   In May, 1997, Steltenpohl reflected on the challenges facing Odwalla:

> Our task now is to rebuild a brand and a name. How you rebuild . . . these are important decisions. You can make what might be good short-term business decisions, but they wouldn't be the right thing. The decisions we make now become building blocks for the [company's] culture. We have to look at what's right and wrong. We need a clear moral direction.

Discussion Questions

1. What factors contributed to the outbreak of E. coli poisoning described in this case? Do you believe that Odwalla was responsible, wholly or in part, for the outbreak? Why or why not?
2. What do you believe Odwalla should have done as of October 30, 1996? As of November 11, 1996? In each instance, please list at least three options and state the arguments for and against each.
3. What steps, if any, should Odwalla take as of the point the case ends?
4. Do you consider Odwalla's voluntary recall decision to be an act of corporate social responsibility? Why or why not?
5. What is the appropriate role for public policy in the area of food safety? Assess the role of government authorities in this case. In your view, did they act properly?

Case Study:
UNUM CORPORATION AND THE MAINE COALITION FOR EXCELLENCE IN EDUCATION

There are things you can do as a group, things that you can do as a collaborative entity, that you could never do as a single company, no matter how powerful you are, no matter how small your state is, no matter how much money you spend.
—Kevin Healey

Kevin Healey, director of public involvement initiatives for Unum Corporation, considered what steps the company should take next in its role as a central player in the Maine Coalition for Education. A comprehensive coalition of primary stakeholders promoting systemic change throughout Maine's kindergarten through twelfth grade (K-12) education system, the Maine Coalition for Excellence in Education (MCEE) had played a critical role in the passage of statewide education reform legislation. Now, in 1997 and seven years into the process, Healey wondered what the future of the Coalition should be. More important, he wondered how Unum could continue to participate in the Coalition in a way that fostered the company's core philosophy of finding a better way in all it did.

Unum Corporation

Unum Corporation was chartered in 1848 as Union Mutual, a small life insurance company. Originally headquartered in Boston, Massachusetts, the company moved to Portland, Maine, in 1881. Founder Elisha B. Pratt had been committed to the notion of finding "the better way," a philosophy that became deeply ingrained in Unum's culture. Over the years, the company had grown into one of the leaders in the insurance industry by focusing on disability insurance and special risks. In the mid-1980s, in order to continue to succeed in the intensely competitive insurance industry, Union Mutual reorganized as a publicly held corporation and renamed itself Unum (meaning "one" in Latin). The company concentrated its efforts in three areas: streamlining operations, diversifying in domestic markets, and expanding overseas. The shift from a mutual company into one that was publicly held required Unum's managers to focus on building long-term value for shareholders while still retaining the company's historical values with respect to customers, employees, and the community.

At the time the company went public, Unum created new mission and vision statements, as shown in Exhibit A. These emphasized the company's intention to act with integrity and high ethical standards, to treat employees "as we would like to be treated," and to build long-term relationships with customers.

A Strategic Focus on Education

In the late 1980s, executives recognized that the changing insurance market would increasingly demand greater name recognition for Unum. Although the company had been in existence for almost 150 years, Unum was hardly a household name. In the past, Union Mutual had sold its insurance products mainly through insurance brokers, who in turn sold to end-users. Now, however, this traditional

Note: This case was written by Michael Ames, MBA/MSW, Boston College (May 1998) and Sandra Waddock, Carroll School of Management, Boston College. ©1998 by the authors. Used by permission. All rights reserved.

EXHIBIT A   Unum Corporation: Mission and Vision Statement

Mission

To relieve clients of insurable financial risk. We protect clients from financial hardships that result from retirement, death, sickness and from disability or other casualty events.·

Vision

We will achieve leadership in our businesses. Leadership does not necessarily mean a dominant market share. Rather, we will achieve leadership in areas which are meaningful and important to our business and the market, e.g., profitability, quality, reputation.

We will focus our business on specialty, risk-relieving products for which we can establish and sustain profitable positions. Development of these products will be driven by the needs of customers, in both domestic and international markets.

We will be a products-offered company: Developing products which meet customer needs and leveraging our expertise and strengths. Our product development efforts will focus on providing the right solution. Seeking market segments which are appropriate for our products. Delivering our products in a high-quality and efficient manner utilizing existing and new channels. Our products will be perceived by customers as representing superior value in quality and price, and will consist of a total offering including risk, service, delivery and reliability.

We will be known for: Superior knowledge, expertise and risk management, quality service, being responsive to the needs of customers and intermediaries, being reliable, dependable and trustworthy providing the right solutions to current and emerging needs, implementing good ideas well.

We will be a well-managed company: Consistently-growing profits, an efficient cost structure, leadership returns and financially sound, anticipating, shaping and effectively responding to relevant external forces and events, making decisions in the best long-term interests of our stakeholders, planning well; making clear and sound business decisions.

Values

We take pride in ourselves and the organization's leadership position:

Acting with integrity and high ethical standards.

Achieving leadership in performance, the community and the industry.

Setting and meeting individual goals consistent with business goals, and owning our individual performance.

Being motivated and excited about the organization.

Believing in what we are doing.

Emphasizing the positives, celebrating our successes and strengths, and constantly striving to improve our performance.

Delivering results.

We value and respect people:

Dealing with each other as individuals, and treating each other as we would like to be treated.

Developing people to their fullest potential.

Working together in a common endeavor: recognizing each other as important elements to the success of the whole.

Having a common understanding of each other's role and how we fit with the corporate objectives.

Collaborating with each other and having a sense of team.

Recognizing and accepting differences among people, but sharing the same values.

We value customers:

Building long-term relationships with our customers and intermediaries.

Maintaining a strong orientation to service and the customer.

Delivering what we promise.

We value communications:

Communicating clearly, consistently and openly with everyone we deal with.

Building an environment which encourages open communication, participation, honesty and candor.

Listening.

model was rapidly changing, and Unum intended to sell policies directly to the public. Unum executives knew they needed to increase their profile among potential customers.

Management felt that by addressing a public policy issue Unum could both make a difference within the community and raise the profile of the company and its CEO, James F. Orr. In 1990 Janice Hird, director of the Unum Foundation, began thinking about enhancing Unum's public involvement. Numerous public policy issues were in the spotlight. Orr and Hird quickly focused on public education. According to John Carroll of the Unum Foundation:

> [Unum] picked education purposefully for two reasons. One, because education is obviously critical to the nature of the business. Education's success and workforce quality is critical. [And two,] . . . to help raise the visibility of the CEO. At the time, when you looked around at the issues you might get involved with, and how to do that, there were environmental issues, crime, the economy, a whole host of issues. . . . Education was . . . central to the company's success, it has a lot of public interest and visibility, but it really did provide a good opportunity to influence and raise the profile of the CEO. . . . Education was an issue waiting to be addressed. There wasn't any clear logical [business] leadership that was already in place [in Maine].

At the time that Unum was considering a possible role in education reform, fully one in five students in Maine did not graduate from high school with their class. Fewer than half who went onto college completed their studies. Additionally, a survey of public and private employers conducted in 1992 reported that over 70 percent said that their young employees did not have the skills they expected of an educated worker. These problems had persisted despite significant raises in average teacher salaries in Maine during the 1980s, as well as nearly 50 percent (inflation adjusted) increases in total spending on education. Since spending alone seemed to be ineffective in achieving significant improvements in educational achievement, it was rapidly becoming clear that Maine needed a major shift in educational policy. Unum's Orr decided to take the lead.

Changing the Company First

Orr wisely understood that before a company like Unum would have credibility to ask the schools, the legislature, parents, or anyone else to change, the company needed to start by reforming its own policies. Unum focused initially on parental leave for school-related matters. Healey noted:

> Recently, I was asked to suggest some easy steps other businesses might take to become better partners for education. . . . I came up with a surprising answer, "Let them begin where we did—with their human resources policies."
>
> When we took our first steps for education reform, our Human Resources Department responded by introducing the School Release policy. The policy allows parents to attend parent/teacher conferences, classroom presentations, field trips, or just to join their child in the classroom for a day. We offer this as a paid benefit specifically because we think they have a special obligation to their children's education, and school activities almost always conflict with the workday.

Later, Orr announced that the company would begin asking for "proof of performance in high school" in its hiring process to reinforce the message that all students, not just the college-bound, need to work hard and get good grades in school.

In addition to looking within, Unum undertook a careful strategic planning process for its education reform efforts. According to Healey:

> Too many companies jump right in and they say, "Well, we're business. We know how to get things done, lets just jump right in and fix it." Big mistake! You wouldn't do that if they were launching a product, or if you were thinking about a major change in your organization. What you would do is get smart and ask yourselves a lot of questions around customers, "What the customers expect? What's the market? What's the focus?" The same approach is true for the education initiative. We took a look at learning everything we could about education, about what attempts had been made, who are our partners, what had happened nationally, what does the department of education do [before acting].

Unum's analysis led it to conclude that systemic change in education was needed. Since the mid-1980s, hundreds of school-business partnerships had been established throughout the United States. Most of them, Unum's analysis concluded, could be characterized as "feel good" partnerships. That is, the companies gave money to always-needy school systems, felt good about it, washed their hands of involvement, and went on to other more pressing business matters. And nothing much changed within the schools, because new band uniforms or more funds for trips had no impact on curriculum, structure, or standards. Despite spending considerable amounts of money on partnerships with schools and a variety of reform efforts, many business leaders nationally had expressed frustration at the slowness of change.

In contrast, Unum management understood that real involvement meant change, both internal and external, if the educational system itself were to change. Schools needed to change, but so did standards, structure, and curriculum. So did the relationships among all stakeholders interested in better educational achievement. And, as the parental leave policy suggested, businesses themselves needed to change. For such change to be successful, Unum CEO Orr figured, it needed to be supported and implemented at three different levels: at the grassroots, involving parents and the rest of the community; within the educational system, involving teachers, administrators, and teachers' unions; and in the public policy arena at the state level. Healey later described these levels as being interconnected, building on top of one another as in the levels in a pyramid.

The bottom level, the grassroots, he noted, is comprised of the education system stakeholders. Initiatives directed at the grassroots, alone, do nothing to change the system but can provide the foundation on which change at other levels can be built. Grassroots initiatives range from changing corporate culture to enable parents to attend to their children's educational needs, to providing assistance to schools by volunteering or providing financial and in-kind donations to schools and PTAs.

The second level, the educational system, includes all aspects of the system, from the teachers and the ways they are trained, to the curriculum they teach, how schools and school days are structured, and standards. Initiatives at this level include working with schools and school administrators through the provision of grants and training resources to change the way they teach.

The third level, the public policy arena, includes the laws and regulations that drive and provide mandates for the educational system. This level, Unum felt, provided the greatest opportunity to impact the educational system. Unum realized, however, that without support and ownership of policy change from the grassroots and educational system levels, such change would be doomed, much as similar initiatives had been elsewhere in the country. Thus, Orr concluded that the only way to effectively work toward systemic change was for Unum to work at each level and to integrate initiatives across all three, in order to maximize support for systemic change.

The Maine Coalition for Excellence in Education (MCEE)

Realizing that there was a need for legislative change involving all stakeholders, not simply business, Unum took the lead in forming a coalition aimed at educational reform. With financial support from Unum, the Maine Development Foundation, a Maine-based foundation whose charge is to promote development in Maine, brought together a group that included business leaders, students, parents, educators, and government officials in what became the Maine Coalition for Excellence in Education. One of the coalition's first actions was to hold a symposium in 1990 called "Rethinking Education: Maine's Future in the Balance." At that symposium, James Orr spelled out his vision, derived from the strategic planning effort on education.

In all our talks and studies with these and other experts, we learned . . .

- Measurable improvements . . . demand fundamental changes in the attitudes and practices of educators and in society's attitudes toward and responsibilities to education.
- There are no quick fixes. Real change will not happen quickly. It must happen, ultimately, if our economy and society are to prosper and grow. So we're prepared to make support of education improvements a fundamental component of our corporate public policy. Not just for today, or this year, but for a minimum of five years, with the intention it will carry on much longer.
- Substantive, long-term solutions are going to take not only financial commitment but human and technical resources as well. We will not sit in criticism of you; rather we will work beside you. We will not give only our money, but share with you our many resources. And we will not judge the system, but will, with you, evaluate its results regularly.

After this symposium, Orr convened a meeting of MCEE, with participation by leading educators, businesspeople, citizens, and government officials. MCEE identified three primary means through which it could help restructure the Maine public education system: by developing a comprehensive *vision* for better education along with a plan for achieving that vision; by creating an independent, consistent *voice* for education reform to sustain this effort and by fostering a collaborative spirit and *understanding among stakeholders.*

The first goal of the Coalition was to develop a plan for Maine's educational system that could be used to drive legislative change. All stakeholders were included in the process of formulating this plan. According to Healey:

> [We] made a conscious choice that [the plan] shouldn't be top down. . . . [Rather,] it *should* be driven by the stakeholders. . . . The Maine Coalition for Excellence in Education . . . included people from the legislature—state senators—members from the Department of Education, the state superintendent. We had business leaders from the banks, to Unum, to [L.L.] Bean. We had the president of the teachers union. We had a couple of students. We tried to get everyone we thought had a stake in this on that coalition.

The involvement of multiple stakeholders was important in two critical ways. First, having representatives of all of education's stakeholders meant that the plan received inputs from a range of sources with different perspectives. The result was a plan that represented all viewpoints. Second, representatives from each sector were able to take ownership of the plan and subsequently present it to other members of their particular group, creating support throughout every sector.

Learning to Work Together

Having so many stakeholders work together, however, was not always easy. Stereotypes existed on both sides. Educators were used to asking for a check from business and doing what they wanted with the money. Unum, however, wanted to engage in a real hands-on partnership in which it would have significant involvement over a long period of time. It was difficult for both sides to give up their unique positions of strength to engage in a more equal collaborative partnership.

One issue the Coalition faced early on was that of school choice. Business leaders tended to take a pro-choice position, which would allow parents and students to choose their schools, presumably permitting market forces to operate in what is traditionally a monopoly situation. Educators, on the other hand, tended to say, "School isn't just like business. This is not a business; we are talking about what is best for kids." Educators tended to take the position that all children need to be educated to succeed in the modern world, that choice will "cream off" the best students for the best schools leaving poorer students in weaker schools that are underfunded. Further, educators tended to believe that education is a public good that not only prepares students for work but also enhances citizenship. These positions created tension between two well-meaning groups.

Rather than allow this potentially divisive issue to split the Coalition, members were able to engage in a productive dialogue because of a culture of openness and trust. According to many observers, Unum CEO James Orr played an important role in creating such a culture. Commented school superintendent Robert Kautz, "Orr as an individual created the climate of openness. He personally facilitated the steps as chairman that created an open climate and trusting culture necessary for the coalition to work. His example also set the stage for others in the coalition to take an approach that all voices must be heard." According to Kautz, Orr demonstrated that an ability to listen to all viewpoints, disagree without personalizing the disagreement, and work through difficult issues in an open and trusting fashion.

Legislative Action

After two years of hard work, MCEE finally issued its own vision and reform plan. The plan, called *Success Begins with Education,* outlined 15 goals. Goals focused on four levels. First was creating successful students by developing a common core of learning and a certificate of initial mastery to be earned by all students effective 1998. Next was successful schools through enhanced accountability measures and an integrated school-assessment process based on specified performance standards. In addition, the goals set forth the resources needed to prepare schools for success, including shared vision, collaboration, leadership, and an emphasis on meeting high expectations for student learning, as well as meeting the expectations of the business community for workforce preparedness. Finally, the goals outlined the steps necessary to prepare communities for success, including providing resources to parents, training for collaboration, and support for parents, children, and schools by employers.

The presence of legislators in MCEE proved vital to successful legislative action. Within nine months of the release of *Success Begins with Education*, the Maine Legislature had approved *An Act to Enhance the Role of the State Board of Education*. But this was only a first step. Continued legislative work, with significant political pressures from the Coalition, resulted in 1994 in the passage of a reform package that mirrored MCEE's plan. Throughout 1994, the Legislature's Task Force on Learning Results worked on state standards. By 1996, Coalition members were able successfully to petition the state to appropriate public money for its continued work. Finally, in 1996, the 117th Maine Legislature adopted six guiding principles proposed by the Task Force to define a successfully educated Maine student. It asked the Task Force to return in 1997 with specific learning standards and performance indicators in eight subjects: career preparation, English and language arts, foreign languages, health and physical education, mathematics, science and technology, social studies, and visual and performing arts. These standards were submitted in February 1997 and passed later in the legislative session.

Other Unum Initiatives

Outside of MCEE, Unum developed initiatives to support change at all three levels. At the grassroots, Unum addressed its company culture and the way this affects and is affected by the education system, as illustrated by its policy to encourage employees to go to their children's school meetings. Further, Unum brought in speakers and trainers to speak to employees and their children about educational issues. And the company assigned an employee to coordinate schools' volunteer needs with volunteers from the company. As a result, parents employed at Unum were able to become more involved in their children's schools, employees were encouraged to volunteer in the schools, and employees had more opportunities to learn more about the public school system. Healey commented:

> We have tried very hard . . . to get the mind-set of our employees moved to not only how important education is, but that the company values education and supports the employees as they try to make a difference in their kids education and in the local school systems. . . . A few years ago the Portland school district bought a new cen-

tralized computer system and they wanted to input all of the student records onto the system so they could start tracking student performance better. They didn't have the labor to do that. We were able to go to employees and say Portland needs help. . . . Hundreds of people responded. . . . It didn't cost the school system a dime in labor.

Working within the second level, the education system, Unum supported change through the provision of grants to schools. For example, the Unum Foundation funded a project called the Extended Teacher Education Program (ETEP). ETEP changed the way teachers were trained at the University of Southern Maine, from a traditional four-year program to an innovative five-year program. This program was sponsored by Unum with the understanding that, if the program were successful, it would be institutionalized when the Unum Foundation grant expired. The company hoped that ETEP would create a model within the system of an innovative new way in which to train teachers.

Moving on to New Challenges

In 1997, the Coalition needed to redefine its mission. Initially, MCEE had successfully created a plan for change. It had then redirected itself to focus on lobbying for the passage into law of the plan's goals. Now, with these goals largely accomplished, the Coalition had to address important questions about its future direction. Healey commented:

> We are now working on what the new role [of the Coalition] should be. One of the things we think we need [to do is to play] . . . an oversight role that watches for opportunities and problems and then brings them to the public's mind. . . .

Although MCEE's plan was far from complete, Unum believed that the Coalition was capable of sustaining the effort for as long as necessary. Because it was organized on an assumption of complementary strengths rather than one sole authority in a leadership position, MCEE represented a unique working relationship among many of the state's leading businesses, education organizations, state agencies, and public and private initiatives in higher education. Its members were able to work individually and in small collaborations on issues that matched their expertise and professional responsibilities. For example, coalition members from the state's schools of education could proceed with innovations in teacher education and professional development for educators. The state Department of Education had refined the education assessment system, while the Superintendent's Association had created seminars to enhance knowledge of standards-based learning. This cooperation allowed the group's work to proceed on many fronts with minimal burdens on individual organizations and relieved members of MCEE from the need to work on activities where they had little expertise, insight, or influence.

Plotting the Future

From the company's point of view, Unum's efforts appeared to have been successful on all counts. It had worked successfully within MCEE to improve the state's education system. In the process, Unum had raised the public profile of the company and of its chief executive. Many people believed that CEO James Orr's appointment as chairman of the National Alliance of Business had resulted in large part from the favorable attention he had received through his efforts to reform education. Having achieved its initial goals, it was time for Unum to reassess its role in the education reform movement in Maine. Healey noted:

We have been spending close to $600,000 a year [on educational reform efforts]. As in any product cycle, there comes a time when you have to ask, are there any new products that we should be focusing on. . . .

What, Healey wondered, as 1998 began and the new century loomed, should be the company's position with respect to education reform and its involvement in the MCEE?

Discussion Questions

1. What were Unum's goals in helping establish the Maine Coalition for Excellence in Education? How well did the company achieve these goals?
2. What were the most important stakeholders in this coalition? What were their underlying interests?
3. What made this coalition work? Can you make any generalizations, based on this case, about the conditions under which collaborative partnerships are likely to succeed?
4. From the perspective of Unum and the other stakeholders in this collaboration, what do you think the next steps should be, and why?

Pat Jones   Pat Jones was an engineer at the Hamilton Company, a manufacturer of power transmission products. Hamilton was a highly respected company, offering a quality product with a reputation for ethical business practices. The company had developed and widely distributed a formal code of ethics and regularly provided ethics training for its employees.

Hamilton's management recently introduced a policy of participative management. Management believed that decision-making responsibility should rest with those closest to the decision. Participative management was intended to allow the company to respond quickly to changing market conditions. It was a deliberate move toward a decentralized organizational structure.

Hamilton's sales were running 20 percent below last year's level and were expected to continue to decline. Management attributed the slump to poor economic conditions. Hamilton's president had recently sent a memo to the sales and engineering personnel. The memo expressed concern regarding incoming orders, recommending cost-cutting measures and alluding to possible layoffs. The president also pointed out market niches that Hamilton managers should pursue more aggressively and indicated that all orders should be reviewed for potential sales of additional accessory products. Most of the accessories offered attractive profit margins.

While working on a recent order, Pat Jones noticed that the order included three oil pumps. Oil pumps were not necessary for the intended application for this order. Oil pumps were normally used on variable speed or inclined drives where the standard splash lubrication system was not adequate. For this application the oil pumps offered no advantage to the customer. The oil pump accessories were sold for $5,000 each and were to be provided on each of three gearboxes.

Pat contacted Kelly Long, the sales agent for the order. Kelly indicated that the oil pumps were included in the order because they were often needed and the customer had insisted on a quick quote. Sales agents typically did not have sufficient information to determine when oil pumps would be required.

Kelly was reluctant to approach the customer to discuss removing the oil pumps from the order. Kelly said, "Look Pat, this customer is very difficult to work with. The purchase order specified oil pumps. Unless it has a detrimental effect on the gearbox, let's give the customer what was ordered. Besides, I'd rather put my efforts toward increasing sales than reducing sales." It was Hamilton's policy to have the sales agent handle all communications with the customer.

Pat discussed the matter with two colleagues at Hamilton. One coworker indicated that the oil pumps should be provided as ordered. The other coworker suggested that oil filters should be included with the oil pumps in the order. The oil filters would provide additional value-added to the customer by providing an oil filtration system ordinarily not furnished, although it was not clear that this additional system was essential for the customer's needs.

Note: The organizations and individuals portrayed here are fictional. They are based on the author's discussions of common ethical dilemmas with corporate managers.

Discussion Questions

1. Since the Hamilton Company has introduced a participative style of management, decision-making responsibility rests with Pat Jones. In light of the firm's economic troubles, should Pat approve the order for the oil pumps? What is Pat's responsibility to Hamilton? To the customer? To the sales agent?

2. Is Hamilton's reputation as an ethical business compromised by the sales agent including oil pumps in the order, or by Pat approving the order? What ethical safeguards at Hamilton are being challenged in the case or should be developed by Hamilton to ensure ethical behavior by its employees?

3. The oil pumps provide an additional, although unnecessary, function for the customer. Is it wrong to provide this benefit to the customer? One of Pat's coworkers suggested an additional accessory: oil filters. Should they be added to the order as well?

4. Using the ethical decision-making framework presented in Chapter 6, what is the proper ethical response to the question confronting Pat? Which is a better guide for ethical conduct in this situation: utilitarianism, rights, or justice?

Chris Brown

Lee Samson and Chris Brown had worked for 15 years as entry-level system programmers for Runner Manufacturing, a leading manufacturer of automotive ride control products. Runner was a large, centralized firm with a traditional, formal hierarchy marked by multiple levels of supervision. Typically, important decisions were made by top management. Respect for authority and being a team player were highly valued by the organization's senior management team.

While working at Runner's corporate headquarters, Lee and Chris slowly worked up through the ranks of the large systems department. In the process, they developed a close friendship. As system analysts, Lee and Chris designed, tested, and brought to operational status software that automated payroll, inventory, finance, and operations management.

Eight months earlier, both had been promoted to a supervisory level upon the retirement of their predecessors. Lee became supervisor of the systems group responsible for operations (inventory controls and product plans), while Chris became supervisor of the functional systems group responsible for program maintenance and development for administration and finance areas. Although both were pleased with their promotions, they both felt uneasy at giving up hands-on work with software. They also believed that they had reached the upper limit of career growth given the rigid cultural climate at Runner.

It was Lee Samson who broached the topic of going off on their own. At first, it was simply a little off-duty talk. Eventually, both Lee and Chris recognized they had skills in software programming that could have a real outside demand. The idea took shape of starting an information systems storage and consulting service for small and medium-sized firms. They decided to take the plunge and resign from the firm as soon as they had acquired the necessary hardware.

The new venture required Lee and Chris to convert space in Lee's home into an office for their computer. While recently inspecting new file servers (data storage equipment), Chris was surprised to find sophisticated software already loaded onto their personal systems at the new office. Closer scrutiny proved the software was similar to the operations, payroll, and accounting systems currently in use at Runner's corporate headquarters. When questioned, Lee at first tried to hedge but finally admitted to systematically copying Runner's system programs and routines that would be useful in their new business. Copying was a simple matter since the office in Lee's home was connected by a modem to the company's mainframe computer. Lee assured Chris that great care had been taken to avoid copying any actual data, as this would have been theft of company proprietary information and a violation of Runner's code of ethics. Seeing Chris's dismayed look, Lee said, "Look Chris, we've worked our tails off for 15 years installing, testing and making every one of these systems run. If anyone 'owns' these systems and the right to their use, it's you and me. Runner loses nothing in this, no product or customer data, absolutely nothing."

Discussion Questions

1. From an ethical perspective, who owns the computer software—the developers of the software (Lee and Chris), or the firm that hired the developers (Runner Manufacturing)? What ethical principles support your position?
2. Using Figure 5–3, why did this ethical problem occur for Chris?
3. What action alternatives are available to Chris in this case? Using each of the six stages of moral development and ethical reasoning discussed in Chapter 6, what action do you think Chris will select? What is the best action for Chris?

Jesse Green

Jesse Green worked in the accounting department for Premier Jewelry, Incorporated. Premier Jewelry had been in existence for over 100 years. The company had a written mission statement that emphasized the value of respecting its employees. The company was highly regarded throughout the industry, operating stores in 17 states.

Jesse Green had worked with the company for five years and had been quite successful. The company was going through a time of change in the past three years with many departments downsizing and restructuring to cut costs. It was increasingly important for Premier Jewelry to manage expenses so that profit margins were equivalent or better than other similar companies in the jewelry industry. The accounting function for the company recently had been decentralized and Jesse was in charge of the accounting area for a business unit of Premier Jewelry.

Jesse was given a specific personnel target size during an interim reorganization period. Several permanent positions were decided, but it was determined that several positions should be filled with temporary employees until the organization would know definitely its long-term needs for permanent staffing.

Premier Jewelry had stated in its policy manual that it would hire people permanently or let them go after one year. This policy had generally not been in conflict with everyday business practices in the past, as temporary employees were usually able to complete their work in less than a year. Temporary employees were not typically told that they had no chance of permanent employment with the company.

Jesse's department had two temporary employees. Alex, a secretary, had been an employee for just over one year. Leslie, an accounting clerk, had been employed for just under a year. Both contracts had been extended for an additional six months by the controller for Jesse's business and the director of finance for Jesse's division. The controller told Jesse that making a personnel hiring decision was a million dollar decision for every employee. The controller and director were in favor of limiting the number of permanent employees for cost reasons. Jesse was told that managing division expenses was something considered in the annual employee performance review.

Jesse felt that the current situation was in violation of the company's stated policy not to hire temporary employees for extended periods of time. Additionally, Jesse felt the company was being unfair and deceptive to the individuals involved, as they had not been told they had no opportunity for long-term employment.

Jesse worked with two other managers in the financial accounting area. Both had been in similar situations and suggested that if Jesse wanted to continue on a successful career path that the two temporary employees should be hired for an additional six months and Jesse should not worry about it. "Besides," they said, "everybody is doing it."

Discussion Questions

1. Assess the ethical basis for Premier Jewelry's policy regarding the hiring of temporary employees. Is the policy fair? Does it respect the employees' rights? Does it achieve the greatest good for the greatest number affected?
2. Which of the nine ethical climates, discussed in Chapter 6, reflects Premier Jewelry's ethical climate? Is this climate ethically acceptable? If not, how could it be improved?
3. Assume that Jesse finds it ethically objectionable to extend Alex and Leslie's contracts for an additional six months. What company ethical safeguards could Jesse use or create to avoid taking this action?

On November 10, 1995, world-renowned Nigerian novelist and environmental activist Ken Saro-Wiwa was executed by hanging in a prison courtyard. Just eight days earlier, he had been convicted by a military tribunal on charges that he had ordered the murder of political opponents. Throughout his trial, Saro-Wiwa had vigorously maintained his innocence. Despite protests by many world leaders and human rights organizations, the Nigerian military regime had quickly carried out the death sentence.

Saro-Wiwa's execution provoked a profound crisis for the Royal Dutch/Shell Group of Companies. In its wake, some environmentalists and political leaders called for an international boycott of Shell's gasoline and other products. The World Bank announced it would not provide funding for Shell's liquefied natural gas project in Nigeria. Several groups, including the London Royal Geographic Society, voted to reject the company's charitable contributions. In Canada, the Toronto provincial government refused a major gasoline contract to Shell Canada, despite its low bid. Some even called for the oil company to pull out of Nigeria altogether.

Alan Detheridge, Shell's coordinator for West Africa, told a reporter in February 1996, "Saro-Wiwa's execution was a disaster for us."

Just what was the connection between Saro-Wiwa's execution and Shell Oil? Why did the company find itself suddenly, in the words of the *New York Times,* "on trial in the court of public opinion?" Had the company done anything wrong? And what, if anything, could or should it do in the face of an escalating chorus of international criticism?

The Group

The Royal Dutch/Shell Group was the world's largest fully integrated petroleum company. Upstream, the conglomerate controlled oil and gas exploration and production; midstream, the pipelines and tankers that carried oil and gas; and downstream, the refining, marketing, and distribution of the final product. The company also had interests in coal mining, metal mining, forestry, solar energy, and biotechnology. In all, the Anglo-Dutch conglomerate comprised over 2,000 separate entities, with exploration and production operations, refineries, and marketing in scores of countries. Royal Dutch/Shell was, in both its ownership and scope, perhaps the world's most truly transnational corporation.

In 1994, Royal Dutch/Shell made more money than any other company in the world, reporting astonishing annual profits of $6.2 billion. The same year, the company reported

Note: This is an abridged version of a longer case: Anne T. Lawrence, "Shell Oil in Nigeria," *Case Research Journal* 17, no. 4 (Fall/Winter 1997). Abridged by the author by permission of the *Case Research Journal.* Sources include articles appearing in *The Wall Street Journal, New York Times, Economist, Fortune, Guardian* (London), *Independent,* and *Village Voice;* U.S. congressional hearings, reports by Amnesty International, Greenpeace, and the World Bank; and material posted by Shell Nigeria on its Web site at http://www.shellnigeria.com. The history of Royal Dutch/Shell is based on Adele Hast, ed., *International Directory of Company Histories* (Detroit, MI: St. James Press, 1991); and *World Class Business: A Guide to the 100 Most Powerful Global Corporations* (New York, NY: Henry Holt, 1992). Ken Saro-Wiwa's story is drawn primarily from his memoir, *A Month and a Day: A Prison Diary* (New York: Penguin Books, 1995), and other writings. A full set of footnotes is available in the *Case Research Journal* version. Copyright © 1997 by the *Case Research Journal* and Anne T. Lawrence. All rights reserved.

revenues of $94.9 billion, placing it tenth on *Fortune*'s Global 500 list. Assets were reported at $108.3 billion, and stockholders' equity at $56.4 billion. With 106,000 employees worldwide, it had the largest workforce of any oil company in the world.

This highly successful global corporation traced its history back over more than a century and a half. In the 1830s, British entrepreneur Marcus Samuel founded a trading company to export manufactured goods from England and to import products, including polished sea shells (hence, the name "Shell"), from the Orient. In the early 1890s, Samuel's sons steered the company into the kerosene business, assembling a fleet of tankers to ply the fuel through the Suez Canal to Far Eastern ports. At about the same time, a group of Dutch businessmen launched the Royal Dutch Company to drill for oil in the Dutch East Indies. In 1907, Royal Dutch and Shell merged, with Royal Dutch retaining a 60 percent interest and Shell, 40 percent. The resulting organization came to be known as the Royal Dutch/Shell Group of Companies, or simply the Group.

Over the years, Royal Dutch/Shell had developed a highly decentralized management style, with its far-flung subsidiaries exercising considerable autonomy. The company believed that vesting authority in nationally based, integrated operating companies—each with its own distinctive identity—gave it the strategic flexibility to respond swiftly to local opportunities and conditions. The corporation was governed by a six-person board of directors. Reflecting its dual parentage, the Group maintained headquarters in both London and The Hague. The chairmanship rotated periodically between the president of Shell and the president of Royal Dutch. Decision making was by consensus, with no dominant personality.

Shell Nigeria

The Shell Petroleum and Development Company of Nigeria—usually called Shell Nigeria—stated its corporate objective simply. It was "to find, produce, and deliver hydrocarbons safely, responsibly, and economically for the benefit of our stakeholders."

The Royal Dutch/Shell Group had begun exploring for oil in West Africa in the 1930s, but it was not until 1956 that oil was discovered in the Niger River delta in southeastern Nigeria. In 1958, two years before Nigeria's independence from Britain, Shell was the first major oil company to commence operations there. Nigerian oil was of very high quality by world standards; in the industry, it was referred to as "sweet crude," meaning that only minimal refining was required to turn it into gasoline and other products.

In 1995, Shell Nigeria was the largest oil company in the country. The company itself was actually a joint venture with the Nigerian federal government, which owned a 55 percent stake. Royal Dutch/Shell owned a 30 percent stake in the joint venture; the remaining 15 percent was owned by two European oil companies strategically aligned with Shell. Although the Nigerian government was the majority owner in the joint venture, its role was confined mainly to providing mineral rights; Shell built and managed the lion's share of the oil operations on the ground. Other players in the Nigerian oil industry, including Mobil and Chevron, mainly operated offshore. Of all the multinational oil companies in Nigeria, Shell had by far the most visibility.

Shell Nigeria's operations were huge, not only by Nigerian standards, but even by those of its parent firm. In 1995, Shell Nigeria produced an average of almost one million barrels of crude oil a day—about half of Nigeria's total output—in 94 separate fields spread over 31,000 square kilometers. It owned 6200 kilometers of pipelines and flow lines, much of it running through swamps and flood zones in the Niger delta. In addition, the company operated two coastal export terminals. The Nigerian operation provided about

14 percent of Royal Dutch/Shell's total world oil production—and probably a larger share of its profits, although financial data for Shell's subsidiaries were not separately reported.

Shell Nigeria employed about 2,000 people. Ninety-four percent of all employees, and about half of senior managers, were Nigerian. Few employees, however, were drawn from the impoverished delta communities where most oil facilities were located. For example, by one estimate, less than 2 percent of Shell Nigeria's employees were Ogoni, the delta ethnic group of which Saro-Wiwa was a member. The percentage of local people was higher—20 to 50 percent—on Shell's seismic crews, which did the dirty and dangerous work of drilling and blasting during oil exploration.

The company's financial arrangements with its host country were highly beneficial to the Nigerian government. For every barrel of oil sold by Shell Nigeria, 90 percent of net revenues (after expenses) went to the federal government, in the form of taxes and royalties. Shell and its aligned companies split the remaining 10 percent. Although Shell and the Nigerian government worked hand in glove in the oil industry, relations between the two were often strained. Although usually unwilling to comment publicly, Shell seemed to resent the Nigerian government's large take and was frustrated by its frequent failure to pay revenues due its corporate partners.

The Giant of West Africa

Nigeria, the Group's sometimes troublesome partner, has been called the "giant of West Africa." Located on the North Atlantic coast between Benin and Cameroon, Nigeria was slightly more than twice the size of California, and—with 98 million people—the most populous country on the continent. Nigeria's gross domestic product of $95 billion placed its economy second, smaller only than South Africa's. The economy was heavily dependent on petroleum; oil and natural gas sales produced 80 percent of the federal government's revenue, and over 90 percent of the country's foreign exchange. Thirty-seven percent of all exports—and 50 percent of oil exports—went to the United States, more than to any other single country.

Nigeria was a land of stark socioeconomic contrasts. The nation's military and business elites had grown wealthy from oil revenues. Yet, most Nigerians lived in poverty. The annual per capita income was $250, less than that of Haiti or China, and in the mid-1990s, economic distress in many parts of Nigeria was deepening.

A legacy of colonialism, in Nigeria as elsewhere in Africa, was the formation of states that had little historical basis other than common colonial governance. In the Nigerian case, the modern nation was formed from what had been no less than 250 disparate ethnic groups, many with few cultural or linguistic ties. The nation was comprised of three main ethnic groups: the Hausa-Fulani, the Yoruba, and the Ibo. Together, these three groups made up 65 percent of the population; the remaining 35 percent was made up of scores of smaller ethnic groups, including the Ogoni.

Since its independence from Britain in 1960, Nigeria had been ruled by military governments for all but nine years. Several efforts—all eventually unsuccessful—had been made to effect a transition to permanent civilian rule. In June 1993, military dictator Ibrahim Babangida annulled the presidential election, suspended the newly created national assembly, and outlawed two fledgling political parties. Just five months later, yet another military man, General Sani Abacha, took power in a coup. The Abacha regime quickly developed a reputation as "indisputably the cruelest and most corrupt" government in Nigeria since independence. A specialist in African politics summarized the situation in Nigeria before the Senate Foreign Relations Committee in 1995:

[The] current government appears indifferent to international standards of conduct, while dragging the country into a downward spiral of disarray, economic stagnation, and ethnic animosity. . . . [It] has curtailed political and civil rights to an unprecedented degree in Nigerian history, magnified corruption and malfeasance in an endemically corrupt system, and substantially abandoned responsible economic management.

In 1993, inflation was running close to 60 percent annually, foreign debt was growing, and the country's balance of payments was worsening. Corruption was so rampant in Nigeria, the *Economist* concluded in an editorial, that "the parasite . . . has almost eaten the host."

The Ogoni People

The Ogoni people, Saro-Wiwa's ethnic group, lived in the heart of the Nigerian oil fields. Numbering about half a million in the mid-1990s, the Ogoni spoke four related languages and shared a common animistic religion. Prior to the arrival of the British in 1901, a stable Ogoni society based on fishing and farming had existed for centuries in a small area (a mere 12 by 32 miles) in the delta region near the mouth of the Niger River. It was here that Shell had discovered oil.

Although Ogoniland was the site of tremendous mineral wealth, the Ogoni people had received virtually no revenue from its development. Somewhere on the order of $30 billion worth of oil was extracted from Ogoniland's five major oil fields between 1958 and 1994. Yet, under revenue sharing arrangements between the Nigerian federal government and the states, only 1.5 percent of oil taxes and royalties was returned to the delta communities for economic development, and most of this went to line the pockets of local officials.

The Rivers State, that included Ogoniland, was among the poorest in Nigeria. No modern sanitation systems were in place, even in the provincial capital. Raw sewage was simply buried or discharged into rivers or lakes. Drinking water was often contaminated, and water-related diseases such as cholera, malaria, and gastroenteritis were common. Ogoniland's population density was among the highest of any rural area in the world. Housing was typically constructed with corrugated tin roofs and cement or, more commonly, dirt floors. Approximately 30–40 percent of delta children attended primary school, compared with about three-quarters in Nigeria as a whole; three-quarters of adults were illiterate. Unemployment was estimated at 30 percent. A British engineer who later returned to the delta village where oil was first discovered commented, "I have explored for oil in Venezuela, I have explored for oil in Kuwait, [but] I have never seen an oil-rich town as completely impoverished as Olobiri."

In 1992, in response to pressure from the Ogoni and other delta peoples, the Nigerian government established a commission, funded with 3 percent of oil revenues, to promote infrastructure development in the oil-producing regions. In 1993, the group spent $94 million, with about 40 percent going to the Rivers State. Shell Nigeria also gave some direct assistance to the oil-producing regions. In 1995, for example, the company's community development program in Nigeria spent about $20 million. Projects included building classrooms and community hospitals, paying teacher salaries, funding scholarships for Nigerian youth, and operating an agricultural station. According to one study, however, almost two-thirds of Shell's community development budget was allocated to building and maintaining roads to and from oil installations. Although open to the public, these roads were of little use to most delta residents, who did not own cars. Moreover, Shell made little effort to involve local residents in determining how its community development funds would be spent.

Ken Saro-Wiwa: Writer and Activist

Ken Saro-Wiwa, who became a leader of the Ogoni insurgency, was in many respects an unlikely activist. A businessman who later became a highly successful writer and television producer, he had a taste for gourmet food, sophisticated humor, and international travel. Yet, in the final years of his life he emerged as a world-famous advocate for sustainable development and for the rights of indigenous peoples who was honored by a Nobel peace prize nomination and the Goldman Environmental Prize.

Saro-Wiwa was born in 1941 in an Ogoni village. A brilliant student, he was educated first at missionary-run schools and later, with the aid of a scholarship, at the University of Ibadan, where he studied literature. After a brief stint as a government administrator, Saro-Wiwa left public service to launch his own business. After four years as a successful grocer and trader, he took the proceeds and began investing in real estate, buying office buildings, shops, and homes. In 1983, with sufficient property to live comfortably, Saro-Wiwa turned to what he called his first love, writing and publishing. He proved to be a gifted and prolific writer, producing in short order a critically acclaimed novel, a volume of poetry, and a collection of short stories.

In 1985, Saro-Wiwa was approached by a university friend who had become program director for the state-run Nigerian television authority. The friend asked him to develop a comedy series. The result, "Basi & Co.," ran for five years and became the most widely watched television show in Africa. Reflecting Saro-Wiwa's political views, the program satirized Nigerians' desire to get rich with little effort. The show's comic protagonist was Basi, "a witty rogue [who] hustled on the streets of Lagos and was willing to do anything to make money, short of working for it."

By the late 1980s, Saro-Wiwa had become a wealthy and internationally known novelist and television scriptwriter. His wife and four children moved to London, where his children enrolled in British private schools. Saro-Wiwa joined his family often, making many friends in the London literary community who would later work doggedly, although unsuccessfully, for his release.

In 1988, Saro-Wiwa undertook a nonfiction study of Nigerian history, later published under the title, *On a Darkling Plain.* This work reawakened his interest in politics and in the plight of his own Ogoni people. In a speech in March 1990, marking the study's publication, Saro-Wiwa laid out a theme from the book that was to become central to the rest of his life's work:

> The notion that the oil-bearing areas can provide the revenue of the country and yet be denied a proper share of that revenue because it is perceived that the inhabitants of the area are few in number is unjust, immoral, unnatural and ungodly.

On a Darkling Plain, not surprisingly, ignited a storm of controversy in Nigeria, and "Basi & Co." was canceled shortly after its publication, as was a column Saro-Wiwa had been writing for the government-owned weekly *Sunday Times.*

Movement for the Survival of the Ogoni People

The cancellation of his TV series and newspaper column seemed to propel Saro-Wiwa further into political activism. In August 1990, he met with a group of Ogoni tribal chiefs and intellectuals to draft an Ogoni Bill of Rights. This document called for political autonomy; cultural, religious, and linguistic freedom; the right to control a "fair proportion" of the region's economic resources; and higher standards of environmental protection for the Ogoni people.

Shortly thereafter, drafters of the bill of rights met to form an organization to press their demands. The group chose the name Movement for the Survival of the Ogoni People (MOSOP). From its inception, MOSOP adopted a philosophy of nonviolent mass mobilization. The group's earliest organizational efforts focused on educational work and appeals to the military government and the oil companies. The organization published the Ogoni Bill of Rights and organized a speaking tour of the region to present it to the Ogoni. Saro-Wiwa traveled abroad—to the United States, Switzerland, England, the Netherlands, and Russia—where he met with human rights and environmentalist groups and government officials to build support for the Ogoni cause. MOSOP also issued a propagandistic "demand notice" calling on Shell and its Nigerian partners to pay damages of $4 billion for "destroying the environment" and $6 billion in "unpaid rents and royalties" to the Ogoni people.

Environmental Issues

A central plank in the MOSOP platform was that the oil companies, particularly Shell, were responsible for serious environmental degradation. In a speech given in 1992 to the Unrepresented Nations and Peoples Organization (UNPO), Saro-Wiwa stated MOSOP's case:

> Oil exploration has turned Ogoni into a wasteland: lands, streams, and creeks are totally and continually polluted; the atmosphere has been poisoned, charged as it is with hydrocarbon vapors, methane, carbon monoxide, carbon dioxide, and soot. . . . Acid rain, oil spillages and oil blowouts have devastated Ogoni territory. High-pressure oil pipelines crisscross the surface of Ogoni farmlands and villages dangerously. The results of such unchecked environmental pollution and degradation include the complete destruction of the ecosystem.

Shell disputed these charges, saying that they had been "dramatized out of all proportion." Shell argued that the land it had acquired for operations comprised only 0.3 percent of the Niger delta. Moreover, Shell charged, many of the oil spills in the area had been caused by sabotage, for which they could not be held responsible.

The Niger delta was one of the world's largest wetlands, a vast floodplain built up by sedimentary deposits at the mouths of the Niger and Benue Rivers. In a comprehensive study of environmental conditions in the Niger delta completed in 1995, the World Bank found evidence of significant environmental problems, including land degradation, overfishing, deforestation, loss of biodiversity, and water contamination. The study did find evidence of air pollution from refineries and petrochemical facilities and of oil spills and poor waste management practices at and around pipelines, terminals, and offshore platforms. Most of the delta's environmental problems, however, the World Bank concluded, were the result not of oil pollution but rather of overpopulation coupled with poverty and weak environmental regulation.

Of the environmental problems associated with the oil industry, the World Bank reported, the worst was gas flaring. Natural gas is often produced as a by-product of oil drilling. In most oil-producing regions of the world, this ancillary gas is captured and sold. In Nigeria, however, gas was routinely simply burned off, or flared, in the production fields. In 1991, over three-quarters of natural gas production in Nigeria was flared—

compared with, say, less than 1 percent in the United States or a world average of less than 5 percent. In 1993, Nigeria flared more natural gas than any nation on earth.

Gas flaring had several adverse environmental consequences. The flares produced large amounts of carbon dioxide and methane, both greenhouse gases and contributors to global warming. Residents in the immediate vicinity of the flares experienced constant noise, heat, and soot contamination. The flares, which burned continuously, lit up the night sky in much of the delta with an eerie orange glow. One British environmentalist commented poignantly after a fact-finding visit to the delta that "some children have never known a dark night, even though they have no electricity."

During the early 1990s, Shell Nigeria was involved in a joint venture known as the Nigeria Liquefied Natural Gas project. The aim of this scheme, in which Shell was a 24 percent shareholder, was to pipe natural gas to ocean terminals, liquefy it, and ship it abroad in special ships at supercooled temperatures. In late 1995, the fate of this venture was still unclear.

Contrary to charges made by some of Shell's critics, Nigeria did have some environmental regulations in place, dating from the late 1980s. These laws, which were enforced by the federal Department of Petroleum Resources, required industry to install pollution abatement devices, restricted toxic discharges, required permits for handling toxic wastes, and mandated environmental impact studies for major industrial developments.

Civil Disturbances in Ogoniland

During the early 1990s, civil disturbances in Ogoniland and nearby delta communities, many directed at Shell, escalated. Shell later posted on the Internet descriptions of some of these incidents. Two examples of Shell's posted accounts follow:

> [This] incident happened when armed youths invaded and occupied a rig location and nearby flow station, chasing off staff who were not given the opportunity to make the location safe. The youths demanded N100 million [*naira,* the Nigerian currency, at that time worth about $12.5 million], a new road, and a water scheme. Attempts to talk with the youths, who were armed with guns and machetes, failed.

In response, Shell staff called the Nigerian police, which sent in mobile units. In the ensuing riot, at least one policeman and seven civilians in the local village were killed. Shell concluded its posting, "The Shell response to the threatening situation was made with the best intentions and what happened was a shock to staff, many of whom had friends [in the village]."

In the second incident, as reported by Shell:

> A gang of youths . . . stormed . . . a drilling rig in the Ahia oil field . . . looting and vandalizing the facility and rig camp. Rig workers were held hostage for most of the first day while property worth $6 million was destroyed or stolen. The rig was shut down for 10 days and the Ahia flow station was also shut down. . . . [A protest leader] raised the issue of [distribution] . . . of oil revenues to the oil producing communities by the government, the need for a new road, and rumours of bribery by Shell of a [local] chief.

In this incident as well, Shell called the police; this time, no injuries resulted.

Most of the civil disturbances followed a similar pattern, as these examples suggest. A group of young men, armed with whatever weapons were readily available, would attack one of Shell's many far-flung oil installations in the delta. Employees would be attacked, equipment would be sabotaged, and the group would make demands. The demands would be denied, and the company would call in police. Violence against civilians sometimes followed.

Shell's own data on patterns of community disturbances in the Niger delta, posted on the Internet, revealed a pattern of escalating violence throughout the early 1990s, peaking in 1993. Shell estimated that the company sustained $42 million in damage to its installations in Ogoniland between 1993 and the end of 1995, as a direct result of sabotage.

The relationship between these incidents and MOSOP was complex. Saro-Wiwa's group explicitly rejected violence and repeatedly disavowed vigilante attacks on Shell or other companies, and Saro-Wiwa himself frequently toured Ogoniland to restore calm. Yet, publication of the Bill of Rights and MOSOP campaigns focusing attention on injustices suffered by the Ogoni clearly had the effect of escalating expectations within Ogoni society. In this context, many young unemployed Ogoni men simply took matters into their own hands.

On January 3, 1993, MOSOP held a massive rally to mark the start of the Year of the Indigenous Peoples. Held at successive locations across Ogoniland, the rally was attended by as many as 300,000 people, three-fifths of the Ogoni population. Protesters carried twigs, a symbol of environmental regeneration. Two weeks later, Shell abruptly announced that it would withdraw from Ogoniland. It evacuated all employees and shut down its operations. Company officials gave a terse explanation: "There is no question of our staff working in areas where their safety may be at risk."

The Militarization of Commerce

As civil unrest escalated in Ogoniland, Shell began to work more and more closely with the Nigerian police. Shell defended this practice, saying that it was normal in Nigeria to request police protection in areas where crime rates were high. Shell acknowledged that it provided firearms to police protecting its facilities. Several human rights organizations claimed that Shell provided more than handguns. The Nigerian Civil Liberties Organization reported that Shell-owned cars, buses, speedboats, and helicopters were regularly used to transport police and military personnel to the site of civil disturbances. Human Rights Watch reported that Shell met regularly with representatives of the Rivers State police to plan security operations.

After General Abacha took power in November 1993, he apparently decided to take a hard line with the Ogoni insurgency in an effort to induce Shell to resume operations. One of his first acts as chief of state was to assemble a special paramilitary force, comprised of selected personnel from the army, navy, air force, and police, to restore order in Ogoniland. According to internal memos, later revealed, the purpose of this force was to ensure that those "carrying out business ventures in Ogoniland are not molested." A memo dated May 12, 1994, read in part: "Shell operations still impossible unless ruthless military operations are undertaken for smooth economic activities to commence." It advised the governor of Rivers State to put "pressure on oil companies for prompt regular inputs as discussed."

In May and June 1994, intense violence erupted in Ogoniland. Amnesty International, which collected eyewitness accounts, reported that the government's paramilitary force entered Ogoniland, where it "instigated and assisted" interethnic clashes between previously peaceful neighboring groups. The units then "followed the attackers into Ogoni villages, destroying houses and detaining people." In May and June, the force attacked 30 towns and villages, where its members "fired at random, destroyed and set fires to homes, killing, assaulting, and raping, and looting and extorting money, livestock, and food," according to the Amnesty International report. As many as 2,000 civilians may have been killed.

In 1995, despite the government's efforts to make the area safe for business, Shell had still not returned to Ogoniland. All its other oil production operations in the Niger delta were being conducted under round-the-clock military protection. Claude Ake, a well-known Nigerian political economist, described the situation in a chilling phrase: "This is a process," he wrote, "of the militarization of commerce."

The Arrest, Trial, and Execution of a Martyr

On May 21, 1994, just over a week after the "smooth economic activities" memo, Saro-Wiwa was en route to a MOSOP rally where he was scheduled to speak. On the way, his car was stopped at a military roadblock, and he was ordered to return home. He never attended the rally. Later that same day, a group of Ogoni chiefs, who were political opponents of Saro-Wiwa, held a meeting. Their gathering was interrupted by a crowd of several hundred youths, who denounced the men as vultures who had collaborated with the military government. Four of the chiefs were assaulted and bludgeoned to death.

The following day, Saro-Wiwa and several other leaders of MOSOP were arrested. In a televised press conference, the governor of Rivers State blamed the MOSOP leaders for the murders. Saro-Wiwa and his colleagues were detained in a secret military camp, where they were chained in leg irons and denied access to medical care. It would be eight months before they were formally charged.

During Saro-Wiwa's imprisonment, his brother, Owens Wiwa, met on three occasions with Shell Nigeria's managing director Brian Anderson to seek his help in securing Ken's release. Wiwa later gave an account of these meetings that was posted on the Internet. Anderson told him, Wiwa reported, that it would be "difficult but not impossible" to get his brother out of prison. Anderson allegedly said, "if [MOSOP] can stop the campaign [against Shell] we might be able to do something." Wiwa refused. Wiwa also reported that he had asked Anderson if the company had made payments to the government's paramilitary force. "The answer he gave is that '*I* [emphasis added] have never approved payment to [the force].' He did not deny that Shell was paying. . . . I think he knew about it, and the people in London knew about it." While later acknowledging that meetings between Anderson and Wiwa had taken place as part of an effort at "quiet diplomacy," Shell denied Wiwa's specific allegations as "false and reprehensible."

In November, General Abacha appointed a Civil Disturbances Special Tribunal to try the case of the MOSOP leaders. Established by special decree, this tribunal was empowered to impose the death penalty in cases involving civil disturbances. The decision of the court could be confirmed or disallowed by the military government, but defendants had no right of judicial appeal. Amnesty International and many other human rights organizations denounced the tribunal for violating standards of due process guaranteed by Nigeria's own constitution and by international treaties.

Saro-Wiwa's trial for murder began in February 1995. Government witnesses testified that Saro-Wiwa had relayed a message to his youthful supporters, after the roadblock incident, to "deal with" his opponents. Saro-Wiwa's defense attorneys countered that Saro-Wiwa had been at home at the time and had had nothing to do with the killings. The defense team also presented evidence that two key prosecution witnesses had been bribed by the government with Shell contracts and cash in exchange for their statements implicating Saro-Wiwa. Shell adamantly denied bribing witnesses.

On November 2, the tribunal found Saro-Wiwa and eight other MOSOP leaders guilty of murder and sentenced them to death. Six defendants were acquitted. On November 8, Shell issued this statement, in response to international appeals that it seek a commutation of the sentence:

> We believe that to interfere in the processes, either political or legal, here in Nigeria would be wrong. A large multinational company such as Shell cannot and must not interfere with the affairs of any sovereign state.

Two days later, Saro-Wiwa and eight MOSOP associates were hanged in prison. His last words on the gallows were: "Lord, take my soul, but the struggle continues."

With Deep Regret   Shell issued a statement on the executions that read, in part, "It is with deep regret that we hear this news. From the violence that led to the murder of the four Ogoni leaders in May last year through to the death penalty having been carried out, the human cost has been too high." Shell told reporters that it had approached the government privately after Saro-Wiwa's conviction to appeal for clemency on humanitarian grounds. It would have been inappropriate, however, the company said, to have intervened in the criminal trial. The company also declined to comment further regarding human rights in Nigeria. A spokesperson said, "We can't issue a bold statement about human rights because . . . it could be considered treasonous by the regime and [our] employees could come under attack."

The company also defended its actions in the months leading up to Saro-Wiwa's arrest and trial. Shell representatives stated that it would have been wrong to have tried to influence government policy on environmental protection, Ogoni autonomy, or other issues of concern to MOSOP. With respect to the actions of the Nigerian police, the company argued that it would have been improper to provide its own armed security. An executive told the news media, "Our responsibility is very clear. We pay taxes and [abide by] regulation. We don't run the government." Shell also vigorously resisted demands by some human rights activists and environmentalists that the company withdraw from Nigeria. If it left, the company argued, whatever organization took over its operations would probably operate with lower environmental and safety standards, and the jobs of its Nigerian employees would be imperiled.

Shell's public disclaimers did little to slow down the controversy swirling around the company. By mid-1996, the company was facing a growing international boycott, the possibility that it would have to abandon plans to proceed with its liquefied natural gas project, and persistent demands that it withdraw from Nigeria altogether. The crisis threatened the company's shareholders, employees, franchisees, and customers—not only in Nigeria, but throughout the world.

Discussion Questions

1. What arguments did Shell make in defending its actions in Nigeria? How would Shell's critics counter these arguments? Do you believe Shell could or should have done anything differently in Nigeria?
2. What internal or external factors contributed to the emergence of this crisis for Shell?

3. What, if anything, should Shell do now?
4. Evaluate Shell's actions in Nigeria in reference to an existing code of conduct for multinational organizations. Do you believe that Shell was in compliance with the code you have selected? If not, how not? Do you believe the code you have selected is appropriate and adequate?
5. In your opinion, is it possible to develop a universal set of ethical standards for business, or do cultural differences make universal standards impractical, if not impossible?

On June 20, 1997, at a little after three in the afternoon, tobacco industry attorney Phil Carlton and Arizona attorney general Grant Woods emerged exhausted from a meeting room at the Park Hyatt Hotel in Washington, D.C. From inside the room—where negotiators for the tobacco industry, public health organizations, and state attorneys general had been engaged in days of nearly around-the-clock talks—reporters waiting in the hall could hear applause, then whooping and whistling. Woods flashed a thumbs-up sign to the press corps. "We've got a deal," he announced.

For weeks, the outcome of the delicate tobacco negotiations had been in doubt. Observers had called the talks chaotic and fractious. The talks had nearly broken down several times during the final few days, as negotiations foundered on the issues of document disclosure, government regulation, and whistle-blower protection. At one point, the attorney representing 20 of the 32 states at the table had simply walked out and flown off in his Lear jet. But at the last moment, both sides had made key concessions, and an agreement was reached.

In many respects, the deal struck at the Park Hyatt was astonishing. The big tobacco companies had agreed to pay *369 billion* dollars over the next quarter century and to submit to federal regulations and broad restrictions on cigarette advertising. In exchange, many state lawsuits would be settled, and the industry would be protected from most future litigation.

Never before had the tobacco giants been willing to make such vast concessions to their opponents. And never before had prominent public health advocates been willing to endorse limits on how much money smokers with lung cancer and heart disease could recover from the tobacco industry. The tobacco deal, said Mike Moore, Mississippi attorney general and a lead negotiator—with a bit of enthusiastic redundancy—was "the most historic public health achievement in history."

Many thought the agreement could herald a new era in the relationship between the tobacco industry and its critics in government and the public health community, as well as a model for the settlement of mass liability cases. On the other hand, the agreement itself was just the first step. In order to become law, the tobacco deal required congressional support. For this to happen, it would likely need the backing of the president, several federal agencies, and the many stakeholder groups it affected. None were assured. The historic tobacco deal could easily go up in smoke.

Note: An earlier version of this case, Anne T. Lawrence, "The Tobacco Deal," was presented at the Western Casewriters Association Annual Meeting, Portland, Oregon, March 26, 1998. The author would like to thank Carol Anderson, an MBA student at San Jose State University, for research assistance. This case was prepared from publicly available materials, including newspaper stories appearing in the *New York Times, The Wall Street Journal, Washington Post, Arizona Republic, Louisville Courier-Journal, Business Week, U.S. News & World Report,* and *USA Today;* material published on the Internet by Center for Responsive Politics; a special issue of *Mother Jones* magazine (May 1996); and two book-length studies, Philip J. Hilts, *Smokescreen: The Truth behind the Tobacco Industry Cover-up* (Reading, MA: Addison-Wesley, 1996); and Stanton E. Glantz, John Slade, Lisa A. Bero, Peter Hanauer, and Deborah A. Barnes, *The Cigarette Papers* (Berkeley, CA: University of California Press, 1996). The Brown & Williamson papers are available on the Internet at http://www.library.ucsf.edu/tobacco.

The U.S. Tobacco Industry

In 1997, tobacco was one of the United States' most profitable businesses, as well as one of its most controversial.

The U.S. cigarette industry was dominated by five companies, as shown in Table 1. The industry leader was Philip Morris Companies, Inc. The world's largest tobacco company, Philip Morris controlled almost half of the U.S. market for cigarettes and owned the world's second most valuable brand, Marlboro (the most valuable brand was Coca-Cola). The company's market value in 1996 was slightly under $107 billion. Although over half the company's revenue came from the sale of tobacco products, Philip Morris also owned profitable real estate, financial services, and food and beverage businesses, including Kraft and Miller Brewing.

Second, ranked by U.S. market share, was RJR Nabisco Holdings Corp. The company's tobacco subsidiary, R.J. Reynolds, produced Camel, Winston, and Salem cigarettes, among others. The company's food subsidiary, Nabisco, was a major producer of cereals, crackers, cookies, candy, gum, and other packaged food products. Although sales were split about evenly between tobacco and food products, most of the company's profits came from cigarettes.

Bringing up the rear were three companies with smaller market shares. BAT Industries (formerly, British American Tobacco), based in Britain, was the owner of Brown & Williamson, maker of Lucky Strike and Kool cigarettes, with an 18 percent share. (BAT had acquired another U.S. company, American Tobacco, in 1995.) Loews Corporation, controlled by billionaire brothers Laurence and Robert Tisch, was a holding company that included CNA Financial (an insurance company) and the Loews Hotels. One of Loews' smaller holdings was the Lorillard Tobacco Company, maker of Kent, Newport, and True cigarettes.

The smallest of the big five was Brooke Group Ltd. Brooke's Liggett division (formerly Liggett & Myers) held about 2 percent of the U.S. market with its Chesterfield, L&M, Lark, and some discount varieties of cigarettes. Brooke's chairman and CEO, Ben-

---

Table 1   *The big five tobacco companies, 1997, ranked by U.S. market share*

Company	Subsidiary	Key Brands	Market Share (percent U.S./ percent global)	Market Value	Sales (in U.S. $ millions)	Profits	Assets
Philip Morris	—	Marlboro, Virginia Slims	43/16	$106,580	$54,553	$6,303	$54,871
RJR Nabisco	RJ Reynolds	Camel, Winston	28/6	8,758	17,063	611	31,289
BAT Industries	Brown & Williamson	Lucky Strike, Kool	18/13	27,767	25,721	2,536	76,630
Loews Corp.	Lorillard	Kent, Newport	7	11,188	19,964	1,384	67,683
Brooke Group	Liggett	L&M, Chesterfield	2	93	414	196	135

Note: Market value is the share price on May 30, 1997, multiplied by the latest available number of shares outstanding. Sales is annual net sales reported by the company. Profits is latest after-tax earnings available to common shareholders. Market value, sales, profits, and assets are worldwide.
Sources: "The Business Week Global 1000," *Business Week,* July 7, 1997, pp. 55–92; http://www.hoovers.com/quarterlies/; http://www.sec.gov/archives/edgar/data/.

nett LeBow, owned 57 percent of the company. (UST Holdings, formerly U.S. Tobacco, was normally not included in the big five because it manufactured chewing tobacco and snuff, rather than cigarettes.)

In the United States in 1997, 26 percent of adults smoked. Slightly more men (28 percent) than women (23 percent) used cigarettes.

Domestic sales, however, were slipping, as they had for some time. At the peak of cigarette consumption in the United States in the early 1950s, fully half of American adults smoked; this percentage had been nearly halved in 40 years. All major tobacco companies had responded by moving aggressively to expand overseas sales, especially in the booming overseas markets of Asia, Eastern Europe, South America, Africa, and the Middle East, where American brands had status and consumption was rising. This strategy was to a large degree successful; in 1996, total international tobacco sales were $296 billion (the U.S. accounted for less than 40 percent).

The cigarette industry was phenomenally profitable. Warren Buffett, the well-known investor, explained the matter simply. "I'll tell you why I like the cigarette business," he said. "It costs a penny to make. Sell it for a dollar. It's addictive. And there's fantastic brand loyalty."

The tobacco industry was a major contributor to the U.S. economy. It added over $55 billion annually to the gross domestic product. Federal, state, and local taxes collected from the sale of cigarettes and other tobacco products in the United States totaled $13.1 billion in 1996. The industry was also a major employer in some states. Of the approximately 700,000 people employed in growing, processing, transporting, marketing, and retailing tobacco and its products, most were concentrated in the southeastern states. These workers, of course, contributed to the economy through their spending and income taxes. Tobacco products, a major export, significantly improved the U.S. balance of trade. The industry spent $6.2 billion a year for advertising, a big boost to Madison Avenue, and kept legions of attorneys and public relations people employed.

The tobacco industry also imposed significant economic costs. The total annual costs of smoking-related illnesses were estimated by the Centers for Disease Control in 1996 to run around $50 billion. These costs included health care for persons with emphysema, lung cancer, heart failure, and other tobacco-related illnesses, and lost work time and reduced productivity of smokers. Some of these costs were borne by the federal government, and hence, indirectly, taxpayers, through Medicare and Medicaid. Annual state spending (through various state medical plans) on smoking-related health care varied by population, of course; to cite a few examples, the yearly tab was $250 million in Florida, $240 million in Massachusetts, and $500 million in West Virginia. Individuals also paid, both directly and through their insurance premiums. These figures did not include, of course, the incalculable costs of pain and grief suffered by victims and their families. On the other hand, one study—funded by the tobacco industry—argued that smoking actually *saved* the U.S. health-care system money, for the simple reason that many smokers died early, sparing the system the cost of caring for them in old age.

Public Health Issues

The adverse health effects of cigarettes had been well-known in the public health community since the early 1950s. Smokers are 10 to 20 times more likely to suffer from lung cancer than are persons who do not smoke. Among smokers, the number of cancers rise with the number of cigarettes smoked. Cigarette smoke has been linked with cancer in animal studies, and a specific chemical agent in tobacco tar, *benzo(a)pyrene,* has been found in experiments to cause cancerous mutations in human lung cells. In addition to causing lung cancer, cigarette smoking also causes a number of other ailments. Smokers are at higher risk for coronary heart disease, stroke, throat and bladder cancer, chronic bronchitis, and emphysema. Smoking by pregnant women retards fetal growth. Secondhand smoke can cause lung cancer and heart disease in healthy non-smokers.

Smoking is the leading preventative cause of death in the United States. Each year, about 420,000 smokers and 53,000 nonsmokers die from tobacco-related illnesses, many more times as many as die from all other preventable causes of death (alcohol, auto accidents, AIDS, suicide, homicide, and illegal drugs) combined.

Nicotine, the pharmacologically active component of tobacco, is highly addictive. A member of the alkaloid family, nicotine is chemically related to other well-known addictive substances, including cocaine, heroin, and morphine. In any given year, about a third of smokers try to quit; only about 10 percent succeed, mainly because of the effects of nicotine addiction.

Smoking as a Pediatric Disease

Dr. David Kessler, commissioner of the Food and Drug Administration, frequently referred to smoking as a pediatric disease, that is, a disease of children.

The reasons for Kessler's somewhat startling assertion is that most people take up the cigarette habit in their teens. Among lifelong smokers, 90 percent began smoking by the time they were 18 and over half by the age of 14. The percentage of U.S. high-school students in 1995 who said they had smoked in the past month was 35 percent, up from 28 percent in 1991.

The reasons that smokers start in their teens are complex. Although nicotine is highly addictive, it does not promote an immediate physiologic dependence as do heroin and some other drugs. Rather, nicotine addiction takes on average one or two years of smoking to become fully established. At the same time, the act of smoking itself, for many people, is not particularly pleasurable initially; beginning smokers report that cigarettes burn their throats, make them cough, and don't taste particularly good. Who, then, sticks with the habit long enough to become hooked? The answer is: People in situations where peer pressures to smoke are strong and for whom peer influence is particularly compelling. Study after study has come to the same conclusion: Teens start smoking because their friends do. Once they've smoked regularly for a year or two, many find it extraordinarily difficult to quit, even if they want to.

Every day in the United States, 3,000 new young people take up the smoking habit. One out of three of them will die from tobacco-related illnesses, many in middle-age.

From the perspective of the tobacco companies, these facts about how people start smoking present a vexing problem. Sales of cigarettes to minors are illegal, and tobacco companies would prefer not to break the law or to face the public disapproval caused by peddling an addictive substance to youngsters. However, the industry is also well aware that it loses customers all the time; 1.3 million smokers quit every year, and 420,000 die. Most replacement smokers will be recruited, if they are recruited at all, from the ranks of the young.

Moreover, brand loyalty is exceptionally high among smokers, so the cigarette a smoker begins with often remains his or her brand for life. Cigarette makers thus have a strong financial incentive to market their products to teens, even though it is publicly awkward—not to mention illegal—to do so.

Lines of Defense   Although smoking was well known to cause death and disease, for many years the tobacco industry maintained a remarkable record of defending itself against both lawsuits and government regulation.

Until 1996, the tobacco industry never lost a lawsuit brought by a smoker. The tobacco companies were well funded, hired top attorneys, and defended all lawsuits extremely vigorously. The industry consistently maintained that tobacco had not been proven to cause cancer or other diseases. After warning labels were introduced in 1965, the industry was also able to argue that smokers had been informed of the risk and had assumed those risks and the consequences. Most juries blamed the smoker for not having the willpower to quit. "The American people know smokers can and do quit, and they still believe in individual responsibility," contended a press release distributed by R.J. Reynolds.

Moreover, the tobacco industry successfully used a variety of political strategies to block antismoking legislation and to thwart efforts to impose government regulation. The big five and their political organization, the Tobacco Institute, consistently donated large sums of money both to political parties and, through their political action committees, to individual candidates. Historically, the industry had funneled funds more or less equally to both major parties, but in the mid-1990s—following the Clinton administration's stepped-up efforts to impose regulations on the industry—its support shifted notably to the Republicans. The industry's 1996 contributions to political parties are shown in Table 2. That year, Philip Morris was the top donor of soft money among *all* contributors. Collectively, the tobacco industry was responsible for $6.6 million to both parties, out of the $263 million total for soft-money contributions that year.

In addition, the industry provided financial support to a variety of advocacy groups and think tanks with interests allied to its own—for example, those opposing FDA regulatory authority, promoting smoker's rights, and supporting free-speech rights for advertisers. The industry's powerful corporate lobby, The Tobacco Institute, vigorously promoted its point of view. Individual firms also maintained their own lobbying efforts; in 1996, for example, Philip Morris spent $19.6 million on its Washington, DC, lobbying operation.

Table 2   *Tobacco industry soft-money political contributions, 1996 election year*

Company	Republican	Democrat	Total
Philip Morris	$2,520,518	$496,518	$3,017,036
RJR Nabisco	1,442,931	254,754	1,697,685
Brown & Williamson	635,000	7,500	642,500
U.S. Tobacco	556,603	118,362	674,965
Tobacco Institute	424,790	106,044	530,834
Total	$5,579,842	$983,178	$6,563,020

Note: Soft money refers to funds donated directly to political parties to support party-building efforts such as televised campaign commercials that do not support a specific candidate, get-out-the-vote drives, and other activities in connection with presidential and congressional races. Soft money was legal under U.S. election laws in 1996. Limiting, or banning, soft-money contributions has been a key element of many campaign finance reform proposals.
Source: Center for Responsive Politics, from Federal Election Commission data, based on year-end reports filed by political parties, January 31, 1997.

The industry-funded Council for Tobacco Research (founded in 1954 as the Tobacco Industry Research Committee) sponsored partisan research and publicized the industry's contention that there was no proof that smoking caused cancer and heart disease. Commented the attorney for the National Center for Tobacco-Free Kids, "While [the industry's] PR campaigns were a failure with the public, they accomplished something more important: They gave politicians cover for failing to act."

Tobacco's political and public relations efforts were remarkably successful. For many years, the industry succeeded in avoiding the regulation of nicotine, holding cigarette taxes to a moderate level, blocking many local antismoking ordinances, and retaining mildly worded warning labels. In instance after instance, the tobacco industry actually managed to turn apparent setbacks to its advantage. When Congress banned television advertising of cigarettes, it benefited existing brands because, without television, introducing new brands was prohibitively expensive. The TV ban also meant the end of mandated public interest antismoking television spots, ones that had been hurting sales. When Congress required warning labels on cigarette packs, the industry won a clause in the law that effectively blocked lawsuits, on the grounds consumers had been warned of the risks. When the government has levied taxes on cigarettes, tobacco companies have often raised prices and then blamed government intrusion.

"Without exception, federal legislation designed to favor the public health has worked to the advantage of the industry," commented tobacco policy expert Kenneth E. Warner.

Chinks in the Industry's Armor

By the mid-1990s, however, tobacco's invincibility was weakening, leading some of its key strategists to consider negotiating an agreement with its adversaries. Several factors contributed to the industry's deteriorating position.

Congress Holds Hearings

In April 1994, the Democratic-controlled House of Representatives opened hearings on the health effects of tobacco. In testimony under oath, top executives of the tobacco industry assured Congress that their companies did not manipulate nor independently control the level of nicotine in cigarettes, and that cigarettes did not cause cancer or other illnesses. The hearings served to focus public attention on the industry. The tobacco industry executives' testimony was widely ridiculed; one survey later found that, when shown to the public, videotape of the tobacco chieftains swearing to tell the truth elicited "instant recognition and instant laughter." Grand juries later considered whether tobacco executives illegally conspired to obstruct a Congressional investigation.

Industry Whistle-Blowers Come Forward

Just a few weeks later, an industry whistle-blower made public some highly damaging internal company documents. Merrell Williams was a paralegal working for a law firm in Louisville, Kentucky, that had been hired by Brown & Williamson to review thousands of pages of company documents in connection with its legal defense. Williams, a longtime smoker of Kools who was suffering from heart disease, was shocked at what he saw. Over a several-month period, Williams smuggled documents out of the office and secretly copied them before returning the originals.

In May 1994, Williams mailed these documents to a prominent antitobacco researcher at the University of California–San Francisco, Dr. Stanton Glantz. Glantz subsequently posted the documents on the Internet. In July 1995, Glantz and his colleagues published an initial review of the B&W documents that provided strong evidence that Brown & Williamson was aware of the addictive nature of nicotine and of the health hazards of tobacco.

FDA commissioner Kessler later stated that the publication of the B&W documents was "a major moment, beyond which all went in one direction. It was the first time we had anyone saying, 'We are in the business of selling nicotine, which is an addictive drug.' Before that, it was all indirect evidence."

In November 1995, a second whistle-blower came forward. Dr. Jeffrey Wigand, chief of research for B&W from 1989–1993, gave a deposition in which he confirmed that the company had known that nicotine was addictive and had actively manipulated its levels in the final product.

FDA Moves to Regulate Tobacco

The B&W documents supplied the FDA with a new and powerful rationale for regulation. Under the Food, Drug, and Cosmetics Act, an article or substance is subject to regulation if it "affects the structure or function of the body." The industry had always maintained that, as a natural product—not a drug or device—tobacco should not be controlled by the FDA. The industry's apparent intent to cause addiction through the active manipulation of nicotine levels, however, seemed to qualify cigarettes as a drug-delivery device and hence subject to regulation.

In August 1995, using this reasoning, the FDA proposed far-reaching new rules that called for eliminating cigarette vending machines, billboard advertising near schools, and many forms of promotion aimed at young people, such as ads in youth-oriented magazines. The proposed rules also banned brand-name sponsorship of sporting events, the sale of tobacco-branded merchandise, and the distribution of free samples.

Within days, the tobacco industry and its allies in the advertising industry filed suit in North Carolina, claiming the FDA had no legal authority to regulate tobacco and that the proposed restrictions on cigarette advertising violated First Amendment rights.

State Lawsuits Progress

Several states brought lawsuits against the tobacco companies to recover the costs of health care for citizens with smoking-related illnesses. Mississippi was the first in 1994; it was quickly followed by a slew of others. Eventually, 29 states mounted lawsuits. These cases gradually worked their way through the system, threatening the tobacco companies with the possibility of massive judgments and bad publicity. The Mississippi case was scheduled to go to trial in June 1997.

Brown & Williamson Found Liable

In August 1996, for the first time ever, the tobacco industry lost in court. Brown & Williamson Tobacco Corp. was ordered to pay a landmark $750,000 in a personal-injury case in Florida brought by a man who had contracted lung cancer after 25 years of smoking. The suit charged the tobacco industry with marketing a defective and dangerous product. Invoking the doctrine of strict liability, plaintiff's attorneys had argued that the company should be held liable for damage done by its products whether or not they were aware of the potential dangers. This landmark decision threatened the tobacco industry, for the first time, with a flood of personal-injury lawsuits.

Liggett Breaks Ranks

In March 1996, the Liggett Group Inc.—the smallest and financially weakest of the major tobacco companies—broke ranks, destroying the industry's long-standing united front. As part of an effort to make Liggett more attractive as a possible acquisition, Bennet LeBow, CEO of Liggett's owner, the Brooke Group, cut separate deals with class-action lawyers and states then suing the tobacco companies. As part of the settlement, LeBow acknowledged that cigarettes were addictive and carcinogenic and said manufacturers had targeted youths under age 18 in their marketing. He also agreed to drop opposition to FDA regulation and to turn over documents that the state attorneys general believed would assist them in their litigation against the tobacco industry.

Tobacco Becomes an Issue in the Campaign

In the 1996 presidential campaign, tobacco regulation became a campaign issue. The Clinton administration focused on protecting children from the dangers of smoking. Senator Robert Dole, the Republican nominee, committed an apparent gaff when he stated during an interview that he did not believe nicotine was addictive. By some accounts, the tobacco issue helped the Democrats win the presidential election.

More Whistle-blowers Come Forward

In March 1997, the FDA released affidavits from three former Philip Morris employees that confirmed earlier allegations that their employer had deliberately manipulated nicotine levels in its cigarettes to ensure smokers got a nicotine jolt. One former scientist for the company stated that, "Nicotine levels were routinely targeted and adjusted by Philip Morris. . . . Knowledge about the optimum range for nicotine in a cigarette was developed as a result of a great many years of investigation." A former shift manager at a cigarette manufacturing plant in Richmond, Virginia, outlined for the FDA how Philip Morris carefully calibrated nicotine levels in a key production process.

Philip Morris responded to these allegations by denying that it manipulated the levels of nicotine in its tobacco products. To the contrary, the tobacco company described nicotine as a key component of taste. "At Philip Morris USA, we work hard to ensure the consistency and quality of our products—and quality control, no matter what the product or service, does not constitute 'manipulation.'"

FDA Jurisdiction Upheld

On April 25, 1997, a federal judge in North Carolina, acting in the industry's lawsuit, upheld the FDA's jurisdiction over tobacco. However, the court also ruled that the FDA had exceeded its authority when it banned certain forms of cigarette advertising, including billboard ads.

The Negotiations   The emergence of whistle-blowers and damaging internal documents, encroaching FDA regulation, successful smoker lawsuits, shifting public opinion, and a break in their own ranks combined to put great pressure on the tobacco companies. The industry was plainly concerned about the extent, and uncontrollability, of their liability for tobacco-related illnesses. For the first time, top executives of the leading tobacco companies began talking about a possible settlement. Cigarette makers "can't continue in public as kind of an outlaw industry," declared RJR Nabisco CEO Steven F. Goldstone. "A lot of forces are at work" favoring some broad settlement with industry adversaries, he noted. "In 1997, the most meaningful thing I can do is come to some solution [to] this problem."

From the industry's standpoint, a settlement held some attractions. Although any agreement would be extremely expensive, at least some of the costs could be passed on to consumers through higher prices. A deal would reduce the industry's legal fees, then running around $600 million a year. Stock prices could rise as tobacco shares, long depressed by investor concern over potential liability, emerged from under a cloud of uncertainty. And, in the United States at least, a public admission of the hazards of tobacco would free the industry to produce a new range of "safer" products, such as smoke-free or low-smoke cigarettes, those with lower concentrations of carcinogens, or even those designed to help smokers quit.

In April 1997, a group of state attorneys general, plaintiff attorneys, and representatives of all of the big five (except for Liggett, which had already settled) began the negotiations that led to the June 1997 deal. Also included in the talks were a few representatives of the public health community, including Matthew Myers, general counsel for the National Center for Tobacco-Free Kids. The White House was not directly involved, but Bruce Lindsey, a key presidential aide, monitored the talks closely as they proceeded.

Terms of the Deal

The June 20, 1997, settlement included the following provisions:

- **Tobacco industry payments.** The tobacco industry would be required to pay $368.5 billion for the first 25 years and then $15 billion a year indefinitely. Most of this money would go to the states, to compensate them for the cost of health care for persons with tobacco-related illness. $25 billion would go toward health care for uninsured children. Some funds would also finance antismoking education and advertising and enforcement of the settlement. Some (the percentage was not specified) would pay the fees of attorneys who negotiated the settlement. Passing these costs along to consumers would, by some estimates, result in a 62-cents-a-pack increase in the price of cigarettes.

- **Advertising.** All billboard and outdoor advertising of tobacco products, the use of human and cartoon figures (such as "Joe Camel") in ads, Internet advertising, product placements in movies and TV, and brand-name sponsorship of sporting events and brand-name promotional merchandise would be banned. Tobacco companies would be required to change their advertising to make it less appealing to children.

- **Warning labels.** Warning labels on cigarette packs would include the statements "Cigarettes Are Addictive," "Cigarettes Cause Cancer," "Smoking Can Kill You," and "Tobacco Smoke Causes Fatal Lung Disease in Nonsmokers" in white lettering on a black background over 25 percent of the top front of cigarette packs.

- **Government regulation of nicotine.** The Food and Drug Administration would be allowed to regulate the *quantity* of nicotine in cigarettes. However, the FDA could not *ban* nicotine from cigarettes until 2009. Even then, in order to reduce nicotine yield, the FDA would have to prove its action would result in a significant overall reduction of health risks, was technologically feasible, and would not create a significant demand for more potent black market cigarettes.

- **Cap on liability.** Tobacco companies would be protected from future litigation by a ban on punitive damages, class-action lawsuits, and consolidated litigation. The agreement would also settle the suits of 40 states and Puerto Rico, one class-action suit against the tobacco industry, and 16 others seeking certification. No money was given to plaintiffs in the 17 class-action suits. The agreement would ban class-action suits, consolidation of multiple suits, and punitive damages for past conduct. Medical bills and lost wages of individual claims would be paid from an annual $5 billion tobacco-company fund. Lawsuits by insurers to recover health-care payouts linked to smoking would be restricted. Also, there would be a yearly cap on payments for settlements and judgments.

- **Access to children.** Sale of cigarettes through vending machines would be outlawed, and a nationwide licensing system for tobacco retailers would be required to enable regulators to enforce the prohibition on access to minors.

- **Youth smoking.** The tobacco industry would be subjected to fines if youth smoking did not drop 30 percent in five years, 50 percent in seven years, and 60 percent in 10 years. There would be a penalty of $80 million per percentage point by which the target was missed. The annual fines would begin in 2002. The industry could petition for a 75 percent refund of a fine if it could show it had acted in good faith and in full compliance with the agreement, pursued all reasonable measures, and did nothing to "undermine achievement of required results."

- **Public smoking.** Smoking in public places and most workplaces without separately ventilated smoking areas would be prohibited. However, restaurants, bars, casinos, and bingo parlors would be exempt.

- **Smoker assistance.** Smokers would received modest payments for smoking-cessation treatment and monitoring smoking-related illnesses.

An Agreement under Fire

The tobacco deal was immediately under fire from several quarters.

The Advocacy Committee on Tobacco Policy and Public Health, a panel of experts headed by C. Everett Koop, a former surgeon general, rejected the deal as unacceptable. The panel criticized the proposed penalties for failing to reduce teen smoking as too small and also said that the pact would undercut the FDA's ability to regulate nicotine. Dr. David Kessler, who had recently left his post as FDA chief—and who also served on the Advocacy Committee—argued that the government's right to regulate nicotine as a drug had already been upheld by the courts. Therefore, any rules that would require the agency to "give up authority or jump through a lot of hoops" would be a major step backward, he said.

Some antismoking and public health organizations that had not participated in the negotiations criticized the proposed plan as a sellout to industry. "The public health community has been locked out of this negotiation," charged the director of SmokeFree Pennsylvania. The American Lung Association, which had opposed negotiations in the first place, said that the agreement was not sufficiently punitive to the industry. An ALA representative pointed out that all payments made by the tobacco companies, under the deal, would be tax deductible, costing the federal treasury some $125 billion. "In terms of holding this industry accountable, it's a free ride," she said.

Some thought that the government should simply stay out of the whole business. "Don't you think there are enough regulations out there?" asked Representative Henry Bonilla of Texas. He questioned whether it was wise "to substitute the federal government for the responsibility of a mother and a father to stop kids from smoking."

And while many state attorneys general had been party to the deal, others opposed it. Minnesota attorney general Hubert H. Humphrey III, who had declined the sign the pact, prepared to move forward with a separate trial against the tobacco companies. He believed that new evidence, including thousands of internal industry documents, could produce a much bigger settlement than his colleagues had negotiated.

Others prepared to mount constitutional challenges to the agreement, should it be approved by Congress. Some legal experts believed that the pact's provisions forcing settlement of existing class-action lawsuits and restricting future rights of smokers to sue violated constitutional rights to due process. The pact's limits on advertising might violate free-speech protections. Finally, the pact would override some state laws, for example, those governing retail licensing, potentially violating states' rights. The agreement was a "constitutional minefield," commented the president of the Association of Trial Lawyers of America.

But the tobacco industry and the state attorneys general vigorously defended the agreement. Massachusetts attorney general Scott Harshbarger said, "I am baffled by [the] criticism. . . . [Under the negotiated settlement], the FDA will for the first time have the money, the resources, and the power to control fully the nature and marketing of tobacco." And a representative of the tobacco industry argued, "People should look upon the settlement as a whole package. They should be aware of the enormous compromises made by the industry which will deliver significant progress in public health, especially in the area of reducing smoking by people who are underage."

Before going into effect, the settlement had to pass the scrutiny of several federal agencies including the Department of Health and Human Services, the Justice Department, and the Agriculture Department. It required presidential approval. And, of course, it had to be approved by Congress. The future of the tobacco deal was all but certain.

Discussion Questions

1. Who were the key stakeholders involved in, or affected by, the negotiations for a tobacco deal, and what were their central interests? To what degree were the interests of the various stakeholders met by the negotiated settlement?

2. Should the FDA regulate tobacco? What are the key arguments for and against involvement of the FDA in restricting or banning the sale or promotion of tobacco products?

3. What mechanisms of political influence had the tobacco industry historically used? Do you believe that the tobacco industry influenced the public policy process legitimately, or did it have too much influence?

4. Do you think it was ethical for the tobacco industry to continue to market cigarettes, even after evidence emerged that smoking caused lung cancer and other illnesses? Why or why not? In your answer, please refer to the three main methods of ethical analysis: utilitarianism, rights, and justice.

5. Do you support the tobacco deal? Why or why not? If not, what changes in the agreement, if any, would lead you to support it?

THE SPOTTED OWL, THE FOREST PRODUCTS INDUSTRY, AND THE PUBLIC POLICY PROCESS

On April 2, 1993, an extraordinary day-long conference opened at the Portland Convention Center in Portland, Oregon. Convened and chaired by President Bill Clinton, the conference was designed—as Clinton had promised during his campaign—to bring together key parties to a long-running dispute over protection of the threatened spotted owl and the logging of old-growth forest in the Pacific Northwest. The conference represented a key, early test of Clinton's position that economic growth and environmental protection are compatible and of his administration's ability to solve difficult problems through open, multiparty discussions.

The importance of the event was underscored by the many top government officials in attendance, including the vice president; the secretaries of Commerce, Labor, Agriculture, and the Interior; the administrator of the Environmental Protection Agency; and the governors of the states of Oregon, Washington, California, Idaho, and Alaska. Arrayed at three roundtables were some 50 invited speakers—scientists, industry officials, timber workers, and environmentalists—many of them longtime antagonists in the controversy.

In addition to the hundreds of observers in the convention center itself, perhaps thousands more rallied noisily outside, where industry groups passed out tree seedlings, environmentalists demonstrated to rock music, and loggers rumbled down the street in their trucks. Although some expressed apprehension about the potentially volatile mixture of groups gathered face to face, expectations ran high that the conference might break the gridlock that had gripped the Pacific Northwest since the late 1980s.

The Spotted Owl and Old-Growth Forest

At the center of the controversy was the survival of a reclusive bird that few present at the conference had ever seen: the northern spotted owl. This small, brown and white predator—just 22 ounces when full-grown—lives mainly in old-growth forests west of the Cascade Mountains from British Columbia to Northern California. As once vast, ancient forests were logged from the Pacific Northwest, the spotted owl's habitat declined; by 1993, only about 3,600 breeding pairs of spotted owls remained, scientists estimated.

The survival of the northern spotted owl is closely linked with the fate of the Pacific Northwest's old-growth forest. Old-growth forest is one in which trees are at least 150 to 200 years old. The majestic stands of old growth in the Pacific Northwest are typically dominated by mature Douglas fir and coastal redwood, often spanning 15 feet in diameter at the base and towering as high as 300 feet. Below these "climax" species grow

Note: This is an edited version of a case presented at the North American Case Research Association (NACRA) annual meeting, New Orleans, Louisiana, November 2, 1994: Anne T. Lawrence, "The Forest Conference: The Pacific Northwest Forest Products Industry, the Spotted Owl, and the Public Policy Process." The case is based on articles appearing in the *New York Times, Washington Post, Seattle Post-Intelligencer,* and other daily newspapers. A full account of the events leading up to the Forest Conference may be found in William Dietrich, *The Final Forest: The Battle for the Last Great Trees of the Pacific Northwest* (New York: Penguin Books, 1992); an analysis of the public policy aspects of the spotted owl controversy may be found in Steven Lewis Yaffee, *The Wisdom of the Spotted Owl: Policy Lessons for a New Century* (Washington, D.C.: Island Press, 1994).

smaller trees, creating a dense, multilayered canopy in which a great diversity of plant and animal species thrives.

Old-growth forest provides an ideal habitat for the northern spotted owl. The bird typically nests in snags, trees with broken tops. Fallen, decaying logs on the forest floor support abundant prey; and the multilayered canopy protects the spotted owl from extreme temperatures and from its own predators such as the goshawk and the great horned owl. Because of its close association with old-growth forest, ecologists refer to the northern spotted owl as an *indicator species,* meaning that its survival is a kind of warning light for the survival of the old-growth ecosystem as a whole and for numerous less well-known species of plants and animals that flourish there.

The Forest Products Industry

The old-growth forest on which the spotted owl depends is also a critical resource to a large and powerful industry: the Pacific Northwest forest products industry.

When pioneers first settled the Pacific Northwest in the mid-1800s, somewhere between 17 and 19 million acres of old-growth forest covered the landscape. Much of this land was eventually accumulated by big timber companies such as Weyerhaeuser, Georgia-Pacific, Boise-Cascade, and International Paper, and by holding companies such as railroads and insurance firms.

Throughout the twentieth century and accelerating in the postwar years, old-growth forests were harvested for their high-quality wood. By the 1980s, somewhere between 80 and 90 percent of the ancient forest had been logged. Virtually all privately owned timber, and most on state-owned lands, had been cut; fully 86 percent of remaining spotted owl habitat was in federally owned national forests and 8 percent on the national parks. Just a few patches of private old growth remained, including some owned by Plum Creek Timber Company, a firm divested by Burlington Northern Railroad during a reorganization in the late 1980s.

Beginning in the 1960s, many of the bigger timber companies, led by Weyerhaeuser, began a transition to *managed forestry,* the practice of growing genetically superior seedlings on massive tree farms carved from previously clear-cut forest. These firms introduced mechanical harvesting machines and developed new, high-tech mills designed to process the much smaller second-growth logs. They also pursued strategies of vertical integration, building or acquiring facilities for making pulp and paper and manufactured wood products.

A second segment of the forest products industry consisted of independent sawmills and manufacturers that processed old-growth logs and fashioned them into various finished wood products. In the early years, the independents were supplied mainly by private landowners. Later, as private reserves were exhausted, they turned to national forests as their main source of old-growth logs. Although prohibited from selling timber from *national parks,* the U.S. Forest Service was permitted—in fact, encouraged—to sell timber from *national forests,* since these sales provided revenue to the U.S. Treasury. Although some independents switched to processing second-growth timber, capital costs of this transition were high, and many remained dependent on federal old growth for their timber supplies.

The Environmentalists' Campaign to Protect the Ancient Forest

Environmentalists seeking to preserve remaining ancient forests were quick to seize on the potential value of the spotted owl. "The northern spotted owl is the wildlife species of choice to act as a surrogate for old growth protection," one environmentalist observed.

"I've often thought that thank goodness the spotted owl evolved in the Northwest, because if it hadn't, we'd have to genetically engineer it."

In 1986, environmentalists petitioned the Department of the Interior to list the spotted owl as an endangered species.[1] The petition was initially refused, but in 1990 the department reversed its position, listing the spotted owl as threatened.

In May 1991, in response to further lawsuits brought by environmentalists, U.S. District Court Judge William Dwyer ruled that the evidence revealed "a deliberate and systematic refusal by the [U.S.] Forest Service and the Fish and Wildlife Service to comply with the laws protecting wildlife." Judge Dwyer issued an injunction blocking timber sales in spotted owl habitat in 17 national forests in Washington, Oregon, and Northern California until the Forest Service could develop an acceptable plan for protecting the threatened species.

Impact on the Economy of the Pacific Northwest

The injunction effectively brought federal timber sales to a halt. In 1992, only 0.7 million board feet of timber were sold from national forest lands in the Pacific Northwest (down from a peak of 5 *billion* board feet during the peak year of 1987). (A board foot is equal to one foot square by one inch thick; a typical single-family house uses about 10,000 board feet of lumber.)

The consequences for the rural economy in many areas of the Pacific Northwest were devastating. By 1993, as many as 135 mills had closed, pushing unemployment up to 25 percent in some small communities. Cutters, loggers, truck drivers, and those in businesses serving them were thrown out of work. Tax receipts declined, affecting social services; the incidence of family problems, alcoholism, and other social problems increased. The intense frustration felt by many in rural Washington and Oregon was reflected in such slogans as "Support your local spotted owl—from a rope" and "Save a logger, shoot an owl."

President Clinton appeared fully aware of the intense controversy that had preceded the Forest Conference as he opened the event—and of the difficulty of reaching a resolution. "The process we begin today will not be easy," he observed. "Its outcome cannot possibly make everyone happy. Perhaps it won't make anyone completely happy. But the worst thing we can do is nothing."

Testimony before the Forest Conference, April 2, 1993[2]

Participants were seated at three large roundtables. As the conference proceeded, each roundtable was addressed in turn. Participants were asked to make a three-minute statement; the table was then opened for questions and discussion among those seated at the table and officials in attendance.

---

[1]The Endangered Species Act (ESA) is the most recent of a series of laws protecting wildlife dating back to 1890. Enacted in 1973, the ESA aims to conserve species of animals and plants whose survival is endangered or threatened. The government is required to make a list of such species and to designate critical habitat. Federal agencies must develop programs to conserve listed species and must not do anything that would destroy or modify critical habitat. One of the most important features of the ESA is that, once a species is listed, economic factors may not be considered in deciding what action to take—or not to take. In their lawsuits, environmentalists also relied on the National Forest Management Act of 1976, which requires that national forests be managed as total ecosystems.

[2]The balance of this case consists of edited excerpts from the verbatim transcript of the Forest Conference, held at the Portland Convention Center, Portland, Oregon, April 2, 1993. Not all speakers are included; however, the speakers represented here appear in the same order in which they spoke at the conference. The original transcript runs 123 pages, single spaced, and is available from the library of the University of Oregon, Eugene, Oregon.

The First Roundtable

The first roundtable was designed to give, in President Clinton's words, a "diverse, but . . . representative group of people in the Pacific Northwest the chance to say what they have seen or experienced personally about the impact of the present set of conditions."

Diana Wales, attorney (family law), Roseburg, Oregon

"Historically, federal forests in the Northwest have been managed essentially as though they were an inexhaustible raw material stockpile. The result is an ecosystem on the verge of collapse. It strikes me that past policies have been like buying a car and then never changing the oil, checking the water, or replacing the tires. Sooner or later, there's going to be a major problem.

"The environmental protection laws we have, such as the Endangered Species Act, are like the red idiot lights going on simultaneous with something terrible happening to your car. The spotted owl, marbled murrelet, and numerous wild fish stocks now at risk are the equivalent of all the lights coming on at once.

"When that happens, it's too late to think about a tune-up. You simply have to stop. And the answer is not disconnecting the idiot lights, just as the answer to the forest management dilemma is not suspending or disobeying the laws that let us know we have a serious problem. . . .

"The bottom line is that the 'who' most affected by environmental decisions of this decade will be the grandchildren of our grandchildren. Difficult as it may be, it is vital that all of our vision extends significantly beyond our own lifetimes. We must also recognize that we are simply a part of and dependent upon an ecosystem we do not fully comprehend, but are systematically destroying."

Ken Marson, Marson & Marson Lumber Company

"I'm speaking here on behalf of 9,000 lumber dealers, . . . the lumber prices have gone up substantially since last October, nearly have doubled, and a $5,000 increase or more in the cost of a house eliminates approximately 127,000 people from the housing market every year. In many cases, the increases in prices have gone up much more substantially than just $5,000.

"Housing . . . is an essential component of the economic development and growth of this country, and we're really concerned that we're starting to see areas of the country have a slowdown in housing because the builders can't afford it. . . . I really think lumber is truly the most compatible building material we have with the environment. Aluminum, steel, even masonry, they're never going to be renewable."

Buzz Eades, Eades Forest Products

"I cut trees for a living, just like my father did before me, and my grandfather. I represent a family that has been working actively in the logging and lumbering business for almost 200 years.

"Two hundred years is a long time. . . . That's how long it takes one of these trees to reach that point we call old growth. I like to think that some of those trees that started life when my ancestor first worked in the timber might be old growth someday, and the trees I am so careful to leave might be my grandchildren's old growth. . . . We're getting old growth, some every day."

Bill Arthur, Sierra Club

"It's not an accident that this conference is taking place on the edge of the Pacific Ocean. We have cut our way west from the Atlantic to the Pacific. It took a little bit over a generation to wipe out the great woods of Wisconsin and Michigan and for the logging to move west.

"We are blessed with bigger, larger, vaster forests here in the Northwest. It took a couple of generations to eliminate 90 percent of the once vast ancient forests that we have here. We have only 10 percent left. We're at the edge of the Pacific Ocean, and the timber frontier is over. We have to learn to protect and work with and revive what we have.

"Balance is important, and that's something that we should strive for. But balance means saving the 10 percent we have left. . . . We don't hunt buffalo, we no longer kill whales, and we can't sacrifice the last 10 percent of a remaining ancient forest for the future."

Nat Bingham, commercial fisherman

"This problem is more than just spotted owls. . . . There is another industry that is dependent on a healthy forest, the salmon fishing industry. . . . If we don't do something right now to protect the remaining habitats, we're going to see listings of salmon that will be of an order of magnitude under the Endangered Species Act that will make the spotted owl situation pale by comparison. I don't think that's something any of us want to see happen."

Meca Wawona, New Growth Forestry

"I founded New Growth Forest in 1976 because I was so appalled at the destruction of the magnificent redwood forests in northern California. . . . I thought then that . . . if we figured out a way to make a second-growth forestry sustainable, that would extend the nation's wood supply. So we started the company with a vision of helping small, private landowners practice sustainable forestry.

"Sustainable forestry is guided by natural selection and biological criteria, not short-term profiteering. . . . We've discovered over the years that we're up against a number of economic disincentives. For example, sustainable forestry requires more skills and time in the woods to get the wood out. This means it's more job-intensive, so there's more costs. Since the majority of logging operations on corporate timberlands are quick and dirty extractions, the playing field for sustainable forestry is not level. . . . Wood is simply too cheap, even at today's prices, to afford the practice of sustainable forestry."

John Hampton, Willamina Lumber Company

"I . . . have experience in second-growth forests. . . . Our company hasn't cut an old-growth log since 1950. We have high technology. . . . The cost of modern technology is extraordinary. It takes a leap of faith, under these conditions, to invest the kind of money that one does to modernize a plant. Last year, at our Tillamook Lumber Company plant alone, we invested 5 million private dollars in the renovation of that plant, which was in pretty good shape before that, to get the highest value and quality and volume out of those second-growth logs. It's laser technology; it's scanning; it's computerized positioning, all run by skilled workers who make [an average wage of] $39,000 a year."

Larry Mason, Western Commercial Forest Action Committee

"I can speak as an individual who owned a small sawmill. . . . Our mill was an old-growth mill. The reason it was an old-growth mill was because the only available timber supply that was accessible to us was off of federal lands, and the federal lands where I live, on the Olympic Peninsula [in Washington], are managed on a 100-year rotation, much longer than on some [privately owned land]. And we were 50 years into that rotation. . . . What would have happened . . . was a gradually declining volume of old-growth timber access and a gradually increasing volume of second growth. And we built our mill to make that transition.

"But you don't make those transitions overnight when your timber supply is disrupted by a court injunction. You don't make those transitions overnight when your American dream has turned into a nightmare."

Unidentified participant

"Stop looking at it as a little loaf of bread that can be neatly sliced and passed out to special interest groups, one piece for the spotted owl, one piece for the salmon, one piece for the marbled murrelet, and one piece for the people. That doesn't work. That's like drawing lines on maps with arbitrary disregard for what's really best for the forest.

"How about taking a step back and concentrating on overall forest health? How do the forest ecosystems work best? . . . That's a comprehensive approach that will take us to a road where the future will be more stable."

Phyllis Strauger, mayor of Hoquiam, Washington

"This conference is too late for my city. My city got hit on November 12th with the closure of a three-unit mill, and our unemployment rate is now 19.5 percent and climbing. We expect it to go over 20 percent."

Margaret Powell, Hoopa Valley Indian Tribe

"I . . . serve as a member of the tribe's Integrated Resources Management Committee. It seems ironic that we are required to manage within the parameters of a complex federal legal and regulatory management scheme that [is] intended to protect the environment when, in reality, we have practiced the principles of conservation for thousands of years. In fact, even before the present-day environmental regulations on timber and related development, our tribe imposed similar restrictions on ourselves as a matter of tribal law. . . . I respectfully submit that Indian tribes such as Hoopa may serve as useful models of the problems confronting this conference."

The Second Roundtable

The second roundtable was designed, President Clinton stated, to present "the range of scientific opinions about where we are and where we might go."

John Gordon, Yale University

"Ecosystem management, based on sound integrated knowledge of the whole forest, allows us to do many things at the same time, rather than saving one or two species at a time, and has the potential, I think, to remedy this old-growth deficit.

"It focuses on maintaining the health and productivity of the entire forest asset, rather than on isolating parts of processes. But it's important to recognize that it will probably not anywhere result in the optimization of yield of any single resource commodity or species. . . .

"When we talk about vision, foresters and other professionals can't do a good job unless we have a clear idea of what our clients want. . . . What does society want for and from their forests? How do they want to make a living? How do they want the Pacific Northwest to look? How much assurance do they want that endangered species will survive and flourish?"

Lorin Hicks, Plum Creek Timber Company

"We are applying new forestry techniques to spotted owl habitat. For example, at the Frost Meadows site on the east side of the Cascades in Washington, I have worked with our foresters to design a timber sale that would maintain spotted owl habitat after harvest. We harvested 55 percent of merchantable timber in this unit, while retaining 80 percent of the trees and maintaining functional old-growth habitat characteristics such as snags, large down-logs, and healthy green trees representative of the original stands. Our radio tracking data revealed that owls continue using the Frost Meadows unit following the harvest."

Charles Meslow, U.S. Department of the Interior, Fish and Wildlife Service

"During the course of developing a recovery plan for the northern spotted owl, biologists determined that some 480 other species of plants and animals were importantly associated with old forests. The recovery team identified 36 other species of birds associated with old forests, 22 species of mammals, 17 amphibians, 43 mollusks.

"In addition, more than 200 stocks of fish are considered at risk within the range of the owl. Thus, the northern spotted owl and marbled murrelet are perhaps only the tip of the iceberg. At least 480 other species may be following in their wake."

Jerry Franklin, University of Washington

"What I've been trying to do during the last decade is . . . to try to produce approaches that do a better job of integrating both ecological and economic values. That's fundamentally what new forestry is all about. . . . We can, with the new forestry, grow structurally complex forests. We probably can grow spotted owl habitat. But we do not know, and it's unlikely we're going to know anytime soon, how to grow old-growth forest, because the complexity of these systems is beyond imagination."

Unidentified participant

"My understanding is that folks who deal in mediation say that sometimes when you're dealing with a can of worms, the trick is to open a larger can of worms. Maybe that's what we need to do with this issue, is start taking the big picture, take our focus off the remaining old growth and really start dealing with the forest landscape."

Louise Fortman, University of California, Berkeley

"We need community-initiated and locality-based planning and management units that make ecological sense and social sense. Locally based management will involve local people and others of their choosing in gathering scientific evidence about local social and economic conditions and about local ecosystems. It will involve community members and others meeting to establish community goals and planning and implementing actions to achieve them. . . .

"Two examples from Northern California: the Plumas Corporation in Plumas County has organized an ecosystem restoration and is working on an economic transition strategy. Trinity Alps Botanicals produces nontimber forest products for export and is developing a forest stewardship program. . . .

"I think that the success of . . . community-based experiments in change tell us that facilitating local process is going to be the most important product of this conference."

Bob Lee, University of Washington

"We're moving into a process which looks an awful lot like what happened to the inner city. We're seeing the collapse of families, disintegration of families, disintegration of communities, loss of morale, homelessness, stranded elderly people, people whose lives are in disarray because of substance abuse. It's a very difficult situation."

Ed Whitelaw, University of Oregon

"Timber [is] no longer driving the Northwest economies. . . . We have accumulating evidence . . . that many of those jobs—including jobs in manufacturing that are paying substantially higher than the timber industry is paying—many of those jobs are quite sensitive to the environmental amenities here in the Northwest."

The Third Roundtable

The third roundtable was designed, President Clinton said, "to lay out some very specific suggestions about what we ought to do."

Julie Norman, Headwaters

"We must disturb no more of the last remaining centers of biodiversity. These are the refuges and the seed sources for tomorrow's forests, tomorrow's wildlife, and tomorrow's economy. Therefore, we must establish a permanent forest and watershed reserve system based on the best scientific knowledge.

"We must also establish interim protection for additional areas to preserve our options, while thorough scientific studies are completed. All suitable habitat for threatened species, all roadless areas, key watersheds for salmon, riparian zones, and large blocs of intact forest must serve as our scientific controls during this research period."

Unidentified Participant

"When I come to this issue of [log] exports, I always feel there's something fundamentally wrong if we're hauling items of that magnitude and weight across the Pacific."

Jim Geisinger, Northwest Forest Association

"The first step is to break the legal gridlock that has essentially kept our federal forest agencies from selling any timber during the last two years. If we don't reinstate some federal timber sale program this year, our industry is going to be forced to lay off thousands of workers and curtail production very significantly. Some type of interim ecosystem protection and timber production plan is essential to try to get us from where we are today to when Congress can act on a long-term solution. The alternative is to do nothing and experience economic catastrophe in the Pacific Northwest. . . .

"I want to make one final comment about the allegation that . . . only 10 percent is left. . . . [T]he Forest Service, the Bureau of Land Management, and the National Park Service say that they have about eight million acres of old-growth forest on their ownerships today. Mathematics would tell you then that at some point in time there was 80 million acres of old-growth in existence. Yet I have to tell you there's only 42 million acres of commercial forest in all of Washington and Oregon. So we don't buy that figure."

Gus Kostopulos, Woodnet

"Woodnet is a nonprofit organization . . . it's a network of over 300 very independent wood products manufacturers. . . . Our goal is to get our members to work together in loosely formed networks. They are sometimes called flexible manufacturing networks, and they engage in activities that, by their nature, can be done better in larger groups than they can undertake on their own. It gives them economies of scale that they otherwise wouldn't have."

Roslyn Heffner, vocational counselor

"I found that these workers [unemployed loggers and millworkers] were rugged individuals and proud of their skills and livelihood. . . . [I]n my professional opinion, . . . formal schooling—I'm going to get some flak for this—even in a community college setting does not work well with this group of people. They're not used to sitting in a classroom, and they haven't done it in years. . . . So that in my opinion, [we should be] giving them on-the-job training, even in a new skill, but placing them at the work-site, giving lots of incentives, including targeted jobs [and] tax credit for the employer."

Rich Nafziger, deputy insurance commissioner, State of Washington

"[W]e must adjust our trade policies. Landowners cannot be expected to stop exporting logs when our trading partners put up barriers to finished products but not to raw logs."

Charles W. Bingham, Weyerhaeuser Corporation

"Weyerhaeuser [has] been in business for 93 years. I think if there's one thing that we have learned, it is that we must manage large-scale change. . . . And I would suggest—and this is the big dilemma we're all engaged in—we're going to have to ride the bicycle here for a while, while we repair the tire. We can't just throw everybody out of work."

Andy Kerr, Oregon Natural Resources

"[E]nvironmentalists such as myself were very wary about this event today because, in a situation like this, all the parties are often called upon to compromise a little and give and take something like that, like a labor-management negotiation, and then everybody splits the difference and says there's a deal. But when so little of the virgin forest is left—that 10 percent—environmentalists are not in a position to compromise that, compromise the forest any further . . . the forest has been compromised all it can stand.

"[P]eople do make money off of forests without cutting them down. My organization has appealed a few timber sales in its day, and one of the timber sales that we appealed is a sale where we tried to show the Forest Service that . . . the annual harvest of gourmet mushrooms from that stand of trees each year was worth more than the standing value of the timber."

Irv Fletcher, Oregon AFL-CIO

"We . . . need . . . adequate assistance for displaced workers . . . both wood products workers and those workers that are going to be displaced because of the wood products jobs that are gone. . . . [W]e also need some guaranteed level in place of the timber receipts . . . [and we need] a release of timber now."

Bob Dopplet, Pacific Rivers Council

"[Programs to protect and restore rivers will create] jobs back up in the woods doing things that many of the rural community people have done in the past, like use bulldozers and excavators to treat road systems."

Jack Ward Thomas, U.S. Department of Agriculture Forest Service

"[T]he first paragraph in the Endangered Species Act says it's not the species that's listed, it's the ecosystem on which it depends. . . . [I]t appears, to me at least, that we have a de facto policy of biodiversity protection, particularly for national forest lands. It becomes an overriding objective."

Walter Minnick, TJ International

"We've worked very hard on these reconstituted wood products. This is an example. This is a product that is made out of laminated veneer lumber. . . . [T]he wood fiber can come out of second-growth trees and, because it's got a very high labor content, probably creates twice as many jobs as sawing a round log into rectangular lumber.... Essentially, what we need the government to do is to get out of the way, let the market system work, because we don't know whether to build another plant here or to go to Canada or even whether we should be hiring folk for a month from now, because we can't be assured that our veneer supplies are going to have the raw material we're going to need....

"[T]here is a pretty straightforward and simple answer conceptually.... [W]e've got to set aside ... some forest preserves.... We've got to surround these areas with some buffer areas that are managed with Jerry Franklin's new forestry.... Then, we've got to release the balance—and some of it's old growth—into the commercial timber base."

Jim Coates, International Woodworkers of America
"I represent the voice of those who haven't been heard through most of this, and that's the workers—those of the unemployed.... I hear Andy and some of the other talking about the beauty of the forest. When I go into the beauty of the forest in the Capital Forest and in the Park Service and in the rock quarries, we have people living there. They have no home; they have no water; they have no power. If I was to divulge where these people were, they wouldn't have their children either."

Ted Strong, Columbia River Inter-Tribal Fish Commission
"In actuality, tomorrow we go out and build coalitions across all ideological lines. We unite as a family, and we begin to do the work that lets us leave behind a legacy of love for our natural resources, to be enjoyed in perpetuity by all humans yet to walk this earth."

Bill Clinton, President of the United States
"One of the things that has come out of this meeting to me, loud and clear, is that you want us to try to break the paralysis that presently controls the situation—to move and to act. I hope that, as we leave here, we are more committed to working together to move forward than perhaps we were when we came....

"I intend to direct the cabinet and the entire administration to begin to work immediately to craft a balanced, a comprehensive, a long-term policy; and I will direct the cabinet to report back to me within 60 days to have a plan to end this stalemate."

Discussion Questions

1. Conduct a stakeholder analysis of this case. Who are the primary and secondary stakeholders, and what are the major concerns of each? Draw a stakeholder map, showing the major lines of expected coalition formation.

2. If you were a member of the interagency task force assembled by the president to devise a solution to this problem, what *goals* or *principles* would you establish to guide development of a plan?

3. What key ideas mentioned by participants in the conference provide a basis for an integrative solution to the controversy faced by public policymakers in this case—a solution that would address both economic and ecological concerns? Do you support these ideas? Why or why not?

4. The Endangered Species Act has been criticized for being too extreme and for not permitting policymakers to balance ecological and economic considerations. Do you agree? If so, in your opinion, what other approach to species protection would work better?

DOING BUSINESS IN THE MAQUILADORAS: A SHAREHOLDER CHALLENGE

In the early 1990s, the Coalition for Justice in the Maquiladoras, an international association of more than 60 environmental, religious, community, labor, women's, and Latino organizations, emerged as an important shareholder activist group. The coalition's goal was to convince U.S. multinational corporations to adopt socially responsible business practices in their factories along the northern Mexican border. Many large U.S. corporations had plants in this region, including AlliedSignal, Chrysler, Du Pont, Eastman Kodak, IBM, and Xerox. Both the region and the factories in the Mexican border area were known as the *Maquiladoras.*

Specifically, the coalition urged the adoption of standards of conduct for firms operating in the Maquiladoras region. These standards emphasized responsible practices for hazardous-waste handling, environmental protection, worker health and safety, fair employment practices, and a concern for the impact of the Maquiladoras factories on the surrounding communities. These standards were addressed in a number of social activist shareholder resolutions voted on by company stockholders on annual proxy ballots or at companies' annual stockholder meetings. The resolutions called for comprehensive investigation of companies' Maquiladoras operations, public reporting of the findings of the investigations, and correction of unacceptable company practices if discovered. "We want to send a message into corporate boardrooms," explained Sister Susan Mika, president of the Benedictine Sisters and of the Coalition for Justice in the Maquiladoras. "Moral behavior knows no borders. What is wrong in the United States is wrong in Mexico, too."[1]

Economic and Social Conditions along the Border

The Maquiladoras development represents the fruits of a Mexican government program begun in 1965. To attract capital investment and address high unemployment in the northern border towns, the Mexican government offered lucrative incentives such as preferential tariffs and tax breaks for foreign firms operating plants there. Maquiladoras factories would pay no tariffs on materials and semifinished products imported into Mexico. When Maquiladoras plants shipped finished products out of Mexico, they would pay tariffs only on the value added in Mexico, not on the value of the entire product. Since the 1980s, companies have flooded to this region, establishing factories that produced a variety of goods. By 1996, more than 2,350 factories were located along the northern Mexican border, over 50 percent of them owned by U.S. corporations or part of a U.S.–Mexican joint venture. These plants produced electronic goods, auto parts, chemicals, furniture, machinery, and clothing and employed nearly 750,000 workers.[2]

The Mexican government saw the development project as an economic success. In 1992, it is estimated that the Maquiladoras industries contributed $4.74 billion in value-added worth to the products manufactured or assembled in these factories. The Maquilado-

---

[1] All quotations are from "Environmental, Religious and Labor Organizations Promote Corporate Social Responsibility in the Maquiladora Industry," *The Corporate Examiner* 20, no. 1 (1991), pp. 1–8.
[2] Pamela Varley, Peter DeSimone, and Heidi Welsh, "U.S. Business in Mexico," IRRC Social Issue Service, 1997 Background Report D, January 22, 1997.

ras region became identified as an attractive site for manufacturing facilities, particularly for companies whose products required labor-intensive assembly. Various businesses associated with the construction and maintenance of manufacturing plants—raw materials suppliers, eateries, grocery stores, and so on—provided an additional boost to the region's economy. In addition to the employment of more than a half million people, billions of dollars of investment capital gave the Mexican government a stronger bargaining position when negotiating trade agreements with the United States, Canada, and other trade partners.

Some believed that the benefits of the Maquiladoras development did not justify the costs incurred by Mexican workers, local communities, and the natural environment, however. Timothy Smith, executive director of the Interfaith Center on Corporate Responsibility explained,

> We find a range of corporate behavior in the Maquiladoras . . . from the irresponsible polluter and exploiter of labor to companies which are working to live up to standards of fairness. Though many company and plant officials proudly point to their high standards for wages, health and safety, and environment, until now [1991] most companies seem to be involved in a race to the bottom.

Social watchdog organizations documented abhorrent conditions in the Maquiladoras area. For example, contamination of the water supply affected both U.S. and Mexican residents. Raw sewage from plants located in Mexicali, Mexico, was dumped into the New River, a waterway extending 120 miles into California. In the early 1990s, more than 20 viruses and bacteria were identified in the river along with over 100 industrial chemicals. People in San Elizario, Texas, were at risk of exposure to hepatitis. Ninety percent of 30-year-olds in this border town had contracted the disease. On the Mexican side of the border, the 85,000 residents of the town of Juarez had no running water and stored their water supply in 55-gallon drums that previously contained dangerous chemical compounds used at Maquiladoras plants. As little as 20 percent of the toxic wastes generated by Maquiladoras plants were returned to the United States for proper disposal as required by U.S. and Mexican law.[3]

The Coalition for Justice in the Maquiladoras charged that multinational corporate owners of Maquiladoras factories had failed to improve the living standards of their workers, often migrants from the inland regions of Mexico. According to a 1997 report, the average hourly wage for Maquiladoras workers was $.74 per hour. It would take a Maquiladoras worker more than 2 hours to earn enough to purchase a dozen eggs, 3 hours for a chicken, and nearly 12 hours to buy a box of 30 diapers![4]

Hazardous working conditions in Maquiladoras plants were blamed for a 300 percent increase in the annual low birth weight of babies born to female workers in the early 1990s. Medical records showed that children of mothers who worked at an electronics plant were more vulnerable to being born mentally retarded than other Mexican children. Those women were exposed to highly toxic polychlorinated biphenyl (PCB) compounds

[3]Roberto A. Sanchez, "In the Maquiladora Industry, Health Is Also at Risk: Maquiladora Masquerade," *Business Mexico* 3, no. 1 (1993), pp. 13–15; and "A Maquiladora Case Study: Hazardous Waste Issues," *IRRC News for Investors*, November 1994, pp. 20–23.

[4]"Maquiladora Worker Demands Living Wage," *Cross Border Connection*, October 1996, http:www.pctvi.com/laamn/maquiladora.html.

for long hours, often reaching into deep vats of the chemicals wearing only rubber gloves for protection.

Since Maquiladoras plants paid virtually no taxes in Mexico, local governments did not receive sufficient revenue from the corporations to defray the costs for city roads, sewer systems, utility lines, and other public services incurred from the plants' operations. Corporations operating Maquiladoras were accused of ignoring the deteriorating public services in border towns from Matamoros, Mexico (near Brownsville, Texas) to Tijuana (across the border from San Diego, California). Although plants in the region had electricity, water, sewage disposal, and green grass, only a short distance away, residents in nearby towns had, at best, limited access to such basic services and amenities. The U.S. National Toxics Campaign conducted research in the early 1990s to investigate accusations of careless or illegal transportation or disposal of hazardous waste by-products by the Maquiladoras factories. The investigation found a "clear and consistent pattern . . . of widespread and serious contamination [of the Maquiladoras region] by U.S.-owned firms. They are turning the border into a 2,000-mile long Love Canal [an area in New York contaminated by long-term underground disposal of toxic wastes]."

Social Issues Enter Corporate Boardrooms

In 1990 the Coalition for Justice initiated the Maquiladoras campaign by sponsoring social responsibility shareholder resolutions. These resolutions called on 12 U.S. corporations to describe in detail their environmental practices, health and safety standards, and workers' standard of living in and around their Maquiladoras plants. Ten companies, including AT&T, Ford Motor, Johnson & Johnson, and PepsiCo, agreed to provide the information or allow inspection of their facilities by interested investors. The shareholder resolutions were then withdrawn.

The campaign escalated a year later when the coalition proposed that corporations operating in the Maquiladoras region adopt the Maquiladora Standards of Conduct. These standards called for companies operating Maquiladoras plants to comply with Mexican and U.S. environmental regulations; to observe fundamental workers' rights, including fair wages, a safe and healthy workplace, reasonable hours of work, and decent living conditions; and to support community public service needs, including a commitment to community economic development. The filing of shareholder resolutions targeting Maquiladoras operations continued throughout the 1990s. The coalition's philosophy and an excerpt from a sample shareholder resolution are presented later in this case study.

Companies Respond to the Shareholders

Some U.S. corporations were quick to respond to the shareholder resolutions filed by coalition members. These firms were already in compliance with or exceeded Mexican laws and regulations. Some firms were committed to applying environmental and employee policies and practices worldwide. The same policies governing U.S. operations were used at the Maquiladoras plants. Therefore, some firms already were addressing the various issues emphasized in the shareholder resolutions. A number of these firms drafted statements in response to the shareholder challenges and made these documents available to interested company stakeholders. Highlights from these documents are presented next.

AT&T's Report on their Mexican Operations

AT&T compiled "A Report for AT&T Shareowners: Manufacturing in Mexico." The report, made available to all interested company stakeholders, addressed numerous issues raised by the coalition, such as human resource, environmental, and worker safety policies and practices.

AT&T was committed to "maintain[ing] consistent, equitable and fair human resources policies at all its locations worldwide." The company policies included paying a competitive wage to all employees, participating in salary surveys in each country where it operated to determine what was a "fair wage," and providing each employee with benefits comparable to what other companies in that country were offering their employees.

AT&T complied with the legal expectations in Mexico regarding the maximum number of hours an employee could work in a week, scheduled rest periods within each workday, and vacation benefits provided for employees. For example, AT&T workers at the Maquiladoras plant were paid for 56 hours per week, although the workweek consisted of only 48 hours or less. In addition, the company provided quality of work benefits and programs for its workers. Comprehensive medical care available to AT&T employees exceeded Mexico's legal requirements. Employees were offered educational assistance programs, sports programs, and, in some locations, subsidized plant cafeterias, food and clothing allowances, and free transportation.

AT&T pledged its commitment to support the Mexican government's efforts toward environmental responsibility. The corporation established the following goals for its Maquiladoras operations: reducing manufacturing emissions of chlorofluorocarbons (CFCs), reducing toxic air emissions, reducing amounts of manufacturing process waste sent for disposal, reducing paper use, and increasing recycling efforts.

The company was actively involved in various environmental initiatives, such as the Industry Cooperative for Ozone Layer Protection, Global Environmental Management Initiative, and International Environmental Health and Safety Conference, which was held in 1992. AT&T went beyond legal requirements in Mexico when it established a self-contained water supply and waste-water systems at its Guadalajara plant.

Worker safety was also a key emphasis for AT&T at its Maquiladoras operations. In compliance with Mexican regulation, each manufacturing unit formed a safety committee with representation from the workers' union, management, production, and medical departments. New workers at AT&T's Maquiladoras plants participated in an orientation program that focused on safety procedures, in compliance with Mexican law.

Ford Motor Company's Maquiladoras Facilities Report

Ford Motor Company's report, "Environmental Practices, Health and Safety Standards and Employee Welfare at Ford Motor Company's Maquiladora Facilities in Mexico," was issued on March 19, 1991, and responded to many of the coalition's various concerns. The report stated that Ford required its Maquiladoras operations to meet high standards for responsible environmental, health, safety, personnel, and community relations policies and, whenever possible, to follow the same policies and practices as did Ford operations in the United States.

For example, although not required by Mexican law or regulation, Ford applied its U.S. environmental policies to the Maquiladoras facilities. These policies required the plants to monitor the handling and disposal of any hazardous materials used in manufacturing processes, which included solvents, cleaners, lubricants, and various metals. The Waste Management Program, launched in 1985 and strengthened in 1990 at Ford's U.S. plants, was applied to its Maquiladoras operations. Cross-functional teams within manufacturing, plant engineering, environmental quality, research, occupational safety and health, and others met regularly to explore safety issues and recommend solutions if necessary. In compliance with Mexican regulation, enforced by SEDUE (the Mexican equivalent to OSHA) and the Mexican Department of Labor, random audits of Ford's Maquiladoras facilities were conducted. In addition, self-audits were often conducted at the plants to ensure compliance with Mexican law as well as company policies.

One of Ford Motor Company's basic values is embodied in the statement: Our people are the source of our strength. This value was manifested in the policies and practices affecting the employees at Ford's Maquiladoras plants. To establish a fair wage scale for its employees, Ford utilized the services of two international compensation consultants who advised the company regarding competitive wages and fringe benefits for each plant location. The company took pride in being able to offer employment to over 10,000 Mexican citizens, providing them with competitive wages and benefits that they could not receive elsewhere, according to the company's report on its Maquiladoras operations. Ford had been a part of Mexico and the Mexican people for over 65 years. According to the Maquiladoras facilities report, "Ford has actively participated in the economic, social, and cultural growth of Mexico in many ways. Our active cultural, educational and community participation is a matter of public record of which we are proud."

PepsiCo's Maquiladoras Report

Evidence of corporate social responsiveness to the social activist shareholder resolutions was reflected in PepsiCo's report:

PepsiCo is committed to making a real contribution to Mexican economic, technological and social development. PepsiCo operations are guided by these basic principles.

- PepsiCo companies are committed to the communities they serve, in terms of providing employment opportunity, fair and equitable working conditions and working with local industry suppliers.
- PepsiCo businesses believe in investing in the future, including establishing employee training and research programs and supporting educational and charitable organizations.
- PepsiCo believes in full cooperation with the Mexican government, to ensure that our objectives are in the nation's best interest.
- Finally, PepsiCo is committed to Mexico for the long term and we are projecting continued expansion.[5]

The Future for the Maquiladoras Region

With the signing of the North America Free Trade Agreement by the United States and Mexico in 1994, Maquiladoras lost some of their privileges—for example, wholesale relief from import duties on components—but they also gained some advantages—for example, freedom to sell products domestically in Mexico and general tariff relief on exports to the United States and Canada. Nonetheless, the Coalition for Justice in the Maquiladoras remained committed to challenging U.S. companies to establish safe, healthy, and environmentally sound business operations in the Maquiladoras region. The number of companies receiving shareholder resolutions and requests for entering into dialogue with the coalition dou-

[5]"Maquiladoras PepsiCo, Inc.," reprinted courtesy, © PepsiCo, Inc.

bled from 1992 to 1993. In 1993 and 1994, the Coalition requested adherence to their standards of conduct or disclosure reports from 38 companies with Maquiladoras operations. In 1997, six companies—AlliedSignal, ALCOA, Becton Dickerson, General Electric, Johnson & Johnson, and United Technologies—were asked by religious-affiliated stockholders to initiate a review of their company's Maquiladoras operations. In addition, AlliedSignal, Chrysler, General Electric, and Johnson & Johnson were requested via a shareholder resolution to review or amend their codes or standards governing all international operations, which included Maquiladoras.

Mission Statement and Standards of Conduct of the Coalition for Justice in the Maquiladoras

The Coalition for Justice in the Maquiladoras adopted the following mission statement:

> We are a tri-national coalition of religious, environmental, labor, Latino and women's organizations that seek to pressure U.S. transnational corporations to adopt socially responsible practices within the maquiladora industry, to ensure a safe environment along the U.S./Mexican border, safe work conditions inside the maquila plants and a fair standard of living for the industries workers.
>
> A central vehicle for achieving these goals is the establishment of the "MAQUILADORA STANDARDS OF CONDUCT." This document provides a code through which we demand that corporations alleviate critical problems created by the industry.
>
> Our efforts are grounded in supporting worker and community struggles for social, economic and environmental justice in the maquiladora industry. Moreover, by supporting these struggles, we believe our efforts will serve the interests of workers and communities along the U.S./Mexican border.
>
> We dedicate ourselves to democratic process and unity of action maintaining sensitivity to the diverse representation within our coalition.

The following is a summary of the issues proposed in the Maquiladora Standards of Conduct.[6]

Introduction: Purpose and Scope of the Standards of Conduct

The "MAQUILADORA STANDARDS OF CONDUCT" are addressed to all U.S. corporations which operate subsidiaries, have affiliates, or utilize contractors or shelter plants in Mexico. The objective of these Standards is to promote socially responsible practices, which ensure a safe environment on both sides of the border, safe work conditions inside Maquiladora plants and an adequate standard of living for Maquiladora employees.

United States citizens, who urge U.S. transnational corporations to adhere to these standards, recognize that both Mexico and the U.S. have the inherent right to regulate commerce within their own boundaries. These Standards are designed to help promote international efforts to secure a safe workplace for Maquiladora em-

---

[6] The "Maquiladora Standard of Conduct" is reprinted in a condensed form by permission of the Coalition for Justice in the Maquiladoras, San Antonio, Texas.

ployees, the protection of the environment and the promotion of human rights and economic justice on both sides of the border.

All company disclosures associated with these Standards should be provided in Spanish and English.

Section I: Responsible Practices for Handling Hazardous Wastes and Protecting the Environment

Pollution from the Maquiladora industry is a binational problem which threatens the health of citizens both in Mexico and the United States. Illegal dumping of hazardous wastes pollutes rivers and aquifers and contaminates drinking water on both sides of the border. In addition, accidental chemical leaks from plants or transportation vehicles carrying hazardous materials impact both sides of the border.

In general, corporations operating Maquiladoras will be guided by the principle that they will follow Mexican and United States environmental protection regulations as established by SEDESOL and EPA [the Mexican and United States' environmental regulatory agencies. . . . Corporations operating Maquiladoras, including corporations which utilize contractors or shelter plants, will: (1) Act promptly to comply with Mexican environmental laws (*Ley General del Equilibrio Ecológico y la Protección al Ambiente. . . . .* (2) Annually, provide full public disclosure of toxic chemical discharges and releases into the air, water and land and amounts of hazardous materials stored and utilized. . . . (3) Provide full public disclosure of hazardous waste disposal methods, including the final location of waste disposal. . . . (4) Use state-of-the-art toxics use reduction, chemical accident prevention and pollution control technologies. . . . (5) Ensure safe and responsible transportation of all hazardous materials in Mexico and the United States. . . . (6) Provide public verification of all hazardous materials being returned to the country of origin. . . . (7) Ensure proper disposal of all spent containers used for chemicals and take necessary initiatives to assure that these containers are not used for the storage of drinking water. . . .
(8) Take remedial action to clean up any past dumping which threatens to release hazardous materials into the environment. . . . (9) Provide fair damage compensation to any community or individual, which has been harmed by pollution caused by the corporation or its subsidiary. . . . (10) Discuss environmental concerns with the community . . . .

Section II: Health and Safety Practices

In general, corporations operating Maquiladoras will be guided by the principle that they will follow regulations established by the *Secretaria del Trabajo y Previsión Social* [Secretary of Labor and Social Provision] and the U.S. Occupational Safety and Health Administration (OSHA).

Corporations operating Maquiladoras will: (1) Disclose to employees, their designated representatives and the public the chemical identity of all chemicals used, as well as amounts of chemical materials and wastes stored on premises. Ensure that all chemical containers will have appropriate warning labels in Spanish as well as

English. . . . (2) In accordance with Mexican law, provide employees with written explanation of risks associated with the use of toxic materials. . . . (3) Use chemicals that are the safest and least toxic for employees. . . . (4) Design work operations and tasks to limit repetitive strain injuries and other ergonomic problems. . . . (5) As required by Mexican law, each plant will establish worker/management health and safety commissions. . . . (6) Provide all employees with health and safety training using a qualified instructor approved by the Joint Health and Safety Commission. . . . (7) Provide an adequate ventilation system including local exhaust for all point sources of air contamination, as well as provide employees with appropriate protective equipment and clothing. . . . (8) Arrange health and safety inspections by qualified outside consultants (approved by the Joint Health and Safety Commission) at least once every six months and provide public disclosure of inspection reports. . . . (9) Provide fair damage compensation to any worker who suffers an occupational injury or illness. . . . (10) In accordance with Mexican law and the OSHA Medical Records Rule, provide all employees and their designated representatives access to medical records. . . .

Section III: Fair Employment Practices and Standard of Living

U.S. corporations will respect basic workers' rights and human dignity. (1) U.S. corporations will not engage in employment discrimination based on sex, age, race, religious creed or political beliefs. Equal pay will be provided for equal work, regardless of sex, age, race, religious creed or political beliefs. . . . (2) In general, workers will be provided with a fair and just wage, reasonable hours of work and decent working conditions. . . . (3) U.S. corporations will not interfere with workers' rights to organize and to reach collective bargaining agreements. . . . (4) U.S. corporations will not employ or utilize child labor and will exercise good faith in ensuring that employees are of legal working age. . . . (5) U.S. corporations will distribute profit sharing to employees as required by Mexican law. . . . (6) U.S. corporations will print and distribute a written handbook on company employment policies to all employees as required by Mexican law. . . . (7) In the workplace, U.S. corporations will take positive steps to prevent sexual harassment. . . .

Section IV: Community Impact

U.S. transnational corporations recognize that they have social responsibilities to the local communities in Mexico and the United States where they locate facilities. These responsibilities include a commitment to community economic development, and improvements in the quality of life. Facilities will not be abandoned to avoid these responsibilities. (1) U.S. corporations will not promote barracks-style living arrangements for employees. Where these living arrangements already exist, U.S. corporations will take immediate action to improve living conditions and ensure that workers are provided with basic human rights. . . . (2) Corporations operating Maquiladoras will work to establish special trust funds to finance infrastructure improvements in communities near Maquiladora plants.

Discussion Questions

1. Assume that the Coalition for Justice in the Maquiladoras has introduced a shareholder resolution at a firm where you are on the board of directors. Would you recommend that your firm adopt the practices outlined in the Maquiladora Standards of Conduct? What values or reasons underlie your recommendation? What is your firm's responsibility to your shareholders?

2. The Maquiladora Standards of Conduct also ask companies to disclose operations information. Should your firm agree to make public information about your Maquiladora operations, as requested by the coalition? Why or why not?

3. If you were a shareholder, would you vote for or against the resolution? Why?

4. Some believe that the SEC should permit stockholders to vote on social as well as economic questions related to the business of the corporation; others do not. Do you believe that the issues raised by the Maquiladora Standards of Conduct are appropriate ones for stockholders to consider, or should these issues be better left up to management or public officials?

5. Laws governing such matters as environmental policy, labor standards, and gender and race discrimination often differ among nations. Do you believe that multinational corporations have an obligation to apply standards consistently among all their operations or simply to follow the law in the country or countries in which they are operating?

Case Study:
DOW CORNING AND THE SILICONE BREAST IMPLANT CONTROVERSY

The corporate jet lifted off from Washington's National Airport, en route to Dow Corning Corporation's headquarters in Midland, Michigan. February 19, 1992, had been a grueling day for Keith R. McKennon. Named chairman and chief executive officer of Dow Corning less than two weeks earlier, McKennon had just testified before the Food and Drug Administration's Advisory Committee on the safety of the company's silicone gel breast implants. Although not the only manufacturer of breast implants, Dow Corning had invented the devices in the early 1960s and had been responsible for most of their medical testing. Now, the company was faced with the task of defending the product against numerous lawsuits and a rising tide of criticism from the FDA, Congress, the media, and many women's advocacy organizations.

The company's potential liability was large: as many as two million American women had received implants over the past three decades, perhaps 35 percent of them made by Dow Corning. In December 1991, a San Francisco jury had awarded a woman who claimed injuries from her Dow Corning implants an unprecedented $7.3 million in damages. Although the company believed its $250 million in product liability insurance was adequate to meet any possible claims, some felt that the company's liability exposure could be much, much larger.

The hearings had been contentious. Critics had repeated their allegations, heard often in the press in recent weeks, that the implants could leak silicone into the body, causing pain, scarring, and—most seriously—debilitating autoimmune diseases such as rheumatoid arthritis and scleroderma. The silicone prostheses could also interfere with detection of breast cancer by mammography, they charged. In response, McKennon had testified that implants served an important public health need and did not pose an unreasonable risk to users. On the job less than a month, however, McKennon had had little time to sort through the thousands of pages of relevant documents or to talk with the many managers who had been involved with the product's development over the past 30 years.

The breast implant controversy would surely be a litmus test of McKennon's crisis management skills. Recruited from Dow Chemical Corporation, where he had been executive vice president and head of domestic operations, McKennon came to his new position with a reputation as a seasoned troubleshooter. At Dow Chemical (which owned 50 percent of Dow Corning), McKennon had earlier managed his firm's response to charges that its product Agent Orange, a defoliant widely used during the Vietnam War, had caused

Note: This is an abridged version of a longer case: Anne T. Lawrence, "Dow Corning and the Silicone Breast Implant Controversy," *Case Research Journal* 13, no. 4 (Winter 1993), pp. 87–112. Abridged by the author by permission of the *Case Research Journal.* Sources include articles appearing in the *New York Times, The Wall Street Journal, Business Week, Newsweek, Time, Chemical and Engineering News, American Bar Association Journal, Journal of the American Medical Association, New England Journal of Medicine,* the Public Citizen Health Research Group *Health Letter,* the Command Trust Network *Newsletter,* press reports of the *Federal News Service,* and U.S. congressional hearings. The history of Dow Corning and the development of silicones is based on Don Whitehead, *The Dow Story: The History of the Dow Chemical Company* (New York: McGraw-Hill, 1968); and Eugene G. Rochow, *Silcon and Silicones* (Berlin: Springer-Verlag, 1987). The case also draws on internal Dow Corning documents released to the public in February 1992. A full set of footnotes is available in the *Case Research Journal* version.

lingering health problems for veterans. Later, he had managed Dow Chemical's problems with Bendectin, an antinausea drug alleged to cause birth defects. At the time of his appointment as chairman and CEO, McKennon had served on Dow Corning's board of directors for nearly six years.

The unfolding breast implant crisis showed every sign of being just as difficult—and potentially damaging—as any McKennon had confronted in his long career. Would Dow Corning become known as another Johnson & Johnson, renowned for its skillful handing of the Tylenol poisonings in the 1980s? Or would it become another Manville or A. H. Robins, companies that had declared bankruptcy in the wake of major product liability crises? McKennon was well aware that the future of the company, as well as his own reputation, might well hinge on decisions he and his top managers would make within the next weeks and days.

Dow Corning, Inc.

Dow Corning was founded in 1943 as an equal joint venture of Dow Chemical Company and Corning Glass Works (later known as Corning, Inc.) to produce silicones for commercial applications. The term *silicone* was coined to describe synthetic compounds derived from silicon, an abundant element commonly found in sand. In the 1930s, Corning researchers working on possible applications of silicone in glassmaking developed a number of resins, fluids, and rubbers that could withstand extremes of hot and cold. In 1940, Corning approached Dow Chemical with a proposal for a joint venture, and by 1942 a small plant in Midland, Michigan (Dow's hometown), had begun production of silicones for military applications. At the close of World War II, Dow Corning moved successfully to develop multiple commercial applications for silicone. Within a decade, the company had introduced more than 600 products and doubled in size three times, making it one of the fastest-growing firms in the booming chemical industry. Its varied product line included specialty lubricants, sealants, and resins as well as a variety of consumer items—ranging from construction caulk, to adhesive labels, to Silly Putty.

Although most uses of silicone were industrial, by the mid-1950s Dow Corning scientists had become interested in possible medical applications and developed several implantable devices. In the early 1960s, Dow Corning engineers developed the first prototype of a breast implant by encapsulating a firm-density silicone gel within a silicone rubber bag. First marketed in 1963, this device—known as the Cronin implant—was used initially almost exclusively in reconstructive surgery performed on breast cancer patients following mastectomies (surgical removal of the breast).

When Dow Corning first developed and marketed breast implants (as well as its other medical products), the company was operating with virtually no government oversight. Unlike pharmaceutical drugs, regulations since 1906 under the Pure Food and Drug Act and its several amendments, medical devices—even those designed for implantation in the body—were for all practical purposes unregulated. Under the Food, Drug, and Cosmetics Act of 1938, the FDA had the authority to inspect sites where medical devices were made and could seize adulterated or misbranded devices. The agency could not require premarket approval for the safety or effectiveness, however, and could remove a product from the market only if it could demonstrate that the manufacturer had broken the law.

Although not required to prove its implants safe by law, Dow Corning—in accord with standard "good manufacturing" practices at the time—attempted to determine the safety of its own medical products before releasing them for sale. In 1964, Dow Corning hired an independent laboratory to undertake several studies of the safety of medical-grade silicones, including those used in breast implants. No evidence was found that silicones caused cancer, but two studies found that silicone fluid injected in experimental animals spread widely—becoming lodged in the lymph nodes, liver, spleen, pancreas, and other organs—and created persistent chronic inflammation. The company appeared unconcerned, noting that it did not advocate the direct injection of silicone fluid.

In the early 1970s, Dow Corning's breast implant business for the first time experienced a serious competitive threat. In 1972, five young men—all scientists or salesmen at Dow Corning—left the company to work for Heyer-Schulte, a small medical devices company in California, where they used their experience with silicones to develop a competing breast implant. Two years later, the group left Heyer-Schulte to form their own company, McGhan Medical Corporation. Their idea was to modify the basic technology developed over the past decade by Dow Corning to make a softer, more responsive implant that more closely resembled the natural breast. By 1974, both Heyer-Schulte and McGhan Medical had competing products on the market.

The Heyer-Schulte and McGhan implants quickly gained favor with plastic surgeons, and Dow Corning's market share began to erode. By 1975, Dow Corning estimated its market share had declined to around 35 percent, as plastic surgeons switched allegiance to products offered by the small company start-ups. Dow Corning managers became alarmed.

The Mammary Task Force In January 1975—responding to the challenge from its California competitors—Dow Corning dedicated a special cross-functional team, known as the mammary task force, to develop, test, and bring to market a new generation of breast implants. The group's main goal was to reformulate the silicone gel to create a softer, more pliable implant competitive with the new products recently marketed by McGhan and Heyer-Schulte. The group of about 20—all men—hoped to have the new implants ready for shipment by June 1975. The company believed it was justified in bringing the new implant to market quickly, without extensive medical testing, because the new product would be based on materials substantially similar to those used in the older Cronin implants. The safety of the existing line, management maintained, had already been satisfactorily documented on the basis of earlier studies and the history of their use.

One of the questions that quickly arose in the task force's deliberations—as reported in the minutes of its January 21, 1975, meeting—was: "Will the new gel . . . cause a *bleed through* which will make these products unacceptable?" (emphasis in original). Dow Corning scientists clearly recognized that a more watery gel (dubbed *flo-gel*), while softer to the touch, might also be more likely to permeate its envelope and bleed into surrounding tissue. Two product engineers were assigned to investigate this issue. Three weeks later they reported that their experiments "*to date* indicate that the bleed with new gel is no greater than what we measure from old gel controls." They also added, however, that they viewed their earlier results as inconclusive, and they remained concerned about "a possible bleed situation."

Biomedical tests were contracted out to an independent laboratory, which proceeded with tests in which the new gel was injected into experimental rabbits. Earlier reports back from the lab on February 26 showed "mild to occasionally moderate acute inflammatory reaction" in the test animals around the injected gel, but the pathologist concluded it was probably due to the trauma of insertion, not the product itself. The task force also ordered biomedical testing of migration of gel into the vital organs of monkeys. The laboratory results showed "some migration of the [flo-gel] formulation." However, the task force agreed that the bleed was still not any more or less than standard gel.

Development proceeded so rapidly that, by March 31, 10,000 new flo-gel mammaries were ready for packaging. The task force minutes reported that the products were "beautiful, the best we have ever made." Now six weeks ahead of schedule, the company was able to ship some samples of the new product to the West Coast in time for the California Plastic Surgeons meeting on April 21. However, earlier demonstrations did not go flawlessly. The task force got back the following report: "In Vancouver, and elsewhere on the West Coast introduction, it was noted that after the mammaries had been handled for awhile, the surface became oily. Also, some were bleeding on the velvet in the showcase." The task force ordered samples from the West Coast for examination, but no further discussion of this issue appeared in the subsequent minutes.

As the flo-gel implants came on line, the focus of the task force's discussion shifted from production issues to marketing strategy. The task force debated various aggressive marketing approaches, such as rebates, distribution by consignment, price breaks for big users, and free samples for surgeons known to perform breast enlargement operations. Noting that June and July were the peak months of the "mammary season," managers called for a big push to regain some of Dow Corning's eroding market share. The group felt that their market share, which they estimated had eroded to around 35 percent, could be lifted back to the 50 to 60 percent range if they moved aggressively.

By September, Dow Corning was producing 6,000 to 7,000 units per month and aimed to phase out the older models by early 1976. However, many bugs in the production process remained to be ironed out. The reject rate at inspection was high, as high as 50 percent on some lots. Among the problems: floating dirt, weak bags, and thin spots in the envelopes. Doctors had returned some unused mammaries, citing breakage and contamination. Overall, however, plastic surgeons liked the product. One task force member later recalled that when plastic surgeons saw and felt the new material, "their eyes got big as saucers." Besides feeling more natural to the touch, the new softer devices were easier to insert and were more suitable for small-incision, low-trauma cosmetic procedures.

A Boom in Busts

Although breast implants first became available in the 1960s, it was only in the late 1970s and 1980s that the rate of implant surgery took off. The increase was due entirely to a fast rise in the number of so-called cosmetic procedures; by 1990, fully 80 percent of all implant surgeries performed in the United States were to increase the size of normal, healthy breasts, rather than for reconstruction following mastectomy.

One cause of the rise in cosmetic augmentations, of course, was the availability of the softer, more pliable implants, which could be inserted through smaller incisions with less trauma to the patient in less expensive outpatient procedures. In 1990, 82 percent of all breast augmentation procedures were performed on an outpatient basis. Other, broader trends within the medical profession and the wider culture also played important roles, however.

One factor behind the boom in breast augmentation surgery was the growth of the plastic surgery profession. Although procedures to graft tissue from a healthy part of the body to another that had been damaged or mutilated were developed early in the century, plastic surgery as a distinct subdiscipline within surgery did not emerge until the 1940s. During World War II, military surgeons struggling to repair the wounds of injured soldiers returning from the front pioneered many valuable reconstructive techniques. Many of these surgeons reentered civilian life to start plastic surgery programs in their home communities. Within a couple of decades, plastic surgery had become the fastest-growing specialty within American medicine. Between 1960 and 1983, the number of board-certified plastic surgeons quintupled, during a period when most other medical specialties were growing much less quickly (and the U.S. population as a whole grew by just 31 percent). The draw for the newly minted MDs was regular hours, affluent customers, and high incomes, averaging $180,000 per year after all expenses in 1987.

As their numbers soared, plastic surgeons faced an obvious problem—developing a market for their services. Demand for reconstructive surgery was not fast growing, and cosmetic procedures were often elective and typically not fully covered by medical insurance. In 1983, following approval by the Federal Trade Commission, the American Society for Plastic and Reconstructive Surgery (ASPRS), a professional association representing 97 percent of all board-certified plastic surgeons, launched a major advertising (or, as the society called it, "practice enhancement") campaign. Other ads were placed by individual surgeons. In one appearing in *Los Angeles* magazine, a seductive, well-endowed model was shown leaning against a sports car. The tag line: "Automobile by Ferrari, Body by [a prominent plastic surgeon]."

Plastic surgeons also campaigned to redefine female flat-chestedness (dubbed *micromastia* by the medical community) as a medical disease requiring treatment. In July 1982, the ASPRS filed a formal comment with the FDA that argued:

> There is a substantial and enlarging body of medical opinion to the effect that these deformities [small breasts] are really a disease which in most patients results in feelings of inadequacy, lack of self-confidence, distortion of body image and a total lack of well-being due to a lack of self-perceived femininity. The enlargement of the under-developed female breast is, therefore, often very necessary to insure an improved quality of life for the patient.

The ASPRS later officially repudiated this view.

By 1990, breast augmentation had become the second most common cosmetic procedure performed by plastic surgeons, exceeded only by liposuction (fat removal). Since it was a more expensive procedure, however, breast augmentation was the top money maker for plastic surgeons in 1990. That year, ASPRS members collected almost $215 million in fees from women for breast implant surgery.

Another factor contributing to the rise in cosmetic augmentation may have been changing cultural standards of feminine beauty in the 1980s, a decade characterized by social conservatism and, according to some commentators, by a backlash against feminism and female liberation. In the 1970s, women appearing in the glossy pages of fashion magazines were often tall and lanky, with long, straight hair tied at the nape of the neck, menswear dress-for-success suits, and distinctly boyish figures. The 1980s ideal woman was very different: the typical fashion model by this time was more likely to sport 1940s retro-look fashions, thick, full curls, sweetheart lips—and lots of bosom. In a special 100th anniversary edition, published April 1992, *Vogue* magazine summed up current standards of female beauty in this sentence:

> And in women's bodies, the fashion now is a combination of hard, muscular stomach and shapely breasts. Increasingly, women are willing to regard their bodies as photographic images, unpublishable until retouched and perfected at the hands of surgeons.

Ironically, the same issue also ran an ad, placed by trial attorneys, in which "silicone breast implant sufferers" were invited to come forward with legal claims.

A Stream of Sick and Injured

As the rate of implant surgeries rose in the 1980s, so did the number of women who were sick, injured, and in pain from their breast surgery. Their stories began to be told at medical conferences, in legal briefs, and by women's and consumer's advocacy organizations. As they were, Dow Corning and other implant makers were forced to respond to a growing crisis of confidence in their products.

The most common adverse side effect of implant surgery was a phenomenon known as *capsular contracture,* a painful hardening of the breast that occurs when the body reacts to the implant by forming a wall of fibrous scar tissue around it. The FDA estimated that severe contracture occurred in about 25 percent of all patients; some hardening may have occurred in up to 70 percent. Implants could also rupture, spilling silicone gel into the body and often necessitating repeat surgery to replace the damaged implants. Dow Corning's data, based on voluntary reporting by surgeons, showed a rupture rate of only 1 percent. These figures were challenged by researchers who pointed out that ruptures often did not show up on mammograms; some individual doctors reported rupture rate as high as 32 percent. Once the device had broken, silicone could and did travel via the lymphatic system throughout the body, lodging in a woman's spleen, liver, and other internal organs. Also worrisome was the tendency of silicone implants to obscure cancerous tumors that otherwise would be revealed by mammography.

More controversial and less-well documented were allegations that silicone implants could lead to so-called autoimmune disorders—diseases in which the body's immune system attacks its own connective tissues. According to the FDA, by 1991 around 600 cases of autoimmune disorders, such as rheumatoid arthritis, scleroderma, and lupus erythematosus, had been reported in women with implants. Some scientists speculated that some women were, in effect, allergic to silicone, and that their bodies had attacked their own tissues in an attempt to rid itself of the substance. Such reactions were most likely in the presence of ruptures, but even small amounts of gel bleeding through the envelope, or silicone in the envelope itself, could provoke an autoimmune response.

Other physicians believed, however, that the appearance of autoimmune disorders in women with implants was wholly coincidental. In any substantial population—and 2 million women with implants was clearly substantial—a certain number would develop autoimmune disease purely by chance. In an interview published in the *Journal of the American Medical Association,* one prominent plastic surgeon called the association between autoimmune disorders and breast implants a "crock of baloney. . . . People get immunological diseases and they just happen to have breast implants."

Unfortunately, no long-term controlled studies of the incidence of autoimmune disorders in populations of women with and without implants were initiated or even contemplated until 1991. In fact, no comprehensive registries of women with implants existed. The question about the relationship between implants and autoimmune disease was, on the basis of existing data, wholly unanswerable. Representative Ted Weiss (Democrat-New York), who reviewed data submitted to the FDA in 1991, later angrily concluded: "For 30 years, more than one million women have been subjects in a massive, uncontrolled study, without their knowledge or consent."

Victims Seek Redress

Some women who had suffered from breast implants sued. In 1984, a Nevada woman was awarded $1.5 million by jurors in a San Francisco court, who concluded that Dow Corning had committed fraud in marketing its implant as safe; the case was later settled for an undisclosed amount while on appeal, and the court records were sealed. In a post-trial ruling, a federal judge who had reviewed the case records called Dow Corning's actions "highly reprehensible." In the wake of this case, Dow Corning changed its package insert to include a warning that mentioned the possibility of capsular contracture, silicone migration following rupture, and immune system sensitivity.

As other cases slowly made their way through the courts, victims began to speak out publicly and to organize. Sybil Goldrich and Kathleen Anneken founded the Command Trust Network, an advocacy organization that became instrumental in providing information, support, and legal and medical referrals to implant victims. Other women's and public health advocacy groups also played a role in publicizing the risks of breast implants. One of the most active was the Health Research Group (HRG), a Washington, D.C.–based spin-off of Ralph Nader's Public Citizen. The HRG in 1988 began a systematic effort to pressure the FDA to ban silicone breast implants. The group petitioned the FDA, testified before Congress and other government agencies, issued regular press releases, and distributed information to consumers. The HRG also initiated an information clearinghouse for plaintiffs' attorneys. Another active advocacy organization was the National Women's Health Network, a public-interest group that widely distributed information on silicone-related issues.

Devising Regulation for Devices

The agency in charge of regulating implants—and thus the object of these and other advocacy organizations' pressure—was the Food and Drug Administration. In 1976, the year after Dow Corning's mammary task force developed its new generation of flo-gel implants, Congress passed the Medical Amendments Act to the Food and Drug Act. Enacted in the wake of the Dalkon Shield controversy, in which thousands of women claimed they had been injured by a poorly designed intrauterine device, the amendments for the first time required that manufacturers of new, implantable medical devices be required to prove their products safe and effective before release to the public. Devices already on the market were ranked by risk, with the riskiest ones—designated Class III—being required to meet the same standards of safety and effectiveness as new devices.

In January 1989, after an extensive internal debate, the FDA identified silicone breast implants as Class III devices and gave their manufacturers 30 months, until January 1991, to submit safety and effectiveness data to the agency. Four breast implant manufacturers submitted the required documents to the FDA: Dow Corning, INAMED (formerly McGhan Medical), Mentor (formerly Heyer-Schulte), and Bioplasty. Surgitek, a unit of Bristol-Myers Squibb, withdrew from the implant business, saying it was unable to meet the FDA's deadline. On August 12, the head of the FDA Breast Prosthesis task force submitted a review of Dow Corning's studies, stating that they were "so weak that they cannot provide a reasonable assurance of the safety and effectiveness of these devices."

Finally, on November 13, the FDA convened an advisory panel of professionals to consider the most recent evidence and to take further testimony. The hearings were highly contentious. The panel heard, once again, arguments concerning the dangers of implants. But the hearings also generated intense support for implants from plastic surgeons, satisfied implant recipients, and breast cancer support and advocacy organizations. Among the most vocal defenders of the implants were women who had experienced successful reconstruction following mastectomies, including representatives of such peer support organizations as Y-Me and My Image after Breast Cancer. Several spoke of the positive psychological benefits of reconstruction and warned that if the FDA took implants off the market, some women, knowing that reconstructive surgery was unavailable, would delay regular checkups for breast cancer, endangering their lives. Other witnesses argued that women should be free to choose implants, so long as they were fully informed of the benefits and risks of the devices.

The advisory panel debate was, by all accounts, heated. In the final analysis, the panel split hairs: it voted that although breast implants "did not pose a major threat to the health of users," the data submitted by manufacturers was "insufficient to prove safety." However, citing "a public health need," the panel recommended that the devices be left on the market.

The regulatory decision, at this point, passed to the FDA commissioner, Dr. David A. Kessler. Appointed just a few months earlier, Kessler had brought a new commitment to regulatory activism to an agency marked by what some viewed as a pattern of weak government oversight during the Reagan administration. Now, the fledgling commissioner had two months, until mid-January, to rule on the panel's recommendation on breast implants.

Unauthorized Leaks

Unfolding events, however, forced Kessler's hand sooner. In December, a San Francisco jury returned a verdict in *Hopkins* v. *Dow Corning,* awarding Mariann Hopkins $7.3 million, by far the largest victory ever for a plaintiff in a breast implant suit. Hopkins' attorney claimed that his client's implants (made by Dow Corning in 1976) had ruptured and spilled silicone gel—causing severe joint aches, muscle pain, fatigue, and weight loss—and told the jury that "this case is about corporate greed and outright fraud." Dow Corning immediately moved to have the legal records in the case—which included hundreds of pages of internal company memos Hopkins' attorney had subpoenaed—sealed.

Somehow, however, the documents from the Hopkins trial ended up in Commissioner Kessler's hands. Their contents evidently alarmed him. On January 6, 1992, Kessler abruptly reversed the FDA's November decision and called for a 45-day moratorium on all sales of silicone gel breast implants, pending further study of their safety, and he recalled the advisory panel to consider "new evidence." Both the plastic surgeons and Dow Corning were furious. The president of the American Society of Plastic and Reconstructive Surgeons took the unusual step of calling a press conference to brand Kessler's action as "unconscionable—an outrage" and called on Kessler to reconstitute the advisory panel, which he called unqualified to judge the safety of the devices. For its part, Dow Corning demanded publicly to know what new evidence Kessler had obtained and restated the company's intention to block any release of "non-scientific" internal memoranda. The chief of Dow Corning's health-care business called a press conference to repeat the company's contention that "the cumulative body of credible scientific evidence shows that the implants are safe and effective."

Dow Corning's efforts to block release of the Hopkins documents, however, failed. On January 13, *New York Times* reporter Philip J. Hilts—saying only that he had obtained the material from several sources—broke the Hopkins case memos in a page-one article, under the headline "Make Is Depicted as Fighting Tests on Implant Safety." In a summary of the contents of several hundred internal company memos, Hilts charged that Dow Corning's safety studies were inadequate and that serious questions raised by its own scientific research and by doctors' complaints had not been answered.

More damaging revelations were yet to come. Over the next several weeks, newspaper readers learned of the following incidents, drawn from the company's internal documents:

- In a 1980 memo, a Dow Corning sales representative had reported to his marketing manager that he had received complaints from a California plastic surgeon who was "downright indignant" because the implant envelopes were "greasy" and had experienced "excessive gel bleed." "The thing that is really galling is that I feel like I have been beaten by my own company instead of the competition. To put a questionable lot of mammaries on the market is inexcusable," the sales representative wrote his manager. "It has to rank right up there with the Pinto gas tank."

- A marketing manager had reported in a memo that he had "assured [a group of doctors], with crossed fingers, that Dow Corning had an active study [of safety issues] under way." (The marketing manager later angrily disputed the interpretation given his remarks by the media, saying in a letter to the Associated Press that he had meant the term *crossed fingers* in a "hopeful" rather than a "lying" sense.)

- A Las Vegas plastic surgeon had had an extensive correspondence with the company reporting his dissatisfactions with the product. In one letter, he charged that he felt "like a broken record" and told of an incident in which an implant had ruptured and spilled its contents—which he described as having the "consistency of 50 weight motor oil"—onto the operating room floor.

Whether wholly justified or not, the memos created a strong impression that Dow Corning had been aware of safety concerns about its implants for many years and had failed to act on this knowledge. The press moved in aggressively, attacking Dow Corning for its "moral evasions"; a widely reprinted cartoon depicted a Dow Corning executive apparently deflating as silicone gel oozed from his body.

A Model Ethical Citizen

That Dow Corning was being labeled publicly as "a company adrift without a moral compass"—as one *New York Times* columnist put it several days after the internal memos broke in the press—struck many in and around the company as deeply unjust. Ironically, Dow Corning Corporation was widely regarded in the business community as a model for its efforts to institutionalize ethical behavior.

At the center of Dow Corning's efforts was a formal code of conduct and an unusual procedure for monitoring compliance. In 1976, the first full year of sales for its new generation of breast implants, the company's board of directors had appointed a three-person Audit and Social Responsibility Committee and charged it with developing a corporate code of ethical conduct. Top managers were motivated, in part, by a breaking scandal at that time in which several large companies had been accused of questionable payments to foreign heads of state to secure contracts. With a substantial portion of its operations overseas, Dow Corning wanted its behavior to be above reproach.

In 1977, the company published its first corporate code of conduct, laying out a comprehensive statement of ethical standards. In order to ensure compliance, the company initiated a series of annual audits, in which top managers would visit various cities around the globe to evaluate corporate performance against code standards. In addition, the company held training programs on the code, and its semi-annual employee opinion survey included a second on business ethics.

Yet, for whatever reason, the company's widely admired procedures had failed to flag the safety of breast implants as an ethical concern. A routine 1990 ethics audit of the Arlington, Tennessee, plant that manufactured silicone implants, for example, did not reveal any concerns about the product's safety. When later questioned about the apparent failure of the audit procedure, the chairperson of the conduct committee pointed out that normally product safety issues would come before the relevant management group, not the ethics review.

A Hardball Strategy

As the controversy widened, Dow Corning's response, in the words of one *Wall Street Journal* reporter, was to "play hardball." On January 14, eight days after the FDA had announced its moratorium on implant sales and one day after the first leaked documents appeared in the press, Dow Corning took a $25 million charge against fourth quarter, 1991, earnings to cover costs of its legal liability, unused inventory, and efforts to prove implants safe. The company also suspended implant production and placed workers at the company's manufacturing facilities on temporary layoff, with full pay and benefits. Investors, apparently alarmed by this turn of events, knocked down the stock price of both Corning, Inc., and Dow Chemical as they contemplated the parent firms' potential liability.

Implant recipients and trial lawyers also were contemplating the liability question. By March, as many as 600 lawsuits had been filed against Dow Corning and other breast implant makers, according to a representative of the Association of Trial Lawyers of America. The National Products Liability Database estimated that Dow Corning had been sued at least 54 times in federal court and possibly more than 100 times in state courts. Dow Corning's attorney disputed these figures, saying that there were far fewer than 200 cases pending against his client.

The unauthorized leaks created tremendous pressure on Dow Corning to release its own documents to the public. The FDA publicly called on the company on January 20 to release the material so that women and their doctors could evaluate the new evidence for themselves, rather than simply relying on news reports. (The agency, although in possession of the documents, could not release them because they were still protected under court order.) The company responded two days later by releasing a group of scientific studies—but not the infamous Pinto memo and other internal materials that the company dubbed unscientific.

Suspension of breast implant sales and release of the scientific studies did not slow down the crisis engulfing the company. On January 29, in an apparent acknowledgment of the severity of the situation, the company hired former attorney general Griffin B. Bell—who had performed a similar role at Exxon Corporation following the *Valdez* oil spill and at E.F. Hutton following the check-kiting scandal—to investigate its behavior in making implants.

Finally, on February 10, following a top-level intervention by the chairmen of Corning, Inc., and Dow Chemical, both of whom sat on Dow Corning's board, the board of directors executed a stunning management shakeup. Dow Corning demoted Chief Executive Lawrence A. Reed to the position of chief operating officer and forced longtime board chairman John S. Ludington to retire. Keith R. McKennon was named chairman and CEO. Simultaneously, the board announced that it would release to the public 15 scientific reports and 94 nonscientific memos or letters from company files, including the Pinto and "crossed fingers" memos, as well as other potentially damaging materials that had not yet been reported by the media.

Several top executives of Dow Corning met the press the same day to present the company's perspective. One defended the company's decision not to release the documents earlier, saying:

Our motives are simple. First and foremost, these memos do not answer fundamental questions and concerns that women have about breast implants. And by focusing attention on the memos rather than the science that supports the device, we do nothing but further raise the anxiety level of women and physicians and scientists.

He added that "while we are not happy with the memos, we have nothing to hide, and we believe that each memo put in its proper context can be understood and explained." Many of the memos, he said, were best understood as part of the normal give and take that occurs within a technical organization, "one part of a multifaceted dialogue or communication or discussion that goes on," and did not reflect fundamental problems. By pulling various statements out of context, he implied, the press had misrepresented questions scientists might legitimately raise in the course of their inquiry as final conclusions. The Dow Corning executives closed the press conference by denying categorically that implants could cause autoimmune disease or cancer.

Facing a Crucial Decision

On February 20, the day after his testimony before the FDA, McKennon received word from Washington. After three hours of tense debate, the FDA advisory panel had voted just after 5:00 P.M. to recommend that implants be taken off the market, except for women needing reconstruction following mastectomies or to correct serious deformities. All implant recipients would be required to enroll in clinical studies. Cosmetic augmentations would be strictly limited to those required by the design of the clinical trials. Commissioner Kessler would have sixty days to rule on the panel's recommendation.

McKennon would have to lay a plan of action before his board soon—he certainly could not wait another two months for the FDA's next move. The breast implant business, he had learned, had not made any money for Dow Corning for the past five years. Even in its heyday, it had contributed no more than 1 percent of the company's total revenues. Some of his top executives had urged him just to get out of the implant business altogether and let the attorneys mop up the liability problems. Many in the company felt that the huge settlement in the Hopkins case would be greatly reduced on appeal, and the company's $250 million in insurance would be sufficient to cover their liability. McKennon reflected on these issues as he contemplated his next actions. Certainly, he needed to act decisively to stem Dow Corning's financial losses. But, he pondered, did the company not also have, as he had put it to a reporter a few days earlier, an "overriding responsibility . . . to the women who have our implants"? And what of the company's reputation, so carefully nurtured, for always upholding the highest standards of ethical behavior?

Discussion Questions

1. What internal and external factors contributed to the emergence of the silicone breast implant crisis for Dow Corning?
2. What should CEO McKennon do as of February 20, 1992?
3. What steps can Dow Corning, or other companies, take to prevent this kind of situation from occurring in the future?

The portrait of urban violence, crime, drugs, and poverty displayed in newspapers and on television reflects a frightening reality for millions of Americans. Myriad social problems afflict thousands of neighborhoods in hundreds of American communities. To many observers, these problems have worsened considerably in the past 20 years. Despite millions of dollars and endless political rhetoric, the problems of America's cities seem to be escalating. Many efforts have been launched to save our cities. Often, they have failed; some may have even made the situation worse.

Fear grows as reality worsens. The city has become an even more fearful place as media attention highlights the bizarre, the insane, the dangerous. Perception often is reality, and some who can avoid the city do so, in an effort to immunize themselves from society's problems. But some people fight back, continuing to find new ways of combating the terror of fear. In many cities, volunteer community groups, local government, and law enforcement continue the struggle to make cities safe for citizens.

Businesses are also involved in the struggle to save America's cities. Most businesses do not have the luxury of relocating to "safe harbor" locations where crime does not happen and social ills do not exist. Most businesses, like most people, have to find ways to cope with their problems, face challenges, and continue their daily activities.

Law enforcement, vigilant neighbors, active community groups, and economic development are all needed if communities are to win the fight to save our cities. Big cities like Atlanta, Cleveland, and Boston, as well as small and medium-sized cities and towns, are undertaking new experiments and forging new approaches. Business is a critical part of these efforts. Although it is too early to know if there are best practices that can be imitated in every community, there is reason to believe that some of the new efforts being undertaken are making an impact.

How Businesses Are Involved

The Urban Institute, a research think tank based in Washington, DC, has studied business involvement in cities and concluded that while individual companies are involved in a wide variety of community activities in cities across the nation, three distinct strategic approaches have dominated corporate involvement in rebuilding and strengthening urban communities.

Direct Involvement

The concept of hands-on business activities with neighborhoods is a relatively new form of direct involvement. Traditionally, business has made somewhat passive charitable con-

Note: Sources for discussion of The Atlanta Project include Archie B. Carroll and Gerald T. Horton, "Do Joint Corporate Social Responsibility Programs Work?" *Business and Society Review,* Summer 1994, pp. 24–28; and Archie B. Carroll and Gerald T. Horton, "The Atlanta Project: Corporate Social Responsibility on a Mega Scale," in Steven Wartick and Denis Collins, eds., *1994 Proceedings of Fifth Annual Conference, International Association for Business and Society* (Hilton Head, NC, March 17–20, 1994), pp. 261–266. Primary sources include *The Atlanta Project* (Atlanta, GA: The Carter Center, 1992); *Improving the Quality of Life in Our Neighborhoods: The Atlanta Project, Strategic Plan* (Atlanta, GA: The Carter Center, March 1992); and J. Carter, "Preface," in *Because There Is Hope: Gearing Up to Renew Urban America* (Atlanta, GA: The Carter Center, 1993). Additional data provided by The Atlanta Project. We are grateful for the assistance of Richard Watson and Jason Foss of TAP.

tributions to arts, educational, and community groups. Investments have rarely been neighborhood-focused, except for those in downtown redevelopment projects. Increasingly, however, businesses have made direct investments in urban neighborhoods for the purpose of stabilizing, even reclaiming, areas that were once thought to be in hopeless decline. There are a few models worth studying. One is a landmark effort, the Crown Center Redevelopment Project in Kansas City. The neighborhood around its corporate headquarters was becoming surrounded by abandoned buildings and empty lots when Hallmark Cards Inc. began a neighborhood redevelopment effort. Twenty-five years after the initiative began, Hallmark has invested more than $500 million in what is considered a jewel in Kansas City's development.

In the 1990s, neighborhood needs are being addressed in a more complete or holistic manner. This has led to direct investments that attack a range of community-based problems. Upjohn, a pharmaceutical company based in Kalamazoo, Michigan, recognized the importance of housing as a stabilizing force in the local community. Citizen ownership of a community begins with home ownership, which is seen as critical to convincing residents that they have a stake in the neighborhood. To restore housing and improve home ownership in neighborhoods near its facilities, Upjohn recruited and supported the Local Initiative Support Corporation (LISC), a nonprofit development corporation, to help build home ownership by making mortgage loans to local residents in Kalamazoo. The long-term effect of Upjohn's efforts appears favorable: home ownership has increased in the target neighborhoods, and other social indicators—crime rates, drug use—have declined.

Community Partnership around a Business Core

Some companies have found it possible to integrate community development objectives into their normal business operations. The company pursues its profit-making business but takes on as a partner a comprehensive community organization. For example, Ben & Jerry's Homemade Inc. has collaborated with Larkin Street Youth Center in San Francisco to open an ice cream shop that provides job training to youths (ages 12 to 17) who are mostly runaways. The company helps meet the education, training, and self-esteem needs of youth with the center's staff. Profits from the ice cream store are shared with the Larkin Center.

Ben & Jerry's has expanded this partnership concept to many other cities and locations. In New York City, for example, the company has partnered with the Harlem Ark of Freedom. The organization runs a homeless shelter and is engaged in a range of community development activities. Again, the store partnership helps to train people who lack education and job skills, to stabilize the neighborhood, and to attract additional businesses.

Some retail businesses with large workforces and connections to the community lend themselves to this approach. A number of supermarkets such as Pathmark, Kroger, and First National have created similar community anchors by building stores, employing previously unemployed people, and serving as a magnet for other economic investment.

Use of Intermediary Institutions

In some cities, community leaders have created a separate institution to serve as an umbrella vehicle for development efforts. In Cleveland, for example, the Cleveland Foundation convened a Commission on Poverty in 1990 to devise a long-term comprehensive strategy for bringing together business, government, and community resources to connect the city's poor neighborhoods to mainstream economic opportunity.

Business leaders were recruited to work with the commission, to study its findings, and to devise alternative responses to the problems. Leaders from Cleveland-based businesses such as White Consolidated Industries, The Higbee Company, Reliance Electric, and several leading law firms participated and saw the linkage between altruism and self-interest. Economic revitalization was critical to community improvement and to building Cleveland into a community that could support a modern base of service and manufacturing industries. It required that action be taken in school reform, housing, and community services. In short, a long-term business goal—a well-trained workforce—was intimately connected to comprehensive community involvement. The Cleveland Foundation has played a central role in aligning projects, sponsors, and corporate participation in what are called *villages* or neighborhoods in the city. Four core areas of community need were defined: education, investment, family development, and health. The foundation, and its Community-Building Initiative Council, helped to coordinate the focusing, funding, and delivery of programs to address these needs in each village. In the course of five years, the entire project has begun to achieve measurable improvement in meeting these core needs using a variety of social and economic indicators.

Building Better Communities: Contrasting Approaches

Businesses often become involved in the social issues affecting cities because they are asked to play a role or work with others to tackle a critical problem. Two examples of corporate involvement are discussed next. One is The Atlanta Project, a broad sweeping approach to Atlanta's complex social issues. The macro or comprehensive approach developed in Atlanta contrasts with the narrower, more selective (micro) approach of Boston Against Drugs, which has enlisted companies to tackle drug issues throughout that city.

The Atlanta Project: A Macro Approach to Social Issues

The Atlanta Project (TAP) is one of the best-known and widely studied recent efforts to save America's cities. Atlanta, like many other American cities, displays contrasting faces: one is the face of wealth, prosperity, a positive spirit, and an optimistic view of life; the other is a face of despair, poverty, and fear. Dr. Johnetta Cole, president of Spelman College in Atlanta, said it this way: "We have two cities . . . one rich, one poor." In Atlanta, civic leaders such as Dr. Cole are in the vanguard of a broad effort to turn two cities into a single, prosperous, safe community for all. The Atlanta Project is a coalition of Atlanta-based organizations—businesses, churches, community groups, government agencies, universities—formed to attack the poverty, crime, and community conditions that contribute to the "second city."

The Atlanta Project was launched on October 25, 1991, by a former president of the United States, Jimmy Carter. Carter, a Georgia native, whose presidential library and home base for continuing activities—the Carter Center at Emory University—are located in Atlanta, had been persuaded by Atlanta's civic leaders to lead the campaign to address the city's poverty and related social problems. Carter's natural interest in such an effort was coupled with his own action theory of how social change occurs in any community: *through the full participation of those affected.* It is an approach Carter has put into practice in global affairs as well: his mediation in Haiti helped to peacefully remove General Cedras and restore President Aristide to power; his efforts helped defuse a crisis over North Korea's nuclear capability; and his efforts helped to negotiate a cease-fire agreement to slow ethnic warfare in Bosnia. Carter has called The Atlanta Project the domestic centerpiece of the Carter Center's work. And, as in his international mediation efforts, fear of failure does not deter the former president. "The real failure, for Atlanta and cities like it, would be not to try," according to Carter.

Collaborative Empowerment

Atlanta has a large, successful professional population. But the city also has a much larger (500,000) inner-city population that suffers the problems of chronic poverty, crime, drugs, joblessness, illiteracy, teenage pregnancy, and substandard housing. To tackle these problems, Carter was determined to engage a broad cross-section of community resources. The former president called together leaders from business, local government, and community organizations and created a consortium to engage the issues. The leaders pledged their co-operation and the involvement of their organizations. As one executive said, "Mr. Carter is very persuasive and a good arm-twister." The former president solicited substantial pledges from such Atlanta-headquartered businesses as Marriott, Coca Cola, Delta Airlines, and BellSouth. Each would become an important partner in TAP. As of 1994, Atlanta businesses had contributed more than $30 million.

TAP was organized around Atlanta's local neighborhoods. The idea was to find a natural community around which an integrated approach to social services and economic assistance could be built. The focus turned to Atlanta's high schools which, it was discovered, served as natural focal points for Atlanta's neighborhoods. Each area was designated a *cluster community*. These 20 clusters became the unit of analysis and action for the project, although they often span political boundaries (e.g., parts of three counties are included in TAP's clusters).

The concept of local empowerment is vital to every aspect of TAP. Within each TAP cluster, for example, is a cluster coordinator and assistant coordinator who live in the neighborhood they represent. These coordinators are employed by TAP to work with a cluster steering committee composed of residents, service providers, and representatives from cluster schools, churches, businesses, and community groups. Cluster coordinators are not bosses in this process; rather, they are facilitators who help the community identify its needs, find the tools for tackling the issues, and create possible solutions to the cluster's problems. TAP has a central resource center to which all coordinators can turn for help, but the emphasis is on community-based solutions to community needs. Each cluster coordinator has to be skillful at using corporate partners, local government agencies, and other community resources to address the agenda of issues, needs, and concerns that the cluster community shares. Imagination is crucial to achieving success.

Business involvement in TAP operates at several levels. The chief executives of Atlanta companies met with former president Carter and leaders of other Atlanta organizations to map out strategies and initiatives in broad terms. Individual companies have been paired with one of the clusters, assigning at least one full-time manager to work with the cluster coordinator and his or her team. (TAP requested that the companies commit a full-time manager for up to *five* years in order to build real expertise at community problem solving.) Some companies have taken the lead in specific citywide projects that span the clusters: BellSouth, for example, has had a companywide commitment to improving adult literacy. The company took the lead in creating a program to bring thousands of books to Atlanta's clusters, coupling the book donations with a volunteer program to teach reading throughout the city. Hundreds of BellSouth employees have participated in this adult literacy education effort.

Thousands of employees in TAP companies have volunteered to help in the clusters, undertaking tasks as diverse as providing computer instruction for teachers and students in local schools; offering small business forums to help residents turn ideas into community enterprises; organizing basketball camps; helping students prepare college financial aid applications; and providing local residents with technical training in electrical wiring, plumbing, secretarial skills, and how to meet commercial driver's license requirements.

Collaboration among all of Atlanta's racial, demographic, and economic segments is the essence of the process. That doesn't happen immediately in most situations because trust must be built, a common vision must be developed, and an understanding of how to work together needs to emerge. Once a diverse community starts to work together, however, new ideas emerge, action follows ideas, and visible progress begins to occur. That is the essence of former president Carter's notion of collaborative empowerment.

Problems

The Atlanta Project is not without its problems and its detractors. Some say the project is too ambitious, too costly, and too closely tied to Carter's unique vision of empowerment. Most observers, however, point to Carter's role as one of being a *catalyst,* not a director. TAP's problems, in their view, have to do with the day-to-day challenges of getting people, who may have never been involved in community processes, to participate and trust the cluster approach. There are also the problems of sustaining the "fire" in cluster coordinators and others who show signs of physical and emotional burn-out after several years of hard work and of continuing to find news ways to leverage limited resources against a very formidable list of community issues and needs. In early 1995, as the fifth year of the five-year TAP program began, several clusters were still operating with acting coordinators.

Business involvement has also suffered some problems. Loaned executives from Atlanta companies, for example, have sometimes sought to return to their companies for personal career reasons. Five years on leave in a community job may be too long away from the mainstream of a telecommunications or banking career. And business representatives have sometimes been frustrated by the slow decision-making processes that accompany the empowerment approach. Discussion takes time, and endless meetings of community representatives may be necessary before a consensus is reached on what to do and how to do it. Still, this is an investment in community decision making that supporters believe will be repaid many times over as more complex problems are tackled by the clusters.

Atlanta's businesses seem likely to stay involved for several reasons. First, former president Carter has made it quite clear that he will not let them walk away from so vital a process. The Atlanta Project is scheduled to continue for a full five years, through 1996, and it has drawn such interest from other cities that Carter announced a national rollout of the concept to other cities starting in 1995. Second, the presence of the 1996 Olympic Summer Games in Atlanta has meant that businesses, government agencies, and community groups have to cooperate to meet the city's commitments as host city. TAP objectives and needs mesh nicely into some aspects of Atlanta's Olympic planning efforts. Third, the entire process is reinforcing an ethic in the Atlanta business community that was summarized by former Atlanta mayor and United Nations ambassador, Andrew Young, in this way: "At the end of the day, the success of business depends not on profit and loss, but on the quality of life." Quality of life cannot mean two cities, one rich and one poor; it must mean one community, with opportunity and hope for all.

Boston Against Drugs: A Micro Approach to Social Issues

Illegal drugs have been a part of America's social problems for many years. Since the 1970s, federal, state, and local governments have tried to combat drug distribution and sale through vigorous enforcement efforts. Many experts believe the nation is still losing its battle against drugs and that renewed efforts must be made to address drug sale and use.

Private sector initiatives have also been undertaken to deal with drugs. Many companies have instituted drug testing programs in the workplace to identify workers whose drug abuse may be harmful to others. To the extent drugs undermine workforce productivity, they threaten the competitiveness of companies. Worse, by far, drugs impair a person's judgment and physical actions. This can be fatal for coworkers and innocent bystanders if the impaired employee is operating mechanical equipment, motor vehicles, or airplanes. Public safety and workplace safety considerations have made drug testing and substance-abuse education common among many companies.

A second type of private sector antidrug effort has involved public education campaigns to persuade people, especially young adults, not to experiment with illegal substances. One of the best-known programs is the advertising campaign sponsored by Partnership for a Drug-Free America. Media companies, advertisers, and advertising agencies have teamed up to raise millions of dollars to broadcast the creative, sometimes shocking Partnership ads. (In one, the camera focuses on an egg as a voice says, "This is your brain." The next scene shows a cracked egg frying on a hot griddle as the voice says, "This is your brain on drugs.") The object is to deter people from ever trying drugs.

Business has also become involved in grassroots, community-based efforts to tackle drug use. In Boston, such a program is called Boston Against Drugs (BAD). BAD is a partnership of businesses, nonprofit organizations, and government agencies formed in 1987 when former mayor Ray Flynn called on local businesses to assist in dealing with the city's drug and substance abuse issues. A number of corporate chief executives were willing to become involved because they believed drugs to be a social scourge which their companies were already addressing through drug testing, education, and prevention programs. Others concluded it was not politically smart to say no to a popular mayor who seemed likely to hold political office for years to come.[1]

As in The Atlanta Project, Boston Against Drugs adopted a neighborhood focus. The city was divided into 16 neighborhoods. For each, a team was formed consisting of government officials, community leaders, and a business that had connections to the area. For example, in South Boston, Gillette, the consumer products giant, signed on as the corporate team member. Among the other companies were Bank of Boston; New England Telephone (NYNEX); Group Bull, a computer manufacturer; Boston Edison, an electric utility; and Blue Cross and Blue Shield, a health insurer. *The Boston Herald* (daily newspaper), MassPort (public authority that operates the airport and harbor), the MBTA (subway and bus system), and several law firms also were involved.

Business leadership was key to BAD's activities. The first challenge was to get the cooperation of community groups, government officials, and businesses to actually form the community teams. Because each of these organizations faces many demands on their

---

[1]Victor Forlani, "Boston Against Drugs: An Analysis of Business in the Community," in Steven Wartick and Denis Collins, eds., *1994 Proceedings of Fifth Annual Conference, International Association for Business and Society* (Hilton Head, NC, March 17–20, 1994), pp. 300–4; Boston Against Drugs, *Annual Report* (Boston: Office of The Mayor, 1994).

time, considerable persuasion was necessary to get the proper players on board. An even greater challenge was to get the team members talking in a constructive and positive way. What were the problems in each neighborhood? What could and should be done? How could obstacles be overcome? Would any of their efforts really make a difference? Months passed before the teams developed enough trust and sense of common purpose for initiatives to begin taking shape. Once they did, however, things began to change in the community. In one neighborhood, the need was for a basketball program; in another, classes were offered at a community center; in yet another, a job counseling project was started. By the end of a year, there were signs of progress.

Boston Against Drugs started small but had potential. In 1990, the program received a federal grant to expand the program to all of the city's neighborhoods and to begin a systematic evaluation process to see whether such efforts ultimately influenced drug use by the population of a neighborhood. An evaluation team was created to work with neighborhood teams, to track results, neighborhood by neighborhood, and to facilitate sharing lessons learned. Boston became a model for other antidrug programs throughout the United States.

A Narrow Focus

Drugs are often at the center of a city's social problems. Many experts believe that by focusing sharply on antidrug activities, leverage can be created for addressing issues such as crime, education, and poverty. Some BAD leaders believe it is crucial to keep a clear focus on drugs if anything is to be accomplished. These people fear a loss of focus if other community problems are added to the agenda.

Business played an important role in Boston Against Drugs. By providing leadership, human resources, financial leverage, and demonstrated commitment, the business community has helped make the program an important part of the city's commitment to saving its neighborhoods. When Mayor Flynn resigned in 1993 to assume the position of U.S. ambassador to the Vatican, a city council member named Thomas Menino became acting mayor. Several months later, Menino was elected to a full term as mayor of Boston. Among his early actions, the new mayor endorsed the concept and reinforced the importance of the Boston Against Drugs partnership: "If we are to build a safe city that serves all of our people, we need partnerships like BAD."

The Future

Not all public–private partnerships succeed in solving the problems of America's cities. Some observers believe that many of these efforts fall short of their goals and objectives. Since program evaluation is often weak, however, the truth is hidden.

Given the complexity of the social ills being addressed, and the challenge of coordinating private sector, public sector, and voluntary sector organizations, it is not surprising that saving the cities is a very difficult task. One role business can play is to insist on careful evaluation of programs in a continuing effort to figure out what works best and what works least well. The business community knows a great deal about program evaluation, total quality management concepts, benchmarking, and quantifying the costs, benefits, and value-added of activities. This expertise needs to be brought to bear on saving our cities. As the authors of the Urban Institute report state:

> The difficulty of measuring such abstract concepts as "improved community spirit" and "increased leadership potential," coupled with the fact that many grassroots or-

ganizations do not have access to measurement tools, has made comprehensive evaluation infrequent. However, this trend is slowly changing, partly as a result of increased corporate involvement in distressed communities. As corporations move away from pure philanthropic donations and look at their contributions as investments, they are demanding to see some return on that investment and have increased the demand for measurement of outcomes.[2]

Discussion Questions

1. What factors have helped to make The Atlanta Project a success? Which are unique to Atlanta and which are common to all communities?
2. What factors have helped to make Boston Against Drugs a success? Which are unique to Boston and which are common to all communities?
3. Consider the problems in your own community. Compare the *comprehensive* approach suggested by The Atlanta Project with the *selective* approach of Boston Against Drugs. Which approach has the best potential for success in your community?
4. Dr. Johnetta Cole, president of Spelman College, has been an active participant in TAP. She has said, "If we focus, if we cooperate, if we sacrifice, . . . we can do it." Are focus, cooperation, and sacrifice enough to save our cities? What else is needed? Is there a role for the federal government? the state government?
5. In some states, there are one or two large cities and many small and medium-sized communities. Should businesses that are located in the large cities, but draw employees and customers from smaller communities as well, participate in projects to strengthen all of these communities? How can they decide which ones not to support?
6. Consider the community in which your college or university is located. What kinds of community involvements does it have? How does it participate in projects to improve the community? What organizations provide the leadership?

---

[2]George Peterson and Dana Sundblad, *Corporations as Partners in Strengthening Urban Communities,* Research Report 1079–94 (New York: The Conference Board, 1994), p. 43.

Glossary

This glossary defines technical or special terms used in this book. It may be used by students as a quick and handy reference for terms that may be unfamiliar without having to refer to the specific chapter(s) where they are used. It also can be a very helpful aid in studying for examinations and for writing term papers where precise meanings are needed.

Acid rain.   Rain that is more acidic than normal; occurs when emissions of sulfur dioxide and nitrogen oxides from utilities, manufacturers, and vehicles combine with water vapor in the air.

Acquisition.   (see **Corporate merger.**)

Administrative costs.   The direct costs incurred in running government regulatory agencies, including salaries of employees, equipment, supplies, and other such items. (See also **Compliance costs.**)

Administrative learning.   A stage in the development of corporate social responsiveness during which managers and supervisors learn new practices necessary for coping with social problems and pressures.

Advocacy advertising.   A strategy used by companies to promote their social, political, or economic viewpoint through the media.

Affirmative action.   A positive and sustained effort by an organization to identify, hire, train if necessary, and promote minorities, women, and members of other groups who are underrepresented in the organization's workforce.

Air pollution.   When more pollutants, such as sulfur dioxide or particulates, are emitted into the atmosphere than can be safely absorbed and diluted by natural processes.

Altruism.   Acting for the benefit of others at the risk of sacrificing one's self-interest.

American dream.   An ideal goal or vision of life in the United States, usually including material abundance and maximum freedom.

Annual meeting.   A yearly meeting called by a corporation's board of directors for purposes of reporting to the company's stockholders on the current status and future prospects of the firm.

Anticompetitive merger.   A merger of two or more companies that reduces or eliminates competition in an industry or region; usually illegal under U.S. antitrust laws.

Antitrust laws.   Laws that promote competition or that oppose trusts, monopolies, or other business combinations that restrain trade.

Arbitration.   A method for resolving a dispute between two parties, such as between a business firm and a consumer. In arbitration, a neutral third party, called an arbitrator, hears both sides of the dispute and then makes a final binding decision.

Biodiversity.   The variety of living organisms and the range of their genetic makeup.

Biometrics.   A field of knowledge that integrates knowledge from biological science and computer science to identify living organisms by identifying their unique genetic patterns.

Biotechnology.   The use and combination of various sciences, including biochemistry, genetics, microbiology, ecology, recombinant DNA, and others, to invent and develop new and modified life forms for applications in medicine, industry, farming, and other areas of human life.

Blowing the whistle.   (See **Whistle-blowing.**)

Board of directors.   A group of persons elected by shareholder votes to be responsible for directing the affairs of a corporation, establishing company objectives and policies, selecting top-level managers, and reviewing company performance.

Bottom line.   Business profits or losses, usually reported in figures on the last or bottom line of a company's income statement.

Business.   The activity or organizing resources in order to produce and distribute goods and services for society.

Business and society.   The study of the relationship of business with its entire social environment.

Business ethics.   The application of general ethical ideas to business behavior.

Business legitimacy principle. The view that a company must comply with the law and conform to the expectations of its stakeholders in order to be a corporate citizen in good standing.

Carrying capacity. The maximum population that an ecosystem can support. (See also **Limits to growth hypothesis.**)

Cause marketing. A form of philanthropy in which contributions to a nonprofit organization are tied to the use of the donor organization's products or services by the recipient organization's members.

Central state control. A socioeconomic system in which political, social, and economic power is concentrated in a central government that makes all fundamental policy decision for the society.

CERES Principles. A corporate code of conduct, developed by the Coalition for Environmentally Responsible Economies (CERES), that commits signers to sound environmental policies and sustainable use of natural resources. (Formerly known as the Valdez Principles.)

Charity principle. The idea that individuals and business firms should give voluntary aid and support to society's unfortunate or needy persons, as well as to other (nonprofit) organizations that provide community services.

Child care. The care or supervision of another's child, such as at a day-care center; offered as a benefit by some employers to working parents.

Chlorofluorocarbons (CFCs). Manufactured chemicals, used as refrigerants, insulation, solvents, and propellants in spray cans, that are believed to react with and deplete ozone in the upper atmosphere. (See also **Montreal Protocol, Ozone.**)

Cloning. The process of genetically creating an identical cell or organism.

Coalitions. Groups of organizations or corporate stakeholders who work together to achieve a common goal.

Codetermination. A system of corporate governance providing for labor representation on a company's board of directors.

Collaborative partnerships. Companies joining with their key stakeholders to respond better to an important issue or problem by pooling resources.

Command and control regulation. A regulatory approach where the government "commands" companies to meet specific standards (such as amounts of particular pollutants) and "controls" the methods (such as technology) used to achieve these standards. This approach is often contrasted with market-based regulatory approaches where the government establishes general goals and allows companies to use the most cost-effective methods possible to achieve them.

Commercial piracy. The wrongful use of intellectual property, such as software, musical recordings, or clothing designs, for commercial gain.

Commons. Traditionally, an area of land on which all citizens could graze their animals without limitation. The term now refers to any shared resource, such as land, air, or water, that a group of people use collectively. (See also **Global commons.**)

Community. A company's area of local business influence. This includes the people and other stakeholder residing near a business operation.

Community advisory panels (CAPs). Groups of citizens from a local community who meet with corporate officials to discuss issues of common interest about a company's operations, such as plant safety, traffic patterns, and emergency planning.

Community relations. The involvement of business with the communities in which it conducts operations.

Comparable worth. The idea that different kinds of jobs can be equated with each other in terms of difficulty, training required, skills involved, effort made, responsibility involved, and working conditions, for the purpose of equalizing wages paid to people holding jobs approximately equal in these ways.

Competition. A struggle to survive and excel. In business, different firms compete with one another for customers' dollars.

Competition policies. A term used to describe antitrust laws or policies in some nations and trading groups.

Compliance costs. The costs incurred by business and other organizations in complying with government regulations, such as the cost of pollution control machinery or the disposal of toxic chemical wastes. (See also **Administrative costs.**)

Comprehensive Environmental Response, Compensation, and Liability Act (CERCLA). (See **Superfund.**)

Computer hackers. Individuals who break into company databases or other secure information banks to steal and delete information or cause confusion for those trying to use the information.

Concentration (corporate, economic, industrial, market). When relatively few companies are responsible for a large proportion of economic activity, production, or sales.

Conglomerate merger. The combination, or joining together, of two or more companies in unrelated industries into a single company. (See also **Horizontal merger, Vertical merger.**)

Consumer bill of rights. Four rights of consumers outlined in a well-known speech by President John F. Kennedy. The four consumer rights Kennedy discussed were the right to safety, the right to be informed, the right to choose, and the right to be heard.

Consumer hot-lines. A telephone line or interactive Web site providing consumers with direct access to a company.

Consumer movement. A social movement that seeks to augment the rights and powers of consumers. (Also known as *consumerism.*)

Consumer protection laws. Laws that provide consumers with better information, protect consumers from possible hazards, or encourage competitive pricing.

Consumer rights. The legitimate claims of consumers to safe products and services, adequate information, free choice, a fair hearing, and competitive prices.

Consumerism. (See **Consumer movement.**)

Corporate crime. Illegal behavior by company employees that benefits a corporation.

Corporate culture. The traditions, customs, values, and approved ways of behaving that prevail in a corporation.

Corporate giving. (See **Corporate philanthropy.**)

Corporate governance. Any structured system of allocating power in a corporation that determines how and by whom the company is to be governed.

Corporate legitimacy. Public acceptance of the corporation as an institution that contributes to society's well-being.

Corporate merger. The combination, or joining together, of two or more separate companies into a single company. (See also **Conglomerate merger, Horizontal merger, Vertical merger.**)

Corporate philanthropy. Gifts and contributions made by corporations, usually from pretax profits, to benefit various types of nonprofit community organizations.

Corporate political agency theory. A theory that holds that politicians are the agents of those who elect or appoint them to office.

Corporate political strategy. Those activities taken by organizations to acquire, develop, and use power to achieve a political advantage or gain.

Corporate power. The strength or capability of corporations to influence government, the economy, and society, based on their organizational resources and size.

Corporate restructuring. The reorganization of a corporation's business units and activities, which often involves the closing of current facilities and reduction of workforce.

Corporate social involvement. The interaction of business corporations with society.

Corporate social policy. A policy or a group of policies in a corporation that define the company's purposes, goals, and programs regarding one or more social issues or problems.

Corporate social responsibility. The idea that businesses are accountable for the effects of their actions and should seek socially beneficial results as well as economically beneficial results.

Corporate social responsiveness. The way firms address social demands initiated by their stakeholders, or actions taken by firms that affect their stakeholders.

Corporate social strategy. The social, political, and ethical parts of a company's plans and activities for achieving its goals and purposes.

Corporate stakeholder. A person or group affected by a corporation's policies and actions.

Corporate strategic management. Planning, directing, and managing a corporation for the purpose of helping it achieve its basic purposes and long-term goals.

Corporate strategic planning. A process of formulating a corporation's basic purpose, long-term goals, and programs intended to achieve the company's purposes and goals.

Corporate takeover. The acquisition, usually by merger, of one corporation by another.

Corporate volunteerism. A program wherein a company engages its employees in community service as a way to improve the company's image as well as serve the communities in which the business operates.

Corporation. Legally, an artificial legal "person," created under the laws of a particular state or nation. Socially and organizationally, it is a complex system of people, technology, and resources generally devoted to carrying out a central economic mission as it interacts with a surrounding social and political environment.

Cost-benefit analysis. A systematic method of calculating the costs and benefits of a project or activity that is intended to produce benefits.

Council of Institutional Investors. An organization founded in 1985 that represents the interests of institutional investors.

Crisis management. The use of a special team to help a company cope with an unusual emergency situation that may threaten the company in serious ways.

Cross-media pollution. Pollution that migrates across several different media, such as air, land, or water. For example, hazardous wastes disposed in a dump might leak out, contaminating groundwater, or evaporate, causing air pollution. (Also known as *multimedia pollution.*)

Culpability score. Under the U.S. Corporate Sentencing Guidelines, the degree of blame assigned to an executive found guilty of criminal wrongdoing.

Cultural distance. The amount of difference in customs, attitudes, and values between two social systems.

Cultural shock. A person's disorientation and insecurity caused by the strangeness of a different culture.

Cyberspace. A virtual location where information is stored, ideas are described, and communication takes place in and through an electronic network of linked systems.

Deceptive advertising. An advertisement that is deceptive or misleading; generally illegal under U.S. law.

Defense industry conversion. The process of transforming businesses that once specialized in military production into businesses capable of producing goods and services for civilian or nonmilitary use.

Delaney Clause. An amendment to the Food, Drug, and Cosmetics Act of 1958 that banned all food additives known to cause cancer in humans or animals; repealed in 1996.

Deregulation. The removal of scaling down of regulatory authority and regulatory activities of government.

Design for disassembly. Designing products so that they can be disassembled, and their component parts recycled or reused at the end of their useful life.

Directors. (See **Board of directors.**)

Discrimination (in jobs or employment). Unequal treatment of employees based on *non–job-related* factors such as race, sex, age, national origin, religion, color, and physical or mental handicap.

Diversity (global and cultural). A concept that describes an organization or community composed of people of many racial, cultural, ethnic, religious, and other distinguishing characteristics.

Divestment. Withdrawing and shifting to other uses the funds that a person or group has invested in the securities (stocks, bonds, notes, etc.) of a company. Investors sometimes have divested the securities of companies doing business in countries accused of human rights abuses.

Dividend. A return-on-investment payment made to the owners of shares of corporate stock at the discretion of the company's board of directors.

Downsizing. The reduction of a company's workforce; often part of a corporate restructuring program designed to reduce costs.

Earth Summit. An international conference sponsored by the United Nations in Brazil in 1992 that produced several treaties on global environmental issues. (Also known as the *Conference on Environment and Development.*)

Eco-efficiency. Occurs when businesses or societies are simultaneously economically efficient and environmentally responsible.

Ecologically sustainable organization (ESO). A business that operates in a way that is consistent with the principle of sustainable development. (See also **Sustainable development.**)

Ecology. The study, and the process, of how living things—plants and animals—interact with one another and with their environment.

Ecosystem. Plants and animals in their natural environment, living together as an interdependent system.

Egoist. (See **Ethical egoist.**)

Elder care. The care or supervision of elderly persons; offered as a benefit by some employers to working children of elderly parents.

Electoral politics. Political activities undertaken by business and other interest groups to influence the outcome of elections to public office.

Emissions charges or fees. Fees charged to business by the government, based on the amount of pollution emitted.

Employee stock ownership plan (ESOP). A benefit plan in which a company purchases shares of its own stock and places them in trust for its employees.

Employment-at-will. The principle that workers are hired and retained solely at the discretion of the employer.

Encryption. A type of software that scrambles e-mails and files, preventing eavesdroppers from seeing information sent across the Internet and stored in databases.

Enlightened self-interest. The view that social responsiveness and long-run economic return are compatible and are in the interest of business.

Entitlement mentality. A view that a person or group is guaranteed an economic or social benefit by virtue of being a member of the designated group. (See also **Right [human].**)

Environmental audit. A company audit, or review, of its progress toward meeting environmental goals, such as pollution prevention.

Environmental justice. A movement to prevent unfair or inequitable exposure to environmental risk, such as from exposure to hazardous chemicals; or a situation where exposure to such risk is fair and equitable.

Environmental labeling. When government agencies or private organizations label products or packaging judged to be environmentally acceptable.

Environmental partnership. A voluntary, collaborative partnership between or among businesses, government regulators, and environmental organizations to achieve specific environmental goals.

Environmental Protection Agency (EPA). The United States federal government agency responsible for most environmental regulation and enforcement.

Environmental scanning. Examining an organization's environment to discover trends and forces that could have an impact on the organization.

Environmental standards. Standard amounts of particular pollutants allowable by law.

Equal-access rule. A legal provision that requires television stations to allow all competing candidates for political office to broadcast their political messages if one of the candidates' views are broadcast.

Equal job opportunity. The principal that all persons otherwise qualified should be treated equally with respect to job opportunities, workplace conditions, pay, fringe benefits, and retirement provisions.

Ergonomics. Adapting work tasks, working conditions, and equipment to minimize worker injury or stress.

Ethical climate. The prevailing, often unspoken ethical attitudes and beliefs of an organization that tend to guide the behavior of organization members when confronted with an ethical dilemma.

Ethical egoist. A person who puts his or her own selfish interests above all other considerations, while ignoring or denying the ethical needs and beliefs of others.

Ethical relativism. A belief that ethical right and wrong are defined by various periods of time in history, a society's traditions, the specific circumstances of the moment, or personal opinion.

Ethics. A conception of right and wrong conduct, serving as a guide to moral behavior.

Ethics audit. A systematic effort to discover actual or potential unethical behavior in an organization.

Ethics code. A written statement that describes the general value system and ethical rules of an organization.

Ethics committee. A high-level group of executives who provide ethical guidance for employees and are often empowered to investigate and punish ethical wrongdoing at the firm.

Ethnocentric business. A company whose business standards are based on its home nation's customs, markets, and laws.

Ethnocentric perspective. The view that a company is an extension of its home country and owes its loyalty to the home country.

European Union (EU). The political and economic coalition of European countries.

Executive compensation. The compensation (total pay) of corporate executives, including salary, bonus, stock options, and various benefits.

Export of jobs. A loss of jobs in a business firm's home nation, and a creation of new jobs in a foreign nation, caused by relocating part or all of the business firm's operations (and jobs) to the foreign nation.

Expropriation. (See **Nationalization.**)

Family-friendly corporation. A company that removes sex discrimination from all aspects of its operations and that supports both men and women in their efforts to balance work and family responsibilities.

Family leave. A leave of absence from work, either paid or unpaid, for the purpose of caring for a family member.

Fiduciary responsibility or duty. A legal obligation to carry out a duty to some other person or group in order to protect their interest.

Fiscal policy. The patterns of spending and taxation adopted by a government.

Flextime. A plan that allows employees limited control over scheduling their own hours of work, usually at the beginning and end of the workday.

Foreign direct investment (FDI). The investment and transfer of funds by investors in one nation into business activities or organizations located in another nation.

Foreign investment review board. A national government body that is empowered to review and approve or disapprove proposed investments by foreign owners in a nation.

Fraud. Deceit or trickery due to the pursuit of economic gain or competitive advantage.

Free enterprise ideology. A set of beliefs about one way to organize economic life that includes individualism, freedom, private property, profit, equality of opportunity, competition, the work ethic, and a limited government.

Free enterprise system. A socioeconomic system based on private ownership, profit-seeking business firms, and the principle of free markets.

Free market. A model of an economic system based on voluntary and free exchange among buyers and sellers. Competition regulates prices in all free market exchanges.

Functional-area ethics. The ethical problems that typically occur in the various specialized operational areas of business, such as accounting, marketing, and finance.

Functional regulation. Regulations aimed at a particular function or operation of business, such as competition or labor relations.

Future shock. A human reaction to rapid technological change whereby individuals experience difficulty in coping with new conditions of life brought on by new technology.

Gender pay gap. The difference in the average level of wages, salaries, and income received by men and women.

Genetic engineering. (See **Biotechnology.**)

Geocentric business. A company whose business standards and policies are worldwide in outlook including multinational ownership, management, markets, and operations.

Geocentric perspective. The view that businesses are global citizens that should behave and respect the laws and culture of every country in which they do business.

Glasnost. A Russian term used to describe "openness" during the late 1980s and early 1990s when the Soviet Union began to collapse as a political entity.

Glass ceiling. A barrier to the advancement of women, minorities, and other groups in the workplace.

Glass wall. A barrier to the lateral mobility of women, minorities, and other groups in the workplace, such as from human resources to operations.

Global commons. The idea that certain types of natural resources, such as the earth's atmosphere, tropical rain forests, and oceans, are vital for all living organisms. (See also **Commons.**)

Global village. The most remote places on earth are linked together—like a single village—through technological advances that allow faster and more widespread communications.

Global warming. The gradual warming of the earth's climate, believed by some scientists to be caused by an increase in carbon dioxide and other trace gases in the earth's atmosphere resulting from human activity, mainly the burning of fossil fuels.

Government and business partnership. A subtype of socioeconomic system in which government and business work cooperatively to solve social problems. (See also **Public-private partnerships.**)

Grassroots politics. Political activity directed at involving and influencing individual citizens or constituents to directly contact government officials on a public policy issue.

Green consumerism. An attitude of consumers that considers the ecological effects of their purchase, use, and disposal of consumer goods and services.

Green management. An outlook by managers that emphasizes the importance of considering ecological factors as management decisions are made.

Green marketing. A concept that describes the creation, promotion, and sale of environmentally safe products and services by business.

Greenhouse effect. The warming effect that occurs when carbon dioxide, methane, nitrous oxides, and other gases act like the glass panels of a greenhouse, preventing heat from the earth's surface from escaping into space.

Greenmail. The practice of paying a premium over the market price of a company's stock as part of a settlement with investors who wish to take over a company.

Hazardous waste. Waste materials from industrial, agricultural, and other activities capable of causing death or serious health problems for those persons exposed for prolonged periods. (See also **Toxic substance.**)

Home country.   The country in which a multinational corporation has its headquarters.

Horizontal merger.   The combination, or joining together, of two or more companies in the same industry and at the same level or stage of production or sales into a single company. (See also **Conglomerate merger, Vertical merger.**)

Host country.   A foreign country in which a multinational corporation conducts business.

Human rights code of conduct.   An organization's statement regarding acceptable and unacceptable types of behavior with respect to people's rights to life, liberty, and well-being.

Human rights reasoning.   (See **Right [human].**)

Ideology.   A set of basic beliefs that define an ideal way of living for an individual, an organization, or a society.

Individualism.   A belief that each individual person has an inherent worth and dignity and possesses basic human rights that should be protected by society. Each person is presumed to be a free agent capable of knowing and promoting his or her own self-interest.

Industrial ecology.   Designing factories and distribution systems as if they were self-contained ecosystems, such as using waste from one process as raw material for another.

Industrial policy.   Government action to encourage the growth and development of specific industries.

Industrial resource base.   The minerals, energy sources, water supplies, skilled labor force, and human knowledge necessary for industrial production.

Industrial society.   A society in which the building and mechanical processing of material goods dominates work and employs the largest proportion of the labor force.

Industry-specific regulation.   Regulations aimed at specific industries, such as telephone service or railroad transportation, involving control of rates charged, customers served, and entry into the industry.

Inflation.   Decline in the purchasing power of money.

Information society.   The current phase of technology; emphasizes the use and transfer of knowledge and information.

Insider trading.   The illegal practice of buying or selling shares of corporate securities based on fiduciary information which is known only to a small group of persons, such as executives and their friends ("insiders"), and which enables them to make profits at the expense of other investors who do not have access to the inside information.

Institutional investor.   A financial institution, insurance company, pension fund, endowment fund, or similar organization that invests its accumulated funds in the securities offered for sale on stock exchanges.

Institutionalized activity (ethics, social responsiveness, public affairs, etc.).   An activity, operation, or procedure that is such an integral part of an organization that it is performed routinely by managers and employees. (See also **Organizational commitment.**)

Intellectual property.   Ideas, concepts, and other symbolic creations of human intelligence that are recognized and protected under a nation's copyright, patent, and trademark laws.

Interactive model of business and society.   The combined primary and secondary interactions that business has with society.

Interactive system.   The closely intertwined relationships between business and society.

Intergenerational equity.   A term describing the unfairness of one generation's accumulation of debt and tax burdens that will have to be borne by future generations.

Interlocking directorate.   A relationship between two corporations that is established when one person serves as a member of the board of directors of both corporations simultaneously.

International regulation.   A form of regulation in which more than one nation agrees to establish and enforce the same rules of conduct for international business activities.

Internet (or World Wide Web).   A conduit of information systems revolutionizing how business is conducted, students learn, and households operate.

Intranet.   Private or limited information network systems cordoned off from public access by software programs called firewalls.

Iron law of responsibility.   The belief that those companies who, in the long run, do not use their power in ways that society deems responsible, will tend to lose their power.

Issues management.   The systematic method of identification, analysis, priority setting, and response to public issues.

Justice.   A mode of ethical reasoning that calls for the fair distribution of benefits and burdens among the people in a society, according to some agreed-upon rule.

Knowledge economy. An economy in which new knowledge, in its many forms, is reshaping and transforming old industries and creating new ones.

Labor force participation rate. The proportion of a particular group, such as women, in the paid workforce.

Labor standards. Conditions affecting a company's employees or the employees of its suppliers or subcontractors.

Laissez faire. A french phrase meaning "to let alone," used to describe an economic system where government intervention is minimal.

Laws. A society's formally codified principles that help define right and wrong behavior.

Leveraged buyouts (LBOs). The acquisition of a corporation by a group of investors, often including top executives, that relies on debt financing to pay the purchase price. The value of the company's assets is used as a "lever" to borrow the necessary amount for the purchase.

Life-cycle analysis. Collecting information on the life-long environmental impact of a product in order to minimize its adverse impacts at all stages, including design, manufacture, use, and disposal.

Limits to growth hypothesis. The idea that human society is now exceeding the carrying capacity of the earth's ecosystem and that unless corrective action is taken soon, catastrophic consequences will result. (See also **Carrying capacity.**)

Lobbying. The act of trying to directly shape or influence a government official's understanding and position on a public policy issue.

Market failure. Inability of the marketplace to properly allocate costs to the parties responsible (e.g., of air pollution emissions) or to achieve the benefits associated with free market economics.

Megacorporation. One of the very largest business corporations.

Merger. (See **Corporate merger.**)

Microenvironment of business. The interrelated social, economic, political, and technological segments of society that influence and are affected by a company's actions.

Militarized nondemocratic systems. A socioeconomic system that resembles mixed private and public enterprise, in which the coercive power of the military supports the government.

Mixed state and private enterprise. A socioeconomic system in which government owns some key industrial and financial enterprises but most businesses are owned and operated by private individuals and corporations.

Monetary policy. Government actions to control the supply and demand of money in the economy.

Montreal Protocol. An international treaty limiting the manufacture and use of chlorofluorocarbons and other ozone-depleting chemicals. (See also **Chlorofluorocarbons, Ozone.**)

Moral development stages. A series of progressive steps by which a person learns new ways of reasoning about ethical and moral issues.

Morality. A condition in which the most fundamental human values are preserved and allowed to shape human thought and action.

Most favored nation (MFN). The foreign policy term used to describe any nation with whom the United States has a relationship that is designed to encourage trade by minimizing trade barriers.

Multimedia pollution. (See **Cross-media pollution.**)

Multinational corporation. A company that conducts business in two or more nations, usually employing citizens of various nationalities.

National competitiveness. The ability of a nation to compete effectively with other nations in international markets through the actions of its privately and publicly owned business firms.

National sovereignty principle. A nation is a sovereign state whose laws, customs, and regulations must be respected by people, organizations, and other nations.

Nationalization. Government taking ownership and control of private property with or without compensation. (Also known as *expropriation.*)

New social contract. An evolving view of how a corporation and its stakeholders should act toward one another in light of modern economic and social changes. (See also **Social contract.**)

New World Order. The phrase used to describe relationships among nations following the end of the cold war in the late 1980s.

Nonpoint source. A source of water or air pollution that cannot be easily identified, such as the source of toxic runoff from urban storm drains. (See also **Point source.**)

Nonrenewable resources. Natural resources, such as oil, coal, or natural gas, that once used are gone forever. (See also **Renewable resources.**)

Occupational crime. Illegal activity by a business employee intended to enrich the employee at the expense of the company.

Occupational segregation. The practice of employing predominantly men or women in a particular job category.

Opportunity costs. The various opportunities that cannot be realized because money is spent for one purpose rather than for others.

Organization commitment. A stage in the development of social responsiveness within a company when social responses have become a normal part of doing business. Therefore, the entire organization is committed to socially responsible actions and policies. (See also **Institutionalized activity.**)

Ozone. A gas composed of three bonded oxygen atoms. Ozone in the lower atmosphere is a dangerous component of urban smog; ozone in the upper atmosphere provides a shield against ultraviolet light from the sun. (See also **Chlorofluorocarbons, Montreal Protocol.**)

Parental leave. A leave of absence from work, either paid or unpaid, for the purpose of caring for a newborn or adopted child.

Paternalistic. Caring for others in need, as a father cares for a child.

Patriarchal society. A society in which men hold the dominant positions in organizations, the society's values reflect and reinforce male-oriented privileges, and women tend to hold subordinate positions.

Perestroika. A Russian term used to describe economic reform and reconstruction during the late 1980s and early 1990s when the Soviet Union began to collapse as a political entity.

Performance-expectations gap. The perceived distance between a corporation's actual performance and the performance that is expected by the corporation's stakeholders.

Perpetual political campaign. The continuous process of raising money, communicating with constituents, and running for reelection.

Philanthropy. (See **Corporate philanthropy.**)

Plant closing laws. Legislation that requires employers to notify employees in advance of the closing of a facility in order to allow time for adjustment, including negotiations to keep the plant open, to arrange an employee buyout, to find new jobs, and so forth.

Pluralism. A society in which numerous economic, political, educational, social, cultural, religious, and other groups are organized by people to promote their own interests.

Point source. A source of water or air pollution that can be easily identified such as a particular factory. (See also **Nonpoint source.**)

Policy decision. A stage in the public policy process when government authorizes (or fails to authorize) a course of action, such as by passing (or failing to pass) a law, issuing a court opinion, or adopting a new regulation.

Policy evaluation. The final stage in the public policy process when the results of a public policy are judged by those who have an interest in the outcome.

Policy formulation. A stage in the public policy process when interested groups take a position and try to persuade others to adopt that position.

Policy implementation. A stage in the public policy process when action is taken to enforce a public policy decision.

Political action committee (PAC). A committee organized according to election law by any group for the purpose of accepting voluntary contributions from individual donors and then making contributions in behalf of candidates for election to public office.

Political cynicism. A climate of public distrust of politics and politicians.

Polluter pays principle (PPP). A principle that states that a polluter should be responsible for paying for the full costs of its pollution, such as through taxes.

Pollution charge. A fee levied on a polluting source based on the amount of pollution released into the environment.

Pollution prevention. (See **Source reduction.**)

Pollution rights. A legal right to emit a specified amount of pollution; such rights may be bought, sold, or held for future use with approval of government regulators.

Polygraph. An operator-administered instrument used to judge the truth or falsity of a person's statements by measuring physiological changes that tend to be activated by a person's conscience when lying.

Populism. A political philosophy that favors grassroots democracy and an economy based on small businesses and farms, and that opposes big business concentration.

Predatory pricing. The practice of selling below cost for the purpose of driving competitors out of business; usually illegal under U.S. antitrust laws.

Preferential hiring. An employment plan that gives preference to minorities, women, and other groups that may be underrepresented in an organization's workforce.

Price-fixing. When two or more companies collude to set—or "fix"—the price of a product or service; usually illegal under U.S. antitrust laws.

Primary interactions or involvement. The direct relationships a company has with those groups that enable it to produce goods and services.

Primary stakeholders. The people and groups who are directly affected by a corporation's economic activities and decisions.

Principle of national sovereignty. The idea that the government of each nation is legally entitled to make laws regarding the behavior of its citizens and citizens of other nations who are acting within the nation.

Priority rule. In ethical analysis, a procedure for ranking in terms of their importance the three ethical modes of reasoning—utilitarian, rights, and justice—before making a decision or taking action.

Privacy. (See **Right of privacy.**)

Private property. A group of rights giving control over physical and intangible assets to private owners. Private ownership is the basic institution of capitalism.

Privately held corporation. A corporation that is privately owned by an individual or a group of individuals; its stock is not available for purchase by the general investing public.

Privatization. The process of converting various economic functions, organizations, and programs from government ownership or government sponsorship to private operation.

Product liability. A legal responsibility of a person or firm for the harmful consequences to others stemming from use of a product manufactured, sold, managed, or employed by the person or firm.

Product recall. An effort by a business firm to remove a defective or sometimes dangerous product from consumer use and from all distribution channels.

Productivity. The relationship between total inputs and total outputs. Productivity increases when the outputs of an organization increase faster than the inputs necessary for production.

Profit maximization. An attempt by a business firm to achieve the highest possible rate of return from its operations.

Profit optimization. An attempt by a business firm to achieve an acceptable (rather than a maximum) rate of return from its operations.

Profits. The revenues of a person or company minus the costs incurred in producing the revenue.

Proxy. A legal instrument giving another person the right to vote the shares of stock of an absentee stockholder.

Proxy statement. A statement sent by a board of directors to a corporation's stockholders announcing the company's annual meeting, containing information about the business to be considered at the meeting, and enclosing a proxy form for stockholders not attending the meeting.

Public affairs function. An organization's activities intended to perceive, monitor, understand, communicate with, and influence the external environment, including local and national communities, government, and public opinion.

Public affairs management. The active management of an organization's external relations with such stakeholders as legislators, government officials, and regulatory agencies.

Public issue. A problem or concern of corporate stakeholders that has the potential to become a politicized matter, leading to legislation, regulation, or other formal governmental action.

Public issue life cycle. The sequence of phases through which a public issue may pass.

Public policy. A plan of action by government to achieve some broad purpose affecting a large segment of the public.

Public policy agenda. All public policy problems or issues that receive the active and serious attention of government officials.

Public policy process. All of the activities and stages involves in developing, carrying out, and evaluating public policies.

Public-private partnerships. Community-based organizations that have a combination of businesses and government agencies collaborating to address important social problems such as crime, homelessness, drugs, economic development, and other community issues. (See also **Government and business partnership.**)

Public referendum.   A citizen's initiative to place a question or resolution on the election ballot for a popular vote.

Public trustee.   A concept that a business owner or manager should base company decisions on the interests of a wide range of corporate stakeholders or members of the general public. In doing so, the business executive acts as a trustee of the public interest. (See also **Stewardship principle.**)

Publicly held corporation.   A corporation whose stock is available for purchase by the general investing public.

Questionable payments.   Something of value given to a person or firm that raises significant ethical questions of right or wrong in the host nation or other nations.

Quotas (job, hiring, employment).   An employment plan based on hiring a specific number or proportion of minorities, women, or other groups who may be underrepresented in an organization's workforce.

Rain forest.   Woodlands that receive at least 100 inches of rain a year. They are among the planet's richest areas in terms of biodiversity.

Reengineering.   The concept of redesigning work systems and organizations in ways that enhance productivity and efficient work activities.

Regulation.   The action of government to establish rules by which industry or other groups must behave in conducting their normal activities.

Reinventing government.   A phrase used to describe efforts to reengineer, restructure, and reduce the cost of government.

Relationship investing.   When large stockholders, usually institutions, form a long-term committed link with a company.

Renewable resources.   Natural resources, such as fresh water or timber, that can be naturally replenished. (See also **Nonrenewable resources.**)

Reregulation.   The imposition of regulation on activities that were deregulated earlier.

Reverse discrimination.   The unintended negative impact experienced by an individual or group as a result of legal efforts to overcome discrimination against another individual or group.

Right (human).   A concept used in ethical reasoning that means that a person or group is entitled to something or is entitled to be treated in a certain way. (See also **Entitlement.**)

Right of privacy.   A person's entitlement to protection from invasion of his or her private life by government, business, or other persons.

Rule of cost.   The idea that all human actions generate costs.

Secondary interactions or involvement.   The relationship a company has with those social and political groups that feel the impact of the company's main activities and take steps to do something about it. These relationships are derived from the firm's primary interactions.

Secondary stakeholders.   The people and groups in society who are indirectly affected by a corporation's economic activities and decisions.

Sex-role spillover.   When men continue to think of women mainly as performing traditional roles as sex partners, homemakers, and childbearers, rather than as co-workers and qualified professionals.

Sexual division of labor.   The traditional or accepted allocation of jobs or roles in a society between men and women.

Sexual harassment.   Unwanted and uninvited sexual attention experienced by a person, and/or a workplace that is hostile or threatening in a sexual way.

Shareholder.   (See **Stockholder.**)

Shareholder resolution.   A proposal made by a stockholder and included in a corporation's notice of its annual meeting that advocates some course of action to be taken by the company

Shareholders' lawsuit.   A lawsuit initiated by one or more stockholders to recover damages suffered due to alleged actions of the company's management.

Social accountability.   The condition of being held responsible to society or to some public or governmental group for one's actions, often requiring a specific accounting or reporting on those activities.

Social audit.   A systematic study and evaluation of an organization's social performance. (See also **Social performance evaluation.**)

Social Charter.   Social policy developed by countries in the European Union.

Social contract.   An implied understanding between an organization and its stakeholders as to how they will act toward one another. (See also **New social contract.**)

Social forecasting.   An attempt to estimate major social and political trends that may affect a company's operations and environment in the future.

Social overhead costs.   Public and private investments that are necessary to prepare the environment for effective operation of a new business or other major institutions.

Social performance evaluation.   Information about an organization's social performance, often contained in a company's annual report to stockholders and sometimes prepared as a special report to management or the general public. (See also **Social audit.**)

Social regulation. Regulations intended to accomplish certain social improvements such as equal employment opportunity or on-the-job safety and health.

Social responsibility. (See **Corporate social responsibility.**)

Social responsibility shareholder resolution. A resolution on an issue of corporate social responsibility placed before stockholders for a vote at a company's annual meeting, usually by social activist groups.

Social responsiveness. (See **Corporate social responsiveness.**)

Society. The people, institutions, and technology that make up a recognizable human community.

Socioeconomic system. The combined and interrelated social, economic, and political institutions characteristic of a society.

Soft money. Funds donated to a political party to support party-building activities such as televised commercials that do not specify a candidate, get-out-the-vote drives, and opinion polling. Soft money is often criticized as a loophole in the political campaign finance laws.

Solid waste. Any solid waste materials resulting from human activities, such as municipal refuse and sewage, industrial wastes, and agricultural wastes.

Source reduction. A business strategy to prevent or reduce pollution at the source, rather than to dispose of or treat pollution after it has been produced. (Also known as *pollution prevention.*)

Special economic zones. Industrial areas in the People's Republic of China that are reserved for foreign companies to establish business operations.

Specialized learning. A stage in the development of corporate social responsiveness within a company during which managers and supervisors, usually with the help of a specialist, learn the new practices necessary for coping with social problems and pressures.

Stakeholder. (See **Corporate stakeholder.**)

Stakeholder coalitions. Temporary unions of a company's stakeholder groups in order to express a common view or achieve a common purpose on a particular issue.

Stakeholder power. The ability of one or more stakeholders to achieve a desired outcome in their interactions with a company.

State-owned enterprise. A government-owned business or industry (e.g., a state-owned oil company).

Stateless corporation. A multinational corporation whose activities are conducted in so many nations as to minimize its dependence on any single nation and enable it to establish its headquarters' activities virtually anywhere in the world.

Stewardship principle. The idea that business managers should act in the interest of all members of society who are affected by their business decisions, thus behaving as stewards or trustees of the public welfare. (See also **Public trustee.**)

Sticky floor. When women, minorities, or other groups are unable to advance in the workplace because they become "stuck" in entry-level, low-paying jobs.

Stockholder. A person, group, or organization owning one or more shares of stock in a corporation. (Also known as *shareholder.*)

Strategic philanthropy. A form of philanthropy in which donor organizations direct their contributions to recipients in order to achieve a direct or indirect business objective.

Strategic rethinking. The process of reconsidering critical business assumptions about what an organization does, business activities it conducts, and in which markets, and how, it will compete.

Strategies of response. (See **Corporate social strategy.**)

Strict liability. A legal doctrine that holds that a manufacturer is responsible (liable) for injuries resulting from the use of its products, whether or not the manufacturer was negligent or breached a warranty.

Superfund. A U.S. law, passed in 1980, designated to clean up hazardous or toxic waste sites. The law established a fund, supported mainly by taxes on petrochemical companies, to pay for the cleanup. (Also known as the *Comprehensive Environmental Response, Compensation, and Liability Act [CERCLA].*)

Sustainable development. A concept that describes current economic development that does not damage the ability of future generations to meet their own needs.

Technology. The tools, machines, skills, technical operations, and abstract symbols involved in human endeavor.

Technology cooperation. Long-term cooperative partnerships between companies in developed and developing countries to transfer advanced technologies.

Telecommunications. The transmission of information via electromagnetic signals.

Telecommuting. Performing knowledge work and transmitting the results of that work by means of computer terminal to an organization's central data bank and management center, while the employee works at home or at some other remote location.

Term limits. Limits on the maximum number of terms in office that an elected official can serve.

Third world nations. Developing nations relatively poorer than advanced industrial nations.

Total quality management (TQM). A management approach that achieves high quality and consumer satisfaction through teamwork and continuous improvement of a product or service.

Toxic substance. Any substance used in production or in consumer products that is poisonous or capable of causing serious health problems for those persons exposed. (See also **Hazardous waste.**)

Tradable allowances. A market-based approach to pollution control in which the government grants companies "rights" to a specific amount of pollution (allowances), which may be bought or sold (traded) with other companies.

Trade association. An organization that represents the business and professional interest of the firms or persons in a trade, industry, or profession, such as medical doctors, chemical manufacturers, or used car dealers.

Trade-offs, economic and social. An attempt to balance and compare economic and social gains against economic and social costs when it is impossible to achieve all that is desired in both economic and social terms.

Trade policy. Actions by government to encourage or discourage commerce with other nations.

Transparency. The degree of openness or visibility surrounding a government's—or other organization's—decision-making process.

Unanimity Rule. In ethical analysis, a procedure for determining that all three modes of ethical reasoning—utilitarian, rights, and justice—provide consistent and uniform answers to an ethical problem or issue.

Urban sprawl. The spread of urban activities into areas that were once suburban and rural land. This usually implies business activities, congestion, and other byproducts of more people and activity.

U.S. Sentencing Guidelines. Official rules to help judges determine the appropriate penalty for criminal violations of federal laws.

U.S. Foreign Corrupt Practices Act. A federal law that specifies penalties for companies that make illegal or questionable payments to officials of other countries.

Utilitarian reasoning. An ethical approach that emphasizes the cost-benefit relationship between actions and their consequences.

Utility (social). A concept used in ethical reasoning that refers to the net positive gain or benefit to society of some action or decision.

Values. Fundamental and enduring beliefs about the most desirable conditions and purposes of human life.

Vertical merger. The combination, or joining together, of two or more companies in the same industry but at different levels or stages of production or sales into a single company. (See also **Conglomerate merger, Horizontal merger.**)

Volunteerism. The uncompensated efforts of people to assist others in a community.

Wall Street. A customary way of referring to the financial community of banks, investment institutions, and stock exchanges centered in the Wall Street area of New York City.

Warranty. A guarantee or assurance by the seller of a product or service.

Water pollution. When more wastes are discharged into waterways, such as lakes and rivers, than can be naturally diluted and carried away.

Whistle-blowing. An employee's disclosure to the public of alleged organizational misconduct, often after futile attempts to convince organizational authorities to take action against the alleged abuse.

White collar crime. Illegal activities committed by corporate managers, such as embezzlement or fraud.

Women's movement. A social movement for the rights of women.

Workplace safety team. A group of workers and managers who seek to minimize the occurrence of workplace accidents.

World Business Council for Sustainable Development (WBCSD). A group of over 125 companies from several nations formed in 1995 to encourage high standards of environmental management and to promote cooperation among businesses, governments, and other organizations concerned with sustainable development.

Bibliography

Part One   Chapters 1–2

Academy of Management Review. Special Topic Forum on Shifting Paradigms: Societal Expectations and Corporate Performance, vol. 20, no. 1, January 1995.

Dennis, Lloyd B., ed. *Practical Public Affairs in an Era of Change.* Lanham, MD: Public Relations Society of America and University Press of America, 1996.

Dertouzas, Michael L.; Richard K. Lester; and Robert M. Solow. *Made in America: Regaining the Productivity Edge.* Cambridge, MA: MIT Press, 1989.

Dickie, Robert B., and Leroy S. Rouner, eds. *Corporations and the Common Good.* South Bend, IN: University of Notre Dame Press, 1986.

Drucker, Peter. *The New Realities.* New York: Harper and Row, 1989.

Etzioni, Amitai. *The New Golden Rule.* New York: Basic Books, 1996.

_____. *The Spirit of Community.* New York: Crown Publishers. 1993.

Frederick, William C. *Values, Nature, and Culture in the American Corporation.* New York: Oxford University Press, 1995.

Freeman, R. Edward. *Strategic Management: A Stakeholder Approach.* Marshfield, MA: Pitman, 1984.

Heath, Robert L., ed. *Strategic Issues Management,* 2d ed. San Francisco, CA: Jossey-Bass, 1996.

Kennedy, Paul. *Preparing for the Twenty-First Century.* New York: Vintage/Random House, 1994.

Krugman, Paul. *The Age of Diminished Expectations.* Cambridge, MA: MIT Press, 1994.

Post, James E., ed. *Research in Corporate Social Performance and Policy.* "The Corporation and Public Affairs," Vol. 14. Greenwich, CT: JAI Press, 1994.

Werhane, Patricia H. *Adam Smith & His Legacy for Modern Capitalism.* New York: Oxford University Press, 1990.

Wolfe, Alan. *One Nation, After All.* New York: Viking, 1998.

Part Two   Chapters 3–4

Ackerman, Robert. *The Social Challenge to Business.* Cambridge, MA: Harvard University Press, 1975.

Block, Peter. *Stewardship: Choosing Service over Self Interest.* San Francisco, CA: Berrett-Koehler, 1996.

Bollier, David. *Aiming Higher.* New York: American Management Association, 1996.

Bowen, Howard R. *Responsibilities of the Businessman,* New York: Harper, 1953.

Bradshaw, Thornton, and David Vogel, eds. *Corporations and Their Critics.* New York: McGraw-Hill, 1981.

Chamberlain, Neil W., *The Limits of Corporate Social Responsibility.* New York: Basic Books, 1973.

Himmelstein, Jerome. *Looking Good and Doing Good.* Bloomington, IN: Indiana University Press, 1997.

Houck, John, and Oliver F. Williams, eds. *Is the Good Corporation Dead? Social Responsibility in a Global Economy.* Lanham, MD: Rowman and Littlefield Publishers, 1996.

Kuhn, James W., and Donald W. Shriver, Jr. *Beyond Success: Corporations and Their Critics in the 1990s.* New York: Oxford University Press, 1991.

Miles, Robert. *Managing the Corporate Social Environment: A Grounded Theory.* Englewood Cliffs, NJ: Prentice-Hall, 1987.

Scott, Mary, and Howard Rothman. *Companies with a Conscience: Intimate Portraits of Twelve Firms That Make a Difference.* New York: Citadel Press Book/ Carroll Publishing Group, 1994.

Part Three   Chapters 5–7

Cavanaugh, Gerald F. *American Business Values: With International Perspective,* 4th ed. Englewood Cliffs, NJ: Prentice-Hall, 1998.

Colby, Anne, and William Damon. *Some Do Care: Contemporary Lives of Moral Commitment.* New York: The Free Press, 1992.

Colby, Anne, and Lawrence Kohlberg. *The Measurement of Moral Judgment: Volume 1, Theoretical Foundations and Research Validation.* Cambridge, MA: Harvard University Press, 1987.

Dobson, John. *Finance Ethics: The Rationality of Virtue.* Lanham, MD: Rowman and Littlefield, 1997.

Dunfee, Thomas W., and Yukimasa Nagayasu. *Business Ethics: Japan and the Global Economy.* Dordrecht, Netherlands: Kluwer Academic, 1993.

Estes, Ralph. *Tyranny of the Bottom Line: Why Corporations Make Good People Do Bad Things.* San Francisco, CA: Berrett Kochler, 1996.

Etzioni, Amitai. *The Moral Dimension: Toward a New Economics.* New York: Free Press, 1988.

Freeman, R. Edward, and Daniel R. Gilbert, Jr. *Corporate Strategy and the Search for Ethics.* Englewood Cliffs, NJ: Prentice-Hall, 1988.

Fukuyama, Francis. *Trust: The Social Virtues and the Creation of Prosperity.* New York: The Free Press, 1995.

Harding, Harry. *China's Second Revolution: Reform after Mao.* Washington: Brookings, 1987.

Jackall, Robert. *Moral Mazes: The World of Corporate Managers.* New York: Oxford University Press, 1988.

Kennedy, Paul. *The Rise and Fall of the Great Powers.* New York: Random House, 1987.

Kidder, Rushworth M. *How Good People Make Tough Choices.* New York: William Morrow & Co., 1995.

Korten, David. *When Corporations Ruled the World.* San Francisco, CA: Berrett-Kochler, 1996.

Levine, Marvin J. *Worker Rights and Labor Standards in Asia's Four New Tigers: A Comparative Perspective.* New York: Plenum Press, 1997.

Messick, David M., and Ann E. Tenbrunsel, eds. *Codes of Conduct: Behavioral Research into Business Ethics.* New York: Russell Sage Foundation, 1996.

Nash, Laura L. *Good Intentions Aside: A Manager's Guide to Resolving Ethical Problems.* Boston: Harvard Business School Press, 1990.

——————. *Believers in Business,* Nashville, TN: Thomas Nelson Publishers, 1994.

Neilsen, Richard P. *The Politics of Ethics.* New York: Oxford University Press, 1996.

Rawls, John. *A Theory of Justice.* Cambridge, MA: Harvard University Press, 1971.

Rest, James L., and Darcia Navarez, eds. *Moral Development in the Professions.* Hillsdale, NJ: Lawrence Erlbaum Associates, 1994.

Stone, Christopher D. *Where the Law Ends: The Social Control of Corporate Behavior.* Prospect Heights, IL: Waveland Press, 1975.

Tavis, Lee A. *Power and Responsibility: Multinational Managers and Developing Country Concerns.* South Bend, IN: University of Notre Dame Press, 1997.

Velasquez, Manuel G. *Business Ethics: Concepts and Cases,* 4th ed. Upper Saddle River, NJ: Prentice Hall, 1998.

Part Four *Chapters 8–10*

Ayres, Ian, and John Braithwaite. *Responsive Regulation: Transcending the Regulation Debate.* New York: Oxford University Press, 1992.

Berry, Jeffrey M. *The Interest Group Society.* Boston: Little, Brown, 1985.

Cranston, Ross. *Law, Government and Public Policy.* New York: Oxford University Press, 1987.

Dewey, Donald. *The Anti-Trust Experiment in America,* New York: Columbia University Press, 1990.

Eagleton, Thomas F. *Issues in Business and Government.* Englewood Cliffs, NJ: Prentice-Hall, 1991.

Epstein, Edwin M. *The Corpoation in American Politics.* Englewood Cliffs, NJ: Prentice-Hall, 1969.

Fugate, Wilbur L. (assisted by Lee Simowitz). *Foreign Commerce and the Anti-Trust Laws,* 4th ed., Boston: Little, Brown, 1991.

Galambos, Louis, and Joseph Pratt. *The Rise of Corporate Commonwealth: United States Business and Public Policy in the 20th Century.* New York: Basic Books, 1988.

Garvey, George E., and Gerald J. Garvey. *Economic Law and Economic Growth: Anti-Trust, Regulation, and the American Growth System.* New York: Greenwood Press, 1990.

Lipset, Seymour Martin, and William Schneider. *The Confidence Gap: Business, Labor, and Government in the Public Mind.* Baltimore: Johns Hopkins University Press, 1987.

Lodge, George C. *The New American Ideology.* New York: Alfred A. Knopf, 1978.

——————. *Comparative Business-Government Relations.* Englewood Cliffs, NJ: Prentice-Hall, 1990.

——————. *Perestroika for America: Restructuring Business-Government Relations for World Competitiveness.* Boston: Harvard Business School Press, 1990.

Mahon, John F., and Richard A. McGowan. *Industry as a Player in the Political and Social Arena: Defining the Competitive Environment.* Westport, CT: Quorum Books, 1996.

Maitland-Walker, Julian, ed. *Toward 1992: The Development of International Anti-Trust.* Oxford, England: ESC Publishing, 1989.

Marcus, Alfred A.; Allen M. Kaufman; and David R. Beam. *Business Strategy and Public Policy: Perspectives from Industry and Academia.* Westport, CT: Quorum Books, 1987.

McGowan, Richard. *State Lotteries and Legalized Gambling: Painless Revenue or Painful Mirage.* Westport, CT: Quorum Books, 1994.

——————. *Business, Politics, and Cigarettes: Multiple Levels, Multiple Agendas.* Westport, CT: Quorum Books, 1995.

——————. *Government Regulation of the Alcohol Industry: The Search for Revenue and the Common Good.* Westport, CT: Quorum Books, 1997.

Oxford Analytica. *America in Perspective: Major Trends in the United States through the 1990's.* Boston: Houghton Mifflin, 1986.

Peters, B. Guy. *American Public Policy: Promise and Performance,* 2d ed. Chatham, NJ: Chatham House, 1986.

Porter, Michael. *The Competitive Advantage of Nations.* New York: Basic Books, 1991.

Reich, Robert B. *The Work of Nations.* New York: Free Press, 1991.

Reich, Robert B., ed. *The Power of Public Ideas.* Cambridge, MA: Ballinger, 1988.

Scherer, F. M. *Competition Policies for an Integrated World Economy.* Washington, D.C.: The Brookings Institution, 1994.

Vietor, Richard H. K. *Strategic Management in the Regulatory Environment.* Englewood Cliffs, NJ: Prentice-Hall, 1989.

Weidenbaum, Murray. *Business, Government and the Public,* 4th ed. Englewood Cliffs, NJ: Prentice-Hall, 1990.

Wolf, Charles. *Markets or Government: Choosing between Imperfect Alternatives.* Cambridge, MA: MIT Press, 1988.

Part Five   *Chapters 11–12*

Brown, Lester R., et al. *State of the World, 1997: A Worldwatch Institute Report on Progress toward a Sustainable Society.* New York: W. W. Norton, 1997.

Buchholz, Rogene. *Principles of Environmental Management.* Englewood Cliffs, NJ: Prentice-Hall, 1993.

Buchholz, Rogene; Alfred Marcus; and James E. Post. *Managing Environmental Issues: A Casebook.* Englewood Cliffs, NJ: Prentice Hall, 1992.

Collins, Denis, and Mark Starik, eds. *Research in Corporate Social Performance and Policy.* "Sustaining the Natural Environment: Empirical Studies on the Interface between Nature and Organizations," Vol. 15, Supp. 1. Greenwich, CT: JAI Press, 1995.

Ehrlich, Paul R., and Anne H. Ehrlich. *The Population Explosion.* New York: Simon & Schuster, 1990.

Fischer, Kurt, and Johan Schot. eds. *Environmental Strategies for Industry: International Perspectives on Research Needs and Policy Implications.* Washington, D.C.: Island Press, 1993.

Gore, Al. *Earth in the Balance: Ecology and the Human Spirit.* Boston, MA: Houghton Mifflin, 1992.

Hoffman, W. Michael; Robert Frederick; and Edward S. Petry eds. *The Corporation, Ethics and the Environment.* Westport, CT: Quorum Books, 1990.

Kolluru, Rao V., ed. *Environmental Strategies Handbook: A Guide to Effective Policies and Practices.* New York: McGraw-Hill, 1994.

Lee, Henry, ed. *Shaping National Responses to Climate Change.* Washington, D.C.: Island Press, 1994.

Mann, Charles C., and Mark L. Plummer. *Noah's Choice: The Future of Endangered Species.* New York: Alfred A. Knopf, 1995.

Meadows, Donella H.; Dennis L. Meadows; and Jorgen Randers. *Beyond the Limits: Confronting Global Collapse, Environing a Sustainable Future.* Post Mills, VT: Chelsea Green Publishing Co., 1992.

Schmidheiny, Stephan. *Changing Course: A Global Perspective on Development and the Environment.* Cambridge, MA: MIT Press, 1992.

Stead, W. Edward, and Jean Garner Stead. *Management for a Small Planet.* Newbury Park, CA: Sage Publications, 1992.

Stone, Christopher. *The Gnat Is Older than Man: Global Environment and Human Agenda.* Princeton, NJ: Princeton University Press, 1993.

Part Six   *Chapters 13–16*

Adler, Nancy, and Dafna N. Israeli, eds. *Competitive Frontiers: Women Managers in the Global Economy.* Cambridge, MA: Basil Blackwell, 1995.

Bloom, Paul, and Ruth Belk Smith, eds. *The Future of Consumerism.* Lexington, MA: Lexington Books, 1986.

Caplan, Lincoln. *Up Against the Law: Affirmative Action and the Supreme Court.* New York: Twentieth Century Fund Press, 1997.

Edley, Christopher F. *Not All Black and White: Affirmative Action, Race and American Values.* New York: Hill and Wang, 1996.

Fagenson, Ellen A., ed. *Women in Management: Trends, Issues, and Challenges in Management Diversity.* Newbury Park, CA: Sage, 1993.

Faludi, Susan. *Backlash: The Undeclared War against American Women.* New York: Doubleday, 1991.

Goldin, Claudia. *Understanding the Gender Gap: An Economic History of American Women.* New York: Oxford University Press, 1990.

Gray, Barbara. *Collaborating: Finding Common Ground for Multiparty Problems.* San Francisco: Jossey-Bass, 1989.

Gunderson, Martin; David J. Mayo; and Frank S. Rhame. *AIDS: Testing and Privacy.* Salt Lake City: University of Utah Press, 1989.

Gutek, Barbara A. *Sex and the Workplace: The Impact of Sexual Behavior and Harassment on Women, Men, and Organizations.* San Francisco: Jossey-Bass, 1985.

Herman, Edward S. *Corporate Control, Corporate Power.* Cambridge, England: Cambridge University Press, 1981.

Hochschild, Arlie. *The Second Shift: Working Parents and the Revolution at Home.* New York: Viking, 1989.

Kester, Carl W. *Japanese Takeovers: The Global Contest for Corporate Control.* Boston: Harvard Business School Press, 1991.

Kittrie, Nicholas N., *The War against Authority: From the Crisis of Legitimacy to a New Social Contract.* Baltimore, MD: Johns Hopkins University Press, 1995.

Kuenne, Robert E. *Economic Justice in American Society.* Princeton, NJ: Princeton University Press, 1993.

Linowes, David F. *Privacy in America: Is Your Private Life in the Public Eye?* Urbana, IL: University of Illinois Press, 1989.

Lorsch, Jay William. *Pawns or Potentates: The Reality of America's Corporate Boards.* Boston: Harvard Business School Press, 1989.

Mann, Jonathan M., and Daniel J. M. Tarantola, eds. *AIDS in World War II: Global Dimensions, Social Roots and Responses.* New York: Oxford University Press, 1996.

Matteo, Sherri, ed. *American Women in the Nineties.* Boston: Northeastern University Press, 1993.

Morrison, Ann M.; Randall P. White; and Ellen Van Velsor. *Breaking the Glass Ceiling: Can Women Reach the Top of America's Largest Corporations?* updated ed. Reading, MA: Addison-Wesley, 1992.

Powell, Gary N. *Women and Men in Management,* 2d ed. Newbury Park, CA: Sage Publications, 1993.

Puckett, Same B., and Alan R. Emery. *Managing AIDS in the Workplace.* Reading, MA: Addison-Wesley, 1988.

Rix, Sara E. *The American Woman 1990–91: A Status Report.* New York: Norton, 1990.

Singer, Merrill, ed. *The Political Economy of AIDS.* Amityville, NY: Baywood Publishers, 1998.

United Nations. *The World's Women, 1970–1990: Trends and Statistics.* New York: United Nations Publications, June 1991.

Part Seven   *Chapters 17–18*

Adler, Paul S., ed. *Technology and the Future of Work.* New York: Oxford University Press, 1992.

Barbour, Ian G. *Ethics in an Age of Technology.* San Francisco: Harper, 1993.

Barcus, F. Earl. *Images of Life on Children's Television: Sex Roles, Minorities, and Families.* New York: Praeger, 1983.

Bradley, Stephen P.; Jerry A. Hausman; and Richard L. Nolan. *Globalization, Technology, and Competition: The Fusion of Computers and Telecommunications in the 1990s.* Boston, MA: Harvard Business School Press, 1993.

Corrado, Frank M. *Media for Managers: Communications Strategies for the Eighties.* Englewood Cliffs, NJ: Prentice-Hall, 1984.

Dates, Jannette L., and William Barlow, eds. *Split Image: African-Americans in the Mass Media.* Washington, D.C.: Howard University Press, 1990.

Dertouzas, Michael L.; Richard K. Lester; and Robert M. Solow. *Made in America: Regaining the Productivity Edge.* Cambridge, MA: MIT Press, 1989.

Drlica, Karl. *Double-edged Sword: The Promises and Risks of the Genetic Revolution.* Reading, MA: Addison-Wesley, 1994.

Etzioni, Amitai. *The Spirit of Community: Rights, Responsibilities, and the Communitarian Agenda.* New York: Crown Publishers, 1993.

Hernstein, Richard J., and Charles Murray, *The Bell Curve: Intelligence and Class Structure in American Life.* New York: Free Press, 1994.

Kolata, Gina. *Clone: The Road to Dolly and the Path Ahead.* New York: Morrow Publications, 1998.

Kuenne, Robert E. *Economic Justice in American Society.* Princeton, NJ: Princeton University Press, 1993.

Linowes, David F. *Privacy in America: Is Your Private Life in the Public Eye?* Urbana, IL: University of Illinois Press, 1989.

Oskamp, Stuart, ed. *Television as a Social Issue.* Newbury Park, CA: Sage Publications, 1988.

Reiss, Michael J. *Improving Nature? The Science and Ethics of Genetic Engineering.* New York: Cambridge University Press, 1996.

Schlesinger, Arthur M., Jr. *The Disuniting of America: Reflections on a Multicultural Society.* New York: Norton, 1993.

Steele, Shelby. *Content of Our Character: A New Vision of Race in America.* New York: St. Martin's Press, 1990.

Stoll, Clifford. *Silicon Snake Oil: Second Thoughts on the Information Highway.* New York: Doubleday, 1995.

Ten Berge, Dieudonne. *The First 24 Hours: A Comprehensive Guide to Successful Crisis Communications.* Cambridge, MA: Basil Blackwell, 1990.

Wilson, James Q., and Joan Petersilia, eds. *Crime.* Cambridge, MA: ICS Press, 1994.

Name Index

Subject Index

LIVERPOOL JOHN MOORES UNIVERSITY
Aldham Robarts L.R.C.
TEL. 051 231 3701/3634

Books are to be returned on or before
the last date below.

2 3 MAR 2005

2 0 OCT 2005

1 0 NOV 2005

LIBREX —

WITHDRAWN

LIVERPOOL JMU LIBRARY

3 1111 01109 7472

WITHDRAWN